Lecture Notes in Computer Science 8659

Commenced Publication in 1973
Founding and Former Series Editors:
Gerhard Goos, Juris Hartmanis, and Jan van Leeuwen

Commenced Publication in 1973
Founding and Former Series Editors:
Gerhard Goos, Juris Hartmanis, and Jan van Leeuwen

Shazia Sadiq
Pnina Soffer
Hagen Völzer (Eds.)

Business Process Management

12th International Conference, BPM 2014
Haifa, Israel, September 7-11, 2014
Proceedings

 Springer

Volume Editors

Shazia Sadiq
The University of Queensland
School of Information Technology and Electrical Engineering
St. Lucia, QLD, Australia
E-mail: shazia@itee.uq.edu.au

Pnina Soffer
University of Haifa
Information Systems Department
Haifa, Israel
E-mail: spnina@is.haifa.ac.il

Hagen Völzer
IBM Research - Zurich
Rueschlikon, Switzerland
E-mail: hvo@zurich.ibm.com

ISSN 0302-9743   e-ISSN 1611-3349
ISBN 978-3-319-10171-2   e-ISBN 978-3-319-10172-9
DOI 10.1007/978-3-319-10172-9
Springer Cham Heidelberg New York Dordrecht London

Library of Congress Control Number: 2014946018

LNCS Sublibrary: SL 3 – Information Systems and Application, incl. Internet/Web
and HCI

Typesetting: Camera-ready by author, data conversion by Scientific Publishing Services, Chennai, India

Printed on acid-free paper

Springer is part of Springer Science+Business Media (www.springer.com)

Preface

The 12th International Conference on Business Process Management (BPM 2014) was held in Haifa, Israel, during September 7-11, 2014. BPM 2014 was jointly organized by the University of Haifa and IBM Research – Haifa.

Over the past decade, the conference has built its reputation by showcasing leading-edge research of the highest quality together with talks, tutorials, and discussions by the most renowned thought leaders and innovators in the field. The BPM conference series embraces the diversity and richness of the BPM field and serves as a melting pot for experts from a mix of disciplines, including computer science, information systems management, services science, and technology management.

Given the increasing span of BPM, this year the conference opened up to a number of new topics that add to existing areas of interest and relevance to BPM research and industry. Recognizing the interdisciplinary nature of BPM, eight high-level topic areas were indicated in the call for papers, while specific topics were classified by topic areas. The topic areas were human-centric BPM, management issues and empirical studies, management of process execution data, non-traditional BPM scenarios, process architecture and platforms, process flexibility and evolution, process modeling and theory, and process model management. Each topic was assigned two expert senior Program Committee members as topic champions. The topic champions promoted the topics and lead the review process of papers submitted for their topics.

In response to the call for papers, 123 papers were submitted for review. Each paper was evaluated by at least three Program Committee members, with the senior Program Committee member providing an additional review in most cases. We accepted 21 regular papers (17% acceptance rate) and 10 short papers.

The conference program consisted of six research paper presentation sessions, two short paper sessions, and one industry paper session. The conference program was greatly enhanced by three outstanding keynote speakers. Rob High, IBM Fellow, Vice President, and Chief Technology Officer, Watson Solutions, IBM Software Group. Prior to joining Watson Solutions, Rob championed an open industry architectural definition of the principles of business and IT alignment enabled by SOA and business process optimization, which has had far-reaching impact within and beyond IBM. Keith Swenson, Vice President of Research and Development at Fujitsu North America and Chief Software Architect for the Interstage family of products. As a speaker, author, and contributor to many workflow and BPM standards, Keith is known for having been a pioneer in collaboration software and Web services, and is the current chairman of the Workflow Management Coalition. Yuval Shahar, professor and previous chair of the Information Systems Engineering Department of Ben-Gurion University, and a leading authority on medical informatics. His work on temporal abstraction of clinical time-oriented data is well known and is at the core of the query and interpretation module of Stanford University's EON system for guideline-based medical care and a backbone for many research projects.

BPM 2014 also hosted ten workshops, which contributed significantly to the overall program by attracting additional participants and increasing the opportunities for discussion and intellectual exchange within and beyond the area of BPM. We would like to thank BPM Workshop Chairs Fabiana Fournier and Jan Mendling and all the respective workshop organizers for their outstanding commitment toward ensuring the success of the workshops. We are thankful to General Co-chairs Avigdor Gal and Mor Peleg, who led the organization of BPM 2014. Many thanks to Opher Etzion and Hajo Reijers for their efforts in attracting high-quality industry papers and further contributions in the review process. Demo Chairs Lior Limonad and Barbara Weber, Tutorial and Panel Chair Marcello La Rosa and Doctoral Consortium Chairs Dirk Fahland and Stefanie Rinderle-Ma all made an outstanding contribution to BPM 2014 in their respective roles, for which we are most grateful. Last but not least, we would like to thank Matthias Weidlich for his timely and innovative help with conference publicity and Tsvi Kuflik and Nilly Schnapp for their tireless efforts in the conference organization.

We are particularly thankful to the senior Program Committee, who embraced the role of topic champions this year, and made a concerted and authentic effort to promote and support high-quality research papers within and across the topics. We thank all the Program Committee members and external reviewers for their insightful reviews and discussions.

We also thank the conference sponsors Bizagi (platinum), IBM, and Haifa municipality (gold), Signavio (silver), and PNMSoft (bronze) for their valuable support, the BPM Steering Committee for their guidance, and Springer, the BPM proceedings' publisher, for their continued support of the BPM conference.

Lastly, we would like to congratulate the authors of all submitted and accepted papers for their high-quality work, and thank them for choosing BPM as their outlet for publication. The BPM conference series remains the premier forum for researchers and practitioners in the growing field of BPM and we look forward to seeing your work presented in this conference in future years as well.

September 2014

Shazia Sadiq
Pnina Soffer
Hagen Völzer

Organization

BPM 2014 was organized in Haifa, Israel, by the University of Haifa and IBM Research - Haifa

General Chair

Avigdor Gal   Technion – Israel Institute of Technology, Israel
Mor Peleg   University of Haifa, Israel

Program Chairs

Shazia Sadiq   The University of Queensland, Australia
Pnina Soffer   University of Haifa, Israel
Hagen Völzer   IBM Research – Zurich, Switzerland

Local Organization Chairs

Tsvi Kuflik   University of Haifa, Israel
Nilly Schnapp   University of Haifa, Israel

Industry Chairs

Opher Etzion   Max Stern Academic College of Yezreel Valley, Israel
Hajo Reijers   Eindhoven University of Technology, The Netherlands

Workshop Chairs

Fabiana Fournier   IBM Haifa Research Lab, Israel
Jan Mendling   Vienna University of Economics and Business, Austria

Doctoral Consortium Chairs

Dirk Fahland   Eindhoven University of Technology, The Netherlands
Stefanie Rinderle-Ma   University of Vienna, Austria

Demo Chairs

Lior Limonad   IBM Haifa Research Lab, Israel
Barbara Weber   University of Innsbruck, Austria

Publicity Chair

Matthias Weidlich   Imperial College London, UK

Tutorial and Panel Chair

Marcello La Rosa   Queensland University of Technology, Australia

Program Committee

Rafael Accorsi	University of Freiburg, Germany
Boualem Benatallah	University of New South Wales, Australia
Christoph Bussler	Tropo Inc., USA
Fabio Casati	University of Trento, Italy
Francisco Curbera	IBM Software Group, USA
Krzysztof Czarnecki	University of Waterloo, Canada
Peter Dadam	University of Ulm, Germany
Florian Daniel	University of Trento, Italy
Jörg Desel	FernUniversität Hagen, Germany
Alin Deutsch	University of California San Diego, USA
Remco Dijkman	Eindhoven University of Technology, The Netherlands
Marlon Dumas	University of Tartu, Estonia
Schahram Dustdar	TU Wien, Austria
Johann Eder	University of Klagenfurt, Austria
Dirk Fahland	Technische Universiteit Eindhoven, The Netherlands
Marcelo Fantinato	University of São Paulo - USP, Brazil
Kathrin Figl	Vienna University of Economics and Business (WU), Austria
Hans-Georg Fill	University of Vienna, Austria
Piero Fraternali	Politecnico di Milano, Italy
Avigdor Gal	Technion, Israel
Luciano García-Bañuelos	University of Tartu, Estonia
Christian Gerth	University of Paderborn, Germany
Claude Godart	Université de Lorraine/Loria Laboratory, France
Thomas Hildebrandt	IT University of Copenhagen, Denmark
Richard Hull	IBM T.J. Watson Research Center, USA

Minseok Song	Ulsan National Institute of Science and Technology, Korea
Mark Strembeck	Vienna University of Economics and BA, Institute of Information Systems, New Media Lab, Austria
Harald Störrle	Danmarks Tekniske Universitet, Denmark
Jianwen Su	University of California at Santa Barbara, USA
Stefan Tai	Karlsruhe Institute of Technology, Germany
Samir Tata	TELECOM SudParis; CNRS UMR Samovar, France
Arthur ter Hofstede	Queensland University of Technology, Australia
Farouk Toumani	Limos, Blaise Pascal University, Clermont-Ferrand, France
Alberto Trombetta	Insubria University, Italy
Aphrodite Tsalgatidou	National and Kapodistrian University of Athens, Greece
Roman Vaculín	IBM Research, Thomas J. Watson Research Center, USA
Wil van der Aalst	Eindhoven University of Technology, The Netherlands
Boudewijn van Dongen	Eindhoven University of Technology, The Netherlands
Irene Vanderfeesten	Technische Universiteit Eindhoven, The Netherlands
Hagen Völzer	IBM Research - Zurich, Switzerland
Jianmin Wang	School of Software, Tsinghua University, China
Barbara Weber	University of Innsbruck, Austria
Matthias Weidlich	Technion - Israel Institute of Technology
Lijie Wen	School of Software, Tsinghua University, China
Mathias Weske	HPI, University of Potsdam, Germany
Michael Westergaard	Eindhoven University of Technology, The Netherlands
Petia Wohed	DSV, SU/KTH, Sweden
Karsten Wolf	Universität Rostock, Germany
Liang Zhang	Fudan University, China
Xiaohui Zhao	Unitec Institute of Technology, New Zealand
Michael zur Muehlen	Stevens Institute of Technology, USA

Additional Reviewers

Athanasopoulos, George	Bokermann, Dennis
Aubry, Alexis	Böttcher, Boris
Bergenthum, Robin	Debois, Søren
Binz, Tobias	Fazal-Baqaie, Masud
Bislimovska, Bojana	Fehling, Christoph

Furfaro, Angelo
Garcia, Andres
Garro, Alfredo
Guo, Jianmei
Guzzo, Antonella
Görlach, Katharina
Hahn, Michael
Harten, Clemens
Heindorf, Stefan
Herzberg, Nico
Hewelt, Marcin
Hipp, Markus
Irgang, Thomas
Janiesch, Christian
Kaufmann, Christian
Khovalko, Oleh
Koutrouli, Eleni
Lezoche, Mario
Liu, Rong
Loures, Eduardo
Mach, Werner
Marrella, Andrea
Masciari, Elio
Mayrhofer, Dieter
Meis, Benjamin
Michelberger, Bernd

Milani, Fredrik P.
Pichler, Christian
Pittl, Benedikt
Pontieri, Luigi
Pufahl, Luise
Rembert, Aubrey
Rodriguez, Carlos
Rogge-Solti, Andreas
Russo, Alessandro
Schlömer, Inga
Serra, Edoardo
Skouradaki, Marigianna
Slaats, Tijs
Steyskal, Simon
Sun, Yutian
Suriadi, Suriadi
Tranquillini, Stefano
Tsagkani, Christina
Ul Haq, Irfan
Weiß, Andreas
Werner, Michael
Wimmer, Manuel
Wittern, Erik
Yahya, Bernardo Nugroho
Yongchareon, Sira
Yu, Jian

Table of Contents

Integrative BPM

Resource and Time Management in BPM

Process Analytics

Industry Papers

Short Papers: Process Enabled Environments

Short Papers: Discovery and Monitoring

Monitoring Business Metaconstraints
Based on LTL and LDL for Finite Traces

Giuseppe De Giacomo[1], Riccardo De Masellis[1], Marco Grasso[1],
Fabrizio Maria Maggi[2], and Marco Montali[3]

[1] Sapienza Università di Roma, Via Ariosto, 25, 00185 Rome, Italy
(degiacomo,demasellis)@dis.uniroma1.it
[2] University of Tartu, J. Liivi 2, 50409 Tartu, Estonia
f.m.maggi@ut.ee
[3] Free University of Bozen-Bolzano, Piazza Domenicani 3, 39100 Bolzano, Italy
montali@inf.unibz.it

Abstract. Runtime monitoring is one of the central tasks to provide operational
decision support to running business processes, and check on-the-fly whether they
comply with constraints and rules. We study runtime monitoring of properties
expressed in LTL on finite traces (LTL_f) and its extension LDL_f. LDL_f is a powerful logic that captures all monadic second order logic on finite traces, which
is obtained by combining regular expressions with LTL_f, adopting the syntax of
propositional dynamic logic (PDL). Interestingly, in spite of its greater expressivity, LDL_f has exactly the same computational complexity of LTL_f. We show that
LDL_f is able to capture, in the logic itself, not only the constraints to be monitored, but also the de-facto standard RV-LTL monitors. This makes it possible to
declaratively capture monitoring metaconstraints, i.e., constraints about the evolution of other constraints, and check them by relying on usual logical services
for temporal logics instead of ad-hoc algorithms. This, in turn, enables to flexibly monitor constraints depending on the monitoring state of other constraints,
e.g., "compensation" constraints that are only checked when others are detected
to be violated. In addition, we devise a direct translation of LDL_f formulas into
nondeterministic automata, avoiding to detour to Büchi automata or alternating
automata, and we use it to implement a monitoring plug-in for the PROM suite.

Keywords: Formal methods, runtime verification, declarative business processes, operational decision support, process monitoring, temporal logics.

1 Introduction

Runtime monitoring is one of the central tasks to provide *operational decision support*
[21] to running business processes, and check on-the-fly whether they comply with
constraints and rules. In order to provide well-founded and provably correct runtime
monitoring techniques, this area is usually rooted into that of *verification*, the branch of
formal analysis aiming at checking whether a system meets some property of interest.
Being the system dynamic, properties are usually expressed by making use of modal
operators accounting for the time.

Among all the temporal logics used in verification, Linear-time Temporal Logic
(LTL) is particularly suited for monitoring, as an actual system execution is indeed linear. However, the LTL semantics is given in terms of infinite traces, hence monitoring

S. Sadiq, P. Soffer, and H. Völzer (Eds.): BPM 2014, LNCS 8659, pp. 1–17, 2014.

must check whether the current trace is a prefix of an infinite trace, that will never be completed [7,2]. In several context, and in particular often in BPM, we can assume that the trace of the system is in fact finite [18]. For this reason, finite-trace variant of the LTL have been introduced. Here we use the logic LTL_f (LTL on finite traces), investigated in detail in [4], and at the base of one of the main declarative process modeling approaches: DECLARE [18,16,11]. Following [11], monitoring in LTL_f amounts to check whether the current execution belongs to the set of admissible *prefixes* for the traces of a given LTL_f formula φ. To achieve such a task, φ is usually first translated into a finite-state automaton for φ, which recognizes all those *finite* executions that satisfy φ.

Despite the presence of previous operational decision support techniques to monitoring LTL_f constraints over finite traces [11,12], two main challenges have not yet been tackled in a systematic way. First of all, several alternative semantics have been proposed to make LTL suitable for runtime verification (such as the de-facto standard RV monitor conditions [2]), but no comprehensive technique based on finite-state automata is available to accommodate them. On the one hand, runtime verification for such logics typically considers finite partial traces whose continuation is however infinite [2], with the consequence that the corresponding techniques detour to Büchi automata for building the monitors. On the other hand, the incorporation of such semantics in the BPM setting (where also continuations are finite) has only been tackled so far with effective but ad-hoc techniques (cf. the "coloring" of automata in [11] to support the RV conditions), without a corresponding formal underpinning.

A second, key challenge is the incorporation of advanced forms of monitoring, where some constraints become of interest only in specific, critical circumstances (such as the violation of other constraints). This is the basis for supporting monitoring of compensation constraints and the so-called contrary-to-duty obligations [20], i.e., obligations that are put in place only when other obligations have not been fulfilled. While this feature is considered to be a fundamental compliance monitoring functionality [10], it is still an open challenge, without any systematic approach able to support it at the level of the constraint specification language.

In this paper, we attack these two challenges by studying runtime monitoring of properties expressed in LTL_f and in its extension LDL_f [4]. LDL_f is a powerful logic that captures all monadic second order logic on finite traces, which is obtained by combining regular expressions with LTL_f, adopting the syntax of propositional dynamic logic (PDL). Interestingly, in spite of its greater expressivity, LDL_f has exactly the same computational complexity of LTL_f. We show that LDL_f is able to capture, in the logic itself, not only the usual LDL_f constraints to be monitored, but also the de-facto standard RV conditions. Indeed given an LDL_f formula φ, we show how to construct the LDL_f formulas that captures whether prefixes of φ satisfy the various RV conditions. This, in turn, makes it possible to declaratively capture *monitoring metaconstraints*, and check them by relying on usual logical services instead of ad-hoc algorithms. Metaconstraints provide a well-founded, declarative basis to specify and monitor constraints depending on the monitoring state of other constraints, such as "compensation" constraints that are only checked when others are violated.

Interestingly, in doing so we devise a direct translation of LDL_f (and hence of LTL_f) formulas into nondeterministic automata, which avoid the usual detour to Büchi automata. The technique is grounded on alternating automata (AFW), but it actually avoids also their introduction all together, and directly produces a standard non-deterministic finite-state automaton (NFA). Notably, such technique has been implemented and embedded into a monitoring plug-in for the PROM, which supports the check of LDL$_f$ constraints and metaconstraints.

2 LTL$_f$ and LDL$_f$

In this paper we will adopt the standard LTL and its variant LDL interpreted on finite runs.

LTL on finite traces, called LTL$_f$ [4], has exactly the same syntax as LTL on infinite traces [19]. Namely, given a set of $\mathcal{P}$ of propositional symbols, LTL$_f$ formulas are obtained through the following:

$$\varphi ::= \phi \mid \neg\varphi \mid \varphi_1 \wedge \varphi_2 \mid \varphi_1 \vee \varphi_2 \mid \bigcirc\varphi \mid \bullet\varphi \mid \Diamond\varphi \mid \Box\varphi \mid \varphi_1 \, \mathcal{U} \, \varphi_2$$

where ϕ is a propositional formuala over $\mathcal{P}$, $\bigcirc$ is the *next* operator, $\bullet$ is *weak next*, $\Diamond$ is *eventually*, $\Box$ is *always*, $\mathcal{U}$ is *until*.

It is known that LTL$_f$ is as expressive as First Order Logic over finite traces, so strictly less expressive than regular expressons which in turn are as expressive as Monadic Second Order logic over finite traces. On the other hand, regular expressions are a too low level formalism for expressing temporal specifications, since, for example, they miss a direct construct for negation and for conjunction [4].

To overcome this difficulties, in [4] *Linear Dynamic Logic of Finite Traces*, or LDL$_f$, has been proposed. This logic is as natural as LTL$_f$ but with the full expressive power of Monadic Second Order logic over finite traces. LDL$_f$ is obtained by merging LTL$_f$ with regular expression through the syntax of the well-know logic of programs PDL, *Propositional Dynamic Logic*, [8,9] but adopting a semantics based on finite traces. This logic is an adaptation of LDL, introduced in [22], which, like LTL, is interpreted over infinite traces.

Formally, LDL$_f$ formulas are built as follows:

$$\varphi ::= \phi \mid tt \mid f\!f \mid \neg\varphi \mid \varphi_1 \wedge \varphi_2 \mid \varphi_1 \wedge \varphi_2 \mid \langle\rho\rangle\varphi \mid [\rho]\varphi$$
$$\rho ::= \phi \mid \varphi? \mid \rho_1 + \rho_2 \mid \rho_1;\rho_2 \mid \rho^*$$

where ϕ is a propositional formula over $\mathcal{P}$; tt and $f\!f$ denote respectively the true and the false LDL$_f$ formula (not to be confused with the propositional formula $true$ and $false$); ρ denotes path expressions, which are regular expressions over propositional formulas ϕ with the addition of the test construct $\varphi?$ typical of PDL; and φ stand for LDL$_f$ formulas built by applying boolean connectives and the modal connectives $\langle\rho\rangle\varphi$ and $[\rho]\varphi$. In fact $[\rho]\varphi \equiv \neg\langle\rho\rangle\neg\varphi$.

Intuitively, $\langle\rho\rangle\varphi$ states that, from the current step in the trace, there exists an execution satisfying the regular expression ρ such that its last step satisfies φ. While $[\rho]\varphi$ states that, from the current step, all executions satisfying the regular expression ρ are such that their last step satisfies φ. Tests are used to insert into the execution path checks for satisfaction of additional LDL$_f$ formulas.

As for LTL$_f$, the semantics of LDL$_f$ is given in terms of *finite traces* denoting a finite, possibly empty, sequence of consecutive steps in the trace, i.e., finite words π over the alphabet of $2^{\mathcal{P}}$, containing all possible propositional interpretations of the propositional symbols in $\mathcal{P}$. We denote by n the length of the trace, and by $\pi(i)$ the i-th step in the trace. If $i > n$, then $\pi(i)$ is undefined. We denote by $\pi(i, j)$ the segment of the trace π starting at i-th step end ending at the j-th step (included). If i or j are out of range wrt the trace then $\pi(i, j)$ is undefined, except $\pi(i, i) = \epsilon$ (i.e., the empty trace).

The semantics of LDL$_f$ is as follows: an LDL$_f$ formula φ *is true* at a step i, in symbols $\pi, i \models \varphi$, as follows:

- $\pi, i \models tt$
- $\pi, i \not\models ff$
- $\pi, i \models \phi$ iff $1 \le i \le n$ and $\pi(i) \models \phi$ (ϕ propositional).
- $\pi, i \models \neg\varphi$ iff $\pi, i \not\models \varphi$.
- $\pi, i \models \varphi_1 \wedge \varphi_2$ iff $\pi, i \models \varphi_1$ and $\pi, i \models \varphi_2$.
- $\pi, i \models \varphi_1 \vee \varphi_2$ iff $\pi, i \models \varphi_1$ or $\pi, i \models \varphi_2$.
- $\pi, i \models \langle\rho\rangle\varphi$ iff for some j we have $\pi(i, j) \in \mathcal{L}(\rho)$ and $\pi, j \models \varphi$.
- $\pi, i \models [\rho]\varphi$ iff for all j such that $\pi(i, j) \in \mathcal{L}(\rho)$ we have $\pi, j \models \varphi$.

The relation $\pi(i, j) \in \mathcal{L}(\rho)$ is defined inductively as follows:

- $\pi(i, j) \in \mathcal{L}(\phi)$ if $j = i + 1 \le n$ and $\pi(i) \models \phi$ (ϕ propositional)
- $\pi(i, j) \in \mathcal{L}(\varphi?)$ if $j = i$ and $\pi, i \models \varphi$
- $\pi(i, j) \in \mathcal{L}(\rho_1 + \rho_2)$ if $\pi(i, j) \in \mathcal{L}(\rho_1)$ or $\pi(i, j) \in \mathcal{L}(\rho_2)$
- $\pi(i, j) \in \mathcal{L}(\rho_1; \rho_2)$ if exists k s.t. $\pi(i, k) \in \mathcal{L}(\rho_1)$ and $\pi(k, j) \in \mathcal{L}(\rho_2)$
- $\pi(i, j) \in \mathcal{L}(\rho^*)$ if $j = i$ or exists k s.t. $\pi(i, k) \in \mathcal{L}(\rho)$ and $\pi(k, j) \in \mathcal{L}(\rho^*)$

Observe that for $i > n$, hence e.g., for $\pi = \epsilon$ we get:

- $\pi, i \models tt$
- $\pi, i \not\models ff$
- $\pi, i \not\models \phi$ (ϕ propositional).
- $\pi, i \models \neg\varphi$ iff $\pi, i \not\models \varphi$.
- $\pi, i \models \varphi_1 \wedge \varphi_2$ iff $\pi, i \models \varphi_1$ and $\pi, i \models \varphi_2$.
- $\pi, i \models \varphi_1 \vee \varphi_2$ iff $\pi, i \models \varphi_1$ or $\pi, i \models \varphi_2$.
- $\pi, i \models \langle\rho\rangle\varphi$ iff $\pi(i, i) \in \mathcal{L}(\rho)$ and $\pi, i \models \varphi$.
- $\pi, i \models [\rho]\varphi$ iff $\pi(i, i) \in \mathcal{L}(\rho)$ implies $\pi, i \models \varphi$.

The relation $\pi(i, i) \in \mathcal{L}(\rho)$ with $i > n$ is defined inductively as follows:

- $\pi(i, i) \notin \mathcal{L}(\phi)$ (ϕ propositional)
- $\pi(i, i) \in \mathcal{L}(\varphi?)$ if $\pi, i \models \varphi$
- $\pi(i, i) \in \mathcal{L}(\rho_1 + \rho_2)$ if $\pi(i, i) \in \mathcal{L}(\rho_1)$ or $\pi(i, i) \in \mathcal{L}(\rho_2)$
- $\pi(i, i) \in \mathcal{L}(\rho_1; \rho_2)$ if $\pi(i, i) \in \mathcal{L}(\rho_1)$ and $\pi(i, i) \in \mathcal{L}(\rho_2)$
- $\pi(i, i) \in \mathcal{L}(\rho^*)$

Notice we have the usual boolean equivalences such as $\varphi_1 \vee \varphi_2 \equiv \neg\varphi_1 \wedge \neg\varphi_2$, furthermore we have that: $\phi \equiv \langle\phi\rangle tt$, and $[\rho]\varphi \equiv \neg\langle\rho\rangle\neg\varphi$. It is also convenient to introduce the following abbreviations:

- $end = [true?]ff$ that denotes that the traces is been completed (the remaining trace is ϵ the empty one)
- $last = \langle true\rangle end$, which denotes the last step of the trace.

It easy to encode LTL$_f$ into LDL$_f$: it suffice to observe that we can express the various LTL$_f$ operators by recursively applying the following translations:

- $\bigcirc\varphi$ translates to $\langle true\rangle\varphi$;
- $\bullet\varphi$ translates to $\neg\langle true\rangle\neg\varphi$ $= [true]\varphi$ (notice that $\bullet a$ is translated into $[true][\neg a]ff$, since a is equivalent to $\langle a\rangle tt$);
- $\Diamond\varphi$ translates to $\langle true^*\rangle\varphi$;
- $\Box\varphi$ translates to $[true^*]\varphi$ (notice that $\Box a$ is translated into $[true^*][\neg a]ff$);
- $\varphi_1 \mathcal{U} \varphi_2$ translates to $\langle(\varphi_1?; true)^*\rangle\varphi_2$.

It is also easy to encode regular expressions, used as a specification formalism for traces into LDL$_f$: ρ translates to $\langle \rho \rangle end$.

We say that a trace satisfies an LTL$_f$ or LDL$_f$ formula φ, written $\pi \models \varphi$ if $\pi, 1 \models \varphi$. (Note that if π is the empty trace, and hence 1 is out of range, still the notion of $\pi, 1 \models \varphi$ is well defined). Also sometimes we denote by $\mathcal{L}(\varphi)$ the set of traces that satisfy φ: $\mathcal{L}(\varphi) = \{\pi \mid \pi \models \varphi\}$.

3   LDL$_f$ Automaton

We can associate with each LDL$_f$ formula φ an NFA A_φ (exponential in the size of the formula) that accepts exactly those traces that make φ true. Here, we provide a simple direct algorithm for computing the NFA corresponding to an LDL$_f$ formula. The correctness of the algorithm is based on the fact that (*i*) we can associate each LDL$_f$ formula φ with a polynomial *alternating automaton on words* (AFW) A_φ which accepts exactly the traces that make φ true [4], and (*ii*) every AFW can be transformed into an NFA, see, e.g., [4]. However, to formulate the algorithm we do not need these notions, but we can work directly on the LDL$_f$ formula. In order to proceed with the construction of the AFW A_φ, we put LDL$_f$ formulas φ in negation normal form $nnf(\varphi)$ by exploiting equivalences and pushing negation inside as much as possible, until is eliminated except in propositional formulas. Note that computing $nnf(\varphi)$ can be done in linear time. In other words, wlog, we consider as syntax for LDL$_f$ the one in the previous section but without negation. Then we define an auxiliary function δ that takes an LDL$_f$ formula ψ (in negation normal form) and a propositional interpretation Π for $\mathcal{P}$ (including *last*), or a special symbol ϵ, returning a positive boolean formula whose atoms are (quoted) ψ subformulas.

$$\delta("tt", \Pi) = true$$

$$\delta("ff", \Pi) = false$$

$$\delta("\phi", \Pi) = \begin{cases} true \text{ if } \Pi \models \phi \\ false \text{ if } \Pi \not\models \phi \end{cases} \quad (\phi \text{ propositional})$$

$$\delta("\varphi_1 \wedge \varphi_2", \Pi) = \delta("\varphi_1", \Pi) \wedge \delta("\varphi_2", \Pi)$$

$$\delta("\varphi_1 \vee \varphi_2", \Pi) = \delta("\varphi_1", \Pi) \vee \delta("\varphi_2", \Pi)$$

$$\delta("\langle \phi \rangle \varphi", \Pi) = \begin{cases} "\varphi" \text{ if } last \notin \Pi \text{ and } \Pi \models \phi \quad (\phi \text{ propositional}) \\ \delta("\varphi", \epsilon) \text{ if } last \in \Pi \text{ and } \Pi \models \phi \\ false \text{ if } \Pi \not\models \phi \end{cases}$$

$$\delta("\langle \psi? \rangle \varphi", \Pi) = \delta("\psi", \Pi) \wedge \delta("\varphi", \Pi)$$

$$\delta("\langle \rho_1 + \rho_2 \rangle \varphi", \Pi) = \delta("\langle \rho_1 \rangle \varphi", \Pi) \vee \delta("\langle \rho_2 \rangle \varphi", \Pi)$$

$$\delta("\langle \rho_1; \rho_2 \rangle \varphi", \Pi) = \delta("\langle \rho_1 \rangle \langle \rho_2 \rangle \varphi", \Pi)$$

$$\delta("\langle \rho^* \rangle \varphi", \Pi) = \begin{cases} \delta("\varphi", \Pi) & \text{if } \rho \text{ is test-only} \\ \delta("\varphi", \Pi) \vee \delta("\langle \rho \rangle \langle \rho^* \rangle \varphi", \Pi) & \text{o/w} \end{cases}$$

$$\delta("[\phi]\varphi", \Pi) = \begin{cases} "\varphi" \text{ if } last \notin \Pi \text{ and } \Pi \models \phi \quad (\phi \text{ propositional}) \\ \delta("\varphi", \epsilon) \text{ if } last \in \Pi \text{ and } \Pi \models \phi \quad (\phi \text{ propositional}) \\ true \text{ if } \Pi \not\models \phi \end{cases}$$

$$\delta("[\psi?]\varphi", \Pi) = \delta("nnf(\neg\psi)", \Pi) \vee \delta("\varphi", \Pi)$$

```
1: algorithm LDLf2NFA ()
2: input LTLf formula φ
3: output NFA Aφ = (2^P, S, {s0}, ϱ, {sf})
4: s0 ← {"φ"}                                              ▷ single initial state
5: sf ← ∅                                                  ▷ single final state
6: S ← {s0, sf}, ϱ ← ∅
7: while (S or ϱ change) do
8:    if (q ∈ S and q' ⊨ ⋀("ψ"∈q) δ("ψ", Θ)) then
9:       S ← S ∪ {q'}                                      ▷ update set of states
10:      ϱ ← ϱ ∪ {(q, Θ, q')}                              ▷ update transition relation
```

Fig. 1. NFA construction

$$\delta("[\rho_1 + \rho_2]\varphi", \Pi) = \delta("[\rho_1]\varphi", \Pi) \wedge \delta("[\rho_2]\varphi", \Pi)$$
$$\delta("[\rho_1; \rho_2]\varphi", \Pi) = \delta("[\rho_1][\rho_2]\varphi", \Pi)$$
$$\delta("[\rho^*]\varphi", \Pi) = \begin{cases} \delta("\varphi", \Pi) & \text{if } \rho \text{ is test-only} \\ \delta("\varphi", \Pi) \wedge \delta("[\rho][\rho^*]\varphi", \Pi) & \text{o/w} \end{cases}$$

where $\delta("\varphi", \epsilon)$, i.e., the interpretation of LDLf formula in the case the (remaining fragment of the) trace is empty, is defined as follows:

$$\delta("tt", \epsilon) = true$$
$$\delta("ff", \epsilon) = false$$
$$\delta("\phi", \epsilon) = false \quad (\phi \text{ propositional})$$
$$\delta("\varphi_1 \wedge \varphi_2", \epsilon) = \delta("\varphi_1", \epsilon) \wedge \delta("\varphi_2", \epsilon)$$
$$\delta("\varphi_1 \vee \varphi_2", \epsilon) = \delta("\varphi_1", \epsilon) \vee \delta("\varphi_2", \epsilon)$$
$$\delta("\langle\phi\rangle\varphi", \epsilon) = false \quad (\phi \text{ propositional})$$
$$\delta("\langle\psi?\rangle\varphi", \epsilon) = \delta("\psi", \epsilon) \wedge \delta("\varphi", \epsilon)$$
$$\delta("\langle\rho_1 + \rho_2\rangle\varphi", \epsilon) = \delta("\langle\rho_1\rangle\varphi", \epsilon) \vee \delta("\langle\rho_2\rangle\varphi", \epsilon)$$
$$\delta("\langle\rho_1; \rho_2\rangle\varphi", \epsilon) = \delta("\langle\rho_1\rangle\langle\rho_2\rangle\varphi", \epsilon)$$
$$\delta("\langle\rho^*\rangle\varphi", \epsilon) = \delta("\varphi", \epsilon)$$
$$\delta("[\phi]\varphi", \epsilon) = true \quad (\phi \text{ propositional})$$
$$\delta("[\psi?]\varphi", \epsilon) = \delta("nnf(\neg\psi)", \epsilon) \vee \delta("\varphi", \epsilon)$$
$$\delta("[\rho_1 + \rho_2]\varphi", \epsilon) = \delta("[\rho_1]\varphi", \epsilon) \wedge \delta("[\rho_2]\varphi", \epsilon)$$
$$\delta("[\rho_1; \rho_2]\varphi", \epsilon) = \delta("[\rho_1][\rho_2]\varphi", \epsilon)$$
$$\delta("[\rho^*]\varphi", \epsilon) = \delta("\varphi", \epsilon)$$

Notice also that for ϕ propositional, $\delta("\phi", \Pi) = \delta("\langle\phi\rangle tt", \Pi)$ and $\delta("\phi", \epsilon) = \delta("\langle\phi\rangle tt", \epsilon)$, as a consequence of the equivalence $\phi \equiv \langle\phi\rangle tt$.

Using the auxiliary function δ we can build the NFA A_φ of an LDLf formula φ in a forward fashion as described in Figure 1), where: states of A_φ are sets of atoms (recall that each atom is quoted φ subformulas) to be interpreted as a conjunction; the empty conjunction $\emptyset$ stands for $true$; Θ is either a propositional interpretation Π over $\mathcal{P}$ or the empty trace ϵ (this gives rise to epsilon transition either to true or false) and q' is a set of quoted subformulas of φ that denotes a minimal interpretation such that $q' \models \bigwedge_{("\psi" \in q)} \delta("\psi", \Theta)$. (Note: we do not need to get all q such that $q' \models \bigwedge_{("\psi" \in q)} \delta("\psi", \Theta)$, but only the minimal ones.) Notice that trivially we have $(\emptyset, a, \emptyset) \in \varrho$ for every $a \in \Sigma$.

The algorithm LDL$_f$2NFA terminates in at most exponential number of steps, and generates a set of states $\mathcal{S}$ whose size is at most exponential in the size of φ.

Theorem 1. *Let φ be an* LDL$_f$ *formula and A_φ the* NFA *constructed as above. Then $\pi \models \varphi$ iff $\pi \in \mathcal{L}(A_\varphi)$ for every finite trace π.*

Proof (sketch). Given a LDL$_f$ formula φ, δ grounded on the subformulas of φ becomes the transition function of the AFW, with initial state $"\varphi"$ and no final states, corresponding to φ [4]. Then LDL$_f$2NFA essentially transforms the AFW into a NFA. □

Notice that above we have assumed to have a special proposition $last \in \mathcal{P}$. If we want to remove such an assumption, we can easily transform the obtained automaton $A_\varphi = (2^\mathcal{P}, \mathcal{S}, \{"\varphi"\}, \varrho, \{\emptyset\})$ into the new automaton

$$A'_\varphi = (2^{\mathcal{P}-\{last\}}, \mathcal{S} \cup \{ended\}, \{"\varphi"\}, \varrho', \{\emptyset, ended\})$$

where: $(q, \Pi', q') \in \varrho'$ iff $(q, \Pi', q') \in \varrho$, or $(q, \Pi' \cup \{last\}, true) \in \varrho$ and $q' = ended$.

It is easy to see that the NFA obtained can be built on-the-fly while checking for nonemptiness, hence we have:

Theorem 2. *Satisfiability of an* LDL$_f$ *formula can be checked in PSPACE by nonemptiness of A_φ (or A'_φ).*

Considering that it is known that satisfiability in LDL$_f$ is a PSPACE-complete problem, we can conclude that the proposed construction is optimal wrt computational complexity for satisfiability, as well as for validity and logical implication which are linearly reducible to satisfiability in LDL$_f$ (see [4] for details).

4 Run-time Monitoring

From an high-level perspective, the monitoring problem amounts to observe an evolving system execution and to report the violation or satisfaction of properties of interest at the earliest possible time. As the system progresses, its execution trace increases, and at each step the monitor checks whether the trace seen so far conforms to the properties, by considering that the execution can still continue. This evolving aspect has a significant impact on the monitoring output: at each step, indeed, the outcome may have a degree of uncertainty due to the fact that future executions are yet unknown.

Several variant of monitoring semantics have been proposed (see [2] for a survey). In this paper we adopt the semantics in [11], which is basically the finite-trace variant of the RV semantics in [2]: given a LTL$_f$ or LDL$_f$ formula φ, when the system evolves, the monitor returns one among the following truth values:

– $[\varphi]_{RV} = temp\_true$, meaning that the current execution trace *temporarily satisfies* φ, i.e., it is currently compliant with φ, but a possible system future prosecution may lead to falsify φ;

- $[\varphi]_{RV} = temp\_false$, meaning that the current trace *temporarily falsify* φ, i.e., φ is not current compliant with φ, but a possible system future prosecution may lead to satisfy φ;
- $[\varphi]_{RV} = true$, meaning that the current trace *satisfies* φ and it will always do, no matter how it proceeds;
- $[\varphi]_{RV} = false$, meaning that the current trace *falsifies* φ and it will always do, no matter how it proceeds.

The first two conditions are unstable because they may change into any other value as the system progresses. This reflects the general unpredictability of system possible executions. Conversely, the other two truth values are stable since, once outputted, they will not change anymore. Observe that a stable truth value can be reached in two different situations: *(i)* when the system execution terminates; *(ii)* when the formula that is being monitored can be fully evaluated by observing a partial trace only. The first case is indeed trivial, as when the execution ends, there are no possible future evolutions and hence it is enough to evaluate the finite (and now complete) trace seen so far according to the LDL$_f$ semantics. In the second case, instead, it is irrelevant whether the systems continues its execution or not, since some LDL$_f$ properties, such as eventualities or safety properties, can be fully evaluated as soon as something happens, e.g., when the eventuality is verified or the safety requirement is violated. Notice also that when a stable value is outputted, the monitoring analysis can be stopped.

From a more theoretical viewpoint, given an LDL$_f$ property φ, the monitor looks at the trace seen so far, assesses if it is a *prefix* of a complete trace not yet completed, and categorizes it according to its potential for satisfying or violating φ in the future. We call a prefix *possibly good* for an LDL$_f$ formula φ if there exists an extension of it which satisfies φ. More precisely, given an LDL$_f$ formula φ, we define the set of *possibly good prefixes for* $\mathcal{L}(\varphi)$ as the set

$$\mathcal{L}_{poss\_good}(\varphi) = \{\pi \mid \exists \pi'.\pi\pi' \in \mathcal{L}(\varphi)\} \tag{1}$$

Prefixes for which every possible extension satisfies φ are instead called *necessarily good*. More precisely, given an LDL$_f$ formula φ, we define the set of *necessarily good prefixes for* $\mathcal{L}(\varphi)$ as the set

$$\mathcal{L}_{nec\_good}(\varphi) = \{\pi \mid \forall \pi'.\pi\pi' \in \mathcal{L}(\varphi)\}. \tag{2}$$

The set of *necessarily bad prefixes* $\mathcal{L}_{nec\_bad}(\varphi)$ can be defined analogously as

$$\mathcal{L}_{nec\_bad}(\varphi) = \{\pi \mid \forall \pi'.\pi\pi' \notin \mathcal{L}(\varphi)\}. \tag{3}$$

Observe that the necessarily bad prefixes for φ are the necessarily good prefixes for $\neg\varphi$, i.e., $\mathcal{L}_{nec\_bad}(\varphi) = \mathcal{L}_{nec\_good}(\neg\varphi)$.

Using this language theoretic notions, we can provide a precise characterization of the semantics four standard monitoring evaluation functions [11].

Proposition 1. *Let φ be an* LDL$_f$ *formula and π a trace. Then:*
- $\pi \models [\varphi]_{RV} = temp\_true$ *iff* $\pi \in \mathcal{L}(\varphi) \setminus \mathcal{L}_{nec\_good}(\varphi)$;
- $\pi \models [\varphi]_{RV} = temp\_false$ *iff* $\pi \in \mathcal{L}(\neg\varphi) \setminus \mathcal{L}_{nec\_bad}(\varphi)$;
- $\pi \models [\varphi]_{RV} = true$ *iff* $\pi \in \mathcal{L}_{nec\_good}(\varphi)$;
- $\pi \models [\varphi]_{RV} = false$ *iff* $\pi \in \mathcal{L}_{nec\_bad}(\varphi)$.

Proof (sketch). Immediate from the definitions in [11] and the language theoretic definitions above. □

We close this section by exploiting the language theoretic notions to better understand the relationships between the various kinds of prefixes. We start by observing that, the set of all finite words over the alphabet $2^{\mathcal{P}}$ is the union of the language of φ and its complement $\mathcal{L}(\varphi) \cup \mathcal{L}(\neg\varphi) = (2^{\mathcal{P}})^*$. Also, any language and its complement are disjoint $\mathcal{L}(\varphi) \cap \mathcal{L}(\neg\varphi) = \emptyset$.

Since from the definition of possibly good prefixes we have $\mathcal{L}(\varphi) \subseteq \mathcal{L}_{poss\_good}(\varphi)$ and $\mathcal{L}(\neg\varphi) \subseteq \mathcal{L}_{poss\_good}(\neg\varphi)$, we also have that $\mathcal{L}_{poss\_good}(\varphi) \cup \mathcal{L}_{poss\_good}(\neg\varphi) = (2^{\mathcal{P}})^*$. Also from the definition it is easy to see that $\mathcal{L}_{poss\_good}(\varphi) \cap \mathcal{L}_{poss\_good}(\neg\varphi) = \{\pi \mid \exists\pi'.\pi\pi' \in \mathcal{L}(\varphi) \wedge \exists\pi''.\pi\pi'' \in \mathcal{L}(\neg\varphi)\}$ meaning that the set of possibly good prefixes for φ and the set of possibly good prefixes for $\neg\varphi$ do intersect, and in such an intersection are paths that can be extended to satisfy φ but can also be extended to satisfy $\neg\varphi$. It is also easy to see that $\mathcal{L}(\varphi) = \mathcal{L}_{poss\_good}(\varphi) \setminus \mathcal{L}(\neg\varphi)$.

Turning to necessarily good prefixes and necessarily bad prefixes, it is easy to see that $\mathcal{L}_{nec\_good}(\varphi) = \mathcal{L}_{poss\_good}(\varphi) \setminus \mathcal{L}_{poss\_good}(\neg\varphi)$, that $\mathcal{L}_{nec\_bad}(\varphi) = \mathcal{L}_{poss\_good}(\neg\varphi) \setminus \mathcal{L}_{poss\_good}(\varphi)$, and also that $\subseteq \mathcal{L}(\varphi)$ and $\mathcal{L}_{nec\_good}(\varphi) \not\subseteq \mathcal{L}(\neg\varphi)$.

Interestingly, necessarily good, necessarily bad, possibly good prefixes partition all finite traces. Namely

Proposition 2. *The set of all traces* $(2^{\mathcal{P}})^*$ *can be partitioned into*

$$\mathcal{L}_{nec\_good}(\varphi) \qquad \mathcal{L}_{poss\_good}(\varphi) \cap \mathcal{L}_{poss\_good}(\neg\varphi) \qquad \mathcal{L}_{nec\_bad}(\varphi)$$

such that $\mathcal{L}_{nec\_good}(\varphi) \cup (\mathcal{L}_{poss\_good}(\varphi) \cap \mathcal{L}_{poss\_good}(\neg\varphi)) \cup \mathcal{L}_{nec\_bad}(\varphi) = (2^{\mathcal{P}})^*$
$\mathcal{L}_{nec\_good}(\varphi) \cap (\mathcal{L}_{poss\_good}(\varphi) \cap \mathcal{L}_{poss\_good}(\neg\varphi)) \cap \mathcal{L}_{nec\_bad}(\varphi) = \emptyset$.

Proof (sketch). Follows from the definitions of the necessarily good, necessarily bad, possibly good prefixes of $\mathcal{L}(\varphi)$ and $\mathcal{L}(\neg\varphi)$. □

5 Runtime Monitors in LDL$_f$

As discussed in the previous section the core issue in monitoring is prefix recognition. LTL$_f$ is not expressive enough to talk about prefixes of its own formulas. Roughly speaking, given a LTL$_f$ formula, the language of its possibly good prefixes cannot be in general described as an LTL$_f$ formula. For such a reason, building a monitor usually requires direct manipulation of the automaton for the formula.

LDL$_f$ instead can capture any nondeterministic automata as a formula, and it has the capability of expressing properties on prefixes. We can exploit such an extra expressivity to capture the monitoring condition in a direct and elegant way. We start by showing how to construct formulas representing (the language of) prefixes of other formulas, and then we exploit them in the context of monitoring.

More precisely, given an LDL$_f$ formula φ, it is possible to express the language $\mathcal{L}_{possgood}(\varphi)$ with an LDL$_f$ formula φ'. Such a formula is obtained in two steps.

Lemma 1. *Given a LDL$_f$ formula φ, there exists a regular expression* pref$_\varphi$ *such that* $\mathcal{L}(\text{pref}_\varphi) = \mathcal{L}_{poss\_good}(\varphi)$.

Proof (sketch). The proof is constructive. We can build the NFA A for φ following the procedure described in Section 3. We then set as final all states of A from which there exists a path to a final state. This new finite state machine $A_{poss\_good}(\varphi)$ is such that $\mathcal{L}(A_{poss\_good}(\varphi)) = \mathcal{L}_{poss\_good}(\varphi)$. Since NFA are exactly as expressive as regular expressions, we can translate $A_{poss\_good}(\varphi)$ to a regular expression pref_φ. $\quad\square$

Given that LDL$_f$ is as expressive as regular expression (cf. [4]), we can translate pref_φ into an equivalent LDL$_f$ formula, as the following states.

Theorem 3. *Given a* LDL$_f$ *formula* φ,

$$\pi \in \mathcal{L}_{poss\_good}(\varphi) \text{ iff } \pi \models \langle \text{pref}_\varphi \rangle end$$
$$\pi \in \mathcal{L}_{nec\_good}(\varphi) \text{ iff } \pi \models \langle \text{pref}_\varphi \rangle end \wedge \neg\langle \text{pref}_{\neg\varphi} \rangle end$$

Proof (sketch). Any regular expression ρ, and hence any regular language, can be captured in LDL$_f$ as $\langle \rho \rangle end$. Hence the language $\mathcal{L}_{poss\_good}(\varphi)$ can be captured by $\langle \text{pref}_\varphi \rangle end$ and the language $\mathcal{L}_{nec\_good}(\varphi)$ which is equivalent $\mathcal{L}_{poss\_good}(\varphi) \setminus \mathcal{L}_{poss\_good}(\neg\varphi)$ can be captured by $\langle \text{pref}_\varphi \rangle end \wedge \neg\langle \text{pref}_{\neg\varphi} \rangle end$. $\quad\square$

In other words, given a LDL$_f$ formula φ, formula $\varphi' = \langle \text{pref}_\varphi \rangle end$ is a LDL$_f$ formula such that $\mathcal{L}(\varphi') = \mathcal{L}_{poss\_good}(\varphi)$. Similarly for $\mathcal{L}_{nec\_good}(\varphi)$.

Exploiting this result, and the results in Proposition 1, we reduce runtime monitoring to the standard evaluation of LDL$_f$ formulas over a (partial) trace. Formally:

Theorem 4. *Let π be a (typically partial) trace. The following equivalences hold:*
- $\pi \models [\varphi]_{RV} = temp\_true$ *iff* $\pi \models \varphi \wedge \langle \text{pref}_{\neg\varphi} \rangle end$;
- $\pi \models [\varphi]_{RV} = temp\_false$ *iff* $\pi \models \neg\varphi \wedge \langle \text{pref}_\varphi \rangle end$;
- $\pi \models [\varphi]_{RV} = true$ *iff* $\langle \text{pref}_\varphi \rangle end \wedge \neg\langle \text{pref}_{\neg\varphi} \rangle end$;
- $\pi \models [\varphi]_{RV} = false$ *iff* $\langle \text{pref}_{\neg\varphi} \rangle end \wedge \neg\langle \text{pref}_\varphi \rangle end$.

Proof (sketch). Follows from Proposition 1 and Theorem 3 using the language theoretic equivalences discussed in Secton 4. $\quad\square$

6 Monitoring Declare Constraints and Metaconstraints

We now ground our monitoring approach to the case of DECLARE monitoring. DE-CLARE[1] is a language and framework for the declarative, constraint-based modelling of processes and services. A thorough treatment of constraint-based processes can be found in [17,14]. As a modelling language, DECLARE takes a complementary approach to that of classical, imperative process modeling, in which all allowed control-flows among tasks must be explicitly represented, and every other execution trace is implicitly considered as forbidden. Instead of this procedural and "closed" approach, DECLARE has a declarative, "open" flavor: the agents responsible for the process execution can freely choose how to perform the involved tasks, provided that the resulting execution trace complies with the modeled business constraints. This is the reason why, alongside traditional control-flow constraints such as sequence (called in DECLARE *chain succession*), DECLARE supports a plethora of peculiar constraints that do not impose specific temporal orderings, or that explicitly account with negative information, i.e., prohibition of task execution.

---

[1] http://www.win.tue.nl/declare/

Given a set $\mathcal{P}$ of tasks, a DECLARE model is a set $\mathcal{C}$ of LTL_f (and hence LDL_f) constraints over $\mathcal{P}$, used to restrict the allowed execution traces. Among all possible LTL_f constraints, some specific *patterns* have been singled out as particularly meaningful for expressing DECLARE processes, taking inspiration from [6]. Such patterns are grouped into four families: *(i) existence* (unary) constraints, stating that the target task must/cannot be executed (a certain amount of times); *(ii) choice* (binary) constraints, modeling choice of execution; *(iii) relation* (binary) constraints, modeling that whenever the source task is executed, then the target task must also be executed (possibly with additional requirements); *(iv) negation* (binary) constraints, modeling that whenever the source task is executed, then the target task is prohibited (possibly with additional restrictions). Table 1 reports some of these patterns.

Example 1. Consider a fragment of a purchase order process, where we consider three key business constraints. First, an order can be closed at most once. In DECLARE, this can be tackled with a absence 2 constraint, visually and formally represented as:

$$\boxed{\overset{0..1}{\text{close order}}} \qquad \varphi_{close} = \neg\Diamond(\text{close order} \wedge \bigcirc\Diamond\text{close order})$$

Second, an order can be canceled only until it is closed. This can be captured by a negation succession constraint, which states that after the order is closed, it cannot be canceled anymore:

$$\boxed{\text{close order}}\bullet\!\!-\!\!\|\!\blacktriangleright\!\!\boxed{\text{cancel order}} \qquad \varphi_{canc} = \Box(\text{close order} \rightarrow \neg\Diamond\text{cancel order})$$

Finally, after the order is closed, it becomes possible to do supplementary payments, for various reasons (e.g., to speed up the delivery of the order).

$$\boxed{\text{close order}}\!-\!\!\!\blacktriangleright\!\!\boxed{\text{pay suppl}} \qquad \varphi_{pay} = (\neg\text{pay suppl}\,\mathcal{U}\,\text{close order}) \vee \neg\Diamond\text{close order}$$

Beside modeling and enactment of constraint-based processes, previous works have also focused on runtime verification of DECLARE models. A family of DECLARE monitoring approaches rely on the original LTL_f formalization of DECLARE, and employ corresponding automata-based techniques to track running process instances and check whether they satisfy the modeled constraints or not [11,12]. Such techniques have been in particular used for:

- monitoring single DECLARE constraints so as to provide a fine-grained feedback; this is done by adopting the RV semantics for LTL_f, and tracking the evolution each constraint through the four RV truth values.
- Monitoring the global DECLARE model by considering all its constraints together (i.e., constructing a DFA for the conjunction of all constraints); this is important for computing the *early detection* of violations, i.e., violations that cannot be explicitly found in the execution trace collected so far, but that cannot be avoided in the future.

We now discuss how LDL_f can be adopted for monitoring DECLARE constraints, with a twofold advantage. First, as shown in Section 5, LDL_f is able to encode the RV semantics directly into the logic, without the need of introducing ad-hoc modifications in the corresponding standard logical services. Second, beside being able to reconstruct all the aforementioned monitoring techniques, our approach also provides a declarative, well-founded basis for monitoring metaconstraints, i.e., constraints that involve both the execution of tasks and the monitoring outcome obtained by checking other constraints.

Monitoring Declare Constraints with LDL$_f$. Since LDL$_f$ includes LTL$_f$, DECLARE constraints can be directly encoded in LDL$_f$ using their standard formalization [18,16]. Thanks to the translation into NFAs discussed in Section 3 (and, if needed, their determinization into corresponding DFAs), the obtained automaton can then be used to check whether a (partial) finite trace satisfies this constraint or not. This is not very effective, as the approach does not support the detection of fine-grained truth values as those of RV. By relying on Theorem 4, however, we can reuse the same technique, this time supporting all RV. In fact, by formalizing the good prefixes of each DECLARE pattern, we can immediately construct the four LDL$_f$ formulas that embed the different RV truth values, and check the current trace over each of the corresponding automata. Table 1 reports the good prefix characterization of some of the DECLARE patterns; it can be seamlessly extended to all other patterns as well.

Example 2. Let us consider the absence 2 constraint φ_{close} in Example 1. Following Table 1, its good prefix characterization is pref$_{\varphi_{close}}$ = $o^* + (o^*; \text{close order}; o^*)$, where o is a shortcut for all the tasks involved in the purchase order process but close order. This can be used to construct the four formulas mentioned in Theorem 4, which in turn provide the basis to produce, e.g., the following result:

	start	do "close order"	do "pay suppl."	do "close order"
0..1				
close order		*temp_true*		*false*

Observe that this baseline approach can be extended along a number of directions. For example, as shown in Table 1, the majority of DECLARE patterns does not cover all the four RV truth values. This is the case, e.g., of absence 2, which can never be evaluated to *true* (since it is always possible to continue the execution so as to perform a twice), nor to *temp_false* (the only way of violating the constraint is to perform a twice, and in this case it is not possible to "repair" to the violation anymore). This information can be used to restrict the generation of the automata only to those cases that are relevant to the constraint. Furthermore, it is possible to reconstruct exactly the approach in [11], where every state in the DFAs corresponding to the constraints to be monitored, is enriched with a "color" accounting for one of the four RV truth values. To do so, we have simply to combine the four DFAs generated for each constraint. This is possible because such DFAs are generated from formulas built on top of the good prefix characterization of the original formula, and hence they all produce the same automaton, but with different final states. In fact, this observation provides a formal justification to the correctness of the approach in [11].

Metaconstraints. Thanks to the ability of LDL$_f$ to directly encode into the logic DECLARE constraints but also their RV monitoring states, we can formalize metaconstraints that relate the RV truth values of different constraints. Intuitively, such metaconstraints allow one to capture that *we become interested in monitoring some constraint only when other constraints are evaluated to be in a certain RV truth value*. This, in turn, provides the basis to declaratively capture two classes of properties that are of central importance in the context of runtime verification:

- *Compensation constraints*, that is, constraints that should be enforced by the agents executing the process in the case other constraints are violated, i.e., are evaluated

Table 1. Some DECLARE constraints, together with their prefix characterization, minimal bad prefix charaterization, and possible RV states; for each constraint, o is a shortcut for "other tasks", i.e., tasks not involved in the constraint itself.

	NAME	NOTATION	pref	POSSIBLE RV STATES
EXISTENCE	Existence	a (1..*)	$(a+o)^*$	temp_false, true
EXISTENCE	Absence 2	a (0..1)	$o^* + (o^*; a; o^*)$	temp_true, false
CHOICE	Choice	a ◇ b	$(a+b+o)^*$	temp_false, true
CHOICE	Exclusive Choice	a ◆ b	$(a+o)^* + (b+o)^*$	temp_false, temp_true, false
RELATION	Resp. existence	a ●— b	$(a+b+o)^*$	temp_true, temp_false, true
RELATION	Coexistence	a ●—● b	$(a+b+o)^*$	temp_true, temp_false, true
RELATION	Response	a ●—▶ b	$(a+b+o)^*$	temp_true, temp_false
RELATION	Precedence	a —▶● b	$o^*; (a; (a+b+o)^*)^*$	temp_true, true, false
RELATION	Succession	a ●—▶● b	$o^*; (a; (a+b+o)^*)^*$	temp_true, temp_false, false
NEGATION	Not Coexistence	a ●—‖—● b	$(a+o)^* + (b+o)^*$	temp_true, false
NEGATION	Neg. Succession	a ●—‖▶● b	$(b+o)^*; (a+o)^*$	temp_true, false

to be *false*. Previous works have been tackled this issue through ad-hoc techniques, with no declarative counterpart [11,12].

- Recovery mechanisms resembling *contrary-to-duty obligations* in legal reasoning [20], i.e., obligations that are put in place only when other obligations are not met.

Technically, a generic form for metaconstraints is the pattern $\Phi_{pre} \to \Psi_{exp}$, where:

- Φ_{pre} is a boolean formula, whose atoms are membership assertions of the involved constraints to the RV truth values;
- Ψ_{exp} is a boolean formula whose atoms are the constraints to be enforced when Φ_{pre} evaluates to true.

This pattern can be used, for example, to state that whenever constraints c_1 and c_2 are permanently violated, then either constraint c_3 or c_4 have to be enforced. Observe that the metaconstraint so constructed is a standard LDL$_f$ formula. Hence, we can reapply Theorem 4 to it, getting four LDL$_f$ formulas that can be used to track the evolution of the metaconstraint among the four RV values.

Example 3. Consider the DECLARE constraints of Example 1. We want to enhance it with a compensation constraint stating that whenever φ_{canc} is violated (i.e., the order is canceled after it has been closed), then a supplement payment must be issued. This can be easily captured in LDL$_f$ as follows. First of all, we model the compensation constraint, which corresponds, in this case, to a standard existence constraint over the pay supplement task. Let φ_{dopay} denote the LDL$_f$ formalization of such a compensation constraint. Second, we capture the intended compensation behavior by using the following LDL$_f$ metaconstraint:

$$\{[\varphi_{canc}]_{RV} = false\} \to \varphi_{dopay}$$

which, leveraging Theorem 4, corresponds to the standard LDL$_f$ formula:

$$((\langle \mathsf{pref}_{\neg\varphi_{canc}}\rangle end \wedge \neg\langle \mathsf{pref}_{\varphi_{canc}}\rangle end) \to \varphi_{dopay}$$

A limitation of this form of metaconstraint is that the right-hand part Ψ_{exp} is monitored *from the beginning of the trace*. This is acceptable in many cases. E.g., in Example 1, it is ok if the user already paid a supplement before the order cancelation caused constraint φ_{canc} to be violated. In other situations, however, this is not satisfactory, because we would like to enforce the compensating behavior only *after* Φ_{pre} evaluates to true, e.g., after the violation of a given constraint has been detected. In general, we can extend the aforementioned metaconstraint pattern as follows: $\Phi_{pre} \to [\rho]\Psi_{exp}$, where ρ is a regular expression denoting the paths after which Ψ_{exp} is expected to be enforced.

By constructing ρ as the regular expression accounting for the paths that make Φ_{pre} true, we can then exploit this improved metaconstraint to express that Ψ_{exp} is expected to become true after all prefixes of the current trace that made Φ_{pre} true.

Example 4. We modify the compensation constraint of Example 3, so as to reflect that when a closed order is canceled (i.e., φ_{canc} is violated), then a supplement must be paid *afterwards*. This is captured by the following metaconstraint:

$$\{[\varphi_{canc}]RV = false\} \to [re_{\{[\varphi_{canc}]RV=false\}}]\varphi_{dopay}$$

where $re_{\{[\varphi_{canc}]=false\}}$ denotes the regular expression for the language $\mathcal{L}(\{[\varphi_{canc}] = false\}) = \mathcal{L}(\langle \mathsf{pref}_{\neg\varphi_{canc}}\rangle end \wedge \neg\langle \mathsf{pref}_{\varphi_{canc}}\rangle end)$. This regular expression describes all paths containing a violation for constraint φ_{canc}.

7 Implementation

The entire approach has been implemented as an *operational decision support (OS) provider* for the PROM 6 process mining framework[2]. PROM 6 provides a generic OS environment [23] that supports the interaction between an external workflow management system at runtime (producing events) and PROM. In particular, it provides an OS service that receives a stream of events from the external world, updates and orchestrates the registered OS providers implementing different types of online analysis to be applied on the stream, and reports the produced results back to the external world.

At the back-end of the plug-in, there is a software module specifically dedicated to the construction and manipulation of NFAs from LDL$_f$ formulas, concretely implementing the technique presented in Section 3. To manipulate regular expressions and automata, we used the fast, well-known library `dk.brics.automaton` [13].

Figure 2 shows a graphical representation of the evolution of constraints described in Example 1 and 4 of Section 6 when monitored using our operational support provider. Events are displayed on the horizontal axis, while the vertical axis shows the three constraints expressed as LDL$_f$ formulas, where the literals f, g and d respectively stand for tasks **close order**, **cancel order**, and **pay supplement**. Note that after the violation of the negation succession constraint a compensation meta-constraint is triggered to enforce that pay supplement is required to occur after the violation.

---

[2] http://www.promtools.org/prom6/

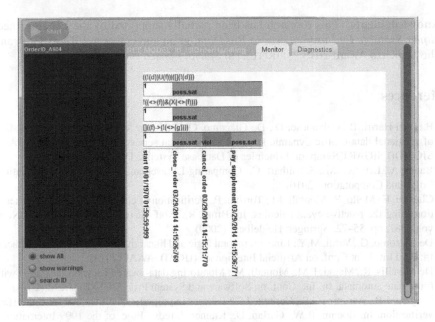

Fig. 2. Screenshot of our operational support provider's output.

8   Conclusion

We have proposed an effective approach for monitoring dynamic (business) constraints on finite traces that represent the executions of running process instances. Our contribution can be seen as an extension of the declarative process specification approach at the basis of DECLARE, in which we tackle the monitoring problem with a more powerful temporal logic: LDL$_f$, i.e., Monadic Second Order logic over finite traces, instead of LTL$_f$, i.e., First Order logic over finite traces. Notably, this declarative approach to monitoring seamlessly supports the specification and monitoring of metaconstraints, i.e., constraints that do not only predicate about the dynamics of task executions, but also about the truth values of other constraints. We have grounded this approach on DECLARE itself, showing how to declaratively specify compensation constraints.

The next step will be to incorporate recovery mechanisms into the approach, in particular providing a formal underpinning to the ad-hoc recovery mechanisms studied in [11]. Furthermore, we intend to extend our approach to *data-aware* business constraints [1,5], mixing temporal operators with first-order queries over the data attached to the monitored events. This setting has been studied using the Event Calculus [15], also considering some specific forms of compensation in DECLARE [3]. However, the resulting approach can only query the partial trace accumulated so far, and not reason upon its possible future continuations, as automata-based techniques are able to do. To extend the approach presented here to the case of data-aware business constraints, we will build on recent, interesting decidability results for the static verification of data-aware business processes against sophisticated variants of first-order temporal logics [1].

Acknowledgments. This research has been partially supported by the EU IP project *Optique: Scalable End-user Access to Big Data*, grant agreement n. FP7-318338, and by the Sapienza Award 2013 "SPIRITLETS: *Spiritlet-based smart spaces*".

References

1. Bagheri Hariri, B., Calvanese, D., De Giacomo, G., Deutsch, A., Montali, M.: Verification of relational data-centric dynamic systems with external services. In: 32nd ACM SIGACT SIGMOD SIGART Symp. on Principles of Database Systems, PODS (2013)
2. Bauer, A., Leucker, M., Schallhart, C.: Comparing LTL semantics for runtime verification. Logic and Computation (2010)
3. Chesani, F., Mello, P., Montali, M., Torroni, P.: Verification of choreographies during execution using the reactive event calculus. In: Bruni, R., Wolf, K. (eds.) WS-FM 2008. LNCS, vol. 5387, pp. 55–72. Springer, Heidelberg (2009)
4. De Giacomo, G., Vardi, M.Y.: Linear temporal logic and linear dynamic logic on finite traces. In: 23rd Int. Joint Conf. on Artificial Intelligence (IJCAI). AAAI (2013)
5. De Masellis, R., Maggi, F.M., Montali, M.: Monitoring data-aware business constraints with finite state automata. In: Int. Conf. on Software and System Proc. (ICSSP). ACM (2014)
6. Dwyer, M.B., Avrunin, G.S., Corbett, J.C.: Patterns in property specifications for finite-state verification. In: Boehm, B.W., Garlan, D., Kramer, J. (eds.) Proc. of the 1999 International Conf. on Software Engineering (ICSE). ACM Press (1999)
7. Eisner, C., Fisman, D., Havlicek, J., Lustig, Y., McIsaac, A., Van Campenhout, D.: Reasoning with temporal logic on truncated paths. In: Hunt Jr., W.A., Somenzi, F. (eds.) CAV 2003. LNCS, vol. 2725, pp. 27–39. Springer, Heidelberg (2003)
8. Fischer, M.J., Ladner, R.E.: Propositional dynamic logic of regular programs. Journal of Computer and System Science (1979)
9. Harel, D., Kozen, D., Tiuryn, J.: Dynamic Logic. MIT Press (2000)
10. Ly, L.T., Maggi, F.M., Montali, M., Rinderle-Ma, S., van der Aalst, W.M.P.: A framework for the systematic comparison and evaluation of compliance monitoring approaches. In: Proc. of the 17th IEEE Int. Enterprise Distributed Object Computing Conf. (EDOC). IEEE (2013)
11. Maggi, F.M., Montali, M., Westergaard, M., van der Aalst, W.M.P.: Monitoring business constraints with linear temporal logic: An approach based on colored automata. In: Rinderle-Ma, S., Toumani, F., Wolf, K. (eds.) BPM 2011. LNCS, vol. 6896, pp. 132–147. Springer, Heidelberg (2011)
12. Maggi, F.M., Westergaard, M., Montali, M., van der Aalst, W.M.P.: Runtime verification of LTL-based declarative process models. In: Khurshid, S., Sen, K. (eds.) RV 2011. LNCS, vol. 7186, pp. 131–146. Springer, Heidelberg (2012)
13. Møller, A.: dk.brics.automaton – finite-state automata and regular expressions for Java (2010)
14. Montali, M.: Specification and Verification of Declarative Open Interaction Models. LNBIP, vol. 56. Springer, Heidelberg (2010)
15. Montali, M., Maggi, F.M., Chesani, F., Mello, P., van der Aalst, W.M.P.: Monitoring business constraints with the event calculus. ACM TIST (2013)
16. Montali, M., Pesic, M., van der Aalst, W.M.P., Chesani, F., Mello, P., Storari, S.: Declarative specification and verification of service choreographies. ACM Trans. on the Web (2010)
17. Pesic, M.: Constraint-Based Workflow Management Systems: Shifting Controls to Users. PhD thesis, Beta Research School for Operations Management and Logistics, Eindhoven (2008)
18. Pesic, M., van der Aalst, W.M.P.: A declarative approach for flexible business processes management. In: Eder, J., Dustdar, S. (eds.) BPM 2006 Workshops. LNCS, vol. 4103, pp. 169–180. Springer, Heidelberg (2006)

19. Pnueli, A.: The temporal logic of programs. In: 18th Ann. Symp. on Foundations of Computer Science (FOCS). IEEE (1977)
20. Prakken, H., Sergot, M.J.: Contrary-to-duty obligations. Studia Logica (1996)
21. van der Aalst, W.M.P.: Process Mining - Discovery, Conformance and Enhancement of Business Processes. Springer (2011)
22. Vardi, M.: The rise and fall of linear time logic. In: 2nd Int. Symp. on Games, Automata, Logics and Formal Verification (2011)
23. Westergaard, M., Maggi, F.M.: Modeling and verification of a protocol for operational support using coloured petri nets. In: Kristensen, L.M., Petrucci, L. (eds.) PETRI NETS 2011. LNCS, vol. 6709, pp. 169–188. Springer, Heidelberg (2011)

Hierarchical Declarative Modelling with Refinement and Sub-processes

Søren Debois[1], Thomas Hildebrandt[1], and Tijs Slaats[1,2]

[1] IT University of Copenhagen, Rued Langgaardsvej 7, 2300 Copenhagen, Denmark
{debois,hilde,tslaats}@itu.dk
[2] Exformatics A/S, Lautrupsgade 13, 2100 Copenhagen, Denmark

Abstract. We present a new declarative model with composition and hierarchical definition of processes, featuring (a) incremental refinement, (b) adaptation of processes, and (c) dynamic creation of sub-processes. The approach is motivated and exemplified by a recent case management solution delivered by our industry partner Exformatics A/S. The approach is achieved by extending the Dynamic Condition Response (DCR) graph model with *interfaces* and composition along those interfaces. Both refinement and sub-processes are then constructed in terms of that composition. Sub-processes take the form of hierarchical (complex) events, which dynamically instantiate sub-processes. The extensions are realised and supported by a prototype simulation tool.

1 Introduction

Business process design technologies today are predominantly based on *flow-oriented* process notations such as the Business Process Model and Notation (BPMN) standard [18], which *imperatively* describes how a process should proceed from start to end. Often, business processes are required to be compliant with regulations and constraints given by busines polices, standards and laws. E.g., a customer must be informed about alternatives and risks before getting a loan in a bank, or a decision on a grant application cannot be made before the deadline for submissions of applications has been reached.

Since the flow-oriented notations only captures *how* to fulfill the compliance rules, the description and verification of compliance rules require other notations and techniques. This leaves the process designers with three modelling tasks: To describe the compliance rules, to describe the process, and to verify that the process is compliant to the rules. Typically, compliance rules are described *declaratively* using a variant of temporal logic such as Linear-time Temporal Logic (LTL) [21]. Compliance can then be verified during execution using run-time verification techniques [12] and, if the flow-diagrams are based on a formal model, also at design time [6]. In most industrial design tools, the flow-diagrams are however *not* based on a formal model, and consequently, design time verification is not supported. This means that the process designers have to figure out manually how to interpret the constraints, and compliance is then subsequently

S. Sadiq, P. Soffer, and H. Völzer (Eds.): BPM 2014, LNCS 8659, pp. 18–33, 2014.

verified informally and approved by, e.g., a lawyer. At best, a formal run-time or post-execution verification is performed against the execution log.

In these situations there is a high risk that processes become either non-compliant or over-constrained by design, to faciliate manual verification. Over-constrained processes, however, rarely fits reality or are simply not suitable for knowledge-intensive processes. A way to avoid these problems is to use the declarative approach (also) for the process design. Several declarative process modelling notations and techniques have been proposed in the last decade, including DECLARE [2,1], CLIMB [13], GSM [11] and Dynamic Condition Response (DCR) graphs [8,14]. However, sometimes the declarative approach makes it less clear from the end-user, how a process will proceed from start to end. Even with a graphical notation (as in DECLARE, GSM and DCR graphs), it may be difficult to comprehend the interactions between different constraints.

The DCR graph process modelling notation stands out by supporting a simple and efficient run-time execution, which mitigates the complexity of comprehending the constraints and allows for run-time adaptation [15], while still being more expressive than (propositional) LTL (and thus DECLARE), in that it allows to describe every union of a regular and an ω-regular language [3,16,14].

DCR Graphs were conceived as both a generalization of event structures [22] and a formalization and generalization of the Process Matrix [17] invented by Danish company Resultmaker. Since its inception, the DCR Graph notation and theory have been developed further in collaboration with Exformatics A/S, a Danish provider of case, document and knowledge management systems. A version of DCR graphs with a simple notion of nesting [9], an additional milestone relation, and support for data now forms the core their workflow engine [20,7]. However, DCR graph models as currently implemented become difficult to comprehend and present at a certain size. They seem to lack encapsulation, modularity and hierarchy; the key techniques to make large models comprehensible in both imperative [19] and declarative settings [23]. Also, practical modelling efforts by Exformatics A/S has revealed that DCR graphs emphatically needs a notion of "dynamically created" or "instantiated" sub-process.

In the present paper, we seek to remedy these shortcomings of DCR graphs. Our contributions are as follows.

1. We introduce refinement-by-composition for DCR graphs.
2. We add to DCR graphs a notion of *dynamically spawned sub-process*, defining Hi-DCR graphs.
3. We demonstrate the use of both incremental process design using an example exctracted from a recent case management solution delivered by Exformatics A/S to a Danish funding agency.
4. We provide a publicly available Hi-DCR graph tool.

The tool allows simulation, model-checking of the finite fragment, automatic visualisation and more. The compositions and refinements presented in examples were not made by hand, they were executed by the tool; all DCR diagrams in this paper has been generated by it, and all examples are fully executable by it.

Hi-DCR graphs are fully formalised; we prove both soundness of refinement—that refinement cannot accidentally remove constraints of the extant model—as well as Hi-DCR being strictly more expressive than ω-regular languages.

1.1   Related Work

Hierarchy for declarative languages was studied in [23], where the authors add *complex activities* to DECLARE [2,1]. The authors make a compelling case that hierarchy is a necessity for constructing understandable declarative models. Our industry partner's experiences fully supports this thesis; this is in part what has led to our investigation of sub-processes.

A complex activity is one which contains a nested DECLARE model governing when that activity may complete. The nested model starts when the complex activity opens, and the complex activity conversely may only close once the nested model completes. Otherwise, there is no interaction between the nested model and the parent model. In the present paper, a sub-process may interact with its parent process: there can be multiple ways to start the sub-process, it can have different observable outcomes, and it is allowed to interact with other activities in the parent process.

Questions about concurrency are left open by [23]: the authors do not report a formal semantics, and the paper has no examples of interleavings of complex activities. In the present approach, sub-process executions are naturally interleaved with other events and even other instances of the same sub-process; we shall see this in examples.

We believe it is straightforward to formalize complex activities of [23] in Hi-DCR Graphs: Use Hi-DCR relations to allow only a single start and end event for each sub-process, and cut off interaction between sub- and super-process by choosing only empty interfaces.

The Guard-Stage-Milestone (GSM) approach [11] to business modelling provides a data-centric notation with declarative flavour. The notation consists of *stages*, which in turn have *guards*, controlling when and how the stage may start, and *milestones*, controlling when and how a stage may close. Stages can contain sub-stages, giving GSM an inherent hierarchy. Where GSM is data-centric, the present formalism is event-based. Nonetheless, the sub-processes of Hi-DCR graphs are strongly reminiscent of GSM stages, with Hi-DCR interface events assuming the rôle of guards and milestones. In future work, we plan to further investigate the similarities between GSM and Hi-DCR Graphs, in the hope of providing a formal connection between them.

2   DCR Graphs

In this section, we recall DCR graphs as introduced in [8,14] and introduce our running example. The example is based on a workflow of a Danish funding agency; our industry partner, Exformatics A/S, has implemented system support for this workflow using the basic DCR graphs of this Section [20]. While vindicating DCR graphs as a flexible and practical modelling tool, that work also highlighted the potential need for refinement and sub-processes, which we introduce in the following Sections. One key idea will be the development of models by *refinement*: start from a very abstract model, then successively refine it until it becomes suitably concrete. In this section, we introduce DCR graphs alongside such a very abstract model.

As the name suggests, DCR graphs are *graphs*, and we tend to represent them visually, as in Fig. 1. This figure depicts a highly abstracted model of the funding agency workflow. Events (boxes) with labels (the text inside them) are related to other events by various arrows. In this model there are only four events: the beginning of the application round Start round; receiving an application (Receive application); the deadline for application submission occurring (Application deadline); and finally the board meeting (Board meeting), at which the board of the funding institution decide which applications warrant grants and which do not.

Relations between these events govern their relative order of occurrence. When not constrained by any relations, events can happen in any order and any number of times.

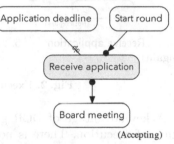

The *condition* relation, $e \rightarrow\bullet e'$, seen between Start round and Receive application indicates that the former must occur before the latter: we do not receive applications before the round has started. In the initial state of the DCR graph, Start round have yet to happen, and so Receive application cannot execute; hence it has been greyed out in the visual representation. The notation and semantics of this relation is similar to the precedence constraint in DE-CLARE [2,1].

Fig. 1. A basic DCR graph

Between Receive application and Board meeting we have a *response* relation, $e \bullet\rightarrow e'$. This indicates that if Receive application happens, then Board meeting must subsequently happen. This does not necessarily mean that each occurrence of the former is followed by a unique occurrence of the latter; it's quite all right to receive seven applications, have a board meeting, receive five more applications, then have a final board meeting. If Receive application has been executed without a following Board meeting, we say that Board meeting is *pending*.

Finally, between the Application deadline and Receive application events we have an *exclusion* relation, $e \rightarrow\% e'$. Once the Application deadline event occurs, the Receive application event becomes excluded, which means that it is from then on considered irrelevant for the rest of the workflow. While excluded, it cannot execute; any response obligations on it are considered void; and if it is a condition for some other event, that condition is disregarded. Dual to the exclusion relation is the *inclusion* relation. It is not exemplified in this DCR graph, but its meaning is straightforward: it re-includes an event in the workflow. DCR graph have also a fifth and final relation, the *milestone* relation $e \rightarrow\diamond e'$; we will postpone explaining that until we use it in the next Section.

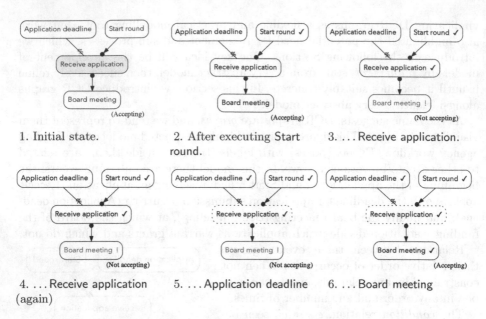

1. Initial state.

2. After executing Start round.

3. ... Receive application.

4. ... Receive application (again)

5. ... Application deadline

6. ... Board meeting

Fig. 2. Execution of the DCR graph of Fig. 1

A key advantage of DCR graphs is that the graph *directly* represents the state of execution. There is no distinction between design-time and run-time. We will illustrate this by example: in Fig. 2 we have a finite execution of Fig. 1. In the upper-left corner, (1) is the initial state, the DCR graph presented in Fig. 1. The Start round event executes, taking us to (2). We can observe events having been executed in the state of the graph: executed events have little check-marks next to them, so in (2), Start round has such a check-mark. Also, with Start round executed, the condition for Receive application is fulfilled; it is now executable and thus no longer greyed out. We execute it to get to (3). Because there is a response from Receive application to Board meeting, that execution puts a pending response on Board meeting. This is indicated in (3) by the red text and the exclamation mark.

We execute Receive application to get to (4). This execution brings no change to the graph, which already had Receive application marked as previously executed, and already had a response on Board meeting. So we execute Application deadline, getting to (5). Because of the exclusion relation from that to Receive application, the latter becomes excluded, indicated by its box being dotted in (5). Even though excluded events cannot be executed, we do not grey them out; the dotted box is enough. Finally, we execute Board meeting to get to (6). This of course fulfils the pending response, which disappears: the text of Board meeting goes back to black, and the exclamation mark disappears.

A DCR graph is *accepting* if it has no included pending responses. (An infinite run is accepting if every incurred response is eventually executed or excluded.) The acceptance state of the graph is indicated in the lower-right corner of each graph. That indication is technically superfluous: the graph will be accepting exactly if it has no red labels/labels with exclamation marks. For large graphs, it can be convenient to have the single indicator anyway.

3   Hierarchy and Refinement

We now come to the core contributions of this paper. We present a notion of "refinement" of DCR graphs, defined in terms of a more primitive notion of "composition" of DCR graphs. Refinement is always achieved by composing an *abstract DCR Graph* with a *refinement DCR Graph*, which introduces new events and/or add additional constraints.

3.1   Refinement

We wish to refine our model to express in greater detail the decision mechanics of the board. We will model board meetings by the DCR graph in Fig. 3. The results of an application round must be gathered in a report. This report is updated and approved repeatedly during the application round. This gives rise to two new events: Update report and Approve report.

Applications are discussed over the course of several board meetings and the results of the board meetings must be worked into the report. To allow the secretary to work efficiently she is *not* required to formally update the report after every single board meeting, but she may combine the outcomes of several of them in a single update. This constraint is represented by the response relation from Board meeting to Update report.

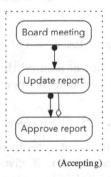

(Accepting)

Fig. 3. Expanded model of the Board meeting

While there are such pending changes to the report, it can of course not be approved. This is modelled using a *milestone* relation Update report →◇ Approve report. This relation means that *while* Update report is pending, Approve report can not execute.

Note that this model does not preclude the board from re-approving a report that has not been updated. While not a particularly sensible thing to do, it is not against the rules, and as such *should* be permitted by the model.

Now, we wish to add these new details about board meetings to our original abstract model of Fig. 1; that is, we wish to *refine* Fig. 1 by Fig. 3. We do so by *composing* them: we fuse together events that are the same in both graphs. In this case only Board meeting. The result can be seen in Fig. 4. (The dashed box in that figure has no semantic ramifications; it is there are simply to make the graph easier to understand. See also [23].)

It is of course important that such a refinement does not accidentally *remove* constraints of the original model. Because of the inclusion and exclusion relations, that might happen, e.g., inclusions in the refining model might cause events excluded in the abstract one to be suddenly allowed. We shall prove in Theorem 4.10 that, roughly, when the two models agree on when fused events are included or excluded, the composition will not admit new behaviour; in this case we call it a refinement. In the present case, the only fused event is Board meeting, which has no inclusions or exclusions going into it in either model, so this composition is really a refinement.

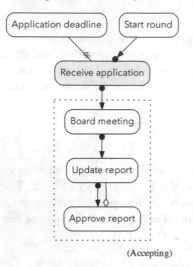

Fig. 4. Refinement of Fig. 1 by Fig.3

Refinement-as-composition in conjunction with DCR graphs having no distinction between design-time and runtime means that we can *refine a running model*. Suppose, for instance, that we have deployed our initial abstract model of Fig. 1, and have reached state (5) in Fig. 2 when it is decided that compliance with the board meeting report procedure of Fig. 3 must be enforced. We may add in these new constraints by refining the running model (Fig. 2, part 5) with the new constraints (Fig. 3). Doing so yields the new DCR graph seen in Fig. 5. Note how the pending state of the fused Board meeting event is preserved. And again, by virtue of the refinement Theorem 4.10, we can be assured that all constraints on execution of the original model is still preserved in this new refined one.

3.2 Subprocesses

Refinement gives us a disciplined method for extending models with new components; thus it gives us a hierarchical notion of process design. However, it does not fully capture the notion of sub-processes in traditional business modelling notations. Here, a sub-processes is a complex activity in the model that has underlying behaviour which is *instantiated* when the sub-process is started and closed when the sub-process ends. Such sub-processes can both be single-instance, meaning that only one instance of the sub-process will be active at any time, or multi-instance, meaning that multiple instances of the sub-processes can execute concurrently.

To enable modelling such sub-processes we extend DCR graphs to Hi-DCR graphs. In these, we may associate with an event an entire *other* Hi-DCR graph which, when the event fires, is composed onto the current graph. We exemplify Hi-DCR Graphs by adding to our funding agency model a more detailed description of the process for an individual application. As many applications may be received and evaluated at the same time, we need a notion of sub-processes (and in particular multi-instance sub-processes) to fully capture this behaviour.

An application must receive some number of reviews, with at least one from a lawyer. The reviews are collected in a review report. Based on the review report, the application is accepted or rejected and the round report is updated with this decision. It is not uncommon that the decision on an application is reverted, changing an "accept" to a "reject" or vice versa, and this may even happen several times as discussions progress. Of course, each change in the decision requires an update to the round report. Finally, each applications cannot remain in limbo and must always eventually be either accepted or rejected.

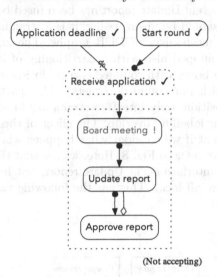

(Not accepting)

Fig. 5. Refinement of Fig. 2 part 5 by Fig. 3

The DCR graph in Fig. 6 models this process. At the top is Lawyer review and Other review. Of these two only Lawyer review is a condition for Review report, with the effect that we cannot write the review report unless we have at least a review from a lawyer.

After the Review report is completed, the reviewers may Accept or Reject the application; as mentioned, there is no restriction that these events happen only once. However, each new verdict requires Update report because of the response relation from Accept and Reject to Update report.

Finally we need to model the fact that either Accept or Reject needs to occur at least once, similar to the *choice* construct in DECLARE. Hi-DCR graphs contain no construct directly analogue to choice; but fortunately, there is a straightforward way—a DCR graph idiom, if you will—to achieve the intended semantics. We explicitly model the fact that a decision is needed as an event Decision. We make this event a condition of itself, meaning that it cannot possibly be executed. We also make it initially included and pending, so that once the application is started, a decision needs to eventually be made. Finally we let both Accept and Reject exclude Decision, indicat-

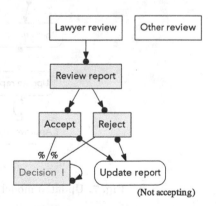

(Not accepting)

Fig. 6. The per-application sub-process

ing that these two both represents a valid decision. Once Decision becomes excluded, it no longer prevents the larger graph from achieving an accepting state.

Now, we wish the entire sub process of Fig. 6 to be instantiated *once per application*. In Hi-DCR graphs this is achieved by associating with the event Receive application in Fig. 5 the entire application processing DCR graph of Fig. 6. After executing Receive application a new copy of the application DCR Graph is composed with the main DCR Graph, and we get the DCR graph of Fig. 7.

Observe that once again, the common event Update report has been fused between the two DCR graphs. So far, this should be unsurprising: it is a straightforward application of the composition mechanism of DCR graphs. The key difference is that a Hi-DCR graphs is equipped also with a partitioning of its events into *interface events* (indicated by boxes with rounded corners in Fig. 6) and *local events* (indicated by boxes with non-rounded corners). This partitioning has the effect that under composition, only interface events are fused, whereas local events are not, even if their labelling overlap. The effect of these interfaces and local events will be apparent if we consider what happens when Receive application executes a *second* time; refer to Fig. 8. Here, we see that the second application process has fused its interface event Update report, but has duplicated its remaining events, which are all local. This has the following two important consequences:

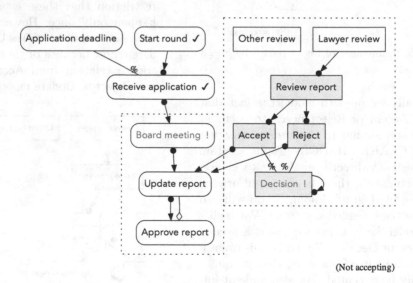

(Not accepting)

Fig. 7. Updated model with one spawned subprocess

1. Each application process is represented separately.
2. Approve report effectively synchronises decisions: whenever the decision on any application is changed, the report needs to be updated.

Connecting local and interface event is a highly expressive mechanism. For instance, if we want to have a review report ready for every application before the

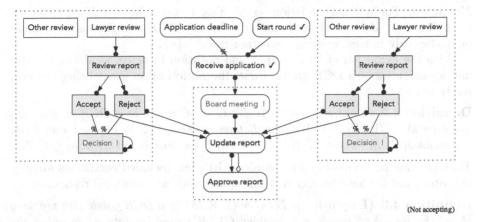

(Not accepting)

Fig. 8. After spawning a *second* subprocess in Fig. 7

board meeting commences, it is enough to have, in the sub-process definition in Fig. 6 a condition from the local event Review report to a new interface event Board meeting.

4 Foundations

In this section, we review the formal theory of DCR graphs, then formally introduce their refinement and their generalisation to Hi-DCR graphs.

We distinguish between events and labels. In a single workflow, the same label may occur multiple times. For instance, the label "Review report" occurs twice in Fig. 8. We accommodate such multiplicity by considering *events* (the boxes), as distinct from their *label* (the text in the boxes). When the distinction between events and labels does not matter, we use the words interchangeably. For instance, in Fig. 1 and 3 we speak of "the event Board meeting", since the label Board meeting uniquely identifies an event. To simplify the presentation we will let the labelling of events remain implicit in the formal definitions.

Definition 4.1 (DCR Graph [8]). *A* DCR *graph is a tuple* (E, R, M) *where*

- E *is a finite set of (labelled) events, the nodes of the graph.*
- R *is the edges of the graph. Edges are partioned into five kinds, named and drawn as follows: The* conditions ($\rightarrow\bullet$), responses ($\bullet\rightarrow$), milestones ($\rightarrow\diamond$), inclusions ($\rightarrow+$), *and* exclusions ($\rightarrow\%$).
- M *is the* marking *of the graph. This is a triple* (Ex, Re, In) *of sets of events, respectively the previously executed* (Ex), *the currently pending* (Re), *and the currently included* (In) *events.*

When G is a DCR graph, we write, e.g., $E(G)$ for the set of events of G, as well as, e.g., $Ex(G)$ for the executed events in the marking of G.

Notation. For a binary relation $\to\ \subseteq X \times Y$ we write "$\to Z$" for the set $\{x \in X \mid \exists z \in Z.\ x \to z\}$, and similarly for "$Z \to$". For singletons we usually omit the curly braces, writing $\to e$ rather than $\to \{e\}$.

With the definition of DCR graphs and notation in place, we define the dynamic semantics of a DCR graph. First, the notion of an event being *enabled*, ready to execute.

Definition 4.2 (Enabled events). *Let $G = (\mathsf{E}, \mathsf{R}, \mathsf{M})$ be a DCR graph, with marking $\mathsf{M} = (\mathsf{Ex}, \mathsf{Re}, \mathsf{In})$. We say that an event $e \in \mathsf{E}$ is* enabled *and write $e \in \mathsf{enabled}(G)$ iff (a) $e \in \mathsf{In}$, (b) $\mathsf{In} \cap (\to \bullet\, e) \subseteq \mathsf{Ex}$, and (c) $\mathsf{In} \cap (\to \diamond\, e) \subseteq \mathsf{E} \backslash \mathsf{Re}$.*

That is, enabled events (a) are included, (b) their included conditions already executed, and (c) have no included milestones with an unfulfilled responses.

Definition 4.3 (Execution). *Let $G = (\mathsf{E}, \mathsf{R}, \mathsf{M})$ be a DCR graph with marking $\mathsf{M} = (\mathsf{Ex}, \mathsf{Re}, \mathsf{In})$. Suppose $e \in \mathsf{enabled}(G)$. We may execute e obtaining the resulting DCR graph $(\mathsf{E}, \mathsf{R}, \mathsf{M}')$ with $\mathsf{M}' = (\mathsf{Ex}', \mathsf{Re}', \mathsf{In}')$ defined as follows.*

1. $\mathsf{Ex}' = \mathsf{Ex} \cup e$
2. $\mathsf{Re}' = (\mathsf{Re} \setminus e) \cup (e \bullet \to)$
3. $\mathsf{In}' = (\mathsf{In} \setminus (e \to \%)) \cup (e \to +)$

That is, to execute an event e one must: (1) add e to the set Ex of executed events. (2) Update the currently required responses Re by first removing e, then adding any responses required by e. (3) Update the currently included events by first removing all those excluded by e, then adding all those included by e.

Definition 4.4 (Transitions, runs, traces). *Let G be a DCR graph. If $e \in \mathsf{enabled}(G)$ and executing e in G yields H, we say that G has* transition *on e to H and write $G \longrightarrow_e H$. A* run *of G is a (finite or infinite) sequence of DCR graphs G_i and events e_i such that: $G = G_0 \longrightarrow_{e_0} G_1 \longrightarrow_{e_1} \cdots$ A* trace *of G is a sequence of labels of events e_i associated with a run of G. We write $\mathsf{runs}(G)$ and $\mathsf{traces}(G)$ for the set of runs and traces of G, respectively*

Not every run or trace represents an acceptable execution of the graph: We need also that every response requested is eventually fulfilled or excluded.

Definition 4.5 (Acceptance). *A run $G_0 \longrightarrow_{e_0} G_1 \longrightarrow_{e_1} \cdots$ is* accepting *iff for all n with $e \in \mathsf{In}(G_n) \cap \mathsf{Re}(G_n)$ there exists $m \geq n$ s.t. either $e_m = e$, or $e \notin \mathsf{In}(G_m)$. A trace is* accepting *iff it has an underlying run which is.*

Acceptance tells us which workflows a DCR graph accepts, its *language*.

Definition 4.6 (Language). *The* language *of a DCR graph G is the set of its accepting traces. We write $\mathsf{lang}(G)$ for the language of G.*

We now know enough to formalise the first DCR graph we saw.

Example 4.7. The DCR graph of Fig. 1 and 2 has events a, s, r, b labelled Application deadline (a), Start round (s), Receive application (r), and Board meeting (b). It has relation R given by $\to \% = \{(a, r)\}$, $\to + = \emptyset$, $\to \bullet = \{s, r\}$, $\bullet \to = \{r, b\}$ and $\to \diamond = \emptyset$. We can find a run of this DCR graph in Fig. 2: $B_1 \longrightarrow_s B_2 \longrightarrow_r B_3 \longrightarrow_r B_4 \longrightarrow_a B_5 \longrightarrow_b B_6$

Here, B_1, B_2 are accepting, whereas B_3–B_5 have b pending and so are not.

4.1 Composition and Interfaces

Composition of DCR graphs was originally introduced in [10].

Definition 4.8 (Composition of DCR graphs). *The composition $G \mid H$ of DCR graphs G and H is defined by taking the union of all components. Formally: $G \mid H = (E \cup E', R \cup R', (Ex \cup Ex', Re \cup Re', In \cup In'))$ The empty or zero DCR graph, $\mathbf{0}$, is the unique DCR graph with no events.*

Composition does not in itself give "refinement" in the classical sense: in DCR graphs, even if G, H share events and labels, the language of $G \mid H$ might actually be *larger* than either G or H. The following definition helps narrow down what are "good" compositions.

Notation. The *projection* of a sequence σ to a set E is obtained by removing every element of σ not in E. For instance, the projection of $\sigma = AABCABC$ to $E = \{A, C\}$ is $\sigma|_E = AACAC$. We lift projection to sets of sequences pointwise.

Definition 4.9 (Refinement). H refines G *iff* $(\mathsf{lang}(G \mid H))|_{E(G)} \subseteq \mathsf{lang}(G)$.

To help establish refinements, we have the following theorem, which states that a DCR graph G is refined by a DCR-graph H if they have no shared event which may be included or excluded unilaterally by H.

Theorem 4.10. *H refines G if in H shared labels are associated only with shared events, and for all $f \in E(G) \cap E(H)$ and $e \in E(H)$ we have that:*

1. *If $e \to\%_H f$ then also $e \to\%_G f$,*   3. $Ex(H) \cap E(G) \subseteq Ex(G)$,
2. *if $e \to+_H f$ then also $e \to+_G f$,*   4. $In(H) \cap E(G) \subseteq In(G)$.

Conditions (1) and (2) mean that H cannot unilaterally include or exclude shared events; conditions (3) and (4) that the marking of H does not change the inclusion- or execution-state of shared events.

Example 4.11. As an example, taking G to be the DCR graphs of Fig. 1 and H to be the one of Fig. 3, then both G, H fulfil the criteria of Theorem 4.10. Thus, we can be sure that when we compose them to obtain $G \mid H$ in Fig. 4, their local behaviour is preserved: the valid execution orders of Application deadline, Start round, Receive application, and Board meeting in Fig. 4 are all also valid according to Fig. 1.

4.2 Hi-DCR graphs

Towards DCR-graphs with sub-processes, we need first DCR graphs with interfaces, i-DCR graphs.

Definition 4.12 (i-DCR graph). *An i-DCR graph is a tuple $G = (E, R, M, I)$ such that (E, R, M) is a DCR graph and $I \subseteq E$. Events $L = E \setminus I$ are local events. An i-DCR graph inherits notions of enabled events, execution, and zero from its underlying DCR-graph.*

We note that once we can speak of *execution*, we have using Definitions 4.4, 4.5, and 4.6 also definitions of transistions, runs, traces, acceptance, and language.

The point of the interface I is to allow us to choose which events should fuse with similar events in composition, and which should be considered private. To avoid fusing of private events, we must sometimes employ renamings.

Definition 4.13 (Freshness, compatibility). *If G, H are i-DCR graphs we say an that G is fresh for H iff $L(G) \cap E(H) = \emptyset$. We say that they are compatible iff they are both fresh for the other. We say that G, H are equivalent if they are structurally identical up to the choice of local events.*

The composition of i-DCR graphs guarantees that local events of compatible graphs do not overlap.

Definition 4.14 (i-DCR composition). *The composition $G \mid H$ of i-DCR graphs G, H is defined as for DCR graphs, taking interfaces of the combined graph to be $I(G) \setminus L(H) \cup I(H) \setminus L(G)$.*

For compatible i-DCR graphs, this definition is equivalent to taking simply $I \cup I'$.

Definition 4.15 (Hi-DCR). *A Hi-DCR graph is a tuple $G = (E, R, M, I, S)$ where S is a map taking events to Hi-DCR graphs and (E, R, M, I) is the underlying i-DCR graph $G|_\iota$ of G. An event e of G is enabled in G iff it is in $G|_\iota$.*

Note that if one wants an event e to *not* spawn any sub-process, one simply maps it to sub-process definition to zero, i.e., takes $S(e) = \mathbf{0}$.

Definition 4.16 (Hi-DCR execution). *Suppose e is an event of the Hi-DCR graph G, that $e \in$ enabled(G) and that $S(e) = H$. Then to execute e in G:*

1. *Pick some H' equivalent to H but fresh for G.*
2. *Execute e in $G \mid H'$ (considered a DCR graph) to obtain H.*

That is, if $G \mid H' = (E, R, M, I, S)$, we execute e in (E, R, M) obtaining (E, R, M'), then declare the execution of e in $G \mid H'$ to be (E, R, M', I, S).

Example 4.17. The notion of i-DCR graph and the definition of Hi-DCR graph execution explains formally why the event Approve decisions is *not* duplicated when a subprocess is spawned between Fig. 7 and 8: it is an interface event, and so is fused in the composition that happens when new sub-processes are spawned. The event Review report in the sub-process, on the other hand, *is* duplicated: It is local, and because execution of Hi-DCR graphs choose fresh names for local events during spawning, it is duplicated.

Theorem 4.18. *Hi-DCR graphs are strictly more expressive then DCR Graphs and therefore also strictly more expressive then ω-regular languages.*

Proof. Hi-DCR graphs conservatively extend DCR graphs, which are known to express exactly ω-regular languages [14]. But in Fig. 8, every time we execute Receive application we are will execute at least one Accept or Reject. This requires *counting* Receive application which is impossible for ω-regular languages.

5 Implementation

For experimentation, we have implemented a prototype tool for working with Hi-DCR graphs. This tool features a simulation engine capable of executing transitions, and of dynamic re-configuration using both unconstrained composition (Definition 4.8) and refinement (Definition 4.9). For finite-state graphs, the tool can do also basic model-checking tasks, such as finding a path to dead-lock, termination, acceptance, or some event being enabled. Whereas in the other sections of this paper, we represented DCR graphs graphically, as figures produced by the tool, the tool inputs a textual representation. As an example of that representation, consider again Fig. 6. Its equivalent textual representation is below.

All events are interface events by default; local events are specified by prefixing them with a slash '/' (line 11-13). Events can also be prefixed '+', '%', and '!', (line 5) indicating that they are initially included, excluded, respectively pending. For convenience, the language allows both chaining of events and relations (line 2–5) as well as relating multiple things (line 7).

The tool uses Graphviz [5] to automatically produce diagrams. The diagrams in the present paper were all so generated. The tool is implemented in F# and runs on the major platforms. The executable and source code can be found at [4].

```
"Other review"                                   1
"Lawyer review"                                  2
-->* "Review report"                             3
-->* ("Accept" "Reject")                         4
-->% !"Decision"                                 5
"Decision" -->* "Decision"                       6
("Accept" "Reject") -->% "Decision"              7
("Accept" "Reject")                              8
*--> "Update report"                             9
                                                 10
/("Other review" "Lawyer review"                 11
  "Review report"                                12
  "Accept" "Reject" "Decision")                  13
```

6 Conclusion

In this paper we first demonstrated how DCR Graphs can be used for incremental, declarative design of processes, by introducing a notion of compositional refinement that guarantees language inclusion (with respect to the labels of events present in the original process) and thus preserves compliance for accepting executions. We then used these techniques to introduce Hi-DCR Graphs, a conservative extension of DCR graphs, which allows events to spawn sub-processes. The extensions have been presented and motivated using as an example an abstraction of a real-world case supplied by our industry partner, Exformatics A/S. We provided a formal semantics for Hi-DCR Graphs and demonstrated by example that they are more expressive then ω-regular languages. Finally we reported on a prototype implementation of Hi-DCR Graphs which supports a programming-like syntax, automatic visualisation, simulation, and rudimentary model-checking.

6.1   Future Work

While the notion of refinement introduced in the present paper preserves compliance for accepting executions, it may in fact introduce errors such as livelocks and deadlocks. The simplest example would be to refine a process with a DCR graph containing a single, included (local) event having itself as condition and being initiatlly required as response. In [15] it is shown how adaptations can be verified for safety and liveness, by relying on the map from DCR Graphs to Büchi-automata [16], which is further mapped to Promela and verified in the SPIN model-checker. However, as demonstrated in [15], this approach is not very efficient. We are therefore currently investigating techniques for more efficient verification of DCR Graphs in the presense of adaptations.

As was mentioned in the related work section the development of Hi-DCR Graphs brings us closer to the GSM notation, and we plan to use this work in the future as a basis for formal mappings between GSM and DCR Graphs models.

The question of the precise expressive power of Hi-DCR graph remains open. We conjecture that they are Turing-equivalent. This points to another relevant question, namely how to constrain Hi-DCR graphs to allow safety and liveness guarantees. An obvious possible constraint would be to bound the number times each sub-process can be spawned by a constant. Because of the formalization of spawning based on composition, it follows that this constrains the model to the expressiveness of standard DCR Graphs, that is, to Büchi-automata.

Formal expressive power aside, in practice many idiomatic constructs, like the "disjunctive responses" used in Fig. 8 could be formalised as derived constructs in their own right, potentially making them more accessible to end-users, much like DECLARE is formalised in terms of LTL. Similarly, other questions regarding the usability of the approach will be investigated in future studies through empirical investigations undertaken in cooperation with our industrial partners and end-users.

Acknowledgments. We gratefully acknowledge fruitful discussions with Rik Eshuis. The work is supported by grant VELUX 33295, 2014-2017 and the Danish Agency for Science, Technology and Innovation.

References

1. van der Aalst, W.M.P., Pesic, M., Schonenberg, H., Westergaard, M., Maggi, F.M.: Declare. Webpage (2010), http://www.win.tue.nl/declare/
2. van der Aalst, W.M.P., Pesic, M.: DecSerFlow: Towards a truly declarative service flow language. In: Bravetti, M., Núñez, M., Zavattaro, G. (eds.) WS-FM 2006. LNCS, vol. 4184, pp. 1–23. Springer, Heidelberg (2006)
3. Carbone, M., Hildebrandt, T., Perrone, G., Wasowski, A.: Refinement for transition systems with responses. In: FIT. EPTCS, vol. 87, pp. 48–55 (2012)
4. Debois, S.: DCR exploration tool v.6. IT University of Copenhagen (2014), http://www.itu.dk/research/models/wiki/index.php/DCR_Exploration_Tool
5. Ellson, J., Gansner, E., Koutsofios, L., North, S.C., Woodhull, G.: Graphviz - open source graph drawing tools. In: Mutzel, P., Jünger, M., Leipert, S. (eds.) GD 2001. LNCS, vol. 2265, pp. 483–484. Springer, Heidelberg (2002), http://dx.doi.org/10.1007/3-540-45848-4_57

6. Groefsema, H., Bucur, D.: A survey of formal business process verification: From soundness to variability. In: Proceedings of the Third International Symposium on Business Modeling and Software Design, pp. 198–203 (2013), http://www.cs.rug.nl/ds/uploads/pubs/groefsema-bmsd.pdf
7. Hildebrandt, T., Marquard, M., Mukkamala, R.R., Slaats, T.: Dynamic condition response graphs for trustworthy adaptive case management. In: Demey, Y.T., Panetto, H. (eds.) OTM 2013 Workshops. LNCS, vol. 8186, pp. 166–171. Springer, Heidelberg (2013)
8. Hildebrandt, T., Mukkamala, R.R.: Declarative event-based workflow as distributed dynamic condition response graphs. In: PLACES. EPTCS, vol. 69, pp. 59–73 (2010)
9. Hildebrandt, T., Mukkamala, R.R., Slaats, T.: Nested dynamic condition response graphs. In: Arbab, F., Sirjani, M. (eds.) FSEN 2011. LNCS, vol. 7141, pp. 343–350. Springer, Heidelberg (2012)
10. Hildebrandt, T., Mukkamala, R.R., Slaats, T.: Safe distribution of declarative processes. In: Barthe, G., Pardo, A., Schneider, G. (eds.) SEFM 2011. LNCS, vol. 7041, pp. 237–252. Springer, Heidelberg (2011)
11. Hull, R., et al.: Introducing the guard-stage-milestone approach for specifying business entity lifecycles (Invited talk). In: Bravetti, M. (ed.) WS-FM 2010. LNCS, vol. 6551, pp. 1–24. Springer, Heidelberg (2011)
12. Maggi, F.M., Westergaard, M., Montali, M., van der Aalst, W.M.P.: Runtime verification of LTL-based declarative process models. In: Khurshid, S., Sen, K. (eds.) RV 2011. LNCS, vol. 7186, pp. 131–146. Springer, Heidelberg (2012)
13. Montali, M.: Specification and Verification of Declarative Open Interaction Models. LNBIP, vol. 56. Springer, Heidelberg (2010)
14. Mukkamala, R.R.: A Formal Model For Declarative Workflows: Dynamic Condition Response Graphs. Ph.D. thesis, IT University of Copenhagen (June 2012)
15. Mukkamala, R.R., Hildebrandt, T., Slaats, T.: Towards trustworthy adaptive case management with dynamic condition response graphs. In: EDOC, pp. 127–136. IEEE (2013)
16. Mukkamala, R.R., Hildebrandt, T.: From dynamic condition response structures to büchi automata. In: TASE, pp. 187–190. IEEE Computer Society (2010)
17. Mukkamala, R.R., Hildebrandt, T., Tøth, J.B.: The resultmaker online consultant: From declarative workflow management in practice to ltl. In: EDOCW, pp. 135–142. IEEE Computer Society (2008)
18. Object Management Group BPMN Technical Committee: Business Process Model and Notation, version 2.0, http://www.omg.org/spec/BPMN/2.0/PDF
19. Reijers, H., Mendling, J., Dijkman, R.: On the usefulness of subprocesses in business process models. BPM Reports 1003, Eindhoven (2010)
20. Slaats, T., Mukkamala, R.R., Hildebrandt, T., Marquard, M.: Exformatics declarative case management workflows as DCR graphs. In: Daniel, F., Wang, J., Weber, B. (eds.) BPM 2013. LNCS, vol. 8094, pp. 339–354. Springer, Heidelberg (2013)
21. Vardi, M.Y.: An automata-theoretic approach to linear temporal logic. In: Moller, F., Birtwistle, G. (eds.) Logics for Concurrency. LNCS, vol. 1043, pp. 238–266. Springer, Heidelberg (1996)
22. Winskel, G.: Event structures. In: Brauer, W., Reisig, W., Rozenberg, G. (eds.) APN 1986. LNCS, vol. 255, pp. 325–392. Springer, Heidelberg (1987)
23. Zugal, S., Soffer, P., Pinggera, J., Weber, B.: Expressiveness and understandability considerations of hierarchy in declarative business process models. In: Bider, I., Halpin, T., Krogstie, J., Nurcan, S., Proper, E., Schmidt, R., Soffer, P., Wrycza, S. (eds.) BPMDS 2012 and EMMSAD 2012. LNBIP, vol. 113, pp. 167–181. Springer, Heidelberg (2012)

Discovering
Target-Branched Declare Constraints

Claudio Di Ciccio[1], Fabrizio Maria Maggi[2], and Jan Mendling[1]

[1] Vienna University of Business and Economics, Austria
{claudio.di.ciccio,jan.mendling}@wu.ac.at
[2] University of Tartu, Estonia
f.m.maggi@ut.ee

Abstract. Process discovery is the task of generating models from event logs. Mining processes that operate in an environment of high variability is an ongoing research challenge because various algorithms tend to produce spaghetti-like models. This is particularly the case when procedural models are generated. A promising direction to tackle this challenge is the usage of declarative process modelling languages like Declare, which summarise complex behaviour in a compact set of behavioural constraints. However, Declare constraints with branching are expensive to be calculated.In addition, it is often the case that hundreds of branching Declare constraints are valid for the same log, thus making, again, the discovery results unreadable. In this paper, we address these problems from a theoretical angle. More specifically, we define the class of Target-Branched Declare constraints and investigate the formal properties it exhibits. Furthermore, we present a technique for the efficient discovery of compact Target-Branched Declare models. We discuss the merits of our work through an evaluation based on a prototypical implementation using both artificial and real-world event logs.

Keywords: Process Mining, Discovery, Declarative Processes.

1 Introduction

Process discovery is the important initial step of business process management that aims at arriving at an as-is model of an investigated process [8]. Due to this step being difficult and time-consuming, various techniques have been proposed to automatically discover a process model from event logs. These log data are often generated from information systems that support parts or the entirety of a process. The result is typically presented as a Petri net or a similar kind of flow chart and the automatic discovery is referred to as process mining.

While process mining has proven to be a power technique for structured and standardised processes, there is an ongoing debate on how processes with a high degree of variability can be effectively mined. One approach to this problem is to generate a declarative process model, which rather shows the constraints of behaviour instead of the available execution sequences. The resulting models

S. Sadiq, P. Soffer, and H. Völzer (Eds.): BPM 2014, LNCS 8659, pp. 34–50, 2014.

are represented in languages like Declare. In many cases they provide a way to represent complex, unstructured behaviour in a compact way, which would look overly complex in a spaghetti-like Petri net. However, simple branching statements like "if you do a, you will do eventually either b or c" cannot be easily mined for Declare models.

In this paper, we address the problem of mining Declare branching constraints. We define the class of Target-Branched Declare and devise efficient mining algorithms for it. The key idea is to exploit dominance relationships, which help to drastically prune the search space. We present formal proofs to demonstrate its merits. A prototypical implementation is used for performance analysis, emphasising feasibility and efficiency for our approach.

Against this background, this paper is structured as follows. Section 2 introduces the essential concepts of Declare. Section 3 provides the formal foundations for mining Target-Branched constraints. Section 4 defines the construction of a knowledge base from which the final constraint set is built. Section 5 describes the performance evaluation. Section 6 investigates our contribution in the light of related work. Section 7 concludes the paper with an outlook on future research.

2 Background on Mining Declarative Process Models

One of the challenges in process mining is the compact presentation of the mined behaviour. It has been observed that procedural models such as Petri nets tend to become overly complex for flexible processes that are situated in a dynamic environment. Therefore, it has been argued to rather utilise declarative models in such a context, in order to facilitate better understanding of the mined process by humans [9,22].

One of the most frequently used declarative languages is Declare introduced by Pesic and van der Aalst in [26]. Instead of explicitly specifying the sequence of events, Declare consists of a set of constraints that are applied to activities. Constraints, in turn, are based on templates that define parametrised classes of properties. Templates have a graphical representation and their semantics can be formalised using formal logics [21,7], the main one being Linear Temporal Logic over finite traces (LTL_f). In this way, analysts work with the graphical representation of templates, while the underlying formulas remain hidden. Table 1 summarises important Declare templates. For a complete specification see [26]. Here, we indicate template parameters with x or y symbols and real activities in their instantiations with a, b or c letters.

The formulas shown in Table 1 can be readily formulated using natural language. The *RespondedExistence* template specifies that if x occurs, then y should also occur (either before or after x). The *Response* template specifies that when x occurs, then y should eventually occur after x. The *Precedence* template indicates that y should occur only if x has occurred before. The templates *AlternateResponse* and *AlternatePrecedence* strengthen the *Response* and *Precedence* templates respectively by specifying that activities must alternate without repetitions in between. Even stronger ordering relations are specified by

Table 1. Graphical notation and LTL_f formalisation of some Declare templates

Template	Formalisation	Notation
$RespondedExistence(x,y)$	$\Diamond x \rightarrow \Diamond y$	x ●——— y
$Response(x,y)$	$\Box(x \rightarrow \Diamond y)$	x ●——→ y
$Precedence(x,y)$	$\neg y \, \mathcal{W} \, x$	x ———● y
$AlternateResponse(x,y)$	$\Box(x \rightarrow \bigcirc(\neg x \, \mathcal{U} \, y))$	x ●═══→ y
$AlternatePrecedence(x,y)$	$(\neg y \, \mathcal{W} \, x) \wedge \Box(y \rightarrow \bigcirc(\neg y \, \mathcal{W} \, x))$	x ═══● y
$ChainResponse(x,y)$	$\Box(x \rightarrow \bigcirc y)$	x ●━━→ y
$ChainPrecedence(x,y)$	$\Box(\bigcirc y \rightarrow x)$	x ━━→ y

templates *ChainResponse* and *ChainPrecedence*. These templates require that the occurrences of the two activities (x and y) are next to each other.

In order to illustrate semantics, consider the *Response* constraint $\Box(a \rightarrow \Diamond b)$. This constraint indicates that if a occurs, b must eventually *follow*. Therefore, this constraint is satisfied for traces such as $t_1 = \langle a, a, b, c \rangle$, $t_2 = \langle b, b, c, d \rangle$, and $t_3 = \langle a, b, c, b \rangle$, but not for $t_4 = \langle a, b, a, c \rangle$ because, in this case, the second instance of a is not followed by a b.

An *activation* of a constraint in a trace is an event whose occurrence imposes some obligations on other *target* events in the same trace. E.g., a is an activation and b is a target for the *Response* constraint $\Box(a \rightarrow \Diamond b)$, because the execution of a forces b to be executed eventually. When a trace is compliant with respect to a constraint, every activation of it leads to a fulfillment. Consider, again, the *Response* constraint $\Box(a \rightarrow \Diamond b)$. In trace t_1, the constraint is activated and fulfilled twice, whereas, in t_3, the same constraint is activated and fulfilled only once. On the other hand, when a trace is not compliant, an activation of it can lead to a fulfillment but also at least to one activation violation. In trace t_4, the *Response* constraint $\Box(a \rightarrow \Diamond b)$ is activated twice: the first activation leads to a fulfillment (eventually b occurs) and the second activation to a violation (b does not occur subsequently). An algorithm to check fulfillments and violations is presented in [2]. To judge the relevance of constraints, we adopt *support* and *confidence* from data mining [1]. The support of a Declare constraint in an event log is defined as the fraction of activations of the constraint that lead to a fulfillment. The confidence of a Declare constraint is the product between the support of the rule and the support of the activation, i.e., the percentage of traces in which the activation occurs.

In spite of its advantages, one of the conceptual limitations of mining Declare constraints at this stage is the lack of support for branching. Branching as supported in the synthesis approach for behavioural profiles [28,24] and for the alpha algorithm [25] try to explicit mine for statements like "if you do a, you will (eventually) do either b or c". Such exclusiveness statements are typically used in experiments on process model understanding, see [18], because of their practical importance. Therefore, we investigate how Declare can be enriched with branching constraints in such a way that mining can still be conducted efficiently.

3   Target-Branched Declare

In this section, we define Target-Branched Declare (TBDeclare). It extends Declare such that the target is not a single activity but a set. This means that $Response(a, \{b, c\})$ is a TBDeclare constraint stating that "if a occurs, b or c must eventually follow". In TBDeclare, a constraint template maps to a LTL_f formula, and a constraint is its interpretation over a log (see Table 2). The models of a constraint are therefore traces that comply with the formula. We consider the class of TBDeclare for the reason that it exhibits interesting properties. First, we prove that a property of set-dominance holds. Then, we discuss implications of this for support. These properties will be exploited in the mining algorithm.

Table 2. LTL_f semantics for Target-Branched Declare constraints, given an activity x and a set of activities $Y = \{y_i | i > 0\}$

TBDeclare template	LTL_f semantics
$RespondedExistence(x, Y)$	$\Diamond x \rightarrow \Diamond \bigvee_{y_i \in Y} y_i$
$Response(x, Y)$	$\Box \left(x \rightarrow \Diamond \bigvee_{y_i \in Y} y_i \right)$
$AlternateResponse(x, Y)$	$\Box \left(x \rightarrow \bigcirc \left(\neg x \, \mathcal{U} \bigvee_{y_i \in Y} y_i \right) \right)$
$ChainResponse(x, Y)$	$\Box \left(x \rightarrow \bigcirc \bigvee_{y_i \subset Y} y_i \right)$
$Precedence(Y, x)$	$\neg x \, \mathcal{W} \bigvee_{y_i \in Y} y_i$
$AlternatePrecedence(Y, x)$	$Precedence(Y, x) \wedge \Box (x \rightarrow \bigcirc Precedence(Y, x))$
$ChainPrecedence(Y, x)$	$\Box \left(\bigcirc x \rightarrow \left(\bigvee_{y_i \in Y} y_i \right) \right)$

3.1   Set-Dominance

In this subsection, we identify that the inclusion property of two branching sets translates into the inclusion of their fulfilment of a constraint template.

Lemma 1. *Given a task x in the process alphabet Σ, two non-empty sets of tasks Y and Y' such that $Y \subseteq Y' \subseteq \Sigma$, and a TBDeclare constraint template $\mathcal{C}$, then $\mathcal{C}(x, Y) \models \mathcal{C}(x, Y')$.*

Proof (sketch). In the base case, $Y = Y' = \{y_1, \ldots, y_n\}$. Therefore, $\mathcal{C}(x, Y) \equiv \mathcal{C}(x, Y')$.

If $Y' = Y \bigcup \{y_{n+1}\}$, with $y_{n+1} \notin Y$, the demonstration proceeds by proving the statement for each constraint template.

$RespondedExistence(x, Y') \equiv \Diamond x \rightarrow \Diamond (\bigvee_{i=1}^n y_i \vee y_{n+1})$. Recalling that, given two non-negated literals φ and ψ:

(a) $\varphi \rightarrow \psi \equiv \neg\varphi \lor \psi$, and
(b) $\Diamond(\varphi \lor \psi) \equiv \Diamond\varphi \lor \Diamond\psi$,

we have that $RespondedExistence(x, Y') \equiv \neg\Diamond x \lor \bigvee_{i=1}^{n} \Diamond y_i \lor \Diamond y_{n+1}$. Consequently, $RespondedExistence(x, Y') \equiv RespondedExistence(x, Y) \lor y_{n+1}$. Given a formula Φ and a non-negated literal ψ, $\Phi \models \Phi \lor \psi$. Therefore, Lemma 1 for *RespondedExistence* is proven. The argument for the other templates has been established in a similar way, which is here omitted for space reasons.   □

3.2   Support Monotone Non-decrement w.r.t. Set-Dominance

Given a constraint C and a log L, the support function $S(C, L)$ returns the number of cases in which the constraint is verified (C_L^+) over the number of cases in which the constraint is activated along the log (C_L^T):

$$S(C, L) = \frac{C_L^+}{C_L^T}$$

Theorem 1 describes the monotonic non-decreasing trend of support for constraints with respect to set-containment of the target set of activities.

Theorem 1. *Given a task a in the process alphabet Σ, two non-empty sets of tasks Y and Y' such that $Y \subseteq Y' \subseteq \Sigma$, a log L and a TBDeclare constraint template C, then $S(C(x, Y), L) \leqslant S(C(x, Y'), L)$.*

Proof. In the following, we name the number of cases in which $C(x, Y)$ and $C(x, Y')$ are verified as, resp., C_L^+ and $C_L'^+$. In the light of Lemma 1, if $Y \subseteq Y'$ then $C(x, Y) \models C(x, Y')$. Therefore, due to the definition of model for a constraint w.r.t. a log, we have $C_L^+ \leqslant C_L'^+$. Since a is the activation for both constraints, the cases in which they are activated are the same, accounting to C_L^T. As a consequence, $\frac{C_L^+}{C_L^T} \leqslant \frac{C_L'^+}{C_L^T}$.   □

4   Discovery

This section describes MINERful for Target-Branched Declare (TB-MINERful), a three step algorithm for: *(i)* building a knowledge base, which keeps statistics on task occurrences; *(ii)* querying the knowledge base for support and confidence of constraints; *(iii)* pruning constraints not having sufficient support and confidence. The input of the algorithm is a log L based on a log alphabet Σ. Three thresholds can be specified: *(i)* *branching factor*, limiting the size of the activity sets for discovered constraints, *(ii)* *support*, and *(iii)* *confidence*.

4.1   The Knowledge Base

The first step is the construction of a knowledge base keeping statistics on task occurrences in the log. It consists of 9 functions listed below along with a semi-formal definition. We indicate parameters for constraints as x, y, z. Y, Z are set-parameters. Consider, e.g., a set of activities $\Sigma = \{a, b, c, d\}$ (log alphabet). While a, b, c, d refers to activity instantiations, a possible instantiation of Y is $\{b, c\}$. As example log we use $L = \{\langle a, a, b, a, c, a\rangle, \langle a, a, b, a, c, a, d\rangle\}$.

- $\overset{\not\times}{\gamma_0}(x)$ counts the traces where x did not occur. For instance, $\overset{\not\times}{\gamma_0}(a) = 0$ for L, because a occurs in every trace. $\overset{\not\times}{\gamma_0}(d) = 1$ instead.
- $\Gamma(x)$ counts the occurrences of x. Therefore, $\Gamma(a) = 8$ in L.
- $\overset{\rightarrow}{\delta_0}(x, Y)$ counts the occurrences of x with no following $y \in Y$ in the traces. In the example, e.g., $\overset{\rightarrow}{\delta_0}(a, \{d\}) = 4$, $\overset{\rightarrow}{\delta_0}(a, \{b\}) = 4$, and $\overset{\rightarrow}{\delta_0}(a, \{b, c\}) = 2$.
- $\overset{\leftarrow}{\delta_0}(x, Y)$ counts the occurrences of x with no preceding $y \in Y$ in the traces. Thus, e.g., $\overset{\leftarrow}{\delta_0}(a, \{d\}) = 8$, $\overset{\leftarrow}{\delta_0}(a, \{b\}) = 4$, and $\overset{\leftarrow}{\delta_0}(a, \{b, c\}) = 4$.
- $\overset{\leftrightarrow}{\delta_0}(x, Y)$ counts the occurrences of x with no $y \in Y$ in the traces. Therefore, $\overset{\leftrightarrow}{\delta_0}(a, \{d\}) = 1$, and $\overset{\leftrightarrow}{\delta_0}(a, \{b, d\}) = 0$ in L.
- $\overset{\rightarrow}{\delta_1}(x, y)$ counts the occurrences of x having y as the next event. Hence, $\overset{\rightarrow}{\delta_1}(a, b) = 2$, $\overset{\rightarrow}{\delta_1}(a, d) = 1$.
- $\overset{\leftarrow}{\delta_1}(x, y)$ counts the occurrences of x having y as the preceding event. In L, $\overset{\rightarrow}{\delta_1}(a, b) = 2$ and $\overset{\rightarrow}{\delta_1}(a, d) = 0$.
- $\overset{\leftrightarrow}{\beta}(x, Y)$ counts how many times x repeats until the first $y \in Y$. If no $y \in Y$ appears in the trace, the count is not further considered. In the example, $\overset{\leftrightarrow}{\beta}(a, \{b\}) = 2$, $\overset{\leftrightarrow}{\beta}(a, \{c\}) = 4$, $\overset{\leftrightarrow}{\beta}(a, \{b, c\}) = 2$, and $\overset{\leftrightarrow}{\beta}(a, \{b, d\}) = 3$.
- $\overset{\leftarrow}{\beta}(x, Y)$ is similar to $\overset{\leftrightarrow}{\beta}(x, Y)$, but reading the trace contrariwise. Thus, $\overset{\leftarrow}{\beta}(a, \{b\}) = 2$, $\overset{\leftarrow}{\beta}(a, \{c\}) = 0$, $\overset{\leftarrow}{\beta}(a, \{b, c\}) = 0$, and $\overset{\leftarrow}{\beta}(a, \{b, d\}) = 2$.

Next, we discuss how this knowledge base is built based on an input log.

4.2   Building the Knowledge Base

Here, we define an algorithm for building the knowledge base, which requires one run over the traces to update it. This makes the algorithm linear w.r.t. the number of traces and their length.

For evaluating $\overset{\rightarrow}{\delta_0}(x, Y)$, the technique executes two steps for each string. As a first step, it computes for every activity $y \in \Sigma \backslash \{x\}$ the value to accumulate in $\overset{\rightarrow}{\delta_0}(x, y)$, i.e., $N_{x,y}^{\delta_0}$. We will also refer to $N_{x,y}^{\delta_0}$ as a pairwise counter. Table 2a shows how this is achieved for $\langle a, a, b, a, c, a\rangle$. $N_{x,y}^{\delta_0}$ is incremented by 1 every time x is read, while parsing the trace. When y is read, $N_{x,y}^{\delta_0}$ is reset to 0. The $\downarrow$ symbol indicates this operation ("flush"). At the end of the trace, the value stored in $N_{x,y}^{\delta_0}$ reports the occurrences of x after which no y occurred. Pairwise counters do not take into account the relation of x with *sets* of activities, though. On the other hand, computing a value for each $Y \in \mathcal{P}(\Sigma \backslash \{a\})$ would be impractical. Therefore, we build *differential cumulative* set-counters, $\Delta N_{x,Y}^{\delta_0}$. If

Table 3. Computation of $N_{a,\cdot}^{\delta_0}$ and $\Delta N_{a,\cdot}^{\delta_0}$, given a sample trace: $\langle a, a, b, a, c, a\rangle$

(a) Computation of $\Delta N_{a,\cdot}^{\delta_0}$.

Trace	a	a	b	a	c	a
$N_{a,b}^{\delta_0}$	1	2	↓	1		2
$N_{a,c}^{\delta_0}$	1	2	3	↓	1	
$N_{a,d}^{\delta_0}$	1	2	3	4		

(b) Computation of $\Delta N_{a,\cdot}^{\delta_0}$, given the values of $N_{a,\cdot}^{\delta_0}$.

$N_{a,\cdot}^{\delta_0}$			$\Delta N_{a,\cdot}^{\delta_0}$
$N_{a,b}^{\delta_0} = 1+$	$N_{a,c}^{\delta_0} = 1$	$N_{a,d}^{\delta_0} = 1+$	$\Rightarrow \Delta N_{a,\{b,c,d\}}^{\delta_0} = 1$
1		1+	$\Rightarrow \Delta N_{a,\{b,\ d\}}^{\delta_0} = 1$
		2	$\Rightarrow \Delta N_{a,\{\ \ d\}}^{\delta_0} = 2$

$Y \subseteq Z$, $\Delta N_{x,Z}^{\delta_0}$ reports the number of times in which none of its elements occurred in the trace after x. $\Delta N_{x,Y}^{\delta_0}$ reports only the difference between *(i)* the number of times in which no $y \in Y$ occurred, and *(ii)* $\Delta N_{x,Z}^{\delta_0}$. Therefore, in $\langle a, a, b, a, c, a\rangle$, we have that $\Delta N_{a,\{b,c,d\}}^{\delta_0} = 1$, $\Delta N_{a,\{b,d\}}^{\delta_0} = 1$, and $\Delta N_{a,\{d\}}^{\delta_0} = 2$. Passing from pairwise counters to differential cumulative set-counters is a linear operation: Table 2b sketches the technique. From this data structure, $\overrightarrow{\delta_0}(x,Y)$ can be extracted as follows:

$$\overrightarrow{\delta_0}(x,Y) = \sum_{Z \supseteq Y} \Delta N_{x,Z}^{\delta_0}$$

Table 4 shows the extraction for the example trace. It is straightforward to see that the differential accumulation ($\Delta N_{x,Y}^{\delta_0}$) allows for keeping fewer values in memory (3 in the example) than the possible entries for the knowledge base ($\overrightarrow{\delta_0}(x,Y)$, which amounts to 6). Every time a new trace is parsed, $N_{x,y}^{\delta_0}$ is reset to 0 for each $x,y \in \Sigma$. At the end of the analysis of every subsequent trace, values for a new structure $\Delta N_{x,Y}^{\delta_0'}$ are calculated. Thereupon, they are added to the preceding results. It might happen that a new Z set was not considered in $\Delta N_{x,\cdot}^{\delta_0}$ for previous traces, but a new $\Delta N_{a,Z}^{\delta_0'}$ is computed. In such case, $\Delta N_{x,Z}^{\delta_0}$ is considered as 0 by the default and the new value in $\Delta N_{x,Z}^{\delta_0'}$ is added. This technique extends to the computation of $\overleftarrow{\delta_0}(x,Y)$ and $\overleftrightarrow{\delta_0}(x,Y)$ with slight modifications. The values of the remaining functions are also determined in a similar way. However, the detailed descriptions are here omitted for the sake of space.

4.3 Querying the Knowledge Base

Once the knowledge base is built, the support of constraints can be calculated. Table 5 lists the functions adopted to this extent, for each TBDeclare constraint. All queries build upon a Laplacian concept of probability with support being computed as the number of supporting cases divided by the total number of cases. In particular, the total number of cases is the count of occurrences of

Table 4. Computation of $\overrightarrow{\delta_0}(a, \cdot)$, given $\Delta N_{a,\cdot}^{\delta_0}$.

$\Delta N_{a,\cdot}^{\delta_0}$				$\Rightarrow$	$\overrightarrow{\delta_0}(a, \cdot)$
$\{b,$	$c,$	$d\} =$	1	$\Rightarrow$	$\overrightarrow{\delta_0}(a, \{b, c, d\}) = \overrightarrow{\delta_0}(a, \{c, d\}) = \overrightarrow{\delta_0}(a, \{c\}) = 1$
$\{b,$		$d\} =$	1	$\Rightarrow$	$\overrightarrow{\delta_0}(a, \{b, d\}) = \overrightarrow{\delta_0}(a, \{b\}) = 2$
$\{$		$d\} =$	2	$\Rightarrow$	$\overrightarrow{\delta_0}(a, \{d\}) = 4$

Table 5. Target-Branched Declare constraints and support functions

TBDeclare constraint	Support
$RespondedExistence(x, Y)$	$1 - \frac{\overleftrightarrow{\delta_0}(x, Y)}{\Gamma(x)}$
$Response(x, Y)$	$1 - \frac{\overrightarrow{\delta_0}(x, Y)}{\Gamma(x)}$
$AlternateResponse(x, Y)$	$1 - \frac{\overrightarrow{\delta_0}(x, Y) + \overset{\curvearrowright}{\beta}(x, Y)}{\Gamma(x)}$
$ChainResponse(x, Y)$	$\frac{\sum_{y \in Y} \overrightarrow{\delta_1}(x, y)}{\Gamma(x)}$
$Precedence(Y, x)$	$1 - \frac{\overleftarrow{\delta_0}(x, Y)}{\Gamma(x)}$
$AlternatePrecedence(Y, x)$	$1 - \frac{\overleftarrow{\delta_0}(x, Y) + \overset{\curvearrowleft}{\beta}(x, Y)}{\Gamma(x)}$
$ChainPrecedence(Y, x)$	$\frac{\sum_{y \in Y} \overleftarrow{\delta_1}(x, y)}{\Gamma(x)}$

the activation in the log, $\Gamma(x)$. For $ChainResponse(x, Y)$, supporting cases are those occurrences of a immediately followed by some $y \in Y$, i.e., $\overrightarrow{\delta_1}(x, y)$. Supporting cases can be summed up because if x is followed by a given $y \in Y$ in a trace, it cannot be immediately followed by any other event $z \in Y$. In other words, the two cases are mutually exclusive. However, this assumption does not hold true, e.g., for $Response(x, Y)$. Therefore, we consider the non-supporting cases, when x is *not* followed by any of the $y \in Y$, i.e., $\overrightarrow{\delta_0}(x, Y)$. We get that $P(E) = 1 - P(\overline{E})$ with $P(E)$ being the probability of E and $\overline{E}$ its negation. Hence, the support of $Response(x, Y)$ is $1 - \frac{\overrightarrow{\delta_0}(x, Y)}{\Gamma(x)}$. Likewise, the support of $RespondedExistence(x, Y)$ is computed on the basis of the non-supporting cases. The support of $AlternateResponse(x, Y)$ is then based on the cases when either *(i)* x is not followed by any $y \in Y$ $(\overleftrightarrow{\delta_0}(x, Y))$, or *(ii)* x occurs more than once before the first occurrence of $y \in Y$ $(\overset{\curvearrowright}{\beta}(x, Y))$. The two conditions are mutually exclusive. Therefore, it is appropriate to sum them up. Similar considerations lead to the definition of support functions for $Precedence(Y, x)$, $AlternatePrecedence(Y, x)$ and $ChainPrecedence(Y, x)$.

Confidence is computed as the constraint's support multiplied by the fraction of traces where the activation occurs. Therefore, given a TBDeclare constraint $\mathcal{C}(x, Y)$, a log L, and the support function $\mathcal{S}(\mathcal{C}(x, Y), L)$, the confidence of $\mathcal{C}(x, Y)$ w.r.t. L, $\mathcal{L}(\mathcal{C}(x, Y), L)$, is defined as

$$\mathcal{L}(\mathcal{C}(x, Y), L) = \mathcal{S}(\mathcal{C}(x, Y), L) \times \left(1 - \frac{\overset{\nearrow}{\gamma_0}(x)}{\Gamma(x)}\right)$$

4.4 Pruning the Returned Constraints

The power-set of activities in the log alphabet amounts to $2^{|\Sigma|-1}$. Therefore, if we name the number of TBDeclare constraint templates as N, up to $N \times 2^{|\Sigma|-1}$ constraints can potentially hold true. When a maximum limit to the cardinality of the set is imposed, the number is reduced to

$$|\Sigma| \times N \times \sum_{i=1}^{\min\{\rho, |\Sigma|-1\}} \binom{|\Sigma|-1}{i}$$

However, even with branching factor set to 3 and $|\Sigma| = 10$, already 3087 constraints have to be evaluated. A model including such a number of constraints would be hardly comprehensible for humans [18,26]. In order to reduce this number, we adopt pruning based on set-dominance and on hierarchy subsumption.

Pruning Based on Set-Dominance. The idea of this pruning approach is that if, e.g., $Response(a, \{b, c\})$ and $Response(a, \{b, c, d\})$ have the same support, the first is more informative than the second. Indeed, stating that "if a is executed then either b or c would eventually follow", implies that also "either b, c or d would eventually follow". In general terms, the support of TBDeclare constraints that are instantiations of the same template and share the activation increases according to the set-containment relation of target activities (see Theorem 1). To this end, the mining algorithm distributes the discovered constraints, along with their computed support, on a structure like the Hasse Diagram of Figure 1. This is a Direct-Acyclic Graph, such that a breadth-first search can be implemented. For each constraint, the pruning technique visits the nodes, from the biggest in size to the smallest. For instance, it can start from $Response(a, \{b, c, d, e\})$, i.e., the sink node, if the branching factor is equal to the size of the log alphabet. Given the current node, it checks whether in one of the parent nodes a constraint is stored (i.e., $Response(a, \{b, c, d\})$, $Response(a, \{b, c, e\})$, $Response(a, \{b, d, e\})$, $Response(a, \{c, d, e\})$) with greater or equal support. If so, it marks the current as redundant, and proceeds the visit towards the parent nodes that are not already marked as redundant. Otherwise, it marks all the ancestors as redundant. The parsing ends when either *(i)* the visit reaches the root node, or *(ii)* no parent, which is not already marked as redundant, is available for the visit.

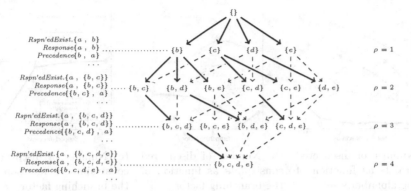

Fig. 1. A Hasse Diagram representing the Partial Order set containment relation. Containing sets are at the head of connecting arcs, contained sets are at the tail.

Pruning Based on Hierarchy Subsumption. As investigated in [7,23,13], Declare constraints are not independent, but partially form a subsumption hierarchy. We consider a constraint $\mathcal{C}(x, Y)$ subsumed by another constraint $\mathcal{C}'(x, Y)$ when all the traces that comply with $\mathcal{C}(x, Y)$ also comply with $\mathcal{C}'(x, Y)$. $Response(x, Y)$, e.g., is subsumed by $RespondedExistence(x, Y)$. Figure 2 depicts the subsumption hierarchy for TBDeclare constraints. It follows that

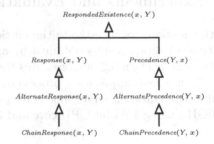

Fig. 2. Diagram showing the subsumption hierarchy relation. Constraints that are subsumed are at the tail.

a subsumed constraint always has a support which is less than or equal to the subsuming one. This pruning technique aims at keeping those constraints that are the most restrictive, among the most supported. Therefore, it labels as redundant every constraint C which is at the same time (i) subsumed by another constraint C', and (ii) having a lower support than C'. Therefore, if, e.g., given a log L, $\mathcal{S}\left(RespondedExistence(x, Y), L\right) > \mathcal{S}\left(Response(x, Y), L\right)$, then $Response(x, Y)$ is marked as redundant. However, if $\mathcal{S}\left(RespondedExistence(x, Y), L\right) = \mathcal{S}\left(Response(x, Y), L\right)$, then $Response(x, Y)$ is preferred. This is due to the fact that more restrictive constraints hold more information than the less restrictive ones. The pruning approach is based on the monotone non-decrement of support (cf. Figure 2). It operates as follows. Starting from the root of the hierarchy tree, if a constraint has a support equal to one of the children, it is marked as redundant and the visit proceeds with the children. If a child has a support which is lower than the parent, it is marked as redundant. All its children will be automatically marked as redundant as well, as they cannot have a higher support.

Both pruning techniques complement one another in reducing the constraint set.

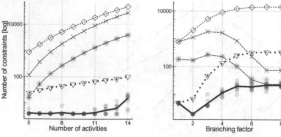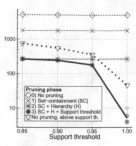

(a) Number of discovered constraints as function of the log alphabet size

(b) Number of discovered constraints as function of the branching factor

(c) Number of discovered constraints as function of the branching factor

Fig. 3. Effectiveness tests performed on synthetic logs

5   Experiments and Evaluation

In this section, we investigate the efficiency and effectiveness of our approach. Section 5.1 shows results obtained by applying the proposed technique on synthetic logs. Section 5.2 demonstrates the effectiveness of our approach for event logs from a loan application process of a Dutch financial institute. All experiments were run on a server machine equipped with Intel Xeon CPU E5-2650 v2 2.60GHz, using 1 64-bit CPU core and 32GB main memory quota.

5.1   Evaluation Based on Simulation

To test the effectiveness and the efficiency of our approach, we have defined a simple Declare model including the following constraints:

- $ChainPrecedence(\{a,b\},\ c)$
- $ChainPrecedence(\{a,b,d\},\ c)$
- $AlternateResponse(a,\ \{b,c\})$
- $RespondedExistence(a,\ \{b,c,d,e\})$
- $Response(a,\ \{b,c\})$
- $Precedence(\{a,b,c,d\},\ e)$

and we have simulated it to generate a compliant event log as described in [7]. In our experiments, we focus on different characteristics of the discovery task including average length of the traces, number of traces, and number of activities. Moreover, we consider characteristics of the discovered model including minimum support and maximum number of branches. In our experiments, we have run the algorithm varying the value of one variable at a time. The remaining variables were fixed and corresponding to 4 and 25 for resp. minimum and maximum trace length, 10,000 for log size, 8 for log alphabet size, 1.0 for support threshold, and 3 for branching factor.

Effectiveness: First, we demonstrate the effectiveness of our approach by investigating the reduction effect of the proposed pruning techniques. In particular, we analyse the trend of the variable "number of discovered constraints" as a function of log alphabet size, branching factor, and support threshold.

Figure 3a shows the trend (in logarithmic scale) of the number of discovered constraints by varying the log alphabet size. Different curves refer to different configurations of the miner: without any pruning (diamonds); with set-containment-based pruning (crosses); with set-containment- and hierarchy-based pruning (asterisks); with set-containment- and hierarchy-based pruning, along with support threshold (points); with support threshold only (triangles). This plot provides evidence that as the number of activities in the log alphabet increases, the number of discovered constraints increases as well. However, we discover a lower increase of constraints as we proceed further in the sequence of pruning techniques. Moreover, there is a significant difference between the number of discovered constraints with filtering based on the minimum support threshold, and based on the pruning techniques presented in this paper. This improvement yields a reduction ratio of 84% (100.3 v. 15.2, on average).

Figure 3b shows the trend (in logarithmic scale) of the number of discovered constraints by varying the branching factor. Here, the trend of the number of discovered constraints is different for different configurations. Without pruning, or with the simple filtering by minimum support threshold, the number of discovered constraints increases as the number of branches increases. On the other hand, when we apply the set-dominance- and hierarchy-based pruning techniques, the number of discovered constraints increases up to a branching value of 3. After this value, the number of constraints decreases. When we apply all the proposed pruning techniques together the number of constraints eventually increases. In addition, the number of constraints obtained by applying set-dominance and subsumption hierarchy converges to the number of constraints discovered when all the pruning techniques are applied together. The difference between the number of discovered constraint with support threshold and the number after using the pruning techniques presented in this paper is quantified (branching factor of 8) in a reduction ratio of 88% (46.2 v. 5.2, on average).

The plot in Figure 3c confirms that for any threshold between 0.85 and 1.0, the number of constraints discovered by applying all the pruning techniques is lower than the one obtained by applying the support-threshold filtering. The reduction ratio is indeed 93% (331.8 v. 22, on average), when the threshold is set to 1.0.

Efficiency: Second, we focus on time efficiency of our approach. We observe that efficiency strongly depends on the template. In particular, the "alternate" templates are less performative. Figure 4a shows this by plotting the computation time as function of the log alphabet size (in logarithmic scale). When the alternate templates are included in the evaluation, the computation time grows exponentially with the growth of the alphabet size.

As a next step, we therefore exclude the alternate templates and get the computation time as a function of log alphabet size (Figure 4b), log size (Figure 5a), and average trace size (Figure 5b). Figure 4b shows the trend (in logarithmic

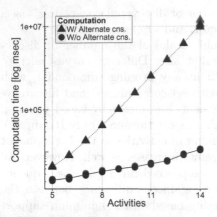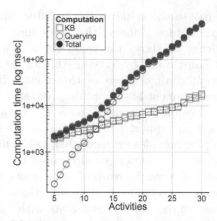

(a) Efficiency test results, including and excluding alternate templates in the evaluation

(b) Efficiency test results, w.r.t. the different phase of the algorithm

Fig. 4. Efficiency tests performed on synthetic logs, considering computation time as function of the log alphabet size

scale) of the computation time by varying the log alphabet size. Different curves refer to the computation time for *(i)* the knowledge base construction, *(ii)* the querying on the knowledge base, and *(iii)* to the total computation time. Notice that there is a break point when the log alphabet is composed of 12 activities in which the query time becomes higher than the knowledge base construction time. Figure 5a shows the trend (in logarithmic scale) of the computation time by varying the log size, whereas Figure 5b depicts the trend (in logarithmic scale) of the computation time by varying the average trace size. In both cases the query clearly outperforms the knowledge base construction time.

5.2   Evaluation Based on Real Data

We have evaluated the applicability of our approach using real-world event logs provided for the BPI challenge 2012 [27]. The event log pertains to an application process for personal loans or overdrafts of a Dutch bank. It contains 262,200 events distributed across 24 different possible event names and includes 13,087 cases.

In this case, it is possible to prune the list of discovered constraints in order to obtain a compact set of constraint, which is understandable for human analysts. By applying the miner with a support equal to 1, confidence equal to 0.85, and branching factor 5, we obtain the following 11 constraints:

$ChainResponse(A\_SUBMITTED, A\_PARTLYSUBMITTED)$

$ChainPrecedence(A\_SUBMITTED, A\_PARTLYSUBMITTED)$

$Response(A\_SUBMITTED, \{A\_PREACCEPTED, A\_DECLINED, A\_CANCELLED\})$

$Response(A\_SUBMITTED, \{A\_PREACCEPTED, A\_DECLINED, W\_Afhandelen\ leads\})$

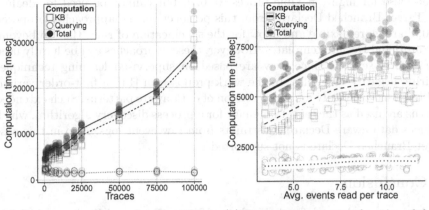

(a) Computation time as function of the   (b) Computation time as function of the
log size   average trace size

Fig. 5. Efficiency tests performed on synthetic logs

Response(A_SUBMITTED, {W_Completeren aanvraag, A_DECLINED, A_CANCELLED})

Response(A_SUBMITTED, {W_Completeren aanvraag, A_DECLINED, W_Afhandelen leads})

RespondedExistence(A_PARTLYSUBMITTED, {A_SUBMITTED})

Response(A_PARTLYSUBMITTED, {A_PREACCEPTED, A_DECLINED, A_CANCELLED})

Response(A_PARTLYSUBMITTED, {A_PREACCEPTED, A_DECLINED, W_Afhandelen leads})

ChainResponse(A_PARTLYSUBMITTED, {A_PREACCEPTED, A_DECLINED, W_Afhandelen leads, W_Beoordelen fraude})

Response(A_PARTLYSUBMITTED, {W_Completeren aanvraag, A_DECLINED, A_CANCELLED})

Response(A_PARTLYSUBMITTED, {W_Completeren aanvraag, A_DECLINED, W_Afhandelen leads})

These results have been derived with a computation time of 7.2 sec for the
construction of the knowledge base, and 25.98 min for constraint mining.

6   Related Work

Several analysis tools for Declare are available in the literature. Some of them
have been implemented as plug-ins of the process mining tool ProM [12].

Some approaches focus on the run-time monitoring of compliance specifications defined through Declare. For example, in [16,11], the authors propose a
technique for monitoring Declare models based on finite state automata. In [29],
the authors define *Timed Declare*, an extension of Declare that relies on timed
automata. In [19], the EC is used for defining a data-aware semantics for Declare. In [20], the authors propose an approach for monitoring data-aware Declare
constraints at run-time based on this semantics. This approach also allows the
verification of metric temporal constraints.

Other works [10,3,5,7,17,15,14] focus on the discovery of Declare models. The
algorithms proposed in [5,17,15] are suitable for discovering standard Declare

models, also for highly flexible processes [6,4], but cannot be used for dealing with Target-Branched Declare. From this perspective, the approaches proposed in [10,3] are more flexible and allow for the specification of rules that go beyond the traditional Declare templates. However, these approaches can be hardly used in real-world settings since they are based on supervised learning techniques requiring negative examples. In the work proposed in [14], a first-order variant of LTL is used to specify a limited version of data-aware patterns. Such extended patterns are used as the target language for a process discovery algorithm, which produces data-aware Declare constraints from raw event logs. Also in this case Target-Branched Declare is not supported.

7   Conclusion

In this paper, we have defined the class of Target-Branched Declare, which exhibits interesting properties in terms of set-dominance. We exploit these properties for the definition of an efficient mining approach. Furthermore, we specify pruning rules in order to arrive at a compact rule set. Our technique is evaluated for efficiency and effectiveness using simulated data and the case of the BPI 2012 challenge. In future research, we aim to investigate potential for improving efficiency. We also plan to extend our technique towards the coverage of data, in order to discern which condition leads to a specific choice.

References

1. Agrawal, R., Srikant, R.: Fast Algorithms for Mining Association Rules in Large Databases. In: VLDB, pp. 487–499. Morgan Kaufmann (1994)
2. Burattin, A., Maggi, F.M., van der Aalst, W.M.P., Sperduti, A.: Techniques for a Posteriori Analysis of Declarative Processes. In: EDOC, pp. 41–50 (2012)
3. Chesani, F., Lamma, E., Mello, P., Montali, M., Riguzzi, F., Storari, S.: Exploiting Inductive Logic Programming Techniques for Declarative Process Mining. In: Jensen, K., van der Aalst, W.M.P. (eds.) ToPNoC II. LNCS, vol. 5460, pp. 278–295. Springer, Heidelberg (2009)
4. Di Ciccio, C., Marrella, A., Russo, A.: Knowledge-Intensive Processes: An Overview of Contemporary Approaches. In: KiBP, pp. 33–47 (2012)
5. Di Ciccio, C., Mecella, M.: Mining Constraints for Artful Processes. In: Abramowicz, W., Kriksciuniene, D., Sakalauskas, V. (eds.) BIS 2012. LNBIP, vol. 117, pp. 11–23. Springer, Heidelberg (2012)
6. Di Ciccio, C., Mecella, M.: Mining Artful Processes from Knowledge Workers' Emails. IEEE Internet Computing 17(5), 10–20 (2013)
7. Di Ciccio, C., Mecella, M.: A Two-Step Fast Algorithm for the Automated Discovery of Declarative Workflows. In: CIDM, pp. 135–142 (2013)
8. Dumas, M., La Rosa, M., Mendling, J., Reijers, H.A.: Fundamentals of Business Process Management. Springer (2013)
9. Fahland, D., Lübke, D., Mendling, J., Reijers, H., Weber, B., Weidlich, M., Zugal, S.: Declarative versus Imperative Process Modeling Languages: The Issue of Understandability. In: Halpin, T., Krogstie, J., Nurcan, S., Proper, E., Schmidt, R., Soffer, P., Ukor, R. (eds.) Enterprise, Business-Process and Information Systems Modeling. LNBIP, vol. 29, pp. 353–366. Springer, Heidelberg (2009)

10. Lamma, E., Mello, P., Riguzzi, F., Storari, S.: Applying Inductive Logic Programming to Process Mining. In: Blockeel, H., Ramon, J., Shavlik, J., Tadepalli, P. (eds.) ILP 2007. LNCS (LNAI), vol. 4894, pp. 132–146. Springer, Heidelberg (2008)
11. Maggi, F.M., Westergaard, M., Montali, M., van der Aalst, W.M.P.: Runtime Verification of LTL-Based Declarative Process Models. In: Khurshid, S., Sen, K. (eds.) RV 2011. LNCS, vol. 7186, pp. 131–146. Springer, Heidelberg (2012)
12. Maggi, F.M.: Declarative Process Mining with the Declare Component of ProM. In: BPM (Demos). CEUR, vol. 1021 (2013)
13. Maggi, F.M., Bose, R.P.J.C., van der Aalst, W.M.P.: A Knowledge-Based Integrated Approach for Discovering and Repairing Declare Maps. In: Salinesi, C., Norrie, M.C., Pastor, Ó. (eds.) CAiSE 2013. LNCS, vol. 7908, pp. 433–448. Springer, Heidelberg (2013)
14. Maggi, F.M., Dumas, M., García-Bañuelos, L., Montali, M.: Discovering Data-Aware Declarative Process Models from Event Logs. In: Daniel, F., Wang, J., Weber, B. (eds.) BPM 2013. LNCS, vol. 8094, pp. 81–96. Springer, Heidelberg (2013)
15. Maggi, F.M., Bose, R.P.J.C., van der Aalst, W.M.P.: Efficient Discovery of Understandable Declarative Process Models from Event Logs. In: Ralyté, J., Franch, X., Brinkkemper, S., Wrycza, S. (eds.) CAiSE 2012. LNCS, vol. 7328, pp. 270–285. Springer, Heidelberg (2012)
16. Maggi, F.M., Montali, M., Westergaard, M., van der Aalst, W.M.P.: Monitoring Business Constraints with Linear Temporal Logic: An Approach Based on Colored Automata. In: Rinderle-Ma, S., Toumani, F., Wolf, K. (eds.) BPM 2011. LNCS, vol. 6896, pp. 132–147. Springer, Heidelberg (2011)
17. Maggi, F.M., Mooij, A.J., van der Aalst, W.M.P.: User-Guided Discovery of Declarative Process Models. In: CIDM, pp. 192–199. IEEE (2011)
18. Mendling, J., Strembeck, M., Recker, J.: Factors of Process Model Comprehension - Findings from a Series of Experiments. Decision Support Systems 53(1), 195–206 (2012)
19. Montali, M., Chesani, F., Maggi, F.M., Mello, P.: Towards Data-Aware Constraints in Declare. In: SAC, pp. 1391–1396 (2013)
20. Montali, M., Maggi, F.M., Chesani, F., Mello, P., van der Aalst, W.M.P.: Monitoring Business Constraints with the Event Calculus. ACM TIST 5(1), 17 (2013)
21. Montali, M., Pesic, M., van der Aalst, W.M.P.: Federico Chesani, Paola Mello, and Sergio Storari. Declarative Specification and Verification of Service Choreographies. ACM Transactions on the Web 4(1) (2010)
22. Reijers, H.A., Slaats, T., Stahl, C.: Declarative Modeling–An Academic Dream or the Future for BPM? In: Daniel, F., Wang, J., Weber, B. (eds.) BPM 2013. LNCS, vol. 8094, pp. 307–322. Springer, Heidelberg (2013)
23. Schunselaar, D.M.M., Maggi, F.M., Sidorova, N.: Patterns for a Log-Based Strengthening of Declarative Compliance Models. In: Derrick, J., Gnesi, S., Latella, D., Treharne, H. (eds.) IFM 2012. LNCS, vol. 7321, pp. 327–342. Springer, Heidelberg (2012)
24. Smirnov, S., Weidlich, M., Mendling, J.: Business Process Model Abstraction Based on Synthesis from Well-Structured Behavioral Profiles. Int. J. Cooperative Inf. Syst. 21(1), 55–83 (2012)
25. van der Aalst, W.M.P., Weijters, T., Maruster, L.: Workflow Mining: Discovering Process Models from Event Logs. IEEE TKDE 16(9), 1128–1142 (2004)

26. van der Aalst, W.M.P., Pesic, M., Schonenberg, H.: Declarative Workflows: Balancing between Flexibility and Support. CSRD 23(2), 99–113 (2009)
27. van Dongen, B.F.: BPI Challenge 2012 (2012)
28. Weidlich, M., Polyvyanyy, A., Desai, N., Mendling, J., Weske, M.: Process Compliance Analysis Based on Behavioural Profiles. Inf. Syst. 36(7), 1009–1025 (2011)
29. Westergaard, M., Maggi, F.M.: Looking into the Future: Using Timed Automata to Provide A Priori Advice about Timed Declarative Process Models. In: Meersman, R., et al. (eds.) OTM 2012, Part I. LNCS, vol. 7565, pp. 250–267. Springer, Heidelberg (2012)

Crowd-Based Mining
of Reusable Process Model Patterns

Carlos Rodríguez, Florian Daniel, and Fabio Casati

University of Trento,
Via Sommarive 9, I-38123, Povo (TN), Italy
{crodriguez,daniel,casati}@disi.unitn.it

Abstract. Process mining is a domain where computers undoubtedly outperform humans. It is a *mathematically complex* and *computationally demanding* problem, and event logs are at *too low a level of abstraction* to be intelligible in large scale to humans. We demonstrate that if instead the data to mine from are *models* (not logs), datasets are *small* (in the order of dozens rather than thousands or millions), and the knowledge to be discovered is *complex* (reusable model patterns), humans outperform computers. We design, implement, run, and test a *crowd-based pattern mining* approach and demonstrate its viability compared to automated mining. We specifically mine *mashup* model patterns (we use them to provide interactive recommendations inside a mashup tool) and explain the analogies with mining business process models. The problem is relevant in that reusable model patterns encode valuable modeling and domain knowledge, such as best practices or organizational conventions, from which modelers can learn and benefit when designing own models.

Keywords: Model patterns, Pattern mining, Crowdsourcing, Mashups.

1 Introduction

Designing good business processes, i.e., *modeling* processes, is a non-trivial task. It typically requires not only fluency in the chosen modeling language, but also intimate knowledge of the target domain and of the common practices, conventions and procedures followed by the various actors operating in the given domain. These requirements do not apply to business processes only. We find them over and over again in all those contexts that leverage on model-driven formalisms for the implementation of process-oriented systems. This is, for instance, the case of data mashups, which are commonly based on graphical data flow paradigms, such as the one proposed by Yahoo! Pipes (http://pipes.yahoo.com).

In order to ease the modeling of this kind of data mashups (so-called *pipes*), in a previous work, we developed an extension of Pipes that interactively recommends mashup model patterns while the developer is modeling a pipe. A click on a recommended pattern automatically weaves the pattern into the partial pipe in the modeling canvas. Patterns are mined from a repository of freely accessible pipes models [11]. We mined patterns from a dataset of 997 pipes

S. Sadiq, P. Soffer, and H. Völzer (Eds.): BPM 2014, LNCS 8659, pp. 51–66, 2014.

Fig. 1. A Yahoo! Pipes data mashup model pattern for plotting news on a map. The mashup logic is expressed as data flow diagram.

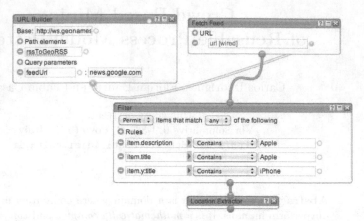

taken from the "most popular" category, assuming that popular pipes are more likely to be functioning and useful. Before their use, patterns were checked by a mashup expert assuring their meaningfulness and reusability (e.g., see Figure 1 for an example of a good pattern). The extension is called Baya [13], and our user studies demonstrate that recommending model patterns has the potential to significantly lower development times in model-driven environments [12].

The approach however suffers from problems that are common to pattern mining algorithms: identifying support threshold values, managing large numbers of produced patterns, coping with noise (useless patterns), giving meaning to patterns, and the cold start problem. Inspired by the recent advent of *crowdsourcing* [6], the intuition emerged that it might be possible to attack these problems with the help of the *crowd*, that is, by involving *humans* in the mining process. The intuition stems from the observation that pure statistical support does not always imply interestingness [2], and that human experts are anyway the ultimate responsibles for deciding about the suitability or not of patterns.

In this paper, we report on the results of this investigation and demonstrate that crowd-based pattern mining can indeed be successfully used to identify meaningful model patterns. We describe our crowd-based mining algorithm, the adopted software/crowd stack, and demonstrate the effectiveness of the approach by comparing its performance with that of the algorithm adopted in Baya. We also show how our results and lessons learned are applicable to and impact the mining of model patterns from business process models.

2   Background and Problem Statement

2.1   Reference Process Models: Data Mashups

Mashups are composite web applications that are developed by integrating data, application logic, and pieces of user interfaces [1]. *Data mashups* are a special type of mashups that specifically focuses on the integration and processing of data sources available on the Web. Typical *data sources* are RSS or Atom feeds, plain XML- or JSON-encoded static resources, or more complex SOAP or RESTful web services. *Data mashup tools* are IDEs for data mashup development. They provide a set of data processing *operators*, e.g., filters or split and join operators, and the possibility to interactively configure data sources and operators (we collectively call them *components*).

In this paper, we specifically focus on the data mashup tool Yahoo! Pipes and our pattern recommender Baya [13]. The components and mashups supported by these tools can be modeled as follows: Let CL be a library of **components** of the form $c = \langle name, IP, IF, OP, emb \rangle$, where *name* identifies the component (e.g., RSS feed or Filter), IP is the set of input ports for data flow connectors, IF is the set of input fields for the configuration of the component, OP is the set of output ports, and $emb \in \{yes, no\}$ tells whether the component allows for the embedding of other components or not (e.g., to model loops). We distinguish three classes of components: *Source* components fetch data from the Web or collect user inputs at runtime. They don't have input ports: $IP = \emptyset$. *Data processing* components consume data in input and produce processed data in output: $IP, OP \neq \emptyset$. A *sink* component (the Pipe Output component) indicates the end of the data processing logic and publishes the output of the mashup, e.g., using JSON. The sink has neither input fields nor output ports: $IF, OP = \emptyset$.

A *data mashup* (a pipe) can thus be modeled as $m = \langle name, C, E, DF, VA \rangle$, where *name* uniquely identifies the mashup, C is the set of integrated components, $E \subseteq C \times C$ represents component embeddings, $DF \subseteq (\cup_i OP_i) \times (\cup_j IP_j)$ is the set of data flow connectors propagating data from output to input ports, and $VA \subseteq (\cup_k IF_k) \times STRING$ assigns character string values to input fields. Generic strings are interpreted as constants, strings starting with "item." are used to map input data attributes to input fields (see Figure 1).

A pipe is considered *correct*, if it (i) contains at least one source component, (ii) contains a set of data processing components (the set may be empty), (iii) contains exactly one sink component, (iv) is connected (in the sense of graph connectivity), and (v) has value assignments for each mandatory input field.

A *mashup model pattern* can thus be seen as a tuple $mp = \langle name, desc, tag, C, E, DF, VA \rangle$, with *name*, *desc* and *tag* naming, describing and tagging the pattern, and C, E, DF, VA being as defined above, however with relaxed correctness criteria: a pattern is *correct* if it (i) contains at least two components, (ii) is connected, and (iii) has value assignments for each mandatory input field.

2.2 Crowdsourcing

Crowdsourcing (CS) is the outsourcing of a unit of work to a crowd of people via an open call for contributions [6]. A *worker* is a member of the crowd (a human) that performs work, and a *crowdsourcer* is the organization, company or individual that crowdsources work. The crowdsourced work typically comes in the form of a *crowd task*, i.e., a unit of work that requires human intelligence and that a machine cannot solve in useful time or not solve at all. Examples of crowd tasks are annotating images with tags or descriptions, translating text from one language into another, or designing a logo.

A *crowdsourcing platform* is an online software infrastructure that provides access to a crowd of workers and can be used by crowdsourcers to crowdsource work. Multiple CS platforms exist, which all implement a specific *CS model*: The *marketplace* model caters for crowd tasks with fixed rewards for workers and clear acceptance criteria by the crowdsourcer. The model particularly suits micro-tasks like annotating images and is, for example, adopted by Amazon Mechanical Turk (https://www.mturk.com) and CrowdFlower (http://crowdflower.com). The *contest* model caters for tasks with fixed rewards but unclear acceptance criteria; workers compete with their solutions for the reward, and the crowdsourcer decides who wins. The model suits creative tasks like designing a logo and is, e.g., adopted by 99designs (http://99designs.com). The *auction* model caters for tasks with rewards to be negotiated but clear acceptance criteria. The model suits creative tasks like programming software and is, e.g., adopted by Freelancer (http://www.freelancer.com).

For the purpose of this paper, we specifically leverage on micro-tasks in marketplace CS platforms. Crowdsourcing a task in this context involves the following steps: The crowdsourcer publishes a *description* of the task to be performed, which the crowd can inspect and possibly express interest for. In this step, the crowdsourcer also defines the reward workers will get for performing the task and how many answers he would like to collect from the crowd. Not everybody of the crowd may, however, be eligible to perform a given task, either because the task requires specific capabilities (e.g., language skills) or because the workers should satisfy given properties (e.g., only female workers). Deciding which workers are allowed to perform a task is commonly called *pre-selection*, and it may be done either by the crowdsourcer manually or by the platform automatically (e.g., via questionnaires). Once workers are enabled to perform a task, the platform creates as many *task instances* as necessary to collect the expected number of answers. Upon completion of a task instance (or a set thereof), the crowdsourcer may inspect the collected answers and *validate* the respective correctness or quality. Work that is not of sufficient quality is not useful, and the crowdsourcer *rewards* only work that passes the possible check. Finally, the crowdsourcer may need to *integrate* collected results into an aggregated outcome of the overall CS process.

2.3 Problem Statement and Hypotheses

This paper aims to understand whether it is possible to crowdsource the mining of mashup model patterns of type mp from a dataset of mashup models $M = \{m_l\}$ with $l \in \{1...|M|\}$ and $|M|$ being "small" in terms of dataset sizes required by conventional data mining algorithms (dozens rather than thousands or millions). Specifically, the work aims to check the following hypotheses:

Hypothesis 1 (Effectiveness). *It is possible to mine reusable mashup model patterns from mashup models by crowdsourcing the identification of patterns.*

Hypothesis 2 (Value). *Model patterns identified by the crowd contain more domain knowledge than automatically mined patterns.*

Hypothesis 3 (Applicability). *Crowd-based pattern mining outperforms machine-based pattern mining for small datasets.*

It is important to note that the above hypotheses and this paper as a whole use the term "mining" with its generic meaning of "discovering knowledge," which does not necessarily require machine learning.

3   Crowd-Based Pattern Mining

The core **assumptions** underlying this research are that (i) we have access to a *repository* of mashup models (the dataset) of limited size, like in the case of a cold start of a modeling environment; (ii) the identification of patterns can be crowdsourced as *micro-tasks* via maketplace-based CS platforms; and (iii) the interestingness of patterns as judged *subjectively* by workers has similar value as that expressed via minimum support thresholds of automated mining algorithms.

3.1   Requirements

Crowdsourcing the mining of mashup model patterns under these assumptions asks for the fulfillment of a set of requirements:

R1: Workers must pass a *qualification test*, so as to guarantee a minimum level of familiarity with the chosen mashup modeling formalism.
R2: Mashup models *m* must be *represented* in a form that is easily intelligible to workers and that allows them to conveniently express patterns *mp*.
R3: It must be possible to input a *name*, a *description* and a list of *tags* for an identified pattern, as well as other *qualitative* feedback.
R4: To prevent *cheating* (a common problem in CS) as much as possible, all inputs must be checked for formal correctness.
R5: The crowdsourced pattern mining algorithm should make use of *redundancy* to guarantee that each mashup model is adequately taken into account.
R6: Workers must be *rewarded* for their work.
R7: Collected patterns must be *integrated and homogenized*, and repeated patterns must be merged into a set of patterns *MP*.
R8: Collected patterns must undergo a *quality check*, so as to assure the reusability and meaningfulness of identified patterns.

Given a set of crowd-mined patterns *MP*, accepting or rejecting our hypotheses then further requires comparing the quality of *MP* with that of patterns that are mined automatically (we use for this purpose our algorithm described in [11]).

3.2   Approach

Figure 2 provides an overview of our approach to crowdsource the mining of mashup model patterns using CrowdFlower (http://www.crowdflower.com) as the crowdsourcing platform. Starting from the left-hand side of the figure, the

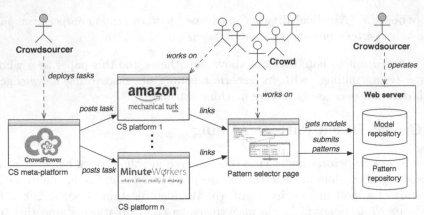

Fig. 2. Approach to crowd-based pattern mining with CrowdFower

crowdsourcer deploys the task on CrowdFlower. Doing this requires the creation of the forms to collect data from the crowd, the uploading of the dataset that contains the units of work (i.e., the mashup models), the preparation of the qualification tests (**R1**), among other tasks that are specific to CrowdFlower. Once the tasks are deployed, CrowdFlower posts them to third-party platforms such as Amazon Mechanical Turk and MinuteWorkers where the *crowd* can actually perform the requested work. Each mashup model is configured to be shown to at least three workers, in order to guarantee that each model gets properly inspected (**R5**), and a monetary reward is set for each pattern provided by the crowd (**R6**). We will discuss more about this last aspect in Section 4.

Each task points to an external *Pattern Selector* page where the crowd can select patterns from the mashups in the dataset. The Pattern Selector page consists in a standard web application implemented in Java, HTML, CSS and Javascript, which displays the image of a pipe in its original representation (screen shot) and allows the worker to define patterns on top (**R2**). In addition, the worker can provide a name, a description and a list of tags that describe the pattern (**R3**). All inputs provided by the worker are validated, e.g., to check that the worker indeed selects a pattern within the mashup (**R4**).

The web application for the Pattern Selector page is hosted on a *web server* operated by the crowdsourcer. The web server hosts a *model repository* where the mashup models are stored and from where the Pattern Selector page gets the models. It also hosts a *pattern repository* where the patterns selected by the crowd are submitted and stored for further analysis, which includes the filtering, validation and integration of the collected patterns (**R7** and **R8**)

3.3   Algorithm

Algorithm 1 (we call it the *Crowd* algorithm) illustrates a *generic* algorithm that brings together human and machine computation for the mining of patterns from mashup models. The algorithm receives as input:

Algorithm 1. Crowd

Data: input dataset IN, pattern mining tasks PMT, data partitioning strategy DPE, data
partition size DPS, answers per partition APP, per-task reward rw, time alloted ta
Result: set MP of mashup model patterns $\langle name, desc, tag, C, E, DF, VA \rangle$

1 $\overline{IN}$ = initializeDataset(IN);
2 DP = partitionInputDataset($\overline{IN}, DPE, DPS$);
3 T = mapDataPartitionsToTasks(DP, PMT, APP);
4 distributeTasksToCrowd(T, rw, ta);
5 $rawPatterns$ = collectPatternsFromCrowd();
6 MP = filterResults($rawPatterns$);
7 **return** MP;

- The dataset IN of *mashup models* from which to identify patterns,
- The design of the parameterized *pattern mining task* PMT to be executed
  by the crowd (the parameters tell which mashup model(s) to work on),
- The *data partitioning strategy* DPE telling how to split IN into sub-sets to
  be fed as input to PMT,
- The *data partition size* DPS specifying the expected size of the input datasets,
- The *number of answers* APP to be collected per data partition,
- The *per-task reward* rw to be paid to workers, and
- The *time allotted* ta to execute a task.

The algorithm consists of seven main steps. First, it initializes the input
dataset IN (line 1) and transforms it into a format that is suitable for the
crowdsourcing of pattern mining tasks (we discuss this step in the next subsection). Then, it takes the initialized input dataset $\overline{IN}$ and partitions it according
to parameters DPE and DPS (line 2). In our case, DPE uses a random selection of mashup models, $DPS = 1$ and $APP = 3$. Next, the algorithm maps the
created partitions of mashup models to the tasks PMT (line 3) and distributes
the tasks to the workers of the crowd (line 4). Once tasks are deployed on the
crowdsourcing platform, it starts collecting results from the crowd until the expected number of answers per model are obtained or the allotted time of the task
expires (line 5). Finally, it filters the patterns according to predefined quality
criteria (line 6), so as to keep only patterns of sufficient quality (we provide more
details of this last step in Section 4).

Note that the core of the approach, i.e., the identification of patterns, is not
performed by the algorithm itself but delegated to the crowd as described next.

3.4 Task design

In order to make sure that only people that are also knowledgeable in Yahoo!
Pipes perform our tasks, we include a set of five multiple choice, pre-selection
questions such as *"Which of the following components can be embedded into a
loop?"* and *"What is the maximum number of Pipe Output modules permitted
in each pipe?"* In order for a worker to be paid, he/she must correctly answer
these questions, for which we already know the answers (so-called *gold data*).

Name and description of pipe sources from Yahoo! Pipes

The pipe model to be analyzed by the worker. The model is a clickable image map that allows the worker to define a pattern by selecting its components.

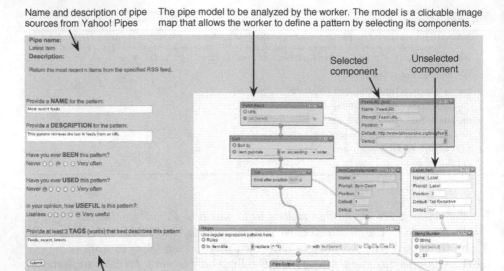

Additional input fields for the specification of pattern name, description and meta-data

Fig. 3. Task design for the selection, description and rating of mashup model patterns

Another core decision when crowdsourcing a task is the UI used to interact with workers. In general, all crowdsourcing platforms available today allow a crowdsourcer to design form-based user interfaces directly inside the crowdsourcing platform. For the crowdsourcing of simple tasks, such as the annotation of images or the translation of a piece of text, this is sufficient to collect useful feedback. In more complex crowdsourcing tasks, such as our problem of identifying patterns inside mashup models, textual, form-based UIs are not enough and a dedicated, purposefully designed graphical UI is needed. The task that workers can perform through this UI corresponds to the implementation of the *collectPatternsFromCrowd*() function in Algorithm 1, i.e., the actual mining.

In order to make workers feel comfortable with the selection of patterns inside pipes models, we wanted the representation of the pipes to be as close as possible to what real pipes look like. In other words, we did not want to create an abstract or simplified representation of pipes models (e.g., a graph or textual description) and, instead, wanted to keep the full and realistic expressive power of the original representation. We therefore decided to work with screen shots of real pipes models, on top of which workers are able to select components of the pipe and to construct patterns by simply clicking on the respective components. Figure 3 shows a screen shot of the resulting GUI for selecting patterns, in which we show a pipe with a total of 9 components, of which 5 have been selected by the worker to form a pattern (see the green-shaded components).

As shown in the figure, next to selecting a pattern, the worker must also provide information about the pattern such as the *name*, *description* and list of *tags* (at least 3 tags). In addition, the worker may also rank the pattern regarding to how often he/she has already *seen* or *used* the pattern before, and to how *useful* he/she thinks the pattern is.

4 Evaluation and Comparison

To study the described *Crowd* algorithm, we performed a set of experiments with CrowdFlower and compared the results with those obtained by running our original automated pattern mining algorithm [11] with different minimum support levels and dataset sizes. We refer to this latter as to the *Machine* algorithm.

4.1 Evaluation Metrics

While for automated mining it is clear by design how the output of an algorithm looks like, this is not as clear if the identification of patterns is delegated to the crowd. As described earlier, it is very common that workers cheat and, hence, do not provide meaningful data. To filter out those patterns that we can instead reasonably trust, we define a set of minimum criteria for crowd-mined patterns: a **good mashup pattern** is a pattern that consists of *at least two modules* and where the modules are *connected*, the name and description of the pattern are *not empty*, and the description and the actual pattern structure *match semantically*. The first three criteria we enforce automatically in the pattern identification UI illustrated in Figure 3. Whether the description and pattern structure match semantically, i.e., whether the description really tells what the pattern does, is assessed manually by experts (us). The result of this analysis is a Boolean: either a pattern is considered *good* (and it passes the filter) or it is considered *bad* (and it fails the filter). Note that with "good" we do not yet assert anything about the actual value of a pattern; this can only be assessed with modelers using the pattern in practice. The same expert-based filter is usually also applied to the outputs of automated mining algorithms and does not introduce an additional subjective bias compared to automated mining scenarios.

In order to compare the performance of the two algorithms and test our hypotheses, we use three metrics to compare the sets of patterns they produce in output: the **number of patterns found** gives an indication of the effectiveness of the algorithms in finding patterns; the **average pattern size**, computed as the average number of components of the patterns in the respective output sets, serves as an indicator of how complex and informative identified patterns are; and the **distribution of pattern sizes** shows how diverse the identified patterns are in terms of complexity and information load.

4.2 Experiment Design and Dataset

The **Crowd algorithm** is implemented as outlined in Algorithm 1 using the popular CS platform CrowdFlower. Running the algorithm is a joint manual and automated effort: our Pattern Selector application takes care of initializing the dataset (the pipes models), partition it, and map partitions to tasks at runtime.

The actual tasks are deployed manually on CrowdFlower and executed by the crowd. Filtering out good patterns is again done manually. For each pipe, we request at least 3 judgments, estimated a maximum of 300 sec. per task, and rewarded USD 0.10 per task.

The **Machine algorithm** is based on a frequent sub-graph mining algorithm described in [11] and implemented in Java. The core parameter used to fine-tune the algorithm is the *minimum support* that the mined sub-graphs must satisfy; we therefore use this variable to test and report on different test settings.

The **dataset** used to feed both algorithms consists of 997 pipes (with 11.1 components and 11.0 connectors on average) randomly selected from the "most popular" pipes category of Yahoo! Pipes' online repository. We opted for this category because, being popular, the pipes contained there are more likely to be functional and useful. The pipes are represented in JSON. The dataset used for the *Crowd* algorithm consists in a selection of 40 pipes out of the 997 (which represents a small dataset in conventional data mining). The selection of these pipes was performed manually, in order to assure that the selected pipes are indeed runnable and meaningful. In addition to the JSON representation of these 40 pipes, we also collected the screen shots of each pipe through the Yahoo! Pipes editor. The JSON representation is used in the automated input validators; the screen shots are used to collect patterns from the crowd as explained earlier.

For our comparison, we run *Machine* with datasets of 997 (big dataset) and 40 pipes (small dataset). We use $Machine^{997}$ and $Machine^{40}$ to refer to the former and the latter setting, respectively. We run *Crowd* only with 40 pipes and, for consistency, refer to this setting as to $Crowd^{40}$.

4.3 Results and Interpretation

Figure 4 summarizes the task instances created and the patterns collected by running $Crowd^{40}$. The crowd started a total of 326 task instances in CrowdFlower, while it submitted only 174 patterns through our Pattern Selector application. This means that a total of 152 task instances were abandoned without completion. Out of the 174 patterns submitted, only 42 patterns satisfied our criteria for *good mashup patterns*. These data testify a significant level of noise produced by workers who, in the aim of finishing tasks as quickly as possible and getting paid, apparently selected random fragments of pipes and provided meaningless descriptions. The cost of this run was USD 17.56, including administrative costs.

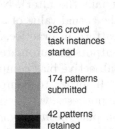

326 crowd task instances started

174 patterns submitted

42 patterns retained

Fig. 4. Task instances and patterns in $Crowd^{40}$

The charts in Figures 5–7 report on the numbers of patterns, average pattern sizes and the distribution of pattern sizes obtained by running $Machine^{997}$ and $Machine^{40}$ with different minimum relative support levels sup_{min}. The bars in gray are the results of the *Machine* algorithm; the black bars represent the results of $Crowd^{40}$. For comparison, we placed $Crowd^{40}$ at a support level of $sup_{min} = 0.025$, which corresponds to $1/40 = 0.025$, in that we ask workers to identify patterns from a single pipe without the need for any additional support.

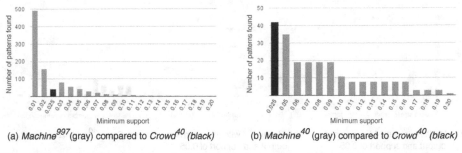

Fig. 5. Number of patterns produced by the two automated mining algorithms under varying minimum support levels. For comparison, the charts also report the number of pattern produced by the crowd-based mining algorithm (in black).

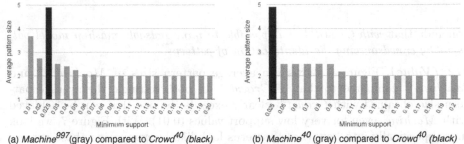

Fig. 6. Average size of the patterns produced by the two automated mining algorithms under varying minimum support levels. For comparison, the charts also report the average size of patterns produced by the crowd-based mining algorithm (in black).

H1 (Effectiveness). Figure 5(a) illustrates the number of patterns found by $Machine^{997}$. The number quickly increases for $Machine^{997}$ as we go from high support values to low values, reaching almost 500 patterns with $sup_{min} = 0.01$. Figure 5(b) shows the results obtained with $Machine^{40}$. The lowest support value for $Machine^{40}$ is $sup_{min} = 0.05$, which corresponds to an absolute support of 2 in the dataset. It is important to note that only very low support values produce a useful number of patterns. In both figures, the black bar represents the 42 patterns identified by $Crowd^{40}$.

The two figures show the typical problem of automated pattern mining algorithms: only few patterns for high support levels (which are needed, as support is the only criterion expressing significance), too low support levels required to produce useful output sizes with small datasets (our goal), and an explosion of the output size with large datasets. As illustrated in Figure 4, $Crowd^{40}$ is instead able to produce a number of patterns in output that is similar to the size of the dataset in input. Notice also that, while Figure 5 reports on *all* the patterns found by $Machine$, the data for $Crowd^{40}$ include only *good patterns*. This means that not only $Crowd^{40}$ is able to find patterns, but it is also able to find practically meaningful patterns. We thus *accept* Hypothesis 1 and

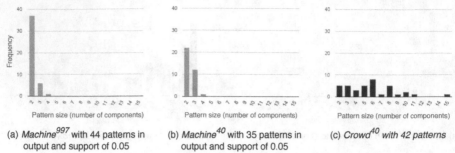

(a) $Machine^{997}$ with 44 patterns in output and support of 0.05

(b) $Machine^{40}$ with 35 patterns in output and support of 0.05

(c) $Crowd^{40}$ with 42 patterns

Fig. 7. Size distribution of the patterns by the three algorithms. To ease the comparison, the histograms of $Machine^{997}$ and $Machine^{40}$ refer to the run with the minimum support level that produced an output dataset close to the one produced by $Crowd^{40}$.

conclude that *with $Crowd^{40}$ it is possible to mine reusable mashup model patterns by crowdsourcing the identification of patterns.*

H2 (Value). Figure 6 shows the average pattern sizes of $Machine^{997}$ and $Machine^{40}$ compared to that of $Crowd^{40}$. In both settings, the average pattern size obtained with $Crowd^{40}$ clearly exceeds the one that can be achieved with $Machine$, even for very low support values (0.01). With Figure 7, we look more specifically into how these patterns look like by comparing those runs of $Machine^{997}$ and $Machine^{40}$ with $Crowd^{40}$ that produce a similar number of patterns in output. In both settings this happens for $sup_{min} = 0.05$ and produced 44 and 35 patterns, respectively. Figures 7(a) and (b) show that automatically mined patterns are generally small (sizes range from 2–4), with a strong prevalence of the most simple and naïve patterns (size 2).

Figure 7(c), instead, shows that the results obtained with $Crowd^{40}$ present a much higher diversity in the pattern sizes, with a more homogeneous distribution and even very complex patterns of sizes that go up to 11 and 15 components. $Crowd^{40}$ is thus able to collect patterns that contain more complex logics and that are more informative, and thus, possibly contain more domain knowledge. These patterns also come with a characterizing name, description and list of tags. These annotations not only enrich the value of a pattern with semantics but also augment the domain knowledge encoded in the pattern and its reusability. We thus *accept* Hypothesis 2 and conclude that *patterns mined with $Crowd^{40}$ contain more domain knowledge than the automatically mined patterns.*

H3 (Applicability). The above assessment of the *effectiveness* and *value* of $Crowd^{40}$ shows that *crowd-based pattern mining outperforms machine-based mining for small datasets*, that is, we *accept* Hypothesis 3. For large datasets, automated mining still represents a viable solution, but for small datasets crowd-based ming is not only applicable but also more effective. With a cost per pattern of USD 0.42 and a running time of approximately 6 hours, crowd-based mining proves to be a very competitive alternative to hiring a domain expert, which would be the alternative to attack a cold start in our small dataset scenario.

5   Discussion and Analogy with BPM

Regarding the above results, we performed a set of additional experiments to analyze the *robustness* of $Crowd^{40}$ along two dimensions: reward and task design. We did not notice any reduction of the number of tasks instantiated by the crowd or the number of patterns collected if we lowered the *reward* from USD 0.10 down to USD 0.05. We essentially got the same response as described in Figure 4, which indicates that we could have gotten the same results also for less money without any loss of quality. Instead, we noticed that there is a very strong sensitivity regarding the *task design*, but only on the number of patterns that can be collected, not on the number of task instances. Concretely, we tried to introduce a minimum level of support (at least 2 times in 3, respectively, 10 pipes shown to the worker). The result was only a strong reduction of the number of patterns submitted. The lesson learned is thus to keep the task as simple as possible, that is, to apply the KISS (Keep It Simple, Stupid) principle, and to concentrate the effort instead on the validation of collected data.

There are two key aspects when designing a CS task: input validation and intuitiveness. We have seen that it is strongly advised to check all inputs for *formal validity* (e.g., no empty strings), otherwise workers may just skip inputs or input fake content (e.g., a white space). As for the *intuitiveness*, we considered collecting patterns via textual input (e.g., the list of component names in the pattern) or via abstract data flow graphs (automatically constructed from the JSON representation of pipes), but in the end we opted for the screen shots. This has proven to be the representation workers are most familiar with; in fact, screen shots do not introduce any additional abstraction.

In order to filter out workers that had some minimum knowledge of Pipes, we performed a *pre-selection* in the form of *gold data*. Yet, our questions were too tough in our first tests, and we had to lower our expectations. Interestingly, however, this did not affect much the quality of the patterns (but workers that did not pass the test, did not get paid). We also noticed a *natural selection* phenomenon: the majority of patterns was submitted by only few workers. We assume these were workers with good knowledge in Pipes that simply liked this kind of modeling tasks and, therefore, submitted patterns not only for the sake of the reward but also for personal satisfaction. We believe that, with the right quality criteria in place, the pre-selection could be omitted, and the "experts" (and good patterns) emerge automatically, at the cost/speed of simple CS tasks.

As for the *quality of patterns*, we carefully analyzed each of the 42 patterns identified by the crowd and conclude with confidence that *all* patterns that satisfy our criteria for *good* patterns are indeed meaningful. Particularly important in this respect are the additional annotations (name, description, tags) that equip the patterns with semantics. It is important to notice that assessing the quality of patterns is non-trivial in general and that the annotations do not only allow one to grasp better the meaning and purpose of patterns; they also allow one to tell serious workers and cheaters apart, which increases quality.

In this paper, we specifically focus on *mashup model patterns*, as we use them to provide interactive recommendations in Baya. Yet, the approach and findings are general enough to be applicable almost straightway also to **business process models**. A *business process* (BP) is commonly modeled as $P = \langle N, E, type \rangle$, with N being the set of nodes (events, gateways, activities), E being the set of control flow connectors, and *type* assigning control flow constructs to gateway nodes. Our definition of *mashups* is not dissimilar: $m = \langle name, C, E, DF, VA \rangle$. The components C correspond to N, and the data flow connectors DF correspond to E. These are the constructs that most characterize a pattern. In fact, our task design requires workers only to mark components to identify a pattern (connectors, embeddings and value assignments are included automatically). If applied to BP models, this is equivalent to ask workers to mark tasks.

Our mashup model is further *data flow* based, while BP models are typically *control flow* based (e.g., BPMN or YAWL) and contain control flow constructs (gateways). If identifying patterns with the crowd, the question is whether gateways should be marked explicitly, or whether they are included automatically (as in the current task design). In our case, for a set of components to form a pattern it is enough that they are connected. In the case of BP patterns, this may no longer be enough. Commonly, BP fragments are considered most reusable if they are well structured, i.e., if they have a single entry and a single exit point (SESE). It could thus be sensible to allow workers to select only valid SESE fragments, although this is not a strict requirement.

As for the comparison of $Crowd^{40}$ with $Machine^{997}$ and $Machine^{40}$, it is important to note that the automated mining algorithm would very likely produce *worse* results if used with BP models. In fact, mashup models are particularly suited to automated mining: the components they use are selected from a predefined, limited set of component *types* (e.g., several dozens). Similarities can thus be identified relatively easily, which increases the support of patterns. BP models, instead, are more flexible in their "components" (the tasks): task labels are *free text*, and identifying "types" of tasks is a hard problem in itself [7]. For instance, the tasks "Pay bill", "Pay" and "Send money" can all be seen as instances of a common task type "Payment." This, in turn, means that the value of $Crowd^{40}$ could be even more evident when mining BP models.

6   Related Work

Crowdsourcing has been applied so far in a variety of related areas. In the specific context of *machine learning*, Sheng et al. [14] collect training labels for data items from the crowd to feed supervised induction algorithms. In the same context, von Ahn et al. [17] propose an interactive *game* that requires multiple players to agree on labels for images, enhancing the quality of labels. In [10], Sheng et al. propose *CrowdMine*, a game that leverages on the crowd to identify graphical patterns used to verify and debug software specifications.

In the context of BPM, the term "patterns" is commonly associated with the **workflow patterns** by van der Aalst et al. [16]. Initially, the focus of these patterns was on control flow structures, but then the idea evolved and included all the aspects (control flow, data flow, resources, exception handling) that characterize workflow languages (http://www.workflowpatterns.com). The proposed patterns are an analytical approach to assess the strengths and weaknesses of workflow languages, more than an instrument to assist developers while modeling, although Gschwind et al. [4] also explored this idea.

The *automated identification* of process models or fragments thereof is commonly approached via *process mining*, more specifically **process discovery** [15]. Process discovery aims to derive model patterns from *event logs*, differently from the problem we address in this paper, which aims to find patterns in a set of *process models*. The main assumptions of process discovery techniques are: (i) each process instance can be identified as pertaining to a process, (ii) each event in the log can be identified as pertaining to a process instance, (iii) each event in the log corresponds to an activity in the process, (iv) each event in the log contains the necessary information to determine precedence relationships. Derived process models thus represent patterns of the dynamics of a single process and generally do not have cross-process validity. Examples of process discovery algorithms are the α-algorithm [15], Heuristic miner [18], and Fuzzy mining [5].

Only few works focus on **mining patterns** from process models. Lau et al. [8] propose to use frequent sub-graph and association rules discovery algorithms to discover frequent sub-graphs (patterns) to provide modeling recommendations. Li et. al [9] mine process model variants created from a given reference process model, in order to identify a new, generic reference model that covers and represents all these variants better. The approach uses a heuristic search algorithm that minimizes the average distance (in terms of change operations on models) between the model and its variants. Greco et al. [3] mine workflow models (represented as state charts) using two graph mining algorithms, *c-find* and *w-find*, which specifically deal with the structure of workflow models.

We would have liked to compare the performance of our *Crowd* algorithm also with that of the above algorithms, yet this would have required either adapting them to our mashup model or adapting *Crowd* to process models. We were not able to do this in time. However, the works by Lau et al. [8] and Greco et al. [3] are very close to our *Machine* algorithm: they share the same underlying frequent sub-graph mining technique. We therefore expect a very similar performance. The two algorithms also advocate the use of a support-based notion of patterns and thus present the same problems as the one studied in Section 4.

7 Conclusion

Mining model patterns from a dataset of mashup or process models is a hard task. In this paper, we presented a crowd-based pattern mining approach that advances the state of the art with three contributions: we demonstrate that *it is possible to crowdsource a task as complex as the mining of model patterns*, that *patterns identified by the crowd are rich of domain knowledge*, and that *crowd-based mining particularly excels with small datasets*. We further explained how the *Crowd* algorithm can be adapted to mine patterns from BP models. To the best of our knowledge, this is the first investigation in this direction.

In our future work, we would like to study how crowdsourcing can be leveraged on for big datasets, e.g., by using pattern similarity metrics and the notion of support, and how the quality of patterns on the reward given. We also intend to adapt the *Crowd* algorithm to BPMN, to compare it with other BPMN-oriented approaches in literature [8,3], and to study if the crowd can also be used for quality assessment (to automate the complete pattern mining process).

References

1. Daniel, F., Matera, M.: Mashups: Concepts, Models and Architectures. Springer (2014)
2. Geng, L., Hamilton, H.: Interestingness measures for data mining: A survey. ACM Computing Surveys 38(3), 9 (2006)
3. Greco, G., Guzzo, A., Manco, G., Sacca, D.: Mining and reasoning on workflows. IEEE Transactions on Knowledge and Data Engineering 17(4), 519–534 (2005)
4. Gschwind, T., Koehler, J., Wong, J.: Applying Patterns during Business Process Modeling. In: Dumas, M., Reichert, M., Shan, M.-C. (eds.) BPM 2008. LNCS, vol. 5240, pp. 4–19. Springer, Heidelberg (2008)
5. Günther, C.W., van der Aalst, W.M.P.: Fuzzy mining – adaptive process simplification based on multi-perspective metrics. In: Alonso, G., Dadam, P., Rosemann, M. (eds.) BPM 2007. LNCS, vol. 4714, pp. 328–343. Springer, Heidelberg (2007)
6. Howe, J.: Crowdsourcing: Why the Power of the Crowd Is Driving the Future of Business, 1st edn. Crown Publishing Group, New York (2008)
7. Klinkmüller, C., Weber, I., Mendling, J., Leopold, H., Ludwig, A.: Increasing Recall of Process Model Matching by Improved Activity Label Matching. In: Daniel, F., Wang, J., Weber, B. (eds.) BPM 2013. LNCS, vol. 8094, pp. 211–218. Springer, Heidelberg (2013)
8. Lau, J.M., Iochpe, C., Thom, L., Reichert, M.: Discovery and analysis of activity pattern cooccurrences in business process models. In: ICEIS (2009)
9. Li, C., Reichert, M., Wombacher, A.: Discovering reference models by mining process variants using a heuristic approach. In: Dayal, U., Eder, J., Koehler, J., Reijers, H.A. (eds.) BPM 2009. LNCS, vol. 5701, pp. 344–362. Springer, Heidelberg (2009)
10. Li, W., Seshia, S.A., Jha, S.: CrowdMine: towards crowdsourced human-assisted verification. In: DAC, pp. 1250–1251. IEEE (2012)
11. Rodríguez, C., Chowdhury, S.R., Daniel, F., Nezhad, H.R.M., Casati, F.: Assisted Mashup Development: On the Discovery and Recommendation of Mashup Composition Knowledge. In: Web Services Foundations, pp. 683–708 (2014)
12. Roy Chowdhury, S., Daniel, F., Casati, F.: Recommendation and Weaving of Reusable Mashup Model Patterns for Assisted Development. ACM Trans. Internet Techn. (2014) (in print)
13. Roy Chowdhury, S., Rodríguez, C., Daniel, F., Casati, F.: Baya: assisted mashup development as a service. In: WWW Companion, pp. 409–412. ACM (2012)
14. Sheng, V.S., Provost, F., Ipeirotis, P.G.: Get another label? improving data quality and data mining using multiple, noisy labelers. In: SIGKDD, pp. 614–622. ACM (2008)
15. van der Aalst, W.M.P., Weijters, T., Maruster, L.: Workflow mining: Discovering process models from event logs. IEEE Transactions on Knowledge and Data Engineering 16(9), 1128–1142 (2004)
16. van der Aalst, W.M.P., ter Hofstede, A.H.M., Kiepuszewski, B., Barros, A.P.: Workflow patterns. Distributed and Parallel Databases 14(1), 5–51 (2003)
17. Von Ahn, L., Dabbish, L.: Labeling images with a computer game. In: SIGCHI, pp. 319–326. ACM (2004)
18. Weijters, A., van der Aalst, W.M.P., De Medeiros, A.A.: Process mining with the heuristics miner-algorithm. TU Eindhoven, Tech. Rep. WP, 166 (2006)

A Recommender System for Process Discovery

Joel Ribeiro[1], Josep Carmona[1], Mustafa Mısır[2], and Michele Sebag[2]

[1] Universitat Politècnica de Catalunya, Spain
{jribeiro,jcarmona}@lsi.upc.edu
[2] TAO, INRIA Saclay - CNRS - LRI, Universite Paris Sud XI, Orsay, France
{mustafa.misir,michele.sebag}@lri.fr

Abstract. Over the last decade, several algorithms for process discovery and process conformance have been proposed. Still, it is well-accepted that there is no dominant algorithm in any of these two disciplines, and then it is often difficult to apply them successfully. Most of these algorithms need a close-to expert knowledge in order to be applied satisfactorily. In this paper, we present a recommender system that uses portfolio-based algorithm selection strategies to face the following problems: to find the best discovery algorithm for the data at hand, and to allow bridging the gap between general users and process mining algorithms. Experiments performed with the developed tool witness the usefulness of the approach for a variety of instances.

Keywords: Process Mining, Recommender Systems, Algorithm Selection.

1 Introduction

The ability of monitoring process executions within information systems yields large-scale event log files. These files can be processed using the so-called *process mining* approaches, at the crossroad of *business intelligence* and *data mining* techniques. Process mining is positioning as the perfect candidate to support information systems in the *big data* era.

Process mining is defined as the extraction of valuable information from event logs, aimed at strategic insight into the business processes [13]. Process mining mainly includes *process discovery, conformance checking* and *enhancement*. Discovery techniques aim at the behavioral modeling of the business process underlying the event logs. Conformance techniques check the compatibility of a process model with regard to a set of event logs. Enhancement techniques enrich a process model based on additional process information available in the event log.

This paper focuses on process discovery, acknowledged to be the most challenging issue in process mining. While several algorithms have been proposed for process discovery (e.g., the reader can find a complete summary in [13]), there is no algorithm dominating all other algorithms. Furthermore, these algorithms are built on different formalisms (e.g., Petri nets, BPMN, EPC, Causal nets).

The selection of the process discovery algorithm and formalism most appropriate to (a set of) event logs is left to the user, hindering the deployment of the process mining approach in two ways. On the one hand, inexperienced users can

S. Sadiq, P. Soffer, and H. Völzer (Eds.): BPM 2014, LNCS 8659, pp. 67–83, 2014.

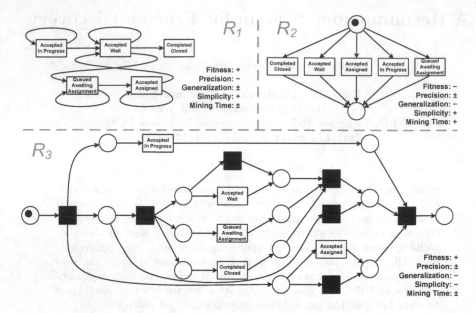

Fig. 1. The process discovery problem: three discovered models for a given log. R_1 is a Causal net discovered by the Flexible Heuristic Miner (FHM), while R_2 and R_3 are Petri nets, discovered by the Alpha and Inductive miners, respectively. These control-flow algorithms are available in the ProM 6 framework [16].

hardly get the best of an algorithm portfolio. On the other hand, experienced users might have to manually inspect the event log to select the appropriate algorithm, along a tedious, time-consuming and error-prone procedure. Figure 1 illustrates the problem: three different models were discovered by three different techniques using the same log. Each model is annotated with a set of generic quality measurements (+: good, ±: average, −: poor; for an overview of quality measures see Section 3.3). Depending on the measurements in consideration, one model may be preferred with respect to the others. If all measurements were considered, the technique presented in this paper would recommend model R_1 (i.e., recommend the FHM). However, if only fitness and precision were considered, model R_3 (Inductive miner) would be recommended by our technique.

The contribution of the paper is an integrated process discovery framework achieving algorithm selection based on machine learning techniques. Formally, this framework elaborates on the *Algorithm Recommender System* (ARS) approach [5], based on using a dataset that reports the results of some algorithms in the portfolio on a set of problem instances; its generality is witnessed as it has been applied successfully in domains such as *Constraint Satisfaction* and *Optimization*.

ARS is integrated within a framework to evaluate process discovery algorithms [14]. We have developed a server-client architecture along the training-test principle used in machine learning. The server achieves lifelong learning, continuously running process discovery experiments to enrich its database reporting the performances of algorithms on case studies (event logs). This database is exploited using ARS, continuously increasing the system knowledge. This knowledge is then disseminated to the clients, that use it to predict the best algorithm on their current event log. The client is implemented as a ProM [16] plugin (Nightly Build version)[1], named RS4PD under the Recommendation package. Experiments using real-life and artificial logs confirm the merits of the proposed approach.

The remainder of this paper is organized as follows. Section 2 presents background and discusses related work. Section 3 presents an overview of the recommender system; its implementation is detailed in Section 4. Section 5 provides an experimental validation of the approach. Section 6 contains a preliminary study about the selection of parameters for discovery algorithms, while Section 7 concludes the paper with some discussion and perspectives for further research.

2 Related Work

Over the last decade, recommender systems became present in a significant number of applications of information systems [2]. In spite of this, few attempts have been done on recommending process mining algorithms. In this paper, the main goal is to build a system for recommending process discovery algorithms. The proposed recommender system requires the combination of three different disciplines. We overview them now in the following subsections.

2.1 Evaluation of Process Discovery Algorithms

Control-flow discovery algorithms focus on finding the causality of activities within a process, e.g., order, conflict, concurrency, iteration, among others. Several approaches can be found in the literature [13]. These algorithms (or the resulting models) can be evaluated using conformance techniques [10], which may reveal mismatches between observed and modeled behavior. Rozinat et al. [9] identified the need of developing a methodology to benchmark process mining algorithms. A conceptual framework was then proposed to evaluate and compare process models. Weber et al. [18] proposed a methodology for assessing the performance of process mining algorithms. This approach assumes the generation of event logs from reference models for applying conformance analysis. Also assuming the existence of reference models, Wang et al. [17] proposed a framework for evaluating process mining algorithms based on the behavioral and structural similarities between reference and mined process models. In this approach, the information gathered from the evaluation (i.e., the similarities between process models) is then used to support a recommender system for process mining algorithms. A different evaluation approach for analyzing the quality of process models was introduced by vanden Broucke et al. [14]. In this approach, several conformance checking metrics can be computed over an event log and a process model in an integrated environment.

---

[1] http://www.promtools.org/prom6/nightly/

2.2 Collaborative Filtering

Due to a large number of choices regarding an item, it is hard to determine possible personal choices without checking the available options throughly. Recommender systems are automated methods to efficiently perform this task. One way to do it is by using item or user related content data given beforehand. This sub-field of recommender systems is studied as content-based filtering methods. Instead of directly using such data, it is possible to employ users' earlier preferences on items. In this way, finding users with similar taste or items with similar user preferences is practical to make user-item predictions. *Collaborative filtering* is the field approaching the recommendation problems from this perspective [12]. The underlying motivation is that if some users share similar preference characteristics on a set of commonly known items, it is likely that these users will have similar taste on other items.

Algorithm Recommender System (ARS) [5] is an algorithm portfolio selection tool that uses collaborative filtering. ARS takes the user-item matrix idea into an instance-algorithm matrix indicating the performance of each algorithm on each instance. The *Algorithm Selection Problem* [8] has been targeted in different areas such as *Constraint Satisfaction* and *Optimization*. The methods developed on these contexts using algorithm selection, like SATZilla [20] and CPHydra [7], need a full performance dataset showing how well a set of algorithms performed on a set of problem instances. Besides that some of these methods were designed in a way that they can only be used for the problems with a specific performance criterion, such as runtime. Unlike these existing methods, ARS does not require a full performance matrix, thanks to collaborative filtering. In addition, ARS has a generic structure that can be used as a black-box method, thus it can be used for any algorithm selection task as the one we have in this paper. This is provided by using a rank-based input scheme. In particular, the performance database involves relative performance, i.e., ranks of tested algorithms on each instance.

2.3 Information Retrieval

Information Retrieval (IR) is a discipline that considers finding information that best satisfies some given criteria (e.g., keywords) on documents. Among the many techniques available, *top-k queries* is a technique used in the framework proposed in this paper. These queries can be defined as the search of the k most relevant (or interesting) entries in a multidimensional dataset. The first algorithms for efficient top-k queries are the so-called *threshold* algorithms [4]. Considered the reference algorithms in the subdomain, threshold algorithms rely on sequential and random accesses to information to compute the exact top-k results. Using an index-based approach to access information, Akbarinia et al. proposed two algorithms [1] that exploit the position of the entries in the dataset to compute the exact top-k results. From these algorithms, the BPA2 algorithm is used in this study for retrieving the top-k discovery techniques, due to its efficiency.

3   Overall Framework

A recommender system for process discovery can follow the same strategy as the portfolio-based algorithm selection [20]. Basically, this selection relies on a set (portfolio) of algorithms, which are executed over a repository of input objects (e.g., datasets or problems). Information about the executions (e.g., performance or results) is used to identify the best algorithms with regard to specific input objects. By characterizing these objects as sets of features, it is possible to build a *prediction model* that associates a ranking of algorithms with features. So, the prediction of the best-performing algorithms on a given input object can be achieved by first extracting the features of that object and then using the prediction model to compute the ranking of algorithms. This approach can be used to build a recommender system for process discovery, with event logs as input objects and discovery techniques as algorithms.

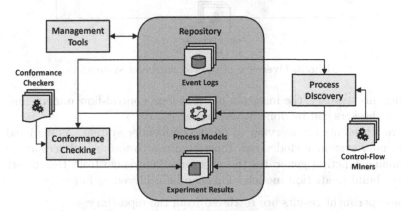

Fig. 2. Outline of the evaluation framework

Figure 2 presents a framework for evaluating process discovery techniques, which can be used to support a recommender system. The *Process Discovery* and the *Conformance Checking* nodes represent the execution of a process mining experiment. These experiments can be defined as follows.

Discovery experiment: consists of executing a control-flow algorithm on an event log in order to produce a process model. The mined model as well as information about the algorithm performance are stored in the repository.

Conformance experiment: consists of computing a conformance measurement on a process model and the event log used to mine that model. The experiments results are stored in the repository.

The *Management Tools* allow (i) the execution of discovery and conformance experiments and (ii) the management of the repository as well as the collection of discovery and conformance techniques (i.e., the control-flow miners and the conformance checkers). The execution of an experiment is selected randomly.

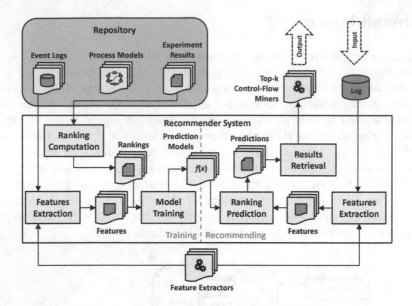

Fig. 3. Overview of the recommender system

Applying this strategy, the insertion of event logs, control-flow miners, and conformance checkers can be done at any moment.

Figure 3 presents an overview of our recommender system. As depicted, the recommender system includes two functionalities: *training* and *recommending*. The training function generates the necessary knowledge from the experiment results to build prediction models. This can be achieved as follows.

i. The experiment results are retrieved from the repository.
ii. For each event log and measurement (performance or conformance) in the results, the ranking of discovery techniques is computed. A ranking of techniques must contain all control-flow miners used in the experiments. In the case a ranking is incomplete (i.e., there is not enough experiment results to compute a complete ranking), a machine learning algorithm (e.g., SVM or Neural Networks) is applied to predict the missing ranking values [5].
iii. The features of the log are extracted for each event log in the results.
iv. For each measurement in the results, the corresponding prediction model is trained using the rankings of discovery techniques and the features of the logs.

The recommending function uses the prediction models to obtain the top-k best-performing discovery techniques for an event log. This can be achieved as follows.

a. The features of the given event log are extracted.
b. For each prediction model, the ranking of techniques with respect to a measurement is predicted using the extracted features.
c. All the predicted rankings are combined into a final ranking.
d. The top-k techniques are retrieved from the final ranking.

The following sections describe in detail the key elements used in the training and recommending parts of the proposed system.

3.1   Features

A *feature* is a numerical function defined on event logs. A set of features therefore induces a (semi-)distance on event logs. In practice, a feature can be defined as a specific characteristic of the event log. By characterizing two logs as two sets of features, it is possible to assess whether or not the logs are different with regard to those features. This means that the execution of discovery techniques and the corresponding results can be associated to features of logs. Importantly, these associations can be used to identify which techniques perform better over logs characterized by specific features. A feature can be defined under one of three different scopes: *trace, event,* and *flow.*

Trace features: focus on characteristics of sequences of events. The average trace length is an example of a trace feature.

Event features: focus on characteristics of single events. The number of distinct events in the log is an example of an event feature.

Flow features: focus on characteristics of causal dependencies (i.e., pairs of consecutive events in the same trace). The number of one-length loops in the log is an example of a flow feature.

A challenge for building a recommender system for process discovery is the definition or selection of a representative set of features, supporting the algorithm selection. A representative set of features is described in Section 4; the validation, extension and improvement of the feature set is left for further study.

3.2   Techniques

A (discovery) *technique* consists of a control-flow algorithm for process discovery.[2] As in the portfolio-based algorithm selection, a set of techniques can be executed over a repository of event logs. The information gathered from the execution can be used to analyze which techniques perform best with regard to the performance of discovery techniques and the quality of their results. Remark that different techniques may produce different types of process models (e.g., the ILP miner produces a Petri net, while the FHM mines a Causal net). Since the conformance checking algorithms used in this study work only on Petri nets, a model conversion may be necessary in order to enable the results of a technique to be evaluated.

3.3   Measures

A *measure* can be defined as a measurement that evaluates the performance of discovery techniques and the quality of their results. By evaluating the execution

---

[2] Remark that other process discovery perspectives such as the *resource,* the *time,* and the *data* perspectives are not considered in the present work. The integration of these perspectives in the recommender system is identified as future work.

of two discovery techniques over the same log (as well as the produced results), it is possible to identify which technique performs better with regard to some measures. The recommender system proposed in this paper considers either a particular measure (aiming at identifying the best algorithm with regard to this measure), or an aggregation of these measures using an information retrieval algorithm (cf. Section 3.4). Together with the characteristics of the logs (i.e., the sets of features), this information can be used to build prediction models for supporting a recommendation system. A measure can be categorized as follows [13].

Performance measure: quantifies a discovery algorithm in terms of execution on a specific event log. The runtime is an example of a performance measure.

Simplicity measure: quantifies the results of a discovery algorithm (i.e., the process model mined from a specific event log) in terms of readability and comprehension. The number of elements in the model is an example of a simplicity measure.

Fitness measure: quantifies how much behavior described in the log complies with the behavior represented in the process model. The fitness is 100% if the model can describe every trace in the log.

Precision measure: quantifies how much behavior represented in the process model is described in the log. The precision is 100% if the log contains every possible trace represented in the model.

Generalization measure: quantifies the degree of abstraction beyond observed behavior, i.e., a general model will accept not only traces in the log, but some others that generalize these.

3.4   Recommending the Top-k Best-Performing Techniques

The recommendation of the top-k best-performing techniques for a specific event log is based on a set of ranking predictions. A ranking prediction identifies the techniques that are expected to perform better with regard to a specific measure. This information is computed using prediction models (i.e., functions that map a set of features to a ranking of techniques), which are built using the results of discovery and conformance experiments. The top-k best-performing techniques are then determined by a final ranking in which one or more ranking predictions are taken into account. The selection of the top-k techniques from the final ranking can be seen as a typical information retrieval problem.

4   Implementation

The implementation of the recommender system proposed in this paper is based on a server-client architecture. The main function of the server is to generate knowledge about the performance of techniques on different event logs. The server includes also both the evaluation framework and the repository, which support the training function of the recommender system. The training function as well as the evaluation framework are implemented as a package in the CoBeFra framework [15], while the repository is supported by a transactional database. The main function of the client is based on the knowledge generated in the server, and consists of predicting (recommending) the best-performing techniques for a given event log. This function is implemented as a ProM plugin (available in ProM 6).

As depicted in Figure 2, the evaluation framework relies on a collection of discovery and conformance algorithms. The current portfolio consists of 9 discovery techniques, which can be evaluated using 8 conformance checking algorithms. Table 1 presents the initial collection of techniques of the recommender system. The conformance checking algorithms are used to assess the quality of the results of the techniques (i.e., the measures as defined in Section 3.3). Table 2 presents the initial set of measures that can be assessed in the recommender system. Remark that performance measures are generated in the discovery experiments, while all the other measures are computed in conformance experiments.

Table 1. Portfolio of control-flow algorithms. These algorithms are available in the ProM 6 framework [16].

Technique	Result
Alpha Miner	Petri Net
Flexible Heuristics Miner	Causal Net
Flower Miner	Petri Net
Fuzzy Miner	Fuzzy Model
Heuristics Miner	Causal Net
Inductive Miner	Petri Net
ILP Miner	Petri Net
Passage Miner	Petri Net
TS Miner	Transition System

Table 2. Set of measures. The conformance checking algorithms that support these measures are available in CoBe-Fra [15]

Category	Measure
Performance	Runtime
	Used Memory
Simplicity	Elements in the Model
	Node Arc Degree
	Cut Vertices
Fitness	Token-Based Fitness
	Negative Event Recall
Precision	ETC Precision
	Negative Event Precision
Generalization	Neg. Event Generalization

As depicted in Figure 3, both training and recommending functions rely on a set of feature extractors. A feature extractor consists of a relatively simple function that can be used to compute specific features of event logs. An initial collection of 12 extractors was implemented and integrated in the system. Table 3 describes the set of features that can be computed using these extractors. Remarkably, experiments presented in Section 5 suggest that, although simple, these features are very effective in the characterization of event logs.

To enable flexibility and extensionality, any technique, measure, or feature can be added to (or removed from) the system at any moment, even when some experiment is being executed. The modification (addition or removal of techniques, measures, or features) will have effect in the succeeding iteration of the training.

4.1   Evaluation Framework

The evaluation framework is implemented as a package of the CoBeFra framework and supported by a MySQL database management system (DBMS). The different functionalities of the framework can be described as follows.

Table 3. The set of features. The causal matrix consists of the counting of direct successors for each pair of events in the log.

Scope	Feature	Description
Trace	Distinct Traces	The number of distinct traces in the log.
Trace	Total Traces	The number of traces in the log.
Trace	Trace Length	The average length of all traces in the log.
Trace	Repetitions Intra Trace	The average number of event repetitions intra trace.
Event	Distinct Events	The number of distinct events in the log.
Event	Total Events	The number of events in the log.
Event	Start Events	The number of distinct start events in the log.
Event	End Events	The number of distinct end events in the log.
Flow	Entropy	The average of the proportion of direct successors and predecessors counts between two events in the log.
Flow	Concurrency	Based on the dependency measures of [19], the percentage of concurrent relations in the causal matrix.
Flow	Density	The percentage of non-zero values in the causal matrix.
Flow	Length-One Loops	The number of length-one loops in the causal matrix.

Management function: controls the repository as well as the collection of discovery and conformance algorithms. The repository consists of a database storing information about event logs, process models, and experiments. The discovery and conformance algorithms consist of executables (e.g., ProM plugins) that can be used for process discovery or conformance checking.

Execution function: executes a single evaluation by selecting randomly an event log, a control-flow algorithm (i.e., a technique), and a conformance algorithm from the repository and the collection of algorithms. An evaluation starts with either executing a discovery experiment in order to mine a process model using the selected discovery technique on the selected log or, if this discovery experiment was executed in a previous evaluation, retrieving this process model from the database. The execution of a discovery experiment consists of running the selected control-flow algorithm on the selected log in which a process model and the performance measures (cf. Table 2) are computed. Both mined model and measures are stored in the database.[3] The evaluation then continues with the

---

[3] Only Petri net models are stored in the repository. If the result of a discovery experiment is not a Petri net then a conversion is necessary. For some model formalisms such as Causal nets, this can be achieved by invoking some ProM plugins. For other formalisms like Fuzzy models, no model will stored in the repository. This means that only performance measures can be computed for these cases.

execution of the conformance experiment (if possible), which consists of running the selected conformance algorithm on the selected log and mined model. As a result, a measure is computed and stored in the database.

4.2 Recommender System

Training. The system's training function is implemented as a Java application. Invoked by a trigger (e.g., every Friday), this application retrieves all the information about the experiments by querying the database. Then, the set of event logs referred in the query results is retrieved from the repository. For each log in the set, it is extracted the set of features (cf. Table 3) that characterizes the log. Next, the entries of the query results are grouped by measure. For each measure and log, a list of experiments results is created, ordered by the result value (e.g., the runtime).[4] This list is then used to build a ranking of techniques. A matrix containing the rankings of the measure is finally built. Each column of the matrix represents a technique, while each row refers to the log from which the ranking was computed. Next, the matrix completion of the ARS algorithm [5] is applied on the matrix to predict eventual unknown values. The matrix as well as the sets of features of the logs described in the matrix can then be used to build a model for predicting the ranking of techniques from a set of features.

Recommending. The system's recommending function is implemented as a ProM plugin (cf. Figure 4). Invoked in the ProM framework, this plugin takes an event log as input and produces a *recommendation* of the best-performing discovery techniques for the given log. The recommendation is based on the knowledge produced by the system's training function. First, the given log is characterized as a set of features. Then, using these features and for each measure, it is applied the prediction function of the ARS algorithm [5] on the matrices generated in the training. As a result, a list of predicted rankings is returned, where each entry represents the expected best-performing techniques for a specific measure. The recommendation is based on a final ranking combining all the predicted rankings. The combined score of a technique $t \in T$ is defined by

$$score(t) = \sum_{m \in M} w_m \times rank(t, m),$$

where $m \in M$ is a measure, w_m is the weight of m, and $rank(t, m)$ is the position of t in the predicted ranking of m. Giving a list of prediction rankings and the weights of each measure, the top-k entries of the final ranking can be efficiently computed by applying the BPA2 algorithm [1].

5   Experiments

A set of experiments was conducted in order to evaluate the recommender system proposed in this paper. Using the implemented evaluation framework and recom-

---

[4] For performance and simplicity measures, the list follows an ascending order. For the other measures, the list follows a descending order. One-element lists are discarded once that they do not hold enough comparative information.

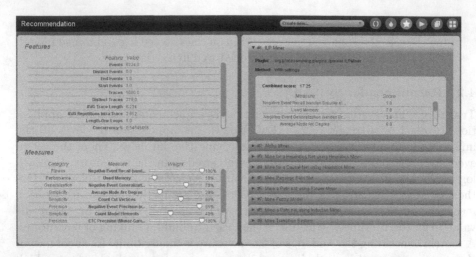

Fig. 4. RS4PD: the client as a ProM plugin. Top-left panel shows the features computed for the uploaded event log. Bottom-left panel allows the user to provide weights to each one of measures. Right panel shows the recommendation.

mender system, we first executed a number of experiments over a set of event logs in order to build the system's prediction models. For these experiments, 130 event logs (112 synthetic and 18 real life) were collected from several sources[5] and uploaded into the repository. As described in Section 4, the portfolio consisted of 9 discovery techniques (cf. Table 1), which can be evaluated using 8 conformance checking algorithms. These conformance algorithms were used to compute the non-performance measures of Table 2. Remark that the performance measures are computed during the execution of the discovery experiments. The set of feature extractors used in the experiments is described in Table 3. The system's evaluation started with the continuous execution of experiments during one week. As a result, 1129 discovery experiments were executed, from which 882 process models were generated. In total, 5475 measures were computed.

Using the prediction models built from the experiments, we then used a set of testing event logs in order to compare the accuracy of the system's recommendations. The testing dataset consists of 13 event logs from the 3TU repository[6] and the testing dataset of [19]. From these logs, 4 are the real life logs used in the *Business Process Intelligence* (BPI) workshop challenges of 2012 and 2013. For each of the testing event logs, we executed all the possible discovery and conformance experiments. Then, using the system's recommending function, we computed the top-9 best-performing techniques for each measure. The *accuracy* of the recommendation is defined by the matching of the predicted technique with the actual best-performing technique measured in the experiments.[7] The

---

[5] Several process mining groups were invited to share their event logs.

[6] http://data.3tu.nl/repository/collection:event_logs

[7] Remark that, unlike rank correlations such as Spearman's or Kendall's, this accuracy measurement does not consider the worst-performing techniques in the rankings, which are unlikely to be taken into account by the user.

accuracy is 1 if the predicted best-performing technique matches the measured best-performing technique. The accuracy is 0 if the predicted best-performing technique matches the measured worst-performing technique. An accuracy value between 0 and 1 is defined by the min-max normalization of the measure value of the predicted best-performing technique, where min and max are the values of the measured worst- and best-performing techniques. The results of the assessment of the system's accuracy are shown in the figures bellow.

The figure on the right presents the average accuracy of the prediction of the best-performing technique for each measure category, discriminated by event log type. These results show that the system's accuracy varies from 0.67 (for precision measures on real life logs) to 1.0 (for fitness measures). Considering both all measures and all event log types, the global system's accuracy is 0.854.

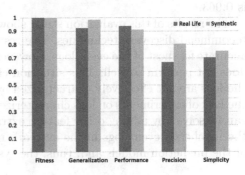

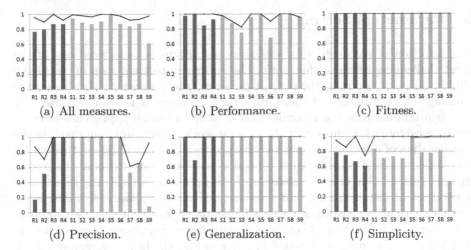

(a) All measures.   (b) Performance.   (c) Fitness.

(d) Precision.   (e) Generalization.   (f) Simplicity.

Fig. 5. Average accuracy of the system's recommendation for each event log

Figure 5 presents the average accuracy of the system's recommendation for each event log. The average accuracy of the prediction of the best-performing technique (i.e., the top-1 technique) is represented by the bars; these accuracy values are discriminated by event log type (dark gray bars represent real life logs, while synthetic logs are identified by the light gray bars). The average accuracy of the prediction of the best-performing technique taking into account the top-3 techniques is represented by the lines. The accuracy values for these cases are defined by the best matching between these three techniques and the actual best-performing technique measured in the experiments (i.e., one of the top-3 techniques should be the actual best-performing technique). Figure 5a shows the global system's accuracy, while the remaining figures show the system's accuracy for each measure category. These results show that for some logs the recommendation of a specific measure may not be accurate (e.g., precision measures on logs $R1$ and $S9$). Nevertheless, the global system's accuracy varies from 0.612 and 1.0. Taking into account the top-3 techniques instead of the top-1, the lower bound of this accuracy interval increases to 0.898. Considering both all measures and all logs, the global system's accuracy considering the top-3 techniques is 0.963.

The results of this evaluation study show that RS4PD can effectively be used to recommend discovery techniques. The results suggest that the system is highly accurate for most of the event logs. However, there are cases for which the system does not perform so well. This situation can be explained either (i) by the fact the logs are not effectively characterized by the current set of features or (ii) by the lack of experiments on logs characterized by specific features. Eventually, this can be solved by adding other feature extractors to the system. Also, increasing the number of event logs in the system's repository should enhance the quality of the prediction models and, thus, the system's accuracy.

6   Parameters Setting

The selection of parameters for discovery algorithms is considered one of the most challenging issues of this work. The current implementation of the RS4PD simply takes into account the default parameters of discovery algorithms when running the experiments (if there are some). However, it is acknowledged that this is a limitation of the recommender system and some approaches were already considered for improving the current work. One simple approach is the instantiation of different versions of the same technique with different values for its parameters, and consider each version as a different algorithm in the recommender system. One of the challenges of this approach is (still) the selection of a good set of instantiations that effectively covers the parameter space. Also, considering multiple instances imply a higher number of experiments to support the recommender system. Another approach is the *parameter optimization* in which parameter space is searched in order to find the best parameters setting with respect to a specific quality measure. The main challenge of this approach is to select a robust strategy to search the parameter space. Traditional strategies such as genetic algorithms have proven to be effective in optimization problems, but they are usually computationally costly. A third approach, which may also be used to facilitate the parameter optimization, is known as *sensibility analysis* and consists of assessing the influence of the inputs of a mathematical model (or system) on the model's output. This information may help on understanding the relationship between the inputs and the output of the model, or identifying redundant inputs in specific contexts. Sensibility methods range from variance-based methods to screening techniques. One of the advantages of screening is that it requires a relatively low number of evaluations when compared to other approaches.

Screening experiments based on the *Elementary Effect* (EE) method [6,3] can be applied to identify non-influential parameters of control-flow algorithms, which usually are computationally costly for estimating other sensitivity analysis measures (e.g., variance-based measures). Rather than quantifying the exact importance of parameters, the EE method provides insight into the contribution of parameters to the results quality.

One of the most efficient EE methods is based on Sobol's quasi-random numbers [11] and a radial OAT strategy [3].[8] The main idea is to analyze the parameter space by performing experiments and assessing the impact of changing parameters with respect to the results quality. A Sobol's quasi-random generator is used to determine a uniformly distributed set of points in the parameter space. Radial OAT experiments [3] are executed over the generated points to measure the impact of the parameters. This information can be used either (i) to guide the users of the RS4PD on the parameters setup by prioritizing the parameters to be tunned, or (ii) as a first step towards parameter optimization in the RS4PD.

The figure on the right presents the results of a preliminary study about the impact of the parameters of the FHM. Using the testing dataset described in Section 5, several radial OAT experiments were executed to measure the impact of the FHM's parameters on the four quality measures. The results suggest that, although the FHM has seven parameters, it mainly relies on three pa-

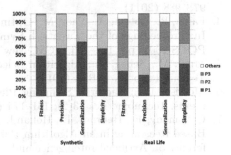

rameters: *dependency threshold* (P1), *relative-to-best threshold* (P2), and *all tasks-connected heuristic* (P3). For more structured logs (the synthetic logs), the quality of the process model depends mainly on P1 and P2. For less structured logs (i.e., real-life), other parameters may be needed for improving the quality of the process model.

7   Conclusions and Future Work

This paper describes a recommender system for process discovery using portfolio-based algorithm selection techniques. To the best of our knowledge, it is the first attempt to incorporate machine learning and information retrieval techniques for recommending process discovery algorithms. Also, the approach is very general and allows for the easy incorporation of new techniques, measurements and log features. Due to its continuous learning principle that makes the system to be decoupled in a server-client architecture, the initial promising results obtained are expected to be even better when a larger training set will be available.

As future work, besides the ideas presented in Section 6, several lines will be pursued. First, research is required to improve and extend the current log features. Second, the incorporation of other discovery and conformance techniques

---

[8] OAT stands for One (factor) At a Time.

will be considered. Third, the encapsulation of the presented recommender system as a pure discovery plugin will be considered, to deliver the user of navigating through the results and thus simplifying the discovery task. Fourth, the incorporation of user-feedback into the training loop will be considered (e.g., usefulness of results or user goals), to improve the usage of the provided recommendations. This feedback may also be used to qualitatively assess the recommender system.

References

1. Akbarinia, R., Pacitti, E., Valduriez, P.: Best Position Algorithms for Top-k Queries. In: Proceedings of the 33rd International Conference on Very Large Data Bases, VLDB 2007, pp. 495–506 (2007)
2. Bobadilla, J., Ortega, F., Hernando, A., Gutiérrez, A.: Recommender Systems Survey. Knowledge-Based Systems 46, 109–132 (2013)
3. Campolongo, F., Saltelli, A., Cariboni, J.: From Screening to Quantitative Sensitivity Analysis. A Unified Approach. Computer Physics Communications 182(4), 978–988 (2011)
4. Fagin, R., Lotem, A., Naor, M.: Optimal Aggregation Algorithms for Middleware. In: Proceedings of the Twentieth Symposium on Principles of Database Systems, PODS 2001, pp. 102–113. ACM, New York (2001)
5. Mısır, M., Sebag, M.: Algorithm Selection as a Collaborative Filtering Problem. Technical report, INRIA (2013)
6. Morris, M.D.: Factorial Sampling Plans for Preliminary Computational Experiments. Technometrics 33(2), 161–174 (1991)
7. O'Mahony, E., Hebrard, E., Holland, A., Nugent, C., O'Sullivan, B.: Using Case-Based Reasoning in an Algorithm Portfolio for Constraint Solving. In: Irish Conference on Artificial Intelligence and Cognitive Science (2008)
8. Rice, J.R.: The Algorithm Selection Problem. Adv. in Computers 15, 65–118 (1976)
9. Rozinat, A., de Medeiros, A.K.A., Günther, C.W., Weijters, A.J.M.M., van der Aalst, W.M.P.: Towards an Evaluation Framework for Process Mining Algorithms. Technical Report 224, Eindhoven University of Technology (2006)
10. Rozinat, A., van der Aalst, W.M.P.: Conformance Checking of Processes Based on Monitoring Real Behavior. Information Systems 33(1), 64–95 (2008)
11. Sobol, I.M.: Uniformly Distributed Sequences With an Additional Uniform Property. USSR Computational Mathematics and Mathematical Physics 16(5), 236–242 (1976)
12. Su, X., Khoshgoftaar, T.M.: A Survey of Collaborative Filtering Techniques. Advances in Artificial Intelligence (2009)
13. van der Aalst, W.M.P.: Process Mining: Discovery, Conformance and Enhancement of Business Processes. Springer, Berlin (2011)
14. van den Broucke, S., Delvaux, C., Freitas, J., Rogova, T., Vanthienen, J., Baesens, B.: Uncovering the Relationship between Event Log Characteristics and Process Discovery Techniques. In: Proceedings of the 9th Workshop on Business Process Intelligence, BPI 2013 (2013)
15. van den Broucke, S., Weerdt, J.D., Baesens, B., Vanthienen, J.: A Comprehensive Benchmarking Framework (CoBeFra) for conformance analysis between procedural process models and event logs in ProM. In: IEEE Symposium on Computational Intelligence and Data Mining, Grand Copthorne Hotel, Singapore. IEEE (2013)
16. Verbeek, H.M.W., Buijs, J.C.A.M., van Dongen, B.F., van der Aalst, W.M.P.: ProM 6: The Process Mining Toolkit. In: Demo at the 8th International Conference on Business Process Management. CEUR-WS, vol. 615, pp. 34–39 (2010)

17. Wang, J., Wong, R.K., Ding, J., Guo, Q., Wen, L.: On Recommendation of Process Mining Algorithms. In: 2012 IEEE 19th International Conference on Web Services (ICWS), pp. 311–318 (2012)
18. Weber, P., Bordbar, B., Tino, P., Majeed, B.: A Framework for Comparing Process Mining Algorithms. In: IEEE GCC Conference and Exhibition, pp. 625–628 (2011)
19. Weijters, A.J.M.M., Ribeiro, J.T.S.: Flexible Heuristics Miner (FHM). In: Proceedings of the IEEE Symposium on Computational Intelligence and Data Mining, CIDM 2011, Paris, France. IEEE (2011)
20. Xu, L., Hutter, F., Hoos, H.H., Leyton-Brown, K.: SATzilla: Portfolio-Based Algorithm Selection for SAT. J. of Artif. Intelligence Research 32(1), 565–606 (2008)

Listen to Me: Improving Process Model Matching through User Feedback

Christopher Klinkmüller[1], Henrik Leopold[2], Ingo Weber[3,4],
Jan Mendling[2], and André Ludwig[1]

[1] Information Systems Institute, University of Leipzig, Leipzig, Germany*
{klinkmueller,ludwig}@wifa.uni-leipzig.de
[2] Wirtschaftsuniversität Wien, Augasse 2-6, A-1090 Vienna, Austria
{henrik.leopold,jan.mendling}@wu.ac.at
[3] Software Systems Research Group, NICTA, Sydney, Australia**
ingo.weber@nicta.com.au
[4] School of Computer Science & Engineering,
University of New South Wales, Australia

Abstract. Many use cases in business process management rely on the identification of correspondences between process models. However, the sparse information in process models makes matching a fundamentally hard problem. Consequently, existing approaches yield a matching quality which is too low to be useful in practice. Therefore, we investigate incorporating user feedback to improve matching quality. To this end, we examine which information is suitable for feedback analysis. On this basis, we design an approach that performs matching in an iterative, mixed-initiative approach: we determine correspondences between two models automatically, let the user correct them, and analyze this input to adapt the matching algorithm. Then, we continue with matching the next two models, and so forth. This approach improves the matching quality, as showcased by a comparative evaluation. From this study, we also derive strategies on how to maximize the quality while limiting the additional effort required from the user.

Keywords: BPM, process similarity, process model matching.

1 Introduction

More and more organizations use process models as a tool for managing their operations. Typical use cases for process models range from process documentation to enactment through a workflow system. Once a repository of process models reaches a certain size, there are several important use cases which require the comparison of process models. Examples include validating a technical

* The work presented in this paper was partly funded by the German Federal Ministry of Education and Research under the projects LSEM (BMBF 03IPT504X) and LogiLeit (BMBF 03IPT504A).
** NICTA is funded by the Australian Government through the Department of Communications and the Australian Research Council through the ICT Centre of Excellence Program.

S. Sadiq, P. Soffer, and H. Völzer (Eds.): BPM 2014, LNCS 8659, pp. 84–100, 2014.
© Springer International Publishing Switzerland 2014

implementation of a business process against a business-centered specification [2], process model search [6,13,10], or identifying clones in process models [7].

The demand for techniques that are capable of comparing process models has led to the development of a variety of *process model matchers*. These matchers, e.g. [24,14,11], are usually designed for universal applicability. That is, they are based on common matching metrics used to assess pairs of activities and define classification rules which are believed to provide meaningful indications of similarity for activities in any pair of process models. However, the insufficient accuracy of these approaches [3] suggests that the assumption of universal applicability is too strict, and might hinder effective application in practice.

For this reason, we seize the idea of an adaptive matcher. A related idea was discussed in [23] where characteristics of a certain process model collection are analyzed to select well-suited matchers for the collection. In contrast to this approach, we devise an *iterative, mixed-initiative approach that utilizes user feedback to constantly adapt the matching algorithm*. It works by presenting automatically determined correspondences between two models to the user, and asking her to add missing and remove incorrect ones. The matching algorithm is then adjusted by analyzing the feedback and the next model pair is matched.

The contributions of this paper are threefold. First, we investigate which information in process models can reliably be used for feedback analysis. For this purpose, we derive indicators from the literature which provide information on whether activities correspond or not and assess their correlation to the classes of corresponding and non-corresponding activity pairs. The results also offer insights into the challenges that process model matching faces. Second, based on this analysis we introduce an approach that integrates user feedback to improve the matching quality. Third, we perform a comparative evaluation and, based on the results, derive strategies to minimize the user workload while maximizing the quality improvements.

The rest of the paper is organized as follows. Section 2 defines process model matching and introduces the state of the art. Section 3 provides an overview of correspondence indicators derived from related research and investigates their potential for user feedback analysis. Based on this survey, Section 4 defines our approach that incorporates feedback. Section 5 evaluates the approach using simulated feedback from gold standards. Finally, Section 6 concludes the paper.

2   Foundations: Problem Illustration and Related Work

This section introduces the problem of process model matching in Section 2.1 and reviews the state of the art in Section 2.2.

2.1   Problem Illustration

In accordance with ontology matching [8], process model matching is the process of identifying an *alignment* between two process models. In this paper, a process model is regarded as a *business process graph* as defined in [4]: a process model consists of labeled nodes of different types and directed edges connecting them. While the edges define the control flow of the process, the nodes express activities, gateways, etc. This abstract notion of process models permits the application of our work to different notations like Petri nets, Event-driven Process Chains (EPCs) or Business Process Model and Notation (BPMN).

Definition 1 (Process model, Set of activities). *Let $\mathcal{L}$ be a set of labels and $\mathcal{T}$ be a set of types. A process model p is a tuple (N, E, λ, τ), in which:*

- *N is the set of nodes;*
- *$E \subseteq N \times N$ is the set of edges;*
- *$\lambda : N \to \mathcal{L}$ is a function that maps nodes to labels; and*
- *$\tau : N \to \mathcal{T}$ is a function that assigns types to nodes.*

For a given process model $p = (N, E, \lambda, \tau)$ the set $A = \{a | a \in N \land \tau(a) = activity\}$ is called the set of activities, where we require $\forall a \in A, n \in N : |\{n|(a,n) \in E)\}| \leq 1$ and $|\{n|(n,a) \in E)\}| \leq 1$. Furthermore, we require that there only exists one start $(\exists n \in N, \forall n_i \in N : (n_i, n) \notin E)$ and one end node $(\exists n \in N, \forall n_i \in N : (n, n_i) \notin E)$.

Given two process models p_1, p_2 and their activity sets A_1, A_2, an *alignment* is a set of *correspondences*, i.e. activity pairs (a_1, a_2) with $a_1 \in A_1$ and $a_2 \in A_2$ that represent similar functionality. Correspondences between sets of activities (A_1^*, A_2^*) with $A_1^* \subseteq A_1$ and $A_2^* \subseteq A_2$ are expressed as sets of correspondences between all activity pairs in A_1^*, A_2^*: $\{(a_1^*, a_2^*)|(a_1^* \in A_1^* \land a_2^* \in A_2^*)\}$.

Fig. 1 shows an alignment between two university admission process models which will be used as a running example throughout the paper. Both processes represent the scenario of receiving, evaluating, and deciding about an application. Hence, activities from one process related to one of these tasks are matched with activities dealing with the same task in the other process. While α_2 and β_2 constitute a one-to-one correspondence, β_6 is not matched. Moreover, there are two complex correspondences: a one-to-many correspondence formed by α_1, β_1 and β_2 and a many-to-many correspondence comprised of α_3, α_4, α_5, β_4 and β_5.

Applying a matcher to automatically determine alignments will only be useful if it is of high quality, i.e. if it meets the user's expectations. This will be the

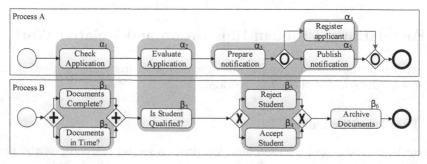

Fig. 1. An example for a process model alignment

case when the number of correctly identified correspondences (*true positives*) is high. Consequently, as few correspondences as possible should be missed (*false negatives*), while the results of a good matcher also contain few erroneous correspondences (*false positives*).

2.2 Related Work

The foundations for research in process model matching can be found in various works on schema and ontology matching [1,8] as well as in research on process model similarity. Such process similarity techniques exploit different sources of information such as text [5,12], model structure [9,4], or execution semantics [13,26]. An overview is provided in [5].

Approaches for process model matching typically derive attributes of activity pairs from these techniques and aggregate these attributes in a predefined static classifier in different ways (see e.g. [24,14,11]). In [23], the idea of a more dynamic assembly of matchers is discussed. Therefore, matchers are allocated to properties of process model pairs. By evaluating these properties within a model collection, appropriate matchers are selected and composed.

However, up until now there is no automated technique for process matching available that achieves results comparable to those in the field of ontology matching. In fact, a comparison of techniques developed by different researchers revealed that the best matcher achieved an f-measure of 0.45 on the test data sets [3]. This calls for improving precision and recall of existing techniques. To this end, we investigate suitable matching indicators and user feedback.

3 Information for User Feedback Analysis

The goal of analyzing user feedback is to find models that can predict user decisions with high success. Therefore, indicators whose values are highly correlated to the decisions, i.e., whether activity pairs correspond or not, are needed [19]. For example, label similarity is seen as a good indicator: activity pairs with a high similarity tend to correspond; pairs with a low similarity tend to not correspond. As various information sources, e.g. structure and execution semantics, can be considered, we systematically identify suitable indicators in a two-step approach: we first present indicators from the literature and own prior work (Section 3.1) and investigate their potential for feedback analysis (Section 3.2).

3.1 Indicator Definitions

Matching approaches rely on various characteristics of activities to judge whether they correspond. From analyzing related work, especially the approaches evaluated in the matching contest 2013 [3], we identified five categories: *position* and *neighborhood* based on the model structure, *label specificity* and *label semantics* referring to the labels, and *execution semantics*. Thereby, some approaches rely on a certain modeling notation or do not explicitly define the characteristics.

In order to be able to assess if these characteristics can be used for feedback analysis, we present indicators adapted to our process model definition.

To this end, we define indicators as similarity functions from the set of activity pairs (A_1, A_2) to the interval $[0,1]$: a value of 0 indicates total dissimilarity, a value of 1 identity, and values in between a degree of similarity. Most of the presented indicators utilize an attribute function $at : A \to \mathbb{R}_{\geq 0}$, which returns a value measured with regard to a certain activity property. Those indicators are referred to as *attribute indicators*. Given an activity pair, they indicate the similarity of these activities with regard to a certain attribute.

Definition 2 (Attribute indicator). *Let A_1, A_2 be two sets of activities and $a_1 \in A_1$, $a_2 \in A_2$ be two activities. The attribute indicator i_{at} is then defined as:*

$$
i_{at}(a_1, a_2) = \begin{cases} 0 & \max_{a \in A_1}(at(a)) = 0 \vee \max_{a \in A_2}(at(a)) = 0 \\ 1 - |\frac{at(a_1)}{\max\limits_{a \in A_1}(at(a))} - \frac{at(a_2)}{\max\limits_{a \in A_2}(at(a))}| & else \end{cases}
$$

In the following, we describe various attributes with regard to the general attribute indicator and define other indicators for each of the five categories.

Position. Process models might represent the same abstract process. In such cases, it is more likely for activities at similar positions to correspond than for activities whose positions differ. This idea is pursued in the *Triple-S* approach, which takes the relative position of nodes in the process models as a similarity indicator [3]. According to our definition, each process model has one start and one end node. Thus, we view these nodes as anchors and consider the distances to these nodes, i.e. the smallest number of activities on paths from a node to the start or end node, as attributes to define the attribute indicators $\sigma_{pos}^{start}, \sigma_{pos}^{end}$.

The position of an activity can also be defined with reference to the *Refined Process Structure Tree* (RPST) [23,24]. The RPST is a hierarchical representation of a process model consisting of single-entry-single-exit fragments [20]. Each RPST fragment belongs to one of four structured classes: trivial fragments (T) consist of two nodes connected with a single edge; a Bond (B) represents a set of fragments sharing two common nodes; polygons (P) capture sequences of other fragments; in case a fragment cannot be classified as trivial, bond, or polygon, it is categorized as a rigid (R). Fig. 2 presents the RPST of the Process A.

The idea is to view the depth of the non-trivial fragments that contain the activity as an attribute for the position of the model structure (σ_{pos}^{rpst}), i.e., the deeper an activity is located in the RPST the more decision points need to be

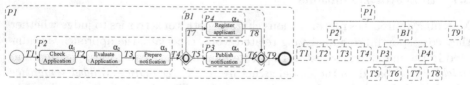

Fig. 2. The fragments of the admission process of university A and the RPST

Table 1. Attribute indicators for an activity pair from the running example

	α_1	$\max\limits_{a\in A_A}$	β_1	$\max\limits_{a\in A_B}$	(α_1,β_1)		α_1	$\max\limits_{a\in A_A}$	β_1	$\max\limits_{a\in A_B}$	(α_1,β_1)
σ_{pos}^{start}	0	3	0	3	1.00	$\sigma_{|label|}$	2	2	2	3	0.67
σ_{pos}^{end}	3	3	3	3	1.00	$\sigma_{\rightsquigarrow}$	4	4	4	4	1.00
σ_{pos}^{rpst}	2	3	3	3	0.67	σ_{+}	0	0	0	1	0.00
σ_{neigh}^{model}	1	3	2	4	0.83	$\sigma_{\parallel}$	0	1	1	1	0.00
σ_{neigh}^{rpst}	2	2	0	0	0.00						

passed to get to the activity. Activities have at most one incoming and at most one outgoing edge. Thus, they cannot be an entry or exit node of a non-trivial fragment and the trivial fragments they belong to have the same depth.

Table 1 illustrates the position indicators for (α_1, β_1) from the running example. Both activities have a distance to the start event of 0. As the structure of both processes is similar they also have the same distance to the end node. Thus, both attribute indicators are 1. As activity β_1 is located in a parallel block and α_1 is not, their RPST positions differ leading to an indicator value of 0.67.

Neighborhood. Whereas the position attributes consider the global location of activities in a model, we next consider the local structure. In this regard, the Triple-S approach [3] considers the ratios of incoming and outgoing edges. As our definition requires activities to have at most one incoming and at most one outgoing edge, these ratios would not provide much information. Instead, we define the structural neighborhood indicator (σ_{neigh}^{model}) based on the undirected version of the process model. We count the activities that are connected to an activity by at least one sequence of distinct edges not containing any activities.

We also consider the RPST for comparing the local structure of activities and define the RPST neighborhood indicator (σ_{neigh}^{rpst}). Therefore, we determine the trivial fragments an activity is part of and count their sibling fragments.

Table 1 also shows examples for the neighborhood indicators. α_1 has one structural neighbor (α_2) and in Process A, α_3 has the most neighbors $(\alpha_2, \alpha_4, \alpha_5)$. Similarly, β_1 has two neighbors (β_2, β_3) and the maximum is four neighbors for β_3 $(\beta_1, \beta_2, \beta_4, \beta_5)$. Thus, the structural neighborhood of both activities is similar (0.83). The RPST neighborhood indicator is 0, because for each activity in Process B there are two trivial fragments forming a polygon. As each of these polygons does not comprise any further fragments, all activities in Process B have an RPST neighborhood size of 0.

Label Specificity. According to an analysis of matching challenges in [11], label specificity (i.e., one label containing more detailed information than another) had a big impact on the correct identification of correspondences. Thus, we assume activities with a similar specificity to correspond more likely than those with different specificities. An attribute indicator in this regard is defined upon the label length $(\sigma_{|label|})$, i.e., the more words a label contains, the more specific information it provides. It is considered for matcher selection in [23] and for label pruning in [11]. The label length is defined as the number of individual words in a label without common *stop words* like "the", "if", and "to". The individual words of an activity label are returned by the function $\Omega : \mathcal{L} \to \mathcal{P}(\mathcal{W})$. Table 1 shows that $|\Omega(\alpha_1)| = |\Omega(\beta_1)| = 2$. Moreover, the maximum label length in Process A is 2. In Process B β_3 ("Is student qualified") has the longest label of length 3 whereas β_2 ("Documents in Time?") consists of two individual words, because "in" is a stop word. Thus, the label length indicator is 0.67.

We further assume frequently occurring words to be more specific than less frequently occurring words. This idea is also pursued for label pruning in [11]. Thus, we rely on the term frequency which is well known in information retrieval. It is defined as the number of occurrences of a certain word in a document. On the one hand, we take the union of all activity labels in the model collection as a document and define the function $tf_{coll} : \mathcal{W} \to [0,1]$ to return the number of a word's occurrences in the model collection divided by the maximum number determined for a word in the collection. On the other hand, we define $tf_{2p} : \mathcal{W} \to [0,1]$ by using all activity labels in the examined model pair to create the document. Based thereon, we define the term frequency indicators σ_{tf}^{coll} and σ_{tf}^{2p}.

Definition 3 (Term frequency indicators). *Let a_1, a_2 be two activities. Then, the term frequency indicators σ_{tf}^{coll} and σ_{tf}^{2p} are defined as:*

$$\sigma_{tf}^{coll}(a_1, a_2) = 1 - |\tfrac{1}{|\Omega(a_1)|} * \sum_{\omega \in \Omega(a_1)} tf_{coll}(\omega) - \tfrac{1}{|\Omega(a_2)|} * \sum_{\omega \in \Omega(a_2)} tf_{coll}(\omega)|$$

$$\sigma_{tf}^{2p}(a_1, a_2) = 1 - |\tfrac{1}{|\Omega(a_1)|} * \sum_{\omega \in \Omega(a_1)} tf_{2p}(\omega) - \tfrac{1}{|\Omega(a_2)|} * \sum_{\omega \in \Omega(a_2)} tf_{2p}(\omega)|$$

Table 2 illustrates the model pair based indicator. "Documents" occurs most often in the pair. Thus, the term frequencies are yielded by dividing the occurrence values with 3. As the average term frequency of α_1 ("Check Application") is 0.50 and for β_2 ("Documents Complete?") it is 0.67, the indicator yields 0.83.

Label Semantics. Every matching approach relies on the calculation of label similarities as an indicator to which degree activities constitute the same functionality. Prior research has shown that the basic bag-of-words similarity [11] yields good results [3]. It calculates a symmetric similarity score $\sigma.\omega : \mathcal{W}^2 \to [0..1]$ for each pair of individual words (ω_1, ω_2) with $\omega_1 \in \Omega(a_1)$ and $\omega_2 \in \Omega(a_2)$. Based thereon, it is then defined as the mean of the maximum similarity score each individual word has with any of the individual words from the other label.

Definition 4 (Basic bag-of-words similarity). *Let a_1, a_2 be two activities. The basic bag-of-word similarity $\sigma.\lambda$ is then defined as:*

$$\sigma.\lambda(a_1, a_2) = \frac{\sum_{\omega_1 \in \Omega(a_1)} \max_{\omega_2 \in \Omega(a_2)} (\sigma.\omega(\omega_1, \omega_2)) + \sum_{\omega_2 \in \Omega(a_2)} \max_{\omega_1 \in \Omega(a_1)} (\sigma.\omega(\omega_1, \omega_2))}{|\Omega(a_1)| + |\Omega(a_2)|}$$

Table 3 illustrates the computation of the basic bag-of-words similarity for α_1 ("Check Application") and β_2 ("Documents complete?"). To compute the similarity of a pair of words, we relied on the maximum of the Levenshtein similarity [15] and the Lin similarity [16]. This measure sees high values in both, syntax (Levenshtein) and semantics (Lin), as evidence for similarity.

Table 2. Word occurrences and term frequencies in the admission processes

	check	application	documents	complete
occurrences	1	2	3	1
term frequency	0.33	0.67	1.00	0.33

Table 3. Example for the basic bag-of-words similarity

	documents	complete	max
check	0.78	0.25	0.78
application	0.11	0.18	0.18
max	0.78	0.25	$\sigma.\lambda = \mathbf{0.50}$

Behavior. Lastly, there are approaches that account for the behavioral context of activities within a process model. Such behavioral attributes are proposed as indicators for matcher selection [23], considered for probabilistic match optimization [14] and also implemented in the ICoP framework [21]. The idea is that corresponding activity pairs show similar characteristics during process execution, whereas non-corresponding pairs do not. Therefore, we rely on the notion of *behavioral profiles* [22] which comprise three relations between activities in a process model defined upon the set of all possible execution sequences. Two activities are in *strict order* ($a_1 \rightsquigarrow a_2$) if a_2 is executed after a_1 in all execution sequences. They are *exclusive* ($a_1 + a_2$) if no sequence contains both activities. Lastly, they are *interleaving* ($a_1 \parallel a_2$) if there are sequences in which a_1 occurs before a_2 and there are sequences in which a_2 occurs before a_1. For each type of relation, we count the number of relations the given activity participates in. Based on these counts, we define the attribute indicators $\sigma_{\rightsquigarrow}$, σ_+ and $\sigma_{\parallel}$ which are illustrated in Table 1, too. While α_1 and β_1 have an identical number of strict order relations (their execution can be followed by the execution of up to four activities), they do not share similar characteristics with regard to the other behavioral attributes. On the one hand, there are no exclusive activities in Process A at all. Thus, the maximum in Process A and the according attribute indicator yield a value of 0. On the other hand, there is one interleaving relation in each process ($\alpha_4 \parallel \alpha_5$ and $\beta_1 \parallel \beta_2$). As β_1 is part of one of these relations and α_1 not, the according indicator is 0.

3.2 Applicability Assessment

We now use these indicators to analyze whether the information sources are suitable to derive models that can predict a user's decisions. Thus, we examine whether there is a correlation between an indicator's values and the classes.

As the suitability of an indicator cannot be predicted in general, it must be estimated with regard to particular data sets (i.e., process collections) for which the set of correspondences is known (i.e., a *gold standard* of correspondences exists). To this end, we used the two process collections and respective gold standards from the matching contest in 2013 [3]: processes on birth certificates and university admission. More precisely, we took the set of all corresponding and

Table 4. p-values of the Kolmogorov–Smirnov test for the birth certificate (gray rows) and the university admission (white rows) data sets

σ_{pos}^{start}	σ_{pos}^{end}	σ_{pos}^{rpst}	σ_{neigh}^{model}	σ_{neigh}^{rpst}	$\sigma_{|label|}$	σ_{tf}^{coll}	σ_{tf}^{2p}	$\sigma.\lambda$	$\sigma_{\leadsto}$	σ_{+}	$\sigma_{\parallel}$
0.001	**0.010**	0.967	0.054	**0.010**	0.581	**0.000**	0.111	**0.000**	**0.000**	0.111	0.211
0.000	0.367	0.155	0.286	0.468	0.210	0.016	0.699	**0.000**	**0.001**	0.864	0.393

the set of all non-corresponding activity pairs for both data sets as representative samples for both classes. At this point, it should be noted that some of the process models in the university admission data set are not sound, which is a necessary prerequisite for computing the behavior attributes. Thus, we only considered the sound university admission models for these attributes.

To assess the correlation of classes and indicator values, we first examined the distributions of indicator values within both classes. The rationale is that classes can only be assigned to value ranges if the values are distributed differently across the classes. Therefore, we randomly drew 100 activity pairs from each class per attribute. The reason is that the number of non-corresponding activity pairs is roughly 30 times as high as the number of corresponding pairs in both data sets, which would distort our analysis. Next, we conducted a two-sided Kolmogorov-Smirnov [17] test at a significance level of 0.01 with these samples. The neutral hypothesis of this test is that the examined distributions are equal and will be rejected if the yielded p-value is lower than the significance level. Table 4 summarizes the p-values yielded for each attribute. Bold values highlight p-values that are below the significance level.

As can be seen from the table, there are only three attributes (σ_{pos}^{start}, $\sigma.\lambda$, and $\sigma_{\leadsto}$) for which the null hypothesis is rejected in both cases. From this analysis, these three attributes seem suitable for classification, but we will also consider σ_{tf}^{coll} as its p-values only marginally infringe the test conditions.

We further substantiated our analysis by investigating how well each class can be assigned to a value range of an indicator. Therefore, we measured the *information gain* [19], a well established measure from statistics, as an indicator for the entropy of class assignments within subsets of activity pairs with regard to all pairs. More precisely, we calculated the values of all activity pairs for each of the four attributes (σ_{pos}^{start}, $\sigma.\lambda$, σ_{tf}^{coll}, $\sigma_{\leadsto}$). We then determined two subsets of pairs with regard to one of the attributes and to a threshold. For all pairs in the first subset the attribute value is smaller than the threshold, whereas the values of pairs in the second subset are larger. We considered all possible separations of activity pairs that satisfied this rule and chose the separation with the highest information gain for each attribute. The rationale is that the respective subsets constitute the best separation of corresponding and non-corresponding pairs with

Table 5. Information gains for the selected attributes for the birth certificate (gray rows) and the university admission (white rows).

$\sigma.\lambda$	σ_{tf}^{coll}	$\sigma_{\leadsto}$	σ_{pos}^{start}
0.056	0.023	0.016	0.005
0.027	0.010	0.007	0.002

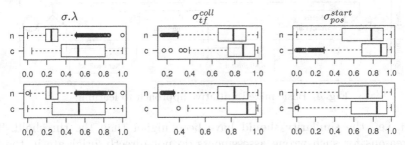

Fig. 3. Box plots for corresponding (c) and non-corresponding (n) activity pairs representing three indicators for the birth certificate (upper row) and the university admission (lower row) data sets.

regard to the considered attribute. As can be seen from Table 5, $\sigma.\lambda$ yields the highest and σ_{pos}^{start} the lowest information gain, σ_{tf}^{coll} and $\sigma_{\leadsto}$ are in between. To convey a better intuition for this measure, Fig. 3 shows the distribution of the relative value frequencies for $\sigma.\lambda$ and σ_{pos}^{start} as well as for σ_{tf}^{coll} as a representative for the indicators with medium information gains.

According to these box plots a threshold at about 0.4 would yield a good classifier for $\sigma.\lambda$ as many corresponding and only a few non-corresponding activity pairs have values larger than this threshold. For the other indicators, whose distributions differ only slightly, there is no threshold which would classify that well. Thus, *we only consider label similarity in terms of $\sigma.\lambda$ for user feedback analysis* and introduce a mixed-initiative approach which aims at increasing the applicability of $\sigma.\lambda$ for separating activity pairs in the next section.

4   Word Similarity Adaptation

The incorporation of user feedback opens the opportunity to analyze the user's decisions and adjust the matching process accordingly. Here, we rely on corrections made by the user to proposed alignments. Therefore, we let the user select a pair of process models and automatically determine an alignment. Presenting it to the user, she is asked to remove incorrect and add missing correspondences. These corrections are passed to the algorithm which examines the feedback and adapts its classification mechanism. Afterwards, the next matching process can be started by the user. Fig. 4 illustrates this basic approach.

As outlined in Section 3, we only consider the basic bag-of-words similarity $\sigma.\lambda$ for correspondence identification. Given a predefined threshold we classify all activity pairs with a basic bag-of-words similarity score higher than or equal to the threshold as correspondences.

Although our analysis shows this indicator to have the most desirable properties, there will still be false positives and false negatives leading to an unsatisfactory matching quality [3]. Hence, it is the goal of the feedback analysis to understand why mistakes were done and how they could have been avoided.

With regard to the matching process, a false positive was suggested because the similarity of the activity pair was estimated too high, i.e., it should have been lower than the threshold. In case of a false negative, it is the other way

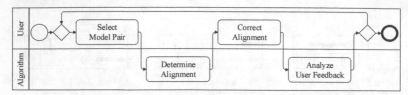

Fig. 4. Basic mixed-initiative approach to learning

around, i.e., the similarity should have been higher than the threshold. The main reasons for such wrong assessments do not directly originate in the basic bag-of-words similarity, but in the underlying word similarity measure $\sigma.\omega$. Those measures are either syntactic, not considering word meaning, or semantic being based on external sources of knowledge like lexical databases or corpora [18]. As the creation of such databases or corpora incurs huge manual effort, matchers usually rely on universal ones. In both cases, i.e. syntactic matching or semantic matching using universal corpora, the word similarity measures do not sufficiently account for domain-specific information, e.g., technical vocabulary or abbreviations, and thus introduce errors.

Consequently, when the user feedback indicates a misclassification of an activity pair, our learning approach checks which pairs of words contributed to that misclassification. According to the definition of the basic bag-of-words similarity, a word pair contributes to an activity pair classification each time it yields the highest similarity score for one word in the respective activity labels. Therefore, in order to adjust the word similarities to the domain characteristics of the considered process model collection, we decrease the similarity of a pair of words whenever it contributed to a false positive, and increase the similarity for a false negative. We do so by defining two counting functions: $\gamma_{fp} : (\omega_1, \omega_2) \to \mathbb{N}$ returns the number of counted false positive contributions for a word pair, and $\gamma_{fn} : (\omega_1, \omega_2) \to \mathbb{N}$ analogously for false negative contributions. Based on these counters, we introduce a word similarity correction term.

Definition 5 (Word similarity correction). *Let ω_1, ω_2 be two words. Furthermore, let $\rho_{fp}, \rho_{fn} \in \mathbb{R}$ be two predefined learning rates. The correction function $\delta : \mathcal{W}^2 \to \mathbb{R}$ is then defined as:*

$$\delta(\omega_1, \omega_2) := \rho_{fp} \times \gamma_{fp}(\omega_1, \omega_2) + \rho_{fn} \times \gamma_{fn}(\omega_1, \omega_2)$$

Note that the counts are multiplied with learning rates; together with the threshold these are the control parameters of the approach.

Given this correction term and an ordinary word similarity measure $\sigma.\omega_o$, we introduce the *adaptive word similarity* $\sigma.\omega_\alpha$.

Definition 6 (Adaptive word similarity). *Let ω_1, ω_2 be two words. Furthermore, let $\delta : \mathcal{W}^2 \to \mathbb{R}$ be a function that returns a correction value for a word pair. The adapting word similarity function $\sigma.\omega_\alpha : \mathcal{W}^2 \to [0..1]$ is then defined as:*

$$\sigma.\omega_\alpha(\omega_1, \omega_2) := \begin{cases} 1 & \sigma.\omega_o(\omega_1, \omega_2) + \delta(\omega_1, \omega_2) > 1 \\ 0 & \sigma.\omega_o(\omega_1, \omega_2) + \delta(\omega_1, \omega_2) < 0 \\ \sigma.\omega_o(\omega_1, \omega_2) + \delta(\omega_1, \omega_2) & else \end{cases}$$

Since $\sigma.\omega_o(\omega_1, \omega_2) + \delta(\omega_1, \omega_2)$ might return a value outside the interval $[0,1]$, but any $\sigma.\omega$ function is expected to stay within these bounds, we enforce the bounds as per the first and second case in the above definition. We then use $\sigma.\omega_\alpha$ as $\sigma.\omega$ in the basic bag-of-words similarity when determining the alignment between two process models.

To illustrate this approach, we refer to Table 3, which outlines the computation of $\sigma.\lambda$ for (α_1, β_1). In previous work [11], we found that a threshold above 0.6 yields good results. In this case, the (α_1, β_1) will be classified as non-corresponding. Collecting user feedback, this will be revealed as a wrong classification. Thus, the false negative counter will be increased by 2 for ("check", "documents") as this word pair yielded the highest value for both words and by one for ("check", "complete") and for ("application", "complete"). Having ρ_{fp} set to 0.1, the adaptive word similarity will now roughly be 0.6. Thus, an activity pair with the labels of α_1 and β_1 will now be classified as corresponding.

5   Evaluation

This section has two objectives. First, we analyze if our mixed-initiative approach improves the results of existing matchers with regard to the amount of missing and incorrect correspondences. Second, we aim to derive strategies to minimize the amount of user feedback required to achieve a high matching quality.

Experiment Setup. Our evaluation utilizes the birth certificate and the university admission data sets from the matching competition [3]. The gold standards serve a dual purpose here: (i) assessing the matching quality and (ii) simulating user feedback. Therefore, going through a sequence of model pairs, we first determine an alignment for the current pair and assess the quality of this alignment. That is, we determine the number of true positives (TP), false positives (FP) and false negatives (FN) given the gold standard. We then calculate the standard measures of precision (P) $(TP/(TP + FP))$, recall (R) $(TP/(TP + FN))$, and f-measure as their harmonic mean (F) $(2 \times P \times R/(P + R))$. Next, we pass the sets of false positives and false negatives to the algorithm which adapts the word similarities accordingly. Then, we move on to the next pair. The average (AVG) and the standard deviation (STD) of all measures and model pairs are used to assess the approach's quality. These are calculated either as a running statistics *during* learning, or as an overall quality indicator *after* all model pairs have been matched and the respective feedback has been considered.

We sampled the space of possible threshold values over the interval $[0,1]$ in steps of 0.05 as well as the space of possible false positive and false negative learning rates over the interval $[0,0.2]$ in steps of 0.01. Moreover, we randomly generated different model pair sequences in order to check the influence of the model pair order on the quality. We used the maximum of the Levenshtein [15] and the Lin [16] similarities as the ordinary similarity measure.

Matching Results. Table 6 compares the results of our mixed-initiative approach to a baseline comprised of the best results from the matching competition

Table 6. Best results from matching contest and for word similarity adaptation

	Birth Certificate					University Admission					
	Precision		Recall		F-Measure		Precision		Recall		F-Measure	
Approach	AVG	STD	AVG	STD	AVG	STD	AVG	STD	AVG	STD	AVG	STD
Baseline	.68	.19	.33	.22	.45	.18	.56	.23	.32	.28	.41	.20
Adaptive	.73	.15	.67	.24	**.69**	.18	.60	.20	.56	.25	**.58**	.21

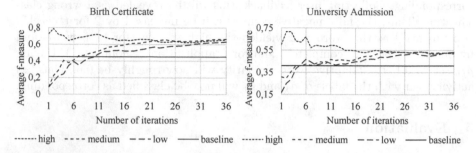

Fig. 5. Running average f-measure after ith iteration

[3], i.e., the RefMod-Mine/NSCM results for the birth certificate and the bag-of-words similarity with label pruning for the university admission data set. The results for the mixed-initiative approach were determined for collecting user feedback over all model pairs. We observed an increase of the f-measure by 0.24 for the birth certificate and by 0.17 for the university admission data set. While the precision remained stable, there was a dramatic improvement in the recall.

Deriving strategies. To derive strategies for minimizing the user workload, we first investigated if the order in which process model pairs are considered had impact on the overall quality. For this purpose, we determined the quality of the basic bag-of-words similarity for each model pair. Then, we split the model pairs for each data set into three equal-sized classes, i.e., model pairs with a high, a medium, and a low f-measure. We generated three sequences (*high, medium,* and *low*) where each sequence starts with 12 model pairs of the respective class, randomly ordered, followed by the remaining 24 model pairs, also in random order. Fig. 5 shows the running average f-measure after the ith iteration for all three sequences per data set. The results suggest that the order only has a small impact on the final quality, since the average f-measures converge to roughly the same value as the number of iterations increases. However, the running average can be misleading: if we start learning with pairs that are already matched well before learning (as in the *high* case), how much can we learn from them? To examine this aspect, we ran a different experiment, where learning is stopped after the ith iteration, and the f-measure over *all* pairs is computed. The results are shown in Fig. 6, left. Looking at the data, one might hypothesize that here the user workload *per model pair* is lower in the *high* case than for the other

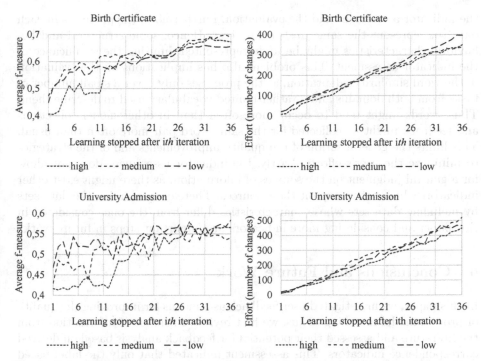

Fig. 6. Overall average f-measure over all 36 model pairs and the user workload after learning for i iterations

sequences. Thus, we also counted the number of changes a user has to do until learning is stopped. These effort indicators are shown in Fig. 6, right.

First of all, it can be seen that – regardless of the order – the amount of corrections is roughly growing linearly without big differences across the sequences. Furthermore, the f-measure curves for all three sequences approach each other with a growing number of iterations used to learn. When learning is stopped early, the best results are yielded for the *low* and the *medium* sequences: feedback on models has a larger impact if matching quality is low beforehand. Finally, regardless of the order, 2/3rds of the improvements are obtained from analyzing about half the model pairs ($i = 16$). In practice it is not possible to sort model pairs with regard to the f-measure upfront. But as feedback collection is progressing, the relative improvements can be measured. As soon as the improvements from additional feedback level off, analyzing can be stopped.

Discussion. The evaluation shows that the incorporation of user feedback leads to strong improvements compared to the top matchers of the matching competition [3]. When feedback is collected for all model pairs, the f-measure increases by 41% and 53% for the two data sets. Even when reducing the workload by only collecting feedback for half of the model pairs, big improvements are obtained.

The main concern about experiments on process model matching relates to external validity, i.e., in how far the results of our study can be generalized [25]. In this regard, the size of the two data sets restricts the validity of both, the indicator assessment and the evaluation. Furthermore, the processes in each data set represent the same abstract process. Hence, some structural and behavioral characteristics might be underrepresented, limiting the significance of the indicator assessment. This problem also has implications on the evaluation of the word similarity adaptation, as the processes only cover a small number of tasks from both domains and a rather limited vocabulary used to describe them. Thus, words might tend to occur more often than in other model collections and feedback might be collected for the same word pair more often than usual. This limits the generalization of the quality improvements and of the strategies to minimize the user's efforts. Lastly, the indicator assessment does not allow for a general judgment on the sources of information, as there might exist other indicators which better exploit these sources. Therefore, enlarging the data sets by including data sets whose characteristics differ from the once considered in this paper and considering more indicators are important steps in future work.

6 Conclusions and Future Work

In this paper, we investigated user feedback as a means for improving the quality of process model matching. Thus, we first reviewed sources of information from the literature and assessed their potential for feedback analysis based on derived correspondence indicators. This assessment indicated that only the label based similarity of activities can reliably be applied to decide whether an activity pair corresponds or not. In a next step, we designed a mixed-initiative approach that adapts the word similarity scores based on user feedback. We evaluated our approach with regard to established benchmarking samples and showed that user feedback can substantially improve the matching quality. Furthermore, we investigated strategies to reduce the user workload while maximizing its benefit.

In future research, we plan to investigate further strategies for decreasing the user workload while maximizing the matching quality. This comprises guidelines for choosing model pairs (or activity pairs) the user needs to provide feedback on. Another direction we plan to pursue is the extension of our approach to better account for semantic relations and co-occurrences of words within labels.

References

1. Bellahense, Z., Bonifati, A., Rahm, E.: Schema Matching and Mapping. Springer, Heidelberg (2011)
2. Branco, M.C., Troya, J., Czarnecki, K., Küster, J., Völzer, H.: Matching business process workflows across abstraction levels. In: France, R.B., Kazmeier, J., Breu, R., Atkinson, C. (eds.) MODELS 2012. LNCS, vol. 7590, pp. 626–641. Springer, Heidelberg (2012)
3. Cayoglu, U., Dijkman, R., Dumas, M., Fettke, P., García-Bañuelos, L., Hake, P., Klinkmüller, C., Leopold, H., Ludwig, A., Loos, P., Mendling, J., Oberweis, A., Schoknecht, A., Sheetrit, E., Thaler, T., Ullrich, M., Weber, I., Weidlich, M.: The process model matching contest 2013. In: PMC-MR (2013)

4. Dijkman, R., Dumas, M., García-Bañuelos, L.: Graph matching algorithms for business process model similarity search. In: Dayal, U., Eder, J., Koehler, J., Reijers, H.A. (eds.) BPM 2009. LNCS, vol. 5701, pp. 48–63. Springer, Heidelberg (2009)
5. Dijkman, R., Dumas, M., van Dongen, B., Käärik, R., Mendling, J.: Similarity of business process models: Metrics and evaluation. Inf. Syst. 36(2), 498–516 (2011)
6. Dumas, M., García-Bañuelos, L., Dijkman, R.M.: Similarity search of business process models. IEEE Data Eng. Bull. 32(3), 23–28 (2009)
7. Ekanayake, C.C., Dumas, M., García-Bañuelos, L., La Rosa, M., ter Hofstede, A.H.M.: Approximate clone detection in repositories of business process models. In: Barros, A., Gal, A., Kindler, E. (eds.) BPM 2012. LNCS, vol. 7481, pp. 302–318. Springer, Heidelberg (2012)
8. Euzenat, J., Shvaiko, P.: Ontology Matching. Springer, Berlin (2013)
9. Grigori, D., Corrales, J.C., Bouzeghoub, M.: Behavioral Matchmaking for Service Retrieval. In: IEEE ICWS, pp. 145–152 (2006)
10. Jin, T., Wang, J., Rosa, M.L., ter Hofstede, A.H., Wen, L.: Efficient querying of large process model repositories. Computers in Industry 64(1), 41–49 (2013)
11. Klinkmüller, C., Weber, I., Mendling, J., Leopold, H., Ludwig, A.: Increasing recall of process model matching by improved activity label matching. In: Daniel, F., Wang, J., Weber, B. (eds.) BPM 2013. LNCS, vol. 8094, pp. 211–218. Springer, Heidelberg (2013)
12. Koschmider, A., Blanchard, E.: User assistance for business process model decomposition. In: IEEE RCIS, pp. 445–454 (2007)
13. Kunze, M., Weidlich, M., Weske, M.: Behavioral similarity – A proper metric. In: Rinderle-Ma, S., Toumani, F., Wolf, K. (eds.) BPM 2011. LNCS, vol. 6896, pp. 166–181. Springer, Heidelberg (2011)
14. Leopold, H., Niepert, M., Weidlich, M., Mendling, J., Dijkman, R., Stuckenschmidt, H.: Probabilistic optimization of semantic process model matching. In: Barros, A., Gal, A., Kindler, E. (eds.) BPM 2012. LNCS, vol. 7481, pp. 319–334. Springer, Heidelberg (2012)
15. Levenshtein, V.I.: Binary codes capable of correcting deletions, insertions and reversals. Soviet Physics Doklady 10(8), 707–710 (1966)
16. Lin, D.: An information-theoretic definition of similarity. In: ICML, pp. 296–304 (1998)
17. Massey, F.J.: The kolmogorov-smirnov test for goodness of fit. Journal of the American Statistical Association 46(253), 68–78 (1951)
18. Navigli, R.: Word sense disambiguation: A survey. ACM Comput. Surv. 41(2), 10:1–10:69 (2009)
19. Tan, P.-N., Steinbach, M., Kumar, V.: Introduction to Data Mining, 1st edn. Addison-Wesley Longman Publishing Co., Inc., Boston (2005)
20. Vanhatalo, J., Völzer, H., Koehler, J.: The refined process structure tree. Data Knowl. Eng. 68(9), 793–818 (2009)
21. Weidlich, M., Dijkman, R., Mendling, J.: The iCoP framework: Identification of correspondences between process models. In: Pernici, B. (ed.) CAiSE 2010. LNCS, vol. 6051, pp. 483–498. Springer, Heidelberg (2010)
22. Weidlich, M., Mendling, J., Weske, M.: Efficient consistency measurement based on behavioral profiles of process models. IEEE Trans. Softw. Eng. 37(3), 410–429 (2011)
23. Weidlich, M., Sagi, T., Leopold, H., Gal, A., Mendling, J.: Predicting the quality of process model matching. In: Daniel, F., Wang, J., Weber, B. (eds.) BPM 2013. LNCS, vol. 8094, pp. 203–210. Springer, Heidelberg (2013)

24. Weidlich, M., Sheetrit, E., Branco, M.C., Gal, A.: Matching business process models using positional passage-based language models. In: Ng, W., Storey, V.C., Trujillo, J.C. (eds.) ER 2013. LNCS, vol. 8217, pp. 130–137. Springer, Heidelberg (2013)
25. Wohlin, C., Runeson, P., Höst, M., Ohlsson, M.C., Regnell, B., Wesslén, A.: Experimentation in Software Engineering: An Introduction. Kluwer Academic Publishers (2000)
26. Zha, H., Wang, J., Wen, L., Wang, C., Sun, J.: A workflow net similarity measure based on transition adjacency relations. Computers in Industry 61(5), 463–471 (2010)

Beyond Tasks and Gateways:
Discovering BPMN Models with Subprocesses, Boundary Events and Activity Markers

Raffaele Conforti[1], Marlon Dumas[2],
Luciano García-Bañuelos[2], and Marcello La Rosa[1,3]

[1] Queensland University of Technology, Australia
{raffaele.conforti,m.larosa}@qut.edu.au
[2] University of Tartu, Estonia
{marlon.dumas,luciano.garcia}@ut.ee
[3] NICTA Queensland Lab, Australia

Abstract. Existing techniques for automated discovery of process models from event logs generally produce flat process models. Thus, they fail to exploit the notion of subprocess, as well as error handling and repetition constructs provided by contemporary process modeling notations, such as the Business Process Model and Notation (BPMN). This paper presents a technique for automated discovery of BPMN models containing subprocesses, interrupting and non-interrupting boundary events and activity markers. The technique analyzes dependencies between data attributes attached to events in order to identify subprocesses and to extract their associated logs. Parent process and subprocess models are then discovered using existing techniques for flat process model discovery. Finally, the resulting models and logs are heuristically analyzed in order to identify boundary events and markers. A validation with one synthetic and two real-life logs shows that process models derived using the proposed technique are more accurate and less complex than those derived with flat process discovery techniques.

1 Introduction

Process mining is a family of techniques to extract knowledge of business processes from event logs [19]. It encompasses, among others, techniques for automated discovery of process models. A range of such techniques exist that strike various tradeoffs between accuracy and understandability of discovered models. However, the bulk of these techniques generate flat process models. When contextualized to the standard Business Process Model and Notation (BPMN), they produce BPMN models consisting purely of tasks and gateways. In doing so, they fail to exploit BPMN's constructs for modular modeling, most notably subprocesses and associated markers and boundary events.

This paper presents an automated process discovery technique that generates BPMN models with subprocesses, interrupting and non-interrupting boundary events, event subprocesses, and loop and multi-instance activity markers. An example of a BPMN model discovered using the implementation of the proposed technique in the ProM framework is shown at the top of Figure 1. At the bottom is shown a flat BPMN model obtained from the Petri net discovered from the same log using the InductiveMiner [11].

S. Sadiq, P. Soffer, and H. Völzer (Eds.): BPM 2014, LNCS 8659, pp. 101–117, 2014.

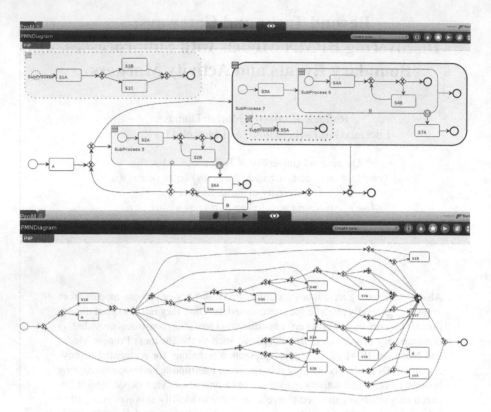

Fig. 1. BPMN model obtained with and without applying the proposed technique on a synthetic log of an order-to-cash process (using InductiveMiner to generate flat models).

The technique takes as input a set of event records, each including a timestamp, an event type (indicating the task that generated the event), and a set of attribute-value pairs. Such logs can be extracted from appropriately instrumented information systems [19]. For example, we validated the technique using logs with these characteristics from an insurance claims system and a grant management system, while [15] discusses a log with similar characteristics from an Enterprise Resource Planning (ERP) system.

The technique analyzes dependencies between event attributes to identify subprocesses. Next, it splits the log into parent and subprocess logs and applies existing discovery techniques to each log to produce flat models. Finally, the resulting models and logs are analyzed heuristically to identify boundary events, event subprocesses and markers.

The technique has been validated on real-life and synthetic logs. The validation shows that, when combined with existing flat process discovery methods, the technique produces more accurate and less complex models than the corresponding flat models.

The paper is structured as follows. Section 2 discusses techniques for automated process discovery. Section 3 outlines the subprocess identification procedure while Section 4 presents heuristics to identify boundary events, event subprocesses and markers. Section 5 discusses the validation and Section 6 concludes and discusses future work.

2 Background and Related Work

This section provides an overview of techniques for discovery of flat and hierarchical process models, and criteria for evaluation of such techniques used later in the paper.

2.1 Automated Discovery of Flat Process Models

Various techniques for discovering flat process models from event logs have been proposed [19]. The α-algorithm [20] infers ordering relations between pairs of events in the log (direct follows, causality, conflict and concurrency), from which it constructs a Petri net. The α-algorithm is sensitive to noise, infrequent or incomplete behavior and cannot handle complex routing constructs. Weijters et al. [25] propose the Heuristics Miner, which extracts not only dependencies but also the frequency of each dependency. These data are used to construct a graph of events, where edges are added based on frequency heuristics. Types of splits and joins in the event graph are determined based on the frequency of events associated with those splits and joins. This information can be used to convert the output of the Heuristics Miner into a Petri net. The Heuristics Miner is robust to noise due to the use of frequency thresholds. Van der Werf et al. [21] propose a discovery method where relations observed in the logs are translated to an Integer Linear Programming (ILP) problem. Finally, the InductiveMiner [11] aims at discovering Petri nets that are as block-structured as possible and can reproduce all traces in the log.

Only few techniques discover process models in high-level languages such as BPMN or Event-Driven Process Chains (EPCs). ProM's Heuristics Miner can produce flat EPCs from Heuristic nets, by applying transformation rules similar to those used when transforming a Heuristic net to a Petri net. A similar idea is implemented in the Fodina Heuristics Miner [22], which produces flat BPMN models. Apart from these, the bulk of process discovery methods produce Petri nets. Favre et al. [7] characterize a family of (free-choice) Petri nets that can be bidirectionally transformed into BPMN models. By leveraging this transformation, it is possible to produce flat BPMN models from discovery techniques that produce (free-choice) Petri nets.

Automated process discovery techniques can be evaluated along four dimensions: fitness (recall), appropriateness (precision), generalization and complexity [19]. Fitness measures to what extent the traces in a log can be parsed by a model. Several fitness measures have been proposed. For example, *alignment-based fitness* [1] measures the alignment of events in a trace with activities in the closest execution of the model, while the *continuous parsing measure* counts the number of missing activations when replaying traces against a heuristic net. *Improved Continuous Semantics* (ICS) fitness [4] optimizes the continuous parsing measure by trading off correctness for performance.

Appropriateness (herein called precision) measures the additional behavior allowed by a discovered model not found in the log. A model with low precision is one that parses a proportionally large number of traces that are not in the log. Precision can be measured in different ways. *Negative event precision* [23] works by artificially introducing inexistent (negative) events to enhance the log so that it contains both real (positive) and fake (negative) traces. Precision is defined in terms of the number of negative traces parsed by the model. Alternatively, *ETC* [14] works by generating a prefix automaton from the log and replaying each trace against the process model and the automaton simultaneously. ETC precision is defined in terms of the additional behavior ("escaping" edges) allowed by the model and not by the automaton.

Generalization captures how well the discovered model generalizes the behavior found in the log. For example, if a model discovered using 90% of traces in the log can parse the remaining 10% of traces in the logs, the model generalizes well the log.

Finally, process model complexity can be measured in terms of size (number of nodes and/or edges) or using structural complexity metrics proposed in the literature [13]. Empirical studies [13,2,17] have shown that, in addition to size, the following structural complexity metrics are correlated with understandability and error-proneness:

- Avg. Connector Degree (ACD): avg. number of nodes a connector is connected to.
- Control-Flow Complexity (CFC): sum of all connectors weighted by their potential combinations of states after a split.
- Coefficient of Network Connectivity (CNC): ratio between arcs and nodes.
- Density: ratio between the actual number of arcs and the maximum possible number of arcs in any model with the same number of nodes.

An extensive experimental evaluation [24] of automated process discovery techniques has shown that the Heuristics Miner provides the most accurate results, where accuracy is computed as the tradeoff between precision and recall. Further, this method scales up to large real-life logs. The ILP miner achieves high recall – at the expense of a penalty on precision – but it does not scale to large logs due to memory requirements.

2.2 Automated Discovery of Hierarchical Process Models

Although the bulk of automated process discovery techniques produce flat models, one exception is the two-phase mining approach [12], which discovers process models decomposed into sub-processes, each subprocess corresponding to a recurrent motif observed in the traces. The two-phase approach starts by applying pattern detection techniques on the event log in order to uncover *tandem arrays* (corresponding to loops) and *maximal repeats* (maximal common subsequence of activities across process instances). The idea is that occurrences of these patterns correspond to "footprints" left in the log by the presence of a subprocess. Once patterns are identified, their significance is measured based on their frequency. The most significant patterns are selected for subprocess extraction. For each selected pattern, all occurrences are extracted to produce subprocess logs. Each occurrence is then replaced by an *abstract activity*, which corresponds to a subprocess invocation in the parent process. This procedure leads to one parent process log and a separate log per subprocess. A process model can then be discovered separately for the parent process and for each subprocess. The procedure can be repeated recursively to produce process-subprocess hierarchies of longer depth.

A shortcoming of the two-phase approach is that it cannot identify subprocesses with (interrupting) boundary events, as these events cause the subprocess execution to be interrupted and thus the subprocess instance traces do not show up neither as tandem arrays nor maximal repeats. Secondly, in case multiple subprocess instances are executed in parallel, the two-phase approach mixes together in the same subprocess trace, events of multiple subprocess instances spawned by a given parent process instance. For example, if a parent process instance spawns three subprocess instances with traces $t_1 = [a_1, b_1, c_1, d_1]$, $t_2 = [a_2, c_2, b_2]$, and $t_3 = [a_3, b_3, c_3]$, the two-phase approach may put all events of t_1, t_2 and t_3 in the same trace, e.g. $[a_1, a_2, b_1, c_1, a_3, c_2, \ldots]$. When the resulting subprocess traces are given as input to a process discovery algorithm, the output is a model where almost every task has a self-loop and concurrency is confused with loops. For example, given a log of a grant management system introduced later, the two-phase approach combined with Heuristics Miner produces the subprocess model depicted in Figure 2(a), whereas the subprocess model discovered using the Heuristics Miner after segregating the subprocess instances is depicted in Figure 2(b).

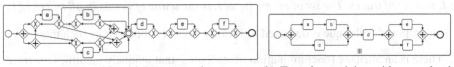

(a) Two-phase mining approach   (b) Two-phase mining with manual sub-
                                         process instance separation

Fig. 2. Sample subprocess model discovered using the two-phase mining approach

Another related technique [10] discovers Petri nets with *cancellation regions*. A cancellation region is a set P of places, where a given *cancellation* transition may fire, such that this transition firing leads to the removal of all tokens in P. The output is a *reset net*: a Petri net with *reset arcs* that remove tokens from their input place if any token is present. Cancellation regions are akin to BPMN subprocesses with interrupting events. However, generating BPMN models with subprocesses from reset nets is impossible in the general case, as cancellation regions may have arbitrary topologies, whereas BPMN subprocesses have a block-structured topology. Moreover, the reset nets produced by [10] may contain non-free-choice constructs that cannot be mapped to BPMN [7]. Finally, the technique in [10] does not scale up to logs with hundreds or thousands of traces due to the fact that it relies on analysis of the full state space.

Other techniques for discovering hierarchical collections of process models, e.g. [8], are geared towards discovering processes at different levels of generalization. They produce process hierarchies where a parent-child relation indicates that the child process is a more detailed version of the parent process (i.e. *specialization* relations). This body of work is orthogonal to ours, as we seek to discover *part-of* (parent-subprocess) relations.

The SMD technique [6] discovers hierarchies of process models related via specialization but also part-of relations. However, SMD only extracts subprocesses that occur in identical or almost identical form in two different specializations of a process.

Another related work is that of Popova et al. [16], which discovers process models decomposed into artifacts, where an artifact corresponds to the lifecycle of a business object in the process (e.g. a purchase order or invoice). This technique identifies artifacts in the event log by means of functional dependency and inclusion dependency discovery techniques. In this paper, we take this idea as starting point and adapt it to identify process hierarchies and then apply heuristics to identify boundary events and markers.

3 Identifying Subprocesses

In this section we outline a technique to extract a hierarchy of process models from an event log consisting of a set of traces. Each trace is a sequence of events, where an event consists of an event type, a timestamp and a number of attribute-value pairs. Formally:

Definition 1 (Event (record)). *Let* $\{A_1,\ldots,A_n\}$ *be a set of* attribute names *and* $\{D_1,\ldots,D_n\}$ *a set of attribute* domains *where* D_i *is the set of possible values of* A_i *for* $1 \leq i \leq n$. *An event* $e = (et, \tau, v_1, \ldots, v_k)$ *consists of*

1. $et \in \Sigma$ is the event type *to which e belongs, where Σ is the set of all event types*
2. $\tau \in \Omega$ is the event timestamp, where Ω is the set of all timestamps,
3. *for all* $1 \leq i \leq k$ $v_i = (A_i, d_i)$ *is an attribute-value pair where A_i is an attribute name and $d_i \in D_i$ is an attribute value.*

Definition 2 (Log). *A trace $tr = e_1 \ldots e_n$ is a sequence of events sorted by timestamp. A log L is a set of traces. The set of events E_L of L is the union of events in all traces of L.*

The proposed technique is designed to identify logs of subprocesses such that:

1. There is an attribute (or combination of attributes) that uniquely identifies the trace of the subprocess to which each event belongs. In other words, all events in a trace of a discovered subprocess share the same value for the attribute(s) in question.
2. In every subprocess instance trace, there is at least an event of a certain type with an attribute (or combination thereof) uniquely identifying the parent process instance.

These conditions match closely the notions of key and foreign key in relational databases. Thus, we use relational algebra concepts [18]. A *table* $T \subseteq D_1 \times \ldots \times D_m$ is a relation over domains D_i and has a *schema* $\mathscr{S}(T) = (A_1, \ldots, A_m)$ defining for each *column* $1 \leq i \leq m$ an *attribute name* A_i. The domain of an attribute may contain a "null" value $\perp$. The set of timestamps Ω does not contain $\perp$. For a given *tuple* $t = (d_1, \ldots, d_m) \in T$ and column $1 \leq i \leq m$, we write $t.A_i$ to refer to d_i. Given a tuple $t = (d_1, \ldots, d_m) \in T$ and a set of attributes $\{A_{i_1}, \ldots, A_{i_k}\} \subseteq \mathscr{S}(T)$, we define $t[A_{i_1}, \ldots, A_{i_k}] = (t.A_{i_1}, \ldots, t.A_{i_k})$ Given a table T, a key of T is a minimal set of attributes $\{K_1, \ldots K_j\}$ such that $\forall t, t' \in T$ $t[K_1, \ldots K_j] \neq t'[K_1, \ldots K_j]$ (no duplicate values on the key). A primary key is a key of a table designated as such. Finally, a foreign key linking table T_1 to T_2 is a pair of sets of attributes $(\{FK_1, \ldots, FK_j\}, \{PK_1, \ldots, PK_j\})$ such that $\{FK_1, \ldots, FK_j\} \subseteq \mathscr{S}(T_1)$, $\{PK_1, \ldots, PK_j\}$ is primary key of T_2 and $\forall t \in T_1 \exists t' \in T_2$ $t[FK_1, \ldots, FK_j] = t'[PK_1, \ldots, PK_j]$. The latter condition is an *inclusion dependency*.

Given the above, we seek to split a log into sub-logs based on process instance identifiers (keys) and subprocess-parent references (foreign keys). This is achieved by splitting event types into clusters based on keys, linking these clusters hierarchically via foreign keys, extracting one sub-log per node in the hierarchy, and deriving a process hierarchy mirroring the cluster hierarchy (Figure 3). Below we outline each step in turn.

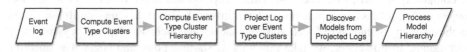

Fig. 3. Procedure to extract a process model hierarchy from an event log

Compute event type clusters We start by splitting the event types appearing in the log into clusters such that all event types in a cluster (seen as tables consisting of event records) share a common key K. The intuition of the technique is that the key K shared by all event types in a cluster is an identifying attribute for all events in a subprocess. In other words, the set of instances of event types in a cluster that have a given value for K (e.g. $K = v$ for a fixed v), will form one trace of the (sub-)process in question. For example, in an order-to-cash process, all event types that have POID (Purchase Order Identifier) as primary key, will form the event type cluster corresponding to the root process. A given trace of this root process will consist of instances of event types in this cluster that share a given POID value (e.g. all events with POID = 122 for a trace). Meanwhile, event types that share LIID (Line Item Identifier) as primary key will form the event type cluster corresponding to a subprocess dealing with individual line items (say a "Handle Line Item" subprocess). A trace of this subprocess will consist of events of a trace of the parent process that share a given value of LIID (e.g. LIID = "122-3").[1]

To find keys of an event type et, we build a table consisting of all events of type et. The columns are attributes appearing in the attribute-value pairs of events of type et.

Definition 3 (Event type table). *Let et be an event type and $\{e_1,\ldots,e_n\}$ the set of events of type et in log L, i.e. $e_i = (et, \tau_i, v_{i_1}, \ldots, v_{i_m})$ where $v_{i_j} = (A_j, d_{i_j})$ and A_j is an attribute for e_i. The event type table for et in L is a table $ET \subseteq (D_1 \cup \{\bot\}) \times \ldots \times (D_m \cup \{\bot\})$ with schema $\mathscr{S}(ET) = (A_1, \ldots, A_k)$ s.t. there exists an entry $t = (d_1, \ldots, d_m) \in ET$ iff there exists an event $e \in ET$ where $e = (et, \tau, (A_1, d_1), \ldots, (A_k, d_k))$ s.t. $d_i \in D_i \cup \{\bot\}$.*

Events of a type et may have different attributes. Thus, the schema of the event type table consists of the union of all attributes that appear in events of this type in the log. Therefore there may be null values for some attributes of some events.

For each event type table, we seek to identify its key(s), meaning the attributes that may identify to which process instance a given event belongs to. To detect keys in event type tables, we use the TANE [9] algorithm for discovery of functional dependencies from tables. This algorithm finds all candidate keys, including composite keys. Given that an event type may have multiple keys, we need to select a primary one. Two options are available. The first is based on user input: The user is given the set of candidate keys discovered for each event type and designates one as primary – and in doing so chooses the subprocesses to be extracted. Alternatively, for full automation, the lexicographically smallest candidate key of an event type is selected as the primary key $pk(ET)$, which may lead to event types not being grouped the way a user would have done so.

All event tables sharing a common primary key are grouped into an event type cluster. In other words, an event type cluster ETC is a maximal set of event types $ETC = \{ET_1, \ldots, ET_k\}$ such that $pk(ET_1) = pk(ET_2) = pk(ET_k)$.

Compute event type cluster hierarchy We now seek to relate pairs of event clusters via foreign keys. The idea is that if an event type ET_2 has a foreign key pointing to a primary key of ET_1, every instance of an event type in ET_2 can be uniquely related to one instance of each event type in ET_1, in the same way that every subprocess instance can be uniquely related to one parent process instance.

With scalability in mind, we use the SPIDER algorithm [3] to discover inclusion dependencies across event type tables. SPIDER identifies all inclusion dependencies between a set of tables, while we specifically seek dependencies corresponding to foreign keys relating one event type cluster to another. Thus we only retain dependencies involving the primary key of an event type table in a cluster corresponding to a parent process, and attributes in tables of a second cluster corresponding to a subprocess. The output is a set of candidate parent process-subprocess relations as follows.

Definition 4 (Candidate process-subprocess relation between clusters). *Given a log L, and two event type clusters ETC_1 and ETC_2, a tuple $(ETC_1, \mathscr{P}, ETC_2, \mathscr{F})$ is a candidate parent-subprocess relation if and only if:*

---

[1] It may happen alternatively that the key of the "Handle Line Item" subprocess is $(POID, LIID)$.

1. $\mathscr{P} = pk(ETC_1)$ and $\forall ET_2 \in ETC_2, \exists ET_1 \in ETC_1 : ET_2[\mathscr{F}] \subseteq ET_1[\mathscr{P}]$ where $ET_1[\mathscr{P}]$ is the relational algebra projection of ET_1 over attributes in $\mathscr{P}$ and similar for $ET_2[\mathscr{F}]$. In other words, ETC_1 and ETC_2 are related, if every table in ETC_2 has an inclusion dependency to the primary key of a table in ETC_1 so that every tuple in ETC_2 is related to a tuple in ETC_1.

2. $\forall tr \in L \forall e_2 \in tr : e_2.et \in ETC_2 \Rightarrow \exists e_1 \in tr : e_1.et \in ETC_1 \wedge e_1[\mathscr{P}] = e_2[\mathscr{F}] \wedge e_1.\tau < e_2.\tau$. This condition ensures that the direction of the relation is from the parent process to the subprocess by exploiting the fact that the first event of a subprocess instance must be preceded by at least one event of the parent process instance.

The candidate process-subprocess relations between clusters induces a directed acyclic graph. We extract a directed minimum spanning forest of this graph by extracting a directed minimum spanning tree from each weakly connected component of the graph. We turn the forest into a tree by merging all root clusters in the forest into a single root cluster. This leads us to a hierarchy of event clusters. The root cluster in this hierarchy consists of event types of the root process. The children of the root are event type clusters of second-level (sub-)processes, and so on.

Project logs over event type clusters We now seek to produce a set of logs related hierarchically so that each log corresponds to a process in the envisaged process hierarchy. The log hierarchy will reflect one by one the event cluster hierarchy, meaning that each event type cluster is mapped to log. Thus, all we have to do is to define a function that maps each event type cluster to a log. This function is called log projection.

Given an event type cluster ETC, we project the log on this cluster by abstracting every trace in such a way that all events that are not instances of types in ETC are deleted, and markers are introduced to denote the first and last event of the log of a child cluster of ETC. Each of these child clusters corresponds to a subprocess and thus the markers denote the start and the end of a subprocess invocation.

Definition 5 (Projection of a trace over an event type cluster). *Given a log* $L = \{tr_1, \ldots tr_n\}$, *an event cluster* ETC, *and the set of children cluster of* ETC *children(ETC)* $= \{ETC_1, \ldots ETC_n\}$, *the projection of* L *over* ETC *is the log* $L_{ETC} = \{tr'_1, \ldots tr'_n\}$ *where* tr'_k *is the log obtained by replacing every event in* tr_k *that is also first event of a trace in the projected child log* L_{ETC_i} *by an identical event but with type* $Start_{ETC_i}$ *(start of cluster* ETC_i*), replacing every event in* tr_k *that is also last event of a trace in the projected child log* L_{ETC_i} *by an identical event but with type* End_{ETC_i} *(end of cluster* ETC_i*), and then removing from* tr_k *all other events of a type not in* ETC.

This recursive definition has a fix-point because the relation between clusters is a tree. We can thus first compute the projection of logs over the leaves of this tree and then move upwards in the tree to compute projected logs of parent trace clusters.

Generate process model hierarchy Given the hierarchy of projected logs, we generate a hierarchy of process models isomorphic to the hierarchy of logs, by applying a process discovery algorithm to each log. For this step we can use any process discovery method that produces a flat process model (e.g. the Heuristics Miner). In the case of a process with subprocesses, the resulting process model will contain tasks corresponding to the subprocess start and end markers introduced in Definition 5.

Complexity The complexity of the first step of the procedure is determined by that of TANE, which is in the size of the relation times a factor exponential on the number of attributes [9]. This translates to $O(|E_L| \cdot 2^a)$ where a is the number of attributes and $|E_L|$ is the number of events in the log. The second step's complexity is dominated by that of SPIDER, which is $O(a \cdot m \log m)$ where m is the maximum number of distinct values of any attribute [3]. If we upper-bound m by $|E_L|$, this becomes $O(a \cdot |E_L| \log |E_L|)$. In this step, we also determine the direction of each primary-foreign key dependency. This requires one pass through the log for each discovered dependency, thus a complexity in $O(|E_L| \cdot k)$ where k is the number of discovered dependencies. If we define N as the number of event type clusters, $k < N^2$, this complexity becomes $O(|E_L| \cdot N^2)$. The third step requires one pass through the log for each event type cluster, hence $O(|E_L| \cdot N)$, which is dominated by the previous step's complexity. The final step is that of process discovery. The complexity here depends on the chosen process discovery method and we thus leave it out of this analysis. Hence, the complexity of subprocess identification is $O(|E_L| \cdot 2^a + a \cdot |E_L| \log |E_L| + |E_L| \cdot N^2)$, not counting the process discovery step.

4 Identifying Boundary Events, Event Subprocesses and Markers

This section presents heuristics to refactor a BPMN model by i) identifying interrupting boundary events, ii) assigning these events a type, iii) extracting event subprocesses, and iv) assigning loop and multi-instance markers to subprocesses and tasks. The overall refactoring procedure is given in Algorithm 1, which recursively traverses the process models hierarchy starting from the root model. This algorithm requires the root model, the set of all models PS, the original log L and the logs for all process models LS, plus parameters to set the tolerance of the heuristics as discussed later.

For each activity a of p that invokes a subprocess s (line 2), we check if the subprocess is in a self loop and if so we mark s with the appropriate marker and remove the loop structure (line 1 – refactoring operations are omitted for simplicity). We then check if the subprocess is triggered by an interrupting boundary event (line 1), in which case the subprocess is an exception flow of the parent process. If so, we attach an interrupting boundary event to the border of the parent process and connect the boundary event to the subprocess via an exception flow. Then we identify the type of boundary event, which can either be timer or message (line 1). Next, we check if the subprocess is an event subprocess (line 1). Finally, we check if the subprocess is multi-instance (line 1), in which case we discover from the log the minimum and maximum number of instances. If activity a does not point to a subprocess (i.e. it is a task), we check if this is a loop (line 16) or multi-instance task (line 17), so that this task can be marked accordingly. Each of these constructs is identified via a dedicated heuristic.

Identify interrupting boundary events Algorithm 2 checks if subprocess s of p is triggered by an interrupting event. It takes as input an activity a_s corresponding to the invocation of subprocess s. We check that there exists a path in p from a_s to an end event of p without traversing any activity or AND gateway (line 2). We count the number of traces in the log of p where there is an occurrence of a_s (line 2), and the number of those traces where a_s is the last event. If the latter number is at least equal to the former, we tag the subprocess as "triggered by an interrupting event" (line 2). The heuristic uses threshold tv_{int}. If $tv_{int} = 0$, we require all traces containing a_s to finish with a_s to tag s as triggered by an interrupting event, while if $tv_{int} = 1$, the path condition is sufficient.

Identify interrupting boundary timer events Algorithm 3 detects if a subprocess s of p is triggered by a timer boundary event. We first extract from the log of p all traces t

---

Algorithm 1. UpdateModel

---

input: Process model p, set of all process models PS, original log L, set of all process logs LS, tolerance values tv_{int} and tv_{timer}, percentages pv_{timer} and pv_{MI}

1 **foreach** *Activity a in p* **do**

2   **if** *there exists a process s in PS such that label(a)* = *Start$_s$* **then**

3   s := updateModel($s, PS, L, LS, tv_{int}, tv_{timer}, pv_{timer}, pv_{MI}$);

4   L_p := getLog(p, LS);

5   **if** *s is in a self loop* **then** mark s as Loop;

6   **if** *isInterruptingEvent(a, p, L_p, tv_{int})* **then**

7   set s as exception flow of p via new interrupting event e_i;

8   **if** *isTimerInterruptingEvent(a, L_p, tv_{timer}, pv_{timer})* **then** mark e_i as Timer;

9   **else** mark e_i as Message;

10   **else if** *isEventSubprocess(a, p)* **then** mark s as EventSubprocess of p;

11   **if** *isMultiInstance(s, L, pv_{MI})* **then**

12   mark s as MI;

13   s_{LB} := discoverMILowerBound(s, L);

14   s_{UB} := discoverMIUpperBound(s, L);

15   **else**

16   **if** *a is in a self loop* **then** mark a as Loop;

17   **if** *isMultiInstance(a, L, pv_{MI})* **then**

18   mark s as MI;

19   a_{LB} := discoverMILowerBound(a, L);

20   a_{UB} := discoverMIUpperBound(a, L);

21 **return** p

---

containing executions of a_s (line 3). For each of these traces we compute the average time difference between the occurrence of a_s and that of the first event of the trace (lines 4-9). We then count the number of traces where this difference is equal to the average difference, modulo an error determined by the product of the average difference and tolerance value tv_{timer} (line 3). If the number of traces that satisfy this condition is greater than or equal to the number of traces containing an execution of a_s, we tag subprocess s as triggered by an interrupting boundary timer event (line 3). The heuristic can be adjusted using a percentage threshold pv_{timer} to allow for noise.

Identify event subprocesses A subprocess s of p is identified as an event subprocess if it satisfies two requirements: i) it needs to be repeatable (i.e. it has either been marked with a loop marker, or it is part of a while-do construct), and ii) can be executed in parallel with the rest of the parent process (either via an OR or an AND block).

Identify multi-instance activities Algorithm 4 checks if a subprocess s of p is multi-instance. We start by retrieving all traces of p that contain invocations to subprocess s (line 4). Among them, we identify those where there are at least two instances of subprocess s executed in parallel (lines 6-7). As per Def. 5, an instance of s is delimited by events of types $Start_s$ and End_s sharing the same (PK, FK). Two instances of s are in parallel if they share the same FK and overlap in the log. If the number of traces with parallel instances is at least equal to a predefined percentage pv_{MI} of the total number of traces containing an instance of s, we tag s as multi-instance. Finally, we set the lower (upper) bound of instances of a multi-instance subprocess to be equal to the minimum

---

Algorithm 2. isInterruptingEvent

---

input: Activity a_s, process model p, log L_p, tolerance tv_{int}

1 **if** *there exists a path in p from a_s to an end event of p without activities and AND gateways* **then**

2   *#BoundaryEvents* := 0;

3   *#Traces* := 0;

4   **foreach** *trace tr in L_p* **do**

5   **if** *there exists an event e_1 in tr such that $e_1.et = label(a_s)$* **then**

6   **if** *there not exists an event e_2 in tr such that $e_2.et \neq label(a_s)$ and $e_2.\tau \geq e_1.\tau$* **then** *#BoundaryEvents* := *#BoundaryEvents* + 1;

7   *#Traces* := *#Traces* + 1;

8   **if** *#BoundaryEvents* $\geq$ *#Traces* $\cdot (1 - tv_{int})$ **then return** *true*

9 **return** *false*

Algorithm 3. isTimerInterruptingEvent

---

input: Activity a_s, log L_p, tolerance tv_{timer}, percentage pv_{timer}

1 *#TimerEvents* := 0;

2 *timeDiff$_{tot}$* := 0;

3 *timeDifferences* := $\varnothing$;

4 **foreach** *trace tr in L_p* **do**

5   **if** *there exists an event e_1 in tr such that $e_1.et = label(a_s)$* **then**

6   e_2 := first event of *tr*;

7   *timeDiff$_{tot}$* := *timeDiff$_{tot}$* + $(e_1.\tau - e_2.\tau)$;

8   *timeDifferences* := *timeDifferences* $\cup \{(e_1.\tau - e_2.\tau)\}$;

9 *timeDiff$_{avg}$* := *timeDiff$_{tot}$* / |*timeDifferences*|;

10 **foreach** *diff* $\in$ *timeDifferences* **do**

11   **if** *timeDiff$_{avg}$* $-$ *timeDiff$_{avg}$* $\cdot tv_{timer} \leq diff \leq$ *timeDiff$_{avg}$* $+$ *timeDiff$_{avg}$* $\cdot tv_{timer}$ **then** *#TimerEvents* := *#TimerEvents* + 1;

12 **return** *#TimerEvents* $\geq$ |*timeDifferences*| $\cdot pv_{timer}$

(maximum) number of instances that are executed among all traces containing at least one invocation to s. Note that $e[PK]$ is the projection of event e over the primary key of $e.et$ and $e[FK]$ is the projection of e over the event type of the parent cluster of $e.et$.

Complexity Each heuristic used in Algorithm 1 requires one pass through the log and for each trace, one scan through the trace, hence a complexity in $O(|E_L|)$. The heuristics are invoked for each process model, thus the complexity of Algorithm 1 is $O(p \cdot |E_L|)$, where p is the number of process models. This complexity is dominated by that of subprocess identification.

5 Validation

We implemented the technique as a ProM plugin called *BPMNMiner*. We also implemented utility plugins to: (i) measure model complexity; (ii) convert Petri nets to BPMN to compare models produced by flat discovery methods with those produced by BPMN

Algorithm 4. isMultiInstance

input: Subprocess s, original log L, percentage pv_{MI}

1   **if** s *is* Loop **then**
2   #Traces$_{MI}$:= 0;
3   #Traces := 0;
4   **foreach** *trace tr in L* **do**
5   **if** *there exists an event e in tr such that* $e.et = Start_s$ **then**
6   **if** *there exist two events* e_1, e_2 *in t such that* $e_1.et = Start_s$, $e_2.et = Start_s$,
                  $e_1[PK] \neq e_2[PK]$ *and* $e_1[FK] = e_2[FK]$ **then**
7   **if** *there exists an event* e_3 *in tr such that* $e_3.et = End_s$, $e_3[PK] = e_1[PK]$,
                     $e_3[FK] = e_1[FK]$, $e_1.\tau \leq e_2.\tau < e_3.\tau$ **then**
8   #Traces$_{MI}$:= #Traces$_{MI}$ + 1;
9   #Traces := #Traces + 1;
10   **return** *#Traces$_{MI}$* $\geq$ *#Traces* $\cdot pv_{MI}$;
11 **return** *false*

Miner (adapted from the Petri Net to EPCs converter in ProM 5.2); (iii) convert BPMN models to Petri nets to compute accuracy (based on [5]); and (iv) simplify the final BPMN model by removing trivial gateways and turning single-activity subprocesses into tasks.[2] Using this implementation, we conducted tests to assess the benefits of the technique in terms of accuracy and complexity of discovered process models.

5.1 Datasets

We used two real-life logs and one artificial log. The first log comes from a system for handling project applications in the Belgian research funding agency IWT (hereafter called FRIS), specifically for the applied biomedical research funding program (2009-12). This process exhibits two multi-instance subprocesses, one for handling reviews (each proposal is reviewed by at least five reviewers), the other for handling the disbursement of the grant, which is divided into installments. The second log (called Commercial) comes from a large Australian insurance company and records an extract of the instances of a commercial insurance claims handling process executed in 2012. This process contains a non-interrupting event subprocess to handle customer inquires, since these can arrive at any time while handling a claim, and three loop tasks to receive incoming correspondence, to process additional information, and to provide updates to the customer. Finally, the third log (called Artificial) is generated synthetically using CPN Tools,[3] based on a model of an order-to-cash process that has one example of each BPMN construct supported by our technique (loop marker, multi-instance marker, interrupting and non-interrupting boundary event and event subprocess). Table 1 shows the characteristics of the datasets, which differ widely in terms of number of traces, events and duplication ratio (i.e. the ratio between events and event types).

---

[2] All plugins, the artificial log and the experimental results are in the BPMN Miner package of the ProM 6 nightly-build – http://processmining.org
[3] http://cpntools.org

Table 1. Characteristics of event logs used for the validation

Log	Traces	Events	Event types	Duplication ratio
FRIS	121	1,472	13	113
Commercial	896	12,437	9	1,382
Artificial	3,000	32,896	13	2,530

5.2 Setup

We measured accuracy and complexity of the models produced by BPMN Miner on top of five process discovery methods, and compared them to the same measures on the corresponding model produced by the flat discovery method alone. We selected the following flat discovery methods: Heuristics Miner (abbreviated as H) and ILP (I) as they provide the best results in terms of accuracy according to [24]; the InductiveMiner (N) as an example of a method intended to discover block-structured models with high fitness; Fodina Heuristics Miner, which generates flat BPMN models natively; and the α-algorithm, as an example of a method suffering from low accuracy, according to [24].

Following [24], we measured accuracy in terms of *F-score* – the harmonic mean of recall (fitness – f) and precision (appropriateness – a), i.e. $2\frac{f \cdot a}{f+a}$. We measured complexity using size, CFC, ACD, CNC and density, as justified in Section 2.

We computed fitness using ProM's Alignment-based Conformance Analysis plugin, and appropriateness using the Negative event precision measure in the CoBeFra tool.[4] The choice of these two particular measures is purely based on the scalability of the respective implementations. These measures operate on a Petri net. We used the mapping in [5] to convert the BPMN models produced by BPMN Miner and by Fodina to Petri nets. For this conversion, we treated BPMN multi-instance activities as loop activities, since based on our tests, the alignment-based plugin could not handle the combinatorial explosion resulting from expanding all possible states of the multi-instance activities. We set all tolerance parameters of Algorithm 1 to zero.

5.3 Results

Table 2 shows the results of the measurements. We observe that BPMN Miner consistency produces BPMN models that are more accurate and less complex than the corresponding flat models. The only exception is made by BPMN$_I$ on the artificial log. This model has a lower F-score than the one produced by the baseline ILP, despite improving on complexity. This is attributable to the fact that the artificial log exhibits a high number of concurrent events, which ILP turns into interleaving transitions in the discovered model (one for each concurrent event in the log). After subprocess identification, BPMN Miner replaces this structure with a set of interleaving subprocesses (each grouping two or more events), which penalizes both fitness and appropriateness.

In spite of the α-algorithm generally producing the least accurate models, we observe that BPMN$_A$ produces results comparable to those achieved using BPMN Miner on top of other discovery methods. In other words, BPMN Miner thins off differences between the baseline methods. This is attributable to the fact that, after subprocess extraction, the discovery of ordering relations between events is done on smaller sets of event types (those within the boundaries of a subprocess). In doing so, behavioral errors also tend to get fixed.

---

[4] http://processmining.be/cobefra

Table 2. Models' accuracy and complexity before and after applying BPMN Miner

Log	Method	Accuracy			Complexity				
		Fitness	Appropr.	F-score	Size	CFC	ACD	CNC	Density
FRIS	A	0.855	0.129	0.224	33	25	3.888	1.484	0.046
	BPMN$_A$	**0.917**	**0.523**	**0.666**	32	21	**3.4**	**1.25**	**0.040**
	F	**0.929**	0.354	0.512	35	85	8.5	2.828	0.083
	BPMN$_F$	0.917	**0.644**	**0.756**	26	10	**3.142**	**1.115**	**0.044**
	I	0.919	0.364	0.521	47	48	4.312	1.765	0.038
	BPMN$_I$	**0.987**	**0.426**	**0.595**	42	34	**3.652**	**1.428**	**0.034**
	H	0.567	0.569	0.567	31	26	3.25	1.290	**0.043**
	BPMN$_H$	**0.960**	**0.658**	**0.780**	24	7	**3.2**	**1.083**	0.047
	N	1	0.442	0.613	45	81	3.866	1.6	0.036
	BPMN$_N$	0.977	**0.525**	**0.682**	39	28	**3**	**1.230**	**0.032**
Commercial	A	0.703^5	0.285	0.405	**19**	16	3.5	1.263	0.070
	BPMN$_A$	**1**	**0.382**	**0.552**	23	**11**	3.5	**1.173**	**0.053**
	F	0.928	0.398	0.557	**26**	29	4	1.538	0.061
	BPMN$_F$	**0.982**	**0.407**	**0.575**	37	35	**3.909**	1.540	**0.042**
	I	**1**	0.221	0.361	**41**	54	5.133	2.121	0.053
	BPMN$_I$	0.913	**0.264**	**0.409**	34	**31**	**4.105**	**1.558**	**0.047**
	H	0.399^5	0.349	0.372	35	32	**3.083**	1.342	**0.039**
	BPMN$_H$	**0.935**	**0.425**	**0.584**	17	2	4	**1**	0.062
	N	1	0.448	0.618	25	21	4.571	1.680	0.070
	BPMN$_N$	1	**0.466**	**0.635**	23	14	**4**	**1.260**	**0.057**
Artificial	A	na	0.208	na	38	47	3.636	1.447	0.039
	BPMN$_A$	0.654	**0.222**	0.331	33	11	**3**	**1**	**0.031**
	F	na	0.295	na	46	53	3.677	1.543	0.034
	BPMN$_F$	0.813	**0.413**	0.548	47	31	**3.3**	**1.212**	**0.026**
	I	**0.969**	**0.331**	**0.493**	74	130	7.068	2.982	0.040
	BPMN$_I$	0.870	0.160	0.270	37	21	4.2	1.216	0.033
	H	na	0.290	na	49	47	3.17	1.387	0.028
	BPMN$_H$	0.908	**0.470**	0.619	33	6	**3**	**0.909**	0.028
	N	1	0.182	0.307	50	120	3.828	1.62	0.033
	BPMN$_N$	1	**0.362**	**0.531**	45	18	**3**	**1.022**	**0.023**

This is the case in three instances reported in our tests (A, F and H on Artificial which have "na" for fitness in Table 2), where the alignment-based fitness could not be computed because these flat models contained dead (unreachable) tasks and were not *easy sound* (i.e. did not have an execution sequence that completes by marking the end event with one token). An example of a fragment of such a model discovered by the Heuristics Miner alone is given in Figure 4(a). In these cases, the use of BPMN Miner resulted in simpler models without dead transitions, cf. Figure 4(b).

We also remark that, while density is inversely correlated with size (smaller models tend to be denser) [13], BPMN Miner produces smaller and less dense process models than those obtained by the flat process discovery methods. This is because it replaces gateway structures with subprocesses leading to less arcs, as evidenced by smaller ACD.

In summary, we obtained the best BPMN models using Heuristics Miner as the baseline method across all three logs. BPMN$_H$ achieved the highest accuracy and lowest

---

^{5} Over-approximation, as the fitness can only be computed on a fraction of the traces in the log.

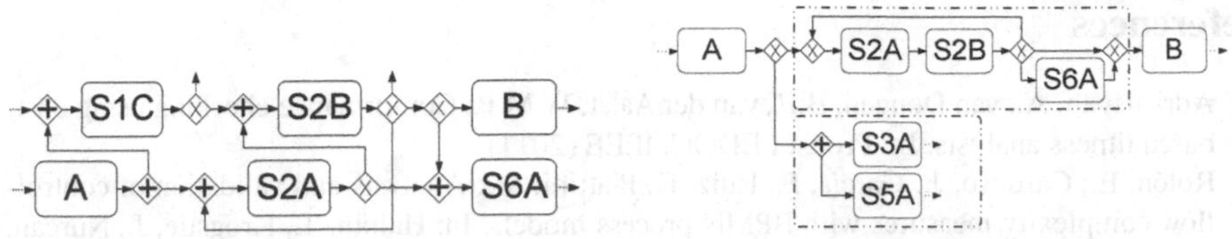

(a) Heuristics Miner   (b) BPMN Miner after Heuristics Miner

Fig. 4. Behavioral error in a discovered flat model not present in the hierarchical one

complexity on FRIS and Artificial, while on Commercial it achieved the second highest accuracy (with the highest being $BPMN_N$) and the lowest complexity.

We conducted our tests on an Intel Xeon 2.93GHz with 16GB RAM, running Windows Server 2008R2 and JVM 7 with 10GB of heap space. Time performance ranged from a few seconds for small logs with few subprocesses (e.g., 4sec for $BPMN_A$ on FRIS) to several minutes for the large log (max. 34.8min for $BPMN_H$ on Artificial while H on Artificial took 14.2sec). The bulk of time is spent in subprocesses identification, while the time required for identifying boundary events and markers is negligible.

6   Conclusion

We have shown that the proposed technique leads to process models that are not only more modular, but also more accurate and less complex than those obtained with traditional flat process discovery techniques. This is a step forward towards the development of methods for discovery of modular and rich business process models from event logs. Naturally, the proposal has its limitations. First, it requires logs with data attributes, such that the set of attributes includes keys to identify (sub)process instances, and foreign keys to identify relations between parent and child processes. One can think of subprocesses where this condition does not hold, for example when subprocesses are used not to encapsulate activities pertaining to a business entity (with its own key) but rather to refactor block-structured fragments with loops – without there being a key associated to the loop body – or to refactor fragments shared across multiple process models. Thus, a potential avenue to enhance the technique is to combine it with the two-phase mining approach [12] and shared subprocess extraction techniques as in SMD [6].

Secondly, it is assumed that data is of sufficient quality to discover the relevant functional and inclusion dependencies. In this respect, more noise-tolerant techniques for functional and inclusion dependency discovery could be employed, but the extent of required noise-tolerance needs to be evaluated against relevant datasets.

A direction for future work is to apply the technique on larger collections of logs, for example logs extracted from ERP systems, where there may be multiple keys for every entity associated with a process and associations may be more complex. A validation of the produced process models with actual users is also needed to assess usefulness.

Acknowledgments. We thank Anna Kalenkova for her BPMN ProM interface and Pieter De Leenheer for enabling access to the FRIS dataset. This work is partly funded by the EU FP7 Program (ACSI Project) and the Estonian Research Council. NICTA is funded by the Australian Department of Broadband, Communications and the Digital Economy and the Australian Research Council via the ICT Centre of Excellence program.

References

1. Adriansyah, A., van Dongen, B.F., van der Aalst, W.M.P.: Conformance checking using cost-based fitness analysis. In: Proc. of EDOC. IEEE (2011)
2. Rolón, E., Cardoso, J., García, F., Ruiz, F., Piattini, M.: Analysis and validation of control-flow complexity measures with BPMN process models. In: Halpin, T., Krogstie, J., Nurcan, S., Proper, E., Schmidt, R., Soffer, P., Ukor, R. (eds.) BPMDS 2009 and EMMSAD 2009. LNBIP, vol. 29, pp. 58–70. Springer, Heidelberg (2009)
3. Bauckmann, J., Leser, U., Naumann, F.: Efficient and exact computation of inclusion dependencies for data integration. Technical Report 34, Hasso-Plattner-Institute (2010)
4. Alves de Medeiros, A.K.: Genetic Process Mining. PhD thesis, Eindhoven University of Technology (2006)
5. Dijkman, R.M., Dumas, M., Ouyang, C.: Semantics and analysis of business process models in bpmn. Information & Software Technology 50(12) (2008)
6. Ekanayake, C.C., Dumas, M., García-Bañuelos, L., La Rosa, M.: Slice, mine and dice: Complexity-aware automated discovery of business process models. In: Daniel, F., Wang, J., Weber, B. (eds.) BPM 2013. LNCS, vol. 8094, pp. 49–64. Springer, Heidelberg (2013)
7. Favre, C., Fahland, D., Völzer, H.: The relationship between workflow graphs and free-choice workflow nets. Information Systems (in press, 2014)
8. Greco, G., Guzzo, A., Pontieri, L.: Mining taxonomies of process models. Data Knowl. Eng. 67(1) (2008)
9. Huhtala, Y., Kärkkäinen, J., Porkka, P., Toivonen, H.: TANE: An efficient algorithm for discovering functional and approximate dependencies. Computer Journal 42(2) (1999)
10. Kalenkova, A., Lomazova, I.A.: Discovery of cancellation regions within process mining techniques. In: Proc. of CS&P Workshop. CEUR Workshop Proceedings, vol. 1032, CEUR-WS.org (2013)
11. Leemans, S.J.J., Fahland, D., van der Aalst, W.M.P.: Discovering block-structured process models from event logs - A constructive approach. In: Colom, J.-M., Desel, J. (eds.) PETRI NETS 2013. LNCS, vol. 7927, pp. 311–329. Springer, Heidelberg (2013)
12. Li, J., Bose, R.P.J.C., van der Aalst, W.M.P.: Mining context-dependent and interactive business process maps using execution patterns. In: zur Muehlen, M., Su, J. (eds.) BPM 2010 Workshops. LNBIP, vol. 66, pp. 109–121. Springer, Heidelberg (2011)
13. Mendling, J., Reijers, H.A., Cardoso, J.: What Makes Process Models Understandable? In: Alonso, G., Dadam, P., Rosemann, M. (eds.) BPM 2007. LNCS, vol. 4714, pp. 48–63. Springer, Heidelberg (2007)
14. Muñoz-Gama, J., Carmona, J.: A fresh look at precision in process conformance. In: Hull, R., Mendling, J., Tai, S. (eds.) BPM 2010. LNCS, vol. 6336, pp. 211–226. Springer, Heidelberg (2010)
15. Nooijen, E.H.J., van Dongen, B.F., Fahland, D.: Automatic discovery of data-centric and artifact-centric processes. In: La Rosa, M., Soffer, P. (eds.) BPM 2012 Workshops. LNBIP, vol. 132, pp. 316–327. Springer, Heidelberg (2013)
16. Popova, V., Fahland, D., Dumas, M.: Artifact lifecycle discovery. CoRR abs/1303.2554 (2013)
17. Reijers, H.A., Mendling, J.: A study into the factors that influence the understandability of business process models. IEEE T. Syst. Man Cy. A 41(3) (2011)
18. Silberschatz, A., Korth, H.F., Sudarshan, S.: Database System Concepts, 4th edn. McGraw-Hill Book Company (2001)
19. van der Aalst, W.M.P.: Process Mining - Discovery, Conformance and Enhancement of Business Processes. Springer (2011)
20. van der Aalst, W.M.P., Weijters, T., Maruster, L.: Workflow mining: Discovering process models from event logs. IEEE Trans. Knowl. Data Eng. 16(9) (2004)
21. van der Werf, J.M.E.M., van Dongen, B.F., Hurkens, C.A.J., Serebrenik, A.: Process discovery using integer linear programming. Fundam. Inform. 94(3-4) (2009)

22. vanden Broucke, S.K.L.M., De Weerdt, J., Vanthienen, J., Baesens, B.: Fodina: a robust and flexible heuristic process discovery technique, http://www.processmining.be/fodina/ (last accessed: March 27, 2014)

23. vanden Broucke, S.K.L.M., De Weerdt, J., Baesens, B., Vanthienen, J.: Improved artificial negative event generation to enhance process event logs. In: Ralyté, J., Franch, X., Brinkkemper, S., Wrycza, S. (eds.) CAiSE 2012. LNCS, vol. 7328, pp. 254–269. Springer, Heidelberg (2012)

24. De Weerdt, J., De Backer, M., Vanthienen, J., Baesens, B.: A multi-dimensional quality assessment of state-of-the-art process discovery algorithms using real-life event logs. Inf. Syst. 37(7) (2012)

25. Weijters, A.J.M.M., Ribeiro, J.T.S.: Flexible Heuristics Miner (FHM). In: Proc. of CIDM. IEEE (2011)

A Genetic Algorithm for Process Discovery Guided by Completeness, Precision and Simplicity

Borja Vázquez-Barreiros, Manuel Mucientes, and Manuel Lama

Centro de Investigación en Tecnoloxías da Información (CiTIUS)
University of Santiago de Compostela, Spain
{borja.vazquez,manuel.mucientes,manuel.lama}@usc.es

Abstract. Several process discovery algorithms have been presented in the last years. These approaches look for complete, precise and simple models. Nevertheless, none of the current proposals obtains a good integration between the three objectives and, therefore, the mined models have differences with the real models. In this paper we present a genetic algorithm (ProDiGen) with a hierarchical fitness function that takes into account completeness, precision and simplicity. Moreover, ProDiGen uses crossover and mutation operators that focus the search on those parts of the model that generate errors during the processing of the log. The proposal has been validated with 21 different logs. Furthermore, we have compared our approach with two of the state of the art algorithms.

Keywords: Process mining, process discovery, Petri nets, genetic mining.

1 Introduction

In the last decade a great effort has been made for developing technologies to automate the execution of processes in different application domains such as industry, education or medicine [3]. In this context, a process is understood as a collection of tasks —or activities— with coordination requirements among them [8]. These tasks are performed by a set of actors to achieve the purpose of the process. Typically, these processes have a detailed description, i.e., there is a design of the process where its activities and the actors participating in these steps are clearly described. However, even in this situation there might be differences between what is actually happening and what is predefined in the process.

Based on this, Process Mining (PM) techniques are needed to get information about *what is really happening* in the execution of a process, and *not what the people think it is happening* [9]. Typically, these techniques use the log files that collect information about the events detected and stored by the information system in which the process has been executed. While PM techniques can be classified in different groups —*process discovery, conformance checking* or *enhancement*— this paper focuses its attention into the process discovery problem, i.e, the control-flow discovery, which aims to retrieve the process model that

S. Sadiq, P. Soffer, and H. Völzer (Eds.): BPM 2014, LNCS 8659, pp. 118–133, 2014.

represents the behavior recorded in an event log. These algorithms are used to discover the underlying process that has been followed by users to achieve an objective.

There has been a lot of work on process discovery [9,13,10,1,12,2,4]. Although some mining techniques use a specific target model for control flow discovery [4], most of the process discovery algorithms are based on Petri nets. These algorithms can be classified depending on the type of technique they applied. Thus *abstraction-based* algorithms [9,13], in general, retrieves simple models but with poor completeness. Other approaches, based on *heuristics* [12], although being robust to noise, do not guarantee optimal results in terms of completeness, as they focus on the main behavior of the log —also, they cannot handle all the common structures at once. Within the *search-based* algorithms, some techniques guarantee sound models [1] —not guaranteeing always the complete model as a solution—, and others can tackle all the different main behavior at once [2], but leaving simplicity aside. Other techniques, based on *theory of regions*, despite guaranteeing complete models [10], cannot handle noise and all the different pattern constructs. Summarizing, very valuable results have been achieved, but it is necessary to deep in the development of algorithms that guide its search towards complete, precise and simple models.

In this paper we present ProDiGen[1] (Process Discovery through a Genetic algorithm), a process discovery algorithm that guides its search towards complete, precise and simple models. The algorithm uses a hierarchical fitness function that takes into account completeness, precision and simplicity —with new definitions for both precision and simplicity— and uses heuristics to optimize the genetic operators: (i) a crossover operator that selects the crossover point from a Probability Density Function (PDF) generated from the errors of the mined model, and (ii) a mutation operator guided by the causal dependencies of the log. The proposal has been tested using 21 unbalanced logs, i.e, logs with many different traces and different frequencies. Furthermore, we have compared our approach with two of the state of the art process mining techniques, using a collection of conformance checking metrics.

The remainder of this paper is structured as follows. Sec. 2 presents the proposed genetic algorithm for process discovery. Sec. 3 shows the obtained results with the 21 logs and, finally, Sec. 4 points out the conclusions.

2   ProDiGen: Process Discovery through a Genetic Algorithm

The proposal of this paper (ProDiGen) is inspired by Genetic Miner [2], albeit there are several differences between them (Tab. 1). Although ProDiGen still codifies each individual[2] of the population[3] using the causal matrix representation [2], almost all of the mains steps of the genetic algorithm (GA) have been

---

[1] http://tec.citius.usc.es/SoftLearn/ProDiGen.html
[2] A candidate solution, i.e., a mined model.
[3] A collection of candidate solutions.

Table 1. Differences between ProDiGen and Genetic Miner

Fitness	The fitness is hierarchical and takes into account the completeness, precision and simplicity of the mined model.
Precision	Definition of a new method to measure the precision of a model.
Simplicity	Definition of a new method to measure the simplicity of a model.
Initialization	The solution of the Heuristics Miner is incorporated to the initial population as well.
Selection	Prodigen uses the binary tournament selection as selection mechanism.
Crossover	The crossover operator is guided by a Probability Density Function (PDF) generated from the errors of the mined model.
Mutation	The mutation operator is guided by the causal dependencies of the log.
Replacement	Steady-state approach, with a reinitialization criterium based on the improvement of the population.

Algorithm 1. ProDiGen

---

1 Initialize population
2 Evaluate population
3 $t = 1$, *timesRun* = *initialTimesRun*, *restarts* = 0
4 **while** $t \leq maxGenerations$ && *restarts* < *maxRestarts* **do**
5   Selection
6   Crossover
7   Mutation
8   Evaluate new individuals
9   Replace population
10    $t = t + 1$
11   **if** *bestInd* (t) == *bestInd* $(t-1)$ **then**
12   *timesRun* = *timesRun* − 1
13   **if** *none of the individuals of the population have been replaced* **then**
14   *timesRun* = *timesRun* − 1
15   **if** *timesRun* < 0 **then**
16   Reinitialize population
17   Evaluate population
18   *timesRun* = *initialTimesRun*, *restarts* = *restarts* + 1

---

modified. More specifically, one of the major changes takes place in the evaluation of the population, where completeness, precision and simplicity are considered in a hierarchical way. ProDiGen also defines (i) a new metric to measure the precision of each individual, and (ii) a new method to measure the simplicity of the model. Furthermore, we introduce heuristics to guide the genetic operators, focusing the search on those parts of the mined model that have errors and, also, reducing the search space to those models that are supported by the information in the log.

Algorithm 1 describes how ProDiGen works. The first three steps correspond to an initialization, where t represents the number of iterations, *timesRun* is used to detect situations in which the search gets stuck, and *restarts* counts the number of reinitializations. The evolution cycle of the algorithm starts at Alg. 1:4. This part will be repeated until the stopping criterion is fulfilled. The mains steps of the iterative part are the selection of the individuals, the crossover and mutation operations to generate new individuals, their evaluation, the replacement of the population, and the analysis of the population to detect blockages in the search process. All these steps are described in detail in the next sections.

2.1   Initialization

In ProDiGen, each individual codifies a workflow using a causal matrix representation [2]. A causal matrix can map any Petri net in terms of dependency relations —which tasks enable the execution of other tasks— as it represents the input and output dependencies of each activity of the model.

ProDiGen uses the same heuristics —based on the causality relations between tasks— described in [2] to generate the initial population. Moreover, we also add to the initial population the solution mined with the Heuristics Miner approach [12]. With this process, the dependency relations are captured using the Heuristics Miner and then, with ProDiGen, the different inputs and outputs bindings are optimized. We have empirically concluded that adding the Heuristics Miner solution to the initial population does not modify the model mined with ProDiGen. Nevertheless, the inclusion of this individual in the initial population *speeds up* the iteration at which the best individual is found: instead of relying only on randomly initialized individuals, ProDiGen also uses the dependency relations mined by Heuristics Miner.

2.2   Evaluation

The individuals of the population are evaluated taking into account completeness, precision and simplicity, combined in a hierarchical fitness function.

Completeness. We use the definition of completeness (C_f) described in [2], which takes into account the number of correctly parsed tasks [4], but also punishes the number of missing and not consumed tokens of the Petri net encoded in the individual —each missing or not consumed token represents a failure.

Precision. A model is precise when it reproduces the event traces of the log, not allowing for too much extra behavior, i.e, behavior that does not exist in the log. Our definition of precision considers all the activities that are enabled —tasks for which their input conditions are met when reproducing the log— while an individual parses the event traces of the log:

---

[4] If a task from an individual does not have the proper input arcs, that task will be incorrectly fired when reproducing the log, as its input conditions are not fulfilled.

$$P_f(L, CM) = \frac{1}{allEnabledActivities\,(L,\ CM)} \tag{1}$$

where *allEnabledActivities* is the sum of enabled activities after firing each activity of the log L by an individual CM. The idea behind this definition is to punish those individuals that enable too many activities during the parsing of the log, as they activate several paths that allow for extra behavior. Contrary to [2], ProDiGen does not consider the rest of the population in order to compute the precision of each individual, which can evolve regardless the precision of the rest of the population.

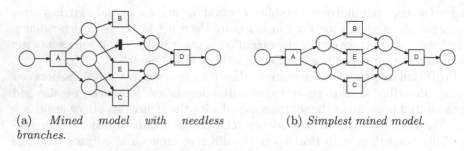

(a) *Mined model with needless branches.*

(b) *Simplest mined model.*

Fig. 1. Two possible solutions with the same completeness and precision

Simplicity. Completeness and precision give, by their own, a good indicator of how good is a mined model, but do not guarantee to find the simplest model. Hence, the third dimension of the fitness is simplicity. Although, there are several metrics that measure the complexity of a directed graph [6], there is no metric to measure the simplicity of a causal matrix. Instead of converting the causal matrix to a Petri net each time we want to measure the complexity of the model, we opted to define a new complexity metric for causal matrices. The new metric measures the complexity of a mined model based on the number of causal relations of an individual:

$$S_f(CM) = \frac{1}{\sum_{t \in CM} \left(\sum_{\Phi \in I(t)} |\Phi| + \sum_{\Psi \in O(t)} |\Psi| \right)} \tag{2}$$

where t is a task of the causal matrix CM, Φ is an element of the input function of t —I(t)—, and Ψ is an element of the output function of t —O(t)—. Therefore, the simplicity counts the number of causal relations of the model using the cardinality of the input and output subsets of the causal matrix.

To illustrate the relevance of simplicity to mine the correct model, lets assume a simple example with three different traces: $<< A, B, C, D >^3, < A, C, B, D >^2, < A, E, D >^4>$. Fig. 1 shows two mined models that have the same completeness and precision: (i) both can parse all the traces, i.e., $C_f = 1.0$; and (ii) they enable exactly the same number of tasks during the parsing (50), thus $P_f = 1/50$. However, the model in Fig. 1a has a $S_f = 1/16$, while the model in Fig. 1b has a $S_f = 1/14$ and, therefore, the second one is a better model[5].

Fitness. ProDiGen uses a hierarchical fitness function that establishes priorities among these three objectives:

$$F(a) > F(b) \iff \{C_f(a) > C_f(b)\} \vee \{C_f(a) = C_f(b) \wedge P_f(a) > P_f(b)\} \quad (3)$$
$$\vee \{C_f(a) = C_f(b) \wedge P_f(a) = P_f(b) \wedge S_f(a) > S_f(b)\}$$

where $F(a)$, $C_f(a)$, $P_f(a)$ and $S_f(a)$, are respectively the *fitness*, *completeness*, *precision* and *simplicity* of a process model a. The advantage of using this hierarchical fitness function over a weighted fitness function is that, during the first stage of the evolutionary process, the GA focuses the search on those individuals that are complete. Once these individuals become representative in the population, the second level of the hierarchy takes the control, modifying the models that are complete in order to improve their precision. Finally, in the third stage, the fitness function guides the GA to improve the simplicity of those models that are both complete and precise.

2.3   Selection

ProdDiGen uses the binary tournament selection as selection mechanism. In a n-tournament selection, n individuals are randomly picked from the population —with replacement— and the best of them is selected. In this case, $n = 2$ —binary tournament selection.

2.4   Crossover

As the process models are represented through causal matrices, and the size of the causal matrix increases with the number of activities in the log, the number of possible crossover points could be really large —increasing significantly the search space. Thereby, we have noticed that picking the crossover point at random produces a poor performance of the crossover operator, as most of *the offspring have a fitness lower than their parents* after the crossover operation —the selected task of the individual to be crossed can be a correctly fired one.

---

[5] The difference between these two solutions —in terms of simplicity— is caused by the output function of the task A: the causal matrix of the model in Fig. 1a has $O(A) = \{\{B\,E\}, \{D\,C\}, \{C\,E\}\}$, which increases its complexity by 6. On the other hand, the causal matrix of the model in Fig. 1b has $O(A) = \{\{B\,E\}, \{C\,E\}\}$, increasing the complexity by 4.

ProDiGen makes the selection of the activity that is going to be crossed using a non uniform Probability Density Function (PDF). This PDF assigns a null probability of being selected to those activities that have been correctly fired during the parsing of the traces in the log. On the other hand, those activities that were incorrectly fired receive a uniform probability —inversely proportional to the number of incorrectly parsed activities— of being crossed.

Algorithm 2. Crossover operator

---

1 $r \leftarrow getRandomNumber()$;   // returns a random number between [0,1)
2 **if** $r < crossoverRate$ **then**
3 | $incorrectlyFiredActivities \leftarrow \emptyset$
4 | **if** $fitness(parent_1) >= fitness(parent_2)$ **then**
5 | └ $incorrectlyFiredActivities \leftarrow$ set of incorrectly fired activities of $parent_1$
6 | **else**
7 | └ $incorrectlyFiredActivities \leftarrow$ set of incorrectly fired activities of $parent_2$
8 | **if** $incorrectlyFiredActivities \neq \emptyset$ **then**
9 | | $crossoverPoint \leftarrow$ randomly select an activity t from
    | └ $incorrectlyFiredActivities$
10 | **else**
11 | | $crossoverPoint \leftarrow$ randomly select an activity t from the bag of all
    | └ possible tasks in the log
12 | $offspring_1$, $offspring_2 \leftarrow doCrossover(parent_1, parent_2, crossoverPoint)$
13 └ Repair $offspring_1$ and $offspring_2$

The selection of the crossover point is summarized in Alg. 2. By incorrectly fired activities we mean (i) activities that need extra tokens in their inputs to be fired, i.e, tasks that do not have the correct input arcs, and (ii) activities that have left tokens in their outputs after the parsing of the traces, i.e, tasks that do not have the correct output arcs. Therefore, during the evaluation process, the algorithm keeps track of the tasks with missing or extra tokens, and generates a bag of *incorrectlyFiredActivities* for each individual. Thereby, the crossover point is selected from the set of *incorrectlyFiredActivities* of the fittest parent (Alg. 2:4). Note that if the set of *incorrectlyFiredActivities* of the fittest individual is empty (Alg. 2:8), i.e, it has a completeness equal to 1, the crossover point is randomly chosen from the bag of all the possible tasks in the log (Alg. 2:11). After the crossover point is selected, the crossover is performed as defined in [2]. Thus, the crossover operator combines —by adding or merging subsets— the inputs for the selected task t of both parents, in order to generate the new inputs for t in the offspring. Finally this process is repeated for the output functions. As the input and output (I/O) functions of the crossover task can change by adding/removing causal dependencies, there may be inconsistencies between the I/O function of the crossover point and the rest of I/O functions of the individual — for example, a task t may have an output dependency with t', but t' does not have the input dependency with t. Thereby, after each crossover, the individual has to be repaired (Alg. 2:13) to avoid these discrepancies between the input and output sets of the tasks. The repair process works as follows. For each task t' that was eliminated from $O(t)$, the process checks if $t' \in O(t)$ —notice that t' can be in several subsets of $O(t)$. If that is false, t has to be eliminated form $I(t')$. This process is repeated also for the input sets. On the other hand, when a task t' is added to $O(t)$, the process checks if $t \in I(t')$. If that is false, then t is added to $I(t)$. A similar process is done for the inputs of t.

2.5   Mutation

The mutation operator modifies the population by (i) adding new material —new relations— to the individuals; (ii) removing causal relations; or (iii) reorganizing an input/output function, for instance, converting an AND-join into an OR-join.

Although ProDiGen uses the three mutation actions defined in [2], there are four major differences between our mutation operator and the one defined in Genetic Miner: (i) the individual is iteratively mutated until it is different from its parent —a mutation could generate an individual equal to its parent due to an useless mutation, for example, redistributing an empty set; (ii) only one task is affected by the mutation operator; (iii) individuals are always forced to mutate —the mutation probability is 1; and (iv) the task t' added to the I/O set of a task t must belong to the set of tasks that have an input/output dependency with t. The major goal of these modifications is to avoid duplicate individuals within the same population, or at least to minimize the duplicates. With these modifications, we have a more diverse population.

The mutation operator is summarized in Alg. 3. It uses two sets for the addition of a new task: *outputDependencies(t)* and *inputDependencies(t)*. ProDiGen uses these sets to reduce the set of tasks that are appropriate to be inserted in an I/O set, preventing the inclusion of a new task t' that never appears in a trace of t within the log. A first approach could be to include in the dependencies sets those tasks that have a dependency with t as calculated in the initialization phase. However, if we only take into account these dependencies, there will be not enough new material to discover all the different constructs. Therefore, *inputDependencies(t)* will be the set of tasks appearing before t in any trace of the log and, in the same way, *outputDependencies(t)* will be the set of activities that appear after t in any trace of the log. In this way, the mutation operator focuses only on those regions of the search space that represent information contained in the log. As a result, the success of the mutation operator increases, finding better offspring. Again, as the mutation operator can add or remove a task from an I/O set of a task t, there may be inconsistencies within the causal dependencies of the individual. Therefore, after each mutation the individual has to be repaired (Alg. 3:15), following the same strategy described in Sec 2.4.

Algorithm 3. Mutation operator

---

1 **while** *the individual does **not** change* **do**
2 | Randomly choose one task t in the individual
3 | $mutationType \leftarrow getRandomNumber()$;   // returns a random number
   | between [0,1)
4 | **if** $mutationType < 1/3$ **then**
5 | | Randomly select a task t' from $inputDependencies(t)$
6 | | **if** $getRandomNumber() < 1/2$ **then**
7 | | | Randomly choose one subset $X \in I(t)$ and add the task t' to X
8 | | **else**
9 | | | Create a new subset X, add the task t' to X, and add X to $I(t)$
10 | **else if** $mutationType < 2/3$ **then**
11 | | Randomly choose one subset $X \in I(t)$ and remove a task t' from X,
   | | where $t' \in X$. If X is empty after this operation, exclude X from $I(t)$
12 | **else**
13 | | Randomly redistribute the elements from $I(t)$
14 | Repeat from line 3, but using $O(t)$ instead of $I(t)$ and
   | $outputDependencies(t)$ instead of $inputDependencies(t)$
15 | Repair the individual

2.6 Replacement

At each iteration, ProDiGen generates N offspring —being N the size of the population— as follows. Tournament selection randomly picks two parents from the current population. These individuals are modified by the genetic operators, creating two new individuals. This process is repeated until N offspring are generated. At this point, the parent population —current population— and the offspring population are joined and sorted —using the fitness. Finally the replacement operator selects the N best individuals. In order to maintain a diverse population, those repeated individuals are placed at the bottom of the ranking —keeping one representative in the original ranking position.

2.7 Reinitialization

A reinitialization takes place when the value of *timesRun* goes under 0 (Alg. 1:15), which indicates that the search process was not improving in the last iterations. This situation is detected in two ways. The first one (Alg. 1:11) is when the new population of an iteration has no new individuals —in comparison with the initial population of that iteration. The second indicator (Alg. 1:13) is the fact that the best individual does not improve. Each time that one of these situations is detected, *timesRun* decreases. The initial population after a reinitialization is generated in the same way as in the initialization stage. Moreover, ProDiGen also includes in the new population a mutation of the

Table 2. Process models used in the experimentation

Model	#Tasks	Sequence	Choice	Parallelism	Length-One Loop	Length-Two Loop	Arbitrary Loop	Structured Loop	Invisible tasks	Unbalanced AND-join/split	#traces	#events
g2 [2]	22	✓	✓	✓		✓	✓		✓		300	4501
g3 [2]	29	✓	✓	✓			✓	✓	✓		300	14599
g4 [2]	29	✓	✓	✓	✓					✓	300	5975
g5 [2]	20	✓	✓	✓				✓	✓		300	6172
g6 [2]	23	✓	✓	✓	✓				✓		300	5419
g7 [2]	29	✓	✓	✓			✓		✓		300	14451
g8 [2]	30	✓	✓	✓		✓	✓		✓	✓	300	5133
g9 [2]	26	✓	✓	✓		✓	✓		✓		300	5679
g10 [2]	23	✓	✓	✓				✓	✓		300	4117
g12 [2]	26	✓	✓	✓		✓		✓	✓		300	4841
g13 [2]	22	✓	✓	✓	✓	✓		✓		✓	300	5007
g14 [2]	24	✓	✓	✓			✓		✓	✓	300	11340
g15 [2]	25	✓	✓			✓	✓		✓		300	3978
g19 [2]	23	✓	✓	✓		✓			✓	✓	300	4107
g20 [2]	21	✓	✓		✓	✓			✓	✓	300	6193
g21 [2]	22	✓	✓				✓		✓	✓	300	3882
g22 [2]	24	✓	✓	✓		✓			✓	✓	300	3095
g23 [2]	25	✓	✓	✓		✓				✓	300	9654
g24 [2]	21	✓	✓	✓				✓	✓	✓	300	4130
g25 [2]	20	✓	✓	✓	✓				✓		300	6312
EMT [1]	7	✓	✓	✓					✓		100	790

best individual of the last iteration. The maximum number of reinitializations is limited, and when it reaches the threshold (*maxRestarts*) ProDiGen ends.

3   Experimentation

This section describes (i) the validation of ProDiGen with 21 different logs using several conformance checking metrics, and (ii) the comparison of ProDiGen performance with two well-known state of the art process mining techniques: Heuristics Miner [12] and Genetic Miner [2].

3.1   Logs

ProDiGen has been validated with 21 different logs from [2] and [1]. Tab. 2 summarizes the structural complexity of these models ranging from 7 to 30 tasks. Some of the models used in the experimentation contain unbalanced AND-split/join points, i.e, there is not a one-to-one relation between the AND-split points and the AND-join points. Moreover, all the logs are imbalanced, i.e., they contain traces with very different frequencies. Thereby, with this experiment we can check whether the algorithm overfits or underfits the data due to the unbalanced frequencies of the traces in the log.

3.2 Metrics

The performance of ProDiGen over the different logs has been measured with two different sets of metrics: (i) metrics based on the original model; and (ii) metrics based on the event log.

Metrics Based on the Original Model. To compare the original and the mined models, we use the metrics defined in [2]:

- To quantify the *behavior similarity* between the original model and the mined one we use the metrics *Behavioral precision* (B_p) and *Behavioral recall* (B_r), which detect, respectively, if the mined model can process traces that cannot be parsed by the original model, and if the original model can parse traces that cannot be processed in the mined model. The mined model is as precise as the original one if $B_p = 1$ and $B_r = 1$: the closer the values of B_p and B_r to 1, the higher the similarity between the original and the mined models.
- On the other hand, to *measure the similarity from the structural point of view* of the mined model with respect to the original one, we use the metrics *Structural precision* (S_p) and *Structural recall* (S_r). They check, respectively, if there are causality relations of the mined model that are not defined in the original model, and if there are causality relations of the original model that are not defined in the mined model. When the original model has connections that do not appear in the mined model, S_r will take a value smaller than 1, and, in the same way, when the mined model has connections that do not appear in the original model, S_p will take a value lower than 1.

Metrics Based on the Log. Additionally to the four previously described metrics, we also use three metrics that do not require the original model as input:

- To measure the completeness we use the proper completion measure [5], which is the fraction of properly completed process instances. *Proper completion* (C) takes a value of 1 if the mined model can process all the traces without having missing tokens or tokens left behind.
- The precision is evaluated with the *alignment precision* (P) defined in [7], which, takes a value of 1 if all the behavior allowed by the model is observed in the log.
- Finally, for the simplicity (S) we use:

$$S = \frac{1}{1 + S'} \qquad (4)$$

where S' is the *weighted P/T average arc degree* defined in [6]. The higher the value of S, the higher the simplicity. To measure these three metrics we used the tool CoBeFra [11].

Table 3. Results for the 21 logs

Method		Metric	g2	g3	g4	g5	g6	g7	g8	g9	g10	g12	g13	g14	g15	g19	g20	g21	g22	g23	g24	g25	EMT
ProDiGen	Model metrics	B_p	1.0	1.0	1.0	1.0	1.0	1.0	1.0	1.0	1.0	1.0	1.0	1.0	1.0	1.0	1.0	1.0	1.0	1.0	1.0	0.96	1.0
		B_r	1.0	1.0	1.0	1.0	1.0	1.0	1.0	1.0	1.0	1.0	1.0	1.0	1.0	1.0	1.0	1.0	1.0	1.0	1.0	0.99	1.0
		S_p	1.0	1.0	1.0	1.0	1.0	1.0	1.0	1.0	1.0	1.0	1.0	1.0	1.0	1.0	1.0	1.0	1.0	1.0	1.0	0.91	1.0
		S_r	1.0	1.0	0.97	1.0	1.0	1.0	0.94	1.0	1.0	1.0	1.0	1.0	1.0	1.0	1.0	1.0	1.0	1.0	0.98	0.91	1.0
	Log metrics	C	1.0	1.0	0.78	1.0	1.0	1.0	0.52	1.0	1.0	1.0	1.0	1.0	1.0	1.0	1.0	1.0	1.0	1.0	1.0	0.98	1.0
		P	0.9	0.82	0.98	0.98	0.95	0.88	0.86	0.92	0.89	0.97	0.93	0.93	0.86	0.92	0.78	0.91	0.9	0.58	0.89	0.74	0.87
		S	0.3	0.3	0.31	0.31	0.31	0.32	0.28	0.31	0.3	0.31	0.3	0.31	0.25	0.3	0.29	0.31	0.3	0.3	0.29	0.31	0.27
GM	Model metrics	B_p	1.0	0.61	0.78	1.0	1.0	1.0	0.84	0.96	0.99	1.0	0.98	0.61	0.8	0.98	1.0	1.0	0.97	0.57	0.83	0.81	1.0
		B_r	1.0	0.97	0.97	1.0	1.0	1.0	1.0	0.97	1.0	0.99	1.0	0.97	0.9	1.0	1.0	1.0	0.88	0.88	0.96	0.83	
		S_p	1.0	0.81	0.81	1.0	1.0	1.0	0.97	0.9	1.0	0.95	0.95	0.88	0.95	1.0	1.0	0.85	0.76	0.75	0.76	0.85	
		S_r	1.0	0.81	0.81	1.0	1.0	1.0	0.94	0.98	0.92	1.0	0.94	0.94	0.87	0.89	1.0	1.0	0.85	0.74	0.75	0.74	0.85
	Log metrics	C	1.0	0.31	0.59	1.0	1.0	1.0	0.26	0.48	0.48	1.0	0.75	1.0	0.15	0.2	1.0	1.0	0.43	0.2	0.72	0.41	0.3
		P	0.9	0.42	0.98	0.98	0.95	0.88	0.0	0.94	0.91	0.97	0.96	0.74	0.0	0.0	0.78	0.91	0.86	0.0	0.88	0.49	0.81
		S	0.3	0.31	0.3	0.31	0.31	0.32	0.26	0.3	0.29	0.31	0.3	0.31	0.24	0.29	0.29	0.31	0.3	0.28	0.3	0.28	0.3
HM	Model metrics	B_p	1.0	1.0	0.94	1.0	0.9	0.97	0.87	1.0	0.96	1.0	1.0	0.97	0.96	0.97	1.0	1.0	0.99	0.6	0.92	0.76	0.81
		B_r	1.0	0.98	0.92	1.0	0.98	0.97	0.99	0.98	0.95	1.0	1.0	0.97	0.98	1.0	1.0	0.99	1.0	0.88	0.94	0.96	
		S_p	1.0	0.97	0.96	1.0	0.93	0.97	0.95	1.0	0.96	1.0	1.0	0.96	1.0	1.0	1.0	0.97	0.91	0.89	0.85	0.76	
		S_r	1.0	0.97	0.86	1.0	0.97	1.0	0.86	1.0	0.96	1.0	1.0	0.92	0.86	0.9	1.0	1.0	0.91	0.94	0.81	0.85	0.74
	Log metrics	C	1.0	1.0	0.78	1.0	0.66	1.0	0.52	0.74	0.78	1.0	1.0	0.91	0.87	0.85	1.0	1.0	0.9	0.0	0.93	0.23	0.37
		P	0.9	0.83	0.99	0.98	0.93	0.9	0.86	0.93	0.9	0.97	0.93	0.92	0.87	0.93	0.78	0.91	0.9	0.0	0.86	0.71	0.85
		S	0.3	0.3	0.32	0.31	0.31	0.31	0.28	0.31	0.3	0.31	0.3	0.32	0.26	0.3	0.29	0.31	0.3	0.29	0.29	0.3	0.29

3.3 Results

Within this scenario, we have conducted an experimentation comparing ProDi-Gen with two of the state of the art most popular algorithms: Genetic Miner [2] and Heuristics Miner [12].

The values that have been used for the parameters of ProDiGen are: *max-Generations* = 1,000, *initialTimesRun* = 35, population size = 100, crossover probability = 0.8 and *maxRestarts* = 5. For the Genetic Miner (GM), we selected the parameters indicated by the authors in [2]: *maxGenerations* = 5,000, population size = 10, crossover probability = 0.8, mutation probability 0.2, elitism rate = 0.2, selection type = tournament 5. For the Heuristics Miner (HM), we used the default parameters established in ProM 6.3 with the option *mine long distance dependencies* enabled.

Table 3 shows the results on the 21 logs. ProDiGen mines the same model as the original model in 17 of the logs —the values of the four model metrics are 1— while in the other four logs the mined model is very similar to the correct one. The difficulties in these 4 logs arise when (i) mining logs with parallel constructs with more than two branches and with two or more tasks in each branch, and (ii) when mining logs that came from models with unbalanced AND-join/split points. These type of patterns are even more difficult to mine considering that not all the possible combinations admitted by the original model are represented in the log, and not all the traces have the same frequency. Therefore, ProDiGen tries to better fit the most frequent behavior of the log, overfitting the data

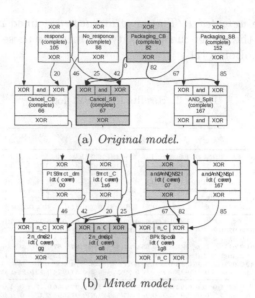

(a) *Original model.*

(b) *Mined model.*

Fig. 2. Detail of the original and mined models for log $g24$

when dealing with these constructs. We now discuss the details of the models incorrectly mined by ProDiGen:

- The results for log $g24$ (Fig. 2) show that the mined model is almost equal to the original one, except the only one relation between two tasks (tasks in grey, Fig. 2b). If we process the log with the original model (Fig. 2b) we can check that the missing relation is never used and, hence, it is impossible to mine that relation with the information of the log.
- The mined model for log $g8$ (Fig. 3) has a behavioral precision and recall equal to 1, i.e., the mined model can parse all the traces from the log and allows the same behavior as the original one with respect to the information contained in the log. However, the model is not complete because it cannot tackle the output dependencies of the tasks *timeout* and *return-contract*, considering them as final tasks —Fig. 3a shows the original output dependencies of these tasks. This results in a incomplete mined model, because all the traces involving these two tasks will have an extra token at the end of the parsing. The main problem with this log is that these two tasks are involved in the unbalanced AND-join/split, which cannot be correctly mined by ProDiGen.
- For log $g25$ the behavioral recall and precision are close to 1. This means that, even when the model is not as precise as the original, it does not allow for more extra behavior than the original one with respect to the log. Despite this model does not have an unbalanced AND-join/split point, it has many interleaving situations, which make very difficult to properly mine the correct relations of the different branches of the parallel construct.

– The mined model for log $g4$ has again a behavioral precision and recall of 1, showing that it expresses the same behavior as the original model with respect to the log. The main problem when mining this log is that ProDiGen cannot find the complete model because it discovers an extra final task due to the unbalanced AND-join/split point —the same problem as in log $g8$.

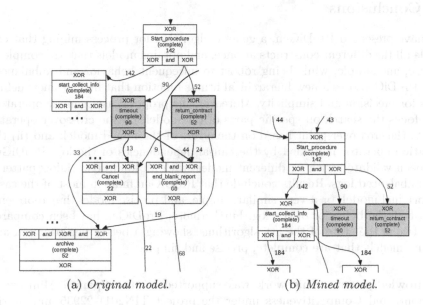

(a) *Original model.*   (b) *Mined model.*

Fig. 3. Detail of the original and mined models for log $g8$

Table 3 also shows the results of the other algorithms. The main problem of GM is that it finds solutions with too many silent transitions[6] generating models with low precision and simplicity. On the other hand, HM focuses its search on the main behavior of the log —finding solutions with high levels of simplicity. Hence, it cannot find the original model on those logs that came from models with many interleaving situations, as it tries to better fit the most frequent behavior recorded in the log —as the logs are unbalanced, *not all the possible relations* have the same frequency.

Comparing the results of the three algorithms: ProDiGen correctly mines, i.e, finds the original model, the 81% (17 out of 21) of the cases; GM finds the original model in the 33% (7 out of 21) of the logs; and HM finds the original model in the 28% (6 out of 21) of the logs. Moreover, Table 3 also shows information about which algorithm retrieves better results for each metric —highlighted in grey. On those logs where ProDiGen did not find the original model —logs $g4$, $g8$, $g24$ and $g25$— it still obtains the best solution of the three algorithms.

---

[6] A silent transition is a type of activity used for routing purposes only, as it does not correspond to any activity in the log.

Based on this experimentation, we can conclude that using a hierarchical fitness function based on completeness, precision and simplicity, shows a great performance when mining unbalanced logs. Moreover, the inclusion of heuristics in the genetic operators also improves the results, as ProDiGen focuses the search over those regions that represent the behavior of the log.

4 Conclusions

We have presented ProDiGen, a genetic algorithm for process mining that can tackle all the different constructs at once, and obtains models that are complete, precise, and simple, while being robust to infrequent behavior and unbalanced logs. ProDiGen uses a new hierarchical fitness function that includes new definitions for precision and simplicity. Moreover, the proposal uses genetic operators that focus the search on specific parts of the model: (i) the crossover operator selects the crossover point based on the errors of the mined model; and (ii) the mutation operator is guided by the causal dependencies of the log. ProDiGen has been validated with 21 different models with all kind of workflow patterns and unbalanced logs. Results conclude that ProDiGen mine in most of the cases the original model, or a very similar, simple, and precise model that represents almost all the behavior of the log. Furthermore, ProDiGen has been compared with two of the state of the art algorithms, showing a better performance, and finding models that are complete, precise and simple.

Acknowledgment. This work was supported by the Spanish Ministry of Economy and Competitiveness under the project TIN2011-22935 and by the European Regional Development Fund (ERDF/FEDER) under the project CN2012/151 of the Galician Ministry of Education.

References

1. Buijs, J., van Dongen, B., van der Aalst, W.M.P.: Quality dimensions in process discovery: The importance of fitness, precision, generalization and simplicity. International Journal of Cooperative Information Systems 23(01) (2014)
2. de Medeiros, A.: Genetic Process Mining. PhD thesis, Technische Universiteit Eindhoven (2006)
3. Dumas, M., ter Hofstede, A., van der Aalst, W.M.P.: Process-aware information systems: bridging people and software through process technology. Wiley-Interscience (2005)
4. Günther, C.W., van der Aalst, W.M.P.: Fuzzy mining – adaptive process simplification based on multi-perspective metrics. In: Alonso, G., Dadam, P., Rosemann, M. (eds.) BPM 2007. LNCS, vol. 4714, pp. 328–343. Springer, Heidelberg (2007)
5. Rozinat, A., van der Aalst, W.M.P.: Conformance checking of processes based on monitoring real behavior. Information Systems 33(1), 64–95 (2008)
6. Sánchez-González, L., García, F., Mendling, J., Ruiz, F., Piattini, M.: Prediction of business process model quality based on structural metrics. In: Parsons, J., Saeki, M., Shoval, P., Woo, C., Wand, Y. (eds.) ER 2010. LNCS, vol. 6412, pp. 458–463. Springer, Heidelberg (2010)

7. van der Aalst, W.M.P., Adriansyah, A., van Dongen, B.: Replaying history on process models for conformance checking and performance analysis. Wiley Interdisciplinary Reviews: Data Mining and Knowledge Discovery 2(2), 182–192 (2012)
8. van der Aalst, W.M.P., Ter Hofstede, A.H., Kiepuszewski, B., Barros, A.P.: Workflow patterns. Distributed and Parallel Databases 14(1), 5–51 (2003)
9. van der Aalst, W.M.P., Weijters, A., Maruster, L.: Workflow mining: Discovering process models from event logs. IEEE Transactions on Knowledge and Data Engineering 16(9), 1128–1142 (2004)
10. van der Werf, J.M.E.M., van Dongen, B.F., Hurkens, C.A.J., Serebrenik, A.: Process discovery using integer linear programming. In: van Hee, K.M., Valk, R. (eds.) PETRI NETS 2008. LNCS, vol. 5062, pp. 368–387. Springer, Heidelberg (2008)
11. vanden Broucke, S., Weerdt, J.D., Vanthienen, J., Baesens, B.: A comprehensive benchmarking framework (CoBeFra) for conformance analysis between procedural process models and event logs in ProM. In: 2013 IEEE Symposium on Computational Intelligence and Data Mining (CIDM), pp. 254–261. IEEE (2013)
12. Weijters, A., van der Aalst, W.M.P., de Medeiros, A.: Process mining with the heuristics miner-algorithm. Technische Universiteit Eindhoven 166 (2006)
13. Wen, L., Wang, J., Sun, J.: Mining invisible tasks from event logs. In: Dong, G., Lin, X., Wang, W., Yang, Y., Yu, J.X. (eds.) APWeb/WAIM 2007. LNCS, vol. 4505, pp. 358–365. Springer, Heidelberg (2007)

Constructs Competition Miner: Process Control-Flow Discovery of BP-Domain Constructs

David Redlich[1,2], Thomas Molka[1,3], Wasif Gilani[1],
Gordon Blair[2], and Awais Rashid[2]

[1] SAP Research Center Belfast, United Kingdom
{david.redlich,thomas.molka,wasif.gilani}@sap.com
[2] Lancaster University, United Kingdom
{gordon,marash}@comp.lancs.ac.uk
[3] University of Manchester, United Kingdom

Abstract. Process Discovery techniques help a business analyst to understand the actual processes deployed in an organization, i.e. based on a log of events, the actual activity workflow is discovered. In most cases their results conform to general purpose representations like Petri nets or Causal nets which are preferred by academic scholars but difficult to comprehend for business analysts. In this paper we propose an algorithm that follows a top-down approach to directly mine a process model which consists of common BP-domain constructs and represents the main behaviour of the process. The algorithm is designed so it can deal with noise and not-supported behaviour. This is achieved by letting the different supported constructs compete with each other for the most suitable solution from top to bottom using "soft" constraints and behaviour approximations. The key parts of the algorithm are formally described and evaluation results are presented and discussed.

Keywords: business process models, business process management, process discovery.

1 Introduction

Due to increasing competition modern organizations need to continuously adapt and improve their business functions. At the heart of these organizations are business processes (BPs) which define the flow of work that needs to be executed to achieve their business goals. Discovering and understanding the actual workflow of the deployed processes from a log of events is the purpose of Process Discovery techniques. This enables further analysis, e.g. identifying bottle necks, thus helping to improve the deployed business processes and increase the overall performance and competitiveness of the whole business.

However, there is a noticeable difference between business process specifications at design-time and the representations of business processes discovered at run-time. Whereas prominent standards for business process models, e.g. BPMN and EPC, are BP-domain-specific, the results of Process Discovery algorithms conform to BP-independent representations like Petri nets as discovered by the alpha-algorithm [11], or Causal nets as discovered by the HeuristicsMiner [10].

S. Sadiq, P. Soffer, and H. Völzer (Eds.): BPM 2014, LNCS 8659, pp. 134–150, 2014.

For a business analyst, the interpretation of these general purpose languages for decision making is a difficult task, because (1) these are of a different representation than what he is familiar with and (2) the mapping between the process modelled at design-time and the discovered process model at run-time can be difficult to establish since they both conform to different languages. One solution to bridge this discrepancy are transformations from and to different possible representations for business processes. A second solution is to directly mine a model conforming to a BP-domain language. This enables the business analyst to formulate requirements directly for the result representation

In this paper we propose an algorithm that follows a top-down approach to discover a business process model which consists of a predefined set of common BP-domain constructs like Sequence, Choice, Loop, Parallelism, etc. and represents the main behaviour of the process according to the requirements of the business analyst. This is achieved by assuming the process is of a nested structure and letting the different constructs compete with each other on each level for the most suitable solution from top to bottom. The competition aspect of the Constructs Competition Miner (CCM) makes it especially suitable for process logs with conflicting or exceptional behaviour.

The remainder of this paper provides a definition of business process elements and event logs (Section 2), a discussion of related work (Section 3), a formal description of the CCM (Section 4), as well as its evaluation (Section 5), and an outlook of future work (Section 6).

2 Process Models and Event Logs

Many different standards for business process models exist. In industry Business Process Model and Notation (BPMN) [7] is a prominent example, in research Yet Another Workflow Language (YAWL) [12] is the most established one. In our work, we focus on a general set of control-flow elements that are supported by the most common standards. These elements include a start and an end event, activities (i.e. process steps), parallel gateways (AND-Split/Join), and exclusive gateways (XOR-Split/Join) (see [7,12]). In Figure 1, an example process containing all considered elements is shown. Formally, we define the control-flow of a business process as follows:

Definition 1. *A business process model is a tuple* $BP = (A, S, J, E_s, E_e, C)$ *where A is a finite set of activities, S a finite set of splits, J a finite set of joins, E_s a finite set of start events, E_e a finite set of end events, and $C \subseteq F \times F$ the path connection relation, with $F = A \cup S \cup J \cup E_s \cup E_e$, such that*

- $C = \{(c_1, c_2) \in F \times F \mid c_1 \neq c_2 \wedge c_1 \notin E_e \wedge c_2 \notin E_s\}$,
- $\forall a \in A \cup J \cup E_s : |\{(a, b) \in C \mid b \in F\}| = 1$,
- $\forall a \in A \cup S \cup E_e : |\{(b, a) \in C \mid b \in F\}| = 1$,
- $\forall a \in J : |\{(b, a) \in C \mid b \in F\}| \geq 2$,
- $\forall a \in S : |\{(a, b) \in C \mid b \in F\}| \geq 2$, *and*
- *all elements* $e \in F$ *in the graph* (F, C) *are on a path from a start event* $a \in E_s$ *to an end event* $b \in E_e$.

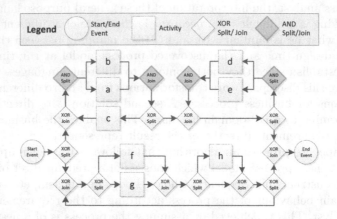

Fig. 1. Example business process with all element types included

A block-structured BP model is a refinement of Definition 1. It is additionally required that the process is hierarchically structured, i.e. every split element is mapped to exactly one join and vice-versa, both representing either a single entry or a single exit point of a non-sequence BP construct, e.g. Choice, Parallel, etc. A very similar representation is the *process tree*, which is defined based on Petri nets/workflow nets in [5].

A computer-aided execution of a business process is recorded in an *event log* containing transaction details for each event. In this paper we only focus on a minimal set of event features necessary for the discovery of the control-flow. Every event needs to have a reference to its *process instance*, e.g. via identifier, and to the corresponding *activity*, e.g. via unique name. All resulting events of a single process instance execution are captured in a *trace*. Accordingly, an event is represented by a pair (t, a) where t links to the trace and a to the activity. Since two traces are assumed to be independent from each other only the order of the activities within a trace is of interest.

Definition 2. *Let A be a finite set of activities then $\sigma \in A^*$ is a trace[1] and $L \subseteq A^*$ is an event log, more specifically L is a multi-set (bag)[2] of traces (sequences of activities). A finite sequence over A of length n is a mapping $\sigma : \{0, 1, ..., n-1\} \rightarrow A$ and is represented in the following by a string, i.e. $\sigma = [a_0, a_1, ..., a_{n-1}]$ where $a_i = \sigma(i)$ for $0 \le i < n$. $|\sigma| = n$ denotes the length of the sequence.*

Traces only consisting of the activity order are called *simple traces* and event logs only consisting of simple traces are called *simple event logs* [13]. An example of a simple event log for the business process in Figure 1 is[3]

---

[1] A^* is the set of finite sequences of elements of A.

[2] Since L is a multi-set each trace can be contained more than once - see [13].

[3] The power values denote the respective occurrences of the traces in the log, e.g. trace $[b, a]$ occurs 4 times in the log.

$$L_1 = \{[b,a]^4, [a,b,d,e]^5, [b,a,e,d]^4, [b,a,c,a,b,c,b,a,d,e,e,d]^6,$$
$$[g,g]^2, [f,h]^3, [f,f,h,f,g,h,g,f,h]^8, [g,h,f]^2\} \tag{1}$$

3 State of the Art

Process discovery is concerned with extracting a business process model from an event log without using any a-priori information [13]. Generally, process discovery is an umbrella term comprising the discovery of all perspectives of a business process, however, in this paper we focus on the discovery of only the control-flow perspective. Usually, the goal of business process standards like BPMN or EPC is to provide a means to build design-time models, and focus on aspects like interoperability, or being a basis for reliable communication between different stakeholders [2]. However, a process model extracted via process discovery instead reflects the actual business process at run-time. Since it is not known beforehand which standard the process to be mined conforms to, process discovery approaches are usually creating models conforming to general purpose representations, e.g. Petri nets [8], Causal nets [10]. A large number of process discovery algorithms exist, each with its own respective strengths and weaknesses. Many of them have in common that at first a *footprint* of the log is created based on which the process is then constructed. In all cases known to the authors, the footprint is represented by a *direct neighbours* matrix containing information about the local relations between the activities, e.g. for the BP of Figure 1: c can only appear after a or b. In this section we want to briefly discuss discovery algorithms that are close to the CCM in concept or purpose.

A few discovery algorithms exist that discover blocked-structured processes: (1) A number of genetic process discovery algorithms restrict the search space to block-structured process models, thus creating structured process trees, e.g. [1]. However, these are non-deterministic and can not guarantee to find a suitable model in finite run-time. (2) Another approach that is conceptually similar to the CCM is proposed in [5], the Inductive Miner (IM). Here a top-down approach is followed to discover block-structured Petri nets. The original algorithm evaluates constraints based on local relationships between activities in order to identify the representing construct. Furthermore, the IM has been extended in order to deal with noise [6]. (3) A third option to create block-structured processes from a log is the discovery of an arbitrary Petri net followed by a transformation into a block-structured process as shown in [9].

Different approaches exist to deal with noise or logs that do not conform to the target process language: (1) a simple technique is to pre-filter the log and remove non-frequent traces. This technique may improve the readability of a general purpose target language like Petri net but is not always applicable for a restricted target language since it could still contain non-expressible behaviour. (2) The fuzzy miner [4] works on a similar principal. Based on correlations and significance it reduces the "exact" model to a simplified model that still supports the main behaviour of the process. (3) A very prominent process discovery algorithm is the HeuristicsMiner which mines a causal net that can be transformed into a more common process representation [10]. Similar to our approach, the footprint used in the HeuristicsMiner is not based on absolute relations between activities but on relative relation values. By increasing certain thresholds a simplification can be achieved.

4   Constructs Competition Miner

In this section we describe the specifics of the Constructs Competition Miner. The motivation to develop a discovery algorithm, which makes different BP constructs compete with each other for the best solution, is derived from the challenge that logs often contain noise or even have frequent but conflicting behaviour. This cannot be expressed by common BP constructs without allowing duplicated activities. In uncertain cases the algorithm should look for the best solution which can support most of the behaviour, i.e. sequence, choice, parallelism, or loop or a combinations of these. Another important part of the CCM is that it is not based on local relationships like *direct neighbours* but rather mines the process structure from global relationships between any two activities, e.g. which activities eventually follow one another in a trace. This approach has the benefit of avoiding a state-space explosion for logs of strongly connected BPs and will be of further benefit for the competition algorithm.

The CCM works in recursive divide-and-conquer fashion. First, a footprint over all activities A from the event log is created. Based on this the suitability between any two activities $x, y \in A$ with regards to each available construct is calculated. The suitability calculation is based on evaluating "soft" constraints for the global activity relations captured in the footprint, e.g. activity x is eventually followed by y. The goal of the subsequent competition algorithm is to find the best combination of (1) the construct type, e.g. Sequence, Choice, or Loop, and (2) the best two subsets A_{first} and A_{second} of A with $A_{first} \cup A_{second} = A$ and $A_{first} \cap A_{second} = \{\}$, that best accommodates all corresponding x, y-pair relations. If it is decided which construct to apply, the corresponding BP structure is created, e.g. AND-split and -join if the winning construct was Parallelism. Via a recursive call the two subsets A_{first} and A_{second} are then analysed in the same way as described before, i.e. a footprint for the subset is created, construct suitability calculated, etc. Note that every supported construct has to split the set in two non-empty subsets. This recursion continues until the set cannot be divided any more, i.e. the set consists of a single activity, in which case this recursively called method successfully returns after creating the construct for the single activity. The block-structured process is completely constructed if the method call at the top of the recursion returns successfully.

4.1   Footprint

The CCM creates multiple footprints during its execution. At the beginning the overall footprint for all occurring activities has to be created.

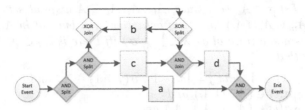

Fig. 2. Example business process with two nested parallel constructs

As the algorithm continues in its divide-and-conquer fashion, new activity subsets are built for each of which a new footprint has to be created, e.g. for $A = \{a, b, c, d, e\}$: $(a, b, c, d, e) \rightarrow ((a, b, c), (d, e)) \rightarrow (((a), (b, c)), ((d), (e))) \rightarrow (((a), ((b), (c))), ((d), (e)))^4$ nine different footprints for sets $\{a, b, c, d, e\}, \{a, b, c\}, \{d, e\}, \{b, c\}, \{a\}, \{b\}, \{c\}, \{d\}, \{e\}$ need to be created. For reasons motivated earlier we focus on global relations between the different activities (e.g. in how many traces will x be followed at some later point in the trace by activity y) and occurrence information about single activities (e.g. how many times does activity x appear in the log). The set of activities the footprint is to be calculated for is denoted by $A_m \subseteq A$. Furthermore, if the elements of A_m are encompassed by one or more parallelism constructs, two more sets need to be specified:

- $A_i \subset A$ is the set of activities that are to be ignored, i.e. the occurrence of these activities do neither directly nor indirectly interfere with the occurrence of the activities in A_m and are to be ignored (e.g. from a distant parallel path).
- $A_t \subset A$ is the set of activities that are to be tolerated, i.e. the occurrence of these activities do not directly interfere with the occurrence of the activities in A_m but indicate that the enclosing parallelism construct has been entered (e.g. from a local parallel path).

Note that A_m, A_i, A_t are disjoint sets of activities. A_i, A_t are empty if the activities in A_m are not on a parallel path. To distinguish between the different activity sets consider the process in Figure 2. If we want to create the footprint for the top path with activity b, the three sets would be configured in the following way: $A_m = \{b\}, A_i = \{a\}, A_t = \{c\}$, because a is on a distant parallel path and c on a local parallel path in relation to b. The distinction between A_i and A_t is that elements in A_i are truly independent from the elements in A_m, but elements in A_t trigger the path in which elements of A_m reside as well. This is important to identify if a parallel path is optional like in our example where b does not appear in every trace.

To enable the CCM to discover the process from top till bottom we require the notion of a sub-trace which later on helps in determining the footprint for a subset A_m of all the activities A in a log:

---

^{4} $(,)$ denote the nested blocks that emerge while splitting the sets recursively.

Definition 3. *Let* $\sigma \in A^*$ *be a trace,* $A_m, A_i, A_t \subseteq A$ *disjoint sets of activities, and* $A_r = A\backslash(A_m \cup A_i \cup A_t)$ *the set of activities in* A *but not in* $A_m, A_i,$ *or* A_t. *Then* $\lambda \in A_m^*$ *is a sub-trace of* σ *($\lambda \sqsubseteq_{A_i,A_t}^{A_m} \sigma$) iff there is* $i, j \in \{0, 1, ..., |\sigma| - 1\}$ *and* $i < j$ *such that*

- $i = 0 \vee \sigma(i-1) \in A_r$ *and* $j = |\sigma| - 1 \vee \sigma(j+1) \in A_r$ *and*
- $\exists_{l \in \{i,i+1,...,j\}} \sigma(l) \in (A_m \cup A_i)$ *and*
- $\forall_{l \in \{i,i+1,...,j\}} \sigma(l) \in (A_m \cup A_i \cup A_t)$ *and*
- $(|\lambda| = 0) \vee$
  $(|\lambda| = 1 \wedge \exists_{l \in \{i,i+1,...,j\}}(\sigma(l) = \lambda(0) \wedge \forall_{n \in \{i,i+1,...,j\}, n \neq l} \sigma(n) \notin A_m)) \vee$
  $(|\lambda| > 1 \wedge \forall_{k \in \{0,1,...,|\lambda|-2\}} \exists_{l,n \in \{i,i+1,...,j\}, l<n}(\sigma(l) = \lambda(k) \wedge \sigma(n) = \lambda(k+1) \wedge$
  $\hspace{5cm} \forall_{p \in \{l+1,l+2,...,n-1\}} \sigma(p) \notin A_m)).$

If we consider again the example in Figure 2 and a corresponding trace $\sigma = [b, c, a, b, d]$ then $\lambda = [b, c, a, b, d]$ is a sub-trace of σ for $\sqsubseteq_{\{\},\{\}}^{\{a,b,c,d\}}$, $\lambda = [b, c, b, d]$ is a sub-trace of σ for $\sqsubseteq_{\{\},\{a\}}^{\{b,c,d\}}$, and $\lambda = [b, b]$ is a sub-trace of σ for $\sqsubseteq_{\{a\},\{c\}}^{\{b\}}$. If we instead consider the trace $\sigma = [c, a, d]$ then only the empty trace $\lambda = []$ represents the sub-sequence of σ for $\sqsubseteq_{\{a\},\{c\}}^{\{b\}}$ because a appeared and indicated that the top path has been enabled as well but exited without any occurrence of b. Note, that $\sigma \sqsubseteq_{\{\},\{\}}^{A} \sigma$, i.e. if the set of activities that are to be monitored is the set of all activities in the trace then the trace itself is the sub-trace. Also, in the case of a loop behaviour contained in a trace, the original trace may produce more than one sub-trace for a subset of activities that reside in the loop, e.g. for trace $\sigma = [b, a, c, a, b, c, b, a, d, e, e, d]$ from L_1 on page 137, the following three sequences are sub-traces of σ for $\sqsubseteq_{\{\},\{\}}^{\{a,b\}}$: $[b, a], [a, b]$, and again $[b, a]$.

The purpose of the definition of a sub-trace is that we can later on discover the best suited BP control-flow construct for the complete traces but also sub-traces corresponding to a subset of all involved activities. In order to build the footprint for sub-traces we furthermore introduce the following notations:

Definition 4. *Let* $L \subseteq A^*$ *be an event log over* A, $A_m, A_i, A_t \subseteq A$ *a disjoint sets of activities specifying the scope of the notations, and* $\Lambda_{A_i,A_t}^{L,A_m} = \{\lambda \mid \lambda \in A_m^* \wedge \lambda \sqsubseteq_{A_i,A_t}^{A_m} \sigma \wedge \sigma \in L\}$ *be a multi-set of all sub-traces in* L *specified by* $A_m, A_i,$ *and* A_t. *Let activity* $x \in A_m$, *then is:*

1. $Once_{A_i,A_t}^{L,A_m}(x) = \{\lambda \in \Lambda_{A_i,A_t}^{L,A_m} \mid \exists_{i \in \{0,1,...|\lambda|-1\}} \lambda(i) = x\},$
2. $Sum_{A_i,A_t}^{L,A_m}(x) = \{(\lambda, l) \mid \lambda \in \Lambda_{A_i,A_t}^{L,A_m} \wedge \lambda(l) = x\},$
3. $Start_{A_i,A_t}^{L,A_m}(x) = \{\lambda \in \Lambda_{A_i,A_t}^{L,A_m} \mid \lambda(0) = x\}.$

Let $x, y \in A_m$, *then is:*

1. $x >_{A_i,A_t}^{L,A_m} y$ *iff a sub-trace* $\lambda \in \Lambda_{A_i,A_t}^{L,A_m}$ *and* $i, j \in \{0, 1, ..., |\lambda| - 1\}$ *and* $i < j$ *exists such that* $\lambda(i) = x$ *and* $\lambda(j) = y$ *and* $\forall_{k \in \{0,1,...,j-1\}} \lambda(k) \neq y,$
2. $x >>_{A_i,A_t}^{L,A_m} y$ *iff a sub-trace* $\lambda \in \Lambda_{A_i,A_t}^{L,A_m}$ *and* $i, j \in \{0, 1, ..., |\lambda| - 1\}$ *and* $i < j$ *exists such that* $\lambda(i) = x$ *and* $\lambda(j) = y,$
3. $|x >_{A_i,A_t}^{L,A_m} y|$ *the number of occurrences of* $x >_{A_i,A_t}^{L,A_m} y$ *in* L,
4. $|x >>_{A_i,A_t}^{L,A_m} y|$ *the number of occurrences of* $x >>_{A_i,A_t}^{L,A_m} y$ *in* L.

For $A_m = A = \{a, b, c, d\}$ consider the following log $L_2 = \{[a, b, c, d]^2, [b, a, c, b, d]^1\}$:

- $|Once_{A_i,A_t}^{L,A_m}(x)|$ determines how many of the sub-traces contained x, e.g.
  $|Once_{\{\},\{\}}^{L_2,\{a,b,c,d\}}(b)| = 3$ (twice from $[a, b, c, d]^2$ and once from $[b, a, c, b, d]^1$);
- $|Sum_{A_i,A_t}^{L,A_m}(x)|$ represents how many x were in all sub-traces, e.g.
  $|Sum_{\{\},\{\}}^{L_2,\{a,b,c,d\}}(b)| = 4$ (2 from $[a, b, c, d]^2$ + 2 from $[b, a, c, b, d]^1$);
- $|Start_{A_i,A_t}^{L,A_m}(x)|$ tells us how many times the sub-trace started with x, e.g.
  $|Start_{\{\},\{\}}^{L_2,\{a,b,c,d\}}(b)| = 1$ (only $[b, a, c, b, d]^1$ started with b)
- $|x >_{A_i,A_t}^{L,A_m} y|$ determines the amount of sub-traces in which x at some point appeared before the first occurrence of y, e.g.
  $|a >_{\{\},\{\}}^{L_2,\{a,b,c,d\}} b| = 2$ (only in $[a, b, c, d]^2$ a appears before the first b)
- $|x >>_{A_i,A_t}^{L,A_m} y|$ determines the amount of sub-traces in which x is occurring at some point before any y, e.g.
  $|a >>_{\{\},\{\}}^{L_2,\{a,b,c,d\}} b| = 3$ (twice from $[a, b, c, d]^2$ and once from $[b, a, c, b, d]^1$).

With the help of these absolute values the footprint can now be calculated by putting them in relation to the number of all sub-traces. Then based on these values the CCM performs a construct analysis which in turn enables the execution of the competition between these constructs.

Definition 5. *Let $L \subseteq A^*$ be an event log over A, $A_m, A_i, A_t \subseteq A$ disjoint sets of activities specifying the scope of the footprint, $|\Lambda_{A_i,A_t}^{L,A_m}|$ be the number of sub-traces in L specified by $A_m, A_i,$ and A_t. Let $x \in A_m$:*

- *The **occurrence once** value $Oon_{A_i,A_t}^{L,A_m}(x)$ and the **occurrence overall** value $Oov_{A_i,A_t}^{L,A_m}(x)$ are calculated as follows:*

$$Oon_{A_i,A_t}^{L,A_m}(x) = \frac{|Once_{A_i,A_t}^{L,A_m}(x)|}{|\Lambda_{A_i,A_t}^{L,A_m}|} \qquad Oov_{A_i,A_t}^{L,A_m}(x) = \frac{|Sum_{A_i,A_t}^{L,A_m}(x)|}{|\Lambda_{A_i,A_t}^{L,A_m}|} \qquad (2)$$

- *The **first element** value $Fel_{A_i,A_t}^{L,A_m}(x)$ is calculated with the following equation:*

$$Fel_{A_i,A_t}^{L,A_m}(x) = \frac{|Start_{A_i,A_t}^{L,A_m}(x)|}{|\Lambda_{A_i,A_t}^{L,A_m}|} \qquad (3)$$

*Let $x, y \in A_m$ then is the **appears before first** value $x \triangleright_{A_i,A_t}^{L,A_m} y$ and the **appears before** value $x \triangleright \triangleright_{A_i,A_t}^{L,A_m} y$ calculated as follows:*

$$x \triangleright_{A_i,A_t}^{L,A_m} y = \frac{|x >_{A_i,A_t}^{L,A_m} y|}{|\Lambda_{A_i,A_t}^{L,A_m}|} \qquad x \triangleright \triangleright_{A_i,A_t}^{L,A_m} y = \frac{|x >>_{A_i,A_t}^{L,A_m} y|}{|\Lambda_{A_i,A_t}^{L,A_m}|} \qquad (4)$$

All values of Oon_{A_i,A_t}^{L,A_m}, Fel_{A_i,A_t}^{L,A_m}, $\triangleright_{A_i,A_t}^{L,A_m}$, and $\triangleright\triangleright_{A_i,A_t}^{L,A_m}$ will be ≥ 0 and ≤ 1 since each of their relation can occur at most once per sub-trace. However, the values of $Oov_{A_i,A_t}^{L,A_m}(x)$ can become greater than 1 if activity x occurs on average more than once per sub-trace. The complete footprint consisting of Oon, Oov, Fel, $\triangleright$, and $\triangleright\triangleright$ is in this paper displayed as labelled vectors for the values of Oon, Oov, and Fel and as labelled matrices for the values of $\triangleright$ and $\triangleright\triangleright$. If we now consider again log L_1 from page 137 then its complete footprint $FP_{\{\},\{\}}^{L_1,A}$ for $A_m = A = \{a, b, c, d, e, f, g, h\}$ is:

$$Oon_{\{\},\{\}}^{L_1,A}(x): \begin{pmatrix} a & b & c & d & e & f & g & h \\ 0.56 & 0.56 & 0.18 & 0.44 & 0.44 & 0.38 & 0.35 & 0.44 \end{pmatrix}$$

$$Oov_{\{\},\{\}}^{L_1,A}(x): \begin{pmatrix} a & b & c & d & e & f & g & h \\ 0.91 & 0.91 & 0.35 & 0.62 & 0.62 & 1.09 & 0.65 & 0.85 \end{pmatrix}$$

$$Fel_{\{\},\{\}}^{L_1,A}(x): \begin{pmatrix} a & b & c & d & e & f & g & h \\ 0.15 & 0.41 & 0.00 & 0.00 & 0.00 & 0.32 & 0.12 & 0.00 \end{pmatrix}$$

$x \triangleright_{\{\},\{\}}^{L_1,A} y :$

	a	b	c	d	e	f	g	h
a	0.18	0.32	0.18	0.44	0.44	0	0	0
b	0.41	0.18	0.18	0.44	0.44	0	0	0
c	0.18	0.18	0.18	0.18	0.18	0	0	0
d	0	0	0	0.18	0.32	0	0	0
e	0	0	0	0.29	0.18	0	0	0
f	0	0	0	0	0	0.24	0.24	0.32
g	0	0	0	0	0	0.29	0.29	0.29
h	0	0	0	0	0	0.29	0.24	0.24

$x \triangleright\triangleright_{\{\},\{\}}^{L_1,A} y :$

	a	b	c	d	e	f	g	h
a	0	0.15	0.18	0.44	0.44	0	0	0
b	0.41	0	0.18	0.44	0.44	0	0	0
c	0	0	0	0.18	0.18	0	0	0
d	0	0	0	0	0.32	0	0	0
e	0	0	0	0.18	0	0	0	0
f	0	0	0	0	0	0	0.24	0.32
g	0	0	0	0	0	0.06	0	0.06
h	0	0	0	0	0	0.06	0.24	0

Definition 6. *Let $L \subseteq A^*$ be an event log over A, $A_m, A_i, A_t \subseteq A$ disjoint sets of activities specifying the scope of the footprint FP, then is*

$$FP_{A_i,A_t}^{L,A_m} = (Oon_{A_i,A_t}^{L,A_m}, Oov_{A_i,A_t}^{L,A_m}, Fel_{A_i,A_t}^{L,A_m}, \triangleright_{A_i,A_t}^{L,A_m}, \triangleright\triangleright_{A_i,A_t}^{L,A_m}) \qquad (5)$$

4.2   Suitability of Supported BP-Constructs

If we consider the footprint from page 142 we can already identify that the activity sets $\{a, b, c, d, e\}$ and $\{f, g, h\}$ are in a Choice construct because all values between the two sets in the $\triangleright\triangleright$ matrix are 0.[5] We can additionally see in the $\triangleright\triangleright$ matrix that $\{a, b, c\}$ and $\{d, e\}$ are in a Sequence construct because d and e are never followed by a, b, or c, but a, b, and c can be followed by d or e. The CCM works similarly to how we identified a Decision and a Sequence construct in the example footprint: Based on the footprint FP_{A_i,A_t}^{L,A_m}, the algorithm identifies the BP construct that best describes the footprint with the help of constraints. The construct which fulfills its respective constraints best will be chosen to be part of the BP model.

As an example, the constraint for the Choice construct (i.e. two activities being mutually exclusive) requires the appears-before values between the respective

---

[5] i.e. none the of activities $\{f, g, h\}$ ever follows or is followed by any of the activities $\{a, b, c, d, e\}$ in a trace.

activities to be "equal to 0". However, in order to handle noise well, the CCM uses the following definition of equality for checking the fulfilment of constraints:

Definition 7. *Let v be the actual value, t be the target value, p be the maximum penalty for a not fulfilled unequal relation, t_t the tolerance which determines the maximum difference so that v and t are still considered equal, and $v, t, p, t_t \in \mathbb{R}^+$:*

$$(v \ncong t) = \begin{cases} p * (\frac{2*t_t}{|v-t|+t_t} - 1)^2 & if \quad |v-t| < t_t \\ 0 & else \end{cases}$$

$$(v \cong t) = \begin{cases} 0 & if \quad |v-t| < t_t \\ |v-t|^2 & else \end{cases}$$

(6)

Note: Since the analysis in the remainder of this section is based on one specific footprint FP_{A_i,A_t}^{L,A_m}, if not otherwise stated we will denote FP_{A_i,A_t}^{L,A_m}, Oon_{A_i,A_t}^{L,A_m}, Oov_{A_i,A_t}^{L,A_m}, Fel_{A_i,A_t}^{L,A_m}, $\triangleright_{A_i,A_t}^{L,A_m}$, and $\triangleright\triangleright_{A_i,A_t}^{L,A_m}$ simply as FP, Oon, Oov, Fel, $\triangleright$, and $\triangleright\triangleright$ for the remainder of this section to support the readability.

Construct Suitability for a Single Activity: If a footprint consists of only one activity, i.e. $|A_m| = 1$, no competition between constructs is necessary. Instead, the correct construct is identified based on the values in the footprint. Four different constructs for a single activity $x \in A_m$ exist[6]:

- *Normal:* if $(Fel(x) \cong 1) = 0$ and $(x \triangleright \triangleright x \cong 0) = 0$ then x is a simple activity.
- *Optional:* if $(Fel(x) \cong 1) > 0$ and $(x \triangleright \triangleright x \cong 0) = 0$ then x is an optional activity, i.e. x may also be skipped.
- *Loopover:* if $(Fel(x) \cong 1) = 0$ and $(x \triangleright \triangleright x \cong 0) > 0$ then x is a looping activity, i.e. x can repeatedly occur after itself ("short loop").
- *Loopback:* if $(Fel(x) \cong 1) > 0$ and $(x \triangleright \triangleright x \cong 0) > 0$ then x is an optional looping activity, i.e. x may be skipped but can also repeatedly occur.

Construct Suitability for Multiple Activities: If a footprint FP consists of more than one activity, i.e. $|A_m| > 1$, a preliminary analysis is carried out to identify the suitability of any two activities $x, y \in A_m$ with regards to each available construct, e.g. activities x and y are in a very strong Parallelism relation but less strong in a Sequence relation. The calculation of this construct's suitability is again based on constraints. If a constraint is not fulfilled there will be a penalty depending on the "level" of the constraint[7] and how strong it has failed.

The first step of the suitability analysis is to identify if the construct represented by the FP is optional, i.e. an optional path exists that allows to bypass this construct. If this is the case the FP needs to be normalized, i.e. removal of the overall optional behaviour. For this purpose it is calculated if and to what extent the FP also recorded empty (sub-)traces, i.e. relative occurrence of an empty (sub-)trace: $op_{FP} = 1 - \sum_{x \in A_m} Fel(x)$. The influence of these empty

---

[6] $>$ is in this case the common greater relation, not the one specified in Definition 4.
[7] The levels of constraints will be discussed later in this section.

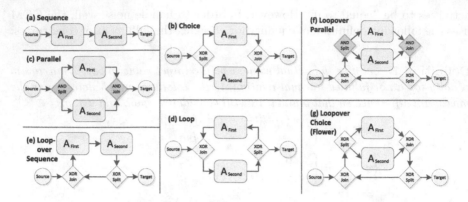

Fig. 3. Supported Business Process Constructs

traces is removed from the FP by multiplying every value of $Oon, Oov, Fel, \triangleright$, and $\triangleright\triangleright$ with $\frac{1}{1-op}$.

Additionally, the following values are calculated for each $x \in A_m$ and each $x, y \in A_m$ pair:

Definition 8. *Let $x \in A_m$ be an activity recorded in FP then is the repetition of x in FP denoted $rep(x) = \frac{Oov(x) - Oon(x)}{Oov(x)}$.*

Definition 9. *Let $x, y \in A_m$ be activities recorded in FP then is (1) the percentage of (sub-)traces in which both x and y appear: $oc(x, y) = x \triangleright y + y \triangleright x$, (2) the maximum possible occurrence of x and y appearing in the same trace: $moc(x, y) = min(Oon(x), Oon(y))$, and (3) the combined occurrence of x and y: $coc(x, y) = Oon(x) * Oon(y)$.*

The algorithm supports the identification of the BP constructs shown in Figure 3. For each construct a set of constraints have been formulated to determine to which degree a construct represents the global relation between any two activities. In Table 1 the constraints for each construct are listed, sorted by the constraint level. We distinguish between different levels/severities of constraints to highlight the importance of their fulfilment: (1) **Strict**: Constraints of this type can be seen as "iff" requirements on the construct and are thus required to be fulfilled for a construct to apply, e.g. every activity in a Loop construct has to occur at least once repeatedly in a trace, otherwise the observed construct cannot be a Loop. Penalties originating from the failure of constraints of this type have a strong influence on the suitability of a construct relation; (2) **Log-Complete**: A log-complete constraint is fulfilled when all variants are represented in the log, i.e. the log is complete. If the log is incomplete constraints of this type may fail. This is why penalties originating from the failure of log-complete constraints have a medium influence on the suitability of a construct relation; (3) **Indication**: An indication constraint represents default behaviour of the construct but may not be fulfilled even in a complete log. Indication constraints are basically

Table 1. Supported BP-constructs and their constraints sorted by constraint level

Construct	Strict	Log-Complete	Indication
Choice	$x \triangleright \triangleright y \cong 0$, $y \triangleright \triangleright x \cong 0$	-	-
Sequence	$x \triangleright \triangleright y \not\cong 0$, $y \triangleright \triangleright x \cong 0$, $x \triangleright \triangleright y \cong x \triangleright y$	-	-
Parallel	-	$x \triangleright y \not\cong 0$, $y \triangleright x \not\cong 0$, $coc(x,y) \cong oc(x,y)$	$x \triangleright \triangleright y \cong$ $(x \triangleright y + min(rep(x), rep(y)))$ $*(moc(x,y) - x \triangleright y)$
Loop	$rep(x) \not\cong 0$, $rep(y) \not\cong 0$	$x \triangleright \triangleright y \cong coc(x,y)$, $y \triangleright \triangleright x \cong coc(x,y)$	-
Loopover-Sequence	$rep(x) \not\cong 0$, $rep(y) \not\cong 0$	$x \triangleright \triangleright y \cong coc(x,y)$, $y \triangleright \triangleright x \not\cong coc(x,y)$, $x \triangleright \triangleright y \not\cong y \triangleright \triangleright x$	-
Loopover-Parallel	$rep(x) \not\cong 0$, $rep(y) \not\cong 0$	$x \triangleright y \not\cong 0$, $y \triangleright x \not\cong 0$, $coc(x,y) \cong oc(x,y)$	$x \triangleright \triangleright y \cong$ $(x \triangleright y * Oon(y) + Oov(y) - Oon(y))$ $/ Oov(y)$
Loopover-Choice (Flower)	$rep(x) \not\cong 0$, $rep(y) \not\cong 0$, $coc(x,y) \not\cong 1$	$x \triangleright y \not\cong 0$, $y \triangleright x \not\cong 0$	$x \triangleright \triangleright y \cong y \triangleright \triangleright x$, $coc(x,y) \cong max(0,$ $Oon(y) + Oon(y) - 1)$

not constraints in the common sense but rather approximations of default behaviour in order to distinguish between two very similar constructs, e.g. Parallel and Loopover-Parallel. Penalties originating from the failure of constraints of this type have a low influence on the overall suitability.

Based on the constraints listed in Table 1 and their respective constraint level the suitability of each construct for any activity pair $x, y \in A_m, x \neq y$ is calculated. Exemplary, we show how values for the constructs Choice $Ch(x,y)$ and Sequence $Ch(x,y)$ are calculated ($w_s \in \mathbb{R}$ is the weight of Strict constraints):

(1) $Ch(x,y) = w_s * \frac{1}{2} * (x \triangleright \triangleright y \cong 0 + y \triangleright \triangleright x \cong 0)$,

(2) $Se(x,y) = w_s * \frac{1}{3} * (x \triangleright \triangleright y \not\cong 0 + y \triangleright \triangleright x \cong 0 + x \triangleright \triangleright y \cong x \triangleright y)$.

The values for the other constructs are similarly calculated, with $w_{lc}, w_i \in \mathbb{R}$ further specifying the weights for Log-Complete and Indication constraints, respectively. Let us now consider again $FP^{L_1,A}_{\{\},\{\}}$ on page 142: The resulting suitability matrices Ch and Se for $w_s = 0.6$ are:

$Ch(x,y):$

	a	b	c	d	e	f	g	h
a	-	0.26	0.6	0.3	0.3	0	0	0
b	0.26	-	0.6	0.3	0.3	0	0	0
c	0.6	0.6	-	0.3	0.3	0	0	0
d	0.3	0.3	0.3	-	0.29	0	0	0
e	0.3	0.3	0.3	0.29	-	0	0	0
f	0	0	0	0	0	-	0.34	0.39
g	0	0	0	0	0	0.34	-	0.34
h	0	0	0	0	0	0.39	0.34	-

$Se(x,y):$

	a	b	c	d	e	f	g	h
a	-	0.13	0.2	0	0	0.2	0.2	0.2
b	0.07	-	0.2	0	0	0.2	0.2	0.2
c	0.4	0.4	-	0	0	0.2	0.2	0.2
d	0.4	0.4	0.4	-	0.09	0.2	0.2	0.2
e	0.4	0.4	0.4	0.14	-	0.2	0.2	0.2
f	0.2	0.2	0.2	0.2	0.2	-	0.14	0.12
g	0.2	0.2	0.2	0.2	0.2	0.18	-	0.18
h	0.2	0.2	0.2	0.2	0.2	0.22	0.22	-

4.3   Competition Algorithm

The goal of the competition algorithm is to find the best combination of (1) the construct type, e.g. Sequence, Choice, or Loop, and (2) the best two subsets A_{first} and A_{second} of A with $A_{first} \cup A_{second} = A$ and $A_{first} \cap A_{second} = \{\}$, that best accommodates all corresponding x, y-pair relations. We will show the principal of operation of the competition algorithm for the Choice construct, i.e. for the explanation the construct is fixed and the two subsets A_{first} and A_{second} have to be determined. A naive solution would be to create and compare all possible split ups. With regards to the execution time of the CCM, this is not desirable since we would have to check all $2^{|A|} - 1$ possible split ups. Instead we want to take advantage of the fact that our relations, in this case only Ch, represent the global relation of x and y. That means it is irrelevant for the calculation of the penalty what the relations between the elements in the same set are (either A_{first} and A_{second}). In Algorithm 1 is presented how the competition algorithm works if we only consider Ch to be part of the competition. Note that the priority queue is ordered firstly by the penalty value and secondly by how even the split up is (since we want to split as evenly as possible to quickly reduce the number of activities). For Ch from the example log with $A_m = A = \{a, b, c, d, e, f, g, h\}$ the algorithm functions as follows: in first step an "empty" combination tuple $(A_{first}, A_{second}, A_{left}, p)$ is inserted into the priority queue with (1) A_{first} and A_{second}, the both disjunct sets of activities - empty at the beginning; (2) the set of the activities A_{left} which contains the activities that still have to be assigned to either the first or second set - $A_{left} = A = \{a, b, c, d, e, f, g, h\}$; (3) the current penalty $p = 0$. With this one element in the priority queue the while-loop is entered. There, the tuple with the highest priority (the one that was just inserted) is removed from the queue and further processed. That means in our case an activity is removed from A_{left} and assigned to x. Now, two more tuples are created, one with x in A_{first} and one with x in A_{second}. According to the set x was inserted into, all Ch values from x to elements from the other set are checked and the average of these is added to the respective penalty value p. Both newly created tuples are then inserted into the priority queue. This continues until the best combination tuple has no activities left, i.e. $A_{left} = \{\}$. In Figure 4 the different created combinations for our example are shown: the light grey combinations are still in the queue when the algorithm terminates, the grey combinations are already processed and the number next to them represents the order in which they were processed; the black combination is the winner of the competition algorithm.

More BP Constructs can enter the competition by three simple modifications of the algorithm: (1) the tuple in the priority queue also has to contain the construct type, e.g. Choice, Loopover-Sequence,etc. (2) adding one "empty" tuple per construct to the priority queue before the while loop is entered; (3) The penalty calculation then has to be carried out on the relation matrix corresponding to the currently processed construct type.

Algorithm 1: Competition Algorithm for the Choice Construct

```
    Data: A, Ch
    Result: A_first, A_second
 1  begin
 2  |   PriorityQueue openCases ← {};
 3  |   openCases.add(({}, {}, A, .0));
 4  |   while true do
 5  |   |   (A_first, A_second, A_left, p) ← openCases.poll();
 6  |   |   if A_left = {} then return(A_first, A_second) ;
 7  |   |   x ← A_left·poll();
 8  |   |   if |A_left| > 0 ∨ |A_second| > 0 then
 9  |   |   |   A_new ← A_first ∪ {x};
10  |   |   |   p_new ← 0;
11  |   |   |   foreach y ∈ A_second do p_new ← p_new + Ch(x, y) ;
12  |   |   |   if p_new > 0 then p_new ← p_new / |A_second| + p ;
13  |   |   |   else p_new ← p ;
14  |   |   |   openCases.add((A_new, A_second, A_left, p_new));
15  |   |   end
16  |   |   if |A_left| > 0 ∨ |A_first| > 0 then
17  |   |   |   A_new ← A_second ∪ {x};
18  |   |   |   p_new ← 0;
19  |   |   |   foreach y ∈ A_first do p_new ← p_new + Ch(y, x) ;
20  |   |   |   if p_new > 0 then p_new ← p_new / |A_first| + p ;
21  |   |   |   else p_new ← p ;
22  |   |   |   openCases.add((A_first, A_new, A_left, p_new));
23  |   |   end
24  |   end
25  end
```

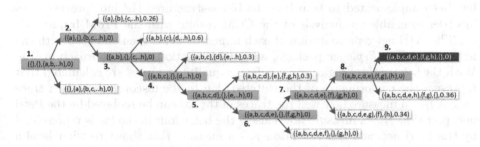

Fig. 4. Competition Algorithm: Traversing to the best split up

5   Evaluation

In this section we evaluate the CCM - first qualitatively and later in comparison to other miners. We have carried out a number of conceptual process rediscover tests, for which we created 67 example processes, each consisting of a small number of activities nested in a combination of BP constructs. These conceptual processes were simulated to produce a corresponding log, which in turn was analysed with the CCM. The tolerance of the CCM was set to $t_t = 0.001$ and the unequal penalty to $p = 1.0$ (see Definition 7). The CCM rediscovered all but 4 of the conceptual processes or found a model with equivalent behaviour. The not successfully rediscovered models were variations of the Loopover-Parallel construct that had at least one loop in the parallel paths.

In the second part of the evaluation, we carried out an analysis of the CCM's performance in comparison to other similar algorithms with the help of the ProM framework [15]. Implementations of the HeuristicsMiner (HM), state-of-the-art

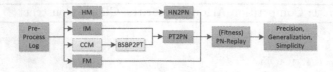

Fig. 5. Experimental Workflow

version of the Inductive Miner (IM), and the Flower Miner (FM) are readily available in the nightly build of ProM and were used to benchmark the quality of the models discovered by the CCM. The experimental setup is conceptually shown in Figure 5: (1) The logs were filtered so that only events with the lifecycle "complete" are considered. These logs are available in the XES-format. (2) In a second step each individual miner discovers the process in its representation language using its default settings, i.e. HM creates a heuristic net, IM creates a process tree, CCM creates a block-structured BP, and FM directly creates a Petri net. (3) In Figure 5 the different transformations from the originally mined language to a Petri net representation are shown. Note, that a transformation has been implemented to translate the block-structured BP into process trees in order to enable an analysis of the CCM results with the ProM framework. (4) The Petri net representation of each mined model is then analysed with the help of the *PNetReplayer* package, an implementation of the approach in [14]. With the help of this plugin, three different quality measures are calculated that represent the conformance of the (filtered) log to the discovered model[8]: trace fitness f_{tf} - a measure how well the traces in the log can be replayed by the Petri net, precision f_{pr} - a measure how closely the behaviour in the log is represented by the Petri net, and generalization f_g - a measure that shows to what level a generalization of the log behaviour was achieved [13]. Additionally, all places, transitions, and arcs of the discovered Petri nets are counted and accumulated to a simplicity measure f_s. The following 10 logs have been used for evaluation: (1) $\mathbf{L_1}$ (8 activities, 34 traces, 204 events): log on page 137 (BP model in Figure 1),
(2) **EX5** $(14, 100, 1498)$: example log of a reviewing process[9],
(3) **REP** $(8, 1104, 7733)$: example log of a repair process[9],
(4) **BE1** $(20, 8204, 189242)$, (5) **BE2** $(20, 8206, 132235)$, (6) **BE3** $(20, 8194, 239318)$, (7) **BE4** $(20, 8153, 253784)$, (8) **BE5** $(20, 8190, 151604)$: large logs of strongly nested BPs - artificially generated by a process simulation tool,
(9) **DF** $(18, 100, 3354)$: an incomplete real-life log of an eHealth process [3], and
(10) $\mathbf{FL_A}$ $(10, 13087, 60849)$: a large real-life log from the finance sector[10].

---

[8] Using "Prefixed based A* Cost-based fitness" algorithm with maximum explored states = 200000.

[9] *Exercise5* (EX5) and *repairExample* (REP) are example logs from the ProM website.

[10] Log from the BPI Challenge of 2012 (http://www.win.tue.nl/bpi/2012/challenge) filtered for events that start with "A", e.g. "A_APPROVED", "A_DECLINED", etc.

Table 2. Conformance results of the different discovery algorithms

Log	Trace Fitness f_{tf}				Precision f_{pr}				Generalization f_g				Simplicity f_s			
	HM	IM	FM	CCM	HM	IM	FM	CCM	HM	IM	FM	CCM	HM	IM	FM	CCM
L₁	0.679	0.863	1.0	1.0	0.532	0.529	0.224	0.550	0.638	0.422	0.949	0.654	86	91	33	81
EX5	0.985	0.935	1.0	1.0	0.495	0.560	0.120	0.529	0.931	0.996	0.999	0.998	155	102	51	80
REP	1.0	1.0	1.0	1.0	0.905	0.955	0.209	0.955	0.998	0.999	0.999	0.999	72	46	33	49
BE1	0.991	1.0	1.0	1.0	0.838	0.814	0.081	0.818	0.999	0.999	1.0	0.999	192	132	69	122
BE2	0.924	0.981	1.0	0.998	0.737	0.594	0.087	0.621	1.0	1.0	1.0	1.0	196	156	69	146
BE3	0.822	0.983	1.0	0.999	0.891	0.443	0.073	0.525	1.0	1.0	1.0	1.0	178	149	69	139
BE4	0.876	1.0	1.0	1.0	0.707	0.406	0.067	0.608	1.0	1.0	1.0	1.0	193	173	69	149
BE5	0.942	0.991	1.0	0.822	0.590	0.668	0.089	0.711	1.0	1.0	1.0	1.0	206	181	69	167
DF	1.0	0.911	1.0	0.970	0.563	0.559	0.060	0.588	0.914	0.906	0.982	0.832	177	136	63	121
FL_A	0.974	1.0	1.0	1.0	0.920	0.695	0.227	0.727	0.925	0.825	0.988	0.818	98	62	39	65

The results of the different discovery algorithms applied to the investigated logs are shown in Table 2. Note, that all algorithms were executed using default settings, i.e. choosing other parameters may result in different results. However, in order to provide comparable results also the parameters for the CCM were fixed to $t_t = 0.001$ and $p = 1.0$ for all runs. Compared with HM and IM the CCM scores a generally high trace fitness for the considered logs (always higher than 0.95) with the exception of BE5 for which a trace fitness of only 0.822 was determined. The precision values of the models discovered by CCM are mostly between the respective values scored by HM and IM but always above 0.5 - as expected FM always scores the lowest for precision. Positive exceptions are L_1, BE5, and DF for which CCM scores the highest precision. In terms of the generalization measure, the CCM scores are average in comparison to HM and IM: yielding a high result for the log L_1 but low results for DF and FL_A. Very positive results are achieved if the simplicity measure is considered: the CCM mostly discovers a model consisting of the lowest number of elements (excluding FM): far smaller than the HM models and slightly smaller than the IM models. Generally, it seems that the CCM tends to favour trace fitness, generalization, and simplicity for the cost of a lower precision.

6   Conclusion

This paper introduces and describes the key parts of the Constructs Competition Miner. The main aspects of the miner are: (1) direct discovery of a block-structured BP model conforming to a BP-domain language, (2) handling of noise due to the relative footprint and the relative constraint interpretation - if conflicting behaviour appears the best suitable construct is chosen, (3) usage of the divide-and-conquer principal to avoid overly complicated models, and (4) usage of global relations between activities to identify BP constructs. The evaluation results showed that the CCM approach is able to discover processes of a similar or sometimes even higher quality than other state of the art approaches (e.g. IM, HM). However, the following points are considered to be future work:

- The Loopover-Parallel construct is not always correctly identified - finding a better constraint could improve the results of the CCM.
- Creating constraints for additional constructs, e.g. OR-Split and -join.
- Adapting the CCM for application on an event stream to continuously monitor a live BP execution, i.e. detection of change over time.

References

1. Buijs, J., Van Dongen, B., Van Der Aalst, W.: A genetic algorithm for discovering process trees. In: Evolutionary Computation (CEC), pp. 1–8. IEEE (2012)
2. Dehnert, J., Van Der Aalst, W.: Bridging The Gap Between Business Models And Workflow Specifications. Int. J. Cooperative Inf. Syst. 13, 289–332 (2004)
3. Galushka, M., Gilani, W.: DrugFusion - Retrieval Knowledge Management for Prediction of Adverse Drug Events. In: Abramowicz, W., Kokkinaki, A. (eds.) BIS 2014. LNBIP, vol. 176, pp. 13–24. Springer, Heidelberg (2014)
4. Günther, C.W., van der Aalst, W.M.P.: Fuzzy Mining – Adaptive Process Simplification Based on Multi-perspective Metrics. In: Alonso, G., Dadam, P., Rosemann, M. (eds.) BPM 2007. LNCS, vol. 4714, pp. 328–343. Springer, Heidelberg (2007)
5. Leemans, S.J.J., Fahland, D., van der Aalst, W.M.P.: Discovering Block-Structured Process Models from Event Logs - A Constructive Approach. In: Colom, J.-M., Desel, J. (eds.) PETRI NETS 2013. LNCS, vol. 7927, pp. 311–329. Springer, Heidelberg (2013)
6. Leemans, S., Fahland, D., Van Der Aalst, W.: Discovering Block-Structured Process Models from Event Logs Containing Infrequent Behaviour, In: Business Process Management Workshops 2013, LNBIP, pp. 66–78, Springer (2013)
7. OMG Inc: Business Process Model and Notation (BPMN) Specification 2.0 (2011), http://www.omg.org/spec/BPMN/2.0/PDF (formal January 03, 2011)
8. Petri, C.A.: Kommunikation mit Automaten. PhD thesis. Rheinisch-Westfälisches Institut f. instrumentelle Mathematik (1962)
9. Polyvyanyy, A., García-Bañuelos, L., Fahland, D., Weske, M.: Maximal Structuring of Acyclic Process Models. The Computer Journal 57(1), 12–35 (2014)
10. Weijters, A., Van Der Aalst, W., Alves de Medeiros, A.: Process Mining with the Heuristics Miner-algorithm. BETA Working Paper Series, WP 166, Eindhoven University of Technology (2006)
11. Van Der Aalst, W., Weijters, A., Maruster, L.: Workflow Mining: Discovering Process Models from Event Logs. IEEE Transactions on Knowledge and Data Engineering 16(9), 1128–1142 (2004)
12. Van Der Aalst, W., Ter Hofstede, A.: YAWL: Yet Another Workflow Language (2003)
13. Van Der Aalst, W.: Process Mining - Discovery, Conformance and Enhancement of Business Processes. Springer (2011)
14. Van Der Aalst, W., Adriansyah, A., Van Dongen, B.: Replaying history on process models for conformance checking and performance analysis. WIREs Data Mining and Knowledge Discovery 2(2), 182–192 (2012)
15. Van Dongen, B., De Medeiros, A., Verbeek, H., Weijters, A., Van Der Aalst, W.: The ProM framework: A new era in process mining tool support. Applications and Theory of Petri Nets 2005, pp. 1105–1116 (2005)

Chopping Down Trees vs. Sharpening the Axe – Balancing the Development of BPM Capabilities with Process Improvement

Martin Lehnert, Alexander Linhart, and Maximilian Röglinger

University of Augsburg, FIM Research Center, Augsburg, Germany
{martin.lehnert,alexander.linhart,
maximilian.roeglinger}@fim-rc.de

Abstract. The management and improvement of business processes is an ever-green topic of organizational design. With many techniques and tools for process modeling, execution, and improvement being available, research pays progressively more attention to the organizational impact of business process management (BPM) and the development of BPM capabilities. Despite know-ledge about the capabilities required for successful BPM, there is a lack of guidance on how these BPM capabilities should be developed and balanced with the improvement of individual business processes. As a first step to ad-dress this research gap, we propose a decision model that enables valuating and selecting BPM roadmaps, i.e., portfolios of scheduled projects with different ef-fects on business processes and BPM capabilities. The decision model is grounded in the literature related to project portfolio selection, process perfor-mance measurement, and value-based management. We also provide an exten-sive demonstration example to illustrate how the decision model can be applied.

Keywords: Business Process Management Capabilities, Process Improvement, Value-based Decision-Making.

1 Introduction

Process orientation is a widely adopted paradigm of organizational design and a rec-ognized source of corporate performance [1, 2]. As a result, business process man-agement (BPM) receives constant attention from industry and academia [3, 4]. As many techniques and tools for process modeling, execution, and improvement are available [5], BPM research is shifting its focus toward the organizational impact of BPM and the development of BPM capabilities [6]. This shift makes emerge novel research questions at the intersection of traditional BPM research and BPM research focused on capability development. In this paper, we investigate one of these novel research questions from a project management perspective, namely how the develop-ment of BPM capabilities should be balanced with the improvement of individual business processes.

S. Sadiq, P. Soffer, and H. Völzer (Eds.): BPM 2014, LNCS 8659, pp. 151–167, 2014.
© Springer International Publishing Switzerland 2014

The BPM literature contains many process improvement approaches [7, 8]. Most improvement approaches, by nature, take on a single-process perspective and neglect how to balance the improvement of a single process with the improvement of other processes or the development of BPM capabilities. From a capability perspective, recent research analyzed which capabilities are necessary for successful BPM. For instance, Rosemann and vom Brocke [9] proposed a framework of six factors (e.g., people, information technology, methods, culture, and governance) each of which is supported by a set of capability areas (e.g., process design, process education, or process improvement planning). A similar framework is authored by van Looy et al. [10]. Jurisch et al. [11] identified which capabilities an organization needs to succeed in process change. Though compiling and structuring BPM capabilities, no approach indicates how these capabilities should be developed. The literature related to the BPM capability areas "process improvement planning" and "process program and project planning" provides no guidance either. A tool that is supposed to provide guidance are process and BPM maturity models [12]. While process maturity models deal with the condition of processes in general or distinct process types, BPM maturity models focus on BPM capabilities [9]. However, maturity models are criticized for adhering to a one-size-fits-all approach, i.e., they typically support a single path of maturation that has to be traversed completely and irreversibly without any possibility for customization [6]. Moreover, maturity models are not suited for decision-making purposes [12]. Other authors take on a project management perspective by using project portfolio selection (PPS) techniques [13]. As process improvement and the development of BPM capabilities are achieved via projects, a project management perspective promises to be a sensible option for balancing both endeavors and for providing more flexible guidance than maturity models do. However, existing quantitative approaches based on PPS only deal with areas of BPM that have nothing to do with BPM capabilities.

The preceding analysis reveals the following research gap: First, organizations require more guidance on how they should develop BPM capabilities. Second, they lack approaches that assist with balancing the development of BPM capabilities and the improvement of individual business processes. From a project management perspective, this research gap refers to a PPS and a project scheduling problem. Therefore, our research question is as follows: *Which projects should an organization implement and in which order should it implement these projects to balance the development of BPM capabilities with the improvement of individual business processes?*

As a first step to answer this question, we propose a decision model for valuating and selecting BPM roadmaps in line with economic principles. A BPM roadmap is a portfolio of scheduled projects with different effects on business processes and BPM capabilities. Thereby, a BPM roadmap indicates which process- or BPM-level projects need to be implemented in which order. As the decision model shows characteristics of a model and a method, we adopt a design science research approach [14]. In line with existing reference processes [15], we cover the following phases of design science research: identification of and motivation for the research problem, objectives of a solution, design and development, and evaluation. In the design and development as well as in the evaluation phase, several industry partners were involved, i.e., an IT service provider, a financial service provider, and an IT consultancy.

The paper is organized as follows: As the decision model is located at the intersection of BPM and project management, we sketch the foundations of BPM, process performance measurement, PPS, and value-based management as theoretical background in section 2. We also derive requirements that a solution to the research question should meet (*objectives of a solution*). In section 3, we propose the decision model (*design and development*). In section 4, we report on the evaluation steps conducted so far, particularly on a demonstration example that builds on a prototypical implementation of the decision model and uses the case of an IT service provider (*evaluation*). We conclude by summing up key results, limitations, and pointing to future research.

2   Theoretical Background and Requirements

2.1   Business Process Management and Process Performance Measurement

BPM is "the art and science of overseeing how work is performed in an organization to ensure consistent outcomes and to take advantage of improvement opportunities" [3]. Therefore, BPM combines knowledge from information technology and management sciences [5]. From a lifecycle perspective, BPM includes the identification, definition, modeling, implementation and execution, monitoring and control as well as continuous improvement of processes [3]. BPM deals with all processes of an organization and, thus, constitutes an infrastructure for efficient work [16].

BPM is closely related to capability development, a field that builds on the resource-based view and dynamic capability theory. According to the resource-based view, capabilities refer to the ability to perform a coordinated set of tasks for achieving a particular result [17]. From a dynamic capability theory perspective, capabilities split into operational and dynamic capabilities [18]. Operational capabilities refer to the basic functioning of an organization [19]. Dynamic capabilities help integrate, build, and reconfigure operational capabilities to increase their fit with the environment as well as their effectiveness and efficiency [20]. Processes and their execution are equated with operational capabilities, whereas BPM is treated as a dynamic capability [21].

As for the BPM lifecycle stages monitoring and control as well as improvement, performance indicators are essential for assessing the performance of a process and the effects of redesign projects [3]. Process performance indicators can be grouped according to the Devil's Quadrangle, a framework that consists of the dimensions time, cost, quality, and flexibility [22]. The Devil's Quadrangle earned its name from the fact that improving one dimension has a weakening effect on at least one other dimension [22]. Thereby, it discloses the trade-offs that have to be resolved during process improvement [22]. To apply the Devil's Quadrangle, its dimensions must be operationalized by performance indicators that account for the peculiarities of the context at hand [3]. As for time, a common indicator is the cycle time, i.e., the time for handling a process instance end-to-end [23]. Typical cost indicators are turnover, yield, or revenue. Quality splits into internal and external quality that can be measured in terms of error rates and customer satisfaction, respectively. Flexibility can be measured via waiting or set-up times [24]. Although there are further non-monetary performance dimensions, we focus on the dimensions of the Devil's Quadrangle. We derive the following requirements:

(R.1) *Capability development*: To determine an optimal BPM roadmap, (a) there must be projects that affect an organization's operational capabilities, i.e., its business processes, and projects that help develop BPM as a dynamic capability. Moreover, (b) there must be projects that influence a single business process and projects that affect multiple business processes.

(R.2) *Process performance measurement*: To evaluate the projects contained in a BPM roadmap, (a) the performance of all processes has to be measured according to typical performance dimensions such as those from the Devil's Quadrangle. (b) It must be possible to operationalize each dimension by one or more performance indicators.

2.2   Project Portfolio Selection

PPS is the activity "involved in selecting a portfolio, from available project proposals [...], that meets the organization's stated objectives in a desirable manner without exceeding available resources or violating other constraints" [25]. The PPS process includes five stages: pre-screening, individual project analysis, screening, optimal portfolio selection, and portfolio adjustment [25]. In the pre-screening stage, projects are checked with respect to whether they align with the organization's strategy and/or are mandatory. During individual project analysis, each project is evaluated stand-alone regarding pre-defined criteria. In the screening stage, all projects are eliminated that do not satisfy the pre-defined criteria. The optimal portfolio selection stage determines the project portfolio that meets pre-defined criteria best. This requires a decision model that integrates all criteria and considers interactions among projects [26]. Finally, decision makers may adjust the optimal portfolio based on their knowledge and experience.

Considering interactions among projects is a challenging, but necessary requirement for making reasonable PPS decisions [27]. The current literature focuses on interactions among information technology/information systems (IT/IS) projects as IT/IS projects typically involve higher-order interactions between three or more projects, whereas, in the capital budgeting or R&D context, mostly interactions between two projects are considered [28]. Higher-order interactions among IT/IS projects can be classified according to three dimensions, i.e., inter-temporal vs. intra-temporal, deterministic vs. stochastic, and scheduling vs. no scheduling [26]. Intra-temporal interactions affect the planning of single portfolios, whereas inter-temporal interactions influence today's decision-making based on potential follow-up projects [29]. Inter-temporal interactions result from effects that depend on the sequence in which projects are implemented [30]. Interactions are deterministic if all parameters are assumed to be known with certainty or were estimated as a single value. If parameters are uncertain and follow some probability distribution, interactions are considered as stochastic [31]. Scheduling interactions occur if projects may start at different points. Otherwise, there are no scheduling interactions. Against this background, we derive the following requirement:

(R.3) *Project portfolio selection*: To determine an optimal BPM roadmap, it is necessary (a) to consider only projects that affect processes or BPM capabilities and align with corporate strategy, (b) to evaluate these projects stand-alone prior to portfolio selection, (c) to consider interactions among these projects.

2.3   Value-Based Management

Value-based management, as a substantiation and extension of the shareholder value concept, sets the maximizing of the long-term, sustainable company value as the primary objective for all business activities [32]. The company value is determined based on future cash flows [33]. Value-based management can only be claimed to be implemented if all business activities and decisions on all management levels are aligned with the objective of maximizing the company value. Therefore, companies must not only be able to quantify the company value on the aggregate level, but also the value contribution of individual activities or decisions.

There is a set of objective functions that are used for making decisions in line with value-based management [34]. In case of certainty, decisions can be based on the net present value (NPV) of the future cash flows [35]. In case of risk with risk-neutral decision makers, decisions can be made based on the expected NPV. If the decision makers are risk-averse, decision alternatives can be valuated using the certainty equivalent method or a risk-adjusted interest rate [36]. To comply with value-based management, decisions must be based on cash flows, consider risks, and incorporate the time value of money [34]. This leads to the following requirement:

(R.4) *Value-based management*: The optimal BPM roadmap is the roadmap with the highest value contribution. To determine the value contribution of a BPM roadmap, one has to account (a) for the cash flow effects of the BPM roadmap, (b) the decision makers' risk attitude, and (c) the time value of money.

3   Decision Model

3.1   General Setting and Basic Assumptions

We consider an organization with multiple business processes. The output of each process is of value to the organization's customers. The demand for each process output depends on quality and time, not on the price. Each performance dimension can be operationalized in terms of case-specific indicators. The organization aims to select the optimal BPM roadmap, i.e., the roadmap with the highest value contribution, from a set of pre-defined project candidates. It thus determines which project candidates should be implemented in which order. The project candidates have been checked for appropriate strategic fit in the pre-screening stage of the PPS process. To unambiguously analyze inter-temporal interactions among projects and processes, only one project can be implemented per period. All projects can be finished within one period such that their effects become manifest at the beginning of the next period. In this context, periods can also be quite short (e.g., quarters or months). When selecting the optimal BPM roadmap, the organization also has to set the relevant planning horizon. If the number of project candidates exceeds the planning horizon, the organization has to make a PPS and a project scheduling decision at the same time. Otherwise, there is only a scheduling decision. Due to the inter-temporal interactions among projects and processes, the absolute effect of a project depends on the projects that have been implemented in prior periods, a phenomenon that is referred to as path dependence [37]. As a result, implementing the same projects in different sequences leads to different absolute effects of each project and to BPM roadmaps with different value contributions. As it is very complex and costly to estimate ex ante the absolute effects of each project candidate considering all possible sequences of implementation [38], we assume that the effects have been assessed in terms of relative numbers independent from other projects during the individual project analysis stage of the PPS process. This setting translates into the following assumptions:

(A.1) Each process $i \in I$ from the set of processes under investigation has a distinct quality $q_{i,y} \in \mathbb{R}^+$ and time $t_{i,y} \in \mathbb{R}^+$ for each period y of the planning horizon $Y \in \mathbb{N}$. The sales price $p_i \in \mathbb{R}^+$ for the output of process i is constant.

(A.2) The demand $n_i(q_{i,y}, t_{i,y}) \in \mathbb{R}^+$ for the output of process i is deterministic and depends on the quality $q_{i,y}$ and time $t_{i,y}$. The demands for different outputs are independent. The customers' sensitivity toward quality and time is constant throughout the planning horizon.

(A.3) One project can be implemented per period. All projects can be finished within one period.

(A.4) The effects of all project candidates have been determined in the individual project analysis stage of the PPS process. These effects are expressed in terms of relative numbers and independent from other projects.

To identify the BPM roadmap with the highest value contribution, all roadmap candidates r must be evaluated. The value contribution of a BPM roadmap is measured in terms of its NPV_r, i.e., the sum of all discounted periodic cash flows using a risk-adjusted interest rate $z \in \mathbb{R}_0^+$. For each period of the planning horizon, the periodic cash flows split into investment outflows $O_y^{inv} \in \mathbb{R}^+$ for implementing the respective project of the roadmap and into operating cash flow from executing the organization's business processes. For a specific period and process, the operating cash flow results from the demand that realizes for the quality and time of the process in that period as well as from a contribution margin, which in turn depends on the price of the process output and the respective periodic operating outflows $O_{i,y}^{\text{op}} \in \mathbb{R}^+$. The investment outflows are assumed to be due at the beginning of each period. The operating cash flow is due at the end of each period. This leads to the following objective function:

$$
\max_{r} : NPV_r = - \sum_{y=0}^{Y} \frac{O_y^{\text{inv}}}{(1+z)^y} + \sum_{i=1}^{|I|} \sum_{y=0}^{Y} \frac{n_i(q_{i,y}, t_{i,y}) \cdot [p_i - O_{i,y}^{\text{op}}]}{(1+z)^{y+1}}
\tag{1}
$$

The remainder of this section is structured along Figure 1, which illustrates how the project archetypes used in our decision model affect the organization's business processes and BPM capabilities as well as the components of the objective function. For increased readability, Figure 1 focuses on one process and a single period.

3.2 Project Archetypes and Their Effects

We distinguish two project archetypes, i.e., process-level and BPM-level projects. Thereby, we deliberately abstract from the large number of projects that may occur in real-world settings as we aim to analyze project effects in general. Process-level projects help develop the organization's operational capabilities by improving a particular business process [19]. BPM-level projects aim at building up BPM as a special dynamic capability that reflects the ability to change existing processes [21]. Due to this effect on dynamic capabilities, BPM-level projects have two different effects on the organization's operational capabilities. Both effects may occur separately or simultaneously, depending on the concrete project at hand. First, BPM-level projects can directly affect operational capabilities as from the next period. In contrast to process-level projects and in line with the infrastructure character of BPM, BPM-level projects influence all business processes [16]. Second, BPM-level projects can affect operational capabilities indirectly by facilitating the implementation of process-level projects in the future.

Process-level projects improve a distinct business process in terms of quality, time, and operating outflows – a value-based substitute for cost – as dimensions of the Devil's Quadrangle [3]. Flexibility is covered indirectly via reduced waiting or set-up times [24]. Depending on the project at hand, each dimension may be influenced positively or negatively or remain unchanged. This allows for covering many different effect constellations. For instance, there are projects that improve the quality of a process, while increasing time with potentially no effect on the operating outflows. Other projects reduce the operating outflows while leaving quality and time unchanged. In addition, all process-level projects cause investment outflows. An example is the hiring of additional workers in the claim settlement process of an insurance company. This project increases the operating outflows of the claim settlement process, reduces the average cycle time, and increases quality in terms of fewer mistakes and undetected cases of fraud. Moreover, consider the adoption of a workflow management system for the claim settlement process. This project reduces the average cycle time due to enhanced resource allocation and increases quality in terms of customer satisfaction. The project also increases the operating outflows of the process due to higher maintenance effort.

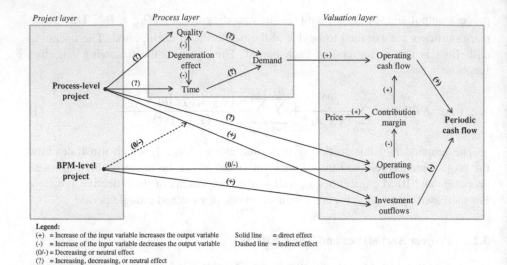

Fig. 1. Effects among projects and processes

BPM-level projects that only have a direct effect on the organization's operational capabilities make all business processes under investigation more cost-efficient [20], e.g., due to a better process culture and awareness. As an example, consider extensive process manager trainings that increase the coordination among processes and ensure an end-to-end mindset. As a result, the operating outflows are likely to drop despite additional periodic training effort. BPM-level projects that only have an indirect effect on operational capabilities make it easier to implement process-level projects. This effect becomes manifest in reduced investment outflows of future process-level projects. That is, implementing such BPM-level projects without subsequent process-level projects only causes investment outflows. As an example, consider training employees in business process reengineering (BPR) methods [39] or process redesign patterns [22]. Based on such trainings, employees are able to implement future process-level projects more easily. Analogous examples that relate to the BPM success factor IT are the adoption of a process modeling or simulation tool. Finally, there are BPM-level projects that combine the direct and indirect effect on operational capabilities. Such projects do not only help implement future process-level projects, but also make all business processes under investigation more cost-efficient as from the next period. Consider, for example, Six Sigma trainings. On the one hand, Six Sigma provides many tools that facilitate process improvement. On the other hand, as an approach to continuous process improvement, Six Sigma sensitizes people to looking for more efficient ways of conducting their daily work. What is common to all BPM-level projects is that they cause investment outflows. We make the following assumptions:

(A.5) Process-level projects enhance the organization's operational capabilities by improving a single process in terms of time, quality, and operating outflows. Considering a distinct project s, u_s denotes the project's relative effect on quality, e_s the relative effect on time, and m_s the relative of effect on the operating outflows. Process-level projects also cause investment outflows $O_s^{inv} \in \mathbb{R}^+$.

(A.6) BPM-level projects enhance operational capabilities directly and/or indirectly. As for the direct effect, a_s denotes a project's relative effect on the operating outflows of all business processes under investigation. As for the indirect effect, b_s denotes the relative effect on the investment outflows of all process-level projects implemented in future periods. BPM-level projects cause investment outflows $O_s^{inv} \in \mathbb{R}^+$.

3.3   Integrating the Project Effects into the Objective Function

With the knowledge about the project archetypes and their effects, we operationalize the objective function (Equation 1). For each period of the planning horizon, we determine the quality, time, and investment outflows as well as the operating outflows of all business processes.

The investment outflows O_y^{inv} in period y depend on which process- or BPM-level project is scheduled for that period (Equation 2). As one project can be implemented per period and each project is finished within one period (A.3), there is a one-to-one relationship between periods and projects. Thus, the index y refers to exactly one project. We use the index s to denote the project that is scheduled for period y in the BPM roadmap r under investigation. If a BPM-level project is scheduled for period y, the investment outflows in that period equal O_s^{inv} as the investment outflows of BPM-level projects are independent of other projects. If a process-level project is scheduled for period y, the investment outflows do not only depend on O_s^{inv}, but also on the indirect effects $b_j \in \;]0; 1]$ of all BPM-level projects that have been implemented until period $y - 1$ (A.6). The set of these BPM-level projects is denoted by $BPM_{r,y-1}$. In our model, the effects b_j are linked multiplicatively due to their relative character (A.4). The combination of multiplicatively linked effects and the discounting of periodic cash effects allows for incorporating inter-temporal interactions. If no project is scheduled for period y, a case that only occurs if the planning horizon exceeds the number of projects in the BPM roadmap, the investment outflows in that period are zero.

$$
O_y^{inv} = \begin{cases} O_s^{inv} & \text{if a BPM-level project is scheduled for } y \\ O_s^{inv} \cdot \displaystyle\prod_{j \in BPM_{r,y-1}} b_j & \text{if a process-level project is scheduled for } y \\ 0 & \text{if no project is scheduled for } y \end{cases} \tag{2}
$$

The operating outflows $O_{i,y}^{op}$ of business process i in period y depend on the BPM-level and the process-level projects that have been implemented until period $y - 1$ (Equation 3). Therefore, the set of previously implemented BPM-level projects, $BPM_{r,y-1}$, and the set of previously implemented process-level projects with an effect on business process i, $PLP_{r,i,y-1}$, have to be considered. Thereby, the effect m_j belongs to process-level projects, whereas a_j refers to the direct cost-efficiency effects of BPM-level projects. As process-level projects may have a positive, negative, or neutral effect on the operating outflows, m_j can take values from the interval $]0; \infty[$ where $m_j = 1$ denotes a neutral effect. As BPM-level projects only reduce the operating outflows (A.6), the effect a_j can take values from the interval $]0; 1]$. As all project effects are relative, we also need the operating outflows of business process i at the decision point ($y = 0$) to calibrate the height of the operating outflows. The operating outflows at the decision point can be reasonably assumed to be known as we consider existing business processes [34].

$$O_{i,y}^{op} = O_{i,0}^{op} \cdot \prod_{j \in PLP_{r,i,y-1}} m_j \cdot \prod_{j \in BPM_{r,y-1}} a_j \tag{3}$$

The quality $q_{i,y}$ of business process i in period y depends on the quality of this process at the decision point ($y = 0$) and on all previously implemented process-level projects that focus on this process (Equation 4). For the quality of process i at the decision point, the same argumentation holds true as for the operating outflows. The relative effect of a process-level project on quality is denoted by u_j. This effect takes values from the interval $]0; \infty[$ as process level-projects may have a positive, negative, or neutral effect on quality. Like all other effects, quality effects are linked multiplicatively. Quality usually has an upper boundary [3]. For example, an error rate ranges from 0 to 100 % or a customer satisfaction index may have maximum of 10. To account for this property, we incorporated an upper quality boundary $q^{max} \in \mathbb{R}^+$. Against this backdrop, it may be the case that investment outflows are wasted if a process-level project with a high quality effect is implemented when the quality of a process is already very close to its upper boundary. In line with the quality management literature, one has to continuously invest to maintain a once-achieved quality level. That is, whenever the organization conducts a BPM-level project or a process-level project that focuses on another process, the quality of process i drops. We therefore integrated a process-specific degeneration effect d_i that takes values from the interval $]0; 1]$. The degeneration effect penalizes if the organization focuses too much on a distinct process or on building up BPM. The exponent of the degeneration effect in Equation (4) indicates the number of periods in which, up to the current period y, the organization did not conduct process-level projects that focus on process i. The extent of the degeneration effect depends on different process characteristics (e.g., complexity, or employee fluctuation).

$$q_{i,y} = \min\left(\left(q_{i,0} \cdot d_i^{y-|PLP_{r,i,y-1}|} \cdot \prod_{j \in PLP_{r,i,y-1}} u_j\right); q^{max}\right) \tag{4}$$

Time and quality can be treated similarly. The difference is that time has no upper boundary and another polarity than quality. The time $t_{i,y}$ of business process i in period y depends on the time of the process at the decision point ($y = 0$) and on all previously implemented process-level projects that focus on this process (Equation 5). The relative time effect of a process-level project is denoted by e_j. This effect takes values from the interval $]0; \infty[$ as process level-projects may have a positive, negative, or neutral effect on time. Analogous to quality, we incorporated a degeneration effect v_i that occurs in all periods where the organization does not conduct process-level projects that focus on process i. As time has a different polarity than quality, the degeneration effect takes values from the interval $[1; \infty[$.

$$t_{i,y} = t_{i,0} \cdot v_i^{y-|PLP_{r,i,y-1}|} \cdot \prod_{j \in PLP_{r,i,y-1}} e_j \tag{5}$$

Having operationalized the objective function using the effects of process-level and BPM-level projects, the decision model can now be employed to valuate and compare roadmaps in terms of their value contribution to identify the optimal BPM roadmap.

4   Evaluation

To evaluate the decision model, we discuss its characteristics against the requirements from the literature. We also built a prototype and provide a demonstration example using the case of an IT service provider. Finally, we are currently applying the decision model in an industry project. We will report on the insights in our future research.

4.1   Feature Comparison

Regarding feature comparison, the characteristics of our decision model are compared with the requirements we derived from the literature in section 2 (Table 1).

Table 1. Results of feature comparison

RQ	Features of the model
(R.1)	The decision model builds on process-level projects, which affect only one business process, and BPM-level projects, which affect all business processes under consideration (R.1b). Process-level projects enhance an organization's operational capabilities, whereas BPM-level projects build up BPM as a dynamic capability. They affect operational capabilities directly by making all business processes more cost-efficient and/or indirectly by facilitating the implementation of process-level projects in the future (R.1a).
(R.2)	The decision model aligns with the Devil's Quadrangle. It directly accounts for the performance dimensions time, quality, and cost, and indirectly for flexibility (R.2a). As value-based substitutes for cost, the decision model relies on operating cash outflows and investment outflows. Each dimension can be operationalized via different performance indicators (R.2b).
(R.3)	We consider a set of pre-defined project candidates. We assume that, in the pre-screening stage of the PPS process, all project candidates were checked for appropriate strategic fit (R.3a) and that, in the individual project analysis stage, the relative effects all of project candidates have been determined as single values independent from other projects (R.3b). The absolute effects of a project depend on the projects that have been implemented in prior periods. Thus, we consider deterministic, scheduling, and inter-temporal interactions among projects (R.3c).
(R.4)	The value contribution of a BPM roadmap is based on its NPV, an appropriate quantity in case of deterministic interactions. The NPV considers all cash effects that result from process- and BPM-level projects as well as from process execution (R.4a). We account for the decision makers' risk attitude using a risk-adjusted interest rate (R.4b). As BPM roadmaps comprise multiple projects implemented at different points in time, we also consider a multi-period planning horizon. The risk-adjusted interest rate also accounts for the time value of money (R.4c).

The requirements that represent the capability development and the process perfor-mance measurement perspectives are met to the full extent. The requirements that account for the PPS and the value-based management perspectives are covered partly. The resulting need for future research is outlined in the conclusion.

4.2   Demonstration Example

For the demonstration example, we consider three service processes that an IT service provider offers to its customers. The demand for a distinct service depends on its quality and time. For the service provider, a planning period lasts one quarter. The interest rate is 2.5% per quarter. The first service is an incident management service that includes the operation of a ticket system and the provision of required service staff. Costumers pay a fixed service fee per ticket. The number of tickets has been identified as a main driver of the service's operational outflows. The quality of this service is measured as the fraction of tickets that is resolved to the customers' satisfaction. Time is operationalized as the average time for reacting upon a ticket. The second service is the operation of an Enter-prise Resource Planning (ERP) system. Costumers pay a fixed license fee per quarter. The quality of the ERP service is expressed as the availability of the ERP system. Time is operationalized as the time necessary to implement minor changes in the ERP system or to conduct related customization. The third service is a backup service. Customers pay a fixed remuneration per license related to their average memory requirements. The perceived quality of this service depends on the agreed service level of the backup ser-vice, i.e., the number of backups per period and the number of periods for which back-ups are stored. For this service, time such as recovery time is not relevant from the customers' point of view.

We consider the three IT service processes just introduced (Table 2) and five dif-ferent projects (Tables 3 and 4), thereof three BPM-level and two process-level projects. The projects and their effects used in this demonstration example were de-rived from projects that were implemented at those industry partners with which we discussed the decision model. Overall, we calculate four scenarios. For each project, we estimated the effects for an optimistic (opt.) and a pessimistic (pess.) scenario. We also consider two planning horizons, i.e., three and eight periods. As for the short planning horizon, the service provider has to solve a PPS and a project scheduling problem. As for the long planning horizon, the service provider has to solve a project scheduling problem. A planning horizon of eight periods leads to 120 different BPM roadmaps to be evaluated, whereas a planning horizon of three periods leads to 60 different BPM roadmaps.

Table 2. IT service processes considered in the demonstration example

i	Name	$q_{i,0}$	$t_{i,0}$	p	$O_{i,0}^{\text{op}}$	d_i, v_i	n_i
1	Incident management service	95 %	60 min	2.50 €	1 €	10.00 %	$11{,}000 \cdot \left(\ln q + e^{\frac{1}{t}}\right)$
2	Operation of an ERP system	91 %	30 d	1,500 €	1,300 €	5.00 %	$200 \cdot \left(\ln q + e^{\frac{1}{t}}\right)$
3	Backup service	80 %	-	220 €	150 €	5.00 %	$1{,}200 \cdot \ln q$

Table 3. BPM-level projects considered in the demonstration example

s	Name	Services influenced	O_s^{Inv}	a_s		b_s	
				pess.	opt.	pess.	opt.
1	Training in BPR methods	All	25,000 €	-	-	0.95	0.8
2	Development of a process performance measurement system	All	100,000 €	0.95	0.85	-	-
3	Training in Six Sigma	All	35,000 €	0.99	0.9	0.95	0.8

Table 4. Process-level projects considered in the demonstration example

s	Name	i	O_s^{Inv}	e_s		u_s		m_s	
				pess.	opt.	pess.	opt.	pess.	opt.
4	Update ticket system	1	110,000 €	0.90	0.70	1.0	1.1	1.3	1.1
5	Increase backup frequency	3	35,000 €	-	-	1.1	1.3	1.2	0.9

The results of all scenarios are shown in Table 5. For each scenario, we list the indices of the included projects and the NPVs for the optimal and the worst BPM roadmaps (Table 5a and 5b). In each scenario, the NPV of the optimal BPM roadmap differs a lot from the NPV of the worst BPM roadmap. For example, in the optimistic scenario with a long planning horizon, the NPV of the optimal BPM roadmap is 1,584,657 € (25 %) higher the NPV of the worst BPM roadmap. This result corroborates the proposition that the concrete set of projects and the inter-temporal interactions implied by the sequence of implementation greatly affect the value contribution.

Apart from the differences in the planning horizon, the projects included in the optimal BPM roadmap and their sequence of implementation are very similar for all scenarios. In three scenarios, the first projects are the projects 2, 3, and 1, i.e., the BPM-level projects. In the fourth scenario, the first two projects are again projects 2 and 3. Project 1 is scheduled for period 4. Though appearing counter-intuitive at first sight, this result is reasonable from the short-term perspective as the projects 2 and 3 influence all processes and, in the case at hand, outperform the process-level projects. Project 1 is implemented in period 3, i.e., the last period of the short planning horizon, because it is much cheaper than the process-level projects. The same argumentation holds true for the long planning horizon. In the pessimistic case, the projects 4 and 5, which are scheduled for period 4 and 5, benefit from the indirect effects caused by projects 1 and 3. In the optimistic scenario, project 5 is scheduled for period 3 because it is rather cheap and has a comparatively strong effect on the quality and the operating outflows of the backup service. In fact, the demand for the backup service is very sensitive toward quality improvements, a circumstance that makes it reasonable from an economic perspective to implement project 5 two periods earlier than in the pessimistic case where its effects are much worse. It is also sensible to implement project 4 the last. The reason is that the quality of the incident management service already is very close to the upper boundary. Thus, project 4 is not fully effective. In addition, with all demand functions having diminishing marginal returns, quality improvements for the incident management service are less effective than for the backup service.

Table 5. Results of the demonstration example

	5 periods	3 periods		5 periods	3 periods
Optimistic	Projects: 2, 3, 5, 1, 4 NPV: 7,892,429 €	Projects: 2, 3, 1 NPV: 2,579,570 €	**Optimistic**	Projects: 4, 1, 5, 3, 2 NPV: 6,307,772 €	Projects: 4, 1, 2 NPV: 1,689,518 €
Pessimistic	Projects: 2, 3, 1, 4, 5 NPV: 4,828,230 €	Projects: 2, 3, 1 NPV: 1,998,147 €	**Pessimistic**	Projects: 5, 4, 1, 3, 2 NPV: 3,805,124 €	Projects: 5, 4, 2 NPV: 1,393,421 €
	(a) Optimal BPM roadmaps			(b) Worst BPM roadmaps	

5   Conclusion and Outlook

Located at the intersection of traditional BPM research and BPM research that focuses on capability development, we investigated the question which projects an organization should implement and in which order it should implement these projects to develop BPM capabilities in a way that is balanced with the improvement of individual business processes. To answer this question, we proposed a decision model that valuates BPM roadmaps, i.e., portfolios of scheduled projects with different effects on processes and BPM capabilities, and selects the roadmap with the highest value contribution in a given planning horizon. The value contribution of a BPM roadmap is expressed in terms of its net present value. The decision model supports two project archetypes, namely process-level and BPM-level projects. Process-level projects help develop an organization's operational capabilities by improving a single process in terms of the dimensions of the Devil's Quadrangle (e.g., time, quality, and cost). BPM-level projects build up BPM as a dynamic capability. They affect an organization's operational capabilities directly by making all business processes more cost-efficient and/or indirectly by facilitating the implementation of process-level projects in the future. As for the evaluation, we discussed the decision model both with industry partners and with respect to the requirements from the literature. We also built a prototype and presented a demonstration example that was also discussed with industry partners.

As the decision model does not meet all requirements derived from the literature to the full extent, it is beset with limitations that may stimulate future research. First, some assumptions of the decision model simplify reality. For example, only one project can be implemented per period. Though being made to analyze the interactions among processes and projects more clearly in a first step, it is worthwhile to relax this assumption in the future. If more than one project can be implemented per period, it is necessary to account for intra-temporal interactions. In its current version, the decision model copes with simple intra-temporal interactions (e.g., budget restrictions or mandatory projects), but not with complex ones (e.g., input-output interactions). The decision model is also based on the assumption of deterministic interactions (e.g., regarding customer demands). Although the risk-adjusted discount rate used for calculating the value contribution of BPM roadmaps implicitly accounts for risks, future research should put more emphasis on stochastic interactions as for example the integration of risks with respective probabilities. Due to the interactions among projects and processes, we assumed that the absolute project effects depend on the previously implemented projects from the BPM roadmap. Thus, project effects were expressed in relative numbers and linked multiplicatively to determine the periodic cash effects. In practice, however, the effects of some projects may be independent of the previously implemented projects, a circumstance that would make an additive linking necessary. Therefore, the decision model should be extended correspondingly.

Second, although we were able to discuss the demonstration example with industry partners, the decision model would benefit from additional case studies. This would help gain more experience with estimating the needed parameters, which is a main difficulty of applying mathematical models. Case studies may also provide further insights into the behavior of the decision model and, for example complemented by additional experiments, serve as foundation for general recommendations for action. To efficiently determine the optimal BPM roadmap in settings of real-world complexity, further research should also search the quantitative project portfolio selection and project scheduling literature for suitable heuristic approaches that avoid the computational expensiveness of exhaustive enumeration.

References

1. Kohlbacher, M., Reijers, H.: The effects of process-oriented organizational design on firm performance. Bus. Proc. Manage. J. 19, 245–262 (2013)
2. Skrinjar, R., Bosilj-Vuksic, V., Indihar-Stemberger, M.: The impact of business process orientation on financial and non-financial performance. Bus. Proc. Manage. J. 14, 738–754 (2008)
3. Dumas, M., La Rosa, M., Mendling, J., Reijers, H.: Fundamentals of Business Process Management. Springer, Heidelberg (2013)
4. vom Brocke, J., Becker, J., Braccini, A.M., et al.: Current and future issues in BPM research: a European perspective from the ERCIS meeting 2010. CAIS 28, 393–414 (2011)
5. van der Aalst, W.M.P.: Business Process Management: A Comprehensive Survey. ISRN Software Eng., vol. 2013 (2013)
6. Niehaves, B., Poeppelbuss, J., Plattfaut, R., Becker, J.: BPM Capability Development–A Matter of Contingencies. Bus. Proc. Manage. J. 20, 90–106 (2014)
7. Sidorova, A., Isik, O.: Business process research: a cross-disciplinary review. Bus. Proc. Manage. J. 16, 566–597 (2010)
8. Vergidis, K., Tiwari, A., Majeed, B.: Business Process Analysis and Optimization: Beyond Reengineering. IEEE Transactions on Systems, Man, and Cybernetics - Part C: Applications and Reviews 38, 69–82 (2008)
9. Rosemann, M.: vom Brocke, J.: The Six Core Elements of Business Process Management. In: Handbook on Business Process Management I. Springer, Berlin (2010)
10. van Looy, A., de Backer, M., Poels, G.: Defining Business Process Maturity: A Journey towards Excellence. Total Qual. Manage. 22, 1119–1137 (2011)
11. Jurisch, M.C., Palka, W., Wolf, P., Krcmar, H.: Which Capabilities Matter For Successful Business Process Change? Bus. Proc. Manage. J. 20, 47–67 (2014)

12. Röglinger, M., Pöppelbuß, J., Becker, J.: Maturity Models in Business Process Management. Bus. Proc. Manage. J. 18, 328–346 (2012)
13. Darmani, A., Hanafizadeh, P.: Business process portfolio selection in re-engineering projects. Bus. Proc. Manage. J. 19, 892–916 (2013)
14. Hevner, A.R., March, S.T., Park, J., Ram, S.: Design Science in Information Systems Research. MIS Quart. 28, 75–105 (2004)
15. Peffers, K., Tuunanen, T., Rothenberger, M.A., Chatterjee, S.: A Design Science Research Methodology for Information Systems Research. J. Manage. Inf. Syst. 24, 45–77 (2008)
16. Harmon, P.: Business Process Change, 2nd edn. Morgan Kaufmann, Burlington (2010)
17. Helfat, C.E., Peteraf, M.A.: The Dynamic Resource-based View: Capability Lifecycles. Strategic Manage. J. 24, 997–1010 (2003)
18. Pavlou, P.A., El Sawy, O.A.: Understanding the Elusive Black Box of Dynamic Capabilities. Decision Sci. 42, 239–273 (2011)
19. Winter, S.G.: Understanding Dynamic Capabilities. Strategic Manage. J. 24, 991–995 (2003)
20. Kim, G., Shin, B., Kim, K.K., Lee, H.G.: IT capabilities, process-oriented dynamic capabilities, and firm financial performance. J. Association Inf. Syst. 12, 487–517 (2011)
21. Ortbach, K., Plattfaut, R., Pöppelbuß, J., Niehaves, B.: A Dynamic Capability-based Framework for Business Process Management: Theorizing and Empirical Application. In: Proceedings of the Hawaii International Conference on System Sciences, Hawaii International Conference on System Sciences, pp. 4287–4296 (2012)
22. Reijers, H.A., Liman Mansar, S.: Best practices in business process redesign: an overview and qualitative evaluation of successful redesign heuristics. Omega 33, 283–306 (2005)
23. Heckl, D., Moormann, J.: Process performance management. In: Handbook on Business Process Management 2. Springer, Berlin (2010)
24. Neuhuber, L.C.N., Krause, F., Roeglinger, M.: Flexibilization Of Service Processes: Toward An Economic Optimization Model. In: Proceedings of the 21st European Conference on Information Systems (ECIS 2013), Paper 66 (2013)
25. Archer, N.P., Ghasemzadeh, F.: An integrated framework for project portfolio selection. Int. J. Project Manage. 17, 207–216 (1999)
26. Kundisch, D., Meier, C.: IT/IS Project Portfolio Selection in the Presence of Project Interactions – Review and Synthesis of the Literature. In: Wirtschaftinformatik Proceedings 2011, Paper 64, pp. 477–486 (2011)
27. Lee, J.W., Kim, S.H.: An integrated approach for interdependent information system project selection. Int. J. Project Manage. 19, 111–118 (2001)
28. Fox, G.E., Baker, N.R., Bryant, J.L.: Economic Models for R and D Project Selection in the Presence of Project Interactions. Manage. Sci. 30, 890–902 (1984)
29. Gear, T.E., Cowie, G.C.: A note on modeling project interdependence in research and development. Decision Sci. 11, 738–748 (1980)
30. Bardhan, I., Bagchi, S., Sougstad, R.: Prioritizing a portfolio of information technology investment projects. Manage. Inf. Syst. 21, 33–60 (2004)
31. Medaglia, A.L., Graves, S.B., Ringuest, J.L.: A multiobjective evolutionary approach for linearly constrained project selection under uncertainty. Eur. J. Oper. Res. 179, 869–894 (2007)
32. Koller, T., Goedhart, M., Wessels, D.: Valuation: Measuring and Managing the Value of Companies. John Wiley, New Jersey (2010)
33. Rappaport, A.: Creating Shareholder Value: The New Standard for Business Performance. Free Press, New York (1986)

34. Buhl, H.U., Röglinger, M., Stöckl, S., Braunwarth, K.: Value Orientation in Process Management - Research Gap and Contribution to Economically Well-founded Decisions in Process Management. Bus. Inf. Syst. Eng. 3, 163–172 (2011)
35. Martin, J.D., Petty, W.J., Wallace, J.S.: Value-Based Management with Corporate Social Responsibility. Oxford University Press, Inc., New York (2009)
36. Berger, J.O.: Statistical Decision Theory and Bayesian Analysis. Springer, New York (2010)
37. Pierson, P.: Not just what, but when: Timing and sequence in political processes. Studies in American Political Development 14, 72–92 (2000)
38. Project Management Institute: A Guide to the Project Management Body of Knowledge. Project Management Institute, Newton Square (2008)
39. Hammer, M., Champy, J.: Reengineering the corporation: a manifesto for business revolution. Nicholas Brealey, London (1993)

Implicit BPM: A Business Process Platform for Transparent Workflow Weaving

Rubén Mondéjar[1,2], Pedro García-López[1], Carles Pairot[1,2], and Enric Brull[2]

[1] Department of Computer Engineering and Maths,
Universitat Rovira i Virgili, Tarragona, Spain
{ruben.mondejar,pedro.garcia,carles.pairot}@urv.cat
[2] Diputació de Tarragona, Spain
enric.brull@dipta.cat

Abstract. The integration of business processes into existing applications involves considerable development efforts and costs for IT departments. This precludes the pervasive implementation of BPM in organizations where important applications remain isolated from the existing workflows.

In this paper, we introduce a novel concept, Workflow Weaving, based on non-intrusive techniques, which achieves transparent integration of business processes into organizational applications. This concept relies on BPM standards, Aspect Oriented Programming, and Web patterns to transparently weave business models among current web applications. A prototype platform is presented, which includes our design of a distributed architecture, and a natural and expressive DSL.

Keywords: Workflow Weaving, Implicit BPM, Distributed Platform, Aspect-Orientation, MVC Architecture.

1 Introduction

There is an increasing demand from organizations to integrate business processes into existing applications. Many of these applications remain apart from the company workflows because they were designed as isolated systems without clear interoperation interfaces. In most cases, the cost of this integration is very high because it implies detailed knowledge of the existing applications, and ad-hoc modifications to provide the required connection with workflow engines. This cost makes it very difficult to adopt BPM strategies in these organizations.

These workflows should provide a way of describing the order of execution and the dependent relationships between the activities of running processes in heterogeneous applications. However, if these processes span existing applications in the organization, their integration implies a costly plumbing and connection development work in every piece of software.

In order to reduce this cost, we introduce a novel concept, namely Workflow Weaving, based on non-intrusive techniques, which achieves transparent integration of business processes into existing web applications. We mainly employ

S. Sadiq, P. Soffer, and H. Völzer (Eds.): BPM 2014, LNCS 8659, pp. 168–183, 2014.

Aspect-Oriented Programming (AOP) [1] to transparently intercept existing web applications and connect them to the workflow system. The novelty of our approach is that we intercept the Model-View-Controller (MVC [2]) pattern in key points in order to avoid a detailed knowledge of the target applications. The MVC pattern enables us to perform black-box [3] wrapping interception and to avoid costly clear-box interception models. The only natural assumption is that any of the intercepted applications must be of an MVC web type.

To simplify application integration, we also provide a Domain Specific Language (DSL [4]) that transparently performs Workflow Weaving. This weaving defines the mechanisms to intercept applications and to inject BPM logic into them. Thus, IT technicians do not need to learn AOP since the simple DSL is responsible for enabling the required interceptors in MVC applications. The major contributions of our approach are:

- Transparent *introspection and interception* of web applications, which benefit from the decoupled nature of the most extended pattern for developing modern web applications (MVC).
- A *natural and expressive* DSL that performs Workflow Weaving by injecting AOP interceptors into web applications. This approach considerably simplifies the integration of business processes into existing applications.
- The design and implementation of a *distributed and implicit* BPM platform, which enables distributed process weaving and management.

The rest of the article is structured as follows. Section 2 shortly introduces the state-of-the-art in BPM integration and implicit techniques fields. In Section 3 we give an overview of our Workflow Weaving technique proposal and its features. In Section 4 we introduce our platform design and implementation. Related work is presented in Section 5, and in Section 6 we draw some conclusions.

2 Background

In this section, we explore relevant background in this area. Firstly, we discuss different topics in the scenarios of BPM integration, including important issues like explicit solutions and support for legacy applications. Secondly, we explore existent techniques to provide transparency and integration concerns.

2.1 BPM Integration

Building systems from the ground up is no longer an acceptable business practice and it is certainly not cost effective. In this setting, Business Process Management (BPM) [5,6] is seen as a mechanism for integrating systems and a way of developing new applications.

Actual BPM solutions are well-known and explicit approaches to implement workflows on top of software applications applicable to a certain business. That approach traditionally supports the separation of the business process from the core application, but presents important drawbacks. Some of these disadvantages include the accommodation of transversal business processes into applications, the combination of different design and execution environments, and the fact of dealing with legacy applications. For these reasons, BPM is in many cases perceived as being expensive and really complex to deploy.

Unanticipated business processes that need to be modelled and incorporated into any operating applications are a common requirement [7,8,9] to accommodate any change in policies, regulations, etc. In addition, business processes should also be easily reused among a variety of applications between the same organization. Such requirements are usually deemed to be painful because existing solutions use explicit techniques.

Since business processes are designed by business analysts, these need to be defined and understood by stakeholders, and they are not typically adept in application development [10]. In this line, the business process must be defined using a high-level domain language, thus hiding technical concerns. As a consequence, business processes are implemented combining standard software engineering approaches, such as object-oriented programming languages (e.g. Java), description languages (e.g. XML), and high-level domain languages (e.g. BPMN).

Finally, another important issue is how to deal with existing legacy applications. Since understanding existing legacy code through reengineering is a challenging task that may consume a lot of resources. Some recent works [11] propose to rewrite them using BPM. Unfortunately, building systems from the ground up can also represent an enormous cost. As an alternative [12] presents a reengineering tool to identify business rules contained in legacy source code. But as authors explain, reengineering using BPM is not easy to apply, because there are no tools that help developers understand the legacy system behaviour.

2.2   Implicit Techniques

Different approaches are taken on implicit middleware [13], like generic wrapping techniques which are normally more intrusive, as well as ad-hoc interception solutions [14] provided by a specific platform in an explicit way.

However, in order to solve transparency or genericity limitations, we can use powerful interception solutions like AOP, which is an established paradigm. Indeed, it enables describing and separating crosscutting system concerns in a modular and highly reusable manner. AOP supports switching on and off new behaviours at a specific point of program execution, while maintaining the system well modularized.

AOP applies to support flexibility and adaptability of applications/services by allowing to switch on and off orthogonal functions, allowing less interdependence and more transparency. The interception is performed in a *join point* (a point in the execution flow), and defined inside a *pointcut* (a set of join points). Whenever the application execution reaches one pointcut, an *advice* (namely a callback) associated with it is executed. The aspect is a module encapsulating pointcuts and advices. It specifies the new functionality to be included and the place in the execution of the original code where this functionality is to be inserted.

In this setting, a weaver is the AOP mechanism that combines code encapsu-
lated in aspects with the original code. There are different weaving mechanisms
that can be classified as static or dynamic. Dynamic weaving enables the inter-
changeability or deactivation of aspects during program execution, while static
weaving disallows such capability, i.e. once defined, aspects cannot be deacti-
vated or exchanged.

Finally, we can distinguish between clear-box and black-box approaches [3] to
AOP. Clear-box approaches to AOP examine the program internals and source
code, producing a combination of program and aspects. Black-box approaches
shroud components with aspect wrappers in strategic points avoiding a detailed
knowledge of the code internals. Obviously, clear-box or white-box approaches
to interception imply more cost and they are more difficult to apply in real
settings. Black-box or wrapper-based techniques [15] can considerably simplify
the distributed interception [16] of existing systems.

3   Workflow Weaving

Commonly, software applications are developed to automate and to make efficient
business processes, which are previously modelled by analysts. Their requirements
are functional and represent activities that the organization is currently trying to
achieve. However, once applications are finally released, functional requirements
inevitably and naturally change in a major or minor degree, evolving to their
clients desires and thus improving their functionalities.

In this section, we introduce a novel technique named Workflow Weaving, that
enables integration of business processes, represented by BPMN models, like true
crosscutting concerns into corporate web applications. Such technique allows integrating business processes with heterogeneous web applications transparently.
In this setting, transparent means that our solution must avoid access, modification and detailed knowledge of the source code of the existing applications.
The major requirements of our so-called transparent integration are:

- A generic code interception of modern web applications using a black-box
  solution (Section 3.2). In addition, it must provide introspection capabilities
  that offer information about models, controllers, and views in the existing
  web applications to be integrated.
- An easy management and deployment of interceptor code. This requires code
  injection using a common interface (Section 3.3), where IT technicians are
  unaware of the application code.
- A high-level domain language and interpreter (Section 3.4) simplifying the
  integration of business processes and web applications. This avoids knowledge of the underlying interception framework (AOP).

The rest of the section explains how the Workflow Weaving technique deals
with each of these requirements itemized above.

3.1   Use Case

Clear examples of real application requirements, are authentication portals or payment gateways, which use web redirections to change the navigation rules and other behaviours of the system.

In Figure 1 we present a use case based on two applications within the same organization: an e-commerce Pet Store application, and a generic Accounting application. The Pet Store is a classic sample application from the Java EE Platform, used to show its features. We have also implemented a generic Accounting application that manages the books, and the customers of an enterprise.

Moreover, a business analyst has designed and modelled a Purchase Workflow in this scenario, limiting itself to a standard BPMN 2.0 design tool. Note that since this is a simple example, the represented tasks are user tasks, although they can be of another type, because our plaftorm provides a full support of BPMN 2.0 activities.

Both applications are implemented on a MVC framework, and their components are: **models**, consisting of persisted domain objects, **controllers**, formed by a set of action to command interactions, and **view** pages, which communicate directly with the end-users. For their graphical representation, we use the UML notation [17] that illustrates interactions among the MVC components of a web application. In addition, the UML notation has the following basic rules: view pages can only interact with controllers, model objects can only interact with controllers, and controllers can interact with any component.

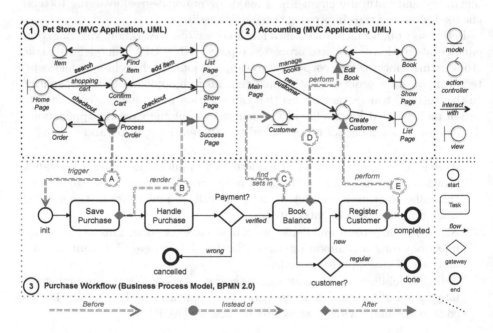

Fig. 1. Workflow Weaving Use Case

Lastly, to interrelate the different diagrams, we use dashed arrows to indicate the existent Workflow Weaving among the business process and the application. Note that each arrow has a tag describing the associated action, and there are three different arrow shapes depending on the interception type: **before**, **instead of**, and **after**.

In Figure 1 we have highlighted the most important spots where Workflow Weaving occurs:

(A) in the PetStore application, **instead of** the *Process* action from the *Order* controller, the *init* event of the Purchase Workflow is triggered.

(B) **After** the *Save Purchase* task is completed, the execution returns to the application to render the *Success Page* view.

Later on, the Purchase Workflow continues its natural execution, until we arrive to the *Book Balance* task. This means that some other participant has claimed and completed the *Handle Purchase* task.

(C) Once the payment is verified, the execution flow moves to the Accounting application. Particularly, **before** the *Book Balance* task is started, the process looks up the *customer* model by its National Identification Number (*NIN*) and sets the result into the *exists* boolean attribute of this task.

(D) **After** the *Book Balance* task is completed, the weaver performs the *Edit* action from the *Book* controller.

(E) Lastly, **after** the *Register Customer* task, the weaver performs the *Create* action from the *Customer* controller.

As seen on the example, the Workflow Weaving technique defines the whole behaviour of the system when the process is running. In the next section, we present how our technique can crosscut MVC applications transparently, providing a true black-box solution.

3.2   MVC Pattern

Web development has changed significantly over the past few years. It has not been long since deploying a web project simply involved uploading static HTML, CSS and JavaScript files to a web server. Nowadays, web application development using web frameworks has become the *de facto* work environment. Furthermore, current frameworks (e.g. Grails [18]) follow common fundamentals and best practise principles like reutilization (i.e. DRY - Don't Repeat Yourself) or productivity (e.g., conventions over configurations, and scaffolding).

Furthermore, the most important of the common features on modern web frameworks is the whole adoption of the MVC pattern. Although MVC was originally developed for desktop computing, it has been widely adopted as an architecture for web applications in all major programming languages. As a result, new MVC frameworks have appeared that provide structure and guidance when developing these applications.

In this work, we mainly focus on MVC based applications, which are mainly those based on modern web frameworks. This restriction allows us to provide a real black-box solution. Thus, even though the entirety of legacy applications

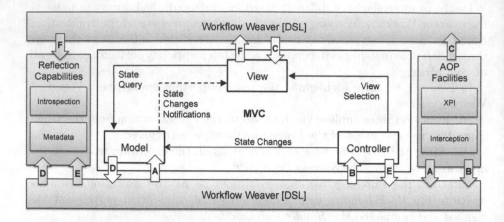

Fig. 2. Black-Box Diagram for the MVC Pattern

may not be included, they can be refactored following some guidelines, like those presented in other works [2].

In our case, we introduce a solution that follows a black-box model injecting code in strategic points of the web application framework. Thanks to the MVC standard pattern, which is used extensively in web frameworks, we are able to intercept models, views and controllers in a transparent and decoupled way. Thus, as we have shown in Figure 2, the MVC pattern enables the use of AOP facilities to intercept code (in points A, B, and C), and to use reflection and introspection techniques to obtain the necessary information (in points D, E, and F).

Indeed, reflection is a well-known self-management technique for providing mechanisms to inspect a system structure and behaviour. Furthermore, the MVC pattern presents a clear facade, standard naming conventions, and inheritance rules to easily perform automatic introspection of the application. In this case, we benefit from this advantage to extract the declared model and attributes (A), the enabled controllers and actions (B), and the deployed views and navigation rules (C) among all of them. Additionally, the workflow weaver also injects new code to add or remove calculated fields to domain classes (D), to change the current behaviour of the controller actions (E), or inject code in compiled versions of the page views (F).

Accordingly, our solution benefits from the MVC pattern to become a generic solution that fulfils the black-box requirement. Furthermore, the limitation of Workflow Weaving to MVC based web applications is not a big constraint, given that MVC is the most common architecture pattern.

3.3   Crosscutting Interfaces

Crosscut Programming Interfaces (XPI) [19] are explicit, abstract interfaces that provide a clear separation between the interceptor logic and the AOP language or

```
1:    public abstract aspect MvcXpi {
2:        public pointcut inController(): within(*..*Controller);
3:        public pointcut controllerAction(): inController() && execution(@Action public * *.*(..));
4:        public pointcut inModel(): within(*.persistence.Entity);
5:        public pointcut saveMethod(): inModel() && execution(public Object save(..));
6:        //More CRUD Methods (...)
7:        public pointcut inView(): within(*..gsp_*_gsp);
8:    }
```

Fig. 3. XPI Example for a MVC Framework

implementation. It allows for their separate and parallel evolution and produces a better correspondence between programs and designs.

In our scenario, each modern web framework uses different implementations and mechanisms to instantiate domain classes, inject controllers, handle the data layer, represent the views, among others. In fact, each of them presents different approaches to implement the MVC pattern and its entities, using different paradigms like object-oriented inheritance, XML configuration, or code annotations.

The idea of the XPI is to create a contract between the platform and the intercepted system. Therefore, the XPI establishes a binding with the MVC Framework which states the pointcuts definition; and it also establishes another binding with the interception platform, namely the advice method definitions. As a result, if the platform uses different XPIs without modifying the advice method definitions, each application is able to be implemented in any MVC framework.

For instance, in Figure 3, we present a crosscutting interface for intercepting each action method, and the persistence model CRUD methods. This example intercepts a specific MVC framework (i.e., Grails [18]) where Controllers follow a name convention (e.g., CartController) and Model domain classes (e.g., Cart) use inheritance from a persistence entity class. Therefore, with a simple but effective variation in the pointcut definition, for instance, intercepting those Controllers marked with a common annotation (e.g., @Controller), we obtain an XPI suitable to intercept another MVC framework.

In addition to this introspection solution, we also need to use the previously explained reflection capabilities to properly extract the system metadata. Thus, we extend this API with the methods to obtain each instance living in the system: models, controllers, among others. For this purpose, we implement interception methods that store these object instances, at model construction and controller injection time.

As a conclusion, we can state that although each MVC implementation requires its own pointcuts, the XPI allows us to maintain the necessary separation between our solution and the framework particularities. Note that this kind of solution allows the platform to intercept at the same time different applications implemented with different MVC frameworks. Therefore, our proposal benefits from the XPI approach to be the abstracted solution that fulfils the second requirement of this section.

```
1:   dsl = name '{' {weaver} '}' ;
2:   weaver = in  application ':' {act ',' behaviour} ';' ;
3:   application = name ;
4    act = when variable element [from controller];
5:   when = Before | Instead of | After ;
6:   element = action | view | event | task | attribute | flow ;
7:   controller = name ;
8:   behaviour = connector variable element [from controller] [by variable] [{another}] ;
9:   connector = perform | find | save | render | trigger | start | sets in ;
10:  another = and behaviour ;
11:  name = { all characters − '"' } ;
12:  variable = '"' , name , '"' ;
13:  all characters = ? all visible characters ? ;
```

Fig. 4. Reduced DSL Grammar

3.4 DSL

It is well known that AOP paradigm has not been adopted by developers and organizations due to its inherent complexity [20]. On the other hand, a Domain Specific Language (DSL) is a reduced language whose main aim is to represent constructions for a given domain. To begin with, a simple and understandable human readable language is required. Thereby, if we are able to provide an adequate DSL, end IT technicians do not need to deal with the underlying AOP facilities.

For our approach, we propose a DSL specification (Figure 4), which provides the way to formalize an abstract descriptor for the Workflow Weaving technique. Basically, this DSL specifies the Workflow Weaving behaviours, and all the interactions among each element in the system (i.e., applications and process model).

The definition of each *dsl* starts with the *name*, which obviously has to be unique in the system once it is deployed, and needs to be the same as the class name (e.g., weaver.PurchaseProcess). We continue with the *workflow-weaver* list. Each workflow weaver determines the target application, and its collection of events, as well as their related behaviours.

In line 4 (Figure 4), the *act* construction is defined, thus establishing when (past, present or future) and how (i.e., basically which is the involved *element*) it is produced in the specified application. Finally, if it is an action, we can specify from which *controller* it comes from. Moreover, in this DSL we specify each *behaviour* bound to an *act*, and it is defined in a similar manner. The *connector* introduces the action that we want to execute (e.g., *render*), and the *element* that will receive it.

Indeed, connectors are the major hook points that bind business processes and MVC web applications. In this line, we have defined a basic set of connectors that allow IT technicians to **start** an event or **trigger** a task from a business processes, access or modify (**find or save**) domain objects from the model, **render** view pages, and **perform** action methods of a controller.

In Figure 5 we show an example of DSL based on the use case described in Section 3.1. This DSL example defines a Workflow Weaving among the *Purchase*

```
1:   PurchaseWorkflow {
2:      in PetStore :
3:         Instead of "process" action from Order, trigger "init" event;
4:         After "Save Purchase" task, render "success" view;
5:      in Accounting :
6:         Before "Book Balance" task, find "customer" by "nin" and sets in "exists" attribute;
7:         After "Book Balance" task, perform "update" action from Book;
8:         After "Register Customer" task, perform "create" action from Customer;
9:   }
```

Fig. 5. Purchase Workflow DSL Example

process and the *PetStore* and *Accounting* applications. As we can see, each workflow weaver is defined simply by following the dotted arrows and the model designed by the business analyst.

Lastly, although this DSL grammar is flexible enough for basic model interactions, in the future we will extend it for executing new actions or accordingly capturing other events with platform implementation functionalities.

Indeed, this use case example demonstrates the usability and expressiveness of our approach. We have shown that our proposal builds a DSL solution including a high-level domain language, which considerably abstracts the use of AOP. Therefore, the main benefit is that the IT department does not need experts in the AOP field.

4 Implicit BPM Approach

In order to materialize the Workflow Weaving technique we have implemented the Implicit BPM approach. We have designed it as a simple, decoupled, and distributed platform. In this section, we introduce our Implicit BPM platform architecture and its life-cycle.

4.1 Architecture

The Implicit BPM platform has already been implemented as a distributed architecture, which consists of two separate parts: the Front-End and the Back-End systems. Both parts of the platform are connected via web standard mechanisms for flexibility and extensibility reasons, as well as due to the suitability of the web paradigm for exposing and consuming remote services.

We can see a diagram of our architecture proposal in Figure 6, where grey coloured components are either newly implemented or extended for our approach and are discussed as follows.

Front-End Side: is where organizational applications are deployed and where they run on servers in a distributed way. In fact, this system provides the interception and reflection components in our MVC black-box solution (as we have shown in Figure 2).

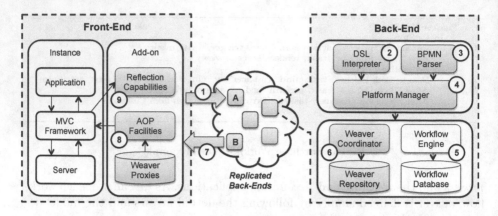

Fig. 6. Implict BPM Platform Architecture

Reflection Capabilities: include all the introspection functionalities. Specifically, this reflective approach retrieves meta-data from the MVC application, for example, the relationship between each model, controller, and view.

Weaver Proxies: live in a container that provides inserting (i.e., deployment) and installing (i.e., activation) them into the distributed and registered applications. In the deployment phase, the weaver proxy is sent to the Front-End container in the same host where the targeted application is running. Whenever the weaver proxy is needed, it has to be loaded from the container (i.e., serialized class) into the application.

AOP Facilities: support and use interceptors intensively, and strictly follow the XPI defined for this purpose. Algorithm 1 shows a workflow weaver example, which is responsible to render a view from a task, after a specific action is performed.

Algorithm 1. $renderTaskView$
Advice: $afterAction$ /* Pointcut */
Input: $resp$ /* Response */
Output: $resp$ /* Response */

1: $acts \leftarrow proxy.getActs()$
2: $action \leftarrow joinPoint.thisMethodName()$
3: **if** $action \in act.getActions()$ **then**
4:     $act \leftarrow proxy.getAct(action)$
5:     $behaviours \leftarrow proxy.getBehaviours(action)$
6:     **for** $beh \in behaviours$ **do**
7:         **if** $beh.connector = render$ **then**
8:             $attrs \leftarrow backEnd.getTaskAttrs(act.task)$
9:             $resp \leftarrow proxy.render(attrs)$
10:        **end if**
11:    **end for**
12: **end if**
13: $return(resp)$

For this purpose, this algorithm intercepts a specified action of a controller, and changes the application behaviour just following the enabled DSL instructions. In addition, it is able to recover the application metadata from the local proxy, and the model information (e.g. task attributes) from remote Back-End instances. We can see an example of this algorithm injection in our use case (Figure 1, Point B) and its DSL code (Figure 5, Line 4) where the Front-End detects the act *After 'Save Purchase' task*, and consequently execute the behaviour *render 'success' view*.

This way, each activated workflow weaver is converted to an AOP interceptor and is loaded in the proper proxy instance. With the XPI, the dynamic and decoupled techniques of the Weaver Proxy produce an important benefit we already explained in the previous section: it supports runtime reconfiguration, although the underlying weaver, from the AOP facilities, does not.

Back-End Side: supports the infrastructure of the system and provides deployment, management, and execution capabilities.

BPMN Parser: transforms the uploaded BPMN 2.0 XML file into a Workflow Engine component. Previously, it verifies the correctness of the model and it saves the necessary data into the platform to allow future Workflow Weavers to be integrated.

DSL Interpreter: is included in the Back-End to allow developers to write accurate DSL codes. It takes advantage of the remote MVC instrospection to facilitate the creation and edition of the Workflow Weaver. Using the communication system, it remotely retrieves all the necessary information from the Front-End reflection capabilities.

Platform Manager: controls, coordinates and consolidates the BPMN models, DSL codes, and registered applications. As a first layer of functionality for the Back-End, administrators are able to deploy models and classes, and manage the registered applications. Finally, it also provides reporting features for the business analysts.

Weaver Coordinator: is responsible for handling the state of each distributed workflow weaver in the platform. In addition, it periodically receives information about the deployed and activated weavers to perform monitoring tasks into the platform.

Weaver Repository: is capable of storing wokflow-weavers remotely. These weavers need to scatter the DSL parts and link them to each business process, which was previously deployed into the Workflow Engine.

Replicated Back-Ends: extend scalability features on this platform side. Application instances are duplicated, since they are mirror images of each other, and running on multiple servers of the organization.

Communication Bus: uses the standard HTTP protocol to expose all the services between the Front-End and the Back-End systems, mainly via REST technology.

4.2 Platform Life Cycle

Figure 6 shows the platform life cycle. First of all, enabling the **Front-End Add-on** an any application automatically registers it (1) into the **Back-End (A) instance**. Once an application is redeployed, the same process is executed in order to detect possible updates, for instance, a simple modification in the application deployed URL. Using remote reflection capabilities, the platform is able to retrieve all the needed information, as the application name, the operating URL, the main domain class (i.e., process instance binding) and the MVC structure and navigation rules.

Later on, in order to perform a new deployment, an administrator user needs: a **DSL** code class (2), and the related **BPMN** model (3) exported from a workflow designer. The **Platform Manager** (4) checks the consistency and coherency between the deployed files, and determines if it can be formally introduced into the system. If it is successfully installed, the generated classes go to the underlying systems (5-6), saving them in their supported **Database** and **Repository**, respectively.

The **Workflow Engine** (5) is wrapped by the **Back-End** system and it is used like a set of services which are exposed in a distributed fashion. Therefore, the engine is completely decoupled from the platform, and it could be easily switched by another BPM compliance implementation (e.g., Activiti[21] or Camunda[22]). In this scenario, tasks are executed within targeted applications, even the service tasks, that have to reference and use code from its corresponding application. Other types of activities, like manual tasks, do not have any special requirements.

Next, the **Weaver Coordinator** (6) controls all remote instances. Following the example in Figure 6, the **Back-End (B) instance** directly (7) deploys, and later injects the specified weaver proxies using the remote **AOP Facilities** (8).

In the end, these **Weaver Proxies** live in each application and they follows the instructions from the deployed DSL. To perform these rules, **Weaver Proxies** use the necessary AOP mechanisms implemented into the **Front-End Add-on** (e.g., Algorithm 1), as a black-box solution.

Finally, since the black-box mechanisms are linked to the XPI contract, they can use **Reflection Capabilities** (9) to return gathered feedback information (1) to any Back-End instance. This information is sent to the **Weaver Coordinator** (6) for monitoring purposes, as well as for reporting tasks to the **Platform Manager** (4).

5 Related Work

Previous works in literature [7,8,9] used AOP interception techniques to integrate applications with BPM platforms or external rule engines. For example, [7] proposed hybrid aspects for integrating object-oriented programming applications and rule-based reasoning. However, this approach relies on the in-depth knowledge of the targeted application to deploy the appropriate interceptors and pointcuts. The adoption of DSLs to simplify the implementation of interceptors have been also proposed in the past [9]. The main disadvantage of these DSLs is that to successfully apply them: they need to know the business classes, relationships among them, the semantics of their methods, and the interactions among instances.

Another related work is [23], where authors propose an AOP approach to separate out the base workflow from addition workflows, which can be weaved into the base when additional features are selected. Again, these works require detailed knowledge of the application that must be intercepted.

Interception approaches for standards such as BPEL have also been proposed before. AO4BPEL [24] and BPEL'n'aspects [25], are specific aspect-oriented language extensions. Each implementation is based on a modified BPEL engine, which checks at all potential join points, if an aspect has specified it in its pointcut. This allows easy and dynamic weaving of BPEL aspects with the drawback of less performance. As we plan to implement generic AOP mechanisms, we will not change the workflow engine but perform weaving on model level prior to workflow execution.

The major difference between all aforementioned previous works is that they follow a clear-box AOP interception model that requires in-depth knowledge of the application that must be intercepted. This clear-box model clearly complicates the adoption of these approaches and reduces their potential uses. In our case, we follow a black-box approach that intercepts code in strategic points using AOP facilities and following a common XPI for MVC frameworks. Thanks to the MVC standard pattern used extensively in web frameworks, we are able to interrogate and manipulate models, views and controllers transparently to the internal code of each application.

As stated before, reengineering legacy applications using BPM [12] is not easy to apply, because there are no tools that help the developers understand the legacy system behaviour. The introspection and wrapping capabilities on top of the MVC pattern enable us to perform black-box interception of any web application using this pattern. This considerably simplifies the integration of Web applications with BPM platforms using our DSL. The users of our DSL do not need to study the code of the existing application, and can thus weave business processes in legacy applications.

We propose the first approach of a distributed platform that interconnects different MVC based applications, and which allows business analysts to observe, proceduralize, and model each process in a holistic way.

6   Conclusions

We outline the importance of integrating business processes into existing applications. Nevertheless, rewriting legacy applications or reengineering them for BPM integration involves important development costs and in-depth knowledge of the targeted applications.

In this paper we present a novel solution (Implicit BPM) for integrating business processes into existing core applications as if they were a whole system.

We introduce a new concept, namely Workflow Weaving, based on non-intrusive techniques, which achieves this kind of integration transparently.

The novelty of our approach is to use black-box AOP techniques that benefit from the MVC web pattern to weave processes in a more transparent way. Previous approaches in literature used clear-box models, which require detailed knowledge of the legacy application. In our previous works [16,26] based on the same underlying distributed AOP principles, we have accurately evaluated that this kind of approach does not impose an additional overhead.

We also provide a natural and easy to use DSL that considerably simplifies the workflow weaving process, while at the same time hiding the underlying AOP complexity. Our prototype implementation is freely available at http://implicit-bpm.sf.net, under a LGPL license. This prototype makes use of the following well-known and widespread technologies: Groovy, Activiti, AspectJ, and Grails. This implementation includes the Front-End Add-on, which includes the MVC weaver, the Back-End system, which contains the DSL interpreter, and the Platform Manager, as well as the mentioned use case applications.

Cloud computing will enable organizations to bypass expensive BPM Enterprise products and start using open BPM platform solutions into their own private clouds. For these, we have designed and implemented our approach to be perfectly suitable for easy deployment and operation into a Cloud. In a close future, we are going to combine our platform with a private PaaS Cloud, like CloudSNAP [26].

Acknowledgments. We thank the BPM chairs and the three anonymous reviewers for their constructive comments, which helped us to improve this work. In addition, we also want to thank to Manuel Bertran for his many helpful review and suggestions.

This work has been partially funded by the EU in the context of the project CloudSpaces: Open Service Platform for the Next Generation of Personal Clouds (FP7- 317555).

References

1. Kiczales, G., Lamping, J., Mendhekar, A., Maeda, C., Lopes, C., Loingtier, J.-M., Irwin, J.: Aspect-oriented programming. In: Akşit, M., Matsuoka, S. (eds.) ECOOP 1997. LNCS, vol. 1241, pp. 220–242. Springer, Heidelberg (1997)
2. Ping, Y., Kontogiannis, K., Lau, T.C.: Transforming legacy web applications to the mvc architecture. In: STEP, Washington, USA, pp. 133–142 (2003)
3. Elrad, T., Filman, R.E., Bader, A.: Aspect-oriented programming: Introduction. Communications of the ACM 44, 29–32 (2001)
4. Dinkelaker, T., Eichberg, M., Mezini, M.: An Architecture for Composing Embedded Domain-specific Languages. In: AOSD, pp. 49–60 (2010)
5. Jablonski, S.: A Software Architecture for Workflow Management Systems. In: DESA, pp. 739–744. IEEE Computer Society (1998)

6. Knuplesch, D., Reichert, M., Fdhila, W., Rinderle-Ma, S.: On enabling compliance of cross-organizational business processes. In: Daniel, F., Wang, J., Weber, B. (eds.) BPM 2013. LNCS, vol. 8094, pp. 146–154. Springer, Heidelberg (2013)
7. D'Hondt, M., Jonckers, V.: Hybrid Aspects for Weaving Object-oriented Functionality and Rule-based knowledge. In: AOSD, pp. 132–140 (2004)
8. Cibran, M., D'hondt, M.: High-Level Specification of Business Rules and Their Crosscutting Connections. In: AOSD (2006)
9. Hnatkowska, B., Kasprzyk, K.: Integration of application business logic and business rules with DSL and AOP. In: Szmuc, T., Szpyrka, M., Zendulka, J. (eds.) CEE-SET 2009. LNCS, vol. 7054, pp. 30–39. Springer, Heidelberg (2012)
10. Geiger, M., Wirtz, G.: Detecting Interoperability and Correctness Issues in BPMN 2.0 Process Models. ZEUS, Rostock, Germany (2013)
11. do Nascimento, G.S., Iochpe, C., Thom, L.H., Reichert, M.: A Method for Rewriting Legacy Systems using Business Process Management Technology. In: ICEIS (3), pp. 57–62 (2009)
12. do Nascimento, G.S., Iochpe, C., Thom, L., Kalsing, A.C., Moreira, Á.: Identifying Business Rules to Legacy Systems Reengineering Based on BPM and SOA. In: ICCSA, pp. 67–82 (2011)
13. Patel, S.R., Gerald, B., Micah, S.: Mastering Enterprise JavaBeans 3.0. John Wiley & Sons, Inc., New York (2006)
14. Schmidt, D., Stal, M., Rohnert, H., Buschmann, F.: Pattern-Oriented Software Architecture, Patterns for Concurrent and Networked Objects, vol. 2. John Wiley & Sons (2000)
15. Mondéjar, R., García-López, P., Fernández-Casado, E., Pairot, C.: TaKo: Providing transparent collaboration on single-user applications. Computer Languages, Systems & Structures 38, 108–121 (2012)
16. Mondejar, R., Garcia-Lopez, P., Pairot, C., Pamies-Juarez, L.: Damon: a Distributed AOP Middleware for Large-Scale Scenarios. Information and Software Technology 54, 317–330 (2012)
17. Rosenberg, D., Scott, K., Matter, F.: Use Case Driven Object Modeling with UML: A Practical Approach (1999)
18. Rocher, G.K., Brown, J., Laforge, G.: The Definitive Guide to Grails. Springer (2009)
19. Griswold, W.G., Sullivan, K., Song, Y., Shonle, M., Tewari, N.: Modular Software Design with Crosscutting Interfaces. IEEE Software 23, 51–60 (2006)
20. Hohenstein, U.D.C., Jäger, M.C.: Using aspect-orientation in industrial projects: Appreciated or damned? In: AOSD, pp. 213–222 (2009)
21. Rademakers, T.: Activiti in Action: Executable business processes in BPMN 2.0. Manning Publications Co. (2012)
22. Freund, J., Rücker, B.: Real-Life BPMN: Using BPMN 2.0 to Analyze, Improve, and Automate Processes in Your Company (2012)
23. Elsner, C.: Towards separation of concerns in model transformation workflows. In: EA, pp. 81–88 (2008)
24. Charfi, A., Mezini, M.: Ao4bpel: An aspect-oriented extension to BPEL. World Wide Web 10, 309–344 (2007)
25. Sonntag, M., Karastoyanova, D.: Compensation of adapted service orchestration logic in bPEL'n'Aspects. In: Rinderle-Ma, S., Toumani, F., Wolf, K. (eds.) BPM 2011. LNCS, vol. 6896, pp. 413–428. Springer, Heidelberg (2011)
26. Mondéjar, R., García-López, P., Pairot, C., Pamies-Juarez, L.: CloudSNAP: A transparent infrastructure for decentralized web deployment using distributed interception. Future Generation Computer Systems 29, 370–380 (2013)

Modeling Concepts for Internal Controls in Business Processes – An Empirically Grounded Extension of BPMN

Martin Schultz[1,*] and Michael Radloff[2]

[1] University of Applied Sciences Wedel, Germany
msz@fh-wedel.de
[2] University of Hamburg, Germany
michael.radloff@wiso.uni-hamburg.de

Abstract. With the increasing number and complexity of legal obligations, ensuring business process compliance presents a major challenge for today's organizations. In this regard, implementing a set of control means and regularly auditing their effectiveness are suitable measures to ensure a compliant design and enactment of a business process. However, common business process modeling languages (PML) do not provide appropriate concepts to comprehensively model such control means. Not surprisingly, common PMLs are not widely used in the audit domain. To address this gap, this paper presents an extension of a PML with modeling concepts for process-integrated control means. As it is based on previous empirical research with auditors, the extension especially considers their requirements. The results of a laboratory experiment with 78 participants demonstrate that the extension supports auditors to gain a more comprehensive understanding of internal controls in a process model compared to current audit practice.

Keywords: Process Modeling Language Extension, Business Process Compliance, Process Audits, BPMN extensibility mechanism, Empirical BPM research.

1   Introduction

Assuring compliance of business processes to internal and external regulations presents a major challenge for today's organizations. The rules and regulations have increased in number and complexity over the last years due to a series of financial scandals (Parmalat 2003, Satyam 2009, Olympus 2011). They stem from diverse sources ranging from voluntary norms or standards (e.g. ISO 38500, COBIT) to policies imposed by active legislation (Sarbanes-Oxley Act, 8th EU directive, Basel I-III) [1]. To ensure a compliant state of their business processes organizations implement and maintain a multitude of different measures collectively referred to as the internal

---

* Corresponding author.

S. Sadiq, P. Soffer, and H. Völzer (Eds.): BPM 2014, LNCS 8659, pp. 184–199, 2014.
© Springer International Publishing Switzerland 2014

control system (ICS). When it comes to auditing the compliance of a business process, internal and external auditors put their focus on the ICS. All control means that are embedded in a process are thoroughly reviewed for their design effectiveness (Is the control means effectively designed to mitigate potential risks?) and their operating effectiveness (Was the control means effectively enacted throughout the time period under audit?). Accordingly, for a comprehensive process assessment, auditors have to collect a large amount of information from diverse sources and various organizational levels [2]. For documenting this information auditors rely on several fundamentally different formats ranging from flexible, less structured narratives over structured aids like control matrices to graphical formats such as flowcharts [3, 4]. Audit standards do not impose binding policies regarding the documentation of processes and related audit-relevant concepts although the format significantly influences the effectiveness and efficiency of an audit [5, 6]. Prior research found that for several audit tasks diagrams lead to higher audit effectiveness than narratives as well as that more elaborate flowchart representations facilitate the audit of business processes [5, 7]. Moreover, empirical research results indicate that auditors would benefit from an integrated representation of the ICS and business process models [8, 9]. However, comprehensive surveys revealed that methods for annotating, and enhancing business process models with compliance/ audit modeling elements are one of the main open issues on the research agenda for business process compliance [10, 11]. Not surprisingly, surveys among auditors show that common process modeling languages (PML)[1] are not widely used in current audit practice [4, 12]. This indicates that common PMLs do not sufficiently meet auditors' requirements for annotating audit-relevant concepts in process models [6, 11, 12].

To close this gap, this paper presents an approach for extending activity-based PMLs with modeling elements for control means. For illustrating the approach, the widely used business process modeling and notation 2.0 (BPMN) is used [13]. The existing BPMN meta-model is extended and notation elements are introduced to provide appropriate means for enriching process models with control means. For constructing the extension, we apply the approach outlined in [14] which recommends involving prospective users and subject-matter experts in such a conceptual modeling task. Accordingly, the presented extension is based on thorough empirical research work in the audit domain, especially focusing on auditors' conceptualization and representation of control means in the context of business process audits. The aim of the extension is to facilitate the creation, interpretation, and analysis of process models from an audit respectively from an internal controls perspective. The utility of the designed extension is evaluated with a laboratory experiment with 78 participants knowledgeable in process modeling and internal controls.

The remainder of this paper is structured as follows. The next section elaborates on related research regarding business process compliance (BPC) and on the conceptualization and representation of audit-relevant concepts in the context of business process audits. Section 3 outlines the applied research method. Section 4 presents a

---

[1] In this paper we use the acronym "PML" to refer to common/ generic business process modeling languages.

detailed description of the proposed PML extension. The results of the evaluation are summarized in section 5. The paper closes with a discussion (section 6) followed by the conclusion along with implications for future research work in section 7.

2   Related Research and Empirical Results

To gain an understanding of a domain, key terms and concepts need to be reconstructed [15]. A key term for the topic at hand is *internal control*. Internal control is broadly defined as a process designed to provide reasonable assurance regarding the achievement of three objectives: 1) effectiveness and efficiency of an entity's operations; 2) reliability of internal and external financial and non-financial reporting; and 3) compliance with applicable laws and regulations [16]. The ICS consists of integrated elements such as people, organizational structures, policies, processes, and procedures [15, 17]. Key elements are *control objective* and *control means*. A control objective describes a desired state of an organization/ process. Control means are recommended courses of action to ensure that a control objective is achieved [15]. They are either directly related to a process (*process-integrated control means*, e.g. invoice approval, reconciliation of invoice and goods receipt) or are independently performed from a particular process (*process-independent control means*, e.g. internal audit) [18, 19].

A few seminal research endeavors have been dedicated to conceptualize internal controls-related concepts and their link to business processes. Rosemann and zur Muehlen [20] are one of first authors who consider the concept *risk* in process modeling. They link *risk* to a conceptual model of business processes. The conceptual model outlined in [21] comprises the concepts *risk, significant account, control objective, control,* and *recovery action*. Karagiannis et al. [22] consider *risk, control objective, control* and *account* as domain specific concepts. These are linked to *BP elements* (information system, process activity, organizational unit). *Control objective, control* and *risk* are also set in relation in [23]. Similarly, Strecker et al. [15] stress *control objective* and *control means* as main concepts to describe an ICS. Sadiq et al. [24] use the concepts *control objective, internal control, risk, process control flow, process task,* and *property* to ontologically align the compliance domain with process modeling. Schumm et al. [25] and Turetken et al. [26] present a conceptual model that focuses on *compliance requirements*. A compliance requirement stems from a *compliance source*, is associated to a *compliance risk* and can be assessed by a *compliance request*. It can be addressed by a *control* that is formally expressible as a *compliance rule* and refers to an abstract *compliance target*. Spies and Tabet [27] present a comprehensive conceptual model for a risk and control taxonomy (GRC-XML) which includes *risk, control objective, control activity, regulation,* and *policy* as key modeling elements for the domain.

To complement these research results with empirical evidence, we derived relevant modeling concepts for process audits by a series of expert interviews (17 interviews) and a subsequent online survey (370 respondents) [8, 28]. 12 modeling concepts were identified: 1) *process control flow, 2) information systems, 3) organization,* 4) *data, 5) Audit/ control objectives, 6) control (means), 7) risk, 8) audit results, 9) standards & regulations, 10) financial statements, 11) materiality, and 12) business objectives.*[2] The results are largely in line with prior research and underline the common understanding among auditors of concepts that need to be considered for process audits. Based on these results, we have constructed a conceptual model for BPC that reflects this audit perspective [29].

Especially for control means diverse characteristics are discussed in audit practice and academia, underlining the wide range of measures available to achieve a particular control objective [15]. Essential attributes for control means are *timing* (preventive or detective), *nature* (manual or automated), and *frequency* (time period a control means has to occur, e.g. daily, monthly) [30]. However, in the context of business processes, the term control means is subject to terminological ambiguity [15]. Audit standards distinguish between *organizational control means* and *procedural control means* [31]. The former are measures that are integrated in the organizational structure of an organization e.g. restricted access, segregation of duties (SoD), and enforcement of approval levels. These means refer to requirements that can be easily expressed as a formal (business/ compliance) rule for a process and/ or process activity [29]. The latter are measures that are directly integrated in the sequence of operations e.g. check for completeness or validity [31]. They represent a target/actual performance comparison enacted as an activity in a process [32].

Our empirical analyses reveal that auditors conceptualize control means mainly as procedural control means [8]. 14 out of 17 experts in our interviews state that control means should be directly integrated into process models as a special activity to facilitates the assessment of processes from an ICS perspective [9]. Hence, although there are semantic differences, for audit purposes control means can be represented as an atomic activity in a process model [33, 34]. However, surveys among auditors reveal that flowcharts and PMLs are only used by a minority of the auditors. When graphically documenting a process, auditors rather rely on firm specific languages or office software instead of PMLs [12]. Narratives and structured aids like control matrices are still the prevalent formats [4]. In this regard, audit standards do not impose binding guidelines although seminal research results demonstrate that documentation formats significantly influence auditors' effectiveness (e.g. increased identification of missing control means and design weaknesses) [5–7, 19, 35, 36]. One explanation for the low dissemination of process modeling/ flowcharts in the audit domain is that existing PMLs do not fully cover relevant concepts of the ICS and thereby not sufficiently meet auditors' requirements [6, 7, 11, 12]. Against this background, the objective of this research is to provide a suitable method for modeling control means in business processes which contributes to a more efficient and effective enactment of process audits. In accordance with our empirical results, the extension focusses on procedural control means.

---

[2] For a description of each audit concept, the concept map, and the methodological details of the expert interviews and the online survey please refer to the respective papers [8, 28].

3   Research Approach

The research presented in this paper follows the design science approach [37, 38]. The designed artefact is an extension to BPMN, a widely used, activity-oriented PML. The BPMN meta-model and the notation are extended to provide suitable modeling concepts for control means. In earlier work we applied a multi-method research approach by combining a qualitative (expert interviews) and a quantitative (online survey) research method to rigorously derive requirements for such an extension for the audit domain. In this paper, the applied research method is conceptual modeling. In accordance to the approach outlined by Ahlemann and Gastl [14], we base our model construction on requirements derived from prospective users and subject-matter experts. The relevance of the artefact stems from the fact that methods for annotating process models with compliance modeling elements are still lacking [11].

There is a consensus in literature that evaluating a designed artefact is an essential step in design science [39]. We choose a 1 x 2 between-group laboratory experiment for evaluating the BPMN extension. Thereby, we focus on the stakeholders' perception of the BPMN extension regarding understandability and appropriateness [40]. The aim is to scrutinize all propositions regarding acceptance of stakeholders (auditors) [14]. Details on the experimental design are outlined in section 5.

4   BPMN+C – A BPMN Extension for Internal Controls

To provide appropriate modeling elements for a particular domain, there are generally two options: 1) developing a new domain specific modeling language (DSML) or 2) extending an existing common modeling language. We opt for the later approach as a large number of concepts that have been identified as relevant for a process audits (process control flow, process activity, data, organizational resources, information systems) are already well-considered in existing common PMLs [41]. BPMN 2.0 is chosen as illustration for two reasons: 1) BPMN provides a standardized meta-model with an extensibility mechanism. 2) In terms of dissemination, BPMN is one of the fastest spreading PMLs worldwide [42, 43]. The latter is especially important in the audit domain which is highly regulated by international audit standards.

The next section presents requirements for the BPMN extension. Subsequently, the extension is outlined on two levels: 1) the semantics of the extension is illustrated in terms of a conceptual model that links domain-specific concepts to the concepts of BPMN (section 4.2). 2) The extension to the notation of the underlying PML is presented in section 4.3. Section 4.4 demonstrates the applicability of the extension by means of an example.

4.1   Requirements for the PML Extension BPMN+C

Based on related research and our empirical research work four requirements are derived that guide the design and implementation of the BPMN extension for control means, subsequently named as 'BPMN+C'. Primary sources for the requirements were seminal research work on modeling languages for audit/ compliance purposes (req. 1, 2, and 4) [15, 29, 44, 45], our empirical research work in the audit domain (req. 1, 2) [8, 12, 28], and the BPMN specification (req. 3 and 4) [13].

- *Requirement 1 – Domain specific modeling elements:* The extension should provide appropriate modeling elements for all concepts that have been indicated as relevant by subject-matter experts. These modeling elements and their relations should be in line with the conceptualization of prospective users. The extension should establish a clear conceptual link between modeling elements of the audit domain and the business process modeling domain and provide a machine-readable format to enable an automated processing of audit information in process models.
- *Requirement 2 – Multiplicity of control means:* The extension should reflect the various types and distinct characteristics of control means that are commonly used in the audit domain.
- *Requirement 3 – Downward compatibility of extended models:* The extension should not alter or contradict the semantics and notation of the underlying PML. An extended process model should be convertible into a process model that only uses the PML standard elements (with a loss of domain specific elements).
- *Requirement 4 – Perceptibility of control means in process models:* The extension should enhance the perceptibility of control means in a process model. The model users should be able to identify and evaluate represented control means with low effort. This requires unique notation elements for control means which are in accordance with symbolic elements of the audit domain. Thereby, the basic look-and-feel of the underlying PML should be taken into account as far as possible.

4.2 BPMN Meta-model Extension

The main challenge for extending BPMN 2.0 is a lack of methodical support for constructing an extension model that complies to the extensibility mechanism of the BPMN specification [46]. Referring to this, Stroppi et al. [46] provide a method to transform a conceptual domain model to a BPMN conform extension model with the help of mapping rules and automated model transformations. This method is applied for this research work. Fig. 1 outlines our proposed conceptual domain model as UML-class diagram. The classes of the BPMN 2.0 meta-model - highlighted in grey - are an excerpt of the BPMN specification. These BPMN classes are associated to further classes. For reasons of clarity, these are omitted in our model. The BPMN specification describes the semantics of these elements in detail [13].

Our extension comprises the classes *ProceduralControlMeans*, *AuditResult*, *Risk*, and *ControlObjective*. These classes represent all control means-related domain concepts that are identified as relevant by the domain experts (*Req. 1*). The core element of this extension is the class *ProceduralControlMeans*. It provides a set of attributes that represent relevant characteristics for control means (*Req. 2*). The *frequency* of the control means, declared by the correspondent property with the enumeration *FrequencyType*, describes the time frame in which the control means should be executed. The *timing* of the control means is declared by the correspondent property with the enumeration *TimingType*. It describes whether a control means is "preventive" or "detective". The property *recommendedAction* defines an action that should be performed to enact the control means. The property *nature* is declared with the enumeration *NatureType* and defines whether a control means is "manual" or "automated".

Our extension is solely linked (via composition) to the BPMN class *Activity* (*Req. 1*). According to BPMN 2.0, an activity is work that is performed within a business process and can be atomic or compound [13]. Accordingly, linking the extension for control means to *Activity* is in line with the conceptualization of auditors (*Req.2*). By means of this composition, a BPMN *Activity* can inherit the attributes of *Procedural-ControlMeans* and is thereby extended. Also, BPMN *Tasks* are atomic activities in the process flow and allow specifying a resource, interface or rule set for the task execution. As BPMN class *Task* inherits from BPMN *Activity* they also can be extended with the control means attributes. In our extension, the different BPMN *Task* types are used to represent the *nature* of a control means. The mapping between *NatureType* and BPMN Task types is as follows: For automated control means BPMN *ScriptTask* or *BusinessRuleTask* are used as they are not require human performer to be executed. Manual control means are represented as *UserTask* or *ManualTask* as they involve a human performer and cannot be executed without a human performer.

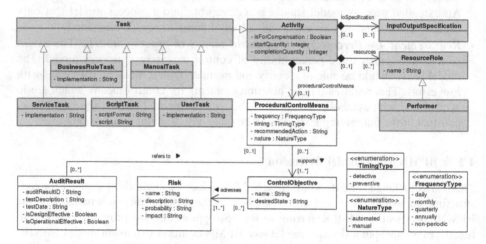

Fig. 1. Domain Model for the BPMN extension

The classes *AuditResult*, *Risk*, and *ControlObjective* are further elements of the audit domain. In our extension, they are included in order to establish references between a specific control means and these concepts. They are solely considered from the control means perspective (e.g. risk is also associated to other BPM concepts). The complete semantics for these concepts is not in the scope of this particular extension.

The conceptual model describes the desired semantics for the BPMN extension. Based on this domain model a transformed model for the BPMN extensibility mechanism is created. The BPMN extensibility mechanism is described in two representations: the MetaObject Facility (MOF) meta-model and an XML schema. The BPMN classes shown in the domain model in Fig. 1 are part of the MOF meta-model. This may not be altered by the extension, but contains classes for the extensibility mechanism. The XML schema enables an interchange of BPMN models between modeling tools. Hence, to add the attributes in a technical implementation, we generate a XML schema definition (XSD) which is linked to the BPMN 2.0 XSD. The generation is based on the 'BPMN+X' UML profile and rule set provided in [46]. The method creates an UML (BPMN+X) extension model, transforms this into an XML schema extension model (model-to-model transformation) and into an XML schema document (model-to-code transformation) [46]. The 'BPMN+X' model for our extension

and excerpts of the corresponding XSD are illustrated in Fig. 2. The BPMN+X model
is enhanced with stereotypes. The *ExtensionDefinition* stereotype describes a container and corresponds to the respective class in the MOF extensibility mechanism. The
ExtensionElement stereotype is defined in the BPMN-X UML profile and matches the
ExtensionAttributeValue class of the MOF extensibility mechanism. This allows illustrating the various elements as class objects for the next transformation step. Finally,
we generate the XSD with the BPMN+X model transformation. This XSD conforms
to the BPMN 2.0 extensibility mechanism *(Req. 3)*. Thereby, the execution semantics
of BPMN 2.0 standard is not altered and a machine-readable format for model interchange is provided *(Req. 1)*. Depending on the underlying PML, the behavior of control means can be further specified, e.g. in BPMN the multi-instance concept can be
used to model a batch processing of many business transactions in one control means.

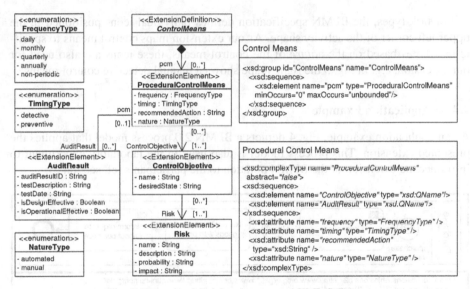

Fig. 2. Extension Model and generated XML Schema

4.3   BPMN Notation Extension

For visualizing the extended modeling elements in a process model, we propose a
corresponding extension of the notation *(Req. 4)*. To describe process models as diagrams, BPMN provides a schema for diagram interchange (BPMN:DI) which is
meant to facilitate interchange between modeling tools. This schema allows specifying the visual attributes of a process model in its XML representation. In this regard,
the BPMN specification provides neither guidelines for the graphical representation
of extension elements nor an extensibility mechanism for new notation elements. The
notation has to be implemented separately to the semantics in a modeling tool [46]. In
general, the notation of an extension must not alter the BPMN notation and should be
as close as possible to it (look and feel) [13]. Our notation extends the shapes of the
BPMN *Activity* respectively the BPMN *Task* and adds an icon to the shape as shown

in Fig. 3. The extended modeling element – the *ProceduralControlMeans* – is represented by a lens icon in the bottom middle anchor of the shape. In this area the BPMN defines three types of markers for activities: a marker for *loop, multi-instance characteristics,* and *compensation.* In the same place, we add a lens icon as marker for control means. Detective control means are denoted by a single lens whereas for preventive control means a lens encircled by a shield icon is chosen. A similar design for both icons shall facilitate the perceptibility of control means in a process model.

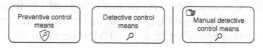

Fig. 3. Notation for the BPMN+C Extension

For task types, the BPMN specification defines individual icons positioned in the upper left corner of the activity shape. As our extension maps control means to specific task types based on the *nature* of the control means, these icons are also used for our extension, e.g. in Fig. 3 the right shape shows a manual detective control means.

4.4   Application Example

As an application example, Fig. 4 depicts a BPMN 2.0 process model that applies the presented extension. This process model is also used in the laboratory experiment to introduce the extension of the BPMN notation to the participants (cf. section 5).

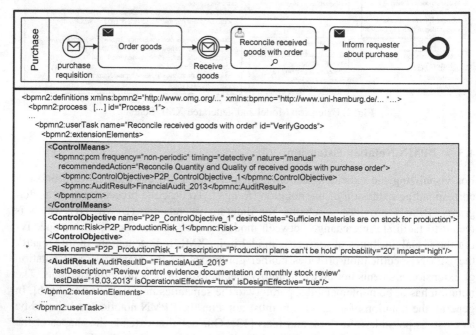

Fig. 4. Sample Process as BPMN model and XML description

In the example, the BPMN user task *'reconcile received goods with order'* is extended with all attributes from class *ProceduralControlMeans*. As illustration, we also add elements for the referenced *ControlObjective, Risk,* and *AuditResult*. To outline the semantics of the extension, the process model is also described as an XML document. We have enhanced a given standard BPMN process model with the modeling elements of our extension. In Fig. 4 these are highlighted in separate boxes.

5   Evaluation

5.1   Experimental Design

In a design science research project, the evaluation step tries to observe and measure how well the designed artifact supports a solution for the addressed problem [47]. For the evaluation of the BPMN extension a 1 x 2 between-group experiment is designed. The two groups receive the same information of a fictitious organization on a purchase-to-pay business process and related control means. One group obtains information on control means (controls matrix) separately from the process models (group BPMN). The other group has access to process models that are enhanced with controls-related information based on the previously presented BPMN extension (group BPMN+C). The provided information has three levels of complexity in terms of process model size and number of control means. By doing so, the external validity of the experiment is increased [48]. The data provided to both groups is designed to be equivalent regarding the informational content [49]. Thus, a transformation of one presentation into the other is possible without loss of information [50].

In process audits there are two main tasks that are related to processes models: 1) model creation and 2) model interpretation. In this evaluation step we focus on model interpretation. For evaluating the quality of model interpretation two perspectives are discussed in academia: *interpretational fidelity* (how faithfully does the interpretation of the model supports the reader to comprehend the domain semantics included in the model?) and *interpretational efficiency* (what resources are required for interpreting the model?) [51, 52]. In similar studies interpretational fidelity is measured by using tasks and questions to test how well a model user comprehends the content of a given model (*comprehension task performance*) [52, 53]. To operationalize interpretational efficiency the time is measured that a model user needs to complete comprehension tasks and questions (*comprehension task efficiency*) [50, 52, 53]. In our experiment following hypothesis are tested:

- **H1:** *Comprehension task efficiency* is positively affected by using the BPMN extension for representing control means in process models.
- **H2:** *Comprehension task performance* is positively affected by using the BPMN extension for representing control means in process models.

The study is implemented as an online accessible experiment using the Qualtrics research suite [54]. Participants are recruited through two channels: 1) master students in information systems are asked for voluntary participation. Due to the master curriculum, the invited students are knowledgeable in process modeling and have a basic understanding of internal control. 2) By utilizing social networks for business professionals (e.g. XING) and large audit associations (e.g. DIIR, ISACA), internal and external auditors as well as process analysts were invited to participate.

In the experiment, the participants have to complete five steps. They first arrive at a landing page which explains the nature of the experiment and introduces the responsible institution (step 1). After the questions referring to demographic characteristics, process modeling knowledge, and ICS knowledge (step 2), a short overview of relevant BPMN standard elements (task types, gateways) is provided. Following this, the participants are randomly assigned to one of the groups (BPMN, BPMN+C) and the elements and notation of the BPMN+C extension are only introduced to the corresponding group. Hereinafter, detailed instructions on the experiment structure and tasks are given to both groups (step 3). Subsequently, three process models (model 1: 3 activities, 3 events; model 2: 10 activities, 7 events; model 3: 11 activities, 4 events, 3 gateways) are consecutively presented to the participants (step 4). As first task for each model, the participants are asked to identify control means by clicking them in the model (*controls identification task*). As second task, the participants have to answer multiple choice questions referring to the process control flow and embedded control means (model 1: 4, model 2: 9, model 3: 15 questions). Finally, the experiment offers an opportunity to evaluate the experiment (step 5).

5.2   Results of the Experiment

In total 78 participants passed the experiment (BPMN = 39 and BPMN+C = 39). 13 students and 65 professional participated (BPMN: 9/30, BPMN+C: 4/35). Based on ten questions, the average self-reported process modeling knowledge on a five-point Likert scale (1 – very poor, 5 – very good) is 3,27 for group BPMN and 3,05 for group BPMN+C. Chi-square tests/ t-tests confirmed that in terms of demographic characteristics (age, education, employment status, working experience, and self-reported process modeling knowledge) the participants are equally represented in both groups and that the results are not biased by the distribution of the participants. Only for the characteristic "gender" there is an unequal distribution (in total: 58 male/20 female, BPMN: 34/5, BPMN+C: 24/15). However, there are no significant differences for the measured variables for male and female participants.

In order to test our hypothesis we conduct a two independent sample t-test (two-tailed) to compare the means of both groups (BPMN, BPMN+C) regarding five variables. For comprehension task efficiency the time is measured (in seconds) the participants need to conduct the controls identification task (Duration - Controls Identification) and to answer the comprehension questions (Duration - Questions). Comprehension task performance is operationalized by the number of correctly identified control means (Correctly Identified Controls), the number of correctly answered questions (Correct Answers), and a score for the perceived ease of understanding derived from five questions with a five-point Likert scale (Perceived Ease of Understanding).

All variables are added up for all three models. Table 1 summarizes the t-test results. The results demonstrate that participants of the group with the extended process models (BPMN+C) require significantly less time to identify the nine control means embedded in the three process models ($p < 0.001$, mean(BPMN) = 99.88 sec., mean(BPMN+C) = 57.88 sec.). Regarding the time for answering the comprehension questions the mean for the BPMN+C group is lower, but the difference is not significant ($p = 0.417$, mean(BPMN) = 521.07 sec., mean(BPMN+C) = 483.82 sec.). In summary, the results of both variables (Duration - Controls Identification, Duration - Questions) support hypothesis H1.

For comprehension task performance the results of the three defined variables (*Correctly Identified Controls, Correct Answers, Perceived Ease of Understanding*) are varying. Participants of the BPMN+C group are more accurate in identifying control means in the process models. At the same time, they answer slightly less comprehension questions correctly. Regarding the perceived ease of understanding the means of both groups only differ marginally. For all three variables the differences between the groups are insignificant. These results are contrary to hypothesis H2 as we expected an improved comprehension task performance.

Table 1. Two-Sample T-Test Results for the Groups BPMN (n=39) and BPMN+C (n=39)[3]

	BPMN		BPMN+C			
	Mean	SD	Mean	SD	t(95)	Sig.
Comprehension Task Efficiency						
Duration - Controls Identification (sec.)	99.88	47.72	57.88	27.05	4.509	**0.000**
Duration - Questions (sec.)	521.07	186.95	483.82	185.95	0.817	0.417
Comprehension Task Performance						
Correctly Identified Controls (0-9)	8.54	1.19	8.79	0.80	-1.117	0.268
Correct Answers (0-28)	23.05	2.65	22.64	3.26	0.610	0.544
Perceived Ease of Understanding (5-25)	19.29	3.32	19.40	3.66	-0.137	0.892

6   Discussion

The experimental results indicate that the BPMN extension has a positive effect on comprehension task efficiency with regard to the representation and the assessment of control means in process models. One potential interpretation is that the integrated documentation of control means and process control flow reduces the cognitive load for model interpretation and thereby increases *interpretational efficiency* and lastly the efficiency of process audits. With respect to interpretational fidelity the experimental results are inconclusive as no significant differences between the groups could be found for comprehension task effectiveness. One potential explanation is that the information and questions provided to both groups allow both groups to gain a relatively high score for effectiveness (approx. 23 from 28). Potentially more complex process models would have led to more significant results. Furthermore, we noticed noteworthy differences regarding different types of questions (process-control flow-related, control means-related, combined). Both aspects require further investigations.

Besides the evaluation results, it is worth to take a closer look on some conceptual and technical aspects. As it is designed in accordance to empirically derived requirements, we believe that the presented extension meet auditors' needs for process audits. However, by including further stakeholder groups like (e.g. compliance managers, process owners) valuable new insights may potentially be derived. In terms of generalizability it can be noted that the extension is instantiated as XSD for BPMN. However, as it is only based on one conceptual link between the PML meta-model (*activity*) and the extension definition (*ProceduralControlMeans*) it is also applicable

---

3 IBM SPSS Statistics Version 21.0.0.0 is used as statistical analysis software.

for other activity- or activity/event-oriented PMLs (e.g. event driven process chains, EPC). In addition, the system-independent data format for information on process-integrated control means allows an alignment with related initiatives in the domain (e.g. GRC XML a schema for sharing and communicating risk and control related information [55]). At the same time, the XML format enables an automated processing of information on control means within process audits. On a broader level the presented extension might contribute to a reconfiguration of complex audit tasks (e.g. process audits) that are largely a matter of auditor's professional judgment in current audit practice [56]. By providing relevant information in a machine-readable format, selected audit task types are reconfigurable to types that can be approached by automated audit procedures which enables a broader software support for auditors.

7   Conclusion and Further Research

Today's organizations have to comply with an ever-increasing number of regulatory requirements in their daily operation. Accordingly, in recent years practitioners and researchers have been paying more attention to management and auditing business process compliance. Nevertheless, recent research results show that methods for an-notating, and enhancing business process models with compliance/ audit modeling elements are still lacking [10, 11]. To address this gap, the paper presented an exten-sion to a common activity-oriented PML that enables an integrated representation of business processes and embedded control means. As illustration, BPMN was ex-tended with domain specific modeling elements and their characteristics that were determined as relevant through previous empirical research work in the audit domain. A laboratory experiment with 78 participants showed that the extension increases interpretational efficiency compared to a separated documentation of process models and control means as it is applied in current audit practice.

However, not only the evaluation results point to several opportunities for further fruitful research directions. Besides control means there are further relevant concepts that need to be considered for a comprehensive process audit. Such a comprehensive modeling method that facilitates an efficient and effective processing of audit-relevant information in the context of process audits remains on our research agenda. Further-more, in this evaluation we focused on model interpretation. The effects of the extension on process model creation also need to be evaluated. We also plan further statistical analysis of the experiment data to gain more insights on the impact of par-ticipants' characteristics on the effectiveness of the BPMN extension. In addition, in current audit practice complex audit assignments such as process audits are to a large extent subject to professional judgment [56]. More structured and automated solutions might have a positive impact on the effectiveness of auditors' decisions. In this re-gard, we believe that the presented extension along with the XML representation of audit relevant information is a useful step towards more comprehensive software solu-tions for process audits. In the long run, not only auditors would benefit from in-creased audit effectiveness and efficiency but all stakeholders of the global economy.

References

1. Ghanavati, S., Amyot, D., Peyton, L.: A systematic review of goal-oriented requirements management frameworks for business process compliance. In: 2011 Fourth International Workshop on Requirements Engineering and Law (RELAW), pp. 25–34 (2011)
2. Maijoor, S.: The Internal Control Explosion. International Journal of Auditing 4, 101–109 (2000)
3. Purvis, S.E.C.: The effect of audit documentation format on data collection. Accounting, Organizations and Society 14, 551–563 (1989)
4. Bierstaker, J., Janvrin, D., Jordan Lowe, D.: An Examination of Factors Associated with the Type and Number of Internal Control Documentation Formats. Advances in Accounting 23, 31–48 (2007)
5. Bryant, S., Murthy, U., Wheeler, P.: The Effects of Cognitive Style and Feedback Type on Performance in an Internal Control Task. Behavioral Research in Accounting 21, 37–58 (2009)
6. Carnaghan, C.: Business process modeling approaches in the context of process level audit risk assessment: An analysis and comparison. International Journal of Accounting Information Systems 7, 170–204 (2006)
7. Alencar, P., Boritz, J.E., Carnaghan, C.: Business Modeling to Improve Auditor Risk Assessment: An Investigation of Alternative Representations. In: Proceedings of the 14th Annual International Symposium on Audit Research, ISAR, Los Angeles, CA (2008)
8. Schultz, M., Müller-Wickop, N., Nüttgens, M.: Key Information Requirements for Process Audits - an Expert Perspective. EMISA, pp. 137–150 (2012)
9. Mueller-Wickop, N., Schultz, M., Nuettgens, M.: Modeling Concepts for Process Audits - An Empirically Grounded Extension of BPMN. In: Proceedings of the 21st European Conference on Information Systems (ECIS), Utrecht, The Netherlands (2013)
10. Abdullah, S.N., Indulska, M., Sadiq, S.: A study of compliance management in information systems research. In: 17th European Conference on Information Systems, pp. 1–10 (2009)
11. Sadiq, S.: A Roadmap for Research in Business Process Compliance. In: Abramowicz, W., Maciaszek, L., Węcel, K. (eds.) BIS Workshops 2011 and BIS 2011. LNBIP, vol. 97, pp. 1–4. Springer, Heidelberg (2011)
12. Schultz, M., Mueller-Wickop, N.: Towards Auditors' Preferences on Documentation Formats in Business Process Audits. In: Modellierung 2014, Vienna, Austria (2014)
13. OMG (Object Management Group): Business Process Model and Notation (BPMN) - version 2.0 (2011)
14. Ahlemann, F., Gastl, H.: Process model for an empirically grounded reference model construction. In: Fettke, P., Loos, P. (eds.) Reference Modeling for Business Systems Analysis, pp. 77–97. IGI Global, Hershey (2007)
15. Strecker, S., Heise, D., Frank, U.: Prolegomena of a modelling method in support of audit risk assessment. Enterprise Modelling and Information Systems Architectures: An International Journal 6, 5–24 (2011)
16. COSO: Internal Control - Integrated Framework (2013), http://www.coso.org
17. Gelinas, U.: Business processes and information technology. Thomson/South-Western, Mason Ohio (2004)
18. Elder, R.J., Beasley, M.S., Arens, A.A.: Auditing and assurance services: an integrated approach. Pearson, Boston (2010)
19. IFAC: ISA 315 (Revised), Identifying and Assessing the Risks of Material Misstatement through Understanding the Entity and Its Environment (2012)

20. Rosemann, M., Zur Muehlen, M.: Integrating Risks in Business Process Models. In: ACIS 2005 Proceedings (2005)
21. Namiri, K., Stojanovic, N.: Towards A Formal Framework for Business Process Compliance. Multikonferenz Wirtschaftsinformatik 2008, 259 (2008)
22. Karagiannis, D.: A Business process Based Modelling Extension for Regulatory Compliance. Multikonferenz Wirtschaftsinformatik. pp. 1159–1173 (2008)
23. Lu, R., Sadiq, S.K., Governatori, G.: Compliance Aware Business Process Design. In: ter Hofstede, A.H.M., Benatallah, B., Paik, H.-Y. (eds.) BPM Workshops 2007. LNCS, vol. 4928, pp. 120–131. Springer, Heidelberg (2008)
24. Sadiq, W., Governatori, G., Namiri, K.: Modeling Control Objectives for Business Process Compliance. In: Alonso, G., Dadam, P., Rosemann, M. (eds.) BPM 2007. LNCS, vol. 4714, pp. 149–164. Springer, Heidelberg (2007)
25. Schumm, D., Turetken, O., Kokash, N., Elgammal, A., Leymann, F., van den Heuvel, W.-J.: Business Process Compliance through Reusable Units of Compliant Processes. In: Daniel, F., Facca, F.M. (eds.) ICWE 2010. LNCS, vol. 6385, pp. 325–337. Springer, Heidelberg (2010)
26. Turetken, O., Elgammal, A., van den Heuvel, W.-J., Papazoglou, M.: Enforcing Compliance on Business Processes through the Use of Patterns. In: ECIS 2011, Helsinki (2011)
27. Spies, M., Tabet, S.: Emerging Standards and Protocols for Governance, Risk, and Compliance Management. In: Kajan, E., Dorloff, F.-D., Bedini, I. (eds.) Handbook of Research on E-Business Standards and Protocols: Documents, Data and Advanced Web Technologies, pp. 768–790. IGI Global, Hershey (2012)
28. Mueller-Wickop, N., Schultz, M., Peris, M.: Towards Key Concepts for Process Audits – A Multi-Method Research Approach. In: Proceedings of the 10th International Conference on En-terprise Systems, Accounting and Logistics, Utrecht, The Netherlands, pp. 70–92 (2013)
29. Schultz, M.: Towards an Empirically Grounded Conceptual Model for Business Process Compliance. In: Ng, W., Storey, V.C., Trujillo, J.C. (eds.) ER 2013. LNCS, vol. 8217, pp. 138–145. Springer, Heidelberg (2013)
30. Gehrke, N.: The ERP Auditlab - A Prototypical Framework for Evaluating Enterprise Resource Planning System Assurance. In: 43rd Hawaii International Conference on System Sciences (HICSS), pp.1–9 (2010)
31. IDW: 261 Feststellung und Beurteilung von Fehlerrisiken und Reaktionen des Abschlussprüfers auf die beurteilten Fehlerrisiken (2009)
32. Sackmann, S., Hofmann, M., Kühnel, S.: Return on Controls Invest. HMD - Praxis Wirtschaftsinform, 289 (2013)
33. Kittel, K.: Recommendation System for Integrating Controls in Business Process Models
34. Krishnan, R., Peters, J., Padman, R., Kaplan, D.: On Data Reliability Assessment in Accounting Information Systems. Information Systems Research 16, 307–326 (2005)
35. Bierstaker, J.L., Thibodeau, J.C.: The effect of format and experience on internal control evaluation. Managerial Auditing Journal 21, 877–891 (2006)
36. Bierstaker, J.L., Hunton, J.E., Thibodeau, J.C.: Do Client-Prepared Internal Control Documentation and Business Process Flowcharts Help or Hinder an Auditor's Ability to Identify Missing Controls? AUDITING: A Journal of Practice & Theory 28, 79–94 (2009)
37. Hevner, A.R., March, S.T., Park, J., Ram, S.: Design science in information systems research. MIS Quarterly 28, 75–105 (2004)
38. Österle, H., Becker, J., Frank, U., Hess, T., Karagiannis, D., Krcmar, H., Loos, P., Mertens, P., Oberweis, A., Sinz, E.J.: Memorandum on design-oriented information systems research. European Journal of Information Systems 20, 7–10 (2010)

39. Peffers, K., Rothenberger, M., Tuunanen, T., Vaezi, R.: Design science research evaluation. In: Peffers, K., Rothenberger, M., Kuechler, B. (eds.) DESRIST 2012. LNCS, vol. 7286, pp. 398–410. Springer, Heidelberg (2012)
40. Frank, U.: Evaluation of Reference Models. In: Fettke, P., Loos, P. (eds.) Reference Modeling for Business Systems Analysis, pp. 118–140. IGI Global, Hershey (2007)
41. Rosemann, M., Recker, J.C., Flender, C.: Contextualisation of business processes. International Journal of Business Process Integration and Management 3, 47–60 (2008)
42. Recker, J.: Opportunities and constraints: the current struggle with BPMN. Business Process Management Journal 16, 181–201 (2010)
43. Muehlen, M.z., Recker, J.: How much language is enough? Theoretical and practical use of the business process modeling notation. In: Bellahsène, Z., Léonard, M. (eds.) CAiSE 2008. LNCS, vol. 5074, pp. 465–479. Springer, Heidelberg (2008)
44. Elgammal, A., Turetken, O., van den Heuvel, W.-J., Papazoglou, M.: On the Formal Specification of Regulatory Compliance: A Comparative Analysis. In: Maximilien, E.M., Rossi, G., Yuan, S.-T., Ludwig, H., Fantinato, M. (eds.) ICSOC 2010. LNCS, vol. 6568, pp. 27–38. Springer, Heidelberg (2011)
45. Kharbili, M.E., de Medeiros, A.K.A., Stein, S., Aalst, W.M.P.: van der: Business Process Compliance Checking: Current State and Future Challenges. In: MoBIS, pp. 107–113 (2008)
46. Stroppi, L.J.R., Chiotti, O., Villarreal, P.D.: Extending BPMN 2.0: Method and Tool Support. In: Dijkman, R., Hofstetter, J., Koehler, J. (eds.) BPMN 2011. LNBIP, vol. 95, pp. 59–73. Springer, Heidelberg (2011)
47. Peffers, K., Tuunanen, T., Rothenberger, M.A., Chatterjee, S.: A Design Science Research Methodology for Information Systems Research. Journal of Management Information Systems 24, 45–77 (2007)
48. Bodart, F., Patel, A., Sim, M.: Ron Weber: Should Optional Properties Be Used in Conceptual Modelling? A Theory and Three Empirical Tests. Information Systems Research 12, 384–405 (2001)
49. Larkin, J.H., Simon, H.A.: Why a Diagram is (Sometimes) Worth Ten Thousand Words. Cognitive Science 11, 65–100 (1987)
50. Van Der Heijden, H.: Effects of diagram format and user numeracy on understanding cash flow data. In: 37th Annual Congress of the European Accounting Association, Tallinn (2014)
51. Burton-Jones, A., Meso, P.: The Effects of Decomposition Quality and Multiple Forms of Information on Novices' Understanding of a Domain from a Conceptual Model. Journal of the Association for Information Systems 9, 748–802 (2008)
52. Recker, J.: Empirical investigation of the usefulness of Gateway constructs in process models. Eur. J. Inf. Syst. 22, 673–689 (2013)
53. Mendling, J., Strembeck, M., Recker, J.: Factors of process model comprehension—Findings from a series of experiments. Decision Support Systems 53, 195–206 (2012)
54. Qualtrics: Qualtrics Research Suite, Provo, Utah, USA (2013)
55. OCEG: GRC-XML Spec and Schema (2013),
    http://www.oceg.org/resources/grc-xml/
56. Manson, S., McCartney, S., Sherer, M., Wallace, W.A.: Audit Automation in the UK and the US: A Comparative Study. International Journal of Auditing 2, 233–246 (1998)

Mining Resource Scheduling Protocols

Arik Senderovich[1], Matthias Weidlich[2], Avigdor Gal[1], and Avishai Mandelbaum[1]

[1] Technion – Israel Institute of Technology, Israel
{sariks@tx,avigal@ie,avim}@ie.technion.ac.il
[2] Imperial College London
m.weidlich@imperial.ac.uk

Abstract. In service processes, as found in the telecommunications, financial, or healthcare sector, customers compete for the scarce capacity of service providers. For such processes, performance analysis is important and it often targets the time that customers are delayed prior to service. However, this wait time cannot be fully explained by the load imposed on service providers. Indeed, it also depends on resource scheduling protocols, which determine the order of activities that a service provider decides to follow when serving customers. This work focuses on automatically learning resource decisions from events. We hypothesize that queueing information serves as an essential element in mining such protocols and hence, we utilize the queueing perspective of customers in the mining process. We propose two types of mining techniques: advanced classification methods from data mining that include queueing information in their explanatory features and heuristics that originate in queueing theory. Empirical evaluation shows that incorporating the queueing perspective into mining of scheduling protocols improves predictive power.

1 Introduction

Service processes can be viewed as a special case of business processes, in which service consumers (aka customers) compete for the scarce capacity of service providers [1]. Service processes can be found, for instance, in the telecommunications, financial, or medical sectors. The handling of customers by a call center or the treatment of patients in an emergency department at a hospital are examples of a service process.

Service processes often face high volumes of service requests, which are subject to large variations over time and high level of uncertainty in the amount of incoming demand [2]. Therefore, in order to assure successful operation of a service process (e.g. limit the time that customers wait for service), one must set an adequate level of resource capacity. Operational analysis, that is based on Queueing Theory [3,4], is common practice for setting capacity levels that would accommodate the time-varying and random demand. Given that service processes are often supported by information systems, event logs recorded during process execution can be exploited for such performance-driven analyses. Various techniques for operational process mining addressed the prediction of wait times based on characteristics of service requests [5,6]. Recently, it was argued that the load imposed on service providers is essential for performance prediction. To account for delays in processing that stem from queueing of customers, queueing models and related predictors can be constructed from event data [7].

S. Sadiq, P. Soffer, and H. Völzer (Eds.): BPM 2014, LNCS 8659, pp. 200–216, 2014.

In this work, we start with the observation that delays in processing cannot be fully explained by the process load. Rather, delays also originate from service providers. In fact, service providers play a symmetric role in their influence on process performance, when compared to customers. Service providers follow *resource scheduling protocols* that define the order of activities followed when serving customers. Knowledge of these protocols allows for predicting the next task of a service provider, out of a set of feasible tasks, thereby providing a more complete performance analysis and improving the accuracy of wait time prediction.

Following the theme of operational process mining, this paper sets out to mine scheduling protocols of service providers from recorded event data. We hypothesize that queueing information serves as an essential element in mining such protocols and hence, one must utilize the queueing perspective of customers in the mining process. We consider two approaches for mining of resource scheduling protocols. First, we show how data mining methods can be employed when queueing information is considered as part of the explanatory features. Second, we present heuristics that originate in queueing theory and do not require historical data in their application. Both techniques are evaluated empirically using real-world logs of a large Israeli telecommunication company. The data covers three months of operation of a service process, with up to 50,000 requests per day. Our results indicate that queueing heuristics, as well as decision trees and random forests, are superior to other methods. Since queueing heuristics are intuitive and can be facilitated online (without a preliminary learning phase), we argue that these are less time-and-resource consuming than data mining methods.

To conclude, this paper makes the following contributions:

- It puts forward the duality of service consumers and service providers, to reach to a more holistic analysis of the performance of service processes. Resource scheduling protocols at the side of the provider are identified as a major influencing factor.
- It provides a set of mining techniques to extract resource scheduling protocols from event data, recorded during process execution. Those techniques vary in the degree with which they incorporate the queueing perspective of customers.
- It reports on a comprehensive evaluation of the proposed techniques using real-world logs. In particular, we show that simple techniques that include basic queueing information are competitive with respect to advanced data mining techniques that require an offline learning phase.

The remainder of the paper is structured as follows. The next section provides further background on service processes and possible causes for delays. Section 3 introduces our model. Section 4 presents algorithms for mining various types of protocols from event data. We evaluated our approach with real-world data in Section 5. Section 6 reviews our contributions in the light of related work, before we conclude in Section 7.

2 Background

Service Processes as Interacting Processes. Service processes show some inherent duality in the sense that both service consumers and providers execute certain activities to reach a goal. Hence, it is natural to view service processes as a choreography [8], i.e., two interacting processes. An example of this view is given by the BPMN [9] model

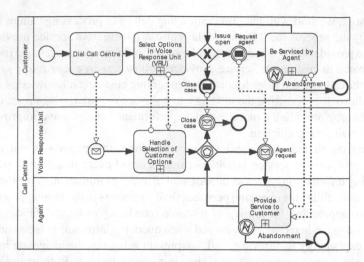

Fig. 1. A call center process modeled as interacting consumer and provider processes

in Fig. 1. It shows a simple call center process in which a customer dials in and first interacts with a Voice Response Unit (VRU). If customers cannot solve their inquiry using the VRU, they are referred to a call center agent. Then, to handle the customer inquiry, multiple iterations with agents may be required.

The model in Fig. 1 highlights the interaction of service consumer and provider processes. However, it focuses only on the activities executed by the service provider that are specifically required to handle a single request of a service consumer. The model neglects the fact that resources at the side of the service provider, i.e., the agent in our example, also follow an explicit process when handling requests of service consumers. This perspective of our example is highlighted in Fig. 2, which depicts how an agent chooses a customer who waits for being served, serves the customer, and then repeats the whole procedure until the shift is finished.

Delays in Service Processes. The various illustrated perspectives on a service process are important when assessing its performance in general, and investigating the causes of delays in processing in particular. Since service consumers typically compete for the scarce capacity of service providers, clearly, unavailability of resources at the service provider is a first cause of delays. In this case, customers are queued and served later when resources become available. The process of the agent in Fig. 2, however, also highlights that there is a particular activity that refers to the choice of the customer to be served. Consequently, the selection strategy applied by an agent is a second cause for delays in processing. Even in case agents are available to handle customer requests, a particular request may be delayed because of this selection strategy.

Resource Scheduling Protocols. Strategies for the selection of resources, commonly referred as *scheduling protocols*, can be grounded on various aspects. Examples include the properties that relate to the processing state of the service provider (e.g., how long a provider was busy or idle), attributes of the process instances (e.g., scheduling based

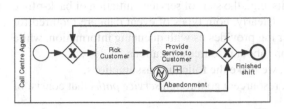

Fig. 2. Process from the perspective of an agent

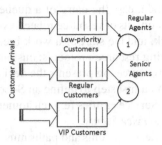

Fig. 3. Queueing perspective for types of customers and agents

on types of customers and service providers), or global context (e.g., scheduling that differs on working days and holidays).

For our example, the call center service process, scheduling based on attributes of process instances is illustrated in Fig. 3. Here, customers are assumed to fall in one out of three groups, 'low-priority', 'regular', or 'VIP'. Customers of either type end up in a separate queue. Agents, in turn, are classified based on their experience, so that agents are 'regular' or 'senior'. In our example, regular agents may serve low-priority or regular customers, whereas senior agents serve regular or VIP customers. This creates a queueing system that is referred to have a W-architecture; see [10]. For this setting, different scheduling protocols may be implemented. As an example, senior agents could always prefer VIP customers and select regular customers only if the VIP queue is empty. A different protocol could define that senior agents prefer VIP customers, but also select the first customer in the regular queue if they waited for more than 15 minutes, and the VIP queue contains at most 2 customers that waited for less than 2 minutes.

These examples illustrate that deriving resource scheduling protocols from process execution data is valuable to achieve more holistic performance analysis. In this work, we hypothesize that queueing information is particularly useful in extracting such protocols.

3   Service Logs and the Protocol Mining Problem

In order to learn allocation of resources to customers from event data, Section 3.1 first defines our model of the *service log* (S-Log). A service log is an event log (c.f. [11, Ch. 4]) that consists of service events and paths that are related to either the customers or the resources of a service process. We then define the problem of mining resource scheduling protocols in Section 3.2. We also provide a brief overview of how to assess the quality of mined protocols in terms of their prediction error.

3.1   Service Logs

For service logs (S-Logs), we present two instantiations that reflect the duality of service processes. The first log contains events that come from the customer's perspective and include, e.g., the entry of a queue, the start of service, and abandonment. The second log consists of resource related events, e.g., the start of service, initiation of back-office work, and the start of a work break. Clearly, both types of event data are required for mining resource protocols: customer log provides us with queueing information, while the resource log presents the decisions about resource allocations.

As a first step to define an S-Log, we make the following assumptions:
- Service entities (e.g. customers, resources) go through *service paths* that consist of *service events*.
- Service events and paths must have unique identifiers (events and paths cannot have the same identifier).
- Service events have attributes.

Below, we first define the essential concepts of service logs, i.e., service events (or events for short) and service paths (or paths), and relate events to their attributes.

Definition 1 (Service event, Service path). *Denote by S the set of all possible service events, i.e. unique event identifiers. Let S^* be the set of all finite sequences over S. We define $\Pi \subseteq S^*$ as the set of all* feasible *service paths, i.e. finite sequences of service events. We require that each service event appears at most once in some path.*

According to this definition, a path $p \in \Pi$ is a finite sequence $(p_1, \ldots, p_n)$ of length n of events, such that $p_i \in S, i = 1, ..., n$. It is worth to mention that, in the literature, paths are often referred to as *cases*. In this work, we wish to capture resource paths as well as customer paths, hence the extension of cases to paths.

Service events are associated with attributes, e.g., *timestamps, service activities, service locations*, and *resources*. We model such an attribute as a function that assigns an attribute value to a service event. A set of such attribute functions, in turn, defines the schema (aka structure) of a set of service events.

Definition 2 (Attribute function, Event schema). *Let A be the domain of an event attribute. Then, the attribute function $\alpha : S \to A$ assigns values of this domain to service events. A finite set $\{\alpha_1, \ldots, \alpha_n\}$ of attribute functions is called an event schema.*

For example, α may be the attribute function for service activities, i.e., the domain of the function is defined as {service start, service end}. A specific service event $s \in S$ then either indicates the start ($\alpha(s) =$ service start) or end of service ($\alpha(s) =$ service end).

Using the introduced concepts, we define the general notion of an S-Log.

Definition 3 (S-Log). *A service log (S-Log) is a tuple (S, G, α_S) where,*
- *$S \subseteq S$ is the set of observed service events.*
- *$G \subseteq \Pi$ is the set of observed service paths.*
- *α_S is the event schema.*

The notion of a service log generalizes the *functional* definition of an event log as presented in [12]. Further, it allows for capturing the duality of service processes, which is reflected in events that stem from the customer's perspective and events that relate to the resources at the service provider. Below, we define service logs of customers and resources as they are recorded in service processes that show a W-architecture, as our example in Figure 3. Either type of log follows the generic structure of a service log, but comes with different event schemas, i.e., different sets of attribute functions.

Customer Log. Recording the behavior of a customer includes information on the time at which an event was observed, the type of the customer, and the type of the executed activity. The latter may refer to the start of queueing, abandonment, the start of service, or the end of service.

Definition 4 (Customer S-Log). *A customer service log is a service log* $(S, G, \{\tau, \eta, \epsilon\})$, *where*

- $\tau : S \to \mathbb{N}^+$ *is a timestamp attribute function.*
- $\eta : S \to \mathbb{N}^+ \cup \{\bot\}$ *is a customer type attribute function, with* $\bot$ *being the null value.*
- $\epsilon : S \to E = \{qEntry, qAbandon, sStart, sEnd\}$ *is an activity attribute function.*

Note that a customer service log does not contain information on the *identity* of particular customers since this information is not expected to be relevant for the operational analysis of service processes. Instead, only the activities performed by a particular type of customer at a certain point in time will be used for extracting queueing information.

Resource Log. The recording of the behavior of a resource captures different information compared to a customer. In addition to the time at which an event was observed, it includes information on the type of a customer served, the type of the resource (i.e., a skill group), the state of a resource, and the start and end of a particular state. In the remainder, we consider four specific resource states: (1) serving a customer, (2) ready to serve a customer (online, waiting for a customer to arrive), (3) performing offline back-office work and (4) idle (e.g. on a break). For each of these states, an event may signal the start or end of the respective state.

Definition 5 (Resource S-Log). *A resource service log is a service log* $(S, G, \{\tau, \eta, \sigma, \phi, \delta\})$, *where*

- $\tau : S \to \mathbb{N}^+$ *is a timestamp attribute function.*
- $\eta : S \to \mathbb{N}^+ \cup \{\bot\}$ *is a customer type attribute function.*
- $\sigma : S \to \mathbb{N}^+$ *is a skill group attribute function.*
- $\phi : S \to A = \{Serving, Ready, Back\text{-}Office, Idle\}$ *is a state attribute function.*
- $\delta : S \to T = \{Start, End\}$ *is a state transaction attribute function.*

We observe that information on timestamps and customer types is included in both, customer and resource logs. However, the reference of a customer type in resource-related events is reasonable only if the resource is actually serving a customer. As a convention, therefore, we assume that $\eta(s) = \bot$ if $\phi(s) \neq Serving$ for all $s \in S$ of a resource log $(S, G, \{\tau, \eta, \sigma, \phi, \delta\})$.

3.2 Problem Statement

We aim at mining resource scheduling protocols. These protocols determine how to allocate resource types to queues of customers, i.e., how to select a certain customer type. Let $\mathcal{D}$ be the set of customer types and, therefore, possible resource allocations. For the

W-architecture in Figure 3, these allocations would be given as $\mathcal{D} = \{$Low, Regular, VIP$\}$. Further, we write $X \in \mathbb{R}^p$ to refer to a random vector of features (explanatory variables) of dimension p, which is used as the basis of allocation. The random variable that is the real allocation of a resource is denoted by $D \in \mathcal{D}$. Using these notions, we are ready to define the problem addressed in this paper.

Problem 1 (Mining Resource-Scheduling Protocols). *The problem of mining resource scheduling protocols is to provide a protocol-function from the features vector space into the decision set, $\pi : \mathbb{R}^p \to \mathcal{D}$, such that π minimizes the expected prediction error with respect to some loss function $L(D, \pi(X))$.*

We choose to represent the loss function as a $K \times K$ matrix $\mathbb{L}$ with K being the cardinality of $\mathcal{D}$. The matrix will be zero in the diagonal and non-negative elsewhere, with $L(k, l)$, corresponding to the cost of (mis)classifying decision $k \in \mathcal{D}$ as $l \in \mathcal{D}$. In the present first-time analysis, we use a $0 - 1$ loss function, i.e. $L(k, l) = 1$ holds if the classification is incorrect and $L(k, l) = 0$ otherwise.

The problem statement requires minimization of the expected prediction error w.r.t. the loss function. In general, the expected prediction error can be written as follows:

$$EPE = E[L(D, \pi(X))] = E_X \sum_{d \in \mathcal{D}} L(d, \pi(X)) \cdot P(D = d | X), \qquad (1)$$

with the first expectation taken over the joint distribution of (D, X). That is, the expected value for the loss function is the expectation of a particular allocation given its probability under the random feature vector. Given a particular realization x of the random feature vector X, and a loss matrix of $0 - 1$, the protocol that minimizes the expected prediction error is given as,

$$\pi(x) = \arg\max_{d \in \mathcal{D}} P(D = d | X = x). \qquad (2)$$

In other words, the best protocol for solving Problem 1 is the one that maximizes the posterior probability of decision D conditioned on a realization of the feature vector, namely x [13, Ch. 2.4]. As we outline in the remainder of this paper, data mining techniques can be used in an attempt to maximize this posterior probability.

4   Discovery of Resource Scheduling Protocols

The goal of resource scheduling protocols is tightly coupled with Quality-of-Service (QoS) that an organization aims to provide. For service processes, two types of QoS are of particular importance: (1) qualitative QoS, e.g. to which extent a customer receives the service that they requested, and (2) operational QoS, e.g. to which extent a customer was not delayed for too long. For illustration of the trade-off between the two types of QoS, consider again the W-architecture shown in Fig. 3. In order to increase operational QoS, regular agents are scheduled to VIP customers, thus inflicting the qualitative QoS. On the other hand, to provide better qualitative QoS, senior agents are often scheduled to serve regular customers.

Considering the above, we hypothesize that scheduling of resources, especially in service processes, is related to both the *skill* of the agent, i.e. the qualitative abilities of the resource, as well as the *system load* that has a direct influence on operational QoS. As discussed in [7], system load can be measured by queue-length or by waiting time of the most delayed customer (the head-of-line, or HOL for short). Based on these insights, our techniques for solving Problem 1 consider four levels of queueing information: (1) no queueing information; (2) lengths of queues of customers; (3) waiting time of the HOL in the customer queues; and lastly (4) a combination of the previous two levels.

Below, we first show how the two service logs, capturing a service process from the perspective of customers and resources respectively, are used to extract allocation decisions, i.e., the moment in time when a resource was allocated to a customer (Section 4.1). Each decision is associated with a vector of features including the skill of the currently allocated resource and the relevant queueing information at the moment of the allocation. Based on that information, we first apply advanced classification methods from data mining to solve Problem 1 (Section 4.2). Our second approach does not require any historical data, but relies on queueing heuristics that originate from optimal control theory for queues operating under heavy-traffic scenarios (Section 4.3). It uses information that is easily observable in service processes, such as the number of customers in each queue.

4.1 Mining Queueing Information from Service Logs

To mine allocation decisions that are associated with queueing information, we extract information on queue lengths and longest waiting time from a customer service log. Let $q(t) = (q_{d_1}(t), \ldots, q_{d_n}(t))$ be a vector of queue lengths at time t, where $d_1, \ldots, d_n \in \mathcal{D}$ are allocation decisions (or customer types, respectively). Given a customer service log $(S, G, \{\tau, \eta, \epsilon\})$ and time t, queue length $q_{d_i}(t)$ is estimated by $\widehat{q_{d_i}(t)}$ as follows:

$$\widehat{q_{d_i}(t)} = |\{(g_1, \ldots, g_m) \in G \mid \epsilon(g_m) = qEntry \wedge \tau(g_m) \leq t \wedge \eta(g_m) = d_i\}| . \quad (3)$$

Similarly, we denote by $h(t) = (h_{d_1}(t), \ldots, h_{d_n}(t))$ the vector of the longest waiting customers in each queue (the delays of the HOL), with $d_1, \ldots, d_n \in \mathcal{D}$ being allocation decisions. For a customer service log $(S, G, \{\tau, \eta, \epsilon\})$ and time t, this vector can estimated from the customer log in a similar manner:

$$\widehat{h_{d_i}(t)} = \min_{s \in \{s \in S \mid \epsilon(s) = qEntry \wedge \eta(s) = d_i \wedge \exists (g_1, \ldots, s) \in G\}} t - \tau(s), \quad (4)$$

Next, we mine allocation decisions from the resource perspective by identifying timestamps in which the resource switched their state to *Serving*. Given a resource service log $(S, G, \{\tau, \eta, \sigma, \phi, \delta\})$, the set of allocation decisions is given by

$$V = \{s \in S \mid \phi(s) = Serving \wedge \delta(s) = Start\}. \quad (5)$$

Finally, we derive a set of explanatory feature vectors, denote by $\mathcal{X}$, for the set of allocation decisions as follows:

$$\mathcal{X} = \{x = (s, \sigma(s), q_{d_1}(t), \ldots, q_{d_n}(t), h_{d_1}(t), \ldots, h_{d_n}(t)) \mid s \in V \wedge t = \tau(s)\}. \quad (6)$$

The vector elements correspond to the skill group of the allocated resource and the queueing information at the time of allocation (queue-lengths and HOL waiting times).

4.2 Data Mining Classifiers

We consider four data mining techniques that are suitable to solve Problem 1 as a classification problem. Namely, we use Linear Discriminant Analysis (LDA), Multinomial Logistic Regression (MLR), decision trees and random forests. These methods provide us with a protocol-function π such that the decision obtained by applying π to a feature vector, $\pi(x) = d$, will have the maximal posterior probability among all other posteriors (see Section 3). Below, we briefly describe these data mining methods and then exemplify mining of resource scheduling protocols with one of the algorithms, i.e., decision trees.

Linear Classifiers: LDA and MLR. The LDA method constructs a discriminant function $\delta_d(x)$ that, given a vector of features x, selects the most probable decision, see Equation (2). The posterior probability $P(D = d|X = x)$ of the decision to select allocation d given feature vector x is rewritten following Bayes theorem:

$$P(D = d|X = x) = \frac{f_d(x) \cdot P(D = d)}{\sum_{l \in \mathcal{D}} f_l(x) \cdot P(D = l)}, \tag{7}$$

with $f_d(x) = P(X = x|D = d)$ and $P(D = d)$ being the prior of decision d. LDA assumes that for $d \in \mathcal{D}$ the density, $f_d(x)$, comes from a Gaussian distribution and that all classes $d \in \mathcal{D}$ have a common covariance matrix. From these assumptions, the discriminant function $\delta_d(x)$ of decision d is *linear* in x and depends on the prior distribution over the classes $P(D = d)$ and the parameters of the Gaussian distribution. Therefore, given a feature vector x, the LDA algorithm 'plugs' the vector into $\delta_d(x)$ for each class d and selects the decision with the highest discriminant function.

Similarly to LDA, the MLR method attempts to model a logic transformation of the posterior probabilities $P(D = d|X = x)$ by linear functions in x. However, unlike the LDA, the MLR ensures that these functions sum up to 1 and stay in the range of $[0, 1]$. Generally, the MLR requires more data observations for accuracy, while the LDA is less robust to outliers. Hence, both models can potentially be valuable (see [13, Ch 4]).

Tree-Based Classifiers: Decision Trees and Random Forests. Classification (decision) trees attempt to find m regions $R_1, \dots, R_m$ in the feature space ($\mathbb{R}^p$) that would best explain the observed outcomes [13, Ch. 9.2]. Decision trees enjoy a low bias, yet suffer from a high variance. In order to handle the large variance of decision trees, the *random forests* algorithm, which has become popular and is considered state-of-the-art in data mining, was introduced by Breiman [14]. The idea is to grow a number of decorrelated decision trees (a forest) and to average on the result, thus reducing variance.

Exemplifying Protocol Mining with Decision Trees. To demonstrate the application and relevance of data mining methods for discovery of resource scheduling protocols, we present a data-based illustration of the method based on decision trees. To this end, we consider real-world data from an Israeli telecommunication company (further details on the data are given when presenting the comparative evaluation of the proposed methods). This company operates a service process that follows the W-architecture as discussed in Section 2 and illustrated in Fig. 3 with the aforementioned three types of customers (low-priority, regular, VIP). For this setting, Fig. 4 presents the histogram

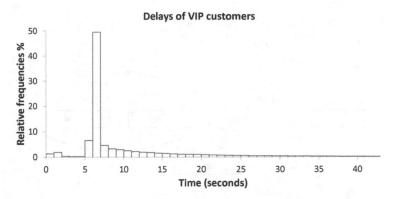

Fig. 4. Histogram of delays for VIP customers, who had to wait for service

of delays for VIP customers, who had to wait prior to being served. We observe that a large proportion of customers experienced a 6 seconds delay. This is an indication of a protocol that causes VIP customers to enter service after a 6 seconds delay.

Applying the outlined approach for this data set leads to the result depicted in Fig. 5. In the graphical representation of the tree, queues (customer types or scheduling decisions, respectively) are denoted by Q_1, Q_2 and Q_3, corresponding to low-priority, regular and VIP customers. The skill groups of agents are 1 and 2, i.e., regular and senior agents. HOL_Q_i represents the waiting time of the longest delayed customer in queue Q_i. Then, the protocol grounded in the decision tree reads as follows:

(1) If no information is available, the best prediction is Q_2, since this relates to the allocation of the most common customer type. In terms of posterior probabilities, we have $P(D|X) = P(D)$ (prior of D), since no feature vector is present.

(2) If the agent has skill 1 (regular agent), then the best prediction is Q_1, since the majority of customers that are allocated to this group stem from the low-priority customer queue. Otherwise, if the skill points to a senior agent, the best prediction is Q_2 based on similar considerations. Note that the first two levels of the tree do not rely on any queueing information.

(3) The second level of the tree does consider queueing information. For regular agents, the prediction is based on the fact whether there are waiting regular customers (Q_2), which should be served first. If this is not the case, prediction is based on HOL waiting times. For senior agents, the prediction is simple. They are allocated to VIP customers that wait 6 seconds or longer (the relevant node is emphasized in Fig. 5). This is exactly the phenomena that is observed in the histogram in Fig. 4.

This example illustrates how the method learns scheduling protocols from event data that are based on features of the resources and queueing information.

4.3 Queueing Heuristics

A complementary approach to the extraction of resource scheduling protocols from historical data, using data mining techniques, is the prediction of scheduling decisions based on queueing heuristics. Here we consider two such heuristics.

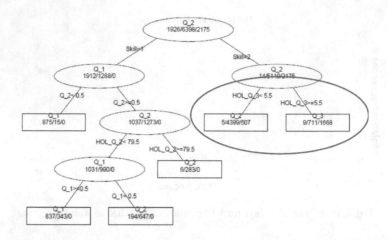

Fig. 5. Decision tree that is constructed from service logs

The first heuristic is based on the length of the queues at the time of the allocation decision. That is, given a time t, a set of feasible allocation decisions $F \subseteq \mathcal{D}$ for a resource (not every type of agent may have the skill to serve every queue), and the observed queue-length vector $q(t) = (q_{d_1}(t), \ldots, q_{d_n}(t))$, the predicted allocation decision is defined as

$$d = \arg\max_{f \in F} q_f(t). \tag{8}$$

We refer to this heuristic as Longest-Queue-First (LQF). This scheduling protocol has its roots in queueing control theory in heavy-traffic scenarios, and is a special case of the Fixed-Queue-Ratio rule proposed in [15]. If there are multiple queues of the same lengths (including the case in which $q(t) = 0$ for every component), the more probable queue in terms of prior probability, is favored. For our running example and the aforementioned data set, this would allocate regular customers to senior agents and low-priority customers to regular agents.

The second heuristic follows a similar idea, but predicts the allocation to the queue with the most delayed head-of-line customer. Given a time t and the head-of-line vector $h(t)$, the predicted allocation decision is defined as

$$d = \arg\max_{f \in F} h_f(t). \tag{9}$$

We refer to this heuristic as Most-Delayed-First (MDF). It can be shown that this heuristic is equivalent up to a constant (asymptotically in heavy-traffic) to the LQF heuristic [16]. Note that both types of heuristics ignore the priorities that exist between the three queues. We later discuss that this has to be seen as one of their limitations.

5   Evaluation

We evaluate our methods using a large-scale real-world data set. We first provide details on the data and experimental setup. Then, we report and discuss the prediction results.

Data Description. The data for our experiments stems from a call center of an Israeli telecommunication company and is gathered and stored in the Technion laboratory for Service Enterprise Engineering (SEELab)[1]. The call center processes up to 50,000 service requests a day, routes requests according to various resource skills, and simultaneously queues requests across multiple sites. The center is operated with around 600-800 agent positions on weekdays and 200-400 agent positions on weekends. Further, several types of services are provided; the most common are Private, Business, Technical and Content Internet. In this paper, we focus on the Private service, which handles requests with low, regular and VIP priorities. For our empirical evaluation we selected three months of data to serve as our service logs, from January 1, 2008 to March 31, 2008. The data features the events of a customer service log as well as those of a resource service log.

Experimental Setup. The controlled variable in our experiments is the *method* we apply to mine a scheduling protocol. As outlined in Section 4, our methods can be divided into: (1) data mining techniques that are based on feature vectors that may depend on queueing information and (2) queueing heuristics that rely on control theory in heavy-traffic. The uncontrolled (responding) variable in the experiments is the *misclassification rate*, i.e., the proportion of incorrect predictions out of total number of predictions. Since we consider the $0 - 1$ loss function, the misclassification rate is essentially an estimator of the expected prediction error (EPE).

The experiments consist of four scenarios that correspond to four levels of queueing information. Scenario I is our baseline scenario, for which the feature vector includes only the skill group of the resource without further queueing information. Scenario II considers queue lengths of the three queues (low-priority, regular and VIP) as additional features. In Scenario III, the queue length is replaced by the waiting time of the head-of-line (HOL) for each queue. Lastly, Scenario IV includes all the above, namely, skill, queue-length and HOL waiting time.

To run the experiments, we first derived the allocation decisions and feature vectors are described in Section 4. For each experiment iteration, we randomly divided the allocation decisions into two subsets: a training set (75% of the data set) and a test set (25%), which is common practice when performing statistical model assessment [13, Ch. 8]. During each iteration the controlled variables were altered, while the misclassification rate was measured. We repeated the process of dividing the data set and running the experiment for 10 times. We used the implementations of LDA, MLR, decision trees and random forests provided by R[2]. For the decision tree algorithm we used the cross-entropy method. For random forests, in order to limit the complexity of the algorithm, we relied on 10 trees, a node size of 50, and disabled recalculations of the proximity matrix.

---

[1] http://ie.technion.ac.il/Labs/Serveng
[2] http://www.r-project.org/

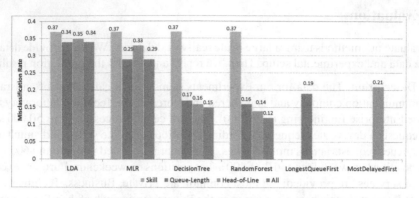

Fig. 6. Misclassification rates of the discovered protocols

Results. The results of our experiments are depicted in Fig. 6, which plots the achieved misclassification rate for the six methods: four data mining methods (LDA, MLR, decision trees and random forests) and two queueing heuristics (Longest-Queue-First (LQF) and Most-Delayed-First (MDF)). For each of the data mining methods, we have four results, one for each type of queueing information (i.e., skill, queue-length, head-of-line, all).

We observe that for the baseline scenario, when the only available information is the skill group of the resource, all data mining algorithms yield the same misclassification rate (of 37%). In Scenarios II-IV, where queueing information is introduced, LDA does not improve beyond the baseline scenario. MLR improves by 8% when queue-length is considered in the prediction. However, this is generally inferior compared to decision trees, random forests, and the Longest-Queue-First heuristic that scored 17%, 16% and 19% misclassification rate, respectively. Considering the influence of the HOL waiting time, none of the linear classifiers (LDA and MLR) improves, whereas decision trees, random forests, and the Most-Delayed-First heuristic achieve 16%, 14% and 21% misclassification. Decision trees and random forests further improve slightly when all types of queueing information is considered.

Discussion. First and foremost, we observe that the linear data mining techniques yield comparably high misclassification rate values. This can be explained by their strong assumptions. For instance, the LDA assumes Gaussian densities of the feature vector conditioned on decisions. As a consequence, the linear methods impose a low computational effort and, when the respective assumptions hold true, provide a precise classification [13, Ch. 4]. However, due to their assumptions, the methods are not applicable to any scenario and, thus, lead to poor performance for our data set.

In contrast, decision trees and random forests do not impose assumptions on the feature vector and therefore, are more robust to various distributions of these vectors. On the downside, tree methods are based on greedy algorithms, which renders it unlikely that they converge to an optimal splitting of the feature vector space. Despite this shortcoming, the tree-based techniques yield the best prediction results in our comparative analysis. In addition, they also allow for decrypting complex scheduling protocols from event data as we exemplified it in Section 4.

Queueing heuristics perform surprisingly well, although their underlying assumption do not hold throughout large portions of the data: the call center is not constantly in heavy-traffic and the three queues do not have the same priorities. The biggest advantage of queueing heuristics is their simplicity; to apply them, one does not need to learn from data or use sophisticated black-box techniques. The information that they require is readily available in any service operation environment, so that they can be easily programmed into any recommendation system. However, our results also indicate that the misclassification rate is not on the level of tree-based methods.

Our results raise the question whether queueing heuristics can be improved, for instance, by incorporating priorities between the various queues. Instead of selecting the longest queue first, or the customer from the most delayed queue, we may consider attaching weights to each of the queues. Suppose that a queue-length vector, $q(t) = (q_{d_1}(t), \ldots, q_{d_n}(t))$, receives corresponding weights, $w_1, \ldots, w_n$ with $\sum_1^n w_i = 1$. Then, with F as the set of feasible allocation decisions at time t, the predicted decision could be defined as:

$$d = \arg\max_{f \in F} q_f(t) \cdot w_f. \tag{10}$$

In fact, this protocol corresponds to the heavy-traffic rule of Fixed-Queue-Ratio (FQR) [15]. The downside of such an extension is that it requires a learning phase for $w_1, \ldots, w_n$, which would inflict the aforementioned advantage of queueing heuristics.

6 Related Work

The work presented in this paper fits under the umbrella of context-aware, operational process mining. Process mining research has seen a remarkable surge lately, providing techniques for the discovery of process-related models from event data, see [11] for a broad overview. Recently, the importance of context information for process mining was highlighted [17]. Our work follows this line by arguing that the most narrow scope, i.e., the context of process instances, is not sufficient for operational analysis of a process. The behavior of resources and allocation protocols as mined in our work are part of the broader process context, beyond single instances.

Operational process mining refers to the creation of models for quantitative analysis. Here, evaluation of temporal properties has received considerable attention, for example, the prediction of processing delays or completion times for running cases by constructing simulation models from event data. In [18], time prediction is grounded on a Coloured Petri net comprising resource and timing information. Other work enriches such predictions with stochastic information [12]. Time prediction based on abstractions of states and state transitions was developed in [5]. It has been argued though, that realistic time prediction requires modeling resource utilization appropriately [19,20]. In [19], the authors used regression analysis to show that speed of service is indeed affected by the workload. To take such context-factors into account, time prediction based on abstractions of states and state transitions was recently extended to consider context information such as system load [6]. We argue that, for service processes, consideration of the system load is not sufficient to explain all delays of processing. Our work highlights the importance of the interplay of customers and resources for performance analysis, and the relevance of queueing information and scheduling protocols in particular.

The application of decision trees to extract resource scheduling rules was also discussed by Li and Olafsson [26], yet only applied to simulated event logs. In contrast, our experiments were conducted on a real-world data set and used a variety of statistical learning and queue mining techniques that go beyond decision trees, which are considered state-of-the-art in mining of scheduling rules.

Further, the duality between a decision problems in processes and classification problems was leveraged for mining of branching conditions [22,23] (falling into the process instance context). Our work relies on similar techniques, but exploits queueing information and works on the broader context of processes to discover protocols.

Despite its importance for performance analysis, only few works analyze behavior of resources. In [21, Ch .2], resource (aka server) networks were defined as directed graphs that depict resource-flow through service activities or customer queues, which can be used to estimate resource absenteeism rates. These rates, in turn, allow for long and short-term workforce planning in service processes. Our work supports this approach by discovering scheduling protocols from event data.

The presented queueing heuristics are grounded in queueing control theory for heavy-traffic scenarios, cf., [16,15]. Given a certain structure of queues and service providers, control theory gives rise to protocols that are provable optimal as the demand reaches system capacity. The two presented heuristics are particularly inspired by delay predictors that do not assume steady-state, but work on wait time information of the current snapshot of a system [24,25]. We follow the same idea when exploiting only the current state of queues instead of historical data.

7   Conclusion

In this paper, we argued that for performance analysis of service processes and estimation of processing delays, it is crucial to understand the resource scheduling protocols that match customers with service providers. Given that in many cases, service processes are supported by information systems that track the execution of activities by customers as well as the behavior of resources, we advocate the discovery of such protocols from event data. Following the hypothesis that queueing information serves as an essential element in mining scheduling protocols, we presented two specific types of mining techniques. First, we showed how classification methods from data mining can be used when including queueing information in their explanatory features. Second, we proposed heuristics that originate in queueing theory and exploit solely the current state of a system. We tested both types of techniques using a large real-world data set from the telecommunications sector. Our results indicate that data mining with decision trees and random forests is able to derive predictors for scheduling decisions with up to 88% precision. In addition, queueing heuristics also perform well reaching levels of up to 81% precision. We conclude that high prediction precision can be achieved already with online methods that do not require a preliminary learning phase on historic data.

As part of future work, we aim at developing and evaluating queueing heuristics that are enriched by a small set of features extracted from historical data and, therefore, allow for a different trade-off of prediction effort and precision. Also, such heuristics should be extended symmetrically to the customer's perspective: upon the arrival of a customer service request, the presence of a set of free resources of various types implies the need to take a routing decision.

References

1. Fitzsimmons, J.A., Fitzsimmons, M.J.: Service Management: Operations, Strategy, Information technology. McGraw-Hill/Irwin, Boston (2004)
2. Gans, N., Koole, G., Mandelbaum, A.: Telephone call centers: Tutorial, review, and research prospects. Manufacturing & Service Operations Management 5(2), 79–141 (2003)
3. Buzacott, J.A., Shanthikumar, J.G.: Stochastic Models of Manufacturing Systems. Prentice Hall, Englewood Cliffs (1993)
4. Hall, R.W.: Queueing Methods: For Services and Manufacturing. Prentice Hall, Englewood Cliffs (1991)
5. van der Aalst, W.M., Schonenberg, M., Song, M.: Time prediction based on process mining. Information Systems 36(2), 450–475 (2011)
6. Folino, F., Guarascio, M., Pontieri, L.: Discovering context-aware models for predicting business process performances. In: Meersman, R., Panetto, H., Dillon, T., Rinderle-Ma, S., Dadam, P., Zhou, X., Pearson, S., Ferscha, A., Bergamaschi, S., Cruz, I.F. (eds.) OTM 2012, Part I. LNCS, vol. 7565, pp. 287–304. Springer, Heidelberg (2012)
7. Senderovich, A., Weidlich, M., Gal, A., Mandelbaum, A.: Queue mining – predicting delays in service processes. In: Jarke, M., Mylopoulos, J., Quix, C., Rolland, C., Manolopoulos, Y., Mouratidis, H., Horkoff, J. (eds.) CAiSE 2014. LNCS, vol. 8484, pp. 42–57. Springer, Heidelberg (2014)
8. Decker, G., Weske, M.: Interaction-centric modeling of process choreographies. Inf. Syst. 36(2), 292–312 (2011)
9. Object Management Group: Business Process Model and Notation (BPMN) 2.0 (2011)
10. Garnett, O., Mandelbaum, A.: An introduction to skills-based routing and its operational complexities. Teaching Notes (2000)
11. van der Aalst, W.: Process Mining: Discovery, Conformance and Enhancement of Business Processes. Springer (2011)
12. Rogge-Solti, A., Weske, M.: Prediction of remaining service execution time using stochastic petri nets with arbitrary firing delays. In: Basu, S., Pautasso, C., Zhang, L., Fu, X. (eds.) ICSOC 2013. LNCS, vol. 8274, pp. 389–403. Springer, Heidelberg (2013)
13. Hastie, T., Tibshirani, R., Friedman, J.: The Elements of Statistical Learning. Springer Series in Statistics. Springer New York Inc., New York (2001)
14. Breiman, L.: Random forests. Machine Learning 45(1), 5–32 (2001)
15. Gurvich, I., Whitt, W.: Service-level differentiation in many-server service systems via queue-ratio routing. Operations Research 58(2), 316–328 (2010)
16. Gurvich, I., Whitt, W.: Scheduling flexible servers with convex delay costs in many-server service systems. Manufacturing & Service Operations Management 11(2), 237–253 (2009)
17. van der Aalst, W., Dustdar, S.: Process mining put into context. IEEE Internet Computing 16(1), 82–86 (2012)
18. van der Aalst, W., Nakatumba, J., Rozinat, A., Russell, N.: Business process simulation: How to get it right. BPM Center Report BPM-08-07, BPMcenter. org (2008)
19. Nakatumba, J., van der Aalst, W.M.P.: Analyzing resource behavior using process mining. In: Rinderle-Ma, S., Sadiq, S., Leymann, F. (eds.) BPM 2009. LNBIP, vol. 43, pp. 69–80. Springer, Heidelberg (2010)

20. Nakatumba, J.: Resource-Aware Business Process Management: Analysis and Support. PhD thesis, Technische Universiteit Eindhoven, Eindhoven (12 (2013)
21. Senderovich, A.: Multi-Level Workforce Planning in Call Centers. Master's thesis, Technion (2012)
22. Rozinat, A., van der Aalst, W.M.P.: Decision mining in prom. In: Dustdar, S., Fiadeiro, J.L., Sheth, A.P. (eds.) BPM 2006. LNCS, vol. 4102, pp. 420–425. Springer, Heidelberg (2006)
23. de Leoni, M., Dumas, M., García-Bañuelos, L.: Discovering branching conditions from business process execution logs. In: Cortellessa, V., Varró, D. (eds.) FASE 2013 (ETAPS 2013). LNCS, vol. 7793, pp. 114–129. Springer, Heidelberg (2013)
24. Whitt, W.: Predicting queueing delays. Management Science 45(6), 870–888 (1999)
25. Ibrahim, R., Whitt, W.: Real-time delay estimation based on delay history. Manufacturing and Service Operations Management 11(3), 397–415 (2009)
26. Li, X., Olafsson, S.: Discovering dispatching rules using data mining. Journal of Scheduling 8(6), 515–527 (2005)

Dealing with Changes of Time-Aware Processes[*]

Andreas Lanz and Manfred Reichert

Institute of Databases and Information Systems, Ulm University, Germany
{andreas.lanz,manfred.reichert}@uni-ulm.de

Abstract. The proper handling of temporal process constraints is crucial in many application domains. Contemporary process-aware information systems (PAIS), however, lack a sophisticated support of time-aware processes. As a particular challenge, the execution of time-aware processes needs to be flexible as time can neither be slowed down nor stopped. Hence, it should be possible to dynamically adapt time-aware process instances to cope with unforeseen events. In turn, when applying such dynamic changes, it must be re-ensured that the resulting process instances are *temporally consistent*; i.e., they still can be completed without violating any of their temporal constraints. This paper presents the ATAPIS framework which extends well established process change operations with temporal constraints. In particular, it provides pre- and post-conditions for these operations that guarantee for the temporal consistency of the changed process instances. Furthermore, we analyze the effects a change has on the temporal properties of a process instance. In this context, we provide a means to significantly reduce the complexity when applying multiple change operations. Respective optimizations will be crucial to properly support the temporal perspective in adaptive PAIS.

1 Introduction

Time is a crucial factor regarding the proper support of business processes [10]. Moreover, in many application areas (e.g., patient treatment, automotive engineering), the handling of *temporal constraints* is vital in order to successfully execute and complete processes [3,4,10]. However, contemporary process-aware information systems (PAIS) lack a comprehensive support of such *time-aware processes* [10]. To remedy this drawback, the proper integration of temporal constraints with both the design and run-time components of a PAIS has been identified as a key challenge [3,4,7]. Our ATAPIS framework aims to provide comprehensive support for the specification, execution and monitoring of time-aware processes in adaptive PAIS.

As a prerequisite for robust process execution in PAISs, the executable *process models* must be *sound* [12]. Moreover, in the context of *time-aware process models*, i.e., process models enriched with temporal constraints, the *consistency* of the

---

[*] A more complete and formally rigor version of this work is described in a technical report [8].

S. Sadiq, P. Soffer, and H. Völzer (Eds.): BPM 2014, LNCS 8659, pp. 217–233, 2014.

temporal constraints must be ensured [1,4,7]. Checking consistency of time-aware process models at design time has been extensively studied in literature [1,3,5]. By contrast, only little attention has been paid to the proper run-time support of time-aware processes [7]. During run time, the temporal consistency of process instances needs to be continuously monitored and re-checked to avoid constraint violations. Particularly, note that activity durations and deadlines are specific to the executed process instance and only become known at run time [7].

As a particular challenge, temporal constraints cannot be considered in isolation, but might interact with each other. Hence, complex algorithms are required for checking the temporal consistency of a process model [7,15]. At run time, however, respective calculations should be reduced to a minimum to ensure scalability of the PAIS [7]. Otherwise, no run-time support of time-aware processes will be possible at the presence of a large number of process instances.

As another challenge, time can neither be slowed down nor stopped. Accordingly, time-aware processes need to be *flexible* to cope with unforeseen events or delays during run time [14]. For example, it is common that deadlines are re-scheduled or temporal constraints are dynamically modified in order to successfully complete a process instance being in trouble. Moreover, in certain scenarios the instances of time-aware processes must be structurally changed (e.g., by moving, deleting or inserting activities) to be able to meet a particular deadline. In the context of such *dynamic process changes*, we must re-ensure that the resulting process instances are sound and temporally consistent. While soundness has been extensively studied in literature [13,12], this work shows how temporal consistency of a time-aware process instance can be efficiently ensured in the context of dynamic changes. Furthermore, we analyse the effects, changes have on the temporal constraints of the respective process instance. In particular, we show how the results of this analysis can be utilized to significantly reduce the complexity when applying multiple change operations. For example, the latter becomes crucial in the context of process evolution, where a possibly large set of process instances needs to be migrated on-the-fly to a changed process model [12].

The remainder of the paper is organized as follows: Sect. 2 considers existing proposals relevant for our work. Sect. 3 provides background information on time-aware processes and defines the notion of *temporal consistency*. Sect. 4 first introduces the set of change operations we consider, followed by an in-depth discussion on how these change operations work in the context of time-aware processes. Sect. 5 analyzes the impact a change has on the temporal constraints of a process and proposes useful optimizations. Sect. 6 evaluates the proposed approach. Finally, Sect. 7 concludes with a summary and outlook.

2   Related Work

In literature, there exists considerable work on managing temporal constraints for business processes [1,3,5,7,11]. The focus of these approaches is on design-time issues like the modeling and verification of time-aware processes. By contrast, only

Table 1. Process Time Patterns TP1 – TP10 [10]

Category I: Durations and Time Lags		Category II: Restricting Execution Times	
TP1	Time Lags between two Activities	TP4	Fixed Date Elements
TP2	Durations	TP5	Schedule Restricted Elements
TP3	Time Lags between Events	TP6	Time-based Restrictions
		TP7	Validity Period
Category III: Variability		**Category IV: Recurrent Process Elements**	
TP8	Time-dependent Variability	TP9	Cyclic Elements
		TP10	Periodicity

few approaches consider run-time issues of time-aware processes [4,7]. In particular, none of the latter considers dynamic changes in this context.

Most approaches dealing with the verification of time-aware processes use a specifically tailored time model to check for the temporal consistency of process models. This becomes necessary since the interdependencies between the various temporal constraints of a process model can be quite complex and cannot be suitably captured in the respective process model. A specific conceptual model for temporal constraints is defined in [11]. In turn, [4,5] use an extended version of the *Critical Path Method* known from project planning. *Simple Temporal Networks* (STN) are used as basic formalism in [1], whereas [7] uses *Conditional Simple Temporal Networks with Uncertainty* for checking the *controllability* of process models, i.e., a more restrictive form of temporal consistency. This paper relies on *Conditional Simple Temporal Networks* (CSTN), an extension of STN that allows for the proper handling of exclusive choices [15].

In [10], we presented 10 empirically evidenced time patterns (TP), that represent temporal constraints of time-aware processes (cf. Tab. 1). In particular, time patterns facilitate the comparison of existing approaches based on a universal set of notions with well-defined semantics [9]. Moreover, [9,10] elaborated the need for a proper run-time support of time-aware processes.

Dynamic process changes were extensively studied in the past. Particularly, there exists considerable work on ensuring structural and behavioural soundness in the context of dynamic process changes [13]. A survey of approaches enabling dynamic changes is provided in [12]. To the best of our knowledge, [14] is the only work considering dynamic changes in the context of time-aware processes. As opposed to our work, however, [14] only provides a high level discussion of the different aspects to be considered when changing time-aware process instances, temporal consistency being one of them.

3   Basic Notions

This section provides basic notions. First, it defines a set of elements for modeling time-aware processes. Second, it introduces the notion of temporal consistency.

3.1   Time-Aware Processes

For each business process exhibiting temporal constraints, a *time-aware process schema* needs to be defined (cf. Fig. 1). In our work, a process schema corresponds to a *process model*; i.e., a directed graph, that comprises a set of *nodes*—representing

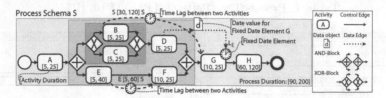

Fig. 1. Core Concepts of a Time-Aware Process Model

activities and *control connectors* (e.g., Start-/End-nodes, XORsplits, or ANDjoins) —as well as a set of *control edges* linking these nodes and specifying precedence relations between them. We assume that process models are well structured [12], e.g., sequences and branchings are specified in terms of nested single-entry single-exit (SESE) blocks. Fig. 1 depicts an example of a well structured process model with the grey areas indicating respective blocks. Each process model contains a unique start and end node, and may be composed of control flow patterns like sequence, parallel split (ANDsplit), synchronization (ANDjoin), exclusive choice (XORsplit), and simple merge (XORjoin) (cf. Fig. 1).

At run time, *process instances* may be created and executed according to the defined process model. We assume that a process instance is logically represented by a clone of the respective process model augmented with instance-specific information. If a process model contains XOR-blocks, uncertainty is introduced since not all instances perform exactly the same set of activities. The concept of *execution path* allows us to identify which activities and control connectors are actually performed during the execution of a particular process instance.

We base our ATAPIS framework on the time patterns (TP) (cf. Sect. 2). Specifically, we focus on the patterns being most relevant in practice [10]. In detail:

An **activity duration** (TP2) defines the minimum and maximum time span $[d_{min}, d_{max}]$ $(0 \leq d_{min} \leq d_{max})$ allowed for executing a particular activity (or node, in general). We assume that each activity has an assigned duration. Since control connectors are automatically executed, we may assume a fixed duration for them (e.g., $[0, 1]$). In turn, a **process duration** $[d_{min}, d_{max}]$ represents the time span allowed for executing a process instance.

Time lags between two activities (TP1) restrict the time span allowed between the starting and/or ending instants of two arbitrary activities of a process model [10]. In Fig. 1, a time lag is visualized through a dashed edge between the source and target activity. The label of the edge specifies the constraint according to the following template: $\langle I_S \rangle [t_{min}, t_{max}] \langle I_T \rangle$ $(-\infty \leq t_{min} \leq t_{max} \leq \infty)$; $\langle I_S \rangle, \langle I_T \rangle \in \{S, E\}$ mark the instant (i.e., starting or ending) of the source and target activity the time lag applies to. In turn, $[t_{min}, t_{max}]$ represents the range allowed for the time span between instants $\langle I_S \rangle$ and $\langle I_T \rangle$. Finally, note that a control edge implicitly represents an $E[0, \infty]S$ time lag between the two activities.

Fixed date elements (TP4) allow restricting activity execution in relation to a specific date (e.g., a deadline). Generally, the value of a fixed date element is specific to a process instance. Fig. 1 visualizes a fixed date element through a clock symbol attached to the activity. Thereby, label $\langle D \rangle \in \{E_S, L_S, E_E, L_E\}$

represents the activity's earliest start date (E_S), latest start date (L_S), earliest completion date (E_E), or latest completion date (L_E).

Fig. 1 shows an example of a process model exhibiting temporal constraints. Note that, although some of the symbols used for visualizing the temporal constraints resemble BPMN timer events, their semantics is quite different and should not be mixed up.

3.2 Temporal Consistency of Time-Aware Processes

A time-aware process model is executed by performing its activities and control connectors, while obeying a set of temporal constraints. We denote a process model as *temporally consistent* if it is possible to perform all *execution paths* without violating the temporal constraints involved. Temporal consistency of a time-aware process model (and its instances) constitutes a fundamental prerequisite for its robust and error-free execution [1,4]. For any PAIS supporting time-aware processes, therefore, a crucial task is to check temporal consistency of the process model at design time as well as to monitor and re-check corresponding instances during run time. This is particularly challenging since temporal constraints might interact with each other resulting in complex interdependencies (e.g., a future deadline might restrict the duration of some or all preceding activities).

Whether a time-aware process model is temporally consistent can be checked by mapping it to a *conditional simple temporal network* (CSTN)—a problem known from artificial intelligence [6]. In ATAPIS, we use CSTN since it allows us to exploit and reuse *checking algorithms* for a well founded model representing temporal constraints. Finally, CSTN allows capturing the complex interdependencies between constraints, which cannot be captured in process models.

Definition 1 (Conditional Simple Temporal Network). *A Conditional Simple Temporal Network (CSTN) is a 6-tuple $\langle \mathcal{T}, \mathcal{C}, L, \mathcal{OT}, \mathcal{O}, P \rangle$, where:*

- *$\mathcal{T}$ is a set of real-valued variables, called time-points;*
- *P is a finite set of propositional letters (or propositions);*
- *$L : \mathcal{T} \to P^*$ is a function assigning a label to each time-point in $\mathcal{T}$; a label is any (possibly empty) conjunction of (positive or negative) letters from P.[1]*
- *$\mathcal{C}$ is a set of labeled simple temporal constraints (constraint in the following); each constraint $c_{XY} \in \mathcal{C}$ has the form $c_{XY} = \langle [x, y]_{XY}, \beta \rangle$, where $X, Y \in \mathcal{T}$, $-\infty \leq x \leq y \leq \infty$, and $\beta \in P^*$ is a label.*
- *$\mathcal{OT} \subseteq \mathcal{T}$ is a set of observation time-points;*
- *$\mathcal{O} : P \to \mathcal{OT}$ is a bijection that associates a unique observation time-point to each propositional letter from P.*

Time-points represent instantaneous events that may be, for example, associated with the start / end of activities. In turn, at *observation time-points* a decision regarding possible execution paths is made. More formally, when executing observation time-point P, the truth-value of the associated proposition

---

[1] In the following we use small Greek letters $\alpha, \beta, \ldots$ to denote arbitrary labels. The empty label is denoted by ⊡.

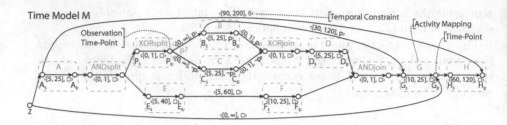

Fig. 2. CSTN Representation of the Process Model from Fig. 1

(i.e., $O^{-1}(P)$) is determined. A *constraint* $c_{XY} = \langle [x, y]_{XY}, \beta \rangle$ expresses that the time span between time-points X and Y must be at least x and at most y, i.e., $Y - X \in [x, y]$. The *label* attached to each time-point (constraint) indicates possible executions of the CSTN, i.e., a particular time-point (constraint) will be only considered if the corresponding label is satisfiable in the respective instance. Fig. 2 depicts the CSTN corresponding to the process model from Fig. 1.

The solution to a CSTN can be defined as follows [6]:

Definition 2 (Scenario and Solution). *Given a CSTN $S = \langle \mathcal{T}, \mathcal{C}, L, \mathcal{OT}, \mathcal{O}, P \rangle$, a scenario over set P is a function $s_P : P \to \{true, false\}$ that assigns a truth-value to each proposition in P.*

A solution for CSTN S under scenario s_P then corresponds to a complete set of assignments to all time-points $X \in \mathcal{T}$ with $s_P(L(X)) = true$, which satisfies all constraints $\langle [x, y]_{XY}, \beta \rangle \in \mathcal{C}$ for which $s_P(\beta) = true$ holds.

We denote the CSTN corresponding to a time-aware process model as its *time model*. The required mapping can roughly be described as follows [7]: First, the control flow of the process model is mapped to a CSTN. Particularly, each control flow element implicitly represents a temporal constraint. Each activity, AND-split, ANDjoin, and XORjoin n_i is represented as a pair of time-points N_{iS} and N_{iE}, corresponding to the starting / ending instant of the respective node. In turn, for an XORsplit, the ending instant (i.e., N_{iE}) is represented by an observation time-point. Next, a constraint $\langle [d_{min}, d_{max}]_{N_{iS}N_{iE}}, \square \rangle$ is added between N_{iS} and N_{iE} representing the duration $[d_{min}, d_{max}]$ of the node. Further, for any control edge between nodes n_i and n_j, a constraint $\langle [0, \infty]_{N_{iE}N_{jS}}, \square \rangle$ is added between the time-points representing the ending instant of n_i and starting instant of n_j. If the source of the edge is an XORsplit, in addition, the label of the constraint is augmented by proposition $p = O^{-1}(P)$. The latter represents the decision made at the corresponding observation time-point P, i.e., the label of the constraint $\langle [0, \infty]_{N_{iE}N_{jS}}, \beta \rangle$ belonging to the "true"-branch is set to βp and the one of the "false"-branch to $\beta \neg p$.[2] Further, the labels of all constraints and time-points corresponding to activities, connectors and control edges in the XOR-block are augmented by either p or $\neg p$ depending on the branch they belong to.

---

[2] Note that this can be easily extended to consider more than two branches, but for the sake of simplicity, we only consider two branches in this paper.

Next, temporal constraints are mapped to the CSTN. A *time lag* $\langle I_S \rangle [t_{min}, t_{max}]$ $\langle I_T \rangle$ corresponds to a constraint $\langle [t_{min}, t_{max}]_{N_{i \langle I_S \rangle} N_{j \langle I_T \rangle}}, L(N_{i \langle I_S \rangle}) \wedge L(N_{j \langle I_T \rangle}) \rangle$ between the two time-points representing the respective instants of nodes n_i and n_j. In turn, a *fixed date element* is initially represented as a constraint $\langle [0, \infty]_{Z N_{\langle D \rangle}}, L(N_{\langle D \rangle}) \rangle$ with Z being a special time-point representing time "0". During run time, value $[0, \infty]$ of the constraint will be updated according to the actual fixed date chosen. Finally, process duration $[d_{min}, d_{max}]$ is represented as constraint $\langle [d_{min}, d_{max}]_{N_{0S} N_{kE}}, \square \rangle$ between the time-points representing the starting instant N_{0S} of the first and the ending instant N_{kE} of the last node of the process.

As example consider Fig. 2. Note that the labels of the constraints representing the XOR-block are either set to p or $\neg p$. For the sake of readability, all edges without annotation are assumed to have bounds $\langle [0, \infty], \square \rangle$.

Based on Def. 2, we formally define the notion of *temporal consistency* for time-aware process models.

Definition 3 (Temporal Consistency). *A CSTN $\langle \mathcal{T}, \mathcal{C}, L, \mathcal{OT}, \mathcal{O}, P \rangle$ is called weakly consistent iff for each scenario s_P at least one solution exists [15].*

A time-aware process model is denoted as temporally consistent iff the corresponding time model (i.e., its CSTN representation) is weakly consistent.

When executing a time-aware process model, temporal consistency of the respective instances needs to be continuously monitored and re-checked. For this purpose, the *minimal network* of a CSTN must be determined.

Definition 4 (Minimal Network). *The minimal network of a CSTN $S = \langle \mathcal{T}, \mathcal{C}, L, \mathcal{OT}, \mathcal{O}, P \rangle$ is the unique CSTN $M = \langle \mathcal{T}, \mathcal{C}', L, \mathcal{OT}, \mathcal{O}, P \rangle$ having the same set of solutions as S and each value allowed by any constraint $c \in \mathcal{C}'$ being part of at least one solution of S.*

For any CSTN S a minimal network exists iff S is *weakly consistent*. In particular, such a minimal network provides a restricted set of constraints: As long as the value of each time-point is consistent with all constraints referring to it, we can guarantee that the entire CSTN is weakly consistent. Besides *explicit constraints* $c \in \mathcal{C}$ we obtain when mapping the process model to the CSTN, the minimal network contains *implicit constraints* between any pair of time-points that may occur in the same execution path. Note that these implicit constraints represent the effects the explicit constraints have on the overall CSTN (i.e., they represent interdependencies between explicit constraints). The implicit constraints are derived from the explicit ones when determining the minimal network. How to determine the minimal network is described in [15].

When executing a process instance, the minimal network of the time model created at design time is cloned. This *instance time model* is then kept up-to-date with the actual temporal state of the process instance (e.g., deadline, activity start and completion times). Further, it is used to monitor and re-check temporal consistency of the instance [7]. Cloning the time model becomes necessary as the temporal state of each process instance is unique; i.e., no two instances have exactly the same instance time model.

4   Change Operations for Time-Aware Processes

Standard change patterns adapting process instances without temporal constraints have been extensively studied in literature [12]. This section discusses how respective change operations may be transferred to time-aware processes. Sect. 4.1 presents the change operations applicable to time-aware processes. Sect. 4.2 then provides an in-depth discussion of these operations and shows how they can be extended to ensure temporal consistency of a changed process instance.

4.1   Basic Change Operations

When changing a process instance or—more generally—its process model, soundness must be ensured. To achieve this, ATAPIS abstracts from low-level *change primitives* (e.g., adding an edge or node) to higher-level *change operations* with well-defined pre- and post-conditions (e.g., inserting a node serially between two succeeding nodes) [12]. Applied to a sound process model, such a high-level change operation guarantees that the modified process model is structurally and behaviourally sound as well [12]. The upper part of Tab. 2 shows selected change operations required for structurally modifying a process instance. Note that respective operations may be combined to realize more complex change patterns [12] (e.g., move activity). ATAPIS extends the set of structural change operations by change operations that allow modifying the temporal constraints of a process model, e.g., inserting a time lag (see the bottom of Tab. 2). Altogether, the operations allow changing a time-aware process instance, while guaranteeing soundness of the corresponding process model. Due to lack of space, this paper restricts itself to insert operations. A detailed presentation of delete operations is provided in a technical report [8].

4.2   Applying Change Operations to Time-Aware Processes

When modifying the model of a time-aware process instance, it must be ensured that the resulting process instance is temporally consistent. This section defines basic criteria ensuring that the application of a change operation does not result in a temporally inconsistent process instance. We further analyze the local impact a particular change operation has on the temporal properties of the respective process model, i.e., its temporal constraints.

When applying a change operation to a process instance, state-specific pre- and post-conditions must be met [12]. Although these are not explicitly considered in this paper, they apply to time-aware processes as well. Furthermore, any time-related, instance-specific data (e.g., activity start and completion times) is maintained in the corresponding *instance time model* (cf. Sect. 3.2), i.e., it is sufficient to only consider the current instance time model of the process instance.

Inserting an Activity Serially. *InsertSerial*$(n_1, n_2, n_{new}, [d_{min}, d_{max}])$ is the first change operation we consider. It allows inserting node n_{new} with duration $[d_{min}, d_{max}]$ between directly succeeding nodes n_1 and n_2 (cf. Fig. 3). Regarding

Table 2. Basic Change Operations

Operation	Informal Description
Control Flow Changes	
$InsertSerial(n_1, n_2, n_{new},$ $[d_{min}, d_{max}])$	Inserts node n_{new} with duration $[d_{min}, d_{max}]$ between directly succeeding nodes n_1 and n_2.
$InsertPar(n_1, n_2, n_{new},$ $[d_{min}, d_{max}])$	Inserts node n_{new} with duration $[d_{min}, d_{max}]$ in parallel to the SESE block defined by n_1 and n_2.
$InsertCond(n_1, n_2, n_{new},$ $[d_{min}, d_{max}], c)$	Inserts node n_{new} with duration $[d_{min}, d_{max}]$ and condition c as well as an XOR block between succeeding nodes n_1 and n_2.
$DeleteActivity(n)$	Deletes activity n.[†]
Temporal Constraints Changes	
$InsertTimeLag(n_1, n_2, type_{tl},$ $[t_{min}, t_{max}])$	Inserts a time lag $[t_{min}, t_{max}]$ between nodes n_1 and n_2. Thereby, $type_{tl} \in$ {start-start, start-end, end-start, end-end} describes whether the time lag is inserted between the start of the two activities, the start of n_1 and the end of n_2, the end of n_1 and the start of n_2, or the end of the two activities.
$InsertFDE(n, type_{fde})$	Adds a fixed date element of type $type_{fde} \in \{E_S, L_S, E_E, L_E\}$ to node n.
$DeleteTimeLag(n_1, n_2, type_{tl})$	Deletes the time lag of type $type_{tl}$ between nodes n_1 and n_2.[†]
$DeleteFDE(n, type_{fde})$	Deletes a fixed date element of type $type_{fde}$ from node n.[†]

[†] Delete operations are not considered in this paper, but are discussed in a technical report [8].

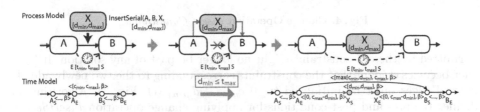

Fig. 3. Change Operation *Insert Serial*

the temporal properties of the resulting process model, the insertion of n_{new} might first and foremost increase the minimum time distance between n_1 and n_2 to d_{min}. By contrast, the maximum distance between the two nodes is not affected by the change as the newly added control connectors do not constrain it. Accordingly, if for the instance time model the minimum duration d_{min} is compliant with any implicit or explicit constraint $\langle [c_{min}, c_{max}]_{N_{1E} N_{2S}}, \beta \rangle$ between the ending instant of n_1 and the starting instant of n_2 (i.e., $d_{min} \leq c_{max}$), the node insertion will not affect temporal consistency of the process instance.[3] Remember that each value of each constraint in the instance time model is part of at least one solution (cf. Def. 4), i.e., one viable execution of the process model. After adding the node to the process instance, the mapping of this node and the control edges must be added to the instance time model as well. Further, the instance time model must be locally adapted to properly reflect the changes. In particular, the constraint between the ending instant of n_1 and the starting instant of n_2 must be updated to $[\max\{c_{min}, d_{min}\}, c_{max}]$ in order to consider the new minimum distance between the two nodes (cf. Fig. 3), i.e., certain values

---

[3] Note that any implicit constraint $\langle [c_{min}, c_{max}]_{N_{1E} N_{2S}}, \beta \rangle$ is always at least as restrictive as any explicit time lag $E[t_{min}, t_{max}]S$ between n_1 and n_2.

InsertSerial(n_1, n_2, n_{new}, $[d_{min}, d_{max}]$)*	
Pre	$succ(n_1) = n_2$, $\forall([c_{min}, c_{max}]_{N_{1E}N_{2S}}, \beta) \in C : c_{max} \geq d_{min}$
Init	$\gamma = L(N_{1E}) \wedge L(N_{2S})$
Post	// Update process model:
	...
	// Add mapping to instance time model:
	$AddTimePoint(N_{newS}, \gamma)$, $AddTimePoint(N_{newE}, \gamma)$,
	$AddConstraint(N_{newS}, N_{newE}, [d_{min}, d_{max}], \gamma)$,
	$AddConstraint(N_{1E}, N_{newS}, [0, \infty], \gamma)$, $AddConstraint(N_{newE}, N_{2S}, [0, \infty], \gamma)$,
	// Adapt instance time model:
	$\forall([c_{min}, c_{max}]_{N_{1E}N_{2S}}, \beta) \in C : UpdateConstraint(N_{1E}, N_{newS}, [0, c_{max} - d_{min}], \beta)$,
	$UpdateConstraint(N_{newE}, N_{2S}, [0, c_{max} - d_{min}], \beta)$,
	$UpdateConstraint(N_{1E}, N_{2S}, [\max\{c_{min}, d_{min}\}, c_{max}], \beta)$

*The complete version of the algorithm is provided in [8].

Algorithm 1. *InsertSerial*

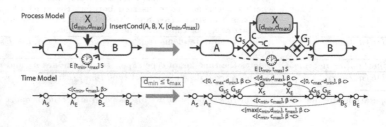

Fig. 4. Change Operation *Insert Conditional*

permitted by the old constraint might no longer be part of any solution. It further becomes evident that the constraints corresponding to the two newly added control edges must be initialized to $[0, c_{max} - d_{min}]$ (cf. Fig. 3). Algorithm 1 defines the pre- and post-conditions for applying change operation *InsertSerial* to a process instance.

The changes applied to the instance time model need to be propagated to all other constraints in order to remove values no longer contributing to any solution. Note that this must be accomplished before performing any other change or resuming the execution of the process instance. Practically, this means that the minimality of the changed instance time model needs to be restored. This may be achieved by applying the same algorithm as the one initially used for determining the minimal time model (cf. Sect. 3.2).

Inserting an Activity in Parallel. From a temporal point of view, change operation *InsertPar* (cf. Tab. 2) is similar to *InsertSerial*. Node n_{new} (together with ANDsplit and ANDjoin nodes) is inserted "serially" between nodes n_1 and n_2—the temporal effects of the enclosed SESE block are already considered in the implicit constraint between n_1 and n_2. A detailed discussion is provided in [8].

Inserting an Activity Conditionally. Change operation $InsertCond(n_1, n_2, n_{new}, [d_{min}, d_{max}], c)$ inserts node n_{new} conditionally between succeeding nodes n_1 and n_2. This change is accomplished by first inserting XORsplit g_s and XORjoin g_j sequentially between n_1 and n_2 and then n_{new} conditionally between g_s and g_j (cf. Fig. 4). The transition conditions of the control edges linking g_s and its successors are set to c and $\neg c$, respectively. When adding XORsplit g_s and condition $c/\neg c$ to the process model, a set of additional execution paths

InsertCond($n_1, n_2, n_{new}, [d_{min}, d_{max}], c$)*		
Pre	$succ(n_1) = n_2, \forall \langle [c_{min}, c_{max}]_{N_{1E}N_{2S}}, \beta \rangle \in C : c_{max} \geq d_{min}$	
Init	$\gamma = L(N_{1E}) \wedge L(N_{2S})$	
Post	// Update process model:	

    ...

    // Add mapping to instance time model:

    $AddTimePoint(G_{sS}, \gamma), AddObservationTimePoint(G_{sE}, c, \gamma),$

    $AddConstraint(G_{sS}, G_{sE}, [0, 1], \gamma),$

    $AddTimePoint(N_{newS}, \gamma), AddTimePoint(N_{newE}, \gamma c),$

    $AddConstraint(N_{newS}, N_{newE}, [d_{min}, d_{max}], \gamma c),$

    ...

    $AddConstraint(G_{sE}, G_{jS}, [0, \infty], \gamma \neg c),$

    // Adapt instance time model:

    ...

    $\forall \langle [c_{min}, c_{max}]_{N_{1E}N_{2S}}, \beta \rangle \in C : UpdateConstraint(N_{1E}, N_{2S}, [c_{min}, c_{max}], \beta \neg c),$

    $AddConstraint(N_{1E}, N_{2S}, [\max\{c_{min}, d_{min}\}, c_{max}], \beta c)$

*The complete version of the algorithm is provided in [8].

Algorithm 2. *InsertCond*

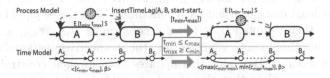

Fig. 5. Change Operation *Insert Time Lag*

results; i.e., each execution path of the old process model, which contains n_1 and n_2, can now be mapped to two execution paths: one with $c = false$ (i.e., $\neg c$) representing the previous execution path and one with $c = true$ representing the new path containing n_{new} between n_1 and n_2. Hence, for any execution path containing n_{new}, *InsertCond* has similar effects as *InsertSerial*. In turn, any execution path not containing n_{new} remains unchanged (except for the added XORsplit and XORjoin, that constitute silent nodes). Altogether, for *InsertCond* similar pre-conditions as for *InsertSerial* hold (cf. Algorithm 1).

In the context of a process instance change, the corresponding instance time model needs to be adapted by adding the mappings of the inserted elements as shown in Fig. 4. Note that this results in a new observation time-point G_{sE} and proposition c to the instance time model (cf. Sect. 3.2). Accordingly, the labels of the temporal constraints representing n_{new} and the two control edges connecting it with g_s and g_j must be set to βc with β being the label of the original constraint between N_{1E} and N_{2S}. In turn, the label of the constraint corresponding to the control edge between g_s and g_j must be set to $\beta \neg c$. Finally, the constraint between the ending instant of n_1 and the starting one of n_2 needs to be updated: The label of the original constraint must be augmented by proposition $\neg c$ resulting in constraint $\langle [c_{min}, c_{max}]_{N_{1E}N_{2S}}, \beta \neg c \rangle$. Further, another constraint $\langle [\max\{c_{min}, d_{min}\}, c_{max}]_{N_{1E}N_{2S}}, \beta c \rangle$ containing proposition c must be added between the two time-points. The latter corresponds to the case n_{new} is executed between the two nodes. Algorithm 2 defines the pre- and post-conditions of *InsertCond*. When applying this operation, again the minimality of the adapted instance time model must be restored. This is required before performing any other change or resuming the execution of the process instance.

Inserting a Time Lag. Operation $InsertTimeLag(n_1, n_2, type_{tl}, [t_{min}, t_{max}])$ allows adding a time lag between activities n_1 and n_2. The instants the time lag

InsertTimeLag(n_1, n_2, $type_{tl}$, [t_{min}, t_{max}])

Pre	$\langle I_S \rangle = \begin{cases} S & type_{tl} = \text{start-}^* \\ E & type_{tl} = \text{end-}^* \end{cases}$, $\langle I_T \rangle = \begin{cases} S & type_{tl} = {}^*\text{-start} \\ E & type_{tl} = {}^*\text{-end} \end{cases}$
	$(L(N_{1\langle I_S \rangle}) \wedge L(N_{2\langle I_T \rangle}))$ is satisfiable
	$\forall ([c_{min}, c_{max}]N_{1\langle I_S \rangle} N_{2\langle I_T \rangle}, \beta) \in C : c_{min} \leq t_{max} \wedge t_{min} \leq c_{max}$

Post // **Update process model:**
  $AddTimeLag(n_1, n_2, \langle I_S \rangle [t_{min}, t_{max}] \langle I_T \rangle)$
// **Add mapping to instance time model:**
  $AddConstraint(N_{1\langle I_S \rangle}, N_{2\langle I_T \rangle}, [t_{min}, t_{max}], L(N_{1E}) \wedge L(N_{2S}))$
// **Adapt instance time model:**
  $\forall ([c_{min}, c_{max}]N_{1E} N_{2S}, \beta) \in C :$
    $UpdateConstraint(N_{1\langle I_S \rangle}, N_{2\langle I_T \rangle}, [\max\{c_{min}, t_{min}\}, \min\{c_{max}, t_{max}\}], \beta)$

Algorithm 3. *InsertTimeLag*

refers to are specified by parameter $type_{tl}$. Adding a time lag is only possible if there exists at least one execution path containing both nodes [9]. The instance time model is then adapted by adding a constraint $\langle [t_{min}, t_{max}]N_{1\langle I_S \rangle} N_{2\langle I_T \rangle}$, $\beta \rangle$ between the time-points representing the respective instants (start vs. end) of the two nodes. Basically, this updates each implicit constraint $\langle [c_{min},$ $c_{max}]N_{1\langle I_S \rangle} N_{2\langle I_T \rangle}, \beta \rangle$. Note that this is only possible if the resulting constraint $[\max\{c_{min}, t_{min}\}, \min\{c_{max}, t_{max}\}]$ in the adapted instance time model still permits at least one value, i.e., it allows for at least one possible solution. Accordingly, in order to apply the operation it must hold $c_{min} \leq t_{max} \wedge t_{min} \leq c_{max}$. Algorithm 3 defines the pre- and post-conditions. After updating the temporal constraints, minimality of the adapted instance time model must be restored.

Inserting a Fixed Date Element. Inserting a fixed date element (i.e., operation *InsertFDE*) is equivalent to adding a time lag between the special time-point Z (indicating time "0") and the respective instant of the node (cf. Sect. 3.2) [8].

5   Analyzing the Effects of Change Operations

When changing a time-aware process instance both the process model and the instance time model must be updated. In this context, the minimality of the instance time model must be restored after each change operation. Only then it can be ensured that another change within the same change transaction may be applied without violating temporal consistency of the process instance. However, calculating the minimal network of a CSTN is expensive regarding computation time, i.e., its complexity is $O(n^3 2^k)$ with n being the number of time-points and k the number of observation time-points in the CSTN. Consequently, there might be significant delays when applying multiple change operations to large time-aware process instances. This becomes even more pressing in the context of process schema evolution [12] when migrating a potentially large set of process instances to a new schema version (i.e., process model). Hence, the maximum effect a particular change has on the instance time model must be estimated. Based on this estimation, it becomes possible to decide whether another change operation may be applied without need to restore minimality of the instance time model first.

When applying the change operations from Sect. 4.2 to the respective instance time model, two types of changes result: adding a temporal constraint or making an existing one more restrictive. Hence, it is sufficient to consider the effects a basic change has on a minimal time model. Regarding changes that make an existing constraint more restrictive, Theorem 1 shows how their maximum effects can be estimated.

Theorem 1 (Restricting a constraint in a minimal network). *Let* $M = \langle \mathcal{T}, \mathcal{C}_M, L, \mathcal{OT}, \mathcal{O}, P \rangle$ *be a minimal CSTN and* $M^* = \langle \mathcal{T}, \mathcal{C}_{M^*}, L, \; \mathcal{OT}, \mathcal{O}, P \rangle$ *the CSTN derived from* M *by replacing constraint* $c_{AB} = \langle [x, y]_{AB}, \beta \rangle \in \mathcal{C}_M$ *with the more restrictive constraint* $c^*_{AB} = \langle [x + \sigma, y - \rho]_{AB}, \beta \rangle$; $\sigma, \rho \geq 0$; *i.e.,* $\mathcal{C}^*_M = \mathcal{C}_M \setminus c_{AB} \cup \{c^*_{AB}\}$.

Then: For the minimal network $N = \langle \mathcal{T}, \mathcal{C}_N, L, \mathcal{OT}, \mathcal{O}, P \rangle$ *of* M^* *it holds: for any constraint* $c'_{XY} = \langle [x', y']_{XY}, \gamma \rangle \in \mathcal{C}_N$ *the lower bound is increased by at most* $\delta = \max\{\sigma, \rho\}$ *and the upper bound is decreased by at most* δ *compared to the original constraint* $c_{XY} = \langle [x, y]_{XY}, \gamma \rangle \in \mathcal{C}_M$. *Formally:*

$$\forall \langle [x, y]_{XY}, \gamma \rangle \in \mathcal{C}_M, \langle [x', y']_{XY}, \gamma \rangle \in \mathcal{C}_N : (x \leq x' \leq x + \delta) \wedge (y \geq y' \geq y - \delta)$$

A proof of Theorem 1 can be found in [8]. Assume that due to a change a constraint $[x, y]_{XY}$ in the time model is restricted to $[x^*, y^*]_{XY} = [x + \rho, y - \sigma]_{XY}$ and afterwards minimality of the time model is restored. Theorem 1 now states that any constraint $[u, v]_{UV}$ in the original time model is restricted to at most $[u', v']_{UV} = [u + \delta, v - \delta]_{UV}$ with $\delta = \max\{\rho, \sigma\}$ in the new time model.

Reconsider operation *InsertSerial*. Assume that the instance time model is adapted as described by Algorithm 1. The next step would be to restore minimality of this instance time model. First of all, note that the constraints introduced by the newly added activity and control edges do not affect the other constraints when restoring minimality. By construction, their effects are already incorporated in the constraint between time-points N_{1E} and N_{2S}, which is updated in the context of the operation (cf. Algorithm 1; see [2] for details). The only change having an effect on the resulting instance time model is the one restricting constraint $[c_{min}, c_{max}]$ between N_{1E} and N_{2S} to $[\max\{c_{min}, d_{min}\}, c_{max}]$. Note that if the constraint is not changed (i.e., $d_{min} \leq c_{min}$), the existing constraints of the instance time model also need not be changed. Otherwise, the lower bound of the constraint is increased by $\delta = d_{min} - c_{min}$. Theorem 1 implies that the upper and lower bound of any other constraint in the new instance time model will be restricted by at most δ as well. Thus we are able to approximate the maximum difference between the new instance time model and the original one.

From this we can conclude that when applying another insert operation, it will be sufficient to verify that any precondition referring to a constraint $\langle [x, y]_{XY}, \beta \rangle$ of the instance time model is satisfied for the respective approximated constraint $\langle [x + \delta, y - \delta]_{XY}, \beta \rangle$ as well. In this case, the insert operation may be applied without violating the temporal consistency of the process instance. In particular, and this is a fundamental advantage of ATAPIS, we need not restore minimality of the modified instance time model prior to the application of the operation. By contrast, if the precondition is not met for the approximated constraint, it might

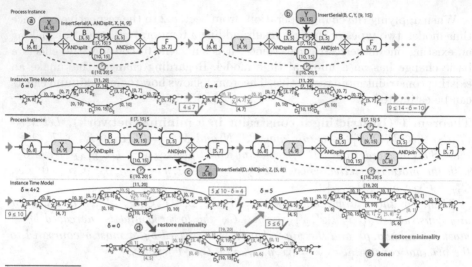

*Note that for sake of compactness only relevant constraints and no labels are shown for the instance time models.

Fig. 6. Applying Multiple Change Operations to a Process Model

still be possible to apply the change without violating temporal consistency. In this case, however, minimality of the modified instance time model must be first restored before deciding whether the change may be applied.

Similar rules apply to all other insert operations. Regarding *InsertCond* (cf. Algorithm 2), in particular, the change relevant to the instance time model is the one restricting the constraint between time-points N_{1E} and N_{2S} to $[\max\{c_{min}, d_{min}\}, c_{max}]$, i.e., the impact on the other constraints is at most $\delta = \max\{0, d_{min} - c_{min}\}$. Finally, for *InsertTimeLag*, the maximum impact corresponds to $\delta = \max\{0, t_{min} - c_{min}, t_{max} - c_{max}\}$ (cf. Algorithm 3).

Based on these observations it becomes possible to apply a sequence of change operations to a process instance within the same transaction without need to restore minimality of the instance time model after each change. If a sequence of change operations $op_1, \ldots, op_n$ with impacts $\delta_1, \ldots, \delta_n$ shall be applied to a process instance, it will be sufficient to consider the aggregated impact of the previously applied operations. Practically speaking, for operation op_i, approximated constraint $[x + \sum_{j=1}^{i-1} \delta_j, y - \sum_{j=1}^{i-1} \delta_j]_{XY}$ needs to be considered to determine whether the operation may be applied. Note that this will significantly reduce complexity when applying multiple change operations. However, the actual savings depend on the strictness of the constraints of the time-aware process model; if the latter is "heavily" constrained, only few change operations can be applied without need to restore minimality of the instance time model. In turn, if the constraints are "weak", multiple change operations may be applied at once, without having to restore minimality of the instance time model between changes.

We illustrate our approach along the example from Fig. 6. It depicts a process instance and corresponding instance time model to which a series of three change operations ⓐ-ⓒ shall be applied. First, activity X with duration $[4, 9]$ shall be inserted between A and ANDsplit (Fig. 6 ⓐ). This is possible without violating the temporal consistency of the process instance since the minimum duration of X is lower than the maximum time distance between A and ANDsplit (i.e., $4 \leq 7$). After performing the change, the value used for approximating the instance time model becomes $\delta = 4 - 0 = 4$. Next, Y shall be inserted between B and C (Fig. 6 ⓑ). Again this is possible since the minimum duration is lower than the approximated maximum time distance (i.e., $9 \leq 14 - \delta = 10$). Afterwards δ is increased to $\delta = 4 + (9 - 7) = 6$. However, inserting Z with duration $[5, 8]$ between D and ANDjoin (Fig. 6 ⓒ) is then not possible based on the approximated instance time model as the precondition of the respective change operation cannot be met (i.e., $5 \nleq 10 - \delta = 4$). Hence, minimality of the instance time model must be restored (Fig. 6 ⓓ). Afterwards, inserting Z becomes possible as for the new instance time model the precondition of the operation is met. Finally, minimality of the last instance time model must be restored (Fig. 6 ⓔ).

6   Proof of Concept

The presented approach was implemented as a proof-of-concept prototype in our ATAPIS Toolset, which is based on the AristaFlow BPM Suite [12]. This prototype enables users to create time-aware process models and to automatically generate respective time models based on CSTN. Further, the presented change operations may be applied to both process models and corresponding instances. Particularly, they are based on AristaFlow's well-founded set of change operations [12]. Overall, the prototype demonstrates the applicability of our approach.

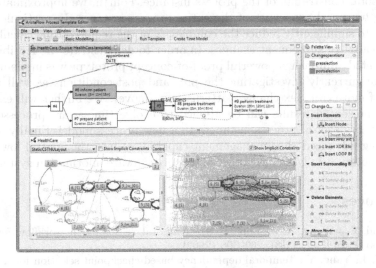

Fig. 7. Screenshot of the Prototype (based on the AristaFlow BPM Suite)

The screenshot from Fig. 7 shows the ATAPIS Toolset[4]: at the top, a process model from the healthcare domain comprising several temporal constraints is shown. At the bottom, the automatically generated time model and its minimal network are depicted. Finally, the right side displays the available set of change operations. Whether a particular change operation may be applied is decided by checking both structural and temporal preconditions. When applying an operation to the process model (i.e., schema or instance) all three models are updated simultaneously as described in Sect. 4.1. A first simulation based on our prototype shows a significantly improved performance of our approximation-based approach for applying multiple change operations compared to the "classical approach" [8].

7   Conclusion

Time constitutes a fundamental concept for the operational support of business processes in PAISs. In business, where missed deadlines and violations of temporal constraints might cause significant problems, it is crucial for enterprises to be able to efficiently control and monitor these temporal constraints during run time. Since process execution does not always stick to the plan, enterprises must be further able to flexibly react to deviations in a time-aware process instance without affecting other properties of the instance. This paper considered dynamic changes of time-aware process instances. First, we defined change operations for time-aware processes. Second, we specified pre- and post-conditions for these operations, which ensure that changed process instances remain temporally consistent. Third, we analyzed the effects respective change operations have on the temporal constraints of the process instance. Fourth, we approximated the resulting temporal properties of the entire process instance. In particular, this allows us to significantly reduce the complexity of the required time calculations in the context of subsequent changes. In order to demonstrate the feasibility of the presented approach, a powerful proof-of-concept prototype was implemented.

We are currently investigating the pre- and post-conditions as well as the impact of more complex change patterns (e.g., move). We further will examine how the presented results can be applied to evolve time-aware processes and migrate a large set of process instances to a new process model. Finally, we are integrating advanced time-management capabilities into the AristaFlow BPM Suite to obtain a fully-fledged time- and process-aware information system.

References

1. Bettini, C., Wang, X.S., Jajodia, S.: Temporal reasoning in workflow systems. Distrib. Para. Dat. 11(3), 269–306 (2002)
2. Chen, J., Yang, Y.: Temporal dependency based checkpoint selection for dynamic verification of temporal constraints in scientific workflow systems. ACM Trans. on Soft Eng. and Methodol. 20(3), 9:1–9:23 (2011)

---

[4] A screencast demonstrating the toolset is available at dbis.info/atapis

3. Combi, C., Gozzi, M., Posenato, R., Pozzi, G.: Conceptual modeling of flexible temporal workflows. TAAS 7(2),19:1–19:29 (2012)
4. Eder, J., Euthimios, P., Pozewaunig, H., Rabinovich, M.: Time management in workflow systems. In: Proc. BIS 1999, pp. 265–280 (1999)
5. Ede, J., Gruber, W., Panagos, E.: Temporal modeling of workflows with conditional execution paths. In: Ibrahim, M., Küng, J., Revell, N. (eds.) DEXA 2000. LNCS, vol. 1873, pp. 243–253. Springer, Heidelberg (2000)
6. Hunsberger, L., Posenato, R., Combi, C.: The dynamic controllability of conditional STNs with uncertainty. In: Proc. PlanEx 2012 (2012)
7. Lanz, A., Posenato, R., Combi, C., Reichert, M.: Controllability of time-aware processes at run time. In: Proc. CoopIS 2013, pp. 39–56 (2013)
8. Lanz, A., Reichert, M.: Process change operations for time-aware processes. Tech. Rep. UIB-2014-01, University of Ulm (2014), http://dbis.eprints.uni-ulm.de/1027/
9. Lanz, A., Reichert, M., Weber, B.: A formal semantics of time patterns for process-aware information systems. Tech. Rep. UIB-2013-02, University of Ulm (2013)
10. Lanz, A., Weber, B., Reichert, M.: Time patterns for process-aware information systems. Req. Eng. 19(2), 113–141 (2014)
11. Marjanovic, O., Orlowska, M.E.: On modeling and verification of temporal constraints in production workflows. Knowl. and Inf. Syst. 1(2), 157–192 (1999)
12. Reichert, M., Weber, B.: Enabling Flexibility in Process-aware Information Systems: Challenges, Methods, Technologies. Springer (2012)
13. Rinderle, S., Reichert, M., Dadam, P.: Correctness criteria for dynamic changes in workflow systems: A survey. Data & Knowl. Eng. 50(1), 9–34 (2004)
14. Sadiq, S.W., Marjanovic, O., Orlowska, M.E.: Managing change and time in dynamic workflow processes. Int'l J. Coop. Inf. Syst. 9(1-2), 93–116 (2000)
15. Tsamardinos, I., Vidal, T., Pollack, M.: CTP: A new constraint-based formalism for conditional, temporal planning. Constraints 8(4), 365–388 (2003)

Temporal Anomaly Detection in Business Processes*

Andreas Rogge-Solti[1] and Gjergji Kasneci[2]

[1] Vienna University of Economics and Business, Austria
andreas.rogge-solti@wu.ac.at
[2] Hasso Plattner Institute, University of Potsdam, Germany
gjergji.kasneci@hpi.uni-potsdam.de

Abstract. The analysis of business processes is often challenging not only because of intricate dependencies between process activities but also because of various sources of faults within the activities. The automated detection of potential business process anomalies could immensely help business analysts and other process participants detect and understand the causes of process errors.

This work focuses on temporal anomalies, i.e., anomalies concerning the runtime of activities within a process. To detect such anomalies, we propose a Bayesian model that can be automatically inferred form the Petri net representation of a business process. Probabilistic inference on the above model allows the detection of non-obvious and interdependent temporal anomalies.

Keywords: outlier detection, documentation, statistical method, Bayesian networks.

1 Introduction

Business process management is the key to aligning a company's business with the needs of clients. It aims at continuously improving business processes and enabling companies to act more effectively and efficiently. The optimization of business processes often reveals opportunities for technological integration and innovation [21]. Despite these positive aspects, business processes are often complex by containing intricate dependencies between business activities. Moreover, the activities are enacted in a distributed fashion and in environments where faults can occur [22]. Thus the analysis of business processes is a highly challenging task [11], even for experts.

Automated mining of process patterns out of event data can reveal important insights into business processes [2]. However, the performance of process mining algorithms is highly dependent on the quality of event logs [3], which in turn are also crucial for documentation purposes [17]. Most data mining algorithms build on the unrealistic assumption that the recorded training data is valid and representative of the data expected to be encountered in the future. In process mining such an assumption makes sense only if documentation correctness is guaranteed. Most work on documentation correctness deals with only structural aspects, i.e., with the *order* of execution of activities [18,4,7].

* This work was partially supported by the European Union's Seventh Framework Programme (FP7/2007-2013) grant 612052 (SERAMIS).

S. Sadiq, P. Soffer, and H. Völzer (Eds.): BPM 2014, LNCS 8659, pp. 234–249, 2014.

This work proposes a novel approach to detect temporal outliers in activity durations. Outliers can have various causes; they can be obvious, e.g., in case of non-typical measurement or execution errors [10], and they can be hidden, e.g., in case of latent or propagated errors that do not reveal themselves as such during the execution. Often, however, it is sufficient to detect potential anomalies and not the exact errors. When presented with such anomalies, expert analysts or other process participants can dig deeper into the problem and fix any present error. Hence, detecting potential anomalies can immensely simplify the task of finding potential errors in business processes [5].

The focus of this work is on temporal anomalies, where a group of interdependent activities has a non-typical runtime or delay pattern. Note that this is different from the detection of delay for a single activity, as a group of activities may still show a regular overall runtime, even if the single activities have anomalous delays. Hence we go beyond the detection of delay for single activities and are generally interested in implausible delay patterns within a group of activities. Our goal is to detect such anomalies from event traces and to extrapolate from the investigation of delay for single activities to the detection of temporal anomalies in the entire case.

The main achievements of this work are:
- An extensive analysis of general properties of temporal anomalies based on event logs and the formalism of stochastic Petri Nets
- A principled formalization of temporal anomalies based on approximate distributions of activity durations
- A probabilistic approach for reliably detecting temporal anomalies in sequences of consecutive activities by analyzing the corresponding event logs
- An extensive evaluation of the approach based on synthetic as well as real-world datasets with labeled error occurrences.

The remainder of the paper is organized as follows. Section 2 introduces the main concepts this work builds on. Section 3 gives an overview of related work and sets the context for the achievements presented in this paper. The approach for temporal anomaly detection is presented in Section 4. An extensive experimental evaluation of the approach is presented in Section 5, before concluding in Section 6.

2   Preliminaries

Understanding the business processes of an organization can be facilitated by business process models. We assume that a business process model is available and accurately describes the behavior of a process. There exist many competing modeling languages for business processes, of which we abstract by relying on the Petri net [15] representation of the models [12], which are able to capture the most important workflow-patterns used in different languages. We define Petri nets according to the original definition [15] as follows.

Definition 1 (Petri Net). *A Petri net is a tuple* $PN = (P, T, F)$ *where:*
- *P is a set of places.*
- *T is a set of transitions.*
- $F \subseteq (P \times T) \cup (T \times P)$ *is a set of connecting arcs representing flow relations.*

We also define paths in Petri nets as follows. Let F^+ denote the transitive closure over F, then a *path* exists between any two nodes $l, n \in (P \cup T)$, iff $(l, n) \in F^+$. We assume that the models are *sound* workflow nets [1], i.e., that they have a dedicated start place p_i and an end place p_o, each node lies on a path between p_i and p_o, there are no deadlocks, and whenever a marking with $p_o > 0$ is reached, all other places $p \in \{P \setminus p_o\}$ are empty, i.e., the process is properly terminated. We do not put further restrictions on the supported model class and explicitly also support non-structured and non-free-choice parts in the models.

During execution of single instances of business processes, information regarding the state and progress of these process instances are recorded in various information systems. For example, a logistics service provider tracks the position of its transport means, or a financial institute tracks the status of customer loan requests. We assume that the progress information for each case is available and collected in event logs [2]. Therefore, we use the established notion of event logs that contain executed traces.

Definition 2 (Event Log). *An event log over a set of activities A and time domain TD is defined as* $L_{A,TD} = (E, C, \alpha, \beta, \gamma, \geq)$, *where:*
- *E is a finite set of events.*
- *C is a finite set of cases (process instances).*
- $\alpha : E \rightarrow A$ *is a function assigning each event to an activity.*
- $\beta : E \rightarrow C$ *is a surjective function assigning each event to a case.*
- $\gamma : E \rightarrow TD$ *is a function assigning each event to a timestamp.*
- $\geq \subseteq E \times E$ *is the succession relation, which imposes a total ordering on the events in E.*

We require that the time of occurrence is recorded for event entries in an event log. For example, in a hospital, where nurses record the timestamps of certain treatment steps in a spreadsheet, we can derive an event log of that spreadsheet, where each case is associated to a row in the spreadsheet and each activity corresponds to a column.

In previous work, we have provided an algorithm to enrich PN models with statistical execution information in event logs [16]. The statistical information that we learn from historical executions is associated with transitions that capture decision probabilities, and with transitions that capture process activities and their corresponding durations. We revisit the definition of the enriched stochastic model [16].

Definition 3 (Generally Distributed Transition Stochastic Petri Net). *A generally distributed transition stochastic Petri net (GDT_SPN) is a tuple:*
$GDT\_SPN = (P, T, \mathcal{W}, F, \mathcal{D})$, *where* (P, T, F) *is the basic underlying Petri net. Additionally:*
- *The set of transitions* $T = T_i \cup T_t$ *is partitioned into immediate transitions T_i and timed transitions T_t.*
- $\mathcal{W} : T_i \rightarrow \mathbb{R}^+$ *assigns probabilistic weights to the immediate transitions.*
- $\mathcal{D} : T_t \rightarrow D$ *is an assignment of arbitrary probability density functions D to timed transitions, reflecting the duration of each corresponding activity.*

Probability density functions represent the relative number of occurrences of observations in a continuous domain. In most real business processes, analytical expressions for probability density functions will not be available, and we resort to *density estimation* techniques [19]. For example, kernel density estimation techniques as described by Parzen [13] are a popular method to approximate the real distribution of values.

Once we extracted the stochastic properties of past executions, we can check whether new traces match the *regular* and *expected* behavior, or if they are *outliers* and deviate from the stochastic model. We are interested in finding temporal anomalies to assist business analysts in root-cause analysis of outliers. Further, we aim at separation of outliers that can occur and are expected during execution from *measurement errors*, e.g., when in the above example a nurse enters a wrong time for an activity by mistake.

The idea of this paper is to exploit knowledge that is encoded in the process model for this task. The problem that we encounter, if we only have an event log that traces the execution of activities, is that it is not made explicit, which activities are dependent on which predecessors, because of possible parallel execution and interleaving events. Therefore, we extract structural information from the *GDT_SPN* model—in fact, the underlying *PN* model already contains this information.

To ease the discussion of temporal outlier detection in the main section, we introduce the concepts of control flow and temporal dependence.

Definition 4 (Control-flow Dependence). *Let $t_1, t_2 \in T$ be two transitions. A control-flow dependence exists between t_1 and t_2, iff there is a path between t_1 and t_2.*

We further define *temporal dependencies* on a process instance level. That is, we want to identify the transitions that are immediately enabled after the current activity finished. We therefore replay the cases from the event log, as proposed in [18,4], and additionally keep track of the global clock during replay [16].

Definition 5 (Temporal Dependence, Direct Dependence). *Let $t_1, t_2 \in T_t$ be two transitions of a GDT_SPN model. There is a temporal dependence in a case between t_1 and t_2, iff the timestamp of termination of t_1 is equal to the global clock, when t_2 becomes enabled. That is, there is no other timed transition firing between the firing of t_1, and the enabling of t_2.*

A direct dependence between t_1, and t_2 exists, iff there is a temporal dependence between t_1, and t_2 and there is a control-flow dependence between t_1, and t_2.

For notational convenience, we define the dependence relation $dep : A \times A$ on the corresponding process activities of the model that contains all pairs of activities, of which the timed transitions in the model are in a *direct dependence* in a case. This simple definition of *dep* works well for process models without loop constructs. If there exist loops in a process model, there could be a *direct dependence* between a transition and itself (in the next iteration), and likewise the corresponding activity would be in a self-dependence. Therefore, we will use the dependence relationship dep_a on individual instances of activities, instead of on the activity model. It is straightforward to see that we can enumerate multiple instances of the same activity and thus limit the direct dependencies of an activity instance to the activity instances that follow directly. Note that the number of the set of activities that directly depends on an activity is in most cases 1, unless there is a parallel split after the activity. In the latter case, the number of directly dependent activities equals the number of parallel branches in the process that are triggered with the termination of the activity. Also note that if we restrict our attention to activity instances in executed process instances, an activity instance followed by an exclusive choice between several alternative branches in the control flow still only has 1 activity with which it is in a direct dependence. Latter is the first activity on the path that was chosen.

Given different instances of activities and the dependence relation dep_a, one can represent their duration dependencies by means of a Bayesian network. In such a network, nodes represent duration variables that follow an estimated prior distribution that is encoded in the *GDT_SPN* model, or they represent points of occurrence of events, such as the termination of an activity. It is straight-forward to see that such a network can be directly derived from an instantiation of the activity model, which in turn can be created during replay of each case of the event log. Later on, we will show that because of the simple structure of this Bayesian network, effectively we only need a window-based analysis of the events and their direct dependencies in the event log.

Definition 6 (Bayesian Network). *Let* $\{X_1, \ldots, X_k\}$ *be a set of random variables. A Bayesian network BN is a directed acyclic graph* (N, F), *where*
- $N = \{n_1, \ldots, n_k\}$ *is the set of nodes assigned each to a random variable* $X_1, \ldots, X_k$.
- $F \subset N \times N$ *is the set of directed edges.*

Let $(n_i, n_j) \in F$ *be an edge from parent node* n_i *to child node* n_j. *The edge reflects a conditional dependence between the corresponding random variables* X_i *and* X_j.

Each random variable is independent from its predecessors given the values of its parents. Let π_i *denote the set of parents of* X_i. *A Bayesian network is fully defined by the probability distributions of the nodes* n_i *as* $P(X_i \mid \pi_i)$ *and the conditional dependence relations encoded in the graph. Then, the joint probability distribution of the whole network factorizes according to the chain rule as* $P(X_1, \ldots, X_N) = \prod_{i=1}^{N} P(X_i \mid \pi_i)$.

Although nodes are most commonly used for capturing random behavior, it is not difficult to introduce deterministic nodes in a Bayesian network. A node in a Bayesian network can be assigned a single value with probability 1 or a (deterministic) function of the values of the parent nodes. For the purposes of this paper, we limit our attention to the most common workflow structures: *sequence*, *exclusive choice*, *parallelization* and *synchronization* of control flow. Because exclusive choices are removed during execution, two deterministic constructs are sufficient to capture the dependencies between durations of activity instances and timestamps of events: we need the *sum* operation to capture sequential dependencies and the *max* operation to model the synchronization of parallel activities. Latter two nodes deterministically assign probability 1 to the sum (resp. max) of the parent variables' values and probability zero to other values.

An example model from a hospital process shall serve to illustrate this point. Figure 1 shows a scenario, where a patient arrives at the operating room (t_A) and is then treated with antibiotics (t_B), while the induction of anaesthesia (t_C) is conducted in parallel. After both these activities are completed, the surgery t_D can be performed. In this example, depending on the current case, the direct dependence relation is $dep_a = \{(a, b), (a, c), (b, d)\}$, if activity b takes longer than c, or $dep_a = \{(a, b), (a, c), (c, d)\}$ in the other case. Note that the faster of the parallel activities has no temporal dependence to activity d, and is thus not included in the dependence relation.

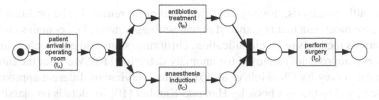

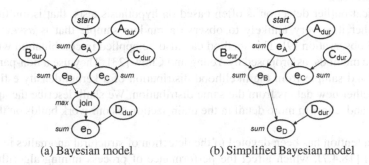

Fig. 1. Surgery example *GDT_SPN* model depicting dependencies between activity durations in a process model with sequence and parallel split and merge constructs.

(a) Bayesian model   (b) Simplified Bayesian model

Fig. 2. Bayesian network models for the surgery example depicted in Figure 1. If we know that e_B happens after e_C in case (b), we can simplify the dependencies by removing the max node and the dependence from e_C to e_D, and only maintain the dependence between e_B and e_D.

The resulting Bayesian model is shown in Figure 2a. The process is started at a certain point in time, which can be aligned to zero in the model. The duration of activity a is modeled as A_{dur}, and influences the value of e_A that captures the observed timestamp of the corresponding termination event. Latter is the last activity before the control flow is split into two parallel branches. For each, we add the corresponding activity duration to the resulting events. Then, the maximum of the parallel branches is selected by the deterministic max node *join* and the final event e_D is the sum of latter and the duration of activity d captured in D_{dur}.

Given the dependency relation dep_a, we can further simplify the Bayesian network, as shown in Figure 2b. In this example, the max node is resolved due to the knowledge that the branch with activity b finished after the branch with activity c. The dependency from e_C to e_D can be removed as well. Note that in general it is not always the case that there will be a single transition in the model for a process activity. If there is more information available about the activity lifecycle of an activity [21] (e.g., if we know when the activity has been enabled, started, and completed), the model can more accurately capture the different phases. Therefore, an extension by replacing a single timed transitions by a sub-net that captures fine grained activity lifecycle transitions is possible.

3 Related Work

The problem of anomaly detection is to identify data that does not conform to the general behavior or the model of the data. Different flavors of the general problem are also known as outlier analysis, novelty detection, and noise removal. The problem is relevant, because most data that is gathered in real settings is *noisy*, i.e., contains outliers or errors. Various methods (e.g., classification, clustering, statistical approaches, information theoretic approaches) are used for anomaly detection [10]. We refer the interested reader to the survey by Chandola et al. [5] for an overview of different approaches to the problem, and to the text book by Han and Kamber [10] for details on classification and clustering approaches. For this paper, we limit the discussion to statistical methods of outlier detection as well as proposed anomaly detection techniques in the domain of business processes.

Statistical outlier detection is often based on hypothesis tests, that is, on the question whether it is very unlikely to observe a random sample that is *as extreme* as the actual observation [9]. This method can also be applied in combination with non-parametric methods, as proposed by Yeung and Chow [23]. They use a non-parametric approach and sample from the likelihood distribution of a kernel density estimate to check whether new data is from the same distribution. We shall describe the approach by Yeung and Chow in more detail in the main section, as our work builds on the same idea.

Much attention has been devoted to the detection of structural anomalies in process event logs [18,4,7], which affect the performance of process mining algorithms [2]. Sometimes, these anomalies are considered harmful, i.e., if they violate compliance rules [8]. Techniques range from algorithmic replay [18], to cost-based fitness analysis [4] that is able to guarantee to find an optimal solution to the alignment of model and log based on distinct costs for not synchronized parts.

Cook et al. integrate time boundaries into conformance checking by using a formal timed model of a system [6]. They assume that a timed model is already present and specified, and consider time boundaries instead of probability density functions, while we strive to detect anomalies that differ from usual behavior and also want to distinguish measurement errors from regular outliers. Hao et al. analyze business impact of business data on key performance indicators and visualize them either in aggregated or single views in the model [11]. In contrast, our work leverages information encoded in the structure of the model to find related variables and to detect outliers in continuous space.

4 Anomaly Detection in Business Processes

The approach presented in this section builds on intuitive assumptions derived from practical observations. For example, we assume that anomalous event durations are rare when compared to normal execution times. Moreover, we assume that the actual (i.e., typical) activity durations are independent; the observed duration of an activity, on the other hand, depends only on its actual (i.e., typical) duration and the observed duration of the preceding activity. Another important assumption is that the whole process itself is in a so-called "steady state", that is, we do not consider trends or seasonality in the model. Finally, we assume that all events are collected in an event log that contains both information about the activity as well as the point in time of occurrence. In practice, such logs are maintained for most business process routines. In [16], it was shown that these kinds of logs can be directly used to infer probabilistic models of business processes, for example *GDT_SPN* models. We assume that a *GDT_SPN* model is enriched from a plain Petri net representation of a business process model.

4.1 Detection of Outliers

Most work on detecting deviations from specified control flow only focuses on structural deviations, e.g., whether the activities were performed in the correct order, or whether activities were skipped [18,4,7]. In this work, we would like to go one step further and also consider the execution time of activities to detect cases that do not conform with the expected duration. The latter is encoded in form of statistical information that is encoded in the probability density function of timed transitions in *GDT_SPN*. First, let us recall a simple procedure to detect outliers.

A common rule to find outliers in *normally* distributed data is to compute the z-score of an observation ($z = \frac{x-\mu}{\sigma}$, i.e., the deviation about the mean normalized in units of standard deviations) and classify an observation as an outlier iff $|z| > 3$. This simple method depends on the assumption that the data is normally distributed, which is often not the case.

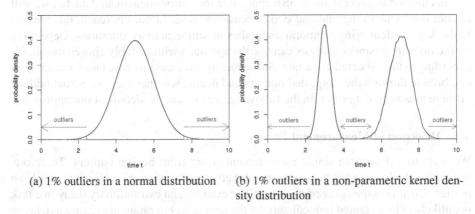

(a) 1% outliers in a normal distribution   (b) 1% outliers in a non-parametric kernel density distribution

Fig. 3. Classification of 1 percent outliers. The areas containing the most unlikely 1 percent are highlighted as outliers.

To gain more flexibility and to not depend on measures in units of standard deviation, it is also possible to specify the threshold for outliers in terms of percentage of the observations. Let us assume we want to find the most extreme 1 percent of a normally distributed observations. Then the we can compute the theoretical 0.5 percent quantile, and the 99.5 percent quantile of the normal distribution and if the observed value falls in the region below the 0.5 percent quantile (or equivalently falls above the 99.5 percent quantile), we classify the observation as an outlier. Figure 3a depicts the region of 1 percent of the most unlikely values in a normal distribution with a mean of 5 and a standard deviation of 1. Note that this more flexible test that is based on lower and upper quantiles is only valid for *symmetric* probability distributions, like the normal distribution.

In reality, the assumption of normally distributed values durations is often inappropriate. When dealing with real data, simple parametric models might not be able to capture the probability distributions in sufficient detail. The observations could belong to distinct classes with different behavior (e.g., due to differences in processing speed), which can result in two modes in the probability density function. An example is depicted in Figure 3b, where two peaks in the data are observable at $t = 3$ and $t = 7$. Note that in such cases, the z-value is not suitable any more, and we rely on more robust classification methods, as described by Yeung and Chow [23].

The main idea for the outlier detection is based on a hypothesis test that tries to identify the probability that an observation x is from a particular model M. Therefore, the distribution $L(y) = \log P(y \mid M)$ of the log-likelihoods of random samples y from the model M is computed. This can be done by sampling and approximating the probability density function of the log-likelihood of each sample point. The log-likelihood of the event that x was generated by the same model M is $L(x) = \log P(x \mid M)$. The hypothesis that needs to be tested is whether $L(x)$ is drawn from the same distribution of log-likelihoods as $L(y)$, i.e., $P(L(y) \leq L(x)) > \psi$ for a threshold parameter $0 < \psi < 1$. The null hypothesis is rejected if the probability is not greater than ψ, implying that x is an outlier with respect to M.

This method is general and is also applicable for multidimensional data, but we will restrict our focus to the one and two dimensional case. In our approach, this method is the key to identifying temporal anomalies in single activity durations. Depending on the domain, business analysts can use the approach with suitably chosen thresholds according to the expected error rate. Subsequently, on a case-to-case basis, the analysts can browse through the suggested outliers and decide whether they are actual outliers or mere measurement errors. In the following, we present the details of our approach.

4.2   Detection of Measurement Errors

We want to differentiate single measurement errors from benign outliers. Therefore, we exploit the knowledge that measurement errors only affect a *single* event, while an outlier also affects the *succeeding* events. For example, an extraordinary delay in a task is unlikely to be regained immediately by the next task, but rather also cause a delay in the latter. This means that if there is a measurement error in a single activity, usually two activities are affected: the activity, of which the event is describing the completion time, as well as the following activity that is enabled immediately afterwards. We expect that a positive measurement error that indicates a long duration to yield a negative error (too short duration) for the following activity. Figure 4 highlights the difference between single outlier detection and measurement error detection. In Fig. 4a a measurement error can happen for a single activity, where we can only hint at the error by identifying it as an outlier. On the other side, we see two dependent activity durations in Fig. 4b, where we can be more certain that a measurement error occurred, if the data point is better explained by the diagonal error model that shows a high negative correlation between the durations.

A typical assumption when designing an outlier detection model is that outliers will not follow the distribution of the benign data points. However, when dealing with the detection of anomalous sequences of data points, e.g., consecutive durations of

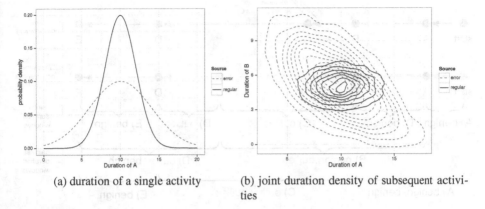

(a) duration of a single activity

(b) joint duration density of subsequent activities

Fig. 4. Expected behavior (solid black curve) and measurement errors (dotted red curve) in the univariate (single activity) and the bivariate case (two directly depending activities).

activities, the problem is that an anomalous sequence may look benign (e.g., anomalous durations may add up to expected runtimes) until the single data points are analyzed in detail. This problem is related to Simpson's paradox [20], where the signal obtained from an aggregated set of data points coming from at least two different distributions can be corrupted, in the sense that it would hide the signal that one might have obtained by analyzing the data points grouped by their distributions. In [14], Pearl defined a set of specific conditions, i.e., precise criteria for selecting a set of "confounding variables" – that yield correct causal relationships if included in the analysis – to avoid Simpson's paradox. Basically, Pearl advocates the analysis of variable dependencies and their representation by means of Bayesian networks; with probabilistic inference on the networks yielding unbiased signals from the data. We follow this recipe and model a sequence of activity durations as a Bayesian network that is directly derived from the dep_a relation that we introduced in Section 2 for each case.

Basically, our Bayesian network contains activity duration variables (e.g., A_{dur}), and timestamps of events (e.g., e_A), see Section 2. For every pair of dependent activity instances $(a, b) \in dep_a$, we examine their durations A_{dur}, and B_{dur}. Thereby, we reason about the probability of an error having occurred at that pair. More specifically, we compare the bivariate distribution of $P(A_{dur}, B_{dur} \mid error)$ with $P(A_{dur}, B_{dur} \mid no\_error)$ and their marginalized versions (including an error), i.e., $P(A_{dur} \mid error) = \int_{B_{dur}} P(A_{dur}, B_{dur} \mid error)$, and $P(B_{dur} \mid error) = \int_{A_{dur}} P(A_{dur}, B_{dur} \mid error)$, to identify certain error patterns in consecutive events. Specifically, we are interested in the relative likelihood of each of the above conditionals (i.e., relative to the sum of the likelihoods of the four available models). This allows us to select the most plausible model that might have generated A_{dur} and B_{dur}.

The simplicity of the above approach allows us to effectively move a window of size 2 over directly dependent events (which must not be direct neighbors in the log) and analyze the plausibility of their joint runtime as well as their durations in separation. The dependencies gathered from the *GDT_SPN* model are leveraged to find successors

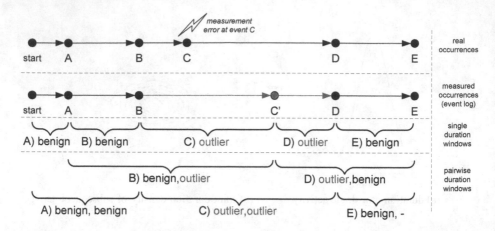

Fig. 5. Window-based measurement error detection approach. First row shows original events, where the timestamp of event C has been corrupted due to an error. By this example error, the duration of C and D are affected. The approach that uses a single duration window has difficulties localizing the error and will usually yield too many false positives. Pairwise comparison of subsequent durations can pinpoint the error location, i.e., if both durations are erroneous and negatively correlated.

of the current event. When the current activity is the last in a dependency chain (i.e., last activity in the process, or last activity in a "fast" parallel branch, where the next activity is not waiting for the fast branch, but for the slow one), we cannot exploit further information to identify outliers as errors. In such cases, we fall back to outlier detection, as described in Section 4.1. If there exists a direct dependency between to the activity and another (i.e., the two activity instances are contained in dep_a), we distinguish 4 cases and probabilistically infer the most plausible one. The four cases are:

benign, benign neither the duration of current event nor the duration of its successor are outliers.
benign, outlier the duration of the successor is an outlier, but not the duration of the current event.
outlier, outlier both durations are outliers and the outliers are strongly correlated negatively. This indicates a measurement error at the current event.
outlier, benign the duration of the current event is an outlier, but not the duration of its successor.

When an activity instance effectively starts multiple activities in parallel (i.e., is contained more than once in dep_a), we simply compute the weighted average of the activity pairs, where by default the weights are distributed evenly. Domain experts could set the weights according to the reliability of single activities error rate.

The most plausible case is decided, based on the likelihood ratios, as described above. Figure 5 gives an overview of this window-based error detection approach. It shows that considering only single activity durations in isolation cannot distinguish between an error of the current activity caused by a local measurement error, or a previous measurement error. The figure also depicts the four cases that we try to distinguish in the pairwise duration window approach.

5   Evaluation

We implemented the anomaly detection mechanism as a plug-in to the process mining framework ProM[1]. Figure 6 shows the graphical user interface of the plug-in. The plug-in allows the user to select a *GDT_SPN* model and an event log to identify the outliers in a case by case fashion. The cases are ordered by the number of outliers per case and by their outlier scores, such that business process analysts ideally only have to scan the top of the list for outliers. In the center of the screen, the model is presented, while the analyst can select individual activities and see the corresponding duration distributions with the current duration marked as a vertical line (top right). Additionally, the log-likelihood distribution of the duration is shown to visually judge the probability that such a value—or a more extreme one—arises assuming that the distribution model in the *GDT_SPN* model is correct.

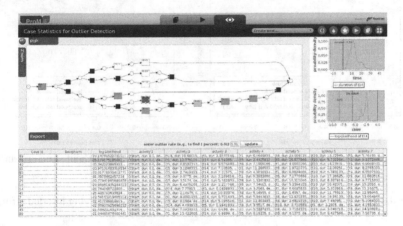

Fig. 6. User interface to the outlier detection plug-in in ProM

To also evaluate our approach with real data, we analyze the accuracy to detect measurement errors in the event log of a Dutch hospital. We depicted the surgery process model in Figure 7. The event log contains 1310 cases. Each event describes the progress of an individual patient. The timestamps are recorded for events. The log contains errors of missing events and also imprecisions in documentations (e.g., the timestamps are sometimes rounded to 5-minutes). Our assumption is that we can detect deviations from the control flow with conformance checking techniques [18,4,7], and therefore limit our evaluation to the subset of 570 structurally fitting cases. The 570 cases contain 6399 events, which are assigned a timestamp each.

---

[1] See StochasticNet package in http://www.promtools.org

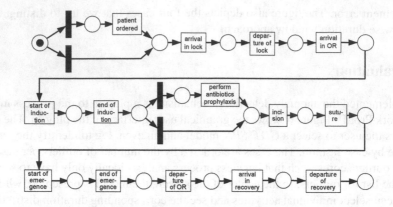

Fig. 7. Surgery model of a Dutch hospital. Most activities are in a sequential relationship.

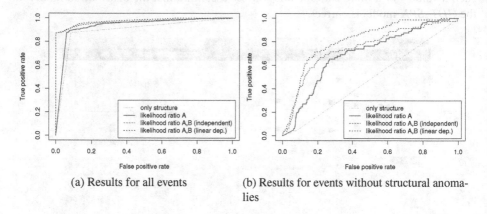

(a) Results for all events   (b) Results for events without structural anoma-
                                              lies

Fig. 8. Receiver operating characteristic (also ROC curve) for identifying inserted errors

We cannot be sure from the dataset alone, which outliers are due to measurement errors, and therefore perform a controlled experiment. We insert manual errors according
to a Gaussian normal distribution with mean=0, sd=1/3 of the average process duration. We perform a 10-fold cross validation, to make sure that the duration distributions
do not contain the original values. In the evaluation phase, we apply our approach to
identify these errors. As described in the previous section, the approach should be able
to identify errors based on the probability density of the original distribution. Furthermore, it should be able to identify many errors as obvious outliers, as a measurement
error often causes a change in the ordering of events, i.e., leading to structural errors.
Finally, some errors should not be detectable, because they may be very low or even 0.
Other errors will be detected depending on the density region that they fall into. Here,
chances are better, if their value becomes an outlier according to the error distribution.

Figure 8 shows the different receiver operating characteristic (ROC) curves for different prediction models:

- The solid line (in red) represents a model that predicts an error based on the likelihood that A is erroneous in two consecutive events A, B. This model ignores B and corresponds to a single-window approach.
- The dashed line (in blue) corresponds to model that predicts an error based on the likelihood that A is erroneous and B is erroneous, independently of each other.
- The dotted line (in green) stands for a model that predicts based on the likelihood that both A and B are erroneous, when linear dependency is assumed.
- The baseline model can predict only structural anomalies

The plot in Figure 8a, is computed from all events (with and without structural anomalies). In Figure 8b, events with structural anomalies are excluded. As it can be seen, the model that assumes a linear relationship between the errors of A and B (e.g., a positive error in one event is a negative error in the following event) performs best. This model achieves an astounding area under the curve (AUC) of 97.5%, when applied to all events (i.e., with and without structural anomalies, see plot on the left).

The next predictor with satisfactory performance is the one that assumes independence between A and B given the possibility of an error. This model corresponds to a Naive Bayes prediction model. Despite its good performance its ROC curve is consistently below the more advanced predictor that takes dependencies into account.

The single duration window model that is based on the likelihood ratio of A being erroneous is already quite good, but it cannot distinguish between the error being caused locally or by a neighbor event.

Finally, the baseline predictor recognizes that two (or more) activities have been swapped in order, but it cannot determine which one is causing the error. This highlights once again the need for more advanced methods that solve this issue by using timing information and reasonable dependency assumptions. In this sense, the suggested method is a considerable improvement over state-of-the art techniques in conformance checking.

Note that the assumption of a normally distributed error turns out to be quite reasonable, because the variance is quite high, i.e., ~ 60 minutes (which on average corre-

Table 1. Areas under the curve (AUC) for Figure 8. The AUC is a prediction quality measure that represents the ranking accuracy with respect to a specific scoring function. An ideal ranking (i.e., with AUC = 100%) would rank all positives on top of all negatives, thus enabling a clear separation between the two classes. As it can be seen, the score corresponding to the likelihood ratio of A and B, when they are assumed to be linearly dependent, yields the highest ranking accuracy. Moreover, when applied to all events (i.e., with and without structural anomalies, see plot on the left), the same method achieves an astounding AUC of 97.5%.

	All events	Without structural anomalies
only structure	0.8953294	0.4823185
likelihood ratio A	0.9337065	0.6960063
likelihood ratio A,B (independent)	0.9671142	0.7490936
likelihood ratio A,B (linear dep.)	0.9753948	0.8122718

sponds to one third of the entire process duration). Furthermore, in the boundary of an activity, if the Gaussian representing its duration is flat enough to resemble a uniform distribution from the previous event to the successor event, the reasoning remains sound from a probabilistic perspective. Therefore, we do not expect major differences when using a uniform error distribution instead of a Gaussian.

We conducted further experiments with different kinds of distributions, of which we only present condensed insights due to space restrictions. The exponential distribution has only one tail, which makes detection of measurement errors more difficult than in the normally distributed case, where it is possible to detect positive as well as negative measurement errors. The general insight is that the stronger the signal-to-noise ratio becomes, the easier it is to detect measurement errors. For example, we can detect all measurement errors > 0, if the timed model is deterministic. It is almost impossible, however, to detect measurement errors of a uniformly distributed activity. Fortunately, real processes are seldom so extreme and when manual process activities are conducted, these activities tend to be rather normally or log-normally distributed.

6 Conclusion

In this work we focused on temporal aspects of anomalies in business processes. Preliminary evaluation on synthetic and real process data shows that the suggested method reliably detects temporal anomalies. Furthermore, it is capable of identifying single measurement errors by exploiting knowledge encoded in the process model. In the experimental evaluation, a large share of inserted errors were detected, even in real process data. The application of our approach to resources should be relatively straight-forward, but standard outlier detection techniques already yield good results [11]. The method is implemented in the open source framework ProM.

We expect the experimental findings to generalize to sensor-based measurements with corresponding changes in the assumed delay distributions. For example, in the case of sensors, an exponential distribution of delays might be more meaningful. However, an exact investigation of the impact of such distributions on the reliability of the suggested method is part of our future work. Other points on our future work agenda are the comparison of the method with other machine learning techniques and its extension to detect multiple erroneous events.

References

1. Wil, M.P.: van der Aalst. Verification of Workflow Nets. In: Azéma, P., Balbo, G. (eds.) ICATPN 1997. LNCS, vol. 1248, pp. 407–426. Springer, Heidelberg (1997)
2. van der Aalst, W.M.P.: Process Mining: Discovery, Conformance and Enhancement of Business Processes. Springer (2011)
3. van der Aalst, W., et al.: Process Mining Manifesto. In: Daniel, F., Barkaoui, K., Dustdar, S. (eds.) BPM Workshops 2011, Part I. LNBIP, vol. 99, pp. 169–194. Springer, Heidelberg (2012)
4. Adriansyah, A., van Dongen, B.F., van der Aalst, W.M.P.: Conformance Checking Using Cost-Based Fitness Analysis. In: EDOC 2011, pp. 55–64. IEEE (2011)

5. Chandola, V., Banerjee, A., Kumar, V.: Anomaly Detection: A Survey. ACM Comput. Surv. 41(3), 1–58 (2009)
6. Cook, J.E., He, C., Ma, C.: Measuring Behavioral Correspondence to a Timed Concurrent Model. In: ICSM 2001, pp. 332–341. IEEE (2001)
7. de Lima Bezerra, F., Wainer, J.: Algorithms for Anomaly Detection of Traces in Logs of Process Aware Information Systems. Inf. Syst. 38(1), 33–44 (2013)
8. Governatori, G., Milosevic, Z., Sadiq, S.: Compliance Checking between Business Processes and Business Contracts. In: EDOC 2006, pp. 221–232 (2006)
9. Grubbs, F.E.: Procedures for Detecting Outlying Observations in Samples. Technometrics 11(1), 1–21 (1969)
10. Han, J., Kamber, M.: Data Mining: Concepts and Techniques, 2nd edn. Morgan Kaufmann (2006)
11. Hao, M.C., Keim, D.A., Dayal, U., Schneidewind, J.: Business Process Impact Visualization and Anomaly Detection. Information Visualization 5(1), 15–27 (2006)
12. Lohmann, N., Verbeek, E., Dijkman, R.: Petri Net Transformations for Business Processes – A Survey. In: Jensen, K., van der Aalst, W.M.P. (eds.) Transactions on Petri Nets and Other Models of Concurrency II. LNCS, vol. 5460, pp. 46–63. Springer, Heidelberg (2009)
13. Parzen, E.: On Estimation of a Probability Density Function and Mode. The Annals of Mathematical Statistics 33(3), 1065–1076 (1962)
14. Pearl, J.: Causality: Models, Reasoning, and Inference. Cambridge University Press, New York (2000)
15. Petri, C.A.: Kommunikation mit Automaten. PhD thesis, Technische Hochschule Darmstadt (1962)
16. Rogge-Solti, A., van der Aalst, W.M.P., Weske, M.: Discovering Stochastic Petri Nets with Arbitrary Delay Distributions From Event Logs. In: Lohmann, N., Song, M., Wohed, P. (eds.) BPM 2013 International Workshops. LNBIP, vol. 171, pp. 15–27. Springer, Heidelberg (2014)
17. Rogge-Solti, A., Mans, R.S., van der Aalst, W.M.P., Weske, M.: Improving Documentation by Repairing Event Logs. In: Grabis, J., Kirikova, M. (eds.) PoEM 2013. LNBIP, vol. 165, pp. 129–144. Springer, Heidelberg (2013)
18. Rozinat, A., van der Aalst, W.M.P.: Conformance Checking of Processes Based on Monitoring Real Behavior. Inf. Syst. 33(1), 64–95 (2008)
19. Silverman, B.W.: Density Estimation for Statistics and Data Analysis. Chapman and Hall, London (1996)
20. Simpson, E.H.: The Interpretation of Interaction in Contingency Tables. Journal of the Royal Statistical Society, Series B, 238–241 (1951)
21. Weske, M.: Business Process Management: Concepts, Languages, Architectures, 2nd edn. Springer (2012)
22. Wombacher, A., Iacob, M.-E.: Estimating the Processing Time of Process Instances in Semistructured Processes–A Case Study. In: 2012 IEEE Ninth International Conference on Services Computing (SCC), pp. 368–375. IEEE (2012)
23. Yeung, D.-Y., Chow, C.: Parzen-Window Network Intrusion Detectors. In: ICPR 2002, vol. 4, pp. 385–388. IEEE (2002)

A General Framework for Correlating Business Process Characteristics

Massimiliano de Leoni[1,2*], Wil M.P. van der Aalst[2], and Marcus Dees[3]

[1] University of Padua, Padua, Italy
[2] Eindhoven University of Technology, Eindhoven, The Netherlands
[3] Uitvoeringsinstituut Werknemersverzekeringen (UWV), The Netherlands
{m.d.leoni,w.m.p.v.d.aalst}@tue.nl,marcus.dees@uwv.nl

Abstract. Process discovery techniques make it possible to automatically derive process models from event data. However, often one is not only interested in discovering the control-flow but also in answering questions like "What do the cases that are late have in common?", "What characterizes the workers that skip this check activity?", and "Do people work faster if they have more work?", etc. Such questions can be answered by combining process mining with classification (e.g., decision tree analysis). Several authors have proposed ad-hoc solutions for specific questions, e.g., there is work on predicting the remaining processing time and recommending activities to minimize particular risks. However, as shown in this paper, it is possible to unify these ideas and provide a general framework for deriving and correlating process characteristics. First, we show how the desired process characteristics can be derived and linked to events. Then, we show that we can derive the selected dependent characteristic from a set of independent characteristics for a selected set of events. This can be done for any process characteristic one can think of. The approach is highly generic and implemented as plug-in for the *ProM* framework. Its applicability is demonstrated by using it to answer to a wide range of questions put forward by the UWV (the Dutch Employee Insurance Agency).

1 Introduction

The interest in process mining is fueled by the rapid growth of event data available for analysis. Moreover, there is increasing pressure to make Business Process Management (BPM) more "evidence based", i.e., process improvements and innovations are more and more driven by facts. Process mining often starts with *process discovery*, i.e., automatically learning process models based on raw event data. Once there is a process model (discovered or made by hand), the events can be replayed on the model to *check conformance* and to *uncover bottlenecks* in the process. However, such analyses are often only the starting point for providing initial insights. When discovering a bottleneck or frequent deviation, one would like to understand why it exists. This requires the correlation of different *process characteristics*. These characteristics can be based on the control-flow (e.g., the next activity going to be performed), the data-flow (e.g., the

---

* The work of Dr. de Leoni is supported by the Eurostars - Eureka project PROMPT (E!6696).

S. Sadiq, P. Soffer, and H. Völzer (Eds.): BPM 2014, LNCS 8659, pp. 250–266, 2014.

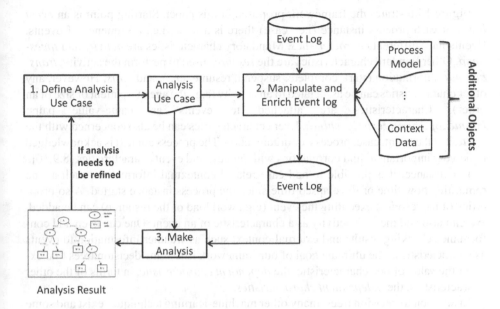

Fig. 1. The general framework proposed in this paper: based on an analysis use case the event log is preprocessed and used as input for classification. Based on the analysis result, the use case can be adapted to gather additional insights.

amount of money involved), the time perspective (e.g., the activity duration or the remaining time to the end of the process), the organization perspective (e.g., the resource going to perform a particular activity), or, in case a normative process model exists, the conformance perspective (e.g., the skipping of a mandatory activity).

The study of these characteristics and how they influence each other is of crucial importance when an organization aims to improve and redesign its own processes. Many authors have proposed techniques to relate specific characteristics in an ad-hoc manner. For example, several approaches have been proposed to predict the remaining processing time of a case depending on characteristics of the partial trace executed [1,2,3]. Other approaches are only targeted to correlating certain predefined characteristics to the process outcome [4,5,6] or the violations of business rules [7].

These problems are specific instances of a more general problem, which is concerned with *relating any process or event characteristic to other characteristics associated with single events or the entire process.* This paper proposes a framework to solve the more general correlation problem and provides a very powerful tool that unifies the ad-hoc approaches described in literature. This is achieved by providing *(1)* a broad and extendable set of characteristics related to time, routing, ordering, resource allocation, workload, and deviations, and *(2)* a generic framework where any characteristic (dependent variable) can be explained in term of correlations with any set of other characteristics (independent variables), For instance, the involvement of a particular resource or routing decision can be related to the elapsed time, but also the other way around: the elapsed time can be related to resource behavior or routing.

Figure 1 illustrates the framework proposed in this paper. Starting point is an *event log*. For each process instance (i.e., case) there is a trace, i.e., a sequence of events. Events have different *characteristics*. Mandatory characteristics are *activity* and *timestamp*. Other standard characteristics are the *resource* used to perform the activity, *transactional* information (start, complete, suspend, resume, etc.), and *costs*. However, any other characteristics can be associated to an activity (e.g., the age of a patient or size of an order). Characteristics are attached to events as name-value pairs: (*name_of_characteristic*, *value*). Event characteristics can be also concerned with the *context* of the event, case, process, or organization. The process context is acknowledged to be very important to find correlations with process and event characteristics [8,9,10].

For instance, it is possible to add case-related contextual information, such as the remaining flow time or the elapsed time since the process instance started. Also properties of the resource executing the event (e.g., workload of the resource) can be added. We can also add the next activity as a characteristic of an event. One can even add conformance checking results and external context such as weather information to events as characteristics. The ultimate goal of our framework is to mine decision trees that explain the value of one characteristic, the *dependent characteristic*, in terms of the other characteristics, the *independent characteristics*.

In addition to decision trees, many other machine-learning techniques exist and some have already been applied in BPM, such as Bayesian Networks [11], Case-Based Reasoning [12] and Markov Models [3]. These are certainly valuable but they are only able to make correlations for single instances of interest or to return significant examples of relevant instances. Conversely, we aim to aggregate knowledge extracted from the event logs and return it as decision rules. Association rules [8] could have been an alternative, but decision trees have the advantage of clearly highlighting the characteristics that are most discriminating. Regression analysis [13] would be only applicable to find numerical correlations and, hence, it could not be employed if the dependent characteristic is nominal or boolean.

The approach is fully supported by a new package that has been added to the open-source process mining framework *ProM*.[4] The evaluation of our approach is based on a case study involving UWV, a Dutch governmental institute in charge of supplying benefits. In particular, we have employed the approach to answer process-related questions that were relevant for the institution. The results were extremely positive: we could answer the UWV's questions regarding the causes of observed problems (e.g., reclamations of customers). For some problems, we could show surprising root causes. For other problems, we could only show that some suspected correlations were not present.

Section 2 presents the framework and highlights that several well-studied problems are specific instances of the more general problem considered in this paper. Section 3 shows the application of our framework and implementation in the context of UWV. Finally, Section 4 concludes the paper.

2   The Framework

The main input of our framework is an event log.

---

[4] The *FeaturePrediction* package, see http://www.promtools.org.

Definition 1 (Events, Traces and Log). *Let C and U be the universe of characteristics and the universe of possible values respectively. An* event e *is an assignment of values to characteristics, i.e. $e \in C \to U$. In the remainder $\mathcal{E} = C \to U$ is the universe of* events. *A* trace $T \in \mathcal{E}^*$ *is a sequence of events. Let $\mathcal{T} = \mathcal{E}^*$ be the universe of traces. An* event log L *is a multi-set of traces, i.e. $L \in \mathbb{B}(\mathcal{T})$*

For each characteristic $c \in C$, $type(c) \subseteq U$ denotes the set of possible values. We use a special value $\perp$ for any characteristic c which an event e is not assigning a value to, i.e. $e(c) = \perp$ if $c \notin dom(e)$. Typically, an event refers to an activity that is performed within a certain case by a resource at a given timestamp. In our framework, these are merely treated as any event characteristics: *Activity*, *Case*, *Resource*, *Timestamp*, respectively. The occurrence of an event, i.e. the execution of an activity, can assign new values to any subset of characteristics.

Our framework aims to support so-called *analysis use cases*.

Definition 2 (Analysis Use Case). *An* analysis use case *is a triple (C_d, c_r, F) consisting of*

- *a dependent characteristic $c_r \in C \setminus C_d$,*
- *a set $C_d \subset C$ of independent characteristics,*
- *an event-selection filter $F \subseteq \mathcal{E}$, which characterizes the events that are retained for the analysis.*

The output of an analysis use case is a decision tree. Decision trees classify instances (in our case events) by sorting them down in a tree from the root to some leaf node. Each non-leaf node specifies a test of some attribute (in our case, an independent characteristic) and each branch descending from that node corresponds to a range of possible values for this attribute. Each leaf node is associated to a value of a class attribute (in our case, the dependent characteristic). A path from root to a leaf represents a classification rule. There exist many algorithms to build a decision tree starting from a training set [13]. Our framework is agnostic with respect to specific algorithms used for decision-tree learning. In our implementation we rely on the C4.5 algorithm, which can handle continuous attributes efficiently and is good at pruning the final decision tree [13]. However, any other classification algorithm could have been used. In the remainder, given a set of instances (i.e. events) $\mathcal{I} \in 2^{(C \to U)}$, a set $C_d \subset C$ of independent variables (i.e., the independent characteristics) and a dependent variable $c_r \in C \setminus C_d$, the procedure to train a decision tree is denoted as *generateTree*$(\mathcal{I}, C_d, c_r)$.

Algorithm 1 describes our approach to build a decision tree based on an event log and an analysis use case. The input consists of an event log and an analysis use case. At the end, set $\mathcal{I}$ contains all instances that are used to train the decision tree. This set is populated with every event e of the log that is not filtered out by the event-selection filter F.

If the dependent characteristic c_r is defined over a continuous domain, value $e(c_r)$ is discretized before event e is added to the instance set $\mathcal{I}$. Decision trees do not support continuous class variables. Therefore, continuous characteristics need to be discretized to be used as dependent. In the algorithm, the procedure of discretization is abstracted as a function *discretize*(val, c, L, n) that, given a characteristic c, a value $val \in type(c)$, the set of values observed in an event log L, and a number n of discretization intervals,

---

Algorithm 1: Generate Decision Tree

Input: Event Log $L \in \mathbb{B}(\mathcal{T})$, An analysis use case $(\mathcal{C}_d, c_r, F)$, the number n of discretization intervals.
Result: Decision Tree

$\mathcal{I} \leftarrow \varnothing$
foreach $T \in L$ **do**
    foreach $e \in L$ **do**
        if $e \in F$ **then**
            if $type(c_r)$ *is continuous* **then**
                | $e(c_r) \leftarrow discretize(e(c_r), c_r, L, n)$
            end
            $\mathcal{I} \leftarrow \mathcal{I} \cup \{e\}$
        end
    end
end
$generateTree(\mathcal{I}, \mathcal{C}_d, c_r)$

---

returns a value over a discrete domain. Literature provides several ways to discretize dependent variables. While our approach can use any discretization technique, our implementation provides two specific ones: *equal-width binning* and *equal-frequency binning* [14]. Given a number n of intervals, the former divides the set of possible values $type(c)$ into n equal-width intervals, assigning a discrete value to each of them. Continuous values are transformed into discrete values according to the intervals they fall into. The *equal-frequency binning* approach tries to transform values more evenly: intervals are of different sizes, choosing them such that (roughly) the same number of observed values falls into each one.

As mentioned before, for many analysis use cases we need dependent or independent characteristics that are not readily available in the event log. Similarly, using business domain knowledge, an analyst may want to verify a reasonable hypothesis of the existence of a correlation to a given set of independent characteristics, which may not be explicitly available in the event log. However, values for many interesting characteristics can easily be derived from the event data in the event log. In some cases we will even derive characteristics from information sources outside the event log (weather information, stock index, etc.).

We provide a powerful framework to manipulate event logs and obtain a new event log that suits the specific analysis use case, e.g. events are enriched with additional characteristics.

Definition 3 (Trace and Log Manipulation). *Let $\mathcal{T}$ be the universe of traces and event logs and let $L \in \mathbb{B}(\mathcal{T})$ be an event log. A* trace manipulation *is a function $\delta_L \in \mathcal{T} \to \mathcal{T}$.*

In the remainder, given a trace-manipulation function δ_L, we also allow δ_L to be applied to an entire log L, thus returning a new log obtained by applying the trace-manipulation function to all traces in L.

Table 1 shows a taxonomy of trace manipulations, grouping them by the process perspective that they take into account. All manipulations shown have been implemented

Table 1. A Taxonomy of Trace Manipulations currently available in the operationalization

Perspective	Trace Manipulations
Control-flow	Number of Executions of Activity a, Next Activity in the Trace, Previous Activity in Trace.
Resource	Workload per Resource, Total Workload.
Time	Time Elapsed since the Start of the Case, Remaining Time Until the End of Case, Activity Duration.
Data-flow	Latest Recorded Value of Characteristic c Before Current Event e, Latest Recorded Value of Characteristic c After Event e, Case-Level Abstraction.
Conformance	Trace Fitness, Number of Not Allowed Executions of Activity a Thus Far (moves on log in alignment), Number of Missing Executions of Activity a Thus Far (moves on model in alignment), Number of Correct Executions of Activity a Thus Far (synchronous moves), Satisfaction of Formula F Considering the Prefix Trace Until Current Event e.

in ProM; the generality of the framework also makes it easy to add new manipulations. Due to space limitations, we can only discuss some of them:

- **Next Activity in the Trace.** It augments each event with an extra attribute that contains the name of the next activity in the trace (or $\perp$ for the last event)
- **Latest Recorded Value of Characteristic c Before Current Event e.** It enriches each event e with the latest value assigned to characteristic c before e in the trace.
- **Latest Recorded Value of Characteristic c After Current Event e.** It enriches each event e with the latest value assigned to characteristic c after e in the trace. It differs from the manipulation *Latest Recorded Value of Characteristic c Before Current Event e* in that the value is taken after the execution of e. If e does not write a value for c, the value before and after e coincides.
- **Case-Level Abstraction.** This replaces all the events the trace with two events, the *case-start* and *case-complete* event. The case-start event is associated with the same values of the characteristics as the first event of the trace. The case-end event is associated with the last recorded values for all characteristics. For both events, the value of the *Activity* characteristic is overwritten with value "Case".
- **Workload per Resource.** It associates each event e with the work-load for the resource that has triggered the event, i.e. the number of activities under execution by $e(Resource)$, at the time the event occurred.
- **Total Workload.** It associates events with the number of activities being executed at the time the event occurred.
- **Activity Duration.** Each (complete) event is associated with a (integer-typed) characteristic that indicates the duration of completing the activity associated with the event.

The last three characteristics in the list require an analysis of the entire log, i.e., the scope is not limited to a single trace. This is the reason why trace-manipulation function $\delta_L(T)$ depends not just on trace T but also L.

Indeed, the values to associate with each event can be derived by replaying the event log and counting the number of activities being executed in each moment in time. It is

Table 2. Fragment of a hospital's event log with four traces. The gray columns have been added after applying two of the trace manipulations in Table 1: Next Activity in the Trace and Time Elapsed since the Start of the Case. NextActivityInTrace and ElapsedTime are the names of the characteristics that are added as result of these manipulations.

Case	Timestamp	Activity	Resource	Cost	NextActivityInTrace	ElapsedTime
1	1-12-2011:11.00	Preoperative Screening	Giuseppe	350	Laparoscopic Gastrectomy	0 days
1	2-12-2011:15.00	Laparoscopic Gastrectomy	Simon	500	Nursing	1.16 days
1	2-12-2011:16.00	Nursing	Clare	250	Laparoscopic Gastrectomy	1.20 days
1	3-12-2011:13.00	Laparoscopic Gastrectomy	Paul	500	Nursing	2.08 days
1	3-12-2011:15.00	Nursing	Andrew	250	First Hospital Admission	2.16 days
1	4-12-2011:9.00	First Hospital Admission	Victor	90	⊥	3.92 days
2	7-12-2011:10.00	First Hospital Admission	Jane	90	Laparoscopic Gastrectomy	0 days
2	8-12-2011:13.00	Laparoscopic Gastrectomy	Giulia	500	Nursing	1.08 days
2	9-12-2011:16.00	Nursing	Paul	250	⊥	2.16
3	6-12-2011:14.00	First Hospital Admission	Gianluca	90	Preoperative Screening	0 days
3	8-12-2011:13.00	Preoperative Screening	Robert	350	Preoperative Screening	1.96 days
3	10-12-2011:16.00	Preoperative Screening	Giuseppe	350	Laparoscopic Gastrectomy	4.08 days
3	13-12-2011:11.00	Laparoscopic Gastrectomy	Simon	500	First Hospital Admission	6.88 days
3	13-12-2011:16.00	First Hospital Admission	Jane	90	⊥	7.02 days
4	7-12-2011:15.00	First Hospital Admission	Carol	90	Preoperative Screening	0 days
4	9-12-2011:7.00	Preoperative Screening	Susanne	350	Laparoscopic Gastrectomy	0.66 days
4	13-12-2011:11.00	Laparoscopic Gastrectomy	Simon	500	Nursing	5.84 days
4	13-12-2011:13.00	Nursing	Clare	250	Nursing	5.92 days
4	13-12-2011:19.00	Nursing	Vivianne	250	⊥	6.16 days

Table 3. The results after applying the Case-Level Manipulation to the event log shown in Table 2

Case	Timestamp	Activity	Resource	Cost	NextActivityInTrace	ElapsedTime
1	1-12-2011:11.00	Case	Giuseppe	350	Laparoscopic Gastrectomy	0 days
1	4-12-2011:9.00	Case	Victor	90	⊥	3.92 days
2	7-12-2011:10.00	Case	Jane	90	Laparoscopic Gastrectomy	0 days
2	9-12-2011:16.00	Case	Paul	250	⊥	2.16 days
3	6-12-2011:14.00	Case	Gianluca	90	Preoperative Screening	0 days
3	13-12-2011:16.00	Case	Jane	90	⊥	7.02 days
4	7-12-2011:15.00	Case	Carol	90	Preoperative Screening	0 days
4	13-12-2011:19.00	Case	Vivianne	250	⊥	6.16 days

not necessary that the event log records the starting and completion of each activity. Although that would be preferred as the workload would be calculated exactly, we have implemented algorithms that can estimate the workload by only using the activity completion events. In our implementation, we estimate the start time of activities as proposed in [15]: assuming no waiting time, the start time of an activity is the latest between the time of completion of the previous activity within the same process instance and the time of completion of the previous activity by the same resource (possibly in a different process instance).

Tables 2 and 3 illustrate the application of some of the manipulation functions of Table 1 to a fragment of an event log. In general, when multiple trace-manipulation functions are applied, the order of application may be important. Table 3 shows the result of the application of the case-level abstraction manipulation after applying *Next Activity in the Trace* and *Time Elapsed since the Start of the Case*. If case-level abstraction was applied before the other two, the final result would be different: characteristic *Next Activity in the Trace* would be given either value "Case" or ⊥.

Table 1 also illustrates a number of trace manipulations that require additional sources/inputs, such as a process model, declarative or procedural, or a (temporal) logical formula F:

- **Trace Fitness.** Given a process model, it augments each event with a continuous value between 0 and 1, denoting the level of the fitness of the model and the trace to which the event belongs. Values 1 and 0 denote perfect and extremely poor fitness, respectively.
- **Number of Not Allowed Executions of Activity a Thus Far, Number of Missing Executions of Activity a Thus Far, and Number of Correct Executions of Activity a Thus Far.** These manipulations augment each event with an integer characteristic that denotes the number of "moves on logs" (occurs in reality but disallowed according to the model), "moves on model" (should have occurred according to the model but did not), and "synchronous moves" (model and reality agree) respectively in the prefix until the current event.
- **Satisfaction of Formula F Considering the Prefix Trace Until Current Event e.** It augments each event with a boolean value that states whether a given formula F was satisfied after the event occurred.

The third manipulation in the above list builds on the ProM operationalization of the technique described in [16]. Here Linear Temporal Logic (LTL) is used to specify F. The others rely on the ProM implementation of the techniques discussed in [17,18], which are concerned with finding an alignment of traces in the log with, respectively, procedural and declarative process models.

Tables 4 and 5 show how six examples of correlation problems can be formulated as analysis use cases. In the tables, the original log denotes the log before any trace manipulation. Trace manipulations are applied in the exact order as they are enumerated in the list. As the examples show, prediction problems are, in fact, correlation problems. When a correlation is observed in the past, one can predict that the same correlation is going to be observed for future process instances, as well.

For most of the problems shown in Tables 4 and 5, research work has already been conducted, yielding ad-hoc solutions. Our framework attempts to solve the more general problem, i.e., finding any type of correlation among arbitrary process characteristics at any level (event, case, process, resource, etc.). By solving the more general problems, we can support existing analyses but also many more.

Some of the analysis use cases in Tables 4 and 5 have been used as intermediate results to solve other problems. For instance, Ghattas et al. [4] uses the answer to Problem #2 as information to drive how to redesign the process to improve the process' outcomes. Similarly, the solutions of Problems #1 and #4 are used in [7] and [6], respectively, as input to provide a run-time support to suggest the next activities to work on.

3 Evaluation with a Real-Life Case Study

This section illustrates how our framework can be used to help UWV. UWV (Employee Insurance Agency) is an autonomous administrative authority to implement employee

Table 4. Five example analysis use cases illustrating the generic nature of the framework presented.

Problem #1: Run-time predictions of violations of formula *F*.
Description: The aim is to predict, given the current status of the process instances, the next activities to work on to maximize the chances of achieving certain business goals expressed as formula F. In [7], an ad-hoc solution is proposed for this problem where formulas are expressed in LTL.
Dependent Characteristic: Satisfaction of Formula F Considering the Prefix Trace Until Current Event.
Independent Characteristics: For each characteristic c of the original event log, the Latest Recorded Value of c Before the Current Event; Activity Name; the resource name.
Event Filter: Every event is retained.
Trace Manipulation: Satisfaction of Formula F Considering the Prefix Trace Until Current Event; for each characteristic c of the original event log, the Latest Recorded Value of c Before the Current Event.

Problem #2: Prediction of the outcomes of the executions of process instances.
Description: The aim is to predict the outcome of a case. Predictions are computed using a set of complete process instances that are recorded in the event log. The last event of each trace is associated with a characteristic *Outcome* to which it is assigned a numeric value that indicates the quality of the outcome. The prediction is done at case level: one instance for learning is created for each trace in the event log. The outcome of the entire trace is predicted rather than of single activities. In [4], an ad-hoc solution is proposed for this problem.
Dependent Characteristic: *Outcome*
Independent Characteristics: Each characteristic c of the original event log, except *Outcome*.
Event Filter: Every case-complete event is retained.
Trace Manipulation: Case-level Abstraction.

Problem #3: Mining of decisions that determine the activity to execute after the execution of an activity a.
Description: The purpose is to predict the conditions that discriminate which activity is executed after a given activity a. Predictions are computed using a set of complete process instances that are recorded in the event log. In particular, only the events referring to activity a are used. In [19], an ad-hoc solution is proposed for this problem.
Dependent Characteristic: Next Activity In the Trace.
Independent Characteristics: For each characteristic c of the original event log, the Latest Recorded Value of c After the Current Event.
Event Filter: Every event e for activity a is retained, i.e. every event e such that $e(Activity) = a$.
Trace Manipulation: For each characteristic c of the original event log, the Latest Recorded Value of c After the Current Event; Next Activity In the Trace.

Problem #4: Prediction of faults during business process executions.
Description: The purpose is to predict whether or not a running instance is going to complete with a fault. If completed with a fault, its magnitude is also predicted. Predictions are computed using a set of complete process instances that are recorded in the event log. If a fault has occurred for a given completed instance, the first event of the corresponding trace is associated with a characteristic *Fault* to which a value is assigned that indicates the magnitude. If no fault is occurred, the first event is associated with a characteristic *Fault* to which a value 0 is assigned. In [6], an ad-hoc solution is proposed for this problem.
Dependent Characteristic: The value of *Fault* after the Current Event.
Independent Characteristics: For each characteristic c of the original event log besides *Fault*, the Latest Recorded Value of c After the Current Event; for each activity a, the Number of Executions of a; Elapsed Time Since the Start of the Case; Activity Name; Resource Name.
Event Filter: Every event is retained.
Trace Manipulation: For each characteristic c of the original event log, the Latest Recorded Value of c After the Current Event; for each activity a, the Number of Executions of Activity a; the Elapsed Time since the Start of the Case.

Problem #5: Prediction of the executor of a certain activity a.
Description: The purpose is to mine the conditions that determine which resource is going to work on a given activity a at a certain moment during the process execution.
Dependent Characteristic: *Resource Name*
Independent Characteristics: Potentially, any characteristic of the original event log as well as any characteristic with which events can be augmented. Every characteristic can be relevant for this prediction.
Event Filter: Every event for activity a is retained, i.e. every event e such that $e(Activity) = a$.
Trace Manipulation: Depending on the scenario, any manipulation but Case-Level abstraction can be relevant.

Table 5. An additional analysis use case illustrating the generic nature of the framework presented

---

Problem #6: Prediction of the Remaining Time to the end of process instances.
Description: The purpose is to predict the remaining time until the end of process instances on the basis of the current state, which consists of the number of executions of each process activity and the current values of process variables. It is similar to [2] when a multi-set abstraction is used, with, additionally, the current values of process variables are also taken into account.
Dependent Characteristic: Remaining Time Until The End of the Case.
Independent Characteristics: For each process activity a, the number of executions of activity a; for each characteristic c of the original event log, the Latest Recorded Value of c After the Current Event.
Event Filter: Every event is retained.
Trace Manipulation: For each characteristic c of the original event log, the Latest Recorded Value of c After the Current Event; for each process activity a, the Number of Executions of Activity a; the Remaining Time Until The End of the Case.

---

insurances and provide labor market and data services. One of the core tasks of UWV is ensuring that benefits are provided quickly and correctly when a Dutch resident, hereafter customer, cannot immediately find a new job after ceasing the previous. UWV is facing various undesired process executions and is interested in discovering the root-causes of a variety of problems identified by UWV's management. In these analysis use cases, we are looking at the process to deal with requests of unemployment benefits. An instance of this process starts when a customer applies. Subsequently, checks are performed to verify the entitlement conditions. If the checks are positive, the instance is being executed for the entire period in which the customer receives the monetary benefits, which are paid in monthly installments. Entitled customers receive as many monthly installments as the number of years for which they were working. Therefore, an instance can potentially be executed for more than one year. During the entire period, customers must comply with certain duties, otherwise a customer is sanctioned and a reclamation is opened. When a reclamation occurs, this directly impacts the customer, who will receive lower benefits than expected or has to return part of the benefits. It also has negative impact from UWV's viewpoint, as this tends to consume lots of resources and time. Therefore, UWV is interested to know the root causes of opening reclamations to reduce their number. If the root causes are known, UWV can predict when a reclamation is likely going to be opened and, hence, it can enact appropriate actions to prevent it beforehand. In order to discover the root causes, UWV formulated four questions:

Q1 Are customer characteristics linked to the occurrence of reclamations? And if so, which characteristics are most prominent?
Q2 Are characteristics concerned with how process instances are executed linked to the occurrence of reclamations? And if any, which characteristics matter most?
Q3 If the prescribed process flow is not followed, will this influence whether or not a reclamation occurs?
Q4 When an instance of the unemployment-benefit payment process is being handled, is there any characteristic that may trigger whether a reclamation is going to occur?

Table 6 enumerates some of the analysis use cases that have been performed to answer the questions above. The analyses have been performed using a UWV's event log containing 2232 process instances and 77551 events. Since the original event log contains

Table 6. Some of the analysis use cases analyzed to provide an answer to the correlation problems raised by UWV

U1. Are customer characteristics linked to the occurrence of reclamations?
Description: We aim to correlate the number of executions of activity *Reclamation* to the customer characteristics. We are interested in all decision-tree paths that lead to a number of executions of activity Reclamation greater than 0.
Dependent Characteristic: Number of Executions of Activity *Reclamation*.
Independent Characteristics: All characteristics of the events in the original log that refer to customers properties.
Event Filter: Every case-complete event is retained.
Trace Manipulation: Number of executions of Activity *Reclamation*; Case-Level Abstraction

U2. Are characteristics concerned with how process instances are executed linked to the occurrence of reclamations?
– Iteration 1
Description: We aim to correlate the number of execution of activity *Reclamation* to process characteristics, the number of executions of all activities and the elapsed time, i.e., the time to complete a process instance. We are interested in all decision-tree paths that lead to a number of executions of activity Reclamation greater than 0.
Dependent Characteristic: Number of Executions of Activity *Reclamation*.
Independent Characteristics: For each process activity a besides *Reclamation*, Number of Executions of a; Time Elapsed Since the Start of the Case; all characteristics of the events of the original log that refer to the outcomes of process instances; Timestamp.
Event Filter: Every case-complete event is retained.
Trace Manipulation: For each process activity a, Number of Executions of a; Time Elapsed Since the Start of the Case; Case-Level Abstraction.

U3. Are characteristics concerned with how process instances are executed linked to the occurrence of reclamations?
– Iteration 9
Description: We aim to correlate the number of execution of activity *Reclamation* to process characteristics and the number of executions of most of activities. We are interested in all decision-tree paths that lead to a number of executions of activity Reclamation greater than 0.
Dependent Characteristic: Number of executions of activity *Reclamation*.
Independent Characteristics: For each process activity a besides *Reclamation* and *Call Contact door HH deskundige*, Number of Executions of a; All characteristics of the events in the original log that refer to the outcomes of process instances, besides *Soort Vaststelling* and 49 more.
Event Filter: Every case-complete event is retained.
Trace Manipulation: For each process activity a, Number of Executions of a; Case-Level Abstraction.

U4. If the prescribed process flow is not followed, will this influence whether or not a reclamation occurs?
Description: We aim to correlate the number of execution of activity *Reclamation* to process characteristics, the number of executions of most of activities as well as to the deviations wrt. the prescribed process model. We are interested in all decision-tree paths that lead to a number of executions of activity Reclamation greater than 0.
Dependent Characteristic: Number of executions of activity *Reclamation*.
Independent Characteristics: Trace Fitness; for each process activity a besides *Reclamation*, the Number of Not-Allowed Executions of a, the Number of Missing Executions of a and the Number of Correct Executions of a; Number of Executions of Activity *Reclamation*.
Event Filter: Every event is retained.
Trace Manipulation: Trace Fitness; for each process activity a, the Number of Not-Allowed Executions of a Thus Far, the Number of Missing Executions of a Thus Far and the Number of Correct Executions of a Thus Far; Number of Executions of Activity *Reclamation*.

U5. When an instance of the unemployment-benefit payment process is handled, is there any characteristic that may trigger whether a reclamation is going to occur?
Description: We aim to predict when a reclamation is going to follow any process activity. For this purpose, we predict which activity is going to follow any process activity and, then, we focus on those paths leading to predicting reclamation as next activity in trace.
Dependent Characteristic: Next Activity in Trace.
Independent Characteristics: For each process activity a besides *Call Contact door HH deskundige*, the Number of Executions of a; All characteristics of the events in the original log that refer to the outcomes of process instances
Event Filter: Every event is retained.
Trace Manipulation: For each process activity a, Number of Executions of a; Next Activity in the Trace.

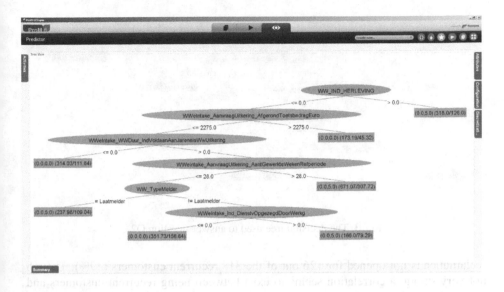

Fig. 2. A screenshot of the framework's implementation in ProM that shows the decision tree used to answer question Q1

more than 100 characteristics, it is not possible to punctually detail single characteristics that have been included or excluded from the analyses. The remainder of this section details how the analysis use cases have been used to answer the four questions above.

Question Q1. To answer this question, we performed the use case **U1** in Table 6. The results of performing this analysis are represented through the decision tree in Figure 2. In particular, the screenshot refers to our implementation in ProM. The implementation allows the end user to configure a number of parameters, such as the level of decision-tree pruning, the minimum number of instances per leaf or the discretization method. In this way, the user can try several configurations, thus, e.g., balancing between over- and under-fitting. In particular, the screenshot refers to the configuration in which the minimum number of instances per leaf is set to 100 and the number of executions of *Reclamation* is discretized as two values: (0.0,0.0) and (0.0,5.0). When the number of executions of *Reclamation* is 0, this is shown as (0.0,0.0); conversely, any value greater than 0 for the number of executions is discretized as (0.0,5.0). The use cases *U2, U3, U4* also use the number of executions of *Reclamation* as dependent characteristic. We used the same discretization for those use cases, as well.

Looking at the tree in Figure 2, some business rules seem to be derived. For instance, if the customer is a recurrent customer ($WW\_IND\_HERLEVING > 0$), a reclamation occurs, i.e. the leaf is labelled as (0.0,5.0).[5] If this correlation really held, it would quite unexpected: recurrent customers tend to disregard their duties. Nonetheless, the label is also annotated with 318.0/126.0, which indicates that a

---

[5] Customers are recurrent if they apply for monetary benefits multiple times because they find multiple temporary jobs and, hence, they become unemployed multiple times.

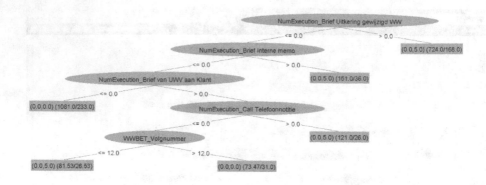

Fig. 3. The decision tree used to answer question Q2

reclamation is not opened for 126 out of the 318 recurrent customers (39%). Though not very strong, a correlation seems to exist between being recurrent customers and incurring in reclamations. Further investigation is certainly needed; perhaps, additional customer's characteristics might be needed to better discriminate but they are currently not present in the event log used for analysis.

Question Q2. Firstly, we performed the analysis use case **U2**. We obtained a decision tree that showed correlations between the number of reclamations and certain characteristics that are judged as trivial by UWV. For instance, there was a correlation of the number of reclamations with *(1.)* the method of payment of the benefit installments to customers and *(2.)* the number of executions of activity *Call Contact door HH deskundige*, which is executed to push customers to perform their duties. Being these correlations considered trivial by UWV, the respective characteristics should be left out of the analysis. So, we excluded these characteristics from the set of independent characteristics and repeated the analysis. We refined the use case analysis multiple times by removing more and more independent characteristics. After 9 iterations, we performed an analysis use case that led to satisfactory results. This use case is denoted as **U3** in Table 6. The results of performing this analysis are represented through the decision tree in Figure 3, which classifies 77% of the instances correctly.

This tree illustrates interesting correlation rules. Reclamations are usually not opened in those process instances in which *(1.)* UWV never informs (or has to inform) a customer about changes in his/her benefits (the number of executions of *Brief Uitkering gewijzigd WW* is 0), *(2.)* UWV's employees do not hand over work to each other (the number of executions of *Brief Interne Memo* is 0) and *(3.)* either of the following conditions holds:

- No letter is sent to the customers (the number of executions of *Brief van UWV aan Klant* is 0);
- At least one letter is sent but UWV never calls the customer (the number of executions of *Call Telefoonnotitie* is equal to 0) and, also, the number of months for which the customer is entitled to receive a benefit is more than 12.

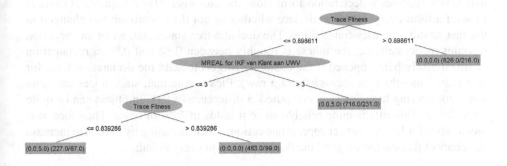

Fig. 4. The decision tree used to answer question Q3

From this analysis, we can conclude that UWV should reduce the hand-over of work. Moreover, it should pay more attention to customers when their situation changes, e.g. they find a new job. When customers find a job, they start having a monetary income, again. The problem seems to be related to the customers who often do not provide information about the new job on time. In these cases, their benefits are not stopped or reduced when they should. Consequently, a reclamation needs to be opened because these customers need to return the amount that was overpaid to them. Conversely, if a customer has already received benefits for 12 months, it is unlikely that a reclamation is going to occur. This can be motivated quite clearly and it is again related to the presence of changes of the customer's job situation. If benefits are received for more than 12 months, the customer has not found a job in latest 12 months and, thus, it is probably going to be hard for him to find one. So, UWV does not have to pay much attention to customers entitled to long benefits when they aim to limit the number of reclamations.

Question Q3. The answer to this question is given by performing the analysis use case **U4**. This use case relies on a process model that describes the normal execution flow. This model was designed by hand, using knowledge of the UWV domain. The results of performing **U4** is represented by the decision tree in Figure 4. Trace Fitness is measured as a value between 0 and 1 (see [17]). Values 1 and 0, respectively, denote perfect and poor fitness between the expected behaviour, represented by the process model, and the actual behaviour, which is recorded in the event log. Analyzing the decision tree, a correlation is clear between trace fitness and the number of reclamations. 610 out of the 826 process executions (nearly 70%) with fitness higher than 0.89 do not comprise any reclamation. Therefore, it seems crucial for UWV to make the best to follow the normal flow, although this is often made difficult by a hasty behavior of customers. This rule seems quite reliable and is also confirmed by the fact that 70% of the executions with fitness lower than 0.83 incur in reclamations.

The decision tree contains an intermediate node labelled *MREAL for IKF van Klant aan UWV*. This characteristic refers to the number of missing executions of activity *IKF van Klant aan UWV*. This activity is executed in a process instance every time that UWV receives a declaration form from the customer. UWV requests customers to send a form every month to declare whether or not their condition has changed in the last month, e.g. they found a job. The decision tree states that, when an execution deviates moderately, i.e. the fitness is roughly between 0.83 and 0.89, a reclamation is still unlikely being opened if the customer forgets to send the declaration form for less than 3 months (not necessarily in a row). Please note that, since traces are quite long, considering how fitness is computed, a difference of 0.06 in fitness can be quite remarkable. This rule is quite reliable since it holds in 79% of cases. Therefore, it is worthwhile for UWV to enact appropriate actions (such as calling by phone) to increase the chances that customers send the declaration form every month.

Question Q4. The answer to this question is given by performing the analysis use case **U5**. We built a decision tree for this use case by limiting the minimal number of instances per leaf to 50. We are interested in tree paths that lead to *Reclamation* as next activity in the trace. Unfortunately, the F-measure for *Reclamation* was very low (0.349), which indicates that *it is not possible to reliably estimate if a reclamation is going to occur at a certain moment of the execution of a process instance*. We also tried to reduce the limit of the minimum number of instances per leaf. Unfortunately, the resulting decision tree was not valuable since it overfitted the instance sets: the majority of the leaves were associated to less than 1% of the total number of instances. Conversely, the decision tree with 50 as minimum number of instance per leaf could be useful to predict when a payment is sent out to a customer: the F score for the payment activity is nearly 0.735. Unfortunately, finding this correlation does not answer question Q4.

4   Conclusion

Process mining is not just about discovering the control-flow or diagnosing deviations. It is crucial that certain phenomena can be explained, e.g., "Why are these cases delayed at this point?", "Why do these deviations take place?", "What kind of cases are more costly due to following this undesirable route?", and "Why is the distribution of work so unbalanced". Although numerous analysis approaches have been proposed for specific questions, a generic framework for correlating business process characteristics was missing. In this paper, we presented such a framework and its implementation in ProM. By defining an analysis use case composed of three elements (one dependent characteristic, multiple independent characteristics and a filter), we can create a classification problem. The resulting decision tree aims to describe the dependent characteristic in terms of the independent characteristics. The approach has been evaluated using a case study within the UWV.

Future work aims at making a more extensive taxonomy of analysis use cases. In this paper only a few examples were mentioned. Moreover, we would like to support the user in selecting the right use case using a questionnaire-based approach. This can be done by building on the current framework and implementation. Regarding improving the correlation accuracy, we also plan to investigate random decision forests, where several decision trees are built in multiple steps. We also acknowledge the limitations of our framework when the dependent characteristic is numerical. The results are not very "stable": a small change in how the characteristic is discretized may have large repercussions on the resulting decision tree. We also plan to investigate solutions to overcome this problem.

References

1. Folino, F., Guarascio, M., Pontieri, L.: Discovering context-aware models for predicting business process performances. In: Meersman, R., Panetto, H., Dillon, T., Rinderle-Ma, S., Dadam, P., Zhou, X., Pearson, S., Ferscha, A., Bergamaschi, S., Cruz, I.F. (eds.) OTM 2012, Part I. LNCS, vol. 7565, pp. 287–304. Springer, Heidelberg (2012)
2. van der Aalst, W.M.P., Schonenberg, M.H., Song, M.: Time prediction based on process mining. Information Systems 36(2), 450–475 (2011)
3. Lakshmanan, G., Shamsi, D., Doganata, Y., Unuvar, M., Khalaf, R.: A markov prediction model for data-driven semi-structured business processes. Knowledge and Information Systems, 1–30 (2013)
4. Ghattas, J., Soffer, P., Peleg, M.: Improving business process decision making based on past experience. Decision Support Systems 59, 93–107 (2014)
5. Kim, A., Obregon, J., Jung, J.Y.: Constructing decision trees from process logs for performer recommendation. In: van der Aalst, W. (ed.) BPM 2013 International Workshops. LNCS, vol. 171, pp. 224–236. Springer, Heidelberg (2014)
6. Conforti, R., de Leoni, M., La Rosa, M., van der Aalst, W.M.P.: Supporting risk-informed decisions during business process execution. In: Salinesi, C., Norrie, M.C., Pastor, Ó. (eds.) CAiSE 2013. LNCS, vol. 7908, pp. 116–132. Springer, Heidelberg (2013)
7. Maggi, F.M., Di Francescomarino, C., Dumas, M., Ghidini, C.: Predictive monitoring of business processes. In: Jarke, M., Mylopoulos, J., Quix, C., Rolland, C., Manolopoulos, Y., Mouratidis, H., Horkoff, J. (eds.) CAiSE 2014. LNCS, vol. 8484, pp. 457–472. Springer, Heidelberg (2014)
8. Dohmen, A., Moormann, J.: Identifying Drivers of Inefficiency in Business Processes: A DEA and Data Mining Perspective. In: Bider, I., Halpin, T., Krogstie, J., Nurcan, S., Proper, E., Schmidt, R., Ukor, R. (eds.) BPMDS 2010 and EMMSAD 2010. LNBIP, vol. 50, pp. 120–132. Springer, Heidelberg (2010)
9. Zeng, L., Lingenfelder, C., Lei, H., Chang, H.: Event-driven quality of service prediction. In: Bouguettaya, A., Krueger, I., Margaria, T. (eds.) ICSOC 2008. LNCS, vol. 5364, pp. 147–161. Springer, Heidelberg (2008)
10. van der Aalst, W.M.P., Dustdar, S.: Process mining put into context. IEEE Internet Computing 16(1), 82–86 (2012)
11. Sutrisnowati, R.A., Bae, H., Park, J., Ha, B.H.: Learning bayesian network from event logs using mutual information test. In: Proceedings of the 6th International Conference on Service-Oriented Computing and Applications (SOCA), pp. 356–360 (2013)
12. Aamodt, A., Plaza, E.: Case-based reasoning: Foundational issues, methodological variations, and system approaches. AI Communication 7(1), 39–59 (1994)
13. Mitchell, T.M.: Machine Learning, 1st edn. McGraw-Hill, Inc., New York (1997)
14. Dougherty, J., Kohavi, R., Sahami, M.: Supervised and unsupervised discretization of continuous features. In: Proceedings of the Twelfth International Conference on Machine Learning (ICML 1995), pp. 194–202. Morgan Kaufmann (1995)
15. Nakatumba, J.: Resource-Aware Business Process Management: Analysis and Support. PhD thesis, Eindhoven University of Technology (2014) ISBN: 978-90-386-3472-2

16. van der Aalst, W.M.P., de Beer, H.T., van Dongen, B.F.: Process mining and verification of properties: An approach based on temporal logic. In: Meersman, R., Tari, Z. (eds.) OTM 2005. LNCS, vol. 3760, pp. 130–147. Springer, Heidelberg (2005)
17. de Leoni, M., van der Aalst, W.M.P.: Aligning event logs and process models for multi-perspective conformance checking: An approach based on integer linear programming. In: Daniel, F., Wang, J., Weber, B. (eds.) BPM 2013. LNCS, vol. 8094, pp. 113–129. Springer, Heidelberg (2013)
18. de Leoni, M., Maggi, F.M., van der Aalst, W.M.P.: An alignment-based framework to check the conformance of declarative process models and to preprocess event-log data. Information Systems (to appear, 2014), doi: 10.1016/j.is.2013.12.005
19. Rozinat, A., van der Aalst, W.M.P.: Decision Mining in Prom. In: Dustdar, S., Fiadeiro, J.L., Sheth, A.P. (eds.) BPM 2006. LNCS, vol. 4102, pp. 420–425. Springer, Heidelberg (2006)

Behavioral Comparison of Process Models Based on Canonically Reduced Event Structures

Abel Armas-Cervantes[1], Paolo Baldan[2],
Marlon Dumas[1], and Luciano García-Bañuelos[1]

[1] Institute of Computer Science, University of Tartu, Estonia
{abel.armas,marlon.dumas,luciano.garcia}@ut.ee
[2] Department of Mathematics, University of Padova, Italy
baldan@math.unipd.it

Abstract. We address the problem of diagnosing behavioral differences between pairs of business process models. Specifically, given two process models, we seek to determine if they are behaviorally equivalent, and if not, we seek to describe their differences in terms of behavioral relations captured in one model but not in the other. The proposed solution is based on a translation from process models to Asymmetric Event Structures (AES). A naïve version of this translation suffers from two limitations. First, it produces redundant difference diagnostic statements because an AES may contain unnecessary event duplication. Second, it is not applicable to process models with cycles. To tackle the first limitation, we propose a technique to reduce event duplication in an AES while preserving canonicity. For the second limitation, we propose a notion of unfolding that captures all possible causes of each event in a cycle. From there we derive an AES where repeated events are distinguished from non-repeated ones and that allows us to diagnose differences in terms of repetition and causal relations in one model but not in the other.

1 Introduction

Comparing models of business process variants is a basic operation when managing collections of process models [1]. In some cases, syntactic matching of nodes or edges are sufficient to understand differences between two variants. However, two variants may be syntactically different and still be behaviorally equivalent or they may be very similar syntactically but quite different behaviorally, as changes in a few gateways or edges may entail significant behavioral differences.

This paper presents a technique to compare business processes in terms of behavioral relations between tasks. The technique diagnoses differences in the form of binary behavioral relations (e.g., causality and conflict) that hold in one model but not in the other. For example, given the models in Fig. 1[1] we seek to describe their differences via statements of the form: *"In model M_1, after* Prepare transportation quote *it is possible to execute either* Arrange delivery appointment

---

[1] Based on an order fulfillment process presented in [2].

S. Sadiq, P. Soffer, and H. Völzer (Eds.): BPM 2014, LNCS 8659, pp. 267–282, 2014.

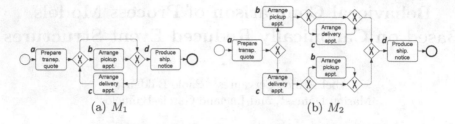

(a) M_1 (b) M_2

Fig. 1. Variants of business process models

and Produce shipment notice, *or only* Produce shipment notice; *whereas in* M_2 *after* Prepare transportation quote, Arrange delivery appointment *is followed by* Produce shipment notice". The diagnosis also considers cyclic behavior, e.g. *"In model* M_1, *activity* Arrange delivery appointment *can be executed many times in a run; whereas in* M_2 *it is executed only once"*.

The key idea of the proposal is to compare abstract representations of the process models based on binary behavioral relations. If two process models have isomorphic abstract representations, then they are behaviorally equivalent and otherwise we can use error-correcting graph matching to diagnose the differences. To this end, we adopt a well-known model of concurrency known as *event structures* [3], where computations are represented via events (activity occurrences) and behavioral relations between events. There are different types of event structures comprising different relations, such as *Prime Event Structures* [3] (PESs) and *Asymmetric Event Structures* [4] (AESs). For the purpose of comparison, more compact representations are desirable as they lead to more concise diagnosis of relations existing in one process and not in the other. In this respect, AESs are more compact than PESs and in prior work [5], we proposed a behavior-preserving folding of AESs. However, the work in [5] shows that in some cases multiple non-isomorphic AESs exist that represent the same behavior.

The contributions of the paper are threefold: (i) we extend our work in [5], by proposing a deterministic order on the folding of AESs that produces a canonical representation of the behavior of a given process model, (ii) we extend our approach to support the differencing of process models with cycles, and (iii) we propose an approach to verbalize differences. For the sake of presentation, we assume that the input process are represented as Petri nets. Transformations from other process modeling notations (e.g. BPMN) to Petri nets are given elsewhere [6].

The paper is structured as follows, Section 2 discusses related work. Section 3 provides definitions of notions used in the rest of the paper. The proposed techniques are presented in Section 4. Finally Section 5 summarizes the contributions and discusses future work.

2   Related Work

Approaches for process model comparison can be divided into those based on node label similarity, process structure similarity and behavior similarity [1]. In this paper we focus on behavioral similarity. Nevertheless, we acknowledge that node label similarity plays an important role in the alignment of nodes (e.g., tasks) across the process models being compared. In our work, we assume that such an alignment is given, i.e. for each node label in one model we are given the corresponding ("equivalent") node label in the other model.

There are many equivalence notions for concurrent systems [7], ranging from trace equivalence (processes are equivalent if they have the same set of traces) to bisimulation equivalence, to finer equivalences which preserve some concurrency features of computations (two models are equivalent if they have same sets of runs taking into account concurrency between events). Few methods have been proposed to diagnose differences between processes based on various notions of equivalence. The paper [8] presents a technique to derive equations in a process algebra characterizing the differences between two *Labeled Transition Systems* (LTSs). The use of a process algebra makes the feedback difficult to grasp for end users (process analysts in our context) and the technique relies on a notion of equivalence that does not take into account the concurrent structure in the process (a process model with concurrency and its sequential simulation are equivalent). In [9], a method for assessing dissimilarity of LTSs in terms of "edit" operations is presented. However, such feedback on LTSs does not tell the analyst what relations exist in one model that do not exist in the other. Also, it is based on a notion of equivalence that does take concurrency into account. The same remarks apply to [10], which presents a method for diagnosing differences between pairs of process models using standard automata theory. In addition, in [10] the set of reported differences is not guaranteed to be complete.

Behavioral Profiles (BP) [11] and *Causal Behavior Profiles* [12] are two approaches to represent processes using binary relations. They abstract a process using a $n \times n$ matrix, where n is the number of tasks in the process. Each cell contains one out of three relations: *strict order*, *exclusive order* or *interleaving*; plus an additional *co-occurrence* relation in the case of causal behavioral profiles. Both techniques are incomplete as they mishandle several types of constructs, e.g., task skipping (silent transitions), duplicate tasks, and cycles. In this case, two processes can have identical BPs despite not being behaviorally equivalent.

Alpha relations [13] are another representation of processes using binary behavioral relations (direct causality, conflict and concurrency), proposed in the context of process mining. Alpha causality is not transitive (i.e. causality has a localized scope) making alpha relations unsuitable for behavior comparison [14]. Moreover, alpha relations cannot capture so-called "short loops" and hidden tasks (including task skipping). *Relation sets* [15] are a generalization of alpha relations. Instead of one matrix, the authors use k matrices (with a variable k). In each matrix, causality is computed with a different look-ahead. It is shown that 1-lookahead matrices induce trace equivalence for a restricted family of Petri nets. The authors claim that using k matrices improves accuracy. But it is unclear how human-readable diagnostics of behavioral differences could be extracted from two sets of k matrices and it is unclear to what notion of equivalence would the diagnostics correspond.

3   Preliminaries

This section introduces some fundamental notions on *Petri nets*, *branching processes* and *event structures* that will be used in subsequent parts of the paper.

3.1   Petri Nets

Definition 1 (Petri net, Net system). *A tuple* $N = (P, T, F)$ *is a* Petri net, *where* P *is a set of* places, T *is a set of* transitions, *with* $P \cap T = \varnothing$, *and* $F \subseteq (P \times T) \cup (T \times P)$ *is a set of arcs. A* marking $M : P \to \mathbb{N}_0$ *is a function that associates each place* $p \in P$ *with a natural number (viz., place tokens). A* net system $S = (N, M_0)$ *is a Petri net* $N = (P, T, F)$ *with an* initial marking M_0.

Places and transitions are conjointly referred to as *nodes*. We write $\bullet y = \{x \in P \cup T \mid (x, y) \in F\}$ and $y \bullet = \{z \in P \cup T \mid (y, z) \in F\}$ to denote the *preset* and *postset* of node y, respectively. F^+ and F^* denote the irreflexive and reflexive transitive closure of F, respectively.

The semantics of a net system is defined in terms of markings. A marking M *enables* a transition t if $\forall p \in \bullet t : M(p) > 0$, denoted as $(N, M)[t\rangle$. Moreover, the occurrence of t leads to a new marking M', with $M'(p) = M(p) - 1$ if $p \in \bullet t \setminus t \bullet$, $M'(p) = M(p) + 1$ if $p \in t \bullet \setminus \bullet t$, and $M'(p) = M(p)$ otherwise. We use $M \xrightarrow{t} M'$ to denote the occurrence of t. The marking M_n is said to be reachable from M if there exists a sequence of transitions $\sigma = t_1 t_2 \ldots t_n$ such that $M \xrightarrow{t_1} M_1 \xrightarrow{t_2} \ldots \xrightarrow{t_n} M_n$. The set of all the markings reachable from a marking M is de-

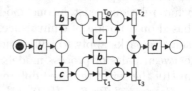

Fig. 2. N_2 of Fig. 1(b)

noted $[M\rangle$. A marking M of a net is *n-safe* if $M(p) \le n$ for every place p. A net system N is said *n-safe* if all its reachable markings are *n-safe*. In the following we restrict ourselves to *1-safe* net systems. Hence, we identify the marking M with the set $\{p \in P \mid M(p) = 1\}$.

A labeled Petri net $N = (P, T, F, \lambda)$ has a function $\lambda : P \cup T \to \Lambda \cup \{\tau\}$ that associates a node with a label. A transition x is said to be *observable* if $\lambda(x) \ne \tau$, otherwise x is *silent*. A labeled net system $S = (N, M_0, \lambda)$ is similarly defined. An example of a labeled net system is shown in Fig. 2, the transitions display their corresponding label inside the rectangle if they are observable.

3.2   Deterministic and Branching Processes

The partial order semantics of a net system can be formulated in terms of runs or, more precisely, prefixes of runs that are referred to as *deterministic processes*[2]

---

[2] Here and in the rest of this section, the term *process* refers to a control-flow abstraction of a business process based on a partial order semantics.

[16]. A process can be represented as an acyclic net with no branching nor merging places, i.e., $\forall p \in P : |{\bullet}p| \leq 1 \wedge |p{\bullet}| \leq 1$. Alternatively, all runs can be accommodated in a single tree-like structure, called *branching process* [3], which can contain branching places and explicitly represents three behavior relations: *causality*, *concurrency* and *conflict* defined as follows.

Definition 2 (Behavior relations). *Let* $N = (P,T,F)$ *be a Petri net and* $x,y \in P \cup T$ *two nodes in* N.
- x *and* y *are in* causal *relation, denoted* $x <_N y$, *iff* $(x,y) \in F^+$. *The inverse causal relation is denoted* $>_N$. *By* $\leq_N$ *we denote the reflexive causal relation.*
- x *and* y *are in* conflict, *denoted* $x \#_N y$, *iff there exist two transitions* $t, t' \in T$ *such that* t *and* t' *are distinct,* ${\bullet}t \cap {\bullet}t' \neq \varnothing$, *and* $(t,x),(t',y) \in F^*$. *If* $x \#_N x$ *then* x *is said to be in self-conflict.*
- x *and* y *are concurrent, denoted as* $x \parallel_N y$, *iff neither* $x <_N y$, *nor* $y <_N x$, *nor* $x \#_N y$.

We can now provide a formal definition for branching process.

Definition 3 (Branching process). *Let* $S = (P,T,F,M_0)$ *be a net system. The* branching process $\mathcal{U}(S) = (B,E,G,\rho)$ *of* S *is the net* (B,E,G) *defined by the inductive rules in Fig. 3. The rules also define the function* $\rho : B \cup E \to P \cup T$ *that maps each node in the branching process* $\mathcal{U}(S)$ *to a node in* S. *We write* $\varrho(B)$ *as a shorthand for* $\bigcup_{b \in B \cup E} \rho(b)$.

In a branching process $\mathcal{U}(S) = (B,E,G,\rho)$, B represents the set of conditions (places) and E the set of events (transitions). Let $\beta = \mathcal{U}(S)$ be a branching process, thus $Min(\beta)$ denotes the set of minimal elements of $B \cup E$ with respect to the transitive closure of G. Henceforth, $Min(\beta)$ corresponds to the set of places in the initial marking of S, i.e., $\varrho(Min(\beta)) = M_0$. A *co-set* is a set of conditions $B' \subseteq B$ such that for all $b,b' \in B'$ it holds $b \parallel b'$. A *cut* is a maximal co-set w.r.t. set inclusion.

$$
\frac{p \in M_0}{b = \langle \varnothing, p \rangle \in B \qquad \rho(b) = p}
$$

$$
\frac{t \in T \quad B' \subseteq B \quad B'^2 \subseteq \parallel_\beta \quad \varrho(B') = {\bullet}t}{e = \langle B', t \rangle \in E \qquad \rho(e) = t}
$$

$$
\frac{e = \langle B', t \rangle \in E \qquad t{\bullet} = \{p_1, \ldots, p_n\}}{b_i = \langle t', p_i \rangle \in B \qquad \rho(b_i) = p_i}
$$

Fig. 3. Branching process, inductive rules

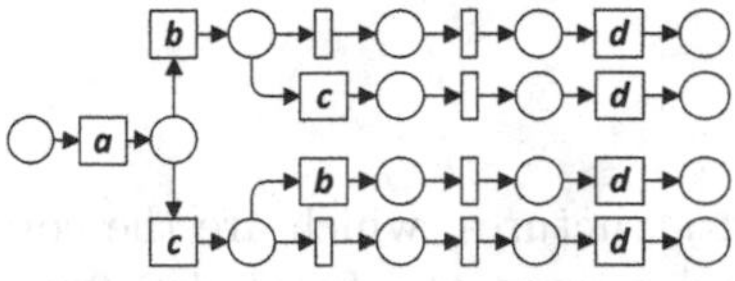

Fig. 4. $\mathcal{U}(N_2)$ (Fig. 1(b))

One characteristic of a branching process is that it does not contain merging conditions. As a result, some nodes in the net system need to be represented more than once in the branching process. For example, the branching process in Fig. 4 contains multiple instances of b, c and d, which come from a single transition in the net system shown in Fig. 2.

Definition 4 (Configuration and deterministic process). *Let* β = (B, E, G, ρ) *be a branching process.*

- *A* configuration C *of* β *is a set of events,* $C \subseteq E$, *which is*
  i) *causally closed, i.e.,* $\forall e' \in E, e \in C : e' \leq_\beta e \Rightarrow e' \in C$, *and*
  ii) *conflict free, i.e.,* $\forall e, e' \in C, \neg(e \#_\beta e')$.
  We denote by $Conf(\beta)$ *the set of configurations of the branching process* β, *whereas* $MaxConf(\beta)$ *refers to the maximal configurations w.r.t. set inclusion.*
- *A* local configuration *of an event* $e \in E$ *is denoted as* $\lfloor e \rfloor = \{e' \mid e' \leq e\}$, *such that it is unique for any event* $e \in E$. *In the same vein, by* $\lfloor e)$ *we denote the set of strict causes of an event* $e \in E$, *i.e.,* $\lfloor e) = \lfloor e \rfloor \backslash \{e\}$
- *A* deterministic process $\pi = (B_\pi, E_\pi, G_\pi, \rho)$ *is the net induced by a configuration* C, *where* $B_\pi = \bigcup_{c \in C} (\bullet c \cup c \bullet)$, $E_\pi = C$, *and* $G_\pi = G \cap (B_\pi \times E_\pi \cup E_\pi \times B_\pi)$.

A cut for a configuration C of a branching process $\beta = \mathcal{U}(S)$ is defined as $Cut(C) = (Min(\beta) \cup \bigcup_{c \in C} c\bullet) \backslash (\bigcup_{c \in C} \bullet c)$; whereas $\varrho(Cut(C))$ is a reachable marking in S, denoted by $Mark(C)$, i.e, $Mark(C) \in [M_0)$. Let C and C' be configurations of β, such that $C \subset C'$, and let π and π' be their corresponding deterministic branching processes. If $X = C' \smallsetminus C$, then we write $\pi' = \pi \oplus X$ and we say that π' is an *extension* of π.

Throughout this paper, we use *visible-pomset equivalence* [17] as the notion of behavioral equivalence. A pomset is a tuple $\langle X, \leq \mid_X \rangle$, where X is a set of events and $\leq \mid_X$ is the projection of the causal relation over X. We use $X^\Lambda = \{e \in X \mid \lambda(e) \neq \tau\}$ to denote the restriction of X to observable events. With abuse of notation, we write X^Λ to denote the restriction of the pomset induced by X, restricted to observable behavior, and it is called the *visible pomset* underlying X. Moreover, we denote by $Conf(\mathbb{P})^\Lambda$ the set of visible pomsets underlying its configurations, i.e., $Conf(\beta)^\Lambda = \{C^\Lambda : C \in Conf(\beta)\}$.

A function f is an *isomorphism* between pomset p and pomset q, iff it is a label-preserving order-isomorphism, i.e., $f : E_p \to E_q$ is a bijection, $\lambda_p = \lambda_q \circ f$, and $e <_p e' \Leftrightarrow f(e) <_q f(e')$ for all $e, e' \in E_p$. Armed with the concepts above, we can now formally define visible-pomset equivalence:

Definition 5 (Visible-pomset equivalence [17]). *Let* β *and* β' *be the branching processes of the net systems* N *and* N'. *Then* N *visible-pomset approximates* N', *written* $N \sqsubseteq_{pt} N'$, *iff every visible-pomset* $X^\Lambda \in Conf(\beta)^\Lambda$ *is isomorphic with at least one visible-pomset* $Y^\Lambda \in Conf(\beta')^\Lambda$. *Moreover,* N *and* N' *are visible pomset equivalent, denoted* $\mathbb{N}_1 \equiv_{vp} \mathbb{N}_2$, *iff each is* $\sqsubseteq_{vp}$ *to the other.*

3.3   Event Structures

This section introduces two variants of event structures, which are the cornerstones of our comparison technique, *prime* and *asymmetric event structures*.

Definition 6 (Prime Event Structure [3]). *Let* $S = (N, M_0)$ *be a net system, where* $N = (P, T, F, \lambda_N)$, *and* $\beta = (B, E, G, \rho)$ *be its branching process. The* *labeled* Prime Event Structure *(PES)* of β is defined as $\mathbb{P} = \langle E, \leq_{\mathbb{P}}, \#_{\mathbb{P}}, \lambda_{\mathbb{P}} \rangle$, where $\leq_{\mathbb{P}} = \leq_{\beta} \cap E^2$ and $\#_{\mathbb{P}} = \#_{\beta} \cap E^2$. Finally, $\lambda_{\mathbb{P}} = \lambda_N \circ \rho$ is a labeling function that associates each event $e \in E$ with the label of its corresponding transition $t \in T$, i.e., $\rho(e) = t \Rightarrow \lambda_{\mathcal{E}}(e) = \lambda_N(t)$.

The conflict relation $\#_{\mathbb{P}}$ is hereditary w.r.t. $\leq_{\mathbb{P}}$, i.e. $e \#_{\mathbb{P}} e' \wedge e' \leq_{\mathbb{P}} e'' \Rightarrow e \#_{\mathbb{P}} e''$ for all $e, e', e'' \in E$.

As stated before, we focus only on observable behavior. Therefore, we use $\bar{\mathbb{P}}$ to denote a PES with observable events, that is, with all its invisible events being abstracted away. Figure 5 shows the PES with all the observable behavior of the net system N_2 from Fig. 2. In this graphical representation, solid arrows represent causality, and annotated dotted lines represent conflict. It is common practice not to include transitive relations in the graphical representation of a PES, for the sake of readability.

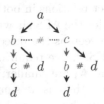

Fig. 5. PES $\bar{\mathbb{P}}$

The set of configurations of a PES $\mathbb{P}$ coincides with the set of configurations of its originative branching process. We will denote this set as $Conf(\mathbb{P})$.

We now turn our attention to *Asymmetric Event Structures* (AESs).

Definition 7 (Asymmetric Event Structure [4]). *An AES is a triplet* $\mathbb{A} = \langle E, \leq, \nearrow \rangle$, *where E represents the set of events, $\leq$ is the causality relation and $\nearrow$ is the asymmetric conflict relation. Moreover, for all $e, e', e'' \in E$ the following holds: (1) $\lfloor e \rfloor = \{ e' \mid e' \leq e \}$ is finite, (2) $e < e' \Rightarrow e \nearrow e'$, (3) if $e \nearrow e'$ and $e' < e''$ then $e \nearrow e''$, (4) $\nearrow \mid_{\lfloor e \rfloor}$ is acyclic, (5) if $\nearrow \mid_{\lfloor e \rfloor \cup \lfloor e' \rfloor}$ is cyclic then $e \nearrow e'$. Finally, let $\Psi_{\mathbb{A}} = (<, \nearrow)$ denote the behavior relations of $\mathbb{A}$.*

This type of event structure replaces the conflict relation in PESs with an asymmetric relation. Graphically, causality is represented by a solid arrow and asymmetric conflict with a dashed arrow. Intuitively, the statement $a \nearrow b$ has two interpretations: (i) the occurrence of b *prevents* the occurrence of a, or (ii) a *precedes* b in all computations where both events occur. By (ii), asymmetric conflict can be seen as a form of weak causality. Interestingly, asymmetric conflict is also hereditary w.r.t. causality. As for PESs, two events are said *concurrent* when they are neither in causal nor in asymmetric conflict relation.

In the case of PESs, the set inclusion relation defines a order over configurations referred to as *configuration extension*. This does not apply to the case of AESs. Consider the AES presented in Fig. 6. Note that $\{a, b, c\}$ is an extension of $\{a, b\}$, but it is not an extension of $\{a, c\}$, because the occurrence of c prevents that of b. Formally, a configuration of $\mathbb{A} = \langle E, \leq, \nearrow, \lambda \rangle$ is a set of events $C \subseteq E$ such that 1) for any $e \in C$, $\lfloor e \rfloor \subseteq C$ (causal closedness) 2) $\nearrow \mid_C$ is acyclic (conflict free). Moreover, if $C_1, C_2 \in Conf(\mathbb{A})$ are cofigurations, we say that C_2 extends C_1, written $C_1 \sqsubseteq C_2$, if

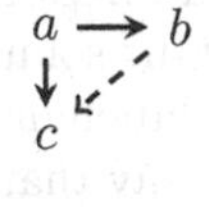

Fig. 6. $\mathbb{A}_0$

$C_1 \subseteq C_2$ and for all $e \in C_1$, $e' \in C_2 \smallsetminus C_1$, $\neg(e' \nearrow e)$. The set of all configurations of $\mathbb{A}$ is denoted by $Conf(\mathbb{A})$.

The AES formalism is more expressive than PESs and it can provide a more compact representation for a given set of configurations. In fact, any PES can be seen as a special case of an AES [4] where the conflict relation is replaced with asymmetric conflict relations in both directions. Consider the AES shown in Fig. 7. $\mathbb{A}_1$ can be seen as the direct translation of a PES, hence requiring duplication. $\mathbb{A}_2$

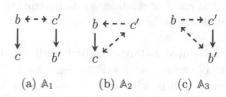

(a) $\mathbb{A}_1$ (b) $\mathbb{A}_2$ (c) $\mathbb{A}_3$

Fig. 7. Equivalent AESs

and $\mathbb{A}_3$ are smaller, but still visible-pomset equivalent, versions of $\mathbb{A}_1$. Observe that there is no smaller AES representation for the same behavior and, in that sense, both $\mathbb{A}_2$ and $\mathbb{A}_3$ are minimal.

In [5], we introduced a technique for behavior-preserving minimization of AESs. Moreover, we found that the technique may lead to different representations for the same behavior, depending on the order on which the folding operation is applied on the input AES. For instance, $\mathbb{A}_2$ (Fig. 7(b)) comes after folding events b and b', whereas $\mathbb{A}_3$ (Fig. 7(c)) comes after folding events c and c'. In the next section, we will address the problem of canonical folding of AESs.

4   Comparison of Process Models

This section describes our approach to process model differencing with Asymmetric Event Structures. The first part addresses the problem of the non-canonicity of the folding of an AES by leveraging the notion of canonical labelling of graphs. The second part extends the method to support the comparison of process models with cycles. Finally, the section presents a differencing operator and an approach to verbalizing the differences found while comparing pairs of processes. The proofs are available at [18].

4.1   Canonicity

Any reliable comparison method requires that its input is provided in a canonical representation. In our context, if we consider that the folding operation is behavior preserving, we would like that the AESs obtained from two isomorphic PESs are also isomorphic. As shown in Fig. 7, this not always the case. In order to address this problem, we leverage some concepts from graph theory.

Our solution to the problem of non-canonicity relies on the concept of canonical labelling of a graph [19], that is an approach to deciding graph isomorphism. We say that $Canon(G)$ is a function that maps a graph G to a canonical label. In this way, if graphs G and H are given, we expect $Canon(G) = Canon(H)$ to hold iff H and G are isomorphic. If we use the string representation of the adjacency matrix of a graph, then a canonical label for a graph G can be determined by computing all permutations of its adjacency matrix and selecting the largest lexicographical exemplar among them[3]. Clearly, this naïve approach is computationally expensive, but state-of-the-art software implement several heuristics to compute canonical labels in a reasonable time. In our context, we are interested in the order of the vertices associated to the adjacency matrix of the canonical exemplar. Formally, let $G = (V, A)$ be a graph, where V is the set of vertices and A the set of arcs. Moreover, let $M(G)$ be the adjacency matrix of G, $\gamma = (0, 1, ... |V|)$ be an order over the set of vertices, and $STR(M(G)^\gamma)$ be the string linear representation of the adjacency matrix G given the order γ. Then the canonical label of G is the string induced by order $\hat{\gamma}$, s.t., $STR(M(G)^{\hat{\gamma}}) \geq_{lex} STR(M(G)^{\gamma_\pi})$ holds for every possible permutation γ_π of γ.

In our implementation, we use **nauty** (http://pallini.di.uniroma1.it/) for computing the graph canonical label and, more precisely, the order on the vertices of the canonical exemplar. Nauty and other similar tools work on graphs with unlabeled edges. To overcome this limitation, we adapted a transformation introduced in [20]. Briefly, this transformation maps a fully labeled graph (both nodes and edges carry a label) into a node-labeled graph and has been proved to be isomorphism preserving. The reader is referred to [20] to get more details about this transformation. By leveraging this result and the notion of canonical label of a graph we can now establish an order on the folding that yields a minimal and canonical AES for a PES.

Intuitively, the folding starts with an AES that is isomorphic to the PES of a business process. Thus, we carry the order $\hat{\gamma}$ computed over the nauty graph of the PES. In every iteration we select a set of events that can be merged without changing the behavior of the AES. We use $\mathbb{A}_{/X}$ to denote the folding of a combinable set of events X on an AES $\mathbb{A}$. In [5] we show that the folding defines a morphism $f : AES \rightarrow AES$ that preserves visible-pomset equivalence. In this context, since there might be multiple candidate sets of events for folding, we use $\hat{\gamma}$ for establishing a total order on the folding operations. For space restriction, we do not include the details on how the whole set of combinable sets of events is computed and refer the reader to [5] for a full description. Therefore, we will assume that the combinable sets of events are given.

Definition 8 (Deterministic folding). *Let $\mathbb{A} = \langle E, \leq, \nearrow, \lambda \rangle$ be an AES, and $\hat{\gamma} : E \rightarrow \mathbb{N}_0$ be the canonical order of events given by nauty. Let $X, Y \subseteq E$ be combinable sets of events. Then the precedence of X over Y in a deterministic folding is defined by the following conditions, listed in decreasing relevance: (i) $\lambda(e) >_{lex} \lambda(e')$ where $e' \in Y$ and $e \in X$, or (ii) $\lambda(e) =_{lex} \lambda(e') \wedge |X| > |Y|$, or (iii) $\lambda(e) =_{lex} \lambda(e') \wedge |X| = |Y| \wedge \hat{\gamma}(X) >_{lex} \hat{\gamma}(Y)$. Hence, $\mathbb{A}_{/X} = \langle E_{/X}, \leq_{/X}, \nearrow_{/X}, \lambda_{/X} \rangle$ is a folding of $\mathbb{A}$, s.t. $e_X \in E_{/X}$ is the event representing $X \subseteq E$, and the canonical labeling function is $\hat{\gamma}_{\mathbb{A}_{/X}} = \hat{\gamma}[e_X \mapsto Ran(\hat{\gamma}) + 1]$. Finally, $f(\mathbb{A})^+_{/X}$ denotes the folding induced by $\hat{\gamma}$ that cannot be further minimized, i.e., the minimal canonical folding.*

---

[3] Some authors prefer the smallest lexicographic string.

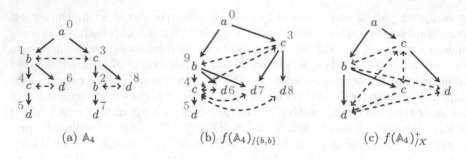

(a) $\mathbb{A}_4$ (b) $f(\mathbb{A}_4)_{/\{b,b\}}$ (c) $f(\mathbb{A}_4)^+_{/X}$

Fig. 8. Canonical labeling and folding

Figure 8 illustrates the canonical folding of $\mathbb{A}_4$, which corresponds to the PES $\bar{\mathbb{P}}$ in Fig. 5. $\mathbb{A}_4$ shows the order $\hat{\gamma}$ assigned by nauty. The combinable sets of events in $\mathbb{A}_4$ are $\{\{b(1),b(2)\},\{c(3),c(4)\},\{d(5),d(6)\},\{d(7),d(8)\}\}$, and from Definition 8 we know that $\{b(1),b(2)\}$ takes precedence over the others. The folding of $\{b(1),b(2)\}$ is depicted in Fig. 8(b). Note that a fresh event b is added, replacing the set $\{b(1),b(2)\}$, and the value 9 is associated to this event in $\hat{\gamma}$. The values added to $\hat{\gamma}$ are monotonically increased. Finally, Fig. 8(c) depicts the minimal and canonical AES. In this particular case, it was necessary to keep two events with label c and two with label d to preserve the behavior. The following proposition shows that the folding of an AES is canonical.

Proposition 1. *Let $\mathbb{A}_1 = \langle E_1, \leq_1, \nearrow_1, \lambda_1 \rangle$ and $\mathbb{A}_2 = \langle E_2, \leq_1, \nearrow_2, \lambda_2 \rangle$ be two iso-morphic AESs and, $\hat{\gamma}_1 : E_1 \to \mathbb{N}_0$ and $\hat{\gamma}_2 : E_2 \to \mathbb{N}_0$ be the canonical order for E_1 and E_2, correspondingly. Then the deterministic folding of $\mathbb{A}_1$ and $\mathbb{A}_2$ produces a canonical AES, such that $f(\mathbb{A}_1)^+_X$ is isomorphic to $f(\mathbb{A}_2)^+_X$.*

4.2   Finite Representation of Cyclic Behavior

A fundamental problem with cyclic process models is that their branching processes may easily get unboundedly large. Engelfriet [16] showed that every Petri net has a unique maximal branching process up to isomorphism, the so-called unfolding of the net. McMillan [21] and then Esparza et al. [22] introduced sophisticated strategies for truncating the unfolding to a finite level, thus getting what is referred to as the *complete unfolding prefix (CP)*. Later, the authors in [23] introduced a framework to generalize previous work and to defined the notion of canonical unfolding prefixes. Our own work relies on such a framework. In the following we restrict ourselves to Petri nets without duplicate tasks.

Consider the net system N_1 and the complete unfolding prefix β_1 presented in Fig. 9. Note that both b_1 and b_4 correspond to the place p_1 in N_1. To compute the complete unfolding prefix, we start applying the inductive rules described in Fig. 3. In this case, however, it is possible to stop unfolding once we reach b_2 and b_4 because any addition to the prefix would duplicate information already represented there. For this reason, events b and c are called *cutoff events*. Although it has been proved that the complete unfolding prefix represents all the

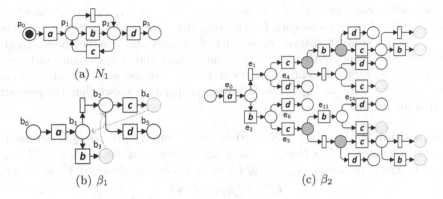

(a) N_1

(b) β_1

(c) β_2

Fig. 9. Petri net and two different unfoldings

behavior of the original net system [22], this prefix does not explicitly contain the information that we require to diagnose the behavioral differences of business processes. For instance, the fact that c causally precedes b and d is not explicitly represented in the prefix. Therefore, we require a larger prefix of the branching process that makes explicit all the causal relations. In the case of the net system N_1 in Fig. 9(a) the required unfolding prefix is β_2, (Fig. 9(c)).

In order to compute a unfolding prefix as the one required for comparison of process models, we define new criteria to identify cutoff events. To this end, we use the notion cutting context introduced in [23]. The cutting context is formally defined as the tuple $\Theta = (\approx, \lhd, \mathcal{C})$ where $\approx$ is an equivalence relation over configurations, $\lhd$ is a total order over configurations, and $\mathcal{C}$ is the set of configurations used at the time of the computation of the unfolding prefix. E.g., the cutting context used in McMillan [21] is $\Theta_{McMillan} = (\approx_{mark}, \lhd_{size}, \mathcal{C}_{loc})$, where $\approx_{mark}$ equates two configurations when they produce the same marking, $\lhd_{size}$ is the total order induced by the size of configurations, and $\mathcal{C}_{loc} = \{\lfloor e \rfloor \mid e \in E\}$ is the set of local configurations. Note that, the complete unfolding prefix β_1 can also be computed by using McMillan's cutting context. In fact, if we consider the local configurations $\lfloor c \rfloor = \{a, \tau, c\}$ and $\lfloor a \rfloor = \{a\}$, then one can easily check that $Mark(\lfloor a \rfloor) = Mark(\lfloor c \rfloor) = \{p_1\}$. Moreover, since $\|a\| < \|c\|$, then one should conclude that event c is a cutoff event. The cutting context in Esparza et al. [22], denoted $\Theta_{ERV} = (\approx_{mark}, \lhd_{slf}, \mathcal{C}_{loc})$, differs from that in [21] only for the definition of the partial order $\lhd_{slf}$, which is refined by considering action labels thus leading to more cut-offs and smaller prefixes (see [22] for details). For our purposes, consider a cutting context which is a modification of Θ_{ERV} with a refined equivalence relation over configurations.

Definition 9 ($\approx_{Pred}$). *Let $\beta = (B, E, G, \rho)$ be a branching process. A pair of configurations $C_1, C_2 \in Conf(\beta)$ are equivalent, represented as $C_1 \approx_{Pred} C_2$, iff $eMark(C_1) = eMark(C_2)$, where*
- $eCut(C) = \{\langle b, \lfloor \bullet b \rfloor \rangle \mid b \in Cut(C)\}$, *and*
- $eMark(C) = \{\langle \rho(b), \rho(\lfloor \bullet b \rfloor) \rangle \mid \langle b, \lfloor \bullet b \rfloor \rangle \in eCut(C)\}$.

We define our cutting context as $\Theta_{Pred} = (\approx_{Pred}, \triangleleft_{slf}, \mathcal{C}_{loc})$. Khomenko et al. [23] also offers a framework for showing that the unfolding prefix generated by a cutting context ensures canonicity, finiteness and completeness. To this end, we need to prove that the equivalence $\approx_{Pred}$ and the adequate order $\triangleleft_{slf}$ are preserved by finite configuration extensions. Esparza et al [22] showed that this property holds for $\triangleleft_{slf}$. The following proposition shows that the property also holds for $\approx_{Pred}$.

Proposition 2. *Let* $\beta = (B, E, G, \rho)$ *be the branching process of a net system* $S = (N, M_0)$ *and* $C, C' \in Conf(\beta)$ *be a pair of configurations, s.t. that* $C \approx_{Pred} C'$. *Therefore, for every suffix* V *of* C, *there exists a finite suffix* V' *of* C' *s.t.:*

$$C' \oplus V' \approx_{Pred} C \oplus V$$

The following proposition shows that the canonical unfolding prefix constructed with Θ_{Pred} contains all the causal relations that would be exhibited in the (possibly infinite) unfolding of a business process with cycles.

Proposition 3 (Completeness of transitive causal relation). *Let* $\beta = (B, E, G, \rho)$ *be the full branching process of a net system* $S = (N, M_0)$, $\Theta_{Pred} = (\approx_{Pred}, \triangleleft_{slf}, \mathcal{C}_{loc})$ *be the cutting context and* $\beta_\Theta = (B', E', G', \rho_\Theta)$ *be the CP unfolding constructed by* Θ_{Pred}. *Finally, let* E''_Θ *be the set of cut-offs computed by the cutting context. Then, the unfolding prefix* β_Θ *contains the distinct transitive causal dependencies, such that for any pair of events* $e_1, e_2 \in E : e_1 < e_2$ *then*

$$\exists e'_1, e'_2 \in E' : e'_1 < e'_2, \text{ where } \rho(e_1) = \rho_\Theta(e'_1) \text{ and } \rho(e_2) = \rho_\Theta(e'_2).$$

Unfortunately, the cutting context Θ_{Pred} does not always produce a prefix that is canonical for business process comparison. For instance, the two net systems presented in Figure 10 are visible-pomset equivalent. However, the presence of silent transitions leads to unfolding prefixes with larger duplication in case of N_4. In the current form, the behavior-preserving folding technique that we rely on will not merge causally related events, e.g. *as* in the unfolding of N_4, because it prevents cycles in the AES. The problem of computing a canonical folding of such cycles is left as future work.

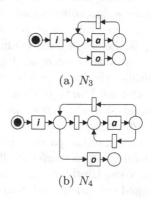

(a) N_3

(b) N_4

Fig. 10. Sample net systems

Repetitions. We now show how to identify the repetitive behavior, given the canonical unfolding prefix induced by Θ_{Pred}. Intuitively, we can say that a transition t in a net system is part of repetitive behavior iff there exists at least one configuration on which two events associated to transition t occur in causal relation. This intuition is captured in the following definition:

Definition 10 (Repetitive behavior). *Let* $\beta = (B, E, G, \rho)$ *be the unfolding prefix induced by* Θ_{Pred} *for a net* $N = (P, T, F, \lambda)$. *The* repetitive behavior *of* N *is defined as* $\mathcal{R} = \{\rho(e_1) \mid \exists C \in Conf(\beta). \ e_1, e_2 \in C \ \wedge \ \wedge \ \rho(e_1) = \rho(e_2) \wedge e_1 < e_2\}$.

It can be easily checked that the sets $\{e_0, e_1, e_4\}$, $\{e_0, e_2, e_6\}$ and $\{e_0, e_2, e_5, e_{11}, e_{14}\}$ are configurations in the unfolding prefix β_2 from Fig. 9(c). From the discussion above, we can conclude that b is part of repetitive behavior, in spite of the fact that there is a configuration that contains a single event carrying the label b. Moreover, we can also see that there exist at least one configuration on which no event labeled b occurs. This means that the task b will be observed zero or more times. In general, tasks participating in repetitive behavior can be observed either "0 or more times" (denoted as "$*$") or "1 or more times" (denoted as "$+$"). We will use the marker "0" for tasks that do not participate in repetitive behavior. The following definition captures the intuition above.

Definition 11 (Partitions of repetitive behavior). *Let* $\beta = (B, E, G, \rho)$ *be the unfolding prefix induced by* Θ_{Pred} *for net system* $S = (N, M_0)$. *The constant behavior* $\mathcal{K}$ *is defined as* $\mathcal{K} = \varrho(\cap MaxConf(\beta))$. *Therefore, the partitions of repetitive behavior are defined as:*

- $0 = \{e \mid e \in E \ \wedge \ \rho(e) \notin \mathcal{R}\}$
- $+ = \{e \mid e \in E \ \wedge \ \rho(e) \in \mathcal{R} \cap \mathcal{K}\}$
- $* = \{e \mid e \in E \ \wedge \ \rho(e) \in \mathcal{R} \ \wedge \ e \notin +\}$

4.3   Comparison

The comparison of process models happens on a subset of events, with the remaining events being discarded. We keep all the events which carry labels that are present in both process models. Moreover, since a single task may have multiple events associated, we compute an optimal matching, with well-known methods [1], on the set of events from both process models and discard the subset of events that does not make part of the matching. As discussed before, if two AESs are isomorphic then they

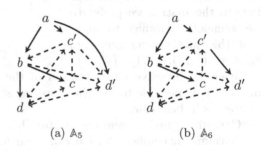

(a) $\mathbb{A}_5$ (b) $\mathbb{A}_6$

Fig. 11. Foldings and optimal matching (hinted by the position) of the AESs of to processes in the running example

must be diagnosed as behaviorally equivalent. In this work we adopt *visible pomset equivalence* [17][4]. It is only when two AESs are not isomorphic that we have to diagnose the differences. Once the optimal matching is computed, the

---

[4] Due to the presence of silent transitions, we use a weaker notion of equivalence than the one adopted in [5].

comparison of business processes happens in three stages: (1) diagnosis over the set of events in the optimal matching, (2) diagnosis on repetitive behavior, and (3) diagnosis on the set of unmatched events.

The diagnostic of the differences of behavior can be represented in a square matrix of order n, where n is the number of events in the optimal matching. To this end, we define the following differencing operator.

Definition 12 (Symmetric difference of AES behavior relations). *Let* $\mathbb{A}_1 = (E_1, \leq_1, \nearrow_1, \lambda_1)$ *and* $\mathbb{A}_2 = (E_2, \leq_2, \nearrow_2, \lambda_2)$ *be labeled event structures, and let* $\Psi_{\mathbb{A}_1}$ *and* $\Psi_{\mathbb{A}_2}$ *be their corresponding behavior relations. Let* $\mathcal{I} : E_1' \to E_2'$ *is the mapping function from* $\mathbb{A}_1$ *to* $\mathbb{A}_2$ *given by the graph matching algorithm, such that* $E_1' \subseteq E_1$ *and* $E_2' \subseteq E_2$.

Let $(e_1, e_2), (e_1', e_2') \in \mathcal{I}$ *be event matchings. The* symmetric difference *of* $\Psi_{\mathbb{A}_1}$ *and* $\Psi_{\mathbb{A}_2}$, *denoted* $\Psi_{\mathbb{A}_1} \triangle \Psi_{\mathbb{A}_2}$, *is defined as follows:*
$$\Psi_{\mathbb{A}_1} \triangle \Psi_{\mathbb{A}_2} [(e_1, e_2), (e_1', e_2')] =$$

$$\begin{cases} \cdot & \text{if } \Psi_{\mathbb{A}_1}[e_1, e_1'] = \Psi_{\mathbb{A}_2}[e_2, e_2'] \\ (\Psi_{\mathbb{A}_1}[e_1, e_1'], \Psi_{\mathbb{A}_2}[e_2, e_2']) & \text{if } \Psi_{\mathbb{A}_1}[e_1, e_1'] \neq \Psi_{\mathbb{A}_2}[e_2, e_2'] \end{cases}$$

Figure 11 shows the AESs of the sample process models in Fig. 1, projected to the subset of events (and behavior relations) in the optimal matching. Figure 12, in turn, shows the symmetric differencing of $\mathbb{A}_5$ and $\mathbb{A}_6$. Since cycles of asymmetric conflict hint a sort of symmetric conflict, in the matrix we prefer to use symmetric conflict to highlight this subtle difference, e.g., $\Psi_{\mathbb{A}_5} \triangle \Psi_{\mathbb{A}_5}[(c, d), (c, d)] = (\#, \nearrow)$.

	a	b	c	c′	d	d′
a	.	.	.	.	.	.
b	.	$(*,0)$	.	.	.	.
c	.	.	$(*,0)$	.	$(\#,\nearrow)$	.
c′	.	.	.	$(*,0)$	.	$(\nearrow,<)$
d	.	.	.	.	.	.
d′	.	.	.	.	.	.

Fig. 12. $\Psi_{\mathbb{A}_5} \triangle \Psi_{\mathbb{A}_6}$

Given the intuitive interpretation of the behavior relations represented in an AES, it is possible to use the following statements to describe the eventual differences in behavior:

- Causality: *"task* **a** *occurs before task* **b** *"*.
- Asymmetric conflict: *"task* **a** *can occur before task* **b**, *or* **a** *can be skipped"*.
- Conflict: *"task* **a** *and task* **b** *are mutually exclusive"*.
- Concurrency: *"task* **a** *and task* **b** *occur in parallel"*.

Similarly, for repetitive activities, we say:

- 0: *"it is not repeated any time"*,
- +: *"activitiy a can occur 1 or more times"*, and
- *: *"activity a can occur 0 or more times"*.

It is often the case that the feedback requires further information to understand the context on which a behavior difference arises. One possibility would be to present the set of runs on which a particular event occurs. However, the amount of information might be overwhelming. Therefore, we include in the feedback only the set of events that are in direct causal relation with the event giving rise to the difference. Based on the above considerations, the following are examples of verbalization for differences encountered from the matrix in Fig. 12:

- $c, d = (\#, \nearrow)$: *In model 1, there is a state after the execution of* c *where* d *and* c *are mutually exclusive; whereas in model 2, there is a state after the execution of* b *where* c *can occur before* d*, or* c *can be skipped*
- $c', d' = (\nearrow, <)$: *In model 1, there is a state after the execution of* a *where* c *can occur before* d*, or* c *can be skipped; whereas in model 2, there is a state after the execution of* a *where* c *precedes* d
- $b(*, 0)$: *Task* b *may occur many times in model 1; whereas in model 2, it is not repeated any time*
- $c(*, 0)$: *Task* c *may occur many times in model 1; whereas in model 2, it is not repeated any time*

In the case of tasks with repetitive behavior, one event is randomly chosen and the feedback is generated with respect to this event (note that the feedback from other instances would be the same). In the last step, we need to produce the feedback for the set of unmatched events. In this case, we also include the set of direct causally preceding events to give a context in the feedback. For the running example, the feedback would be:

- *There is an occurrence of* b *after* c *in model 1 but not in model 2*
- *There is an occurrence of* c *after* b *in model 1 but not in model 2*

5 Conclusions and Future Work

We present a method for comparing business process models based on behavioral relations, specifically those supported by AES. The contributions of the paper are threefold. First, we propose a method to calculate a canonically reduced AES from an acyclic Petri net. Second, we propose a technique to compute a finite representation for repetitive behavior that preserves casual dependencies, although the latter representation is not canonical as in the acyclic case. Finally, we propose a verbalization technique to generate difference diagnostics between process models. The presented techniques are implemented in a prototype tool available at https://code.google.com/p/fdes/. This tool takes pairs of process models captured in BPMN notation as input and produces a textual diagnostic of their differences.

As avenues for future research, we want fine tune the techniques to improve scalability of the tool. We also foresee an empirical study to assess the usability of the diagnostics produced by our tool. Finally, we aim at investigating further the problem of comparison of process models with cycles.

References

1. Dijkman, R., Dumas, M., van Dongen, B., Käärik, R., Mendling, J.: Similarity of business process models: Metrics and evaluation. Inf. Sys. 36(2), 498–516 (2011)
2. La Rosa, M., Clemens, S., ter Hofstede, A.H.M., Russell, N.: Appendix A. The Order Fulfillment Process Model. In: Modern Business Process Automation 2010 (2010)

3. Nielsen, M., Plotkin, G.D., Winskel, G.: Petri Nets, Event Structures and Domains, Part I. Theoretical Computer Science 13, 85–108 (1981)
4. Baldan, P., Corradini, A., Montanari, U.: Contextual Petri Nets, Asymmetric Event Structures, and Processes. Information and Computation 171, 1–49 (2001)
5. Armas, A., Baldan, P., García-Bañuelos, L.: Reduction of event structures under hp-bisimulation. Technical report, http://arxiv.org/abs/1403.7181
6. Polyvyany, A., García-Bañuelos, L., Dumas, M.: Structuring acyclic process models. Information Systems 37(6), 518–538 (2012)
7. van Glabbeek, R., Goltz, U.: Refinement of actions and equivalence notions for concurrent systems. Acta Informatica 37, 229–327 (2001)
8. Cleaveland, R.: On automatically explaining bisimulation inequivalence. In: Clarke, E., Kurshan, R.P. (eds.) CAV 1990. LNCS, vol. 531, pp. 364–372. Springer, Heidelberg (1991)
9. Sokolsky, O., Kannan, S., Lee, I.: Simulation-Based Graph Similarity. In: Hermanns, H., Palsberg, J. (eds.) TACAS 2006. LNCS, vol. 3920, pp. 426–440. Springer, Heidelberg (2006)
10. Dijkman, R.: Diagnosing Differences between Business Process Models. In: Dumas, M., Reichert, M., Shan, M.-C. (eds.) BPM 2008. LNCS, vol. 5240, pp. 261–277. Springer, Heidelberg (2008)
11. Weidlich, M., Mendling, J., Weske, M.: Efficient Consistency Measurement Based on Behavioral Profiles of Process Models. IEEE TSE 37(3), 410–429 (2011)
12. Weidlich, M., Polyvyanyy, A., Mendling, J., Weske, M.: Causal Behavioural Profiles. Fundamenta Informaticae 113(3-4), 399–435 (2011)
13. van der Aalst, W.M.P., Weijters, T., Maruster, L.: Workflow mining: discovering process models from event logs. IEEE TKDE 16(9), 1128–1142 (2004)
14. Badouel, E.: On the α-Reconstructibility of Workflow Nets. In: Haddad, S., Pomello, L. (eds.) PETRI NETS 2012. LNCS, vol. 7347, pp. 128–147. Springer, Heidelberg (2012)
15. Weidlich, M., van der Werf, J.M.: On Profiles and Footprints – Relational Semantics for Petri Nets. In: Haddad, S., Pomello, L. (eds.) PETRI NETS 2012. LNCS, vol. 7347, pp. 148–167. Springer, Heidelberg (2012)
16. Engelfriet, J.: Branching processes of Petri nets. Acta Informatica 28, 575–591 (1991)
17. van Glabbeek, R., Goltz, U.: Equivalence notions for concurrent systems and refinement of actions.. In: Kreczmar, A., Mirkowska, G. (eds.) MFCS 1989. LNCS, vol. 379, pp. 237–248. Springer, Heidelberg (1989)
18. Armas, A., Baldan, P., Dumas, M., García-Bañuelos, L.: Behavioral comparison of process models based on canonically reduced event structures. Technical report It is, available at, http://math.ut.ee/~abela
19. McKay, B.D.: Practical graph isomorphism. Department of Computer Science, Vanderbilt University (1981)
20. Kant, G.: Using canonical forms for isomorphism reduction in graph-based model checking. Technical report, CTIT University of Twente, Enschede (July 2010)
21. McMillan, K.L., Probst, D.K.: A Technique of State Space Search Based on Unfolding. Formal Methods in System Design 6(1), 45–65 (1995)
22. Esparza, J., Römer, S., Vogler, W.: An Improvement of McMillan's Unfolding Algorithm. Formal Methods in System Design 30(2), 285–310 (2002)
23. Khomenko, W.V., Koutny, M., Vogler: Canonical prefixes of Petri net unfoldings. Acta Informatica 40(2), 95–118 (2003)

Where Did I Go Wrong?
Explaining Errors in Business Process Models

Niels Lohmann[1] and Dirk Fahland[2]

[1] Universität Rostock, Institut für Informatik, 18051 Rostock, Germany
[2] Technische Universiteit Eindhoven, P.O. Box 513, 5600 MB Eindhoven, The Netherlands
`niels.lohmann@uni-rostock.de,d.fahland@tue.nl`

Abstract. Business process modeling is still a challenging task — especially since more and more aspects are added to the models, such as data lifecycles, security constraints, or compliance rules. At the same time, formal methods allow for a detection of errors in the early modeling phase. Detected errors are usually explained with a path from the initial to the error state. These paths can grow unmanageably and make the understanding and fixing of errors very time consuming. This paper addresses this issue and proposes a novel explanation of errors: Instead of listing the actions on the path to the error, only the decisions that lead to it are reported and highlighted in the original model. Furthermore, we exploit concurrency to create a compact artifact to explain errors.

1 Introduction

Business process modeling is a sophisticated task and received a lot of attention in the past decades. With the advent of domain-specific languages and a growing scientific community, the act of creating and managing business process models has become a discipline on its own. Despite all efforts, design flaws may still occur. This can have different impacts, ranging from syntactically incorrect models, which are harder to understand, up to catastrophic faults and down times in the execution that yield to a loss of money or a legal aftermath. Consequently, a large branch of research focuses in the detection, correction, and avoidance of errors in business process models. Whereas plain control flow analysis is now well understood, other aspects such as data, business rules, or security may introduce more subtle flaws that are harder to detect.

The most prominent property of business process models is *soundness* [1], which combines several desirable properties such as proper termination and the absence of deadlocks, livelocks, and dead code. For this fundamental "sanity check", more and more sophisticated techniques and tools have been introduced in the last years. Recent experiments [2] suggest that soundness checks for industrial business process models can be conducted within microseconds. This allows for a tight integration of verification steps into the process of modeling.

Staying with the soundness property, we can classify existing approaches into three classes: (1) Some approaches exploit certain structural constraints of the business process model, for instance by focussing on workflow graphs that only consist of AND/XOR-gateways, for instance [3]. (2) Other approaches rely on the definition of soundness which

S. Sadiq, P. Soffer, and H. Völzer (Eds.): BPM 2014, LNCS 8659, pp. 283–300, 2014.
© Springer International Publishing Switzerland 2014

can be defined in terms of standard Petri net properties such as boundedness, liveness, or the existence of place invariants [4]. The two mentioned approaches are *domain-specific* in the sense that they exploit the fact that they investigate business process models. In contrast, (3) general purpose verification tools (usually called *model checkers* [5,6]) can check all kinds of properties as long as they can be expressed in terms of temporal logics. As this is the case for soundness, these tools are also applicable for the verification of business process models.

By nature, only domain-specific approaches may exploit the special nature of business process models and their correctness criteria are best suited for corresponding verification tasks — in particular, since the approaches are specially tailored to the need of the modelers. In contrast, general purpose verification tools are not "aware" of the background of the property or the model under investigation and hence may only produce results of limited value. At the same time, the ongoing evolution of business process modeling languages, the growing number of aspects that need to be covered by a business process model, or the trend toward executable business process models, makes state-of-the-art business process model verification a moving target. As a consequence, specific approaches may become inapplicable for novel demands, leaving only general purpose approaches as stable tools for the future.

Goal. This paper tries to improve the applicability of general purpose approaches to business process models. We thereby try to combine the advantages of a vast set of supported correctness criteria (and hence, the flexibility to keep up with the fast evolution of novel modeling languages and correctness criteria) with the domain-specific diagnosis results of existing business process verification tools. This paper thereby can be seen as a follow-up to the reports for Fahland et al. [2] where comprehensive diagnosis results where only reported for domain-specific approaches, in particular [3].

Problem description. In principle, a model checker takes a formal model (e.g., a Petri net) and a formal description of the property to check (usually described by temporal logics) as input and tries to proof the property by an exhaustive investigation of the model's states. In case the property is violated (e.g., a deadlocking state is detected), a path to this error state is reported [5,6]. The path contains all actions of the model that need to be executed to reach the error state from the initial state. Due to this operational nature of paths, the scenario that led to the error can be simulated. It is furthermore possible to explain the scenario in terms of the original model; that is, to map the states of the Petri net back to events of a BPMN model.

Unfortunately, the size of the paths correlates with the size of the model and paths of industrial models can thus be very long and hardly understandable. Furthermore, the path can contain a lot of irrelevant or diverting information that makes the comprehension of the error very difficult. For instance, the path usually contains actions that only "set up" the process (e.g., initializations and login procedures). These inevitable actions are certainly *necessary* to be able to reach the error state, but are usually not the *cause* of it. Another aspect that makes paths hard to understand is the fact that business process models may span several components where activities are executed in parallel. On the path, these originally unordered activities are reported in a fixed — and possibly arbitrary — order which may yield confusion due to unintuitive error descriptions.

Contribution. To solve the mentioned problems, this paper makes four contributions. First, we shorten paths by focussing on the choices made rather than on each individual action. Second, we perform additional verification steps to further reduce the path. Third, we exploit the concurrency of the model to undo the aforementioned arbitrary ordering and to express concurrent parts of the error independently of each other. Fourth, we take the investigated property into account to remove aspects of the part which are irrelevant to the detected error. We shall use a large case study as experimental evaluation of our proposed approach.

Organization. The next section introduces the basic concepts we build our approach on, including Petri nets as formal model and a brief introduction to model checking. Section 3 introduces a novel representation of paths by focussing on the made choices. In Sect. 4, we discuss how the path can be further shortened by performing additional verification steps. The combination of paths and concurrency is described in Sect. 5. Section 6 demonstrations how the size of the resulting artifacts can be further reduced. All reduction steps are evaluated by experimental results with more than 1,000 industrial business process models. Finally, Sect. 7 summarizes the results and concludes the paper.

2 Preliminaries

2.1 Petri Nets

Business process modeling languages are usually semiformal and hence are not directly applicable to a mathematically rigorous proof of correctness criteria. However, the operational semantics can be captured in formalisms such as Petri nets or process calculi. With the advent of executable languages such as WS-BPEL 2.0 or BPMN 2.0, such a formalization became much easier, because a precise execution semantics yielded more careful language specifications.

Our framework is based on *Petri nets* [7] and is hence not tied to a specific business process modeling language. In fact, for most of today's languages from industry or academia (including BPMN, WS-BPEL, UML activity diagrams, YAWL, or EPC), translations into Petri nets exists [8]. We chose Petri nets as formalism for two reasons: First, it is a *graphical formalism* that closely resembles languages such as BPMN and allows to easily translate findings from the original model into the Petri net model, and vice versa. Second, *concurrency* (i.e., the independent and yet parallel execution of actions) can be expressed naturally in terms of Petri nets. This is especially helpful as the behavior of a Petri net can be expressed by a set of *distributed runs*, an artifact we shall use in Sect. 5–6 of this paper.

Intuitively, a Petri net is a directed graph, consisting of active components called *transitions* (depicted as squares) which model actions and decisions of business processes and passive components called *places* (depicted as circles) which model locations of resources such as documents, messages, or the current control flow. The flow of resources is modeled by arcs between places and transitions, and vice versa. A state of a Petri net is expressed by a distribution of tokens (depicted by black dots) on the places (called a *marking*) which models the current presence of the respective resource. Formally:

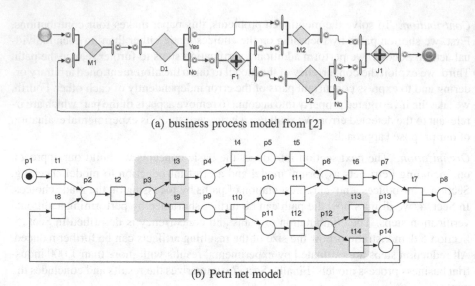

(a) business process model from [2]

(b) Petri net model

Fig. 1. A business process model (a) and its translation into a Petri net (b)

Definition 1 (Petri net). *A Petri net is a tuple* $N = [P, T, F, m_0]$ *where* P *is finite a set of places,* T *is finite a set of transitions* $(T \cap P \neq \emptyset)$, *a flow relation* $F \subseteq (P \times T) \cup (T \times P)$, *and an initial marking* $m_0 : P \rightarrow \mathbb{N}$.

Example. Figure 1(a) depicts a small business process model from [2] which contains two subtle control flow errors: a lack of synchronization and a local deadlock. Its translation into a Petri net is shown in Fig. 1(b). As we see, the structure is very similar to the original model. The concrete mapping from the models from [2] into Petri nets is described in [9].

The initial marking m_0 defines an initial distribution of tokens on the places. The marking can change by *firing* transitions.

Definition 2 (Firing rule). *Let* $N = [P, T, F, m_0]$ *be a Petri net,* $t \in T$ *be a transition, and* $m : P \rightarrow \mathbb{N}$ *be a marking of* N. *Transition* t *is* activated *in* m *(denoted* $m \xrightarrow{t}$) *iff* $m(p) > 0$ *for all* $p \in {}^\bullet t$. *An activated transition can* fire, *yielding a new marking* m' *(denoted* $m \xrightarrow{t} m'$) *with*

$$m'(p) = \begin{cases} m(p) + 1, & \text{iff } p \in t^\bullet \setminus {}^\bullet t, \\ m(p) - 1, & \text{iff } p \in {}^\bullet t \setminus t^\bullet, \\ m(p), & \text{otherwise.} \end{cases}$$

Thereby, let for a node $x \in P \cup T$ *be* ${}^\bullet x = \{y \mid [y, x] \in F\}$ *the* preset *of* x *and* $x^\bullet = \{y \mid [x, y] \in F\}$ *be the* postset *of* x.

The behavior of a Petri net is defined by the *reachability graph* which has all reachable markings as nodes, m_0 as initial node, and a t-labeled edge between node m and

m' iff $m \xrightarrow{t} m'$. The reachability graph is a very versatile tool when investigating the behavior of Petri net models as all interesting properties of Petri nets can be checked using this reachability graph. This includes the most prominent correctness criteria for business process models such as soundness.

2.2 Model Checking

Model checking [5,6] is an approach to proof that a system satisfied a given correctness criterion; for instance soundness, the absence of a deadlocking state, the presence of a sound process configuration, correct data life cycles, or compliance to business rules. In contrast to *theorem provers*, which sometimes need the manual inputs, or *testing*, which can only proof the existence of errors, but never their absence, model checking is an automated and complete way to investigate systems.

In this paper, we assume that the model under investigation is given as a Petri net. The correctness criterion is typically motivated by the domain of the original model (i.e., a business process). For an automated check, this correctness criterion needs to be expressed in terms of a *temporal logics*. Temporal logics extend classical propositional logics by temporal operators that express the relationships of propositions (i.e., that a state B is reached *after* state A is reached) and path quantifiers that express whether some or all successors of a state need to satisfy a property. The most prominent temporal logics used in model checking is CTL*. We refrain from a formal definition, as we shall concentrate on the evaluation of errors in incorrect systems rather than in the correctness criteria and their formalization themselves. Detailed introductions provide [5,6].

For the remainder of the paper, we assume the existence of a model checking tool that takes a Petri net N and a temporal logical formula φ as input. If the formula is satisfied by the Petri net (e.g., if the Petri net is sound), this is reported as "yes" to the modeler. In case the formula is violated (e.g., a deadlocking marking m is found), this is reported as "no" to the modeler. In addition, a path $\pi = t_1 \cdots t_n$ is given to the modeler which explains how m is reachable from the initial marking m_0; that is, $m_0 \xrightarrow{t_1} \cdots \xrightarrow{t_n} m$. Depending on the nature of the formula φ, the marking reached by the reported path either is a proof that the formula is not satisfied by the behavior of the Petri net N and is called a *counterexample* or marking itself is the proof that the formula is satisfied (e.g., if φ expresses the reachability of that marking m) and is called a *witness*. In this paper, we do not distinguish the semantics of the marking m and always refer to m as *goal marking*.

Example (cont.). The business process from Fig. 1(a) has a lack of synchronization. This can be detected by checking the Petri net from Fig. 1(b). The following path π describes how a marking m can be reached which puts two tokens on place p_6.

$$\pi = t_1\, t_2\, t_9\, t_{10}\, t_{11}\, t_{12}\, t_{14}\, t_8\, t_2\, t_3\, t_4\, t_5 \qquad m = \{p_6 \mapsto 2\}$$

The path contains 12 transitions. In the remainder of this paper, we use this path to exemplify the proposed reductions.

It is worthwhile to mention that model checking suffers a devastating worst case complexity due to the well-known state explosion problem which yields reachability graphs with exponential blow-ups compared to the size of the Petri nets. However, even industrial business process models can be model checked in few microseconds, because heuristics that fight the state space explosion proved to be very effective in this domain [2].

3   Representing Paths by Made Choices

3.1   The Problem: Long Paths = Big Problems

In the remainder of the paper, we focus on the following problem:

> Given a path π to a goal marking m of a Petri net model N, how can the reason for the error modeled by m be briefly and comprehensively explained to the modeler of N?

Apparently, π describes how the goal marking m can be reached from the initial marking m_0 of N. Consequently, reporting the transitions of π together with the intermediated markings to the modeler should help to understand the reasons m was reached. Unfortunately, this approach is futile in case π contains dozens of transitions. The reasons for such long paths are:

Detours: Model checkers usually investigate the markings of a Petri net in a depth first search. As a result, the reported paths do not need to be optimal and may contain some transitions that model "detours" in the reachability graph that do not contribute in the actual reaching of the goal marking. Note that breadth-first approaches are not applicable to many classes of formulae.

Interleaving of concurrent transitions: A marking of N may activate two transitions t_1 and t_2 which are not mutually exclusive. That is, firing either transition first does not disable the other one. A typical reason for this is that t_1 and t_2 do not share any resources. Consequently, the order in which t_1 and t_2 occur on the path π is arbitrary. If each transition belongs to different components of the underlying business process model, then these arbitrary interleaving of the transitions may be irritating to the modeler if she tries to understand the path π. In the example path, transition t_{11} and t_{12} are concurrent and the reported order in path π (t_{11} before t_{12}) is arbitrary.

Indisputable parts: Though the path π is an actual proof *that* the goal marking m can be reached in N, not every transition on the path is an actual cause of m. In the example process, *any* path will begin with firing t_1 and hence does not need to be reported to the modeler as reason for an error.

3.2   The Solution: Don't Report the Obvious

To tackle the problem of long paths with redundant or unhelpful information, we shall exploit two aspects to shorten paths in the remainder of this chapter: *progress* and *conflicts*.

Progress is the assumption that the model never "gets stuck" in case a transition is activated. That is, if a marking activates one or more transitions, then this marking is eventually left by firing on of these transitions. Progress is a natural assumption for business process models in which the execution of tasks also cannot be postponed indefinitely. Though the actual occurrence of message or timer events cannot be precisely predicted, the respective states are always assumed to be eventually left by the modeled actions.

A *conflict* is a situation in which there exist more than one possible continuations. In terms of Petri nets, it is a marking in which two transitions t_1 and t_2 are enabled, but after firing either of them, the other transition is disabled. This situation is dual to concurrent transitions (see above) that do not disable each other. A detailed discussion of these aspects can be found in [7].

The combination of these aspects brings us to the following intuitive observation: *Only the conflicts on the path π carry information on how to reach the goal markings.* Any other marking m on the path between the initial and the goal marking either (1) enables no transition: Then this must be the goal marking itself, because it has no successor marking. Alternatively, (2) marking m enables exactly one transition: Then this transition is eventually fired due to the assumption of progress. Consequently, this transition does not need to be reported to the modeler as its firing was already determined by the previous transition on π thad lead to m. Finally, (3) marking m enables several concurrent transitions. These transitions may fire independently, and if all of them are on π, then the exact order is arbitrary.

In the remainder of this section, we shall give a formal definition of conflicts and sketch an algorithm to reduce paths based on these conflicts. Finally, we shall report on experimental results applying this algorithm to thousands of business processes. We shall first formalize a conflict:

Definition 3 (Conflict marking, conflict transition). *Let m be a marking with $m \xrightarrow{t_1}$ and $m \xrightarrow{t_2}$. Marking m is a conflict marking and t_1 and t_2 are conflict transitions iff (1) $m \xrightarrow{t_1} m_1$, (2) $m \xrightarrow{t_2} m_2$, and (3) $m_1 \xarrownot\xrightarrow{t_2}$ or $m_2 \xarrownot\xrightarrow{t_1}$.*

The above definition relies on markings. However, conflict transitions can be approximated using the structure of the Petri net. Intuitively, transitions may be conflict transitions if they share a place in their presets. Desel and Esparza [10] extended this observation toward a decomposition of a Petri net into its *conflict clusters*.

Definition 4 (Conflict cluster). *Let $x \in P \cup T$ be a node of a Petri net. The conflict cluster of x, denoted $[x]$ is the minimal set of nodes such that: (1) $x \in [x]$. (2) If $p \in P$ and $p \in [x]$, then $p^\bullet \subseteq [x]$. (3) If $t \in T$ and $t \in [x]$, then $^\bullet t \subseteq [x]$.*

The conflict clusters of a Petri net can be determined by a union-find-algorithm with effectively constant amortized time complexity.

Note that *free-choice Petri nets* [10] have the following property: If one transition in a conflict cluster is activated in a marking m, then m activates *all* transitions of that conflict cluster. That is, an additional check is not required. However, not all aspects of business process models can be formalized using free-choice Petri nets, for instance errors, complex gateways, or timeouts. To this end, we decided not to constrain our approach to this class of Petri nets, but to make it applicable to arbitrary Petri nets. However, checking whether a transition is activated given a concrete marking has linear complexity in the size of the net and can usually be assumed to be constant as transitions hardly have all places in their preset, but only a very small subset.

Now we can reduce the path π as follows:

1. Calculate the conflict clusters of N.
2. For each transition t of π activated by a marking m reached by a (possibly empty) prefix of π: Report t as part of the reduced path if and only if t is a conflict transition; that is, if and only if $\{t' \in T \mid t' \in [t] \ \wedge \ m \xrightarrow{t'}\} \neq \{t\}$.

We discuss the implementation of this algorithm in Sect. 7.

Example (cont.). The conflict clusters with more than one transition of our running example are shaded gray in Fig. 1(b): transitions t_3 and t_9, as well as t_{13} and t_{14} are conflicting. Consequently, we can reduce the path π as follows:

$$\pi_{reduced} = t_9 \ t_{14} \ t_3 \qquad m = \{p_6 \mapsto 2\}$$

The firing of all other transitions is clear from the context from the intermediate markings and the assumption of progress. Note that the transition names need to be translated back into the terms of the original model. A different representation of $\pi_{reduced}$ could be: "After (1) decision D1: *No*, (2) decision D2: *No*, and (3) decision D1: *Yes*, a lack of synchronization occurs after after merge M2."

3.3   Experimental Results

To evaluate the path reduction algorithm, we applied it to a large collection of industrial process models created by IBM customers using the *IBM WebSphere Business Modeler*. The models were first presented in a report by Fahland et al. [2], where the 1386 process models were checked for soundness using different approaches. As one general-purpose model checker, *LoLA* [11], took part in this investigation, the process models were also translated into Petri nets.[1] The models are partitioned into five libraries (A, B1, B2, B3, C) and stem from different business areas, ranging from financial services, automotive, telecommunications, construction, supply chain, health care, and customer relationship management.

Soundness. Using these models, we repeated the soundness checks to created paths for those Petri nets with unsound behavior. In the original report [2], each Petri net was checked twice to proof soundness: once for weak termination (i.e., whether the final marking is reachable from every reachable marking) to rule out *local deadlocks* and once for unsafe markings (i.e., whether a marking m is reachable with $m(p) > 1$ for a place p) to rule out *lack of synchronization*.

---

[1] The original models and their Petri net translations are available for download at http://service-technology.org/soundness.

Table 1. Paths from the checks for local deadlocks

library	A	B1	B2	B3	C
avg. path length before / after	17.51 / 1.83	17.52 / 2.11	16.06 / 1.54	20.34 / 1.67	13.40 / 2.30
max. path length before / after	53 / 8	66 / 7	56 / 6	54 / 5	21 / 3
sum of path lengths before / after	1699 / 178	1419 / 171	1349 / 129	1688 / 139	134 / 23
reduction	89.52 %	87.95 %	90.44 %	91.77 %	82.84 %

Table 2. Paths from the checks for lack of synchronization

library	A	B1	B2	B3	C
avg. path length before / after	30.83 / 3.17	10.47 / 0.66	12.16 / 0.68	11.50 / 0.59	51.00 / 7.57
max. path length before / after	89 / 13	52 / 7	100 / 8	103 / 14	120 / 17
sum of path lengths before / after	1079 / 111	1047 / 66	1459 / 82	1507 / 77	357 / 53
reduction	89.71 %	93.70 %	94.38 %	94.89 %	85.15 %

Table 3. Paths from the checks for noninterference

library	A	B1	B2	B3	C
avg. path length before / after	12.06 / 2.79	13.82 / 2.55	18.13 / 2.33	14.27 / 2.55	11.27 / 2.33
max. path length before / after	44 / 7	70 / 7	95 / 7	95 / 7	27 / 3
sum of path lengths before / after	19699 / 4557	5707 / 1054	13835 / 1777	17494 / 3130	169 / 35
reduction	76.87 %	81.53 %	87.16 %	82.11 %	79.29 %

From the 1386 models, 642 control-flow errors were found — 355 Petri nets were not weakly terminating and 393 Petri nets contained unsafe markings.[2] Consequently, we could apply our reduction to 748 paths.

Table 1 summarizes the results from the reduction of the paths for Petri nets with local deadlocks. We list, for each library, the average path length, the maximal path length, and the sum of all path lengths for the respective library — once before and once after the reduction. The numbers suggest that the reduction is very effective: The average path length could be reduced from 13–20 transitions to 1.5–2.3 transitions. This means a reduction of 82–91 %.

Table 2 reports similar results for Petri nets with a lack of synchronization. In summary, the longest path for a soundness violation contains at most 17 transitions, compared to 120 before the reduction.

Information Flow Security. Furthermore, the same business process models were used in a recent report [12] on information flow security. In this case study, *noninterference* [13] was verified. This correctness criterion ensures that decisions from a secure domain cannot be reproduced by investigating public runtime information of the business process. To perform this check, each business process model needed to be checked several times: For each participant (i.e., swimlane of the process), one check is required. In that case study, 4050 errors were reported, yielding 4050 paths to investigate.[3]

---

[2] 24 Petri nets had both kind of errors and hence failed both checks.

[3] The original models were not designed with noninterference in mind. However, the authors of [12] decided to use the processes from [2] as case study to investigate their algorithms.

Table 3 summarizes the reduction results for the paths. Again, we can report a reduction between 76–87 %. The maximal reduced path of the whole case study consists only of 7 transitions, whereas it was 95 transitions before the reduction. On average, not more than 2.79 transitions are reported per detected error.

The experiments report promising results. Though the reduced paths consist of Petri net transitions, they can be easily translated back into the nomenclature of the original model. For each model translated from the IBM WebSphere Business Modeler into a Petri net, a file was created that maps the Petri net nodes to a construct of the original model, see [9]. Consequently, conflict transitions can be easily linked to the respective gateways.

4 Further Reduction: Remove Spurious Conflicts

4.1 Motivation and Formalization

In the previous section, we showed how paths to errors in business process models can be reduced by only reporting conflict transitions. This reduction decided, for each marking that activates a transition, whether conflicting transitions are also activated. This check is local in the sense that it is not checked whether those transitions that were not taken in the decisions actually could have avoided the next conflict transition on the path.

We can formalize this idea as follows:

Definition 5 (Spurious conflict). *Let $\pi = t_1 \cdots t_n$ be a reduced path and, for $0 \leq i < n$ be m_i the marking that is reached from m_0 by firing the first i transitions of π. In marking m_i, transition t_i is a spurious conflict iff, for all $t \in [t_i] \cap T$ with $t \neq t_i$ and $m_i \overset{t}{\rightarrow}$ holds: $m_i \overset{t}{\rightarrow} m'_i$ and for all paths beginning with m'_i, marking m_{i+1} is eventually reached, activating the next conflict transition t_{i+1} on π.*

Intuitively, a transition t_i on a reduced path π is a spurious conflict iff every transition t in conflict to t_i eventually reaches the marking m_{i+1} which enables the next transition t_{i+1} on path π. In this case, choosing any transition from the conflict cluster $[t_i]$ will eventually enable the next conflict on the path to the goal state. Consequently, reporting the spurious conflict t_i is of little help to the modeler to understand the error itself.

The check for spurious transitions defined above can be straightforwardly be implemented using a model checker.[4] We integrated this check as postprocessing step after reducing the paths as described in the previous section. Note that executing a model checker can be very time and memory consuming. However, even if a check is not finished with a reasonable amount of resources, we just failed to proof whether a conflict is spurious and can continue with the investigation of the next transition. That said, the postpocessing can be aborted at any time — any intermediate result is still correct.

---

[4] We check whether N with initial marking m'_i satisfies the CTL formula $\varphi = \mathbf{AF}\, m_{i+1}$.

Table 4. Reduced paths from the checks for local deadlocks

library	A	B1	B2	B3	C
avg. path length before / after	1.84 / 0.91	2.11 / 0.67	1.54 / 0.57	1.67 / 0.41	2.30 / 0.90
max. path length before / after	8 / 2	7 / 1	6 / 1	5 / 1	3 / 1
sum of path lengths before / after	178 / 88	171 / 54	129 / 49	139 / 34	23 / 10
reduction	50.56 %	68.42 %	62.79 %	75.54 %	60.87 %
aborted checks	1	0	0	0	0

Table 5. Reduced paths from the checks for lack of synchronization

library	A	B1	B2	B3	C
avg. path length before / after	3.17 / 0.86	0.66 / 0.17	0.68 / 0.14	0.59 / 0.09	7.57 / 1.00
max. path length before / after	13 / 2	7 / 2	8 / 2	14 / 2	17 / 2
sum of path lengths before / after	111 / 30	66 / 17	82 / 17	72 / 12	53 / 7
reduction	72.97 %	54.55 %	79.27 %	84.42 %	86.79 %
aborted checks	1	4	0	0	4

Table 6. Reduced paths from the checks for noninterference

library	A	B1	B2	B3	C
avg. path length before / after	2.79 / 0.99	2.55 / 0.75	2.33 / 0.55	2.55 / 0.63	2.33 / 0.40
max. path length before / after	7 / 2	7 / 2	7 / 2	7 / 2	3 / 1
sum of path lengths before / after	4557 / 1614	1054 / 310	1777 / 423	3130 / 772	35 / 6
reduction	64.58 %	70.59 %	76.20 %	75.34 %	82.86 %
aborted checks	12	4	4	7	0

4.2 Experimental Results

We applied the reduction of spurious conflicts to the case studies described in the previous section. Table 4.2–5 summarize the results. In all three experiments, the paths could be *further* reduced by 50–86%. Now, in all experiments, at most two transitions are reported as to reach the error. All other transitions are either nonconflicting or are spurious conflicts for which *any* resolution eventually reaches the next conflict on the path. Note that in some cases, the check for spurious conflicts has been aborted after more than 2 GB of memory were consumed. In these cases, the conflict was kept in the path and the check proceeded with the next conflict.

5 Combining Paths and Concurrency

5.1 Motivation and Formalization

So far, we focused on reducing paths by removing any transitions whose firing provides no information to the modeler on why the goal state was actually reached. Thereby, we could exploit the Petri net structure to calculate conflict clusters to identify possible conflict transitions. This allowed for a quick check whether a transition is actually a conflict.

However, we still considered paths as a *sequences* of transitions leading to the goal state. As discussed earlier, this sequence may be an arbitrary linearization of originally concurrent behavior. Therefore, communicating paths to the modeler — for instance by means of animation or simulation — still uses this arbitrary and hence unintuitive ordering. This may be especially confusing if the underlying process spans several components (e.g., participants of a choreography or lanes) and the path constantly switches between actions of different components.

To this end, this section aims at exploiting the concurrency of the Petri net model and to use it to reorganize paths. We thereby try to undo the arbitrary ordering and to provide partially-ordered paths, called *distributed runs* in the literature [7]. As sketched earlier, two transitions t_1 and t_2 may fire concurrently in a marking if they do not disable each other; that is, any ordering of t_1 and t_2 are possible. The definition of Petri nets further ensure that firing any order of concurrent transitions yield the same marking. This has one interesting effect: by depicting concurrent transitions as concurrent (i.e., unordered), a distributed run implicitly expresses all possible orderings of these transitions.

Before we continue, we formalize the concept of a distributed run. The underlying structure of such a distributed run is a *causal net*:

Definition 6 (Causal net). *A causal net is a Petri net $C = [P, T, F]$ without initial marking such that (1) for each place p holds: $|{}^\bullet p| \leq 1$ and $|p^\bullet| \leq 1$, (2) the transitive closure F^+ of the flow relation F is irreflexive, and (3) any node has only finitely many predecessors with respect to F^+.*

Intuitively, a causal net is (1) conflict free and begins and ends with places, (2) is acyclic, and (3) the prefix of any element is finite. A causal net does not have an initial marking — its places with empty preset represent initially marked places. This becomes clear in the definition of a distributed run of a Petri net N, defined as follows:

Definition 7 (Distributed run). *Let $N = [P_N, T_N, F_N, m_0]$ be a Petri net, $C = [P_C, T_C, F_C]$ be a causal net, and $\beta \subseteq (P_C \times P_N) \cup (T_C \times T_N)$ be a mapping. Further assume, without any loss of generality, that $m_0(p) \leq 1$ for all $p \in P_N$. The pair $[C, \beta]$ is a distributed run of N iff: (1) for all $p_C \in P_C$ with ${}^\bullet p_C = \emptyset$ holds: $m_0(\beta(p_C)) = 1$ and (2) for each $t_C \in T_C$ with $\beta(t_C) = t_N$ holds: β bijectively maps ${}^\bullet t_C$ to ${}^\bullet t_N$ and $t_C^\bullet$ to $t_N^\bullet$.*

A distributed run is a causal net C whose nodes are mapped to those of a Petri net, such that (1) those places of C without predecessors map to the initially marked places of N and (2) the preset and postset of a transition of C bijectively maps to the preset and postset of the respective transition of N.

5.2 Translating Paths into Distributed Runs

Intuitively, we can translate a path into a distributed run by copying fired transitions with their preset and postset to the distributed run and "glue" those places representing resources created by one transition and consumed by another transition.

In more detail, a path π of a Petri net N can be translated into a distributed run $[C, \beta]$ as follows: First, add, for each initially marked place p_N of N, a place p_C to P_C and define $\beta(p_C) = p_N$. Then, for each firing $m \xrightarrow{t_N} m'$ in π, (1) add a transition t_C to T_C and define $\beta(t_C) = t_N$, (2) for each place $p_N \in {}^\bullet t_N$, find a place p_C of C with

Fig. 2. The path π as a distributed run with highlighted conflict transitions

$\beta(p_C) = p_N$ and $p_C^\bullet = \emptyset$ and add an arc $[p_C, t_C]$ to F_C, and (3) for each place $p_N \in t_N^\bullet$ add a place p_C to P_C and define $\beta(p_C) = p_N$ and add an arc $[t_C, p_C]$ to F_C.

As paths are acyclic, the created distributed run is finite by definition. Furthermore, paths are conflict-free (i.e., every intermediate marking has exactly one successor) such that the created Petri net structure is indeed a causal net.

The translation into a distributed run now allows for a reasoning of the relationship between occurrences of transitions on the path. We distinguish two cases: On the one hand, if there is a directed path between t_1 and t_2, then $\beta(t_1)$ was fired *causally before* $\beta(t_2)$. On the other hand, $\beta(t_1)$ and $\beta(t_2)$ were fired *concurrently*, if there exists neither a path from t_1 to t_2 nor from t_2 to t_1. In this case, the order on path π was arbitrary and should not be reported as such to the modeler.

Example (cont.). Figure 2 depicts path π as distributed run. Note that the cycle in the model is unfolded, yielding two copies of transition t_2. Two places p_6 without successors model the target marking $\{p_6 \mapsto 2\}$. Furthermore, note transition t_{11} is displayed concurrently to all transitions following t_{10}.

5.3 Applying the Conflict Reduction to Distributed Runs

We implemented the translation of paths into distributed runs. This construction algorithm only works for unreduced paths, because it requires that all intermediate markings are used to create places in the underlying causal net. Therefore, the reduction reported in Sect. 3–4 are not directly applicable.

To combine the advantages of both approaches — that is, reducing paths by removing nonconflicting transitions on the one hand and not ordering concurrent transitions on the other hand — we exploit the two relationships (causal order and concurrency) from above and create an artifact (called *reduced distributed run*[5]) with the following properties:

1. For each initially marked place of N, it contains a place with empty preset and the respective labeling.
2. For each place marked by the goal marking reached by π, it contains a place with empty postset and the respective labeling.
3. For each conflict transition (i.e., transitions that were not removed by the reductions in Sect. 3–4), it contains a transition with the respective labeling.
4. For each transition consuming a token from the initial marking or producing a token to the goal marking, it contains a transition with the respective labeling and the respective arcs to the places in the preset and postset.

---

[5] In fact, the described artifact is not a distributed run. Though it shares properties of distributed runs, we decided to stick to the name as it is most intuitive.

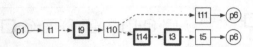

Fig. 3. The reduced path π as a reduced distributed run with highlighted conflict transitions

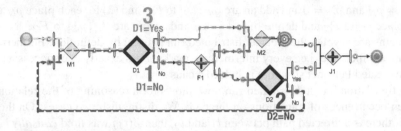

Fig. 4. Mapping back the reduced distributed run to the original process model

5. For each two transitions t_1 and t_2, add a dashed arc $[t_1, t_2]$ if we can derive from the distributed run that t_1 is causally before t_2.
6. Transitively reduce the dashed arcs; that is, remove all dashed arcs $[t_1, t_3]$ for which there exists arcs $[t_1, t_2]$ and $[t_2, t_3]$.

As reduced distributed runs have more or less the same size as the reduced paths, we refrain from a detailed discussion of a case study.

Example (cont.). An example is depicted in Fig. 3. It explains how the initial marking $\{p_1 \mapsto 1\}$ is transformed into the goal marking $\{p_6 \mapsto 2\}$. In case a transition consumes from the initial marking or produces to the goal marking, it is reported explicitly. Furthermore, the resolved conflicts on the original path π are reported, and their causal order is depicted by dashed arcs. Figure 4 further depicts an example how the information of a reduced distributed run can be used for a visualization of a path in a concrete business process model.

6   Cropping Distributed Runs

This section introduces a further reduction for distributed runs, that can be combined to reduced distributed runs as described in the previous section. We shall first concentrate on unreduced distributed runs.

When a path π is translated into a distributed run, it is a precise description on how the initial marking is translated into the target marking. However, usually only a parametrized description of the target marking is given to the model checker, for instance a formula expressing "Find a marking m such that $m(p) > 1$ for a any place p." in case of checking the absence of lack of synchronization. In case a goal marking m is found that does mark a place with more than one token, then m usually also marks other places of the Petri net. These places are, however, not relevant to the proof that unsafe markings are reachable in the Petri net. Therefore, it would be of more value if the distributed run could be "cropped" such that it only contains those places and transitions in the prefix of the unsafe places.

As each node of a causal net only has finitely many predecessors, the cropped prefix of a set of nodes is well-defined. Any other nodes that are not on this prefix can be removed. The result is still a causal net, but violates the definition of a distributed run. For the sake of a uniform nomenclature, we refer to this artifact as *cropped distributed run*. Note that reduced distributed runs can be cropped as well, producing *cropped reduced distributed runs*.

Which places are used to crop the distributed run depends on the property under investigation. We gave a straightforward example for the check for lack of synchronization. For the noninterference check, the marking of a specific goal place signals a security flaw — consequently, this place can be used to crop the distributed run. For local deadlocks, this choice is not straightforward, because the final marking of the Petri net is actually unreachable in the reported goal marking. A starting point to crop distributed runs is subject of future research.

7 Concluding Remarks

7.1 Summary

In this paper, we investigated how the output of model checking tools — usually a path from the initial state to a state modeling an error — can be briefly and comprehensively explained to the modeler. We presented four reductions — each focussing on a different aspect of the problem:

1. In Sect. 3, we removed all transitions whose firing is totally determined by the current marking, because there are no activated conflict transitions. As a result, we explain errors not by the complete path from the initial to the goal state, but only explain which choices on the way lead to the goal state.
2. In Sect. 4, we further removed those choices where any continuation eventually reaches the next choice on the path. This postprocessing step required additional verification runs which can be stopped at any time without jeopardizing correctness. Though the reduction seems technical, it is actually very effective in the investigated case study.
3. The underlying concurrency of the model was exploited in Sect. 5. There, we create a distributed run from the path in which concurrent transitions are not any more artificially ordered. We further demonstrated how distributed runs can be combined with the previous reductions.
4. A final reduction is presented in Sect. 6: The verification problem usually concentrates on few places of the Petri net. Distributed runs allow to remove all aspects that are irrelevant to the goal marking.

All reported reductions were implemented in a tool *Pathify* which bases on the *Petri Net API* [14] to calculate conflict clusters and can process Petri nets and paths from the *LoLA* model checking tool [11]. The tool, together with the Petri nets from the case studies can be downloaded from http://www.pirat.ly/25wg2.

Note that our approach heavily relies on Petri nets and their concise semantics, a natural expression of concurrency and conflict relation, efficient algorithms, and a notion of distributed runs. These features are not available by other formalisms or modeling languages. At the same time, we are not bound to a specific input modeling language as most business process modeling languages can be translated into Petri nets.

7.2 Related Work

The analysis and verification of business process models is a broad field of research. Consequently, there exists a variety of domain-specific approaches (e.g., the decomposition of workflow graphs into SESE regions to check soundness [3]). However, we are not aware of other approaches that postprocess error information from general purpose model checkers to explain these errors to the modelers. In particular, most approaches consider only a subset of the modeling language's features (e.g., BPMN without fault handling). In contrast, our presented approach is applicable to any verification approach that produces witness paths.

Related to the presentation of error information is the automated correction of flawed business process models [15,16]. These approaches use similarity metrics to find a correct business process model which maximally resembles the flawed model. These approaches have the benefit of avoiding lengthy manual correction steps altogether.

Back annotation of execution sequences. The problem studied in this paper is similar to *model-based analysis* in Software Engineering which is the problem of translating a (high-level) domain model (of a generic software system) into a formal model and analyzing for various properties and problems [17]. Also there, the open problem is to make the analysis result obtained on the formal level understandable by a domain expert [18]. One generic approach to relate traces of the formal model to model elements of the domain model is *back annotation* [19]. Here, the model transformation from domain model to formal model is reversed to translate steps of the formal model to steps or elements of the domain model. However, mismatches in granularity and semantics complicate the translation from one to another, requiring customized solution for each case. The technique proposed in this paper is orthogonal: rather than trying to translate entire traces, we have shown that the diagnostic information of the formal trace can be reduced to an essential minimum which is easier to map. Though a systematic integration with the back annotation approach is left open here.

This paper considered traces generated by verification and validation tools from given models. Process mining considers traces recording the actual process execution. Here, *conformance checking* is the problem of detecting how and where traces deviate from process models [20]. Deviations can be highlighted on the traces and the process model directly [21]. Also, branching processes of Petri nets can be used to greatly simplify process models in *process discovery* [22]. It is an open question whether the reduction techniques presented in this paper can used to improve the diagnostic information in conformance checking and results in process mining.

7.3 Future Work

In this paper, we focused on reducing paths to error states and neglected the retranslation into the original business process model. Visualizations such as Fig. 4, possibly enriched with animations, need to be automatized and evaluated by business process modelers. Here, understandability criteria [23] could be of great value. However, this was out of scope of this paper which aimed at evaluating the idea of using conflicts to reduce paths with three experimental setups checking different correctness criteria with thousands of industrial business process models.

Beside better visualizations, also the investigation of further correctness criteria is a direction of future work. In particular the cropping of distributed runs appears to be a promising approach to help the modeler focus on the original causes of an error. Another aspect of this investigation is a better localization of errors — in particular, any behavior where the avoidance of an error is still possible should be left out, allowing to better spot the action or decision in the model that makes the error inevitable.

We see in this paper a first step toward a diagnosis framework which uses general purpose verification tools to verify business process models. As motivated in the introduction, domain-specific approaches are very closely coupled to the structure or the property under investigation, but may become inapplicable for future developments. In contrast, the modularization (a translation into Petri nets as frontend, a general purpose model checking tool as middleware, and a diagnosis framework as backend) may be more flexible when it comes to novel business process languages and properties.

References

1. van der Aalst, W.M.P.: The application of Petri nets to workflow management. Journal of Circuits, Systems and Computers 8(1), 21–66 (1998)
2. Fahland, D., Favre, C., Jobstmann, B., Koehler, J., Lohmann, N., Völzer, H., Wolf, K.: Instantaneous soundness checking of industrial business process models. In: Dayal, U., Eder, J., Koehler, J., Reijers, H.A. (eds.) BPM 2009. LNCS, vol. 5701, pp. 278–293. Springer, Heidelberg (2009)
3. Vanhatalo, J., Völzer, H., Leymann, F.: Faster and more focused control-flow analysis for business process models through SESE decomposition. In: Krämer, B.J., Lin, K.-J., Narasimhan, P. (eds.) ICSOC 2007. LNCS, vol. 4749, pp. 43–55. Springer, Heidelberg (2007)
4. Verbeek, H.M.W., Basten, T., van der Aalst, W.M.P.: Diagnosing workflow processes using Woflan. Comput. J. 44(4), 246–279 (2001)
5. Clarke, E.M., Grumberg, O., Peled, D.A.: Model Checking. MIT Press (1999)
6. Baier, C., Katoen, J.: Principles of Model Checking. MIT Press (2008)
7. Reisig, W.: Petri Nets. EATCS Monographs on Theoretical Computer Science edn. Springer (1985)
8. Lohmann, N., Verbeek, E., Dijkman, R.: Petri net transformations for business processes – A survey. In: Jensen, K., van der Aalst, W.M.P. (eds.) Transactions on Petri Nets and Other Models of Concurrency II. LNCS, vol. 5460, pp. 46–63. Springer, Heidelberg (2009)
9. Fahland, D.: Translating UML2 activity diagrams to Petri nets. Informatik-Berichte 226, Humboldt-Universität zu Berlin, Berlin, Germany (2008)
10. Desel, J., Esparza, J.: Free Choice Petri Nets. Cambridge University Press (1995)
11. Wolf, K.: Generating petri net state spaces. In: Kleijn, J., Yakovlev, A. (eds.) ICATPN 2007. LNCS, vol. 4546, pp. 29–42. Springer, Heidelberg (2007)

12. Accorsi, R., Lehmann, A.: Automatic information flow analysis of business process models. In: Barros, A., Gal, A., Kindler, E. (eds.) BPM 2012. LNCS, vol. 7481, pp. 172–187. Springer, Heidelberg (2012)
13. Busi, N., Gorrieri, R.: Structural non-interference in elementary and trace nets. Mathematical Structures in Computer Science 19(6), 1065–1090 (2009)
14. Lohmann, N., Mennicke, S., Sura, C.: The Petri Net API: A collection of Petri net-related functions. In: AWPN, CEUR Workshop Proceedings 643, CEUR-WS.org, pp. 148–155 (2010)
15. Lohmann, N.: Correcting deadlocking service choreographies using a simulation-based graph edit distance. In: Dumas, M., Reichert, M., Shan, M.-C. (eds.) BPM 2008. LNCS, vol. 5240, pp. 132–147. Springer, Heidelberg (2008)
16. Gambini, M., La Rosa, M., Migliorini, S., ter Hofstede, A.: Automated error correction of business process models. In: Rinderle-Ma, S., Toumani, F., Wolf, K. (eds.) BPM 2011. LNCS, vol. 6896, pp. 148–165. Springer, Heidelberg (2011)
17. Bondavalli, A., Cin, M.D., Latella, D., Majzik, I., Pataricza, A., Savoia, G.: Dependability analysis in the early phases of uml-based system design. Comput. Syst. Sci. Eng. 16(5), 265–275 (2001)
18. Csertán, G., Huszerl, G., Majzik, I., Pap, Z., Pataricza, A., Varró, D.: VIATRA - visual automated transformations for formal verification and validation of uml models. In: ASE 2002, pp. 267–270. IEEE Computer Society (2002)
19. Hegedüs, Á., Bergmann, G., Ráth, I., Varró, D.: Back-annotation of simulation traces with change-driven model transformations. In: SEFM 2010, pp. 145–155. IEEE Computer Society (2010)
20. van der Aalst, W.M.P.: Process Mining - Discovery, Conformance and Enhancement of Business Processes. Springer (2011)
21. van der Aalst, W.M.P., Adriansyah, A., van Dongen, B.F.: Replaying history on process models for conformance checking and performance analysis. Wiley Interdisc. Rew.: Data Mining and Knowledge Discovery 2(2), 182–192 (2012)
22. Fahland, D., van der Aalst, W.M.P.: Simplifying discovered process models in a controlled manner. Inf. Syst. 38(4), 585–605 (2013)
23. Mendling, J., Reijers, H.A., Cardoso, J.: What makes process models understandable? In: Alonso, G., Dadam, P., Rosemann, M. (eds.) BPM 2007. LNCS, vol. 4714, pp. 48–63. Springer, Heidelberg (2007)

User-Friendly Property Specification and Process Verification – A Case Study with Vehicle-Commissioning Processes

Richard Mrasek[1], Jutta Mülle[1], Klemens Böhm[1],
Michael Becker[2], and Christian Allmann[2]

[1] Karlsruhe Institute of Technology (KIT), 76131 Karlsruhe, Germany
{richard.mrasek,jutta.muelle,klemens.boehm}@kit.edu
[2] AUDI AG, 85045 Ingolstadt, Germany
{christian.allmann,michael1.becker}@audi.de

Abstract. Testing in the automotive industry is supposed to guarantee that vehicles are shipped without any flaw. Respective processes are complex, due to the variety of components and electronic devices in modern vehicles. To achieve error-free processes, their formal analysis is required. Specifying and maintaining properties the processes must satisfy in a user-friendly way is a core requirement on any verification system. We have observed that there are few pattern properties that testing processes adhere to, and we describe these patterns. They depend on the context of the processes, e.g., the components of the vehicle or testing stations. We have developed a framework that instantiates the property patterns at verification time and then verifies the process against these instances. Our empirical evaluation with the industrial partner has shown that our framework does detect property violations in processes. From expert interviews we conclude that our framework is user-friendly and well suited to operate in a real production environment.

1 Introduction

The systematic testing and configuration of complex products, e.g., vehicles, is an important step of any production process. To this end, certain tasks need to be executed, automatically or with the help of a human. So-called commissioning tasks test a component or put it into service, e.g., configure the software [33]. Workflows called commissioning processes describe the arrangement of these tasks. Domain experts of the industrial partner develop the commissioning processes. Workflow management systems (WfMS) in the production domain that plan and coordinate the testing and end-of-line manufacturing are referred to as diagnostic frameworks.

Our overall goal is to verify if a given commissioning process is correct. In contrast to validation that ensures if a process meets the needs of a stakeholder, verification checks if a process fulfills the required properties. To this end, one must specify which properties the process must fulfill. We have collected such properties in cooperation with domain experts by analyzing existing processes,

S. Sadiq, P. Soffer, and H. Völzer (Eds.): BPM 2014, LNCS 8659, pp. 301–316, 2014.

and by closely observing these experts when designing processes. To illustrate, if a process uses more connections than available, the process must halt, i.e., process execution time is unnecessarily long. A common definition of correctness of a process is that it observes all properties required. Properties typically are formulated as property rules, similarly to compliance rules [16][18]. For example, a property rule states that before executing Task X another Task Y has to be executed.

Verification itself is a process that consists of several phases, namely specifying the properties of the commissioning process, verifying them, and presenting the results to the users. Our concern is the design and realization of a framework supporting users throughout this entire process. This gives way to the following questions. First, how must processes as well as the properties be specified to facilitate the deployment of verification techniques? Second, how to utilize domain information to support the users specifying the formal properties? Finally, how user-friendly are respective solutions? To verify process models given in a formal representation like Petri nets against properties, there already exist efficient model checking approaches [25][26]. However, deriving and specifying the properties the model must satisfy is a separate issue. A core question is what a user-friendly framework for process verification should look like.

Designing such a framework gives way to several challenges: First, the knowledge on which characteristics a process should fulfill is typically distributed among several employees in different departments. Often a documentation is missing, and properties merely exist in the minds of the process modelers. Second, the properties frequently are context-sensitive, i.e., only hold in specific contexts of a commissioning process. For example, some tasks need different protocols to communicate with control units for testing at different factories. Due to this context-sensitiveness, the number of properties is very large, but with many variants with only small differences. This causes maintenance problems [15]. Third, to apply an automatic verification technique, like model checking, it is necessary to specify the properties in a formal language such as a temporal logic [23]. With vehicle-commissioning processes as well as in other domains, see, e.g., [10], [20], specifying the properties in this way is error-prone and generally infeasible for domain experts. To allow for an automatic verification, the process must be formalized in a notation that allows to directly construct its state space. To this end, it must be easy to let the properties refer to the processes modeled. Fourth, evaluating an approach such as the one envisioned is difficult. One issue is that the evaluation criteria must be specified.

We have addressed these challenges based on the real-world use case of vehicle-commissioning processes. More specifically, we make the following contributions: We have analyzed which properties occur for vehicle commissioning processes and the respective context information. We have observed that there are few patterns these properties adhere to. We propose to explicitly represent these patterns, rather than each individual property. Next, we develop a model of the context knowledge regarding vehicle-commissioning processes. Here *context* is the components of a vehicle, their relationships and the constraints which the

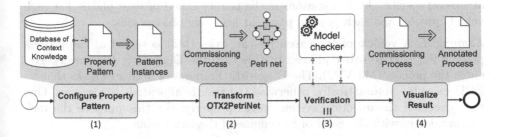

Fig. 1. Steps of the Verification Framework

vehicle currently tested and configured must fulfill. We let a relational database manage the context information. To populate it, we use several sources, e.g., information on the vehicle components from production planning, constraints from existing commissioning processes, and information provided by the process designers themselves. Our framework uses this information to generate process-specific instances of the property patterns, transforms the process to a Petri net, and verifies it against these properties, see Figure 1. Our evaluation has shown that the framework does detect rule violations in actual real-world commissioning processes. Further, we have evaluated whether our model of the context together with the rules is expressive enough for our domain, in two steps. First, we have evaluated whether our framework can indeed find property violations in real-world commissioning processes. Second, we have evaluated the non-functional requirements on our framework by means of expert interviews, as part of an established test. Our evaluation is one of only few studies that collect feedback from domain experts systematically. We conclude that our framework is operational, sufficiently general and usable in a real production environment.

Section 2 describes our scenario *commissioning processes*. Section 3 introduces our notation. Section 4 explains how to specify the properties required, and Section 5 says how to verify them. Section 6 describes our framework. Section 7 features our evaluation. Section 8 reviews related work, Section 9 concludes.

2 Scenario and Requirements

Commissioning processes describe the end-of-line manufacturing and testing of vehicles. This includes, say, to check for each vehicle produced if all its Electronic Control Units (ECU) are integrated correctly and to put the ECUs into service. To check an ECU, several tasks have to be executed. There typically are hundreds of tasks for each vehicle. For example, for an executive-car series there are more than 1650 tasks in 13 processes altogether, and it is necessary to check each of them. Most, but not all tasks communicate with at least one ECU. For instance, a human task tests if the light in the glove compartment functions correctly. This task does not need to communicate with an ECU. Diagnostic Frameworks, i.e., respective workflow management systems, execute the commissioning processes at several specific physical stations in the factory called process places. For each vehicle project and each process place, at least one process exists.

Example 1. A vehicle of the executive-car series (M3) is tested at the process place VP2, next to other places. To this end, the Diagnostic Framework executes the process (M3_VP2). The Diagnostic Framework activates tasks that an ECU executes automatically, otherwise the task is allocated to a worker. One task checks if the injection system works properly. For this purpose the task communicates with the ECU of the engine of the automobile.

Our framework should be able to detect property violations in commissioning processes. Additionally to this functional criteria, the framework must meet the needs of the process developers in practice: The number of *false positives*, i.e., the number of reported violations that are not problematic, and the number of *false negatives*, i.e., the number of undetected rule violations in the processes, should be small. The framework should be general enough to be used in another factory. The handling of the framework should be intuitive and not require the help of a technical person – we have categorized these non-functional requirements into three categories, namely quality, generality and usability.

3 Notation

In this section we introduce the notations used in this paper, i.e., CTL (Computation Tree Logic) as the language to specify properties. Our framework aims to verify whether commissioning processes given fulfill certain rules regarding the commissioning of vehicles, i.e., properties. We transform our processes to Petri nets because their execution semantics is unambiguously defined, and established verification techniques for Petri nets exist. We use CTL because it can express general properties, and efficient model checking algorithms for CTL exist. For a more detailed introduction, see the standard literature, e.g., [2] and [8]. CTL is a temporal logic to specify properties. Model checking algorithms exist to efficiently verify CTL properties [7]. The CTL syntax is as follows:

Definition 1 (Computation Tree Logic:). *Every atomic proposition $p \in AP$ is a CTL formula. If ϕ_1 and ϕ_2 are CTL formulas then $\neg\phi_1$, $\phi_1 \vee \phi_2$, $\phi_1 \wedge \phi_2$, $AX\phi_1$, $EX\phi_1$, $AG\phi_1$, $EG\phi_1$, $AF\phi_1$, $EF\phi_1$, $A[\phi_1 \ U \ \phi_2]$, $E[\phi_1 \ U \ \phi_2]$ are CTL formulas.*

In our domain, AP is a state M of a Petri net. The operators always occur in pairs: a path operator (A or E) and a temporal operator (X,G,F or U). A means that the formula holds in *all* succeeding execution paths, E means that at least one execution path *exists*. X means that the formula holds in the next state, G means that it holds in all succeeding states, F means that it holds in at least one succeeding state, and $[\phi_1 \ U \ \phi_2]$ means that ϕ_1 holds until ϕ_2 is reached.

4 Property Specification

Our overall goal is to develop a verification framework for vehicle commissioning processes which is easy to use, easily adaptable to new vehicle variants and adequate for flexible commissioning process execution. Before verification takes place, it is usually required to specify the properties for a process. To support this step, we have collected so-called property patterns together with engineers who develop diagnostic programs, see Section 4.1. As part of the verification, our framework determines the context of the process first. For instance, the context consists of the process place, the vehicle project and the list of tasks and ECUs used. This concrete process context is used to query a database for the information required to dynamically generate instances of the property patterns. Section 4.2 identifies recurring characteristics of such patterns and proposes a respective database representation. Section 4.3 says how to use the patterns to generate process-specific instances of the patterns.

4.1 Properties and Property Patterns for Commissioning Processes

We have identified typical properties of commissioning processes and character-istics of processes, as follows.

P1 Syntactical Correctness: The commissioning process must be syntacti-cally correct and comply with the naming conventions of the company for tasks.

P2 Resources of the ECUs: Some ECUs require specific resources at the process place for their testing. When a task requires a resource not available at the current process place the process is blocked.

P3 Connections of the ECUs: Each ECU opens a connection to one of two transport protocols supported (**UDS** or **KWP2000**). Each transport protocol can handle a certain number of open connections, in our environment 10 at the same time. In total, 14 connections altogether can be open at the same time. To avoid blocking of a process, the process must not open more connections. Table 1 shows the respective property patterns.

P4 Task Conditions: Some tasks depend on the occurrence of other tasks in the process, e.g., they cannot run in parallel or need to occur in a certain sequential order. Table 1 contains the different property patterns for commis-sioning processes. They are the result of a comprehensive survey of ours to detect all dependencies that are conceivable.

P5 ECU Conditions: Additionally to the conditions on tasks, conditions spe-cific to certain ECUs exist, see Table 1. These conditions hold for any task that communicates with the respective ECU.

Given this list, we conclude that for some properties a model-checking approach is feasible, while for others an algorithmic approach is more efficient. Properties that refer to structural constraints like the occurrence and arrangement of tasks can be expressed in temporal logic and thus call for a model-checking verifica-tion. Violations of those properties can result in undesirable characteristics of the process execution, subsequently referred to as *major disturbance*. An exam-ple is that it may block the execution of the process. This holds for properties P3, P4 and P5. Our approach is to define patterns for these properties. Table 1

Table 1. Property Patterns for Task and ECU Conditions

Prop.	Name	Description	CTL
P3.1	Maximal **UDS** Connections	The number of connections to **UDS** should not exceed 10.	AG(**UDS** $\leq$ 10)
P3.2	Maximal **KWP-2000** Connections	The number of connections to **KWP2000** should not exceed 10.	AG(**KWP2000** $\leq$ 10)
P3.3	Maximal Connections	The number of connections **UDS** and **KWP2000** should not exceed 14.	AG((**UDS** + **KWP2000**) $\leq$ 14)
P4.1	Sequential before	If a task A is in the process, a task B has to occur before A.	A [(**run-A** = 0) W (**run-B** > 0)]
P4.2	Optional Sequential before	If both A and B occur in the commissioning process, B has to occur before A. B can completely be missing.	A [(**run-A** = 0) $\lor$ AG (**run-B** = 0)) W (**run-B** > 0)]
P4.3	Sequential after	The occurrence of task A leads to the occurrence of task B.	AG ((**run-A** > 0) $\rightarrow$ AF (**run-B** > 0))
P4.4	Non-Parallel	Tasks A and B are not allowed to occur in parallel.	AG ($\neg$((**run-A** > 0) $\land$ (**run-B** > 0)))
P5.1	Restricted access	Only one task at the same time can access/test each ECU C.	AG (**C** $\leq$ 1)
P5.3	Non-Parallel	Some ECU C must never be tested in parallel with an ECU C_2.	AG ($\neg$((**C** > 0) $\land$(C_2> 0)))
P5.4	Close Connection	Task close-C must close the connection to an ECU C.	AG ((**C** > 0) $\rightarrow$ AF (**close-C** > 0))

shows the patterns and the respective CTL formulas. The atomic propositions are inequations referring to states of a Petri net. For instance, (**run-A** > 0) refers to all states where the place **run-A** contains more than zero tokens, i.e., A is currently running. We use the term *minor disturbance* accordingly. This holds for properties P1 and P2. They are on a representational level, i.e., the syntax and the environment of the processes. Examples are violations of conventions or deviation from best practice or from guidelines. We use a syntax check and a query-based verification to check these properties, see *Data Reconciliation* in Section 5.

4.2 Database of Context Knowledge

Our goal is to generate properties for checking commissioning processes automatically, based on the information collected a priori. To this end, we have developed a model of the context knowledge on commissioning processes in the automotive industry which supports generating the properties. We then have designed a relational database to manage this context information. The rationale is that the context information is represented in a user-friendly manner. The database

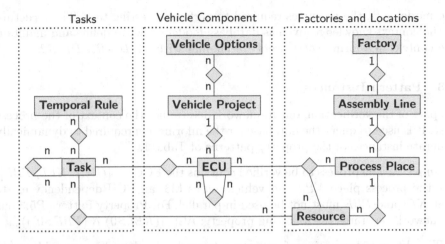

Fig. 2. Excerpt of the Database Schema for Context Knowledge

needs to fulfill the following requirements:

DB-R1 **Representing Contextual Information:** The database should contain the contextual information of the commissioning processes. First, the properties of the processes depend on the vehicle, i.e., on the components built into it which have to be tested, mostly ECUs. The type of the vehicle and its concrete configuration determine the ECUs required. Second, the properties of the processes depend on the process places the component is tested at. The assembly lines for testing and configuring consist of these places. They vary in different factories. Third, there exist dependencies between the commissioning tasks, see Subsection 4.1.

DB-R2 **User-Friendly Specification of the Properties:** Engineers should be able to specify the properties in a comfortable way. To this end, the structure of the database should support the perspective of these experts and not require extensive experience with formal modeling.

DB-R3 **Use of Existing Documents and Information:** Defining the properties should use as much information from previous steps of the production life cycle as is available. Information on the vehicle and its components which have to be tested arises during the production design and production planning. The database should contain this information.

Figure 2 shows an excerpt of our database model illustrating the overall structure, see [27] for more details. Our model consists of three parts, in line with *DB-R2*. One part comprises the vehicle components (e.g., the ECUs), including variants of the component configurations, so-called options of the vehicle. The product planning step delivers such information, which we use to populate the respective part of the database, cf. *DB-R3*. Another part contains the commissioning task objects, dependencies between tasks, and constraints on the tasks, specified as CTL formulas. A third part describes the assembly lines with process places and resources available there. Dependencies between the parts complete the model, e.g., the resources required to perform a testing task. The structure of the context knowledge given as database model allows to define and maintain the context in a form expert users are familiar with, cf. *DB-R1, DB-R2*.

4.3   Pattern Instances

As part of the verification, our framework determines the context of the process first. It is used to query the database for the information required to dynamically generate instances of the property patterns of Table 1.

Example 2. The process to be verified contains the ECUs = $[GWA, KEL, FBE]$. For the process place *VP2* and vehicle series M3, an ECU dependency exists that *KEL* and *FBE* must not be used in parallel. For Property Pattern P5.3 our framework generates the following property: $\mathsf{AG}(\neg((KEL{>}0) \land (FBE{>}0)))$.

The dynamic generation of properties from the database has several benefits compared to their direct specification in, say, CTL. First, for a process given we only consider the properties relevant for it. Second, the maintenance of the properties is simplified. For example, if a new ECU is available for a process place, one only needs to add the information into the database, i.e., to Relation *ECU*. With a direct specification in turn, one might have to specify several hundred properties. The database stores the contextual knowledge in a centralized and non-redundant form, instead of managing all properties specified in CTL. For example, the Pattern "*A* leads to *B*" has a few hundred instances. If, for example, the need to change the pattern to "The first occurrence of *A* leads to *B*" arose, updating would be avoided. Third, domain experts only need to specify properties in CTL when there is a new property type, so the number of these error-prone and complicated tasks is reduced.

5   Verification

We now describe the architecture of our verification framework and how it verifies if a commissioning process fulfills a set of property instances. The industrial partner uses several different process notations, depending on the factory and vehicle project. OTX is an ISO-Standard [13] that is planned as a vendor-independent standard for commissioning processes. A preprocessing step transforms a process file in another format into OTX (Figure 3.1). Next, the context information regarding the process place and the vehicle project are extracted

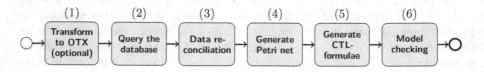

Fig. 3. The Verification Steps

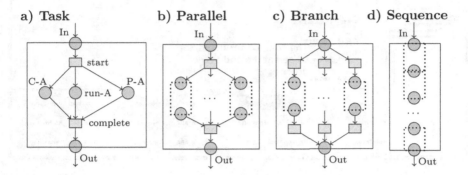

Fig. 4. The Templates for a Task (a), a Parallel-Node (b), a Branch-Node (c) and a Sequence-Node (d).

from the commissioning process (Figure 3.2). Not all properties can be verified with one paradigm. Therefore, our program consists of two modules: the *Data-Reconciliation* (Figure 3.3) and the *Model Checker* (Figure 3.4 to 3.6). In the past, researchers have developed efficient tools for model checking with Petri nets [24][14]. Hence, model checking in the narrow sense of the word is not a topic of this article. Our framework contains an established framework for model checking [24].

5.1   Data Reconciliation

First, our framework tests the syntactical correctness of the OTX process. To do so, the module validates the commissioning process against the XML schema of OTX. Additionally, we check for each task if it complies with the naming conventions of the company. Then, the module checks if the resources are available at the process place of the commissioning process (P2). To this end, our framework queries the database to evaluate if the resources at the process place match the resources used in the process.

5.2   Model Checking

Model Checking is the problem of finding all states s such that the state machine M has a given property ϕ in s. The commissioning processes are given in OTX, a block-based language [17] similar to WS-BPEL [33]. OTX does not allow for a direct construction of the state space. Therefore, we transform the OTX process model into a Petri net and can then analyze its state space.

Transformation: OTX describes the process as tree structure (cf. RPST [31]). Each leaf node corresponds to a task, and each inner node represents a control

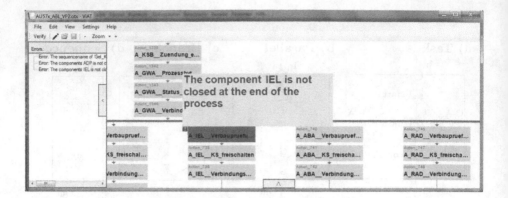

Fig. 5. Screenshot of the Verification Framework

structure, e.g., parallel execution, exclusive execution or sequential execution of the child nodes. For each type of nodes we define a template. A template is a Petri net with an input *In* and an output place *Out*. Figure 4 shows the templates for a task, a parallel node, a branch node and a sequence node. The control structure nodes have specific regions, where to include the child elements (dotted boxes in Figure 4). To transform the OTX process, we parse the process tree in a breadth-first manner and include for each node the respective Petri net template into the net. Our approach is similar to the one of [12] and [29]. Figure 4 a) shows the Petri net template for a task, i.e., a commissioning routine. The place *In* marks that Task A is activated and ready for execution. If a task execution starts, the transition *start* fires and creates a token in each of the places *run-A*, *C-A* and *P-A*. *run-A* represents the actual execution of the task. *C-A* is the place of the ECU A communicates with, and *P-A* gives the bus protocol that A uses, either **UDS** or **KWP2000** [33]. Several tasks use the same place for *C-A* and *P-A*.

Verification: For model checking we have included the LoLA-Framework [24] into our framework. It generates the state space for the Petri net and uses a model-checking algorithm to verify the properties. Note that our framework is not specifically tailored to this concrete model checker. We do not foresee any major difficulties when including other frameworks for state-space generation or model checking.

6   Implementation

We have implemented concepts described so far in our framework called AAAFT (Automatic Arrangement of Working Steps in Production and Testing). The database for context knowledge is a MySQL database. We also have implemented a graphical front-end that can load an OTX process, visualize it, verify the process and highlight any task that relates to the violations detected.

Example 3. Figure 5 shows a screenshot of our framework. The program has loaded an OTX process and has verified it against the database. Dark (red) boxes highlight tasks that cause a rule violation, e.g., the component IEL is not closed at the end of the process. On the left-hand side, the framework lists the violations detected.

7 Empirical Evaluation

In Subsection 7.1 we say how we have evaluated that our framework can identify rule violations in real processes. Additionally to this criterion we want to evaluate that the framework does meet the requirements of the process developers in practice, see Subsection 7.2.

7.1 Functional Evaluation

We have used our prototype to verify 60 commissioning processes, newly generated or modified ones, before their execution. These processes refer to four vehicle series: the middle class car M1, the upper-middle class car M2, the executive car M3, and the sports car M4. They are executed at 34 stations. We have discussed the verification results and have categorized the processes into three categories: correct, with minor process disturbance and with major process disturbance. Figure 6 shows the number of processes in the three categories for each vehicle series. Most of the minor disturbances result from incorrect labels of tasks and missing values in the database. For few processes, the verification framework has reported false positives, due to the fact that we do not consider guard conditions. These false positives have also been categorized as minor. In a significant share of the processes ($\approx 23\%$), we could detect a major disturbance.

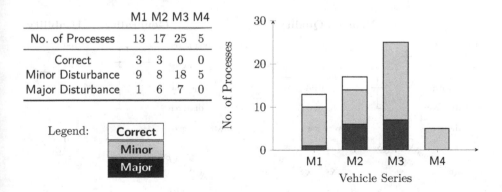

	M1	M2	M3	M4
No. of Processes	13	17	25	5
Correct	3	3	0	0
Minor Disturbance	9	8	18	5
Major Disturbance	1	6	7	0

Legend: Correct Minor Major

Fig. 6. Process Disturbances Found in the Evaluated Processes

7.2 Expert Interviews

To evaluate our approach we have held semi-structured expert interviews. We aim to test the three characteristics: process quality, generality and usability, as explained next. The interview guide is available on our website: http://dbis.ipd.kit.edu/2027.php.

Process Quality: *Has the framework increased the quality of the commissioning processes?* This criterion includes the change in the development time of processes, the number of *false positives* and the number of *false negatives*.

Generality: *Can the framework be used in a different context within the company?* For instance, is the framework general enough to be used in another factory? We have also asked how well the framework can be integrated into the tool chain.

Usability: *Can the framework be used in an intuitive way? Is the help of a technical person needed to use the framework?* For usability we have used the Standard System Usability Test (SUS) [5]. SUS is a 10 item test that is scored on a 5-point scale of strength of agreement or disagreement. The SUS has the advantage that it is technology-agnostic, i.e, it can be used in different application domains. Due to its wide usage, a meta-test and guidelines exist to interpret the results [5].

Participants: Participants in our study are domain experts, i.e., employees who have developed commissioning processes. We have limited our interviews to experts who had used our framework intensively and had enough expertise to give feedback. We have been able to gain four experts who met these requirements for a qualitative interview. Their experience in developing commissioning processes range between 1 and 14 years, with an average of 7 years.

Results and Discussion: Figure 7 shows the results of our qualified interviews. The experts do not think that our framework will influence the development time negatively. The number of false positives and false negatives are acceptable but

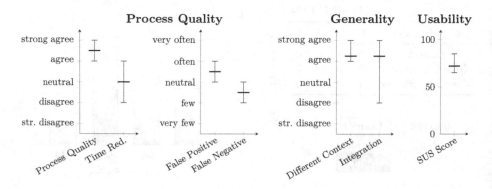

Fig. 7. Results of the Empirical Evaluation

should be improved. Our framework detected slightly more false positives than false negatives. The experts saw a great potential of our framework to be used in other testing environments as well. The rating of how well the framework can be integrated into the tool chains varies between the experts. The SUS score (a measure for the usability) ranges between 65 and 85 with an average of 71.67. This is slightly above the average (69.69) and median (70.91) of reported studies using the SUS score [5]. All experts see great potential in improving the quality of the commissioning processes by means of our framework.

Conclusion: The evaluation has shown that the experts deem our framework very useful and with high potential to enhance process quality. A minor issue is that they have criticized the amount of information presented by our framework. To this end, we plan to have two modes. A debug mode that presents detailed information on the model checking process, and a normal mode that only shows the information required by the domain experts. To improve usability further, the experts had suggested presenting the results in more than one language. Some experts doubt that our framework can be easily integrated into the tool chain. To this end, we currently are reimplementing it in C#. The framework currently is implemented in Java.

8 Related Work

Related work includes the user-friendly specification of properties, their management and the property-specific verification of processes.

Specification: The direct specification of properties in a formalism like CTL is error-prone and not feasible for a user without experience in formal specification. To this end, different approaches have been developed. Most business processes are modeled in a graph-based modeling language like BPMN [32], YAWL [3] or Petri nets [1]. [6] extends the BPMN notation with new elements that directly represent LTL operators. BPMN-Q [4] extends BPMN with new edge types that represent sequential ordering between tasks. Compliance Rule Graphs [20] allow a specification of requirements in a graph-based formal language. Another approach is the use of specification patterns. [10] introduces the property patterns to specify concurrent systems. [28] extends the pattern system to PROPEL (PROPerty ELucidation) to cover variations of the property patterns. [9] uses a question tree to allow specifying PROPEL patterns. In our domain, only a few different property patterns exist. Dependent on the context, many instances are generated. Because of the small number of patterns but many similar instances, we have not found any of the approaches to be very helpful in our specific case.

Management of Properties: [30] builds an ontology for the domain of compliance management. However, it is not sufficient to capture the domain-specific information needed for the instantiation of our patterns. Managing compliance properties includes allocating the properties to the business processes. [15] allocates the compliance properties to the processes using potentially relevant activities. We in turn dynamically generate only the properties relevant for the commissioning processusing the context knowledge directly before verification.

Verification: We aim to check if a business process complies with the properties given. [22] uses an approach that checks if the event log L (a set of execution traces) complies with properties. In our case, there exist violations of properties that are not related to an event during process execution. For example, we do not see how to recognize a violation of a non-parallel property from the log of a process. Further, we use model checking to verify the processes. Most high-level process languages lack the direct construction of the state space required for model checking. To this end, a transformation to a formal language like Petri nets is required. [19] gives an overview of transformations from BPMN, YAWL and WS-BPEL to Petri nets. Our approach is similar to [12]. [21] empirically evaluates different approaches for soundness verification. The criteria include error rates, process size and verification time. [11] evaluates three techniques (Partial-Order-Reduction, Woflan and SESE-Decomposition) to verify the soundness of over 700 industrial processes. Our verification technique is more general than just verifying soundness as in [21] and [11]. It is however interesting to see that some insights at an abstract level are similar to ours. In particular, the size of the processes correlates with the number of rule violations, and a significant share of processes in industrial settings contains rule violations.

9   Conclusions

To avoid property violations in commissioning processes, a framework to verify if a process is correct clearly is helpful. With verification, an important step is specifying which properties a process must fulfill. Given that verification algorithms already exist, a core question is how to arrive at a user-friendly framework for process verification that supports collecting and maintaining the properties.

We have analyzed which properties vehicle commissioning processes in the automotive industry must fulfill and have identified the context information relevant for verification. An important insight has been that there exist only a few types of properties, but the number of properties may be very large. Thus, an important design decision has been to develop a database with contextual information and to focus on property patterns covering all properties relevant for vehicle-commissioning processes. Consequently, we have proposed a transformation of patterns to properties tailored to a certain process model. Our framework then verifies these properties on the commissioning processes. An interview-based evaluation together with domain experts has shown that the framework does enhance the process quality. Ongoing work addresses an even tighter integration of the framework and its database into the tool chain.

References

1. van der Aalst, W.M.P.: The Application of Petri Nets to Workflow Management. Journal of Circuits, Systems and Computers (1998)

2. van der Aalst, W.M.P., van Hee, K.: Workflow Management: Models, Methods, and Systems. MIT Press (2004)
3. van der Aalst, W.M.P., ter Hofstede, A.H.M.: YAWL: Yet Another Workflow Language. Information Systems (2005)
4. Awad, A., Decker, G., Weske, M.: Efficient Compliance Checking Using BPMN-Q and Temporal Logic. In: Dumas, M., Reichert, M., Shan, M.-C. (eds.) BPM 2008. LNCS, vol. 5240, pp. 326–341. Springer, Heidelberg (2008)
5. Bangor, A., Kortum, P.T., Miller, J.T.: An Empirical Evaluation of the System Usability Scale. International Journal of Human-Computer Interaction (2008)
6. Brambilla, M., Deutsch, A., Sui, L., Vianu, V.: The Role of Visual Tools in a Web Application Design and Verification Framework: A Visual Notation for LTL Formulae. In: Lowe, D.G., Gaedke, M. (eds.) ICWE 2005. LNCS, vol. 3579, pp. 557–568. Springer, Heidelberg (2005)
7. Clarke, E.M., Emerson, E.A., Sistla, A.P.: Automatic Verification of Finite-State Concurrent Systems Using Temporal Logic Specifications. ACM Trans. Program. Lang. Syst. (1986)
8. Clarke, E.M., Grumberg, O., Peled, D.A.: Model checking. MIT Press (1999)
9. Cobleigh, R.L., Avrunin, G.S., Clarke, L.A.: User Guidance for Creating Precise and Accessible Property Specifications. In: ACM SIGSOFT International Symposium on Foundations of Software Engineering (2006)
10. Dwyer, M.B., Avrunin, G.S., Corbett, J.C.: Property Specification Patterns for Finite-State Verification. In: 2nd Workshop on Formal Methods in Software Practice (1998)
11. Fahland, D., Favre, C., Jobstmann, B., Koehler, J., Lohmann, N., Völzer, H., Wolf, K.: Instantaneous Soundness Checking of Industrial Business Process Models. In: Dayal, U., Eder, J., Koehler, J., Reijers, H.A. (eds.) BPM 2009. LNCS, vol. 5701, pp. 278–293. Springer, Heidelberg (2009)
12. Hinz, S., Schmidt, K., Stahl, C.: Transforming BPEL to Petri Nets. In: van der Aalst, W.M.P., Benatallah, B., Casati, F., Curbera, F. (eds.) BPM 2005. LNCS, vol. 3649, pp. 220–235. Springer, Heidelberg (2005)
13. ISO, Geneva, Switzerland: Road vehicles – Open Test sequence eXchange format (OTX). ISO 13209 (2012)
14. Jensen, K., Kristensen, L.M., Wells, L.: Coloured Petri Nets and CPN Tools for Modelling and Validation of Concurrent Systems. International Journal on Software Tools for Technology Transfer (2007)
15. Rinderle-Ma, S., Kabicher, S., Ly, L.T.: Activity-oriented clustering techniques in large process and compliance rule repositories. In: Daniel, F., Barkaoui, K., Dustdar, S. (eds.) BPM Workshops 2011, Part II. LNBIP, vol. 100, pp. 14–25. Springer, Heidelberg (2012)
16. Knuplesch, D., Ly, L.T., Rinderle-Ma, S., Pfeifer, H., Dadam, P.: On Enabling Data-Aware Compliance Checking of Business Process Models. In: Parsons, J., Saeki, M., Shoval, P., Woo, C., Wand, Y. (eds.) ER 2010. LNCS, vol. 6412, pp. 332–346. Springer, Heidelberg (2010)
17. Kopp, O., et al.: The Difference Between Graph-Based and Block-Structured Business Process Modelling Languages. Enterprise Modelling and Information Systems Architecture (2009)
18. Liu, Y., Muller, S., Xu, K.: A Static Compliance-Checking Framework for Business Process Models. IBM Systems Journal (2007)
19. Lohmann, N., Verbeek, E., Dijkman, R.: Petri Net Transformations for Business Processes–a Survey. In: Jensen, K., van der Aalst, W.M.P. (eds.) Transactions

on Petri Nets and Other Models of Concurrency II. LNCS, vol. 5460, pp. 46–63. Springer, Heidelberg (2009)

20. Ly, L.T., Knuplesch, D., Rinderle-Ma, S., Göser, K., Pfeifer, H., Reichert, M., Dadam, P.: SeaFlows Toolset – Compliance Verification Made Easy for Process-Aware Information Systems. In: Soffer, P., Proper, E. (eds.) CAiSE Forum 2010. LNBIP, vol. 72, pp. 76–91. Springer, Heidelberg (2011)

21. Mendling, J.: Empirical Studies in Process Model Verification. In: Jensen, K., van der Aalst, W.M.P. (eds.) Transactions on Petri Nets and Other Models of Concurrency II. LNCS, vol. 5460, pp. 208–224. Springer, Heidelberg (2009)

22. Ramezani Taghiabadi, E., Fahland, D., van Dongen, B.F., van der Aalst, W.M.P.: Diagnostic Information for Compliance Checking of Temporal Compliance Requirements. In: Salinesi, C., Norrie, M.C., Pastor, Ó. (eds.) CAiSE 2013. LNCS, vol. 7908, pp. 304–320. Springer, Heidelberg (2013)

23. Schlingloff, H., Martens, A., Schmidt, K.: Modeling and Model Checking Web Services. Electronic Notes in Theoretical Computer Science (2005)

24. Schmidt, K.: LoLA A Low Level Analyser. In: Nielsen, M., Simpson, D. (eds.) ICATPN 2000. LNCS, vol. 1825, p. 465. Springer, Heidelberg (2000)

25. Schmidt, K.: Stubborn Sets for Standard Properties. In: Donatelli, S., Kleijn, J. (eds.) ICATPN 1999. LNCS, vol. 1639, pp. 46–65. Springer, Heidelberg (1999)

26. Schmidt, K.: Stubborn Sets for Model Checking the EF/AG Fragment of CTL. Fundamenta Informaticae (2000)

27. Schneider, T.: Specification of Testing Workflows for Vehicles and Validation of Manually Created Testing Processes. Master's thesis, Karlsruhe Institute of Technology (May 2012) (in German)

28. Smith, R.L., et al.: PROPEL: An Approach Supporting Property Elucidation. In: Conference on Software Engineering (2002)

29. Stahl, C.: A Petri Net Semantics for BPEL, Technical Report 188. Humboldt-Universität zu Berlin (2005)

30. Syed Abdullah, N., Sadiq, S., Indulska, M.: A Compliance Management Ontology: Developing Shared Understanding through Models. In: Ralyté, J., Franch, X., Brinkkemper, S., Wrycza, S. (eds.) CAiSE 2012. LNCS, vol. 7328, pp. 429–444. Springer, Heidelberg (2012)

31. Vanhatalo, J., Völzer, H., Koehler, J.: The Refined Process Structure Tree. In: Dumas, M., Reichert, M., Shan, M.-C. (eds.) BPM 2008. LNCS, vol. 5240, pp. 100–115. Springer, Heidelberg (2008)

32. Wohed, P., van der Aalst, W.M.P., Dumas, M., ter Hofstede, A.H.M., Russell, N.: On the Suitability of BPMN for Business Process Modelling. In: Dustdar, S., Fiadeiro, J.L., Sheth, A.P. (eds.) BPM 2006. LNCS, vol. 4102, pp. 161–176. Springer, Heidelberg (2006)

33. Zimmermann, W., Schmidgall, R.: Bussysteme in der Fahrzeugtechnik – Protokolle, Standards und Softwarearchitektur. Vieweg + Teubner (2010)

Analysis of Operational Data for Expertise Aware Staffing

Renuka Sindhgatta[1,2], Gaargi Banerjee Dasgupta[1], and Aditya Ghose[2]

[1] IBM India-Research, Bangalore, India
[2] University of Wollongong, New South Wales, Australia
{renuka.sr,gdasgupt}@in.ibm.com, aditya.ghose@uow.edu.au

Abstract. Knowledge intensive business services such as IT Services, rely on the expertise of the knowledge workers for performing the activities involved in the delivery of services. The activities performed could range from performing simple, repetitive tasks to resolving more complex situations. The expertise of the task force can also vary from novices who cost less to advanced skill workers and experts who are more expensive. Staffing of service systems relies largely on the assumptions underlying the operational productivity of the workers. Research independently points to the impact of factors such as complexity of work and expertise of the worker on worker productivity. In this paper, we examine the impact of complexity of work, priority or importance of work and expertise of the worker together, on the operational productivity of the worker. For our empirical analysis, we use the data from real-life engagement in the IT service management domain. Our finding, on the basis of the data indicates, not surprisingly, that experts are more suitable for complex or high priority work with strict service levels. In the same setting, when experts are given simpler tasks of lower priority, they tend to not perform better than their less experienced counterparts. The operational productivity measure of experts and novices is further used as an input to a discrete event simulation based optimization framework that model real-life service system to arrive at an optimal staffing. Our work demonstrates that data driven techniques, similar to the one presented here is useful for making more accurate staffing decisions by understanding worker efficiency derived from the analysis of operational data.

Keywords: operational productivity, experience and expertise, IT incident management.

1 Introduction

A key characteristic of Knowledge Intensive Business Services (KIBS)[20] is its reliance on the knowledge of workers for delivering services to customers. The quality and cost of the service delivered depends on the expertise of the workers involved. In IT infrastructure management services (a specific class of KIBS), there are several processes defined to ensure smooth operation and management of the customer's infrastructure. For example. the Service Desk which serves as

S. Sadiq, P. Soffer, and H. Völzer (Eds.): BPM 2014, LNCS 8659, pp. 317–332, 2014.

a contact between service providers and customers and Incident Management to quickly restore normal service operations in the event of failure (Office of Government Commerce 2007). Apart from being process intensive, the operations tend to be resource intensive as well. Hence, it is important to evaluate the efficiency of resources and optimally staff the teams delivering services. In this paper we describe the analysis of data collected within an organization (IBM) to gain insights into various factors that impact the productivity of the workers. These insights influence the staffing decisions of a complex service delivery system.

We focus on the IT Incident Management Process where the failures or events are reported in by customers as Service Requests (SR). The service organization managing the processes is the service provider, and has a team of service workers (SW) who deliver the services. The time taken (completion time) to restore the service or resolve a SR is a critical performance metric, and hence is closely monitored within the IT Management Process. Typically the contracts specifies a minimal percentage of SR (i.e X%) in a month that must be resolved within a target completion time (i.e. Y hrs). On a breach of the terms in the contract, the provider is liable to pay penalties. Hence keeping completion times within contractual target times is the most critical performance metric of this incident management process. Several factors affect completion times in an IT incident management system. The completion time of a SR depends on the (a)queue waiting time in the system and the (b)service time of the worker (time required to do complete a single unit of work). The queue waiting time in turn depends on the amount of work that exists in the system and the resources available for doing that work. In case of an under-staffed system, all workers are busy and the queue waiting times are higher. This leads to overall higher completion times. The service time of the worker on the other hand is independent of the amount of work in the system, and depends on factors such as the worker expertise and the type of request. In this paper we focus on the factors impacting the service time of the worker and their impact on the optimal staffing of the system .

The service time of a worker is known to depend on the expertise of a worker gained through experience [16],[22]. Prior studies also indicate the service times vary with work complexity. Complex work requires more time than simple work [10]. In this paper, we additionally evaluate the impact of work priority (importance of work) and analyze the service time of the workers in the context of the three factors: i.e., on (a) complexity of work (b) the minimum expertise level of the worker required for a work and (c) importance or priority of the work. We observe that, *while experts have lower service time than novices for complex work and important work, they tend to have the same efficiency as novices for less important work*. We use the insights gained to make informed skill-based staffing decisions within the incident management process. A simulation model closely models behavior of experts and novices for varying work complexity and priority. A search based optimizer uses the simulation model to arrive at an optimal staffing.

This work demonstrates that data-driven techniques similar to the ones presented here can be useful in identifying policies governing the optimal matching of service worker to service requests. Our intent here is not to suggest that the specific findings about the correlation between service worker and request profiles should work in all organizational settings and in all instances. Indeed, the validity of these specific findings is restricted to the specific organizational context. These might potentially not hold even in other parts of the same organization. However, the results presented may serve as the basis for methodological guidelines on how data-driven analysis can lead to more effective allocations of workers to tasks.

Rest of the paper is organized as follows: In section 2, we present background on IT incident management process. Section 3 presents details of our data and the model used to simulate and arrive at optimal staffing. Section 4 presents the actual analysis of service times along the dimensions and presents insights that can adopted by staffing solutions. Section 5 summarizes the threats to validity. Section 6 presents related work and section 7 concludes the paper.

2   IT Incident Management Process

This section provides an overview of the IT incident management process of the service system under study. We define commonly used concepts of a service system supporting the incident management process.

Figure 1 illustrates an incident management process. A problem or issue faced by a customer or a business user is **reported as an incident** into an incident management system. The dispatcher reviews the incident and **evaluates the complexity and priority of the incident**. The dispatcher further **identifies a**

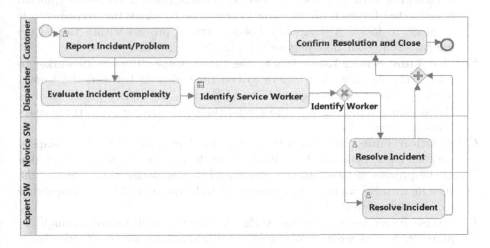

Fig. 1. IT Incident Management Process

service worker suitable for resolving the incident. This task is based on specific rules and policies and hence is a rule based activity. In the IT service system under study, workers are broadly categorized into two distinct classes Experts or experienced service workers and novices or less experienced service workers. If an incident is complex, an expert service worker is assigned the incident and if the incident is simple, a novice service worker is given the incident. An alternate dispatching policy applies when none of the novice workers are free i.e. all are busy resolving other incidents. In such a scenario, a simple ticket is asssigned to a free expert worker. The worker assigned to the incident, **resolves the incident**. Once an incident is resolved, the business user validates and confirms the service provided by the worker and **closes incident**.

2.1 Concepts in the Service System

We define the key concepts underpinning the service system below:

Incident or Service Request Incidents or service requests constitute inputs to the service system and are handled by service workers. Each incident is characterized by its complexity and priority.

Complexity The complexity of an incident is indicative of the "level of difficulty". A finite set of complexities levels X are defined. A complexity level is associated with each incident.

Priority The priority of an incident indicates the urgency and impact of an incident. A finite set of priorities levels P are defined. A priority level is associated with each incident. A higher value of priority indicates that the incident is important and needs faster resolution.

Work Arrivals The arrival pattern of service requests is captured for finite set of time intervals T (e.g. hours of a week). That is, the arrival rate distribution is estimated for each of the time intervals in T, where the arrival rate is assumed to follow a stationary Poisson arrival process within these time intervals (one hour time periods) [11] [2].

Service Time Service time refers to the time taken by the service worker to handle the incident. This refers to the time interval between the time a service worker picks up the incident and the time the service worker resolves the incident. In the Figure 1, the service time is the time spent in the activity "Resolve Incident".

Completion Time Completion time of an incident refers to the time elapsed between the generation of the incident by the customer and the completion of the process of handling the incident. The completion time includes the time an incident waits in the queue for it to be dispatched by the dispatcher to a service worker.

Expertise Expertise of a service worker is based on skill gained through experience. Service workers are categorized into a finite set of expertise levels L.

A mapping $\beta : X \to L$ is a map from the complexity of work to the minimum expertise of service worker required to support an incident. This mapping is used by the dispatcher to evaluate the complexity and decided the expertise of the SW capable of working on the incident. An expert is capable of resolving service request or incidents of all complexities.

Service Level Agreements Service levels are a measure of quality or outcome of service. SLA are given for each customer and priority pair as $\gamma_{ip} = (\alpha_{ip}, r_{ip}), \alpha_{ip}, r_{ip} \subset \mathbb{R}$ is a map from each customer-priority pair to a pair of real numbers representing the SR completion time deadline (time) and the percentage of all the SRs that must be completed within this deadline in a month. For example, $\gamma_{Customer_1, P_1} = <4, 95>$, denotes that 95% of all SRs from $Customer_1$ with priority P_1 in a month be completed within 4 hours.i.e. completion time of 95% of the requests of the $Customer_1 \leq 4$ hours.

2.2   Service System Model for Staffing

There are several complexities involved in modeling a service system as described by the authors in [9]. First, the incidents or service requests are differentiated by their complexities and priorities with request arrival rates varying over hours and days of the week. Second, the service levels vary for each customer and priority of the incident. Finally, the service times of the workers is dependent on multiple factors that we would evaluate through the empirical study in this paper. Due to these inherent complexities, we use a simulation based modeling and optimization framework to determine optimal staffing levels. For simplicity, in our optimization model, we consider a service system supporting one customer. It can be easily extended to support multiple customers by considering different service levels and different volume of requests per customer. The optimization model defined in [9] has been adopted for arriving at the number of workers at each expertise level to meet the service level agreements at minimal costs. We describe the optimization model in brief:

- p, the set of priorities of a service request ; $p := \{1, 2, \ldots, P\}$

- x, the set of complexities $c := \{1, 2, \ldots, X\}$

- l , the set of expertise levels; $l := \{1, 2, \ldots, L\}$

- n_l, the set of workers with expertise level l
- $\overline{n_l}$, the upper bound on the number of workers with expertise level l

- $\underline{n_l}$, the lower bound on the number of workers with expertise level l

- c_l is the cost of a service worker with expertise level l

- v_{px}^t is the volume of requests in the period t with priority p and complexity x

- s_{pxl} is the service time for a request with priority p, complexity x and assigned to worker of expertise l

- β_{xl} is valued 1 if request of complexity x can be addressed by an expertise level l and 0 otherwise

- α_p is the target attainment for priority p during a measurement time
- r_p is the target resolution time for a request of priority p.

Objective Function and Constraints. The objective of the staffing solution is to minimize the cost of the service system as defined:

$$minimize \sum_{l \in L} n_l c_l \tag{1}$$

such that,

$$f_p(v_{px}^t, s_{pxl}, \beta_{xl}, n_l, r_p) \leq \alpha_p \tag{2}$$

$$\underline{n_l} \leq n_l \leq \overline{n_l} \tag{3}$$

Equation (1) is the staffing cost of the solution. Equation (2) is the constraint indicating service level agreements must be satisfied. The function f_p is computed by the simulation model which indicates if the attainment level α_p is met. Equation (3) is the restrictions set on the minimum and maximum staffing levels set for the solution.

The simulation model uses discrete event simulation to generate service request of defined priorities and complexities. The service time of the workers are based on their expertise levels, priority and complexity of the work. The outcome of the simulation model is the service level attainment considering all the factors described in function f_p.

3   Data Setting and Parameters

In this section we look at various factors that impact the service time of a worker. We further present the parameters used in our model to evaluate the impact of these factors on the staffing of the system.

3.1   Setting

We study the data collected from three teams within the organization (IBM). All the three teams were involved in managing incidents of the operating systems (OS) domain -i.e manage OS of servers of customers. The data on service time (worker productivity) was collected for a period of three weeks using time and motion study. There were a total of 60 workers across the three teams. Service time data from approximately 4000 incidents was analyzed. For each incident, we extract the complexity, priority, expertise of the assigned worker and the service time.

Dependent Variable. We examine service time as the dependent variable. *Service Time* is used to evaluate productivity of a worker. As indicated in earlier studies [10], service time follows a log normal distribution as seen in Figure 2. The mean service time is 40.33 minutes and the standard deviation is 37.29.

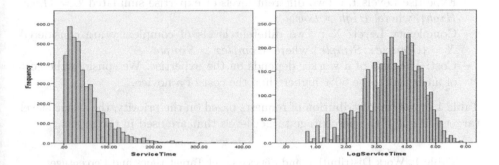

Fig. 2. Service Time Distribution

Independent Variables. Complexity of incident, priority of incident and expertise of the worker are chosen as the independent variables.

Expertise The expertise of the workers in the team is based on the experience of the workers - novice with < 2 years experience, experts with > 2 years, < 7 years experience. Of the 60 workers, 20 are novices and 40 are experts. We refer to an expert having a High expertise and novice having Low expertise.

Complexity The complexity is determined by the dispatcher. Incidents range from handling password reset requests (simple) to verifying security compliance of a server (complex). We have two levels of complexity - Simple and Complex. Simple work can be assigned to novices or experts. We observe 50% of the simple incidents get resolved by experts. While it is not preferable to assign complex work to novices, in the data collected across teams, we observe 10% of the complex incidents assigned to novices.

Priority Priority of an incident determines its urgency and importance. There are 4 levels of priority - Very High(VH), High(H), Medium (M) and Low (L). VH priority incidents are rare and are always treated as exceptions. The low priority incidents also form a small percentage and since their service levels are relaxed, these incidents rarely need to get assigned to a higher skilled worker. i.e. a simple work is assigned to a novices even if they are busy as they have relaxed target time. Hence, in our study, we focus High and Medium priority tickets.

3.2   Model Parameters

Based on the evaluation of complexities, priorities and expertise in the dataset, the parameters used in our simulation model are as follows:

- The finite set of time intervals for arriving work, denoted by T, contains one element for each hour of week. Hence, $|T| = 168$. Each time interval is one hour long.
- Priority Levels P : Two levels of priority are considered $P = \{High, Medium\}$, where $High > Medium$.
- Expertise Levels L : Two different levels of expertise simulated $L = \{Low, High\}$, where, $High > Low$.
- Complexity Levels X : Two different levels of complexity are considered $X = \{Complex, Simple\}$ where, $Complex > Simple$
- Cost: The cost of a worker depends on the expertise. We consider the cost of an expert to be 50% higher than the cost of a novice.

Table 1 shows the distribution of requests based on the priority, the service level target times and the percentage target levels that are used in the model.

Table 1. Work Distribution and Service Level Target times and Percentages

Priority of Incident	Percentage Distribution	Service Level Target Times (minutes)	% Meeting Target Time
VeryHigh	2	240	95
High	20	480	95
Medium	75	720	90
Low	3	1440	90

3.3 Implementation

Our implementation of the IT incident Management process model is built using the AnyLogic simulation software [25] [5] which supports discrete event simulation technique. It also provides optimization package that uses intelligent search procedures in scatter search combined with Tabu search metaheuristics [19][14]. We simulate up to 40 weeks of simulation runs. Measurements are taken at end of each week. No measurements are recorded during the warm up period of first four weeks. In steady state the parameters that are measured include:

- SLA measurements at each priority level
- Completion times of work in minutes (includes queue waiting times and service times)
- Resource utilization (captures the busy-time of a resource)
- Number of resources that is an indication of cost

For all the above parameters the observation means and confidence intervals are reported. Whenever confidence intervals are wider, the number of weeks in simulation is increased and reported values in the paper are within confidence intervals.The simulation model further, does not dispatch a high complexity work to a novice. We arrive at all our results where an expert can do a simple work but a novice doesn't do a complex work in line with the real-life dispatching policy.

4   Empirical Study: Service Time Analysis and Impact on Staffing Solution

4.1   Impact of Work Complexity on Service Time

A commonly used approach in practice is to profile the service time of workers based on the complexity of requests assigned [10]. Figure 3 shows the difference in means of service time and their confidence intervals, with complexity of the request. Statistical techniques such as ANOVA [23], can be used to analyze the variance in the mean of a dependent variable (service time) due to one or more independent variables (here the complexity). However, ANOVA assumes that the data follows Gaussian distribution and has equal variances across means. We verify the homogeneity of variance through Levene's test. The verification of Levene's test for homogeneity of variances fails. Hence, we use non-parametric counterpart test (Kruskal-Wallis test) to compare variance of means across complexities. The Kruskal-Wallis test [23] for analysis of variance by ranks across the two levels of complexity yields a statistically significant difference ($K=44.1$, $p < 0.001$). The results of the Kruskal-Wallis test indicate a significant impact of work complexity on service time. The dispatching policy also indicates that complex work requires an expert to work on it while simple work can be resolved by novices or experts. We observe that, in this setting: *Complex work takes more time to resolve as compared to simple work. Percentage distribution of simple and complex work forms an important input for arriving at the distribution of experts and less experienced workers.*

The service time variance with work complexity is used by the model and the staffing of experts and novices is determined for varying distribution of work complexities. Figure 4 shows the results obtained. As the distribution of complex work increases from 20% to 40% of the workload, the number of workers increases from 4 experts (of total 9 workers) and 7 experts (of the total 11 workers).

Complexity	Mean Service Time	Std. Error	95% Confidence Interval	
			Lower Bound	Upper Bound
Complex	55.283	.944	53.432	57.135
Simple	39.013	1.154	36.752	41.275

Fig. 3. Summary statistics of Service Time Variance with Work Complexity

4.2   Impact of Work Complexity and Expertise of Worker on Service Time

Expertise has a significant impact on the efficiency or productivity of a worker [22]. In our study, we evaluate the variance in service time along the dimensions of the expertise of the worker resolving the request. The Kruskal-Wallis

Complexity	% Distribution	Service Time	Number of Workers		% Utilization	
			Expert	Novice	Expert	Novice
Complex	20	55.28				
Simple	80	39.03	4	5	59.53	86.72
Complex	40	55.28				
Simple	60	39.03	7	4	60.83	89.91

Fig. 4. Staffing of Experts and Novices considering Service Time variance with work complexity

Complexity	Expertise	Mean Service Time	Std. Deviation	N
Complex	High	53.8564	43.81102	1813
	Low	72.4159	59.67647	151
	Total	55.2834	45.47910	1964
Simple	High	34.1284	34.63919	646
	Low	43.7232	36.18852	670
	Total	39.0133	35.74652	1316

Fig. 5. Summary statistics of Service time variance with work complexity and worker Expertise

test statistics for variance in means of service time across the levels of expertise fails to show statistical significance ($p = 0.403$). We attribute this anomaly to the fact, that less experienced workers do not work on complex incidents (only experts are assigned complex incidents). As complex incidents having higher service time, the overall impact of expertise on service time is not evident. We further evaluate the variance in service time considering expertise for low complexity work. The variance in service time means for varying expertise yields a statistically significant difference (K=33.2 ,$p < 0.001$).

Figure 5 shows the variance in service time considering both expertise and complexity of work. Service workers with low expertise level rarely work on complex tickets (as indicated by N=151 of 1964 incidents). However, we observe significant variance in service time means for low complexity work (Means of 43.7 and 34.1 for Low and High expertise of worker respectively).

When the service times derived by analysis of the dimensions of expertise and complexity is used into the simulation model with the staffing results obtained in section 4.1, only 85% of low priority incidents meet the service level required. Hence, the staffing derived in section 4.1 (service time variance with only complexity as a dimension) is lower than what is required for meeting the target service levels. We model the variance in service time accounting for expertise and complexity of work to derive an optimal staffing. Figure 6 indicates the staffing numbers for novice and experts when using the dimensions of complexity and expertise for service time variance. The staffing solution indicates a higher number of novices. This is because, in this setting, *analysis of service time*

Complexity	% Distribution	Expertise	Service Time	Number of Workers		% Utilization	
				Expert	Novice	Expert	Novice
Complex	20	High	53.85				
		Low	Not Assigned				
Simple	80	High	34.12				
		Low	43.72	5	5	69.9	90.1
Complex	40	High	53.85				
		Low	Not Assigned				
Simple	60	High	34.12				
		Low	43.72	8	5	60.83	89.92

Fig. 6. Staffing of Experts and Novices considering service time variance with work complexity and worker expertise

considering expertise only indicates that, the service time of low complexity work is low when experts work on it. Novices take sufficiently longer time to work on low complexity work. Hence, more number of novices are required to meet the service levels.

4.3 Impact of Work Complexity, Priority and Expertise of Worker on Service Time

Prior work on staffing considers priority of work as an important factor for modeling service time variance [9]. We evaluate the impact of all the three factors on service time (worker expertise and work priority for simple and complex incidents). Figure 7 shows the mean service times and the results of Kruskal-Wallis test for different complexities, expertise and priority of the workers. The first four rows show the service times for low complexity requests. Here, less experienced workers have the same service time irrespective of the priority. Experienced workers, tend to have better efficiencies only for high priority tickets. We observe that in our study setting, *the operational efficiency of experts for simple work varies with the importance of work (indicated by priority).* It can also been seen that for less important work, experts take as much time as less experienced workers. This could be attributed to several factors e.g. expert's attention on high priority work, mentoring novices, lower motivation to do less important work, etc. An in-depth analysis of these factors and evaluation through a survey would be needed to understand the variance in expert's efficiency.

The last four rows in Figure 7 depict the service times for high complexity work. Here, the less experienced workers take longer time. The operational efficiency of experts does not change with the importance of work. The study data indicates that: *when the complexity of work matches the minimum skill of the worker, there is no improvement in the operational efficiency irrespective of the importance of work.* The staffing obtained in section 4.2 when used in the simulation model accounting for service time mean variances with work complexity, worker expertise and work priority results in a target service level attainment 86% for low severity work. Hence, the staffing solution in section 4.2 under estimates the number of workers required to meet the service levels.

Complexity	Expertise	Priority	Mean Service Time	Standard Deviation	Kuskal-Wallis Test Statistic
	Low	Medium	47.77	39.39	
		High	42.98	36.32	p>0.05 (0.4)
	High	Medium	43.25	34.46	
Simple		High	32.22	34.64	K=36.6 (*p<0.001)
	Low	Medium	74.4	60.9	High priority work not given to workers with low expertise
		High	–	–	
	High	Medium	54.35	38.01	
Complex		High	53.85	45.33	p>0.05(0.33)

Fig. 7. Service Time Variance with Work complexity , worker expertise and priority

Complexity	% Distribution	Expertise	Priority	Service Time	Number of Workers		% Utilization	
					Expert	Novice	Expert	Novice
Complex	20	High	High	53.3				
		High	Medium	54.5				
		High	High	32.2				
		High	Medium	43.2				
		Low	High	42.98				
Simple	80	Low	Medium	47.77	4	6	61.3	89.3
Complex	40	High	High	53.3				
		High	Medium	54.5				
		High	High	32.2				
		High	Medium	43.2				
		Low	High	42.98				
Simple	60	Low	Medium	47.77	7	6	63.2	87.2

Fig. 8. Staffing of Experts and Novices considering Service Time variance with work complexity, expertise and priority

We use the results of our analysis to determine the staffing of experts and novices. We see that the number of experts reduces as the staffing solution converges at a larger number of novices in this model.

4.4 Observations and Dispatching Recommendations

The efficiency of service workers influences the optimal staffing in terms of cost and quality (adherence to service levels). By evaluating the service time of the worker across various dimensions of expertise, complexity and priority, our simulation and optimization framework reflects the behavior of experts and novices and provides the staffing in the face of these three factors. In section 4.1 when the service time is only based on complexity of work, the model arrives at a specific number of experts (4 and 7 experts as compared to 5 and 4 novices with varying work complexity distribution respectively) as low complexity work indicates lower service time. When the service time is analyzed in the context of the expertise and complexity (section 4.2), the number of novices increases as they take longer time to complete simple requests. The number of experts also increase (5 and 8 experts as compared to 5 and 5 novices respectively) as the experts are found to have better efficiency for simple work. When we further evaluate the experts efficiency in the context of priority (section 4.3), the model further converges with a solution of having lower number of experts (4 and 7) as they perform better than novices for specific case of higher priority work. The number of novices increases in the final solution as they are preferred for all simple and low priority work.

These observations can be used to improve the dispatching policies or rules that are evaluated by a dispatcher when assigning tickets to service workers. As the complex work can only be assigned to experts and the behavior of the experts does not change for complex work, there is no change in the dispatching rule for assigning complex work. However, simple work can have new dispatching rules as indicated in Table 2. Existing dispatching policies in teams primarily evaluate the availability of a service worker. Hence, the rules in the first column check first for the availability of a novice and then dispatch to either a novice or an expert. We recommend that the priority of the incident is also evaluated. If the priority of the incident is high, then an expert can work on it faster and work towards meeting the service levels. If the priority of the ticket is lower, then it should largely be handled by a novice to reduce the cost of the service system as novices and experts have similar service times. These dispatching rules are indicated in the second column of the Table 2.

Table 2. Dispatching Policies for Simple or Low complexity work

Existing Policy in Teams	Recommended Policy in Teams
if (novice *isAvailable*) → assign to novice	if (incident priority *isHigh*) and if(expert *isAvailable*) → assign to expert
if (**not** novice *isAvailable*) and if (expert *isAvailablc*) → assign to expert	if (incident priority *isHigh*) and if(**not** expert *isAvailable*) and if (novice *isAvailable*) → assign to novice
if (**not** novice *isAvailable*) and if (**not** expert *isAvailable*) → wait in queue	if (incident priority *isLow*) and if (novice *isAvailable*) → assign to novice
	if (incident priority *isLow*) and if(**not** novice *isAvailable*) and if (expert *isAvailable*) → wait in queue
	if (incident priority *isLow*) and if(**not** novice *isAvailable*) and if (**not** expert *isAvailable*) → wait in queue
	if (incident priority *isHigh*) and if(**not** expert *isAvailable*) and if (**not** novice *isAvailable*) → wait in queue

5   Threats to Validity

In this section, we identify the limitation of our study with respect of *construct validity, internal validity* and *external validity*.

Construct Validity denotes that the variables are measured correctly. The dependent and the independent variables used in this study have been evaluated by earlier studies described in the Related Work section. However, we realize that the independent variables - expertise levels and work complexity measures can vary across studies. Expertise levels is based on the organization's categorization of its resources. Similarly, categorization of work complexity is relative to type of work being handled and the domain. In our study, this threat is mitigated by considering data from one organization and evaluating teams doing the same type of work i.e IT service management for operating systems.

Internal Validity is established for a study if it is free from systematic errors and biases. We have accessed development data from three teams for a period of 3 weeks. During this measurement interval, issues that can affect internal validity such as mortality (that is, subjects withdrawing from a study during data collection) and maturation (that is, subjects changing their characteristics during the study outside the parameters of the study) did not arise. Thus, we believe the extent of this threat to validity is limited.

External Validity concerns the generalization of the results from our study. We have studied the impact of various factors on the operational efficiency of workers based on data collected from approximately 4000 incidents. While insights can be drawn from our study, we do not claim that these results can be generalized in all instances. These results might not hold even in other parts of the same organization. However, the results serve as the basis of using data driven approach for evaluating worker productivity leading to more effective allocation of service workers to service requests.

6   Related Work

In this section, we situate our work within prior research on team and organizational learning theories, resource planning and service delivery modeling. There has been a significant body of work focused on teams and their learnings. About two decades back researchers[26,12] studied the effects of organizational structure (i.e. hierarchy, team etc.) on metrics like problem solving, cost, competition and drive for innovation and also the effect [7] of learning and turnover on different structures. Carley's [6] theory of group stability postulates a relationship between individual's current knowledge and her behavior. This work builds on previous work to postulate the relationship between individual's current knowledge, the importance of work and her behavior.

Learning has also been looked at in the context of human resource planning [4], [3], where there is a need to forecast the future skill mix and levels required, as well as in context of dynamic environments like call centers[13], where both and learning and turnover are captured to solve the long and medium term staffing problem. In the domain of learning, Guadagnoli et. al [15] formulate a challenge point framework for motor learning where the learning is maximized at an optimal challenge point. According to authors, how much an individual learns when challenged, depends on the skill level of the performer and the task complexity. Jaber et. al present the learning and forgetting models ([18,17,21,24]) for the manufacturing domain. These theories can be applied to service delivery principles as well [8]. Diao et.al present the first detailed model of a complex delivery system. However in this case, the service times are not profiled based on worker expertise. In [1] authors discuss how teams can be formed in accordance with one of the following service delivery models: (a) Customer focused (b) Business Function focused and (c) Technology-focused. Here authors hint that the choice of the delivery model organization should be based on multiple factors one of which is the expertise or skill of knowledge workers. To the best of our knowledge, in the setting of an IT service delivery system this is the first work that attempts to draw insights on the dependency of a worker's efficiency on her skill, work complexity and priority.

7   Conclusion

In this paper, we have evaluated the operational productivity of service workers on multiple factors such as complexity of work, priority or importance of work and expertise of the worker. The analysis of service times is further used to evaluate the staffing solution required to meet the cost and quality requirements of the service system. We observe that, in our operational settings, the behavior of experts varies with the importance of work. The insights gained from our study offer implications for dispatching or ticket assignment policies that consider behavior of experts and novices. We demonstrate that data-driven techniques similar to ours can serve as the basis for methodological guidelines and provide effective dispatching and staffing policies required to meet the contractual service levels (quality) of the service system.

References

1. Agarwal, S., Sindhgatta, R., Dasgupta, G.B.: Does *one-size-fit-all* suffice for service delivery clients? In: Basu, S., Pautasso, C., Zhang, L., Fu, X. (eds.) ICSOC 2013. LNCS, vol. 8274, pp. 177–191. Springer, Heidelberg (2013)
2. Banerjee, D., Dasgupta, G.B., Desai, N.: Simulation-based evaluation of dispatching policies in service systems. In: Winter Simulation Conference, pp. 779–791 (2011)
3. Bordoloi, S.: A control rule for recruitment planning in engineering consultancy. Journal of Productivity Analysis 26(2), 147–163 (2006)
4. Bordoloi, S.K., Matsuo, H.: Human resource planning in knowledge-intensive operations: A model for learning with stochastic turnover. European Journal of Operational Research 130(1), 169–189 (2001)

5. Borshchev, A.: The Big Book of Simulation Modeling. Multimethod Modeling with AnyLogic 6. Kluwer (2013)
6. Carley, K.: A Theory of Group Stability. American Sociological Review 56, 331–354 (1991)
7. Carley, K.M.: Organizational learning and personnel turnover. Organization Science 3, 20–46 (1992)
8. Dasgupta, G.B., Sindhgatta, R., Agarwal, S.: Behavioral analysis of service delivery models. In: Basu, S., Pautasso, C., Zhang, L., Fu, X. (eds.) ICSOC 2013. LNCS, vol. 8274, pp. 652–666. Springer, Heidelberg (2013)
9. Diao, Y., Heching, A.: Staffing optimization in complex service delivery systems. In: CNSM, pp. 1–9 (2011)
10. Diao, Y., Heching, A.: Analysis of operational data to improve performance in service delivery systems. In: CNSM, pp. 302–308 (2012)
11. Diao, Y., Heching, A., Northcutt, D.M., Stark, G.: Modeling a complex global service delivery system. In: Winter Simulation Conference, pp. 690–702 (2011)
12. Roberts, K.H., Jablin, F.M., Putnam, L.L., Porter, L.W. (eds.): Handbook of Organizational Communication: An Interdisciplinary Perspective. Sage (1986)
13. Gans, N., Zhou, Y.-P.: Managing learning and turnover in employee staffing. Oper. Res. 50(6) (2002)
14. Glover, F., Laguna, M.: TABU search. Kluwer (1999)
15. Guadagnoli, M.A., Lee, T.D.: Challenge point: a framework for conceptualizing the effects of various practice conditions in motor learning. Journal of Motor Behavior 36(2), 212–224 (2004)
16. Huckman, R.S., Pisano, G.P.: The firm specificity of individual performance: Evidence from cardiac surgery. In: Management Science, pp. 473–488 (2006)
17. Jaber, M.Y., Kher, H.V., Davis, D.J.: Countering forgetting through training and deployment. International Journal of Production Economics 85, 33–46 (2003)
18. Jaber, M.Y., Sikstrom, S.: A numerical comparison of three potential learning and forgetting models. International Journal of Production Economics 92(3) (2004)
19. Martí, R., Laguna, M., Glover, F.: Principles of scatter search. European Journal of Operational Research 169(2), 359–372 (2006)
20. Miles, I., Kastrinos, N., Flanagan, K., Bilderbeek, R., Den Hertog, P., Huntink, W., Bouman, M.: Knowledge-intensive business services, vol. (15). EIMS Publication (1995)
21. Nembhard, D.A., Uzumeri, M.V.: Experiential learning and forgetting for manual and cognitive tasks. International Journal of Industrial Ergonomics 25, 315–326 (2000)
22. Newell, A., Rosenbloom, P.S.: Mechanisms of skill acquisition and the law of practice, pp. 81–135. MIT Press (1993)
23. Siegel, S., Castellan, N.J.: Nonparametric statistics for the behavioral sciences, 2nd edn. McGraw–Hill, Inc. (1988)
24. Sikstrom, S., Jaber, M.Y.: The power integration diffusion (pid) model for production breaks. Journal of Experimental Psychology 8, 118–126 (2002)
25. XJ Technologies (2011), http://www.xjtek.com
26. Williamson, O.E.: The economics of organization: The transaction cost approach. American Journal of Sociology (1981)

From a Family of State-Centric PAIS to a Configurable and Parameterized Business Process Architecture

Andreas Rulle[1] and Juliane Siegeris[2]

[1] Nexoma GmbH, Paderborn
andreas.rulle@nexoma.de
[2] HTW Berlin University of Applied Sciences
juliane.Siegeris@htw-Berlin.de

Abstract. The paper presents a solution to model and refine processes of long-living business objects. The proposed BPMN model describes the life-cycle of one business object, covering the passed states, the events that invoke state changes and the acitivities that are triggered to perform operations on the object which as a result lead to new states.

Starting from that state-centric operational design model a configurable business process architecture is derived that is controlled by a state automaton and runs on a BPMS that supports BMPN 2.0. Architectural rules are provided to ensure the behavioral correctness of this architecture. The solution emerged from an industrial use case at the transition between two generations of a family of Process Aware Information Systems (PAIS). As a proof of concept the architecture of a platform for the management of delivery times for a wholesaler is described.

Keywords: state-centric process modeling within BPMN 2.0, software product line, PAIS, configurable business process architecture, governance of long-living objects, use cases for BPM.

1 Overview

There are different paradigms in modeling processes. The process can be seen as activity or state driven. In the first paradigm activities have to be accomplished in a certain order to reach a business goal. In the state driven way of thinking, the triggering order of the transitions depends on the current state and the occurrence of events. The application domain of product master data management (MDM) is concerned with the life-cycle of product data. Within this area the state-centered thinking is quite natural: not a specific goal is headed for, but depending on certain events the product data is maintained through-out a, possibly very long, life-cycle.

In the here described stetting, the legacy architecture of the Process Aware Information Systems (PAIS) has been replaced. The new process architecture is based on BPMN 2.0 in order to make use of state of the art open source technology for the execution support. Another request in order to increase competitiveness in a

S. Sadiq, P. Soffer, and H. Völzer (Eds.): BPM 2014, LNCS 8659, pp. 333–348, 2014.

globalized market was the realization of a software product line (SPL). The solution should allow the configuration of processes at design- and the parameterization of processes at run-time.

The problem: the master data management domain is inherently state-centered. The business logic of the objects are so far described and supported with state automata. Hence the following questions had to be answered:

- What is an adequate methodology to analyze and model processes in a domain that has inherently state-centered business objects?
- What is the best alternative to model state-centric information in BPMN 2.0 diagrams?
- How can configurable models be designed that can be enacted on a BPMN 2.0 enabled BMPS?
- How can the behavioral correctness of a business process architecture be made plausible if for example a set of 39 processes can be configured and even parameterized at runtime to dynamically call each other?

These challenges appeared within the application domain of product master data management. Therefore chapter 2 starts with a short introduction to the use case of MDM. It also shows the role of state-centric processes (SCP) during the redesign of a software product line that builds instances of master data management systems (MDMS). In chapter 3 different alternatives for modeling state-based information have been evaluated. From the results a suitable and compact notation, a so-called state-centric operational model (SCOM), was derived. This representation minimizes the artifacts to represent state information and allows to model industry sized but still comprehensible models. To achieve a configurable architecture these operational models are refined to an executable business process architecture whose processes are controlled by a state automaton that is externally realized. The behavioral correctness[1] of this state-centric business process architecture has been made plausible by the application of business process patterns. The derivation of the new process architecture and its description can be found in chapter 4. Chapter 5 gives a short summary of related work on configurable models and on SPLs for business process management. In chapter 6 we argue in that the whole engineering process makes a contribution to the BPM use case catalog of van der Aalst, cf. [21, Ch. 4], adding a special refinement use case that defines a business process architecture as an output. The paper is concluded by a resume in chapter 7. The Fig. 1 shows the relationship between the central concepts of this paper.

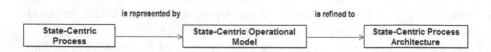

Fig. 1. Concepts for state-centric business processes

---

[1] See chapter 4 for a brief characterization of the term behavioral correctness.

The practical applicability of this solution is shown by the description of a delivery time management portal that has been released by the software product line.

2   Introduction of the Product Data MDM Use Case[2]

Dumas points out that "Master Data Management (MDM) methods provide guidance for managing and governing data across application and organizational boundaries", see [12, p. 20]. In product MDM an electronic catalog comprises structured information such as prices and product dimensions, semi-structured texts and logical references to media files. A supplier might produce such catalogs for different groups of products, countries and in different languages. In this paper the grouping of such product descriptions is denoted as an assortment. It is not uncommon that an assortment of a wholesaler contains 250,000 product descriptions, the corresponding XML-file is larger than 1 GB and the media files comprise 25 GB or much more. Since the data of assortments can be rather large, a component suite that efficiently handles common MDM tasks is needed.

The international master data server (MDS) for a sector of industry, see the sample MDS in Fig. 2, has more than 130 suppliers and about 800 assortments with more than one million product descriptions. It delivers its data to several thousands of business customers. Based on these electronic product data the business customers issue electronic orders that are processed by the suppliers. To minimize the transactional costs of these orders the high quality of the product data is a key success factor. Therefore about 400 audits automatically test the products data und the media files. Human data editors receive delta reports for updates of syntactically correct assortments and manually check the quality of the product data. If the changes for the products have been approved in a staging area then these products are taken over to the shared area and transformed to the output formats and delivered to the customers. The "taking over" of staging area changes of an assortment into the shared area can be decomposed into different smaller steps like "selection of the released product descriptions" or "check the resulting shared area assortment".

A master data management system assists the data editorial in operating of an MDS. As can be seen from the short description the considered MDS has Person-to-Application (P2A) and Application-to-Application (A2A) processes. It is a key characteristic of an assortment in an MDS that it usually has a long lifetime. Many of the assortments in the sample MDS in Fig. 2 live there for more than 9 years, that is since the sample MDS has been updated with MDMS-2. These assortments are "essentially permanent", c. f. [p. 507 in 6]. An MDS for a sector of industry is a strategic investment and it is therefore indispensable that it is based on stable theoretical concepts and a solid technological basis. Fig. 2 shows the influence of academic research and technological trends on two generations of the concrete MDMS.

---

[2] We would like to thank the anonymous reviewers for their invaluable hints to improve this paper as a whole and especially this chapter.

336   A. Rulle and J. Siegeris

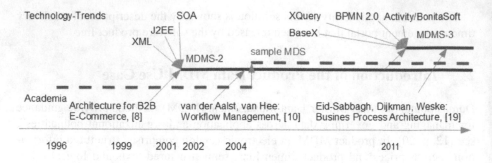

Fig. 2. Influence of academia and technology on the evolution of the product family

The described sample MDS was realized with the second generation of the MDMS, see MDMS-2 in Fig. 2. An A2A-process like "taking over" is there described in a proprietary DSL and enacted on a special purpose processor for this DSL. The domain specific components are triggered by the tasks within the A2A-processes. MDMS-2 has a state controller that triggers the P2A- und A2A-processes, see Fig. 3. This state controller was realized as a J2EE application, see [7]. The workflow in the controller is implemented by a hard-coded state automaton for each instance of an MDS. The design for the interoperation of the state controller and the DSL-processor was influenced by the idea of workflow interoperability, c.f. [p. 157 in 10]. This MDS can be characterized as PAIS.

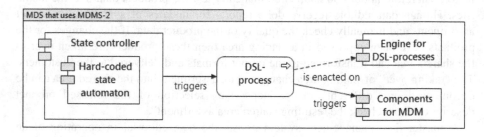

Fig. 3. Architecture of MDMS-2

Besides the strength of the architecture – for example a rollback to earlier states of the assortments - there are weaknesses. Among them are the hard coded state automaton and the hard-coded tasks that trigger the DSL-processes. The auxiliary processes that prepare and post-process the process invocations are hard-coded as well.

The state controller in MDMS-2 implements what we call a state-centric process: it interprets a state automaton and triggers application specific operations accordingly, c.f. Fig. 3.

We want to emphasize that the business logic of an assortment is inherently state-centric[3]. For example it is not a good idea to make a fresh import into an assortment after the human data editorial has approved the changes and before these approved changes are transferred to the shared area. A state-centric workflow makes the states that are part of the business logic a first class citizen. It also supports the idea to separate different concerns, the trigger and their order on the one side (realized in the state controller) and the invoked operations (in Fig. 3 the DSL-processes) on the other. The tasks that perform the state transitions can easily be identified and designed. This separation allows the configuration at design time and the parameterization of the architecture at run-time if the state information within the workflow is specified declaratively, for example in a state transition table.

In the rest of this chapter, we will explain the concept of a state-centric process, its derivation and the benefit in detail.

The MOVE-architecture, see Fig. 2 and [8] and [9], analyzes inter-organizational processes to identify business objects[4]. The central role of the business objects in inter-organizational business processes is highlighted by the meta-model in [9, p. 135]. All the latter modeling is centric on their handling[5].

The business objects of an MDS are the assortments. For an MDS there can be different input and output business objects with different definitions like EDIFACT and BMEcat. It turns out to be a good choice for an MDS for a sector of industry to define a master business object where all input business objects are mapped onto, audits are checked on and output business objects are generated from. The state automaton in Fig. 3 represents the states and state transitions of this master business object over its entire life-cycle. It is this concept of a master business object that makes a state-centric process for an MDS quite effective. This motivates the following informal definition of a state-centric process.

Definition: A state-centric process spans the life-cycle of one business object. It describes the states of the business object, the events that invoke state changes and the operations that transfer the business object into its subsequent states.

Table 1 sets state-centric processes as they are used in this paper informally in relation to data-centric concepts as described in [6]. The comparison points out that an SCP shares common features with a data-centric process but that there are important differences.

---

[3] An objection might be that the steps from an input into the MDS to the output form a chain of activities (CA). But only one CA may operate on an assortment concurrently. Therefore at least two states (CA-running, CA-not-running) and a state controller that maintains these states is needed.

[4] The concept „Informationsobjekt", see [9, p. 140], has been translated to the term business object.

[5] For the definition of a message diagram for business objects see [9, pp. 144-146]. In MDMS-2 the MDM-components for handling the assortments, see Fig. 3, are generated from XML representations of the master business object. In MDMS-3 a master business object is defined by an XML schema.

Table 1. An SCP and aspects of a data-centric process

	SCP in an MDMS	Data-centric processes
Central concept	business object	business artifact
Whole life-cycle covered?	yes	yes
Representation of states	in a SCOM	in a life-cycle model
Definition of processes	graphically in BPMN 2.0	declarative

Looking at the SCPs of various applications it can be stated that sectors of industries differ according to business objects and their structure and the specific audits that check the quality of the data. Still they share common functionality in managing the assortments, which makes it attractive under re-use aspects to view the different applications as a product family, sharing technical components and even processes. A product family is a set of items that have common aspects and predicted variability, see [3, p. 2], and the SEI defines in [4]: "A software product line is a set of software-intensive systems that share a common, managed set of features satisfying the specific needs of a particular market segment or mission and that are developed from a common set of core assets in a prescribed way." In this paper we use the SCP as the central concept to define an SPL for an MDMS.

Now we consider architectural alternatives to enact the state controller and the operations of an SCP on a BPMN 2.0 enabled BPMS. A naïve approach would be to model the state controller of the SCP as one process with one of the alternatives of chapter 3 and the operations as sub-processes of this state controller. But in the context of long-living business objects this would result in one long-running process per one long-living object.

Process evolution and process migration for long-living processes is a well-known topic that is for example discussed in depth in [11, Ch. 9]. Especially if the PAIS does not support automatic instance migration then the uncontrolled instance migration, see [11, Sec. 9.2.3.1], often needs manual intervention, is costly and error-prone, [11, Sec. 9.2.3.1].

Even if business objects in an MDS would not be essentially permanent this naïve approach could not have been chosen because it does not meet the requirement of a configurable state controller. Chapter 5 clarifies why the option to configure a configurable model (BPM use case ConCM) was not attractive for MDMS-3.

Therefore to meet a central design requirement and for practical reasons in MDMS-3 an SCP for a (long-living) business object is refined to an external state automaton on the technical level, see chapter 4. The question how to technically realize state information seems to be similar to that for business rules. Even complex business rules could be expressed in executable BPMN but for practical reasons they are better specified in an external business rules engine. Throughout the rest of the paper the examples are taken from a solution that was released by the software product line for MDMS-3. The delivery times of the wholesaler UDO BÄR[6] are

---

[6] See www.udobaer.com. [accessed: March 15, 2014].

managed by a web portal. By using this portal the wholesaler can review the delivery times for the products of its assortments and the suppliers can maintain them. The verified delivery time information is distributed via a soap web service. In the next chapter 3 we search for the best option to model an SCP on the design level. Since we have already made the decision to refine the states to a transition table of a state automaton this investigation can focus on the complete representation of the states and transitions of the state automaton and the readability of the model for the large number of states that describe the business logic of an MDS for an industrial solution.

3   Modeling of an SCP in BPMN

In this section we discuss and evaluate options of the modeling of states and events in operational BPMN diagrams. In a recent workshop[7] of the BPM offensive Berlin the representation of states within BPMN has been addressed and a consolidation of the workshop results is summarized in Table 2.

This table lists different possibilities for representing state information in BPMN 2.0 diagrams. The collection is likely to be complete as it was the result of an intensive discussion between several BPMN-experts, which was afterwards ensured through an investigation of the OMG-Specification [14].

Table 2. Main alternatives for modeling state /event information in BPMN

ID	BPMN element used to depict state	BPMN element used to model events	Literature
A1	Data objects with state information	-	[13, Fig. 152], [17, p. 32]
A2	Conditional event		BPMN 2.0 Spec. [14, p.251—254]
A3	-	Catching event, e.g. following an event based gateway	See pattern "deferred choice" [16, pp. 17–18]
A4	Edge-labels of XOR-gateway	-	BPMN 2.0 Spec. [14, p. 290]
A5	Activities/Sub-processes	Consecutive XOR gateways for different events	[2, pp. 48–50, 85–98]
A6	Activities/Sub-processes	Attached interrupting events	[17, pp. 83–106, pp. 119–144], [14, pp. 254-257]

---

[7] See [1] for the introductory talk.

Alternative A1 is a good choice if several example states in a process model shall be depicted. Different business objects with their state information can be integrated into the sequence flow by directional data associations. Since the state in this alternative is a textual remark at the business object it is not obvious how to map events that leave the states. Alternative A2 and A3 allow for the integration of state respectively event information into a BPMN model. The interpretation here is that the flow is paused until the event occurs respectively the condition becomes true. By using alternative A4 state information can be integrated into decisions in the process model. This alternative is often used in combination with A1 in order to express the choice made upon some preceding status evaluation. In alternative A5 the state is modeled with the help of an activity/sub-process. The choice of activities that are possible within that state are modeled with a subsequent XOR-gateway. This alternative allows a systematic transformation of UML state automata into BPMN diagrams, see [2]. A6 is a variant of A5. The modeled content is the same, but the description is shortened as attached events avoid gateways for modeling different alternatives.

These alternatives have been evaluated in order to find a suitable modeling for state-centric processes. According to its definition such a process model should: describe the possible states of the business object, depict the events that invoke state changes and line this up with the activities that are operated on the business objects leading to a new state. Additionally it should be a notation that remains understandable also for industry sized examples.

As result, alternative A6 was chosen. The summarized arguments are:

The state-centric processes mainly cope with one object. It would inflate the model unnecessarily if we would use A1 and attach the same data object to every task within the process, depicting the actual state. This alternative is more suitable if different objects are used. A2 and A3 are not considered either, as the splitting of the flow due to alternative state changes would make the use of gateways compelling and again inflate the model. A4 allows selecting an alternative on the base of a state. Still it is not possible (i) to identify the current state of a business object and (ii) it is not obvious how to map events that leave the states. (i.e. various gateways could be labeled with the same state). Modeling alternative A6 is preferred to A5 as fewer elements are needed and as a rule of thumb the clarity of the resulting model is improved if less model elements are used to express it.

Fig. 4 describes (a part of) the main business process of the delivery time portal for the wholesaler with the help of the chosen alternative. Here, states are modeled by activities. For a better distinction, they have been color-coded and a capital S and a number precede the label. The attached catching events model the events that are possible in the state. Their occurrence trigger application specific operations on the business object, here modeled via the subsequent sub-processes. In the case when only one event leaves the state the attached event is replaced by a normal sequence flow leaving the activity. This further reduces the number of model constructs. After an assortment of a supplier has been created in the delivery time portal, it can be updated. The new version of the assortment with the contained delivery data is checked by mandatory audits and quality audits. If both categories of audits are fulfilled then that version of the assortment is taken over into the delivery time information of the wholesaler and the assortment is set to the state "S5: up to date". If the quality audits fail then the result is manually reviewed and the update is released or not. If the reviewer does not release the update or the mandatory audits fail, then the supplier has to maintain the delivery time information of the assortment and the process continues with the checking of the mandatory audits after this maintenance has been completed.

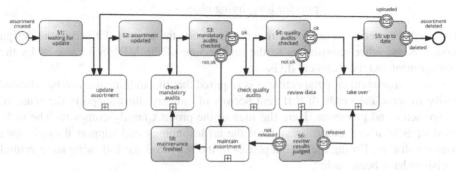

Fig. 4. The state-centric operational model for the wholesaler example using A6

Such a model, describing the life-cycle of a business object in a state-centric manner, is called a state-centric operational model (SCOM). A SCOM is a restricted BPMN model. Except for the source and the sink no other than the described elements, namely state representing activities with boundary events and application specific sub-processes are allowed. Some structural restrictions furthermore suggest:

- that all elements are on a path from the source to the sink, whereas
- any path starts and ends with a state representing activity and
- state representing activities and application specific processes alternate.

The derived model is quite simple and therefore remains comprehensible also for larger numbers of states. The complexity is hidden within the application specific sub-processes and the realization of the state representing activities. For the application specific processes the full expressive power of BPMN can be used within the refinement-level. The state representing activities specify the state controller, see chapter 2, and are refined to the transition table of the state automaton on the executional level.

4   Configuration and Parameterization of the Business Process Architecture

To incorporate the advancing maturity of the BPM as a discipline, see [5], namely to use existing open source solutions for the execution support, the MDMS-3 was designed with the following main objectives.

Target audience:	light weight solutions also suitable for small and medium businesses
Modeling notation:	BPMN 2.0
Database Technology:	native XML database (BaseX) for the efficient handling of large data sets within the component suite[8].
Requirements:	Cloud-ready P2A and A2A, open source components, executable BPMN 2.0, reuse of shared functionality, support for long-living objects

The goal is to derive an architecture which supports the process defined in the design model. Some other impositions to the architecture of the MDMS-3 came in by the management and the technical division:

From a management perspective it is required that the architecture can be adjusted easily to serve the needs of different sectors of industry, thus supports the reuse of components and processes. Here the idea of the product family comes in. The technical division also focused on state of the art technology and support through open source software. During the design phases of the MDMS-3 the following architectural decisions have been made[9]:

- (D1) The processes are enacted on a BPMN 2.0 enabled BPMS.
- (D2) The SCP shall be the central concept of the MDMS-3.
- (D3) The state of the assortments is maintained in an external representation, working like a state automaton.
- (D4) The auxiliary processes in the state controller must be configurable.
- (D5) Long-running processes must be avoided.

Within the architecture the distinction between the application specific processes and the state representing processes is remained. The implementation of the application specific processes is done by a corresponding set P-A of executable processes.

This set can be subdivided into the disjunctive sets of asynchronously started main processes (P-A-M), actually performing the tasks on the assortments and auxiliary processes for the pre- and post-processing/error handling (P-A-AUX). The auxiliary processes (P-A-AUX) are started as a call-activity by the standard processes (P-C).

The information modeled by the state processes is implemented by a state automaton and a set of controlling processes (P-C) that interpret the automaton. The state automaton is saved in a database holding the information of the current state as well as the list of possible state changes and triggered application processes. The controller processes evaluate this table and trigger the application specific processes accordingly. Therefore the state automaton determines the order in which the application specific processes are invoked.

In order to achieve a homogenous environment both controller processes (P-C) and the application specific processes (P-A) are realized by executable BPMN 2.0

---

[8] For the benefits of the BaseX database in the component suite of MDMS-3 see
http://basex.org/customers/nexoma/. [accessed: June 04, 2014].

[9] The reverse engineering of MDMS-2 and the decisions for MDMS-3 have been done by Mr. Redder, Nexoma GmbH, see www.nexoma.de. [accessed: March 17, 2014].

processes in MDMS-3. This comes along with the advantage that existing software, namely open-source software, can be used to support the process execution at run-time. Fig. 5 shows the state controller and application processes for a part of the state-centric operational model of Fig. 2. It demonstrates how the two application specific tasks "update assortment" and "check mandatory audits" are technically realized. An instance of the controlling process "ReadState" reads the current state and checks whether an automatic state transition is possible. It then triggers the processes for the preparation of the update of the assortment and the update itself. The instance of another controlling process "Workflow Response" evaluates the result of the update, triggers the post processing and then triggers an instance of the process "SetState". This process sets the state "S2: assortment updated". A new instance of "ReadState" then again reads the new state and triggers the checking of the mandatory audits. If for example the state "S5: up to date" has been reached, "ReadState" notices that no automatic state transition is possible and ends. There is no running process for this assortment until the web portal calls a rest web service that triggers a new instance of the process "ReadState". This web service call corresponds to the event "updated" or "deleted" in the SCOM, see Fig. 2.

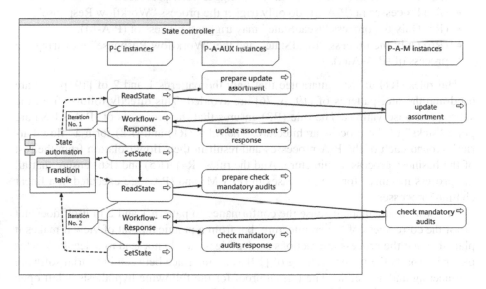

Fig. 5. Process interactions in the state-centric business process architecture

The application specific set of processes (P-A) for the delivery time portal contains 36 processes. Each of these processes has a short lifetime and performs a specific contribution to the assortment handling.

This shows the decoupling of the long lifetimes of the assortments from the life-times of the processes that are handling them although the SCP as a whole spans the total lifetime of the business object. The process evolution can be administered by the usual increasing of the process version number. Since the processes have a short lifetime, an uncontrolled process migration is avoided.

To minimize the data dependencies among the processes an extensible hash map is used as data interface between the processes. This improves the flexibility and variability of the process architecture.

In their paper "Business Process Architecture: Use and Correctness", see [19], Eid-Sabbagh et al. formally define a business process architecture and the concept of behavioral correctness. Based on a formalization of the interdependencies of processes they present structural patterns and anti-patterns for the design and analysis of process architectures. A process architecture is defined to be correct if it is free from deadlocks, livelocks, dead events and lost triggers of flow objects, see [19, p. 6] for the definition of these terms.

To achieve the behavioral correctness of the MDMS-3 process architecture the following restrictions are imposed on the application specific processes.

- (R1) Processes in (P-A) shall not be the source of information flow to other processes.
- (R2) Processes in (P-A) shall not be the sink of information flow from other processes.
- (R3) Processes in (P-A-AUX) may not trigger other processes.
- (R4) Processes in (P-A-M) do only trigger the process "Workflow Response".
- (R5) Only the process "ReadState" may trigger a process of (P-A-M).
- (R6) Only the process "ReadState" and the "Workflow Response" may trigger a process of (P-A-Aux).

The rules (R1) to (R6) guarantee that only the patterns 1 and 2 of [19, p. 73] are used and the anti-patterns of [19, p. 76] are avoided. This directly follows from the subsequent observations. The rule (R3) ensures that the processes of (P-A-AUX) are plain "sinks" of the process architecture. The rules (R1) and (R2) form a "flow barrier" around each of the P-A processes and result in their flow isolation from the rest of the business process architecture. And the rules (R4), (R5) and (R6) ensure that all the process instances for the processes in (P-A-M) and (P-C) are executed in a linear chain of processes.

In a strict mathematical sense the conformance to pattern 1 and 2 in itself does not proof the correctness of the architecture, but from a practical point of view it makes it plausible that the process interactions are harmless, i.e. do not lead to a deadlock. This paper interprets the pattern catalog of [19] as an interface between industrial software engineering and academia. The formal proof for the following hypothesis is left open for academic research: "If only patterns 1 and 2 are used as process interaction patterns and no anti-pattern is present, then the process architecture is correct".

Benefits of the Proposed and Validated Architecture

1. Reuse: The controller processes P-C are stable, in a way that the product family of different applications that are realized with MDMS-3 share the same set of control processes. The application specific processes describe cohesive services in a compact manner and can be used and re-assembled like building blocks to serve different applications.

2. Runtime changes: Modifications to the state automata influence the process execution at runtime. Changing the state automata other (or even new) application specific processes can be invoked. Thus by using the external state automaton a parameterization of the process execution is gained.

3. Separation of Concerns: As can be seen from Fig. 5 the state controller handles the life-cycle of the business objects. It does provide the necessary context for the designer of an application specific process. So they can focus on a single operation between two states of the business object.

4. Governing of long-living objects: Instances of the application specific processes are invoked only if a state change has taken place and a state transition is possible. Long-living processes are avoided.

Fig. 6 uses ArchiMate, see [18], to give an overview on the variation points of the software product line and the project steps that concretize them.

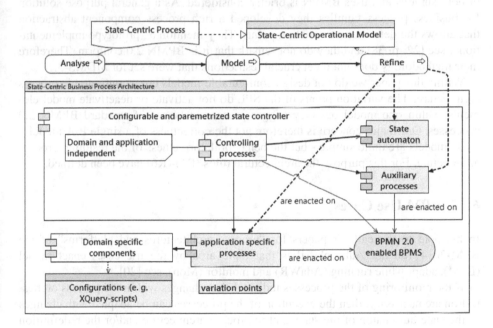

Fig. 6. The state-centric business process architecture and its SPL variation points

5   Related Work

Neglecting the long-living objects, it is possible to refine the model in Fig. 4 to a model that can be enacted on a BPMN 2.0 compliant BPMS. Since the operations of Fig. 4 are quite common for an MDS one might consider designing a configurable model and then adapt the configurable model to meet the particular demands of a specific customer of an MDS.

Under an SPL perspective the adaption points of a configurable process model can be interpreted as the variation points of the SPL. A systematic literature review for the use of SPLs for BPM is given in [15] and a survey for business variability modeling is presented in [23] by La Rosa et al. In that survey the different identified approaches are evaluated by a set of characteristics. Two of them are the process modeling language and the question if the customized models are executable. The authors conclude: "Configurable Workflows approach is in essence the only approach to support customization of executable models (in YAWL, BPEL and SAP Workflow), down to the level of producing models that can be deployed in a BPMS", see [23, p. 46].

Therefore it follows from that study that there is a shortage of variability modeling approaches that enforce the "correctness of individualized models"[10] and can be executed on a BPMN 2.0 enabled BPMS.

To illustrate this point the work of Barat and Kulkarni, see [22], that is mentioned in both surveys and uses BMPN is briefly considered. As a general purpose solution for business process families they developed a rich process component abstraction that allows the definition of variation points. They mention a "prototype implementation", see [22, p. 38] and they do not remark that it is BPMN 2.0 conform. Therefore their methodology does not meet crucial restrictions that were set for MDMS-3.

Within this paper we do not design configurable models but a configurable process architecture. The variation points of the SPL do not activate or deactivate model elements within one model but they trigger process instances of standard BPMN 2.0 processes. Our major concern is therefore not the correctness of a single P-A model – those models are quite simple - but the behavioral correctness of the resulting process architecture. For this purpose the architectural rules (R1)-(R6) have been defined.

6   BPM Use Cases

In his note to the call for papers for "process architectures and platforms" of the BPM-2014 van der Aalst classifies that topic area by the use cases enact model (EnM), adapt while running (AdaWR) and monitor (Mon), see [20].

If the monitoring of the processes indicates that changes within the process orchestration are necessary, then the execution of the processes can be adapted with changes to the state automaton of the state-centric process architecture and/or the redefinition of the application specific processes.

The output of the refinement step in this paper, see Fig. 6, does not really result in a single model but has as output

- the set of the P-A-Models and
- the technical state automaton that controls the business process architecture.

Each of the BPM use cases of van der Aalst in [21, Ch. 4] has a transition from the left (starting point) to the right side (achieved result). A look on the right side of those transition shows that none of the use cases mentioned there results in more than one

---

[10] See [23, p. 46].

model and of course none of these right sides contains a technical state automata. Therefore the solution in this paper, a process architecture that is controlled by a state automaton, can motivate an extension of the use case catalog by a special refinement use case that defines a business process architecture as an output.

7   Conclusion

Master data management systems are probably not first associations that come into mind when one thinks of BPM and BPMS. But the ongoing proliferation of multi-channel commerce increases the importance of high quality product master data. The usage of a BPMS as the core of a master data management system on the one hand brings business process engines to new application areas and stakeholders in contact with BPMN 2.0 who have hardly heard of it before. On the other hand do state-centric long-living business objects and comparable small budgets demand fresh and innovative approaches. Since long-living business objects also occur in other application domains like insurances and banks, the approach to enact them using the proposed architecture may be promising.

This paper has demonstrated that recent trends in business process architecture research form a solid foundation for a state-centric business process architecture and for a software production line that is based on BPMN 2.0.

References

1. Hubl, K.: Model driven configuration, http://www.bpmb.de/images/Hubl.pdf (accessed: February 8, 2014)
2. Borschert, K.: Model-Driven Configuration of Standard Processes, Berlin (November 13, 2012)
3. Weiss, D.M.: Software product-line engineering: a family-based software development process. Addison-Wesley, Reading (1999)
4. SEI, A Framework for Software Product Line Practice, Version 5.0, http://www.sei.cmu.edu/productlines/frame_report/what.is.a.PL.htm (accessed: February 22, 2014)
5. van der Aalst, W.M.P.: A Decade of Business Process Management Conferences: Personal Reflections on a Developing Discipline. In: Barros, A., Gal, A., Kindler, E. (eds.) BPM 2012. LNCS, vol. 7481, pp. 1–16. Springer, Heidelberg (2012)
6. Bhattacharya, K., Hull, R., Su, J.: A Data-Centric Design Methodology for Business Process. In: van der Aalst, W.M.P., Cardoso, J. (eds.) Research on Business Process Modeling. Information Science Reference, Hershey (2009)
7. Java Platform, Enterprise Edition (Java EE) | Oracle Technology Network | Oracle, http://www.oracle.com/technetwork/java/javaee/overview/index.html (accessed: February 08, 2014)
8. Fischer, J., Hammer, G., Kern, U., Rulle, A., Städler, M., Steffen, T.: Verbundprojekt MOVE - Modellierung einer verteilten Architektur für die Entwicklung unternehmensübergreifender Informationssysteme und ihre Validierung im Handelsbereich. In: Statusseminar des BMBF Softwaretechnologie, Berlin, März 23-24, pp. 109–142 (1998)

9. Steffen, T.: Modellierungsmethode zur Integration zwischenbetrieblicher Informations-flüsse. Tenea Verlag, Berlin (2002)
10. van der Aalst, W.M.P., van Hee, K.M.: Workflow management models, methods, and systems. MIT Press, Cambridge (2002)
11. Reichert, M., Weber, B.: Enabling Flexibility in Process-Aware Information Systems Challenges, Methods, Technologies. Springer, Heidelberg (2012)
12. Dumas, M.: On the Convergence of Data and Process Engineering. In: Eder, J., Bielikova, M., Tjoa, A.M. (eds.) ADBIS 2011. LNCS, vol. 6909, pp. 19–26. Springer, Heidelberg (2011)
13. Allweyer, T.: BPMN 2.0: Introduction to the Standard for Business Process Modeling. Books on Demand, Norderstedt (2010)
14. O. M. G. Specification, Business Process Model and Notation (BPMN) Version 2.0. (2011)
15. dos Santos Rocha, R., Fantinato, M.: The use of software product lines for business process management: A systematic literature review. Inf. Softw. Technol., 55(8), 1355–1373 (2013)
16. White, S.A.: Process Modeling Notations and Workflow Patterns, http://www.omg.org/bpmn/Documents/Notations_and_Workflow _Patterns.pdf (accessed: December 13, 2013)
17. Silver, B.: BPMN method and style. Cody-Cassidy Press, Aptos (2009)
18. Lankhorst, M. (ed.): Enterprise architecture at work: modelling, communication and analysis, 3rd edn. Springer, Heidelberg (2013)
19. Eid-Sabbagh, R.-H., Dijkman, R., Weske, M.: Business process architecture: Use and correctness. In: Barros, A., Gal, A., Kindler, E. (eds.) BPM 2012. LNCS, vol. 7481, pp. 65–81. Springer, Heidelberg (2012)
20. van der Aalst, W.M.P.: Plumbers needed! — BPM 2014, http://bpm2014.haifa.ac.il/Topic_Areas/ process-architectures-and-platforms/plumbers-needed (accessed: February 08, 2014)
21. van der Aalst, W.M.P.: Business Process Management: A Comprehensive Survey. In: ISRN Software Engineering, vol. 2013, Article ID 507984, 37 pages (2013), http://dx.doi.org/10.1155/2013/507984
22. Barat, S., Kulkarni, V.: A component abstraction for business processes. Int. J. Business Process Integration and Management 6(1), 29–40 (2012)
23. Rosa, M.L., van der Aalst, W.M.P., Dumas, M., Milani, F.: Business Process Variability Modeling: A Survey. QUT ePrints (2013)

DRain: An Engine for Quality-of-Result Driven Process-Based Data Analytics

Aitor Murguzur[1], Johannes M. Schleicher[2], Hong-Linh Truong[2],
Salvador Trujillo[1], and Schahram Dustdar[2]

[1] Software Production Area, IK4-Ikerlan Research Center, Spain
{amurguzur,strujillo}@ikerlan.es
[2] Distributed System Group, Vienna University of Technology, Austria
{j.schleicher,truong,dustdar}@infosys.tuwien.ac.at

Abstract. The analysis of massive amounts of diverse data provided by large cities, combined with the requirements from multiple domain experts and users, is becoming a challenging trend. Although current process-based solutions rise in data awareness, there is less coverage of approaches dealing with the Quality-of-Result (QoR) to assist data analytics in distributed data-intensive environments. In this paper, we present the fundamental building blocks of a framework for enabling process selection and configuration through user-defined QoR at runtime. These building blocks form the basis to support modeling, execution and configuration of data-aware process variants in order to perform analytics. They can be integrated with different underlying APIs, promoting abstraction, QoR-driven data interaction and configuration. Finally, we carry out a preliminary evaluation on the URBEM scenario, concluding that our framework spends little time on QoR-driven selection and configuration of data-aware processes.

Keywords: Data-aware Processes, Runtime Configuration, Data Analytics, Smart Cities.

1 Introduction

The emergence of the smart city paradigm has created a plethora of new challenges for ICT [1]. Specifically, the analysis of large volumes of diverse data (referred to as Big Data) provided by large cities, combined with disperse requirements from multiple domain experts and stakeholders is becoming challenging [2]. For instance, the task of urban planning in the smart city context needs to collect data from all areas of significance ranging from energy consumption, construction and mobility systems to sociological factors, to just name a few.

Although workflows have been used to compose and execute a series of computational or data manipulation steps, such as scientific workflows [3,4], a few discussions have been focused on the utilization of runtime mechanisms to select and configure data-aware processes based on user-defined Quality-of-Result (QoR) to perform distributed data analytics. This is required in our URBEM[1]

---

[1] http://urbem.tuwien.ac.at/

S. Sadiq, P. Soffer, and H. Völzer (Eds.): BPM 2014, LNCS 8659, pp. 349–356, 2014.

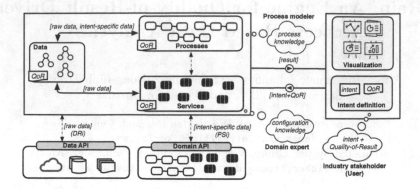

Fig. 1. Artifacts and interactions in process-based data analytics

scenario where large sets of data-aware process variants interact with data services, each with particular quality constraints. Hence, due to the high variability of data-aware analytics processes and data endpoints, it is crucial to provide means of quality-driven process selection and customization at runtime.

1.1 Motivation, Contributions and Paper Structure

In process-based data analytics the data needed to actually execute process activities is much broader than the typical process-related data (see Fig. 1). Although *raw data* (e.g. data from *Data APIs*) can be relevant to several artifacts, such as services and process activities, it is not bound to any specific intent and thus represents general information. On the other hand, the results of remote analytics processes and available services can be offered as *intent-specific data*, exposing the expected result as Data as a Service (DaaS).

Services include computational models (e.g. MATLAB model) from domain experts which are required by activities in a process execution. An data-aware analytics *process*, referred to as Workflow as a Service (WFaaS), represents a particular intent for an industry stakeholder. Such process logic is represented in form of process models (e.g. BPMN2, BPEL), which stands for a particular analytics type, consisting of a number of activities to be executed. Hence, process instances are created on user *intent* request which may indicate a desired QoR.

In this scenario and due to the high variability of related processes and data variety, we need to defer WFaaS selection and configuration to runtime, where process variants are customized and executed based on QoR. This would reduce the complexity of managing large sets of process variants, as well as binding suitable data endpoints and processes ensuring required QoR for analytics. However, although a number of approaches have been focused on data analytics processes, such as scientific workflows [3,4], Quality-of-Service (QoS) based service selection [5,6], and process variant re-configuration [7,8,9], none of them are capable of selecting and configuring data-aware process variants based on QoR at runtime.

In this paper, we therefore present some of the fundamental building blocks of a framework (called DRain) for QoR-driven selection and configuration of data-aware processes. The main contributions (C) are: **C1** - we propose an approach and a prototype framework to select, configure and execute data-aware analytics processes at runtime; and **C2** - we demonstrate through an evaluation on a real example from URBEM that our framework spends little time for selecting analytics processes and data endpoints, as well as configuring variation points (DRi activities) based on data from the data realm.

The rest of the paper is structured as follows: In Section 2 related work is summarized. We present the overall architecture and detail individual framework building blocks in Section 3. Section 4 evaluates the functionality and usefulness of the presented approach by encoding a realistic example in URBEM. Lastly, we conclude the paper and present the direction of future work in Section 5.

2   Related Work

Alternative approaches have been focused on employing workflows for data analytics, such as in scientific workflows [3,4], but without considering QoR, a term originally coined for data analytics [10], or Quality-of-Service (QoS) to drive process selection and configuration. The term QoS is mainly used in the area of service composition. In this light, the Discorso framework [5] facilitates late binding of services by the subsequent selection of applicable Web services based on supervision rules and QoS constrains at runtime. Canfora et al. [6] provide a QoS-aware composite service binding and re-binding approach based on Genetic Algorithms. These latter provide useful methods for QoS-based service (re-)binding; however, they are focused on service selection, rather than enabling process configuration at runtime through QoR-driven data interactions.

On the other hand, process re-configuration [7,8,9] capabilities have been promoted by other authors. For instance, the CEVICHE framework [7] enables BPEL process schema level re-configuration by means of monitoring QoS (service availability and service performance). In a similar vein, Xiao et al. [8] present a constraint-based framework to enable re-configuration (changing relationships among fragments through constraints) and adaptation through adaptation policies to select fragments at runtime. Additionally, in [9] autonomic mechanisms are used to guide the self-adaptation of service compositions according to context changes and variability specification. With respect to the mentioned work, we are not focused on re-configuration, otherwise our approach defers QoR-driven process selection and configuration to runtime.

Last but not least, process configuration abstractions have also been proved by other authors. For instance, a requirements-driven approach [11] enables the configuration of BPEL processes based on quality constraints. Similarly, a questionnaire-driven approach [12] enables a step-wise configuration of reference processes at design-time. However, to the best of our knowledge, no framework is capable of customizing QoR-driven data-aware process variants at runtime.

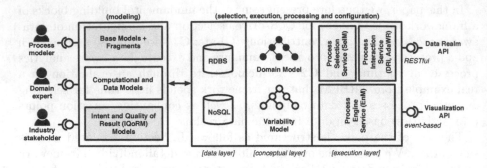

Fig. 2. The DRain framework overview

3   DRain Building Blocks

The DRain framework (see Fig. 2) allows for modeling, configuration, processing and execution of data-aware analytics processes based on user-defined QoR.

3.1   Modeling

Base Models and Fragments. In order to correspond to different user-defined QoR needs (e.g. time and cost constraints), the process modeler may create *base models* and *fragments* using BPMN2 elements (e.g. Service Tasks for invoking available *computational model* services) and custom variation points (the so-called DRi activities). In essence, a base model represents the commonality shared by a process family and variation points that are subjected to change. Variation points identify specific parts in a base model where data interaction and fragment selection occur (in DRi activities). A process fragment, or fragment for short, describes a particular configuration option for each variation point within a base model. For a more detailed discussion of our foundations regarding process variability modeling, we refer to our previous work [13].

IQoRM. The *Intent and Quality of Result Model (IQoRM)* is reflected through an UML diagram, containing intents representing user requests, constraints (QoR) representing user restrictions and analytics scope (see Fig. 3). Those abstractions are used to construct a data analytics task and its strategy, and thus represent constraints for the desired behavior. The analytics range is limited by the Scope class, which delimits the range of an analytics Intent. For example, a user might want to perform the analysis: "determine the energy consumption for the specific district X" (X can be any district of the city). In this case, "energy consumption" is the desired intent which contains "for the specific district X" as a delimiter. Two sub-classes are differentiated: ConfigurationScope which demarcates between different configuration alternatives (e.g. the value variable may determine selection (SelM), configuration (ConCM), discovery (DiscM) or composition (CompM) alternatives, as distinguished

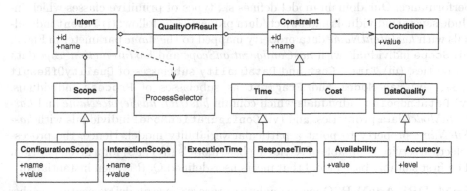

Fig. 3. IQoRM model

by [14]), and `InteractionScope` for limiting available data endpoints (e.g. the `value` variable delimits the range of data endpoints, such as check `ALL` available resources from the data realm). Such parameters delimit data interactions during a base model execution which considers both interaction and configuration scopes, i.e., data endpoints that should be considered for a particular function.

`QualityOfResult` can determine not only the selection of a particular analytics process, but also the binding of inherent data endpoints. A `Constraint` is a basic aspect of our framework which represents some condition, restriction or assertion related to the analytics artifacts. It includes a set of `Conditions` that are atomic formulae or implications (see the code snippet below) for driving process selection and customization. Conditions (`lessThan`, `greaterThan`, `inBetween`) may be applied to different constraint types. In Fig. 3, three constraints are considered: (i) `Time` for the entire time that a process, computational service or data service takes for execution (`ExecutionTime`) and its network channel to ping (`ResponseTime`), (ii) `Cost` which represents the cumulative expected cost of performing action, and (iii) `DataQuality` to exhibit the `Availability` (refers to the availability of data) and `Accuracy` (refers to the level of provided data values confidence) of provided data endpoints. In a simplified version, we consider {`True`,`False`} for the former, and {`Green`,`Orange`,`Red`} for the latter. Once intent, scope and QoR are specified, `ProcessSelector` initializes the search algorithm for finding a relevant analytics process.

Excerpt of a QoR condition

```
quality.addResponseTime(new ResponseTime("responseTime",
    Condition.lessThan(400)));
```

3.2   Selection, Execution, Processing and Configuration

SelM. In DRain, the domain model is defined using ontologies. This type of representation has been widely accepted as a conducive method for domain modeling (knowledge vocabulary) and reasoning, with low impact on scalability and performance. Our domain model defines six types of primitive classes which include several individuals and object/data properties as follow: (i) `Intent` individuals with *hasIntentName* data property mapped to the *name* parameter in Fig. 3, (ii) `Scope` individuals with *hasConfigurationScope* and *hasInteractionScope* data properties, (iii) `Time` , `Cost` and `DataQuality` subclasses of `QualityOfResult` class, (iv) `BaseModel` and `Fragment` as subclasses of `Process` individuals, (v) `DataEndpoint` individuals which contain *hasURI*, *hasServiceName* and *hasDataModel* data properties, and (vi) `ConfigurationModel` individuals with *hasFileName* property to point a particular variability model. Hence, the process selection service is capable of retrieving base models (WFaaS) for a given petition. The first suitable base model that meets user-defined QoR is then instantiated.

EnM, DRi, AdaWR. Once an analytics process (base model) execution reaches a `DRi` activity, the process engine follows several steps. If there is no fragment assignment for the current `DRi` activity execution, this activity throws an event to select a suitable fragment based on context data. Such selection requires two types of processing. In the first *interaction* task, the event coming from a `DRi` execution is triggered by the process interaction service to find a single data endpoint URI that satisfies pre-established QoR constraints (by running a SPARQL query). Data collected from a REST resource (in JSON) is mapped to a data model object (by a *hasDataModel* data property) to automatically perform the base model instance *configuration*. For the latter, the context values gathered from the REST service are mapped to placed attributes in a variability model, in order to get a preferred fragment choice considering pre-established constraints and fragments for each variation point. Once a suitable fragment is resolved using a Solver, `DRain` signals the particular `DRi` activity execution which executes the preferred fragment and then continues its control-flow.

We adopt feature models [15] to model all configuration options for each analytics base model and surrounding `DRi` activities (i.e. variation points) in a variability model. The mapping between a domain model and a variability model is realized by naming compounds as follows: (i) feature names are mapped to `BaseModel` and `Fragment` individuals *hasProcessKey* data property, (ii) variation point features are linked to *hasServiceName* data property of a `DataEndpoint` individual, and (iii) variability model attributes are related to data model variables from each `DataEndpoint`. The latter relation correlates data model variable/-value pairs with feature model attributes.

4   Evaluation

In the following, we briefly describe the evaluation scenario in URBEM and present the results of the evaluation runs on `DRain`. The `DRain` framework was developed in Java and Clojure based on open source technologies.

Provided Models. For the evaluation, we created 30 base model variants (individuals) with different time and cost QoR constraints for an energy consumption intent in URBEM. This analytics process consists of four `DRi` activities (variation points) and two service tasks. Each `DRi` activity contained 2 fragment

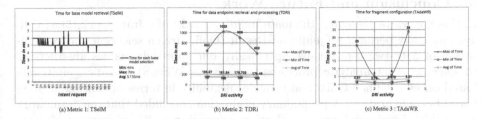

Fig. 4. Evaluation results

alternatives, providing each distinct data quality (availability and accuracy), so we get $2^4 = 16$ variant customizations for the outlined base model. Moreover, we created 24 data endpoints with different QoR and five data values were parsed in a configuration model in each data interaction.

Metrics. In order to obtain a reliable evaluation, we processed the base model 200 times and evaluated the results against three performance-related metrics:

- *Time for base model retrieval (TSelM)*: This metric measures the time required for intent-driven and QoR-based base model searching.
- *Time for data endpoint retrieval (TDRi)*: This metric defines the timespan from DRi activity initialization to the moment when the process interaction service finds a suitable data endpoint for the given QoR and invoked the particular REST resource to collect data.
- *Time for fragment solving (TAdaWR)*: This metrics measures the time required to establish context values and find a suitable fragment once data is gathered from a REST resource.

Results. The results of our evaluation in terms of the average of all evaluation runs are provided as graphics in Fig 4.[2] Overall, we can state that our engine operates with little impact on performance, and slightly affects the execution time required by each analytics process instance. This allows for QoR-driven selection and configuration of data-aware analytics processes that involve a considerable number of variants and data endpoints (i.e. 30 and 24 respectively in the evaluation), offering greater flexibility and abstraction. As shown in Fig. 4 (a), the difference between the minimum and maximum time required for a base model retrieval (TSelM) based on a user-defined QoR is about **3ms**. In a similar vein, the average time for data endpoint selection and processing (TDRi) is reasonable at **184.019ms**, considering both sequential, such as BuildingSpecification and EnergyDemand, and parallel activities, such as ElectricalGridUtilisation and ThermalGridUtilisation (check supplement file). Finally, it is also important to note the overall average time required to complete the runtime configuration, e.g., for (TAdaWR) an average time of **2.986ms** is necessary for putting five context values in the variability model to set a particular fragment for a given DRi.

---

[2] All datasets, a detailed description of the example and additional files are available at: https://github.com/amurguzur/drain

5   Conclusion and Future Work

In this paper, we presented the main building blocks of a framework (DRain) to automatically perform a Quality-of-Result (QoR) driven selection and configuration of data-aware processes. Specifically, our approach enables abstractions to select relevant analytic processes (exposed as WFaaS) and data endpoints based on user-defined QoR, and provides flexibility in terms of runtime process variants configuration. A preliminary evaluation concluded that our framework is capable of high-performance selection, processing and configuration of data-aware processes in subsequent QoR-driven data interactions. For future work, we plan to extend the associated framework and test it against industrial case studies, and adapt the QoR model for a more domain-specific environment. Further, we will explore ranking and selection algorithms/dimensions using QoR.

References

1. Naphade, M., Banavar, G., Harrison, C., Paraszczak, J., Morris, R.: Smarter cities and their innovation challenges. Computer 44(6), 32–39 (2011)
2. Khan, Z., Kiani, A.A.,, S.L.: Cloud based big data analytics for smart future cities. In: UCC Workshops (2013)
3. Altintas, I., Berkley, C., Jaeger, E., Jones, M., Ludascher, B., Mock, S.: Kepler: an extensible system for design and execution of scientific workflows. In: SSDBM, pp. 423–424 (2004)
4. Hauder, M., Gil, Y., Liu, Y.: A framework for efficient data analytics through automatic configuration and customization of scientific workflows. In: e-Science, pp. 379–386 (2011)
5. Ardagna, D., Pernici, B.: Adaptive service composition in flexible processes. IEEE Transactions on Software Engineering 33(6), 369–384 (2007)
6. Canfora, G., Di Penta, M., Esposito, R., Villani, M.L.: A framework for qos-aware binding and re-binding of composite web services. J. Syst. Softw. 81(10) (2008)
7. Hermosillo, G., Seinturier, L., Duchien, L.: Using complex event processing for dynamic business process adaptation. In: SCC, pp. 466–473 (2010)
8. Xiao, Z., Cao, D., You, C., Mei, H.: Towards a constraint-based framework for dynamic business process adaptation. In: SCC, pp. 685–692 (2011)
9. Alférez, G., Pelechano, V., Mazo, R., Salinesi, C., Diaz, D.: Dynamic adaptation of service compositions with variability models. In: JSS (2013)
10. Truong, H.L., Dustdar, S.: Principles of software-defined elastic systems for big data analytics. In: MIE, pp. 10–14 (2014)
11. Lapouchnian, A., Yu, Y., Mylopoulos, J.: Requirements-driven design and configuration management of business processes. In: Alonso, G., Dadam, P., Rosemann, M. (eds.) BPM 2007. LNCS, vol. 4714, pp. 246–261. Springer, Heidelberg (2007)
12. La Rosa, M., Lux, J., Seidel, S., Dumas, M., ter Hofstede, A.H.M.: Questionnaire-driven configuration of reference process models. In: Krogstie, J., Opdahl, A.L., Sindre, G. (eds.) CAiSE 2007 and WES 2007. LNCS, vol. 4495, pp. 424–438. Springer, Heidelberg (2007)
13. Murguzur, A., De Carlos, X., Trujillo, S., Sagardui, G.: Context-aware staged configuration of process variants@Runtime. In: Jarke, M., Mylopoulos, J., Quix, C., Rolland, C., Manolopoulos, Y., Mouratidis, H., Horkoff, J. (eds.) CAiSE 2014. LNCS, vol. 8484, pp. 241–255. Springer, Heidelberg (2014)
14. van der Aalst, W.M.P.: Business process management: A comprehensive survey. ISRN Software Engineering, 37 (2013)
15. Batory, D.: Feature models, grammars, and propositional formulas. In: Obbink, H., Pohl, K. (eds.) SPLC 2005. LNCS, vol. 3714, pp. 7–20. Springer, Heidelberg (2005)

Use Your Best Device!
Enabling Device Changes at Runtime

Dennis Bokermann, Christian Gerth, and Gregor Engels

Department of Computer Science, University of Paderborn, Germany
{dennis.bokermann,gerth,engels}@uni-paderborn.de
http://is.uni-paderborn.de

Abstract. The usage of different computing devices, like desktop computers or smartphones, in our everyday lifes increases continuously. Moreover, smart watches and other wearables are ready to accompany us in our daily habits. As a consequence, applications are developed for a variety of different computing devices, in order to give users the freedom to choose a device that really fits their current situation. If this situation changes, a different device may become more suitable than the chosen one. In most cases, applications do not support changing the executing device at runtime, since this is usually not considered at design time and would require the transferal of the current state. In this paper, we present an approach to define device changes for process-driven applications. To this extent, we enrich process models with deployment information, which allows specifying where it should be possible to change the device while keeping the application's state. Additionally, we have adapted a process engine to support the execution of these enriched process models. Thereby, we take a further step towards human-centric BPM that enables users to use their most suitable device.

1 Introduction

In addition to classic desktop computers, other computing devices like smartphones and tablets entered our everyday lifes. Upcoming technologies such as smart TVs, smart watches, or other wearables will probably increase the computing device diversity and density even more. Consequently, most applications are no longer exclusively available for desktop computers. Instead software vendors provide their applications for a variety of devices.

Depending on their current situation, users choose different devices to use an application. Thereby, the suitability of a device depends on various factors, e.g. a study conducted by Dearman et al. [3] shows that users assign different roles to different devices, such as work computer or private phone. Furthermore, the suitability depends on environmental aspects, like the current location, and on installed software as well as available hardware and peripheral equipment.

Throughout this paper, we use the process of buying a train ticket as an example for an application, which is provided for different devices. Thereby, we focus on two types of computing devices: smartphones and ticket vending

S. Sadiq, P. Soffer, and H. Völzer (Eds.): BPM 2014, LNCS 8659, pp. 357–365, 2014.

machines (TVMs). When buying a ticket at a TVM, the ticket has to be paid in cash and it is printed afterwards. In contrast to that, smartphones do not allow cash payment instead the ticket must be paid online. Moreover, a digital ticket is provided because smartphones usually do not have printer access.

In most cases, changing the device at runtime is not possible because device changes are not considered while the application is developed. Thus, users are forced to stick to a single device. Consequently, by choosing a device users are already limiting the available options. This leads to the fact that users wait until the most suited device for the primary objective is available [5], e.g. if a user wants a printed ticket and the smartphone has no printer access, the user is forced to wait until a TVM is available. Alternatively, if a user starts the process on a smartphone, the current state is lost when changing to a TVM. Consequently, the user has to start again from the beginning and redo already completed steps, like searching for a connection.

Enabling users to change a device and keep the current application state, constitutes a step forward and would result in more flexible applications. Instead of being limited to the capabilities of a single device, users could switch to another device to overcome these limitations. In case of our example, a user should be able to search for an appropriate connection and select the ticket options on the smartphone, and afterwards, may continue on the TVM to pay and print the ticket. We call such an application a *cross-device application* (CDA), since it enables users to change devices while keeping the state. In order to enable such device changes at runtime, several key challenges must be overcome. For instance, possible device changes must be specifiable at design time. This includes that it must be specifiable which part of an application is executed by which device, since not all device have the same capabilities. For these purposes, a description of the available types of devices and their properties is required because concrete devices are usually not known at design time. To actually perform device changes at runtime, it must be explained how to preserve an application's state. Aside from this, device changes introduce new kinds of exceptions, which must be considered at design time, e.g. the failure of a device change.

In this paper, we address the specification of process-driven CDAs. For this purpose, we enrich process models with deployment information, so that device changes can be specified while designing a process. To define deployment information, we build an ontology which describes available device types and their properties. This information is linked to process models to specify which devices are capable of executing certain parts of a process. Afterwards, it can be specified at which points a process supports device changes. By presenting the basic ideas for a process engine, which supports our approach, we take a major step to enable device changes at runtime.

The remainder of this paper is structured as follows: In Section 2, we explain how to describe device types and their properties. Section 3 explains our approach to enrich process models with deployment information. Subsequently, Section 4 discusses related work. Finally, Section 5 concludes the paper and gives an outlook on future work.

2   Device Modeling

As a prerequisite for the specification of process-driven CDAs, it is necessary to have knowledge about the devices, which are present at runtime. This section explains the specification of a device ontology, which describes the available types of devices and their properties. At runtime, this ontology is used to manage information about concrete device. The device ontology can be used to enrich multiple process models with deployment information, since it is defined independently from a concrete process model.

In case of our example, we focus on two device types: TVM and smartphones. Furthermore, we consider properties of these device types, i.e. functional properties like printer access or non-functional properties like mobility. These device types and properties can be specified in terms of an ontology using the Web Ontology Language (OWL)[1]. Based on OWL, we define semantic information like sub class relations of device types. This is used later on to infer additional knowledge about devices and their interrelations. For our example, we only predefine classes for device types and their properties. However, the further content of the ontology is up to the application developer.

The device ontology cannot only be used for the specification of CDAs, it can also serve as basis for managing device information at runtime. For this purpose, the ontology is extended by adding instances of the device types and properties, which represent concrete devices. For instance, a concrete smartphone is represented by an instance of the type smartphone and information about the smartphone's properties is stored, e.g. if it has printer access or not. For the management of the ontology at runtime, we developed a component where devices can register themselves automatically, so that information about them is added to the ontology dynamically. After registration, a device must propagate property changes to the component to keep this information up-to-date. For the implementation of such a component, we use the Resource Description Framework (RDF)[2] as serialization format for our ontology and use the Apache Jena framework[3] to store, manipulate, and query the ontology. The component can be embedded into an existing application or deployed independently as a service.

3   Enabling Device Changes

In this section, we consider the specification of process-driven CDAs. To this extent, we use the device ontology introduced in the previous section, to enrich process models with deployment information. Thereby, we specify where certain devices are required and when device changes are possible. Moreover, we explain how this can be used to enable device changes at runtime.

When building process-driven CDAs, we have to define which part of the process shall be executed by which device. Therefore, we define device requirements for parts of a process. In the following, we focus on doing this for single

---

[1] www.w3.org/TR/owl-ref/

[2] www.w3.org/TR/rdf-primer/

[3] jena.apache.org

tasks, however, we also support the definition of device requirements for arbitrary sub parts of a process, reaching from a single task to the entire process. Figure 1 shows the process to buy a train ticket considering the capabilities of smartphones and TVMs. The process is modeled using the Business Process Model and Notation (BPMN)[4]. The device requirements are visualized by icons attached to the tasks of the process model, e.g. a printer icon is attached to the task "Print Ticket". First, the user has to search for the connection, which requires a device with internet access. Both types of devices, smartphones and TVMs, fulfill this requirement. Next, the user has to select the ticket options and a payment method. Cash payment is offered by devices, which have a cash module, e.g. a TVM. Online payment also requires internet access. This would also be the case smartphones as well as for TVMs. However, we do not want to allow online payment at TVMs because of privacy concerns. Thus, we define for the task "Pay Online" that internet access is required and that it should be a private device. To get a printed ticket, a device with printer access is required and a digital ticket is only useful on mobile devices.

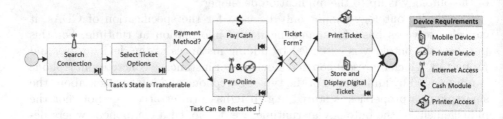

Fig. 1. Process to Purchase a Train Ticket with Deployment Information

For documentation purposes, it would suffice to describe device requirements informally. However, we want to automatically determine, which devices meet the requirements at runtime. Consequently, we need a formal and executable form to specify device requirements. To this extent, we propose mapping device requirements to the device types and properties of the device ontology using SPARQL[5], a querying language for the RDF. We define a special form of SPARQL query called Device Selection Expression (DSE), which retrieves a device list from the device ontology at runtime. The selection criteria of such a DSE can be refined, so that only devices which meet the requirements are returned. As a result, an empty DSE, one where the selection criteria is not refined, returns all available devices. The Apache Jena framework allows evaluating SPARQL queries on RDF ontologies. By focusing on device properties for the specifications of DSEs, we can easily consider other device types, which offer these properties. For instance, we could add desktop computers to our device ontology, which properties include that is a private device and might have internet as well as printer access.

---

[4] www.omg.org/spec/BPMN/2.0/

[5] www.w3.org/TR/rdf-sparql-query/

By assigning device requirements to tasks, we already define *necessary device changes*. Essentially, every time when the execution of a process instance reaches a new task, it must be checked if the current device meets the requirements of the upcoming task. If this is not the case, it becomes necessary to change to another device. For instance in our example, if the current device is a smartphone and cash payment is selected, it is necessary to change to a TVM. Additionally, it is also possible to have *optional device changes*, where a user might want to change the device even though the current device is capable of continuing the process execution. An example for such an optional device change would be if a user searches for connection on his smartphone but wants to change to a TVM to select the ticket options.

Enabling device changes at runtime requires keeping the applications state while the device is changed. If no tasks are active, the complete state of a process-driven CDAs is described by the process' instance. Thus, device changes can be performed by transferring the process instance to another device like in [11]. Alternatively, a process-driven CDA can be executed centrally and just the tasks are executed by end-user devices. Thus, device changes are managed by delegating tasks to different devices, while the process instance is not exchanged between devices. For our implementation, we chose the latter approach, since it allows excluding problems raised by transferring process instances [11].

In addition, if device changes happen while tasks are active, the internal states of the currently active tasks must be considered, too. Consequently, it must be specified what happens to the internal state of a task, when the device is changed. For this purpose, we differentiate between three types of tasks regarding device changes: *continuous, restartable* and *transferable*. Since the BPMN normally does not consider device changes, tasks are expected to run until completion. We consider this to be the default case and call these tasks *continuous*. Also, we do not allow device changes during the execution of these tasks. In our example, the task "Print Ticket" is *continuous* because the internal state is represented by the physical ticket, which is being printed. This cannot be transferred, and thus, we forbid device changes for this task. For *restartable* tasks, the internal state of a task is either discarded or reverted if a device change is invoked. On the new device the task starts again from the beginning. To indicate this behavior we use the rewind symbol (◄◄), e.g. the payment tasks in Figure 1 are *restartable* because a payment is either completed or not done at all. In case of *transferable* tasks, a task's state is serialized and transferred to a new device, so that it can continue the execution. The playpause symbol (►❘❘) marks *transferable* tasks. In case of our example, the task "Search Connection" is declared to be *transferable*. During a device change information like the date of travel or the destination could be transferred to the new device.

The transferal of a task's state requires a serialization format for the internal state, which is understood by all implementations of a task. To this extent, we propose to proceed similar to defining web services using the Web Service Description Language (WDSL)[6]. There, a serialization format for the input and

---

[6] www.w3.org/TR/wsdl/

output parameters is defined. We propose to similarly define a serialization format for the internal states of a task. If a task is suspended, the current state is serialized to the predefined format, and every implementation of the task, which understands the format, must be able to continue the execution based on the serialized state. For instance, such a serialization format for the task "Search Connection" of our example in Figure 1 could describe already entered input values, like origin and destination, and the position inside the internal state space. The creation of such a serialization format will be further addressed in future work.

In our current approach and prototype, we support device changes between tasks (i.e. no task is active) or during the execution of *restartable* and *transferable* tasks. In addition, we support the specification of allowed and forbidden device changes. For instance in our example, we want to allow device changes from a TVM to a smartphone and the other way around. Moreover, a user should be able to change between different smartphones but switching from one TVM to another one should be forbidden because a user cannot be at two TVMs at once. To express this in a process model, all device changes are by default forbidden in our approach and must explicitly be allowed for parts of a process models. This can be done by specifying Device Change Definitions (DCDs), which consists of two DSEs identifying the source and target of a device change as well as a flag, which declares if the change is allowed or not. At runtime, a DCD applies if the device assigned to the currently active part of the process fits the DSE of the source devices. If this is case, it is possible to change to any device matching the target DSE, unless another DCD applies, which forbids this device change. Similar to DSEs, DCDs can be attached to entire sub parts of a process definition. To define the aforementioned device changes for our example, we need to define two DCDs. At first, we need a DCD, which consists of an empty DSEs for the source and target devices. Consequently, this DCD always applies and allows changing to any device. Additionally, we need to define a DCD, which forbids changing from one TVM to another. Thus, this DCD must be marked as forbidden and the DSEs for the source and target devices must describe devices of the type TVM. Both DCDs must be attached to the whole process definition, since they should affect all tasks.

By stating the device requirements and by specifying DCDs, it is possible to define when and where it should be possible to change a device. In order to define device changes for active tasks, the device change must be allowed by the DCDs attached to the corresponding part of the process and the tasks must either be *restartable* or *transferable*. We implemented our approach as a BPMN extension and extended the process engine Activiti[7] to support our approach. Therefore, we added a component to manage information about available devices based on the device ontology (see Section 2) and added a parser for our BPMN extension. The engine executes a CDA centrally and assigns tasks to devices, whose properties match to the device requirements. Additionally, we developed

---

[7] www.activiti.org

a client-side component for the Android platform[8] and as a Node.js[9] web server usable on Windows or Linux. The client-side component informs the engine about device information and handles the client part of a device change, e.g. invoking methods to reset or suspend running tasks.

4   Related Work

One area of related work is concerned with the distributed execution of business processes. Approaches like [9] and [10] split a process into multiple sub parts and use a planing phase at the beginning of the execution to assign these parts to different devices. Afterwards, only limited replanning is possible. Such approaches are not suitable for executing process-driven CDAs, since the device assignments are not flexible enough. The approach of Zaplata et al. [11] distributes the execution of business processes by transferring process instances. Their approach is complementary to our approach because they enable the transferal of process instances but do not consider transferring active tasks. Combining both approaches would lead to an even more flexible execution of business processes. Montagut et al. [7] also developed an approach to distribute the execution of business processes. Similar to our approach they allow specifying device requirements. They define roles, which a device must have, in order to be capable of executing a task. During the execution of a process, a centralized service is used to determine devices having the appropriate roles to execute parts of a process. Unlike our approach, they do not allow device changes for active tasks nor does their approach allow the restriction of device changes. In [8], Pryss et al. present an approach, where a central process engine can delegate parts of a process to mobile devices. These parts can be managed independently by mobile devices and the execution can be migrated from one mobile device to another via a centralized mediator. However, their approach is based on their own process description and is less expressive considering the definition of device changes.

Context-based middleware approaches like [6] collect context information and enable the reaction on context changes. Devices running a part of process can be seen as part of a process' context. However, we believe that not all actions, i.e. device changes, can be inferred by observing the context. Users' needs or preferences are often not measurable. Thus, changing from one device to another cannot always be determined by context information. Instead we must provide users the possibility to change between devices according to their needs. This especially includes the case of device changes for active tasks.

Chakraborty et al. [2] describe an approach to combine business processes and collaboration tools, e.g. instant messengers. They can reach users on different devices by exploiting knowledge about context information to select the best suitable communication channel. However, their approach offers only limited interaction with users and does not cover the migration of tasks.

---

[8] www.android.com
[9] www.nodejs.org

Ghiani et al. [4] developed an infrastructure to migrate existing web applications from one device to another and keep the current state. We are convinced that cross-device interaction must be considered at design time, otherwise an application cannot consider the functionality offered by different types of devices. Nevertheless, a migration platform like the one presented in [4] would also be beneficial for our approach as well.

In [1], an ontology to describe devices is presented, which could be used as initial device ontology for our approach. However, information about a device's user, peripheral equipment, or non-functional aspects, like mobility, is missing.

5   Conclusion and Future Work

In this paper, we presented an approach to enrich process models with deployment information to model and enable process-driven CDAs. For this purpose, we created an ontology to describe device types and their properties at design time. This ontology is later on used to manage information about concrete devices at runtime. Based on the ontology, we introduced a mechanism to specify device requirements for arbitrary parts of a process and we explained how to specify device changes. Furthermore, we implemented our approach by adapting an existing process engine, and thereby, we enable users to change devices

In the future, we want to further improve the specification of devices changes, e.g. by allowing to define that a process part requires the same or a different device as another part of the process. Currently, the schema describing the internal state of transferable tasks must be developed manually. For this reason, we plan to further assist developers in creating such a schema. Moreover, we will address handling exceptions introduced by enabling device changes.

References

1. Bandara, A., Payne, T.R., de Roure, D., Clemo, G.: An Ontological Framework for Semantic Description of Devices (Poster). In: ISWC 2004 (2004)
2. Chakraborty, D., Lei, H.: Pervasive Enablement of Business Processes. In: PerCom 2004, pp. 87–100. IEEE (2004)
3. Dearman, D., Pierce, J.S.: "It's on my other computer!": Computing with Multiple Devices. In: CHI 2008, pp. 767–776. ACM (2008)
4. Ghiani, G., Paternò, F., Santoro, C.: Push and Pull of Web User Interfaces in Multi-device Environments. In: AVI 2012, pp. 10–17. ACM (2012)
5. Karlson, A.K., Iqbal, S.T., Meyers, B., Ramos, G., Lee, K., Tang, J.C.: Mobile Taskflow in Context: A Screenshot Study of Smartphone Usage. In: CHI 2010, pp. 2009–2018. ACM (2010)
6. Kunze, C.P., Zaplata, S., Lamersdorf, W.: Mobile Process Description and Execution. In: Eliassen, F., Montresor, A. (eds.) DAIS 2006. LNCS, vol. 4025, pp. 32–47. Springer, Heidelberg (2006)
7. Montagut, F., Molva, R.: Enabling Pervasive Execution of Workflows. In: CollaborateCom 2005, pp. 10–20. IEEE (2005)

8. Pryss, R., Tiedeken, J., Kreher, U., Reichert, M.: Towards Flexible Process Support on Mobile Devices. In: Ng, K.W. (ed.) CAiSE Forum 2010. LNBIP, vol. 72, pp. 150–165. Springer, Heidelberg (2010)

9. Sen, R., Hackmann, G., Haitjema, M., Roman, G.C., Gill, C.D.: Coordinating Workflow Allocation and Execution in Mobile Environments. In: Murphy, A.L., Vitek, J. (eds.) COORDINATION 2007. LNCS, vol. 4467, pp. 249–267. Springer, Heidelberg (2007)

10. Sen, R., Roman, G.C., Gill, C.D.: CiAN: A Workflow Engine for MANETs. In: Lea, D., Zavattaro, G. (eds.) COORDINATION 2008. LNCS, vol. 5052, pp. 280–295. Springer, Heidelberg (2008)

11. Zaplata, S., Hamann, K., Kottke, K., Lamersdorf, W.: Flexible Execution of Distributed Business Processes based on Process Instance Migration. Journal of Systems Integration (JSI) 1(3), 3–16 (2010)

Specifying Flexible Human Behavior in Interaction-Intensive Process Environments

Christoph Dorn[1], Schahram Dustdar[1], and Leon J. Osterweil[2]

[1] Distributed Systems Group, Vienna University of Technology
{dorn,dustdar}@dsg.tuwien.ac.at
[2] Department of Computer Science, University of Massachusetts Amherst
ljo@cs.umass.edu

Abstract. Fast changing business environments characterized by unpredictable variations call for flexible process-aware systems. The BPM community addressed this challenge through various approaches but little focus has been on how to specify (respectively constrain) flexible human involvement: how human process participants may collaborate on a task, how they may obtain a joint decision that drives the process, or how they may communicate out-of-band for clarifying task-vital information. Experience has shown that pure process languages are not necessarily the most appropriate technique for specifying such flexible behavior. Hence selecting appropriate modeling languages and strategies needs thorough investigation. To this end, this paper juxtaposes the capabilities of representative human-centric specification languages hADL and Little-JIL and demonstrate their joint applicability for modeling interaction-intensive processes.

1 Introduction

Over the past 15 years, process flexibility [15] has been consistently identified as a key aspect for addressing the challenges arising from fast changing business requirements and unpredictable runtime situations. Existing research approaches predominately address flexibility at the process, artifact, and resource level. Little focus has been given to flexible human involvement. Flexible human involvement gains particular importance in interaction-intensive environments. Typical processes occur frequently in the health-care domain or when jointly creating knowledge. These environments exhibit close collaboration among participants, ad-hoc communication, and dynamic decision making while maintaining regions of rigid control-flow constraints. Traditional approaches to process and workflow specification assume a single executing entity per task or activity. Any communication among participants remains implicit, respectively remains outside the specification's scope. CSCW and groupware approaches, on the other hand, offer extensive flexibility but lack sophisticated process support.

We propose a middle ground between these two "extreme" ends of the human interaction spectrum. Specifically, we suggest refining process tasks with human interaction patterns and vice versa. For example, a health-care process could specify that a particular flow-decision may be discussed in a chat room with the head-nurse as moderator. In the opposite direction, authors working on a joint report (i.e., a shared artifact pattern) may incorporate a process specifying steps to safeguard report quality, intellectual property protection, and data anonymity. Experience has shown that pure process

S. Sadiq, P. Soffer, and H. Völzer (Eds.): BPM 2014, LNCS 8659, pp. 366–373, 2014.

languages are not necessarily the most appropriate technique for specifying human interaction patterns. Imagine modeling collection, filtering, distribution, and floor control in a chat room merely in terms of task sequences. Utilizing only process modeling elements quickly becomes tedious, while from a process point of view only the decision outcome (made by the chat room participants) is ultimately of true relevance. Hence interaction-intensive processes require dedicated specification of user behavior beyond current process-centric approaches.

In this paper we consider two mechanisms: (a) the process-centric language *Little-JIL* [7], and (b) the structure-centric *human Architecture Description Language* (hADL) [9] (Sec. 3). Along these lines, we attempt to obtain better insights into jointly utilizing Little-JIL and hADL. Although there is strong support for using either language independently [14,10,9] our hypothesis is that applying both languages in combination will provide more intuitive results in interaction-intensive environments (Sec. 4).

2 Related Work

Work on process flexibility typically focus on adding, removing, replacing process fragments, extending loops, and reconfiguring control dependencies on the process type level and process instance level [16]. Schonenberg et al. [15] provide a taxonomy whereby they distinguish among flexibility *by design*, *by deviation*, *by underspecification*, and *by change*. FLOWer [1] and similar case-based approaches (often denoted as activity-based or ad-hoc work-flows [11]) excel at undoing, repeating, skipping, and including activities. Our work is highly complementary as we specifically focus on the process participants' collaboration flexibility which none of these approaches appropriately address. Further investigations into applying our approach to for example case management or business artifacts are highly appealing.

Recently, the BPM community started exploring the convergence of BPM technology and social media. Brambilla et al. present design patterns for integrating of social network features in BPMN [6]. A social network user may engage in task-centric actions such as voting, commenting, reading a message, or joining a task. Böhringer utilizes tagging, activity streams, and micro-blogging for merging ad-hoc activities into case management [5]. Dengler et al. utilize collaborative software such as Wikis and social networks for coordinating process activities [8]. At best, contemporary Social BPM approaches model collaboration as individual social network user actions; neither the actual collaborative activities nor their structure are explicitly specified. Our work, in contrast, focuses on modeling the actual collaboration among users (well beyond workflow coordinated tasks) in detail. We, thereby, treat the workflow and collaboration structure as equal models.

Also the software engineering community identified the need for combining process technology and collaboration support. Paulo Barthelmess provides an in-depth review of approaches to collaboration and coordination support [3]. Languages and tools primarily target coordination and collaboration via file-centric development artifacts and tasks. Serendipity [12] utilizes events, filters, and actions as the main coordination means among participants. SPADE [2] supports the integration and invocation of collaboration tools, but remains unaware what collaboration type and structure such external tools implement. Oz [4] builds upon a rule-based language for specifying which users are allocated as task executors. Overall, modeling collaboration structures is crude and imprecise, often requiring tedious composition from low-level events. Any tightly integrated collaboration tools provide limited, fixed set of a/synchronous mechanisms that remain outside the process specification's modeling scope. Independent of research domain, we can claim that no process specification approach makes the distinction among collaboration connector and human component, nor provides dedicated decision support (e.g., voting) or information streams (e.g., subscriptions).

3   Specifying Human Flexible Behavior

The overall process specification needs to balance analyzability and flexibility. Orthogonal, the specification needs to differentiate between the three types of human involvement: communication, coordination, and work (co-)execution.

The **human Architecture Description Language** (hADL) [9] describes according to what structure humans interact to achieve a common (sub)goal such as discussing and subsequently jointly deciding upon resource usage (Fig. 2). hADL distinguishes between *HumanComponents* (light green rectangles) and *CollaborationConnectors* (dark green rectangles) to emphasize the difference between the primary collaborating users (e.g., a decision maker) and non-essential, replaceable users that coordinate the collaboration (e.g., a discussion moderator). A CollaborationConnector is thus responsible for the efficient and effective interaction among HumanComponents. Users typically employ diverse means of interaction that range from emails, to chat rooms, shared wiki pages, and Q&A forums, to vote collection. These means implement vastly different interaction semantics: a message is sent and received, a shared artifact can be edited, a vote can be cast. *CollaborationObjects* (rounded rectangles) abstract from concrete interaction tools and capture the semantic differences in subtypes; e.g., *Message* (yellow), *Stream* (light orange), or *SharedArtifact* (dark orange). *HumanActions* (tool icon) specify what capabilities a component or connector requires to fulfill his/her role, e.g., read a discussion thread or cast a vote. Complementary, a CollaborationObject signals its offered capabilities in the form of *ObjectActions* (gear-wheel icon). Both action types distinguish further between *Create*, *Read*, *Update*, and *Delete* (CRUD) privileges. Ultimately, *Links* connect ObjectActions and HumanActions to wire up HumanComponents, CollaborationConnectors, and CollaborationObjects into a collaboration structure. The *Pattern* provides a container for complex, hierarchical CollaborationObjects and interaction patterns composed from the elementary hADL elements. Element types, action CRUD privileges, as well as link cardinalities have no graphical representation and are edited as textual properties. The main motivation for hADL as a dedicated language is the separation between (i) CollaborationConnector and HumanComponent as well as (ii) the distinct CollaborationObjects. Languages such as UML are too vague to unambiguously model these differences. Even with extensions, they might tempt designers into modeling hADL aspects with non-hADL elements or contradict hADL's constraints and thus jeopardize rigorous analysis.

Little-JIL [7] is a visual language, depicting processes as hierarchies of steps (Fig. 1). An edge between a parent and child steps carries specifications of the arguments being passed between the two and an optional annotation specifying the number of child step instances. Little-JIL incorporates four different step execution sequencing specifications: sequential ($\rightarrow$), which specifies that substeps are to executed sequentially from left to right; parallel (=), which specifies fork-and-join for its substeps; choice ($\ominus$), which specifies that only one of the step's substeps is to be executed, with the choice being made by the parent step; and try ($\times\rightarrow$), which specifies that the step's substeps are to be executed in left-to-right order until one of them succeeds by failing to throw an exception. Exception handling is a particularly strong and important feature of Little-JIL. Exceptions may be thrown by a step's prerequisite check or postrequisite check or by the execution agent. Every step can contain one or more exception handlers, each of which may itself be an entire step hierarchy. A step's interface specification incorporates information about whether any arguments are an input, an output, or both, and the types of resources needed in order to perform the task associated with that step. One resource is always designated as the steps agent, namely the resource responsible for the performance of the step, may it be human(s), software, or hardware. This allows for linking Little-JIL steps to hADLs model elements, in a way that allows the two specifications to be orthogonal. Expressive, extensible, orthogonal resource specification and management [14] is thus one of the main reasons for choosing Little-JIL over workflow languages such as BPEL or YAWL. The way in which Little-JIL supports implementation of abstraction, based upon semantics rigorously defined using finite state machines, also facilitates clear specification of both activities and communication, as well as their relations to each other. These give the use of Little-JIL important advantages over other languages such as BPEL, BPMN, and YAWL.

Little-JIL vs. hADL

We analyze the spectrum between rigor and flexibility for multiple aspects as hADL and Little-JIL differ in their focus on where they enable precision, respectively underspecification.

Control flow describes the order relation among multiple actions, specifically interaction, coordination, and work execution steps. hADL assumes no single, dedicated control flow that determines the order of all human actions in a collaboration pattern. Instead, hADL enables specification of object lifecycle actions (CRUD) and who may trigger them. In contrast, Little-JIL offers primitives for rigorously determining the sequence and trigger conditions of steps.

Concurrency dependencies describe the active, simultaneous involvement of multiple users in the system. hADL assumes user behavior concurrent by default, only action sequences determined by an object's lifecycle imply order (i.e., first create, then read). Hence, actions such as multiple users reading a (shared) message or updating a shared artifact are expected to occur in no particular order with no synchronization mechanism involved. Little-JIL provides the "parallel step" primitive for marking a set of substeps explicitly as concurrently executable. Instantiating multiple identical substeps is achieved by annotation a step's edge with a fixed integer, a predicate, or a specification based upon the number of available resources.

Temporal, Cardinal, and Structural constraints provide additional refinement primitives that govern acceptable behaviors. hADL focuses primarily on minimal and maximal interaction cardinality, e.g., whether one or many users may update an artifact, the minimal number of reviewers of a report object, whether a user may create a single or multiple task request objects. Little-JIL provides cardinality constraints for specifying the lower and upper bounds for repeatedly executing a particular step. Temporal constraints determine the maximum duration a step may take for completion. Resource constraints allow the precise selection of agents (filtered by properties), for example, expressing that the same agent must (or may not) execute a particular set of steps.

Communication primitives describe the various means and their properties for establishing unstructured communication among participants. hADL employs the CollaborationObject element (and its subtypes such as Message, Artifact, or Stream) for specifying the nature of communication and which communication role a particular user plays. CollaborationObjects thus may describe synchronous one-to-one video communication as well as asynchronous multiuser information exchange via a blackboard. Little-JIL facilitates communication among agents only via explicit data passing between steps.

Coordination primitives describe the available means for managing work dependencies among participants. hADL distinguishes between work-centric HumanComponents and coordination-centric CollaborationConnectors. Little-JIL relies on the process engine as the sole coordinator of human involvement (in contrast to hADL where multiple CollaborationConnectors are not uncommon). The process description serves as the sole coordination basis. Step output and resource availability determine the flow through the process, however from a human participant's point of view, there is no distinction between coordinating steps and work executing steps.

Execution primitives outline the basic language elements for specifying human behavior. In hADL, a HumanComponent's actions describes all capabilities required to fulfill the collaborative work task. A HumanComponent thereby makes use of actions made available by potentially multiple collaboration objects. Such an object may serve as work input/output, but also for coordination or communication. Little-JIL unambiguously specifies human work in the process' step definitions. Step definitions precisely define all required input data, and exactly what output is expected, respectively what exceptions may occur. Exception handling is a significant aspect of a Little-JIL process specification in contrast to hADL where exceptions have to be modeled as regular collaboration objects.

4   A Hospital Patient Handling Use Case

We evaluate to what degree the above outlined capabilities of hADL and Little-JIL manifest as synergies. We follow a simple strategy: a designer chooses the language(s) that support specifying the kind of details about which she would like to reason upon and understand. Where control is desired, she tends towards process specification in Little-JIL. Where flexibility and human initiative needs to be emphasized and understood, there she opts for hADL. In this use case, we analyze the potential for human flexibility in an exemplary emergency department (ED) process (see also [14]). Efficient and effective ED processes rely on optimal resource allocation. This includes determining the optimal number of personnel such as Physicians, Nurses, Triage Nurses, or Clerks, their activities, and constraints on the combination of activities and personnel. Typically, a hospital determines a-priori the various thresholds which remain unchanged during operation.

Whether a threshold is adequate, however, is highly dependent on the dynamic changing ED context and highlights the potential benefit for ad-hoc involving actual humans in the dynamic resource allocation decisions. We model the main ED process (Fig. 1) in Little-JIL and the flexible collaboration structures (Fig. 2) in hADL. The *EDProcessScope* step assumes registered patients need first placement in a bed. The *NurseOverloadHandler* becomes active when available nurses are unable to carry out *PutPatientInBed* and resource allocation rules yet keep triage nurses from substituting. In this situation, how triage nurses may volunteer upon coordination with the ED supervisor is left for specification in hADL. In case no triage nurse volunteers or the supervisor declines the substitution, the *AssignBedScope* step executes a blocking *PutPatientInBed* step. If a bed is unavailable, a nurse may initiate a swap or, upon failure, will simply wait for a bed blocking. After successful bed placement and subsequent *AssessAndTreatScope*, the *EvalLoad* step determines a switch from *FinalAssessmentSame* to *FinalAssessmentDiff* strategy or vice versa in order to maintain short patient Length-of-Stay (LOS). How the ad-hoc, collaborative decisions come about are generally outside Little-JIL's scope but rather specified in hADL. The integration among Little-JIL and hADL occurs through a step's executing agent; here *EvaluateLoadAgent* and *NurseOverloadHandler*. These agents may be human or software entities.

The hADL model (see Fig. 2) focuses on the coordination among *Physicians, Supervisor, TriageNurses*, and process steps agents when to switch assessment strategies, and when to volunteer for role substitution. The *NurseOverloadHandler* directs *NurseLoadAlerts* messages to the *TaskAllocator* connector. The connector in turn creates a *VolunteerSelection* artifact, invites *TriageNurses*, observes who indicates their availability, waits for *Supervisor* confirmation and only then returns a *ResourceSubstitutionConfig* message to the process. Similarly, the *StrategySwitcher* connector observes resource status and patient LOS, collects *Physicians'* opinions on whether to switch, considers a *Supervisor's* overruling, and notifies the *EvaluateLoadAgent* step instances asynchronously on the agreed *StrategyChange* via a message stream. The connector

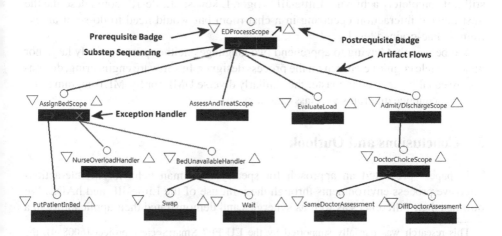

Fig. 1. Describing the adaptive ED process (excerpt) with Little-JIL

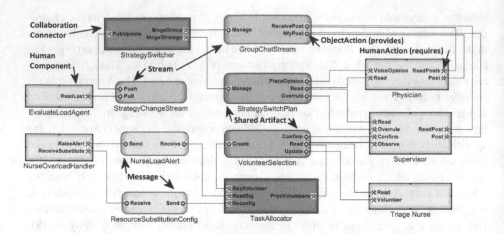

Fig. 2. Modeling collaboration structures in hADL

also manages a *GroupChatStream* that enables Physicians and Supervisor(s) to discuss strategy switching in an asynchronous and distributed manner. The sole purpose of the *TaskAllocator* connector and *StrategySwitcher* connector is coordinating collaboration among humans and integrating the collaboration with the process. Either connector might be implemented in software or by a dedicated user, e.g., a head nurse. The resulting decoupling ensures that process participants neither need to care about how to communicate with all relevant collaborators, nor do collaborators have to be physically collocated. Decoupling also provides the opportunity for establishing collaborations in parallel to multiple process instances.

Previous research [14,10,9] demonstrated the independent applicability of Little-JIL and hADL. Relying on a single language only, however, risks stretching it beyond its comfort zone. Modeling detailed processes in hADL quickly becomes tedious while still not completely achieving Little-JIL's rigor. Likewise, Little-JIL could describe the unstructured interaction occurring in a chat room but would need to do so at an extremely fine-grained level.

We believe that having to apprehend two languages neither puts an overly large nor unacceptable cognitive burden on the process designer. In software engineering, designers are equally expected to master the similarly diverse UML (or SysML) diagram types such as sequence diagrams vs. class diagrams.

5 Conclusions and Outlook

This paper[1] presented an approach for specifying human behavior in interaction-intensive process environments through the joint use of the Little-JIL and hADL. We outlined their differences as well as synergies and demonstrated their applicability in a

---
[1] This research was partially supported by the EU FP7 SmartSociety project (600854), the U.S. NSF under Award Nos. IIS-1239334 and CNS-1258588 and the NIST under grant 60NANB13D165.

use case. The combination of both languages avoids stretching one language beyond its comfort zone. Our approach will ultimately lead to more precisely specified human involvement and thereby enable better analysis of human actions as well as better support of their interaction needs. Our future investigation will focus on deployment issues such as instantiating collaboration patterns from a process engine and vice versa, observing collaborations, and detecting deviations from the initial model.

References

1. van der Aalst, W.M.P., Weske, M.: Case handling: A new paradigm for business process support. Data Knowl. Eng. 53(2), 129–162 (2005)
2. Bandinelli, S., Di Nitto, E., Fuggetta, A.: Supporting cooperation in the spade-1 environment. IEEE Trans. Softw. Eng. 22(12), 841–865 (1996)
3. Barthelmess, P.: Collaboration and coordination in process-centered software development environments: a review of the literature. Inf. and Soft. Tech. 45(13), 911–928 (2003)
4. Ben-Shaul, I., Skopp, P., Heineman, G., Tong, A., Popovich, S., Valetto, G.: Integrating groupware and process technologies in the oz environment. In: Proc. Int. Software Process Workshop, pp. 114–116 (October 1994)
5. Böhringer, M.: Emergent case management for ad-hoc processes: A solution based on microblogging and activity streams. In: zur Muehlen and Su [13], pp. 384–395
6. Brambilla, M., Fraternali, P., Vaca, C.: BPMN and design patterns for engineering social BPM solutions. In: Daniel, F., Barkaoui, K., Dustdar, S. (eds.) BPM Workshops 2011, Part I. LNBIP, vol. 99, pp. 219–230. Springer, Heidelberg (2012)
7. Cass, A.G., Lerner, B.S., Sutton Jr., S.M., McCall, E.K., Wise, A.E., Osterweil, L.J.: Littlejil/juliette: a process definition language and interpreter. In: ICSE, pp. 754–757. ACM (2000)
8. Dengler, F., Koschmider, A., Oberweis, A., Zhang, H.: Social software for coordination of collaborative process activities. In: zur Muehlen and Su [13], pp. 396–407
9. Dorn, C., Taylor, R.N.: Architecture-driven modeling of adaptive collaboration structures in large-scale social web applications. In: Wang, X.S., Cruz, I., Delis, A., Huang, G. (eds.) WISE 2012. LNCS, vol. 7651, pp. 143–156. Springer, Heidelberg (2012)
10. Dorn, C., Taylor, R.N.: Coupling software architecture and human architecture for collaboration-aware system adaptation. In: ICSE, pp. 53–62. IEEE / ACM (2013)
11. Dustdar, S.: Caramba Process-Aware Collaboration System Supporting Ad hoc and Collaborative Processes in Vrtual Teams. Distributed Parallel Databases 15(1), 45–66 (2004)
12. Grundy, J., Hosking, J.: Serendipity: Integrated environment support for process modelling, enactment and work coordination. Automated Software Engineering 5(1), 27–60 (1998)
13. Jones, N.D., Muchnick, S.S.: Business Process Management Workshops - BPM 2010 International Workshops and Education Track, Revised Selected Papers. LNBIP, vol. 66. Springer, Heidelberg (1978)
14. Raunak, M.S., Osterweil, L.J.: Resource management for complex, dynamic environments. IEEE Trans. Software Eng. 39(3), 384–402 (2013)
15. Schonenberg, H., Mans, R., Russell, N., Mulyar, N., Aalst, W.: Process flexibility: A survey of contemporary approaches. In: Dietz, J., Albani, A., Barjis, J. (eds.) Advances in Enterprise Engineering I, LNBIP, vol. 10, pp. 16–30. Springer Berlin Heidelberg (2008)
16. Weber, B., Rinderle, S., Reichert, M.: Change patterns and change support features in process-aware information systems. In: Krogstie, J., Opdahl, A.L., Sindre, G. (eds.) CAiSE 2007 and WES 2007. LNCS, vol. 4495, pp. 574–588. Springer, Heidelberg (2007)

Separating Execution and Data Management: A Key to Business-Process-as-a-Service (BPaaS)

Yutian Sun[1],[*], Jianwen Su[1],[*], and Jian Yang[2]

[1] Department of Computer Science, UC Santa Barbara, USA
[2] Department of Computing, Maquarie University, Australia

Abstract. In most business process management (BPM) systems, the interleaving nature of data management and business process (BP) execution makes it hard for providing "Business-Process-as-a-Service" (BPaaS) due to the enormous effort required on maintaining both the engines as well as the data for the clients. In this paper we formulate a concept of a self-guided artifact, which extends artifact-centric BP models by capturing *all needed data* for a BP throughout its execution. Taking advantage of self-guided artifacts, the SeGA framework is presented to support the separation of data and BP execution.

1 Introduction

The need for business process management (BPM) is ubiquitous as business processes (BPs) or workflows exist in all types of organizations including governments, healthcare, and business. In a traditional setting, to develop a BPM (software) system, required expertise includes application specific knowledge and software development experiences. The development team not only formulates concrete BP models, identifies data and other resources including human, but also decides on computing hardware and software. After a BPM system is installed, in addition to routine maintenance, the system is often required to change in order to adapt to the changes in the environment, regulations and policies, market competitions, etc. Changes are hard technically and cost wise to many organizations. For example, soon after installing its BPM system, the Housing Management Bureau in city of Hangzhou, China decided to design another system due to the changed policies, environment, and requirements [9]. Such incidents caused the State Council of China[1] to urge provincial and lower governments to use/purchase more services available in the market to streamline administration, an essential aspect of this call is to shift towards the "Business-Process-as-a-Service" (BPaaS) paradigm.

Cost effective BPaaS is challenging to achieve. Multi-tenancy for BPM systems is an obvious option for effective BPaaS, but is technically hard to realize. A primary reason is that existing BP design methodologies lack coherent plans for data design. BP execution needs at least the following five types of data: (i) business data for the process logic, (ii) BP models, (iii) execution states (and histories), (iv) correlations among BP instances, and (v) resources and their states (e.g, room reserved). Without coherent data design, current BPM systems handle and manage data in ad hoc manners, data for

---

[*] Supported in part by a grant from Bosch.

[1] http://www.gov.cn/zwgk/2012-07/20/content_2187242.htm

S. Sadiq, P. Soffer, and H. Völzer (Eds.): BPM 2014, LNCS 8659, pp. 374–382, 2014.

BP execution is scattered across databases, auxiliary data stores managed by the BPM systems, and even in files (e.g., BP schemas). It is important to note that artifact-centric BPM systems are similar since their BP models [2,6,9] only focus on data of type (i) but are agnostic of types (ii) to (v).

A fundamental principle needed to support BPaaS is the *independence of data management and execution management*. The principle entails that a BP execution engine should be free of managing *any* data while the manager of data needed for BP executions should not interfere with decisions on BP execution. A technical challenge here is to develop BPM systems that adhere to this principle. In [1], the authors studied how data auditing can be done for BPaaS, where data and execution management are interleaved. In this paper, we observe that the data auditing problem of [1] can be easily solved if data and execution are independently managed.

Rather than developing a new BPM system, in this paper we use "self-guided artifacts" (sg-artifacts) to show that existing systems can be "wrapped" and "mediated" to achieve execution independence. Sg-artifacts extend artifact-centric BP models by capturing *all five types* of data for a BP throughout its execution. Effectively, sg-artifacts make BP engines free of data management.

Technically, we formulate sg-artifacts based on the two artifact systems: Barcelona [5] and EZ-Flow [9]. We not only define sg-artifacts, but also specify correspondence between sg-artifact contents and (effectively) system snapshots in both systems. This paper extends the work in [8], where an earlier ScGA prototype to support process collaboration was reported but the concept of sg-artifact was not clearly formulated.

This paper is related to [4] that focuses on how to hide the business logic of outsourced GSM BPs [6] while still providing the BP services to clients. A generic solution for BP execution analysis with a process data warehouse model and ETL generation mechanism was presented in [3]. In paper [7], a mapping language is proposed for connecting the process data with the data in the persistent store.

Technical contributions of the paper are: (1) while the concept of sg-artifact was introduced in [8], we formulate sg-artifacts for Barcelona and EZ-Flow that include the mappings to snapshots, i.e., translations between sg-artifacts and Barcelona/EZ-Flow, and (2) a framework called SeGA is developed based on the SeGA tool of [8]. This framework takes advantage of sg-artifacts, supports the separation of data and BP execution for the two targeted systems, and is a sound platform for BPaaS.

This paper is organized as follows. Section 2 motivates the need for separating data and execution in order to enable BPaaS. Section 3 reviews Barcelona and EZ-Flow, formulates sg-artifacts including translations from/to Barcelona and EZ-Flow, and outlines the SeGA framework. Section 4 concludes the paper.

2 Motivations

The success of cloud computing has fueled the desire to provide BP execution as service or BPaaS. Consider as an example real estate property management in China. There are roughly 10 to 50 Housing Management Bureaus (HMBs) in each of about 30 provinces for managing titles, permits, licenses etc. Each HMB currently runs/maintains its own BPM system. BPaaS could potentially bring huge savings to HMBs in managing and maintaining BPM systems and is a great business opportunity in the software market.

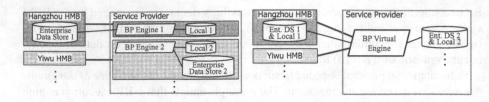

Fig. 1. Running Clients' BP Engines   **Fig. 2.** Shared BP Virtual Engine

Virtualization (i.e., VMs) is a key technology for cloud computing that frees clients from owning and maintaining computing hardware and operating systems. In Fig. 1, a service provider uses VMs to run BPM systems for many HMBs as services. For the large city Hangzhou, its HMB manages its business data in the enterprise database. the service provider can then run and manage the BPM system, including the data store "Local 1" containing data specific to Hangzhou HMB's BP execution. Almost all current BPM systems also manage data related to the processes running in the systems locally within the systems. For the small city Yiwu, the situation is similar except that the provider also manages Yiwu's enterprise data. BPM systems are semantically rich, each BP engine only suits in its local context, its local data store is a main part of the reason. As a result, one BP engine cannot be used to serve multiple HMBs. Thus each HMB's BP engine needs to be managed individually, the total effort of maintenance of all BPM systems for HMB clients is not reduced much excepted that it is simply shifted to the service provider. For example, when the core execution engine is to be upgraded, each installation must be upgraded individually in a seemingly repetitive manner.

Fig. 2 shows a much improved situation. In this case, only one BP virtual engine is running, each HMB's enterprise business data and engine-specific local data are packaged and stored in an extended data store and maintained either by the client (e.g., Hangzhou) or by the service provider (e.g., Yiwu). Both the data and process definition are provided to the virtual engine when it needs to schedule tasks; upon completion, all data is again packaged and stored accordingly for the client. This is far more efficient and scalable as the number of clients grows.

Achieving Fig. 2 turns out to be technically challenging. In order to understand how to separate data from BP execution, we present a concrete example below.

Example 1. Consider a BP model in Hangzhou HMB (HHMB). This BP concerns approval for "Early-sell permits" submitted by developers to allow some apartments in the buildings under construction to be put on the market. Permit approval involves two collaborating BPs carried out by different departments. The primary BP "Early-sell Approval Flow" (EAF) accepts applications from developers, performs reviews in several aspects, processes fee payment, and issues approval certificates. One aspect of the review concerns reserved space for building maintenance functions (total area, accessibility, etc.) and is done by the other BP "Maintenance Space Check" (MSC). An EAF instance launches a MSC instance for all apartments in the EAF instance and located in the same building. If multiple buildings are involved in the EAF instance, one MSC instance for each building will be launched.   ∎

During the execution of an EAF instance, there are at least five types of data involved: (i) the data about the applicant, the apartments, etc., (ii) the EAF model itself, (iii) the current execution status, e.g., the initial review of the applicant is completed and two MSC instances have been spawned, (iv) correlation information of the EAF and two MSC instances, and (v) the building records (owned by Hangzhou's Land Management Bureau) have been checked out for possible update by the EAF instance (an approved apartment will be marked on the building records). Among the above types of data, only business data of type (i) is managed in the HHMB enterprise database, while all others are stored within the HHMB's BPM system. If this BPM system is also to manage executions of BPs from other HMBs, problems will rise since data of types (ii) to (v) from all HMBs are mixed together. HHMB uses a proprietary BPM software but the situation is similar for YAWL and jBPM; the conclusion easily applies to YAWL and jBPM.

A major overhaul of storage and management of data of types (ii) through (v) seems necessary in order to support multi-tenancy. In this paper, we formulate a technique "sg-artifact" to cleanly separate all types of data from the execution management of a BPM system. Based on sg-artifacts, a framework called "SeGA" was developed, SeGA easily allows a single BPM system to serve BP executions from multiple clients.

3   Self-guided Artifacts

Our goal is to develop techniques for separating data from execution in order to support multi-tenancy and BPaaS. We start with introduction of wrappers for data used in BPs called "self-guided artifacts" (or "sg-artifacts") to contain all needed data for execution. We focus on two artifact models, Barcelona [5] (i.e., the execution engine name for GSM [6]) and EZ-Flow [9]. Then we introduce sg-artifacts and how to wrap Barcelona/EZ-Flow into sg-artifacts. Finally, a framework to support sg-artifacts, called "SeGA", is presented. Note that activity-centric BPs and artifact-centric BPs only different in modeling data of type (i) (see Section 2), this technique can be easily extended to other BP models/systems.

GSM and EZ-Flow Artifacts

An artifact stores all business information related to the BP using pairs of *attributes* and values. An *event type* is with an event name and a sequence of distinct attributes as *payload*. Each event type also contains the special attribute "ID" to hold an artifact identifier (that uniquely identifies each artifact instance). An *event* is an instance of an event type that can be either *incoming* or *outgoing* to denote it is to be sent or received.

We now briefly review GSM [5] with an example. Continue with Example 1; Fig. 3 shows the *lifecycle* of a GSM process for MSC that prescribes how the process should be executed. The lifecycle starts from *stage* "Requirements Check". It is opened once the condition in the diamond-shaped *guard* is satisfied. The guard tests if a "Request Maintenance Check" event arrives. Once the stage is activated, some *sub-stages* can open. For example, if HHMB decides to revise the maintenance apartments plan, sub-stage "Partial Apts Check" can be activated. During the execution, outgoing events can be sent out to request execution of actual tasks outside environment (e.g., human-performed). Once the requirement is checked, the circle-shaped *milestone* with name

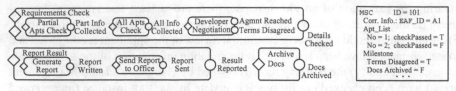

Fig. 3. A GSM Artifact Lifecycle Model of MSC   **Fig. 4.** A MSC Instance

"Details Checked" will automatically close the associated stage. The instance finishes when milestone "Docs Archived" is achieved.

The formal models of GSM artifact schemas and lifecycles are given in [6]. A GSM schema always contains an attribute "ID" to hold the identifier of an artifact instance.

A *GSM artifact instance* records the status of a single run of a GSM artifact at some time point. Fig. 4 shows a MSC artifact instance for the BP described in Fig. 3. Consider the instance with ID = 101. It has two maintenance apartments, in which the one labeled "No. 2" failed to pass the maintenance check. The milestone "Term Disagreed" is achieved to denote that the negotiation with the developer fails at the current moment. There is an attribute called "EAF_ID" in MSC to denote the correlated EAF business processes mentioned in Example 1.

An artifact instance represents a running BP instance (with all data values). Artifact instances can depend on each other through the IDs of instances stored as attribute values of other instances. Quite often, if some attributes of an instance change during execution, other instances referencing this instance may possibly change as well. The BP engine should keep track of all *dependency relationships*.

Based on GSM semantics [6], the Barcelona engine [5] was developed. The communication between the environment and Barcelona is done through events. The incoming events (sent by a task or a user) are handled sequentially. For each event, a "B-step" will be performed to update the correlated artifact instance stored in a DB2 database according to the schema. Some depending artifacts may also change during the same B-step. Once it is done, the engine will process the next event.

The EZ-Flow model is similar to GSM, details can be found in [9].

Self-guided Artifacts

A "self-guided artifact" captures a complete set of data for a BP model so that its instances are independent from execution engine; this is a key enabler for multi-tenancy and BPaaS. In particular, each self-guided artifact instance incorporates both artifact instance (including its snapshot) and its process model that this instance will follow.

Conventional BP modeling languages allow specification of tasks and control flow (BPMN, Activity Diagrams, YAWL, etc.), leaving data modeling to some later stage and/or at a lower conceptual level. Artifact-centric models [2,6] integrate logical data models for business data (i.e., type (i)) and activity/task models. Even current artifact systems still capture context, status, and resource data in an ad hoc manner. For example, Barcelona [5] stores artifact dependency and the execution state directly in its local database. In this paper, we advocate a fundamental principle for BPM systems:

Execution independence *refers to the freedom of making changes to the process execution engine while leaving conceptual BP models unchanged.*

A necessary ingredient to support execution independence is the ability to capture all five types of data in conceptual BP models, including (i) business data for BP execution, (ii) BP schemas, (iii) current execution states (and histories), (iv) correlations among BP instances, and (v) resources and their states.

In database management systems, "physical data independence" was a key enabler for the development of transaction models (concurrency, crash recovery) independently from query optimization. Analogously, execution independence could allow the management/modification of execution and data to be dealt with separately.

We now define the central notion of "self-guided artifacts". Essentially, a self-guided artifact (instance) is a GSM (EZ-Flow) artifact augmented with state and runtime dependency information, and with the artifact schema. (Resource data is not included since neither models represent resources.)

Definition: A *self-guided* (or *sg-*) *artifact schema* is a tuple (A, ID, Att, Sta), where A is a (unique) name, ID is the ID attribute, Att is a set of *data* attributes, and Sta is a set of *state* attributes. Given an sg-artifact schema (A, ID, Att, Sta), a *self-guided (sg-) artifact instance* Σ of A is a tuple $(v, \mathcal{L}, \mathcal{M}, Dep)$ where v assigns values to attributes in $\{ID\} \cup Att \cup Sta$ such that $v(ID)$ is a unique ID, $\mathcal{L}$ is either "GSM" or "EZ" representing a modeling language (GSM or EZ-Flow), $\mathcal{M}$ is an artifact schema in the language $\mathcal{L}$, and Dep is a set of *dependencies* whose representation depends on the language $\mathcal{L}$.

A sg-artifact schema is an abstraction of *running instances* of both GSM and EZ-Flow artifacts. Each sg-artifact instance captures data attribute values, status and dependencies, and (its own copy of) schema or BP model. The inclusion of the schema frees the engine from storing BP models.

To achieve execution independence for GSM (EZ) artifacts, all data concerning BP including data and states are extracted from Barcelona (EZ-Flow) and stored as sg-artifact instances. When Barcelona performs a B-step (EZ-Flow performs a transition), it updates all affected artifact instances. Thus, it is necessary to establish a 1-1 mapping from GSM (EZ) instances to sg-artifact instances so that the fact of sg-artifacts storing the system data/status is transparent to Barcelona (EZ-Flow). We discuss below a few technical notions for the mappings for GSM and EZ-Flow separately.

In Barcelona, once an event comes, it will first affect one GSM instance; during the same B-step, the effect may also ripple to the other depending instances. For each GSM instance, a *dependency closure* can be computed to record all the instances that might be affected during the execution.

Given a sg-artifact instance $\Sigma' = (v, \mathcal{L}, \mathcal{M}, Dep)$, the key notion relating a GSM instance Σ and sg-artifacts is given by mapping (i) the ID, data, and status attributes/values through v, (ii) $\mathcal{L} = $ "GSM", (iii) $\mathcal{M}$ to be the schema of Σ, and (iv) Dep the dependency closure of Σ.

The mapping not only keeps the original ID, data and status attributes, but also includes the execution language and the schema. For the dependency closure, though it can be derived from the data attribute values, it is necessary to raise it as the first-class citizen in order to explicitly denote the relationship with other instances.

Given a sg-artifact instance Σ' that is mapped from a GSM instance Σ, it is straightforward to recover Σ by simply mapping each attribute-value pair from Σ' to Σ.

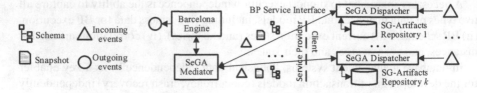

Fig. 5. The SeGA Framework

The mapping from EZ-Flow (schema/instances) to sg-artifact (schema/instances) can be achieved similarly; the logical description of the mapping is omitted.

The SeGA Framework

A sg-artifact instance captures all necessary data for execution, and allows a BP engine to operate without knowing the context of instances. The "SeGA" framework wraps BP engines into "stateless" services to support BPaaS and how sg-artifacts can interact with the provided services. Based on SeGA, a prototype was developed and reported in [8].

Fig. 5 shows the architecture of the SeGA framework (or simply SeGA), which consists of a *SeGA dispatcher* and a *SeGA mediator*. When an external event arrives, the dispatcher fetches the relevant sg-artifact instances from a sg-artifact repository, separates the schema from each sg-artifact instance, maps it back to the original form (GSM or EZ-Flow), and sends the external event, schema, and the original artifact instance to the mediator. When the mediator receives the event, schema, and the instance, it deposits the artifact schema in the appropriate location where the Barcelona/EZ-Flow engine can access, and passes the control over to the Barcelona/EZ-Flow engine by forwarding the event. When the Barcelona/EZ-Flow engine receives the incoming event, it executes the next step and updates the artifact instances according to the schema deposited by the mediator; and outgoing events may also be sent directly from the engine if there exists task invocation during the execution. Once it completes, the mediator fetches the updated artifact instances, together with their schemas and states, and sends them back to the dispatcher. The dispatcher then maps the instances and schemas back to sg-artifacts and stores into the corresponding repository.

SeGA can be used to support BPaaS. The dispatcher would reside at the service *consumer*, where a repository of sg-artifacts is maintained. The mediator is located at the service *provider* who runs a BP engine (or multiple engines). The dispatcher and mediator communicate through service invocations such as WSDL or REST, and work in pairs so that the service provider can use its BP engines to execute BP received from the service consumer in the form of data.

The SeGA framework takes advantage of the execution independence that separates data and execution management. From the engine's perspective, it provides business-process-as-a-service but does not maintain any data. This allows the provider to serve a large number of consumers. From the consumer's view, all BP data are maintained at its site; beyond that, there is no need to manage BP execution.

SeGA requires the dispatcher/service consumer to have a sg-artifact repository so that the dispatcher can fetch (sg-artifact) instances. In general, an enterprise stores the data in a enterprise persistent data store (e.g., a relational database) rather than storing data for each individual BP model. A general approach of a data mapping to bridge the relationships between sg-artifact instances and databases was developed in [7]. As an advantage of [7], one can design artifact storage and map the artifact data to the existing database(s). The mapping in [7] can propagate updates on artifact instances to the database and vice versa. Together with the mapping framework, the SeGA framework provides an effective way of elevating a BPM system for multi-tenancy and BPaaS.

Design Methodology to BPM Systems
Our study on SeGA leads to two suggestions for the future BPM system development. First, existing BPM systems can be extended so that data in the process manager is extracted and packaged with the business data into sg-artifacts. Although we only explored two systems, the same method is applicable to other systems including jBPM and possibly YAWL. Second, more generally it is most desirable to develop future BPM systems that support the independence principle. In this regard, we envision that a BPM system consists of three layers, a *modeling layer* to accept/analyze the data and BP design, and map to sg-artifacts; a *SeGA layer* to manage sg-artifacts and interact with the engine at runtime; an *execution layer* to manage executions with no local data. Such new style BPM systems will provide a tremendous support for BPaaS and process collaboration.

4   Conclusions

The demand for BPaaS is coming. We have seen various vertical BPaaSs in for example HR and procurement. Clearly BPaaS is not just about providing APIs and interfaces for configuration and graphical analysis. The challenges lie in the capability to handle massive scaling, the service must be able to support multiple languages and execution environments, as well as massive customers and processes. We argue that the separation of the data from the execution engine is a good way to achieve this demanded scaling.

References

1. Accorsi, R.: Business Process as a Service: Chances for remote auditing. In: Proc. IEEE 35th Annual COMPSAC Workshops, pp. 398–403 (2011)
2. Bhattacharya, K., Gerede, C.E., Hull, R., Liu, R., Su, J.: Towards formal analysis of artifact-centric business process models. In: Alonso, G., Dadam, P., Rosemann, M. (eds.) BPM 2007. LNCS, vol. 4714, pp. 288–304. Springer, Heidelberg (2007)
3. Casati, F., Castellanos, M., Dayal, U., Salazar, N.: A generic solution for warehousing business process data. In: Proc. 33rd Int. Conf. on Very Large Data Bases (VLDB), pp. 1128–1137 (2007)
4. Eshuis, R., Hull, R., Sun, Y., Vaculín, R.: Splitting GSM schemas: A framework for outsourcing of declarative artifact systems. In: Daniel, F., Wang, J., Weber, B. (eds.) BPM 2013. LNCS, vol. 8094, pp. 259–274. Springer, Heidelberg (2013)
5. Heath III, F(T.), Boaz, D., Gupta, M., Vaculín, R., Sun, Y., Hull, R., Limonad, L.: Barcelona: A design and runtime environment for declarative artifact-centric BPM. In: Basu, S., Pautasso, C., Zhang, L., Fu, X. (eds.) ICSOC 2013. LNCS, vol. 8274, pp. 705–709. Springer, Heidelberg (2013)

6. Hull, R., et al.: Business artifacts with guard-stage-milestone lifecycles: Managing artifact interactions with conditions and events. In: Proc. 5th ACM Int. Conf. on Distributed Event-Based System (DEBS), pp. 51–62 (2011)
7. Sun, Y., Su, J., Wu, B., Yang, J.: Modeling data for business processes. In: Proc. 30th Int. Conf. on Data Engineering (ICDE), pp. 1048–1059 (2014)
8. Sun, Y., Xu, W., Su, J., Yang, J.: SeGA: A mediator for artifact-centric business processes. In: Proc. 20th Int. Conf. on Cooperative Information Systems (CoopIS), pp. 658–661 (2012)
9. Xu, W., Su, J., Yan, Z., Yang, J., Zhang, L.: An artifact-centric approach to dynamic modification of workflow execution. In: Proc. 19th Int. Conf. on Cooperative Information Systems (CoopIS), pp. 256–273 (2011)

Assessing the Need for Visibility of Business Processes – A Process Visibility Fit Framework

Enrico Graupner[1,2], Martin Berner[1,3], Alexander Maedche[1], and Harshavardhan Jegadeesan[3]

[1] University of Mannheim, Institute for Enterprise Systems, Mannheim, Germany
{graupner,berner,maedche}@es.uni-mannheim.de
[2] Commerz Business Consulting GmbH, Frankfurt (Main), Germany
enrico.graupner@commerzbank.com
[3] SAP AG, Walldorf, Germany
{martin.berner,harshavardhan.jegadeesan}@sap.com

Abstract. Real-time visibility of relevant information during process execution becomes increasingly feasible leveraging advanced information technologies. However, it remains vague where organizations should exploit the new, but also cost-intensive opportunities. Theoretically grounded in the Information Processing View (IPV) this paper proposes a decision framework that identifies business processes which need technology investments enabling real-time visibility. The framework considers both, visibility requirements of processes as well as visibility capabilities of information technology.

Keywords: Process Visibility, Information Processing View, Process-centric Business Intelligence & Analytics.

1   Introduction

For a long time data analysis and provisioning has not or has only been loosely coupled to process execution. Traditional Business Intelligence and Analytics (BI&A) has been data-centric, based on historical data and focused on strategic decision support [1]. Accordingly, latest analytical data was not set into its process context and was not usable for daily decisions. Currently, BI&A moves to resolve these limitations and can create visibility into processes that has never existed before [2]: First, BI&A becomes increasingly process-aware and creates visibility by setting data into the process context. This is driven by the complementary increase of process-orientation in enterprises. Second, the shift from managerial task support towards operational decision support marks an additional important movement in BI&A. Organizations perform better if they provide frontline workers with analytical information that increases the visibility of problems and opportunities in daily business [3]. Third, new big data technologies deal with datasets and sources which exceed the abilities of typical databases in terms of capturing, storing, managing, and analyzing [4]. This enables to overcome the technological challenge of correlating millions of

S. Sadiq, P. Soffer, and H. Völzer (Eds.): BPM 2014, LNCS 8659, pp. 383–391, 2014.

events to its underlying processes and the creation of visibility into processes as they are happening [5].

Previously described novelties in BI&A and the associated speed of technological advance are challenging for organizations. Lacking experience with new BI&A trends towards process-centric, operational and big data-based decision support makes it difficult to identify potential areas of use and assess the value added. Considering limited IT budgets, organizations need to establish a careful assessment where business processes benefit from advanced analytics. This leads to the research question:

Which factors determine the need for visibility in business processes?

Even if the processes are identified for which visibility is highly required, it remains vague which technological capabilities are relevant to create it in particular. Accordingly, our paper has a second research question:

Which technological capabilities have to be established to cope with the visibility need of business processes?

2   The Concept of Process Visibility

The concept of visibility is well-established in supply chain management (SCM) research. It is an outcome of information sharing for important activities and processes between supply chain partners [6, 7]. Visibility is essential for appropriate performance and its degree depends on the level to which information is relevant, trustworthy, and timely [7]. Also lean production literature stresses the importance of visual controls and making abnormalities visible: "The most important spur to perfection is transparency, the fact that in a lean system everyone [...] can see everything" [8]. Research generalizes the visibility concept of SCM and the lean transparency concept to a broader business process context [9, 10]. Table 1 outlines our conceptual frame of process visibility which is derived from a comprehensive review of literature [11].

Table 1. Morphological Box of Process Visibility

Characteristic	Attribute Value			
Focus [12]	Process design	Process redesign		Process execution
Management Level [12]	Operational	Tactical		Strategic
Integration Level [12, 13]	Instance	Model / Multiple Instances		Meta Model
Process Phase [12]	Definition/ Modeling	Implementation	Monitoring/ Controlling	Continuous Improvement
Kind of Process [12, 13]	Business		Technical	
Time Relevance [12, 13]	Real-time (live)		Historical (ex-post)	
Range of Users [12]	Small	Middle		Broad
Data Sources [12]	Internal (intra-organizational)		External (inter-organizational)	

Based on these foundations, our paper understands *process visibility* as the sharing, analysis, and access of process information in an operational decision making context in real-time [2]. Thus, the concept exceeds the aspect of visualization and creates end-to-end information visibility about process instances.

3 Process Visibility Requirements

This paper introduces the example of airport hub operations to illustrate the need for process visibility. The example origins from the participation of one of the co-authors in the planning phase of process-centric BI&A implementation project in 2013. Insights were gained from workshops, interviews, and on-site observations in the project. Various activities are involved in the process (Fig. 1) to ensure that approximately 60 airplanes are handled successfully every night. In particular, the hub operations manager needs to know the number of shipments in different phases across the value stream as well as high-level traffic lighting that shows which shipments are in danger of delaying outbound planes. In addition, real-time metrics (such as time taken for loading a plane) are needed to dynamically allot people and collaborate with colleagues to solve problems as they arise.

Fig. 1. High-level phases of an airport hub operations process

To enable a more systematic assessment of the need for process visibility, we derive an evaluation schema based on a theoretical foundation: The Information Processing View (IPV) [14, 15] describes information processing as "the gathering of data, the transformation of data into information, and the communication and storage of information in the organization" [16]. The creation of visibility requires these information processing activities and therefore we adopt the IPV as an appropriate theoretical foundation for our research. Extant information systems research has applied the IPV in the domain of SCM and outsourcing relationships on the organizational level. To the best of our knowledge we are the first to establish IPV on the process level. We use the process as unit of analysis - and thus choose the unit that information technology affects directly and at which its impacts are best observable [17].

Information processing requirements describe the amount of information that must be collected, processed, and disseminated for achieving a certain level of performance [18]. In IPV-related literature the complexity of the task environment, the interdependence of the task environment, and the strategic importance of the outsourced process are identified as determinants for information requirements [18, 19]. In the following, we transform these three determinants to a process-specific perspective.

First, *process intricacy* relates to complexity of the task. To define complexity, this paper adopts the characteristics of big data – namely volume, velocity, and variety [20]. We argue that business processes become more complex, the larger the number of process instances and events that need to be correlated, the faster the required throughput and decision speed, and the higher the diversity of systems, data types, and sources. Accordingly, this paper defines process intricacy as the complexity of a process in terms of volume, velocity, and variety.

Second, *process interdependence* is the degree to which processes and their inherent steps interact. According to the IPV, high inter-unit task dependencies are associated with frequent and unexpected changes in the task environment resulting in high uncertainty [15]. Considering an end-to-end process perspective, dependencies may consist between single process steps as well as across various processes. From an organizational perspective, dependencies between multiple organizational units can arise including a wide range of involved application systems.

Third, *process importance* is the degree to which a process impacts the competitiveness of organizations [19]. In IPV research, high criticality calls for extensive monitoring to cope with uncertainty. Porter's [21] differentiation between core and support processes may provide an initial orientation: Core processes contribute to the value creation and are therefore typically highly important for a firm's competitiveness. However, support processes can also influence a firm's competitiveness; for example when process compliance is crucial due to regulatory liabilities.

In summary, processes are distinguished along a continuum of their process visibility requirements (Table 2). To assess for which processes the BI&A trends are particularly useful, the next section outlines complementary technological capabilities.

Table 2. Process Visibility Requirements

Dimension	Description	Evaluation for Airport Hub Operations
Process Intricacy	Degree to which a process is complex in terms of volume, velocity, and variety	High • Volume: 300,000 shipments per night creating 18 million streaming events • Velocity: 50,000 streaming events per minute • Variety: transactional shipment data as well as stream events
Process Interdependence	Degree to which processes and their inherent steps, participants, organizations, and technical systems interact	High • Interrelations: Many highly interacting sub processes spanning across various systems like shipment scanners, air traffic system, ground operations, warehouse management systems • Dependencies: Various sources, e.g. flight schedule delays and damaged goods
Process Importance	Degree to which a process affects the competitiveness of organizations	High • Criticality: Liabilities if express shipments are delayed. Furthermore loss of reputation and business

4   Technological Capabilities for Process Visibility

There are multiple BI&A system categories which cover relevant aspects of process visibility. Business Activity Monitoring (BAM), Business Process Intelligence (BPI), and Operational Business Intelligence (OpBI) label such decision support technologies that have been established for more than a decade. However, none of these traditional BI&A system categories can deal with all challenges of process visibility such as the rapidly increasing amount of data as well as real-time and process-centric in-formation provisioning   [2]. In response, analysts predict that the boundaries of existing analytical software packages are vanishing by combining them with new technologies: Gartner introduces *Intelligent Business Operations* as generic term for real-time usage of BI&A technologies enhanced with complementary software pack-ages like Complex Event Processing (CEP), Business Rules Management, and BPM [22]. TDWI uses the term *Real-time Operational Intelligence* for "an emerging class of analytics that provides visibility into business processes, events, and operations as they are happening" [5]. Correspondingly, software vendors increasingly offer process-centric BI&A solutions for the operational level and incorporate big data technologies [2]. In summary, technological advance offers new opportunities to make processes visible. The remainder of the section structures these technologies from the perspective of our theoretical basis.

Table 3. Process Visibility Capabilities

Dimension	Description	Evaluation for Airport Hub Operations
Process Information Gathering	Amount of relevant, accurate, timely and concise data that is compiled about a process.	Medium • Events was recorded at different stages of the proc-ess but data not consolidated • Correlation of large data amount to its process con-text: Low
Process Information Analysis	Interpretation and synthesizing of process information for decision-making.	Low • Flexibility at query execution time: Low • Sophisticated predictions based on Big Data: None • Process-awareness: Low
Process Information Dissemina-tion	Availability of actionable infor-mation for process participants to support operational decisions and trigger required actions while process execution.	Low • Real-time information availability: Low • Actionable insights on operational level based on data: Low

Informed by the definition of information processing that refers to the gathering of data, transformation into information and communication of the information [16], we derive the following process visibility capabilities which are of technological nature: Process information gathering, process information analysis, and process information dissemination. Table 3 describes the capabilities and illustrates these for our example.

First, the degree to which technologies enable *process information gathering* re-flects the amount of data that is compiled about a process from different sources. Data become information if relevant, accurate, timely and concise [15]. Process informa-tion must be gathered from large data sets by correlating millions of events to its business process context. Information becomes process-ware by leveraging knowl-edge of the process structure and setting data into relation with process steps.

Second, *process information analysis* refers to the interpretation and synthesizing of necessary information for decision making [15]. It ranges from concise process performance indicators to advanced predictive and prescriptive capabilities. The latter are supported by new database technologies which allow full flexibility at query execution time, whereas classical BI&A technology requires the preparation and optimization of potential queries already at design time [23].

Third, the degree to which technologies enable *process information dissemination* is defined as the access of actionable information for process participants to support operational decision making and trigger required actions in a timely manner. "[T]he best information will be wasted if it is not routed to the people in the organization who need it to perform their jobs" [24]. An easily understandable information presentation is required to derive appropriate actions quickly.

Based on the current trends in BI&A and theoretically grounded in the IPV, we captured information processing capabilities. The next section brings together these capabilities with the corresponding requirements and introduces the concept of fit.

5   The Process Visibility Fit

Based on the IPV we argue that low or high information processing requirements as well as low or high capabilities are not good or bad per se. The fit between both is important for appropriate process visibility (Fig. 2). This paper considers fit as the deviation between process visibility capabilities and requirements.

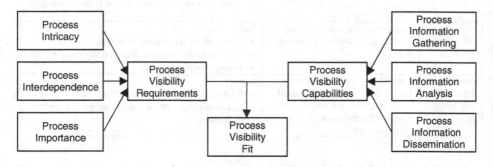

Fig. 2. The Process Visibility Fit Framework

The fit between requirements and capabilities can follow four distinct configurations (Fig. 3). Two refer to a match between requirements and capabilities. The match can either be achieved if both dimensions are low or high. The process visibility is appropriate in both cases. In contrast, two other configurations reflect a mismatch: The requirements might be higher than the available capabilities. As a consequence, flaws in decision making might occur. Furthermore, the requirements can be lower than the existing capabilities (process visibility overload). Inefficient management of resources and decreased operational efficiency are possible consequences.

In our Airport Hub Operations example, high process visibility requirements (Table 2) and low capabilities (Table 3) exist. Consequently, the visibility fit framework identifies a process visibility gap. The negative impact of the visibility gap is confirmed in practice: Hub managers lack transparency into the process and cannot identify important and time-critical shipments in the technical systems. Accordingly, resource bottlenecks and problem areas are not anticipated and are not addressed proactively. To increase the process visibility capabilities, SAP Operational Process Intelligence, a solution based on in-memory HANA technology is currently evaluated in a pilot implementation at the logistics service provider.

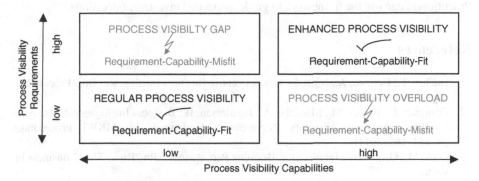

Fig. 3. Process Visibility Fit as Requirements and Capabilities Match

6   Conclusion

The vast majority of data in organizations is used without considering its process context. This paper identifies process visibility as an emerging theme that is driven by the BI&A trends towards process-centric, big data-based, and real-time decision support. Theoretically grounded in the Information Processing View we develop a decision framework to assess the appropriate degree of visibility for business processes. The framework considers the specific process under investigation and assesses its process visibility requirements, process visibility capabilities as well as the fit between both. Throughout the paper, we illustrate the applicability of the framework with a real world example from the logistics service industry and establish more specific determinants for both, requirements and capabilities.

This paper is subject to specific limitations: First, it assesses information processing capabilities solely from a technological perspective. Future research has to include complementary organizational capabilities that are needed to adequately deploy the technical capabilities. Second, this is a conceptual paper that lacks comprehensive empirical evidence, as we only introduce one exemplary process from a logistic service provider to assess the model. Future research has to establish a broader empirical basis to validate the framework. In this regard, design science research can be informed by the framework. Furthermore, empirical studies might identify additional dimensions for process visibility requirements and capabilities beyond those which were derived from IPV-related research.

Despite these limitations, we believe that this paper makes relevant contributions to theory and practice: From a theoretical perspective, this paper contributes to the body of knowledge related to the IPV. Whereas the IPV considered capabilities generally as referring to the organizational structure, we adopted a technological perspective.

Furthermore, we transform the IPV to the process level and thus assess process visibility requirements and capabilities where they are best observable. Another contribution is the conceptualization of process visibility for operational decision making. From a practical perspective, we provide a framework to identify processes that demand high visibility and outline which corresponding technologies can be used to generate it. Practitioners can use the framework to guide associated investment decisions.

References

1. Bucher, T., Gericke, A., Sigg, S.: Process-centric Business Intelligence. Bus. Process Manag. J. 15, 408–429 (2009)
2. Graupner, E., Berner, M., Maedche, A., Jegadeesan, H.: Business Intelligence & Analytics for Processes – A Visibility Requirements Evaluation. In: MKWI Proceedings. pp. 154–166 (2014)
3. Lock, M.: Operational Intelligence: Boosting Performance with "Right-Time" Business Insight,
   http://resources.idgenterprise.com/original/
   AST-0009180_0172-6528-RA-OperationalBI-MDL-NSP-03.pdf
4. Manyika, J., Chui, M., Brown, B., Bughin, J., Dobbs, R., Roxburgh, C., Byers Hung, A.: Big Data: The Next Frontier for Innovation, Competition, and Productivity. McKinsey Global Institute, San Francisco (2011)
5. Russom, P.: Operational Intelligence: Real-Time Business Analytics from Big Data. TDWI Checkl. Rep. 1–8 (2013)
6. Wang, E.T.G., Wei, H.-L.: Interorganizational Governance Value Creation: Coordinating for Information Visibility and Flexibility in Supply Chains. Decis. Sci. 38, 647–674 (2007)
7. Barratt, M., Oke, A.: Antecedents of Supply Chain Visibility in Retail Supply Chains: A Resource-Based Theory Perspective. J. Oper. Manag. 25, 1217–1233 (2007)
8. Womack, J.P., Jones, D.T.: Lean Thinking: Banish Waste and Create Wealth in Your Corporation. Free Press, New York (2003)
9. Klotz, L., Horman, M., Bi, H.H., Bechtel, J.: The Impact of Process Mapping on Transparency. Int. J. Product. Perform. Manag. 57, 623–636 (2008)
10. Berner, M., Graupner, E., Maedche, A., Mueller, B.: Process Visibility – Towards a Conceptualization and Research Themes. In: Proceedings of 33th ICIS, pp. 1–13 (2012)
11. Urbitsch, E.: Process Visibility Capabilities - A Conceptualization and Operationalization (Master Thesis). University of Mannheim (2014)
12. Felden, C., Chamoni, P., Linden, M.: From Process Execution towards a Business Process Intelligence. In: Proceedings of 13th Conference on BIS, pp. 195–206 (2010)
13. Zur Muehlen, M.: Process-driven Management Information Systems - Combining Data Warehouses and Workflow Technology. In: Proceedings of 4th ICECR, pp. 550–566 (2001)
14. Galbraith, J.R.: Designing Complex Organizations. Addison-Wesley, Reading (1973)
15. Tushman, M.L., Nadler, D.A.: Information Processing as an Integrating Concept in Organizational Design. Acad. Manag. Rev. 3, 613–624 (1978)
16. Egelhoff, W.: Strategy and Structure in Multinational Corporations: An Information-Processing Approach. Adm. Sci. Q. 27, 435–458 (1982)
17. Melville, N., Kraemer, K., Gurbaxani, V.: Information Technology and Organizational Performance: An Integrative Model of IT Business Value. MIS Q. 28, 283–322 (2004)

18. Mani, D., Barua, A., Whinston, A.: An Empirical Analysis of the Impact of Information Capabilities Design on Business Process Outsourcing Performance. MIS Q. 34, 39–62 (2010)
19. Mani, D., Barua, A., Whinston, A.B.: Successfully Governing Business Process Outsourcing Relationships. MIS Q. Exec. 5, 15–29 (2006)
20. Russom, P.: Big Data Analytics, ftp://ftp.software.ibm.com/software/tw/Defining_Big_Data_through_3V_v.pdf
21. Porter, M.E.: Competitive Advantage. Free Press, New York (1985)
22. Gartner: Gartner Says Intelligent Business Operations Is the Next Step for BPM Programs, http://www.gartner.com/it/page.jsp?id=1943514
23. Grondelle, J.: Leveraging Big Data Analytics in Business Processes. Be Inf. 1–5 (2013)
24. Davenport, T.H., Beers, M.C.: Managing Information about Processes. J. Manag. Inf. Syst. 12, 57–80 (1995)

The Automated Discovery of Hybrid Processes

Fabrizio Maria Maggi[1], Tijs Slaats[2,3], and Hajo A. Reijers[4,5]

[1] University of Tartu, Estonia
[2] IT University of Copenhagen, Denmark
[3] Exformatics A/S, Lautrupsgade 13, 2100 Copenhagen, Denmark
[4] Eindhoven University of Technology, The Netherlands
[5] Perceptive Software, The Netherlands
f.m.maggi@ut.ee, tslaats@itu.dk, h.a.reijers@tue.nl

Abstract. The declarative-procedural dichotomy is highly relevant when choosing the most suitable process modeling language to represent a discovered process. Less-structured processes with a high level of variability can be described in a more compact way using a declarative language. By contrast, procedural process modeling languages seem more suitable to describe structured and stable processes. However, in various cases, a process may incorporate parts that are better captured in a declarative fashion, while other parts are more suitable to be described procedurally. In this paper, we present a technique for discovering from an event log a so-called *hybrid* process model. A hybrid process model is hierarchical, where each of its sub-processes may be specified in a declarative or procedural fashion. We have implemented the proposed approach as a plug-in of the ProM platform. To evaluate the approach, we used our plug-in to mine a real-life log from a financial context.

1 Introduction

Process models are an important aid to capture how business operations are organized. One direction to simplify the tasks of creating, maintaining, and reading such models involves the use of declarative techniques for process modeling. In contrast to the procedural approach, which is dominant for modeling business processes, a declarative approach leaves implicit in what exact sequences activities must be carried out. Instead, the emphasis is on the constraints that must be respected in carrying out the process – any behavior that respects these goes. In contexts where activities can be executed in highly different combinations, a declarative approach arguably produces simpler representations of the involved process logic. Examples of concrete declarative modeling techniques are Declare, DCR Graphs [3], and SCIFF.

In [10], we reported that a *hybrid* process modeling technique was considered by practitioners as more attractive than a completely declarative or procedural one. Hybrid, in this context, refers to the potential use of both procedural and declarative model elements in the same model. The rationale is that the two types of modeling paradigms allow for a natural fit with different types of process behavior. In places where the process is highly flexible, a declarative modeling approach leads to a compact and simple description of such a "pocket of flexibility" [11]. Instead of describing all the different types of feasible behavior, the focus is then on ruling out what is not allowed (if

S. Sadiq, P. Soffer, and H. Völzer (Eds.): BPM 2014, LNCS 8659, pp. 392–399, 2014.

anything). By contrast, for parts of the process that are highly structured, a procedural description may be the way to go: It is then simpler to describe what is allowed than what is to be ruled out. For processes that both incorporate structured and unstructured pockets, a hybrid model delivers a compact and simple description.

This paper should be seen as a direct follow-up to our earlier work. Specifically, we developed a technique *to automatically generate a hybrid model from an event log*. This is a novel contribution, since existing techniques can only generate a process model that is either procedural or declarative. By contrast, our technique flexibly alternates between employing a procedural or declarative mining approach in accordance with the nature of the traces it processes. By doing so we are able to avoid the "spaghetti"-like process models that are commonly generated by traditional process mining techniques.

Against this background, the paper is structured as follows. In Section 2, we will outline the notion of a hybrid model and pinpoint its semantics. Section 3 describes our core contribution, the discovery approach. We will will evaluate this approach in Section 4 on a real-life log. After a discussion of related work, we conclude this paper with a reflection on the presented work and future steps in Section 6.

2 Semantics of a Hybrid Model

Our interest in this paper is with hybrid models where the procedural and declarative parts are contained in separate sub-processes. In this sense, there is a resemblance with the *pockets of flexibility* concept [11]. A hybrid process consists of a procedural or declarative top-level process, which may contain a number of atomic activities as well as sub-processes. Each sub-process can be either procedural or declarative and may contain sub-processes of its own. Our approach is applicable to any combination of procedural and declarative languages, but in this paper we will apply Petri nets for our procedural models and Declare [9] for our declarative models. Sub-processes are considered atomic, meaning that once a sub-processes is started the control is passed from the parent process to that sub-process. No other activities can be executed until the sub-process has completed. A sub-process can only complete while it is *accepting*. When exactly it is accepting depends on the language used. In the case of a Petri net this means reaching a final marking, while for a Declare model it means having no violated constraints. For the language of a hybrid model we consider the start and completion of sub-processes as silent transitions, which means that there will be no start- and complete-events for the sub-processes in the log. This underlines the fact that the sub-processes are really just a tool for improving the understanding of the process and not a part of the actual enactment of the process.

3 Discovering Hybrid Process Models

Fig. 1 gives an overview of our approach. In the following paragraphs we describe our approach step by step.

Distinguishing Structured and Unstructured Events. We start by separating the events of the log into two distinct sets: one containing those events that occur in a structured

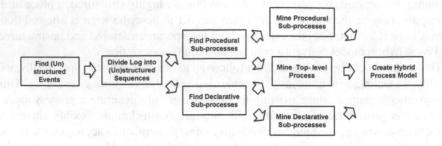

Fig. 1. Overview of our approach

context and one containing those events that occur in an unstructured context. To distinguish structured from unstructured events we use a novel technique, which we refer to as *context analysis*. Our first step is to determine for each event the number of unique predecessors and successors to that event. We then consider an event with a large number of both predecessors and successors to be unstructured (according to a user-defined threshold, in our experimentation we used 4), while an event with a small number of predecessors or a small number of successors is considered to be structured. The reasoning behind these cases is as follows: if an event has a high number of predecessors and a high number of successors, then there are few rules constraining when exactly the event can occur. We then consider it likely to fit well into a declarative model. Similarly, if an event has only a small number of predecessors and a small number of successors, then it is probably more easily modeled procedurally, for example, as a sequence or a choice from a low number of options. In the case that an event has a small number of predecessors, but a large number of successors, we consider it likely that the event is either the last element in a structured sequence, which is followed by an unstructured sequence, or that the event is followed by a choice from a large number of options. In both cases it makes sense to consider this as a structured event and model it procedurally. Similarly, in the case that an event has a small number of successors, but a large number of predecessors we consider it likely that the event is either the first element in an structured sequence, which was preceded by an unstructured sequence, or that the event joins a choice from a large number of options. In both cases it seems fitting to consider this as a structured event and model it procedurally.

Dividing the Log into Structured and Unstructured Sequences. The context analysis gives us two sets: one that contains structured events and one that contains unstructured events. In the following step, we use these events to identify structured and unstructured sequences by parsing the log and starting a new sequence whenever an event does not belong to the same set as its preceding event. After this step, our approach splits into two branches, one handling the structured sub-logs and the other handling the unstructured sub-logs.

Finding and Mining procedural Sub-processes. By grouping together each structured event with all the direct successors and all the direct predecessors, we obtain a set of disjoint clusters of the structured sequences. We then mine procedural sub-processes for each of these clusters. Finally, we abstract the main log by replacing each sequence with the identifier of the sub-process that it belongs to. It should be noted that the clusters of procedural sequences that are discovered could be further split up using existing clustering techniques. This did not seem necessary on basis of the examples we used in our experimentation with the technique.

Finding and Mining Declarative Sub-processes. For finding declarative sub-processes, we first use an indirect association rule mining algorithm on the set of unstructured sequences to find declarative patterns. Recall that an indirect association rule can be used to find events that rarely occur together, yet there are other "mediator events" with which they appear relatively frequently. We use this type of algorithms since it gives us the opportunity to not only discover Declare constraints that express positive relations, but also constraints like, for example, not coexistence constraints, which are more likely to be satisfied when the events involved do not occur together in the same trace. In a second stage, we use a mining algorithm for standard association rules on the remaining sequences. These rules reflect relationships that exist between events that often co-occur in common transactions. For this reason, these rules allow us to group together events that are very likely connected with each other through positive relations in Declare. The patterns are abstracted in the main log, and any remaining event that is at this point not identified as belonging to a declarative pattern is left as an atomic event.

Mining the Top-level Process. When we are done finding (but not necessarily mining) procedural and declarative sub-processes and have all sub-processes abstracted in the main log, we can then either choose to apply the approach iteratively on the abstracted log, starting from the first step where we distinguish structured and unstructured activities based on their context, or we can choose to finalize the approach by mining the main log. In the latter case, we compute the average string edit distance for all traces in the abstract main log and in case of a high similarity among the traces (>50%) we mine the log procedurally using a procedural miner. In case of a lower similarity, we mine it using a declarative miner. The use of the string edit distance is a simple way to distinguish between structured and unstructured logs. We validated this approach based on experiments on synthetic logs. The results of these experiments have shown that traces in structured logs are more similar to each other with respect to traces in an unstructured log. Of course, more sophisticated techniques can be used for discriminating between them.

Creating a Hybrid Process Model. When all mining tasks have finished, we can combine the resulting process models into a single hybrid model, based on which abstract activities in the top-level model correspond to which sub-process. The exact method will depend on the miners used and the languages that they use to generate models. In our implementation, we simply generated separate Petri nets and Declare models. However, to improve usability, a tool that supports the visualization and management of such hybrid models would be needed (for example, to graphically represent a Declare sub-process within a top-level Petri net model). At this point, this is left for future work.

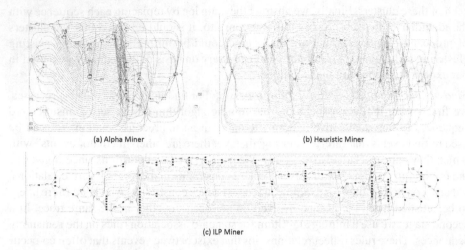

(a) Alpha Miner   (b) Heuristic Miner

(c) ILP Miner

Fig. 2. Procedural Models

4   Evaluation

To evaluate our approach, we have implemented it as a plug-in of the process mining tool ProM.[1] For the evaluation, we turned to the real-life event log, which was made available as part of the BPI Challenge 2012.[2] The process represented in the event log is an application process for a personal loan within a global financing organization. The log itself contains some 262.200 events in 13.087 cases.

Our evaluation took on the following form. We set out to compare a model that would result from a traditional mining approach on the selected log with a hybrid model that is generated as proposed in this paper. We will refer to these as the *procedural* and the *hybrid* models. The aim then is to compare these models specifically with respect to the understandability of the generated models. We decided to create three procedural models of the event log by using the Alpha, Heuristic, and ILP miner, respectively. The resulting procedural models are shown in Fig. 2.

We created the hybrid model by using the Declare miner on the clusters of unstructured sequences, while using the Heuristic miner on the clusters of structured sequences. Since the root model in this case also could be classified as structured, it was mined with the Heuristic miner as well. The hybrid model can be seen in Fig. 3. In this figure, the procedural root net is shown, as well as links to its sub-nets. Note that two sub-nets are of a declarative nature (D1.1 and D2.1); the other sub-nets are procedural.

To make sure that a comparison with respect to the simplicity of the various models is fair, we first reflect on their *fitness* [13]. This expresses how well the model is able to "replay" the observed behavior in the log. The values are provided in Table 1. As can be seen, the fitness values for the procedural models range from 0.01 for the ILP

---

[1] http://www.promtools.org/prom6/HybridMiner
[2] http://dx.doi.org/10.4121/
   uuid:3926db30-f712-4394-aebc-75976070e91f

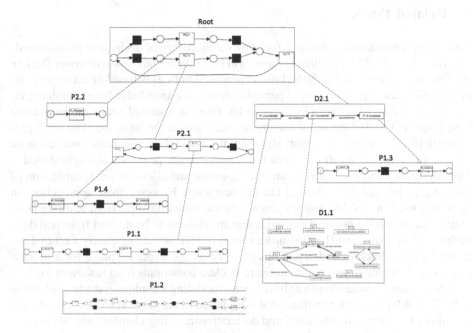

Fig. 3. Hybrid Model

miner to 0.58 for the Alpha miner. For the hybrid model, the fitness values are provided for each of the sub-nets. These values vary from 0.69 to 1.00 (perfect fitness). Without an integrated fitness measure available for hierarchical nets, we propose to take the minimum value as a conservative approximation for the fitness of the hybrid net. On this basis, the replay fitness of the hybrid net can be seen to be at least as good as that of the procedural models. Also, it is not particularly "flower-like", which can be a drawback of aiming at a well-fitting model [13].

A visual inspection of the models seems to indicate that the hybrid model is vastly simpler than the procedural models. All procedural models can be characterized as "spaghetti-like". The hybrid model, by contrast, is composed of 9 different sub-nets, each of which having a fairly simple structure. Arguably the most difficult of these sub-nets are P1.2 and D1.1, which are the largest procedural and declarative sub-nets, respectively. While the modularity of the hybrid model to some extent seems to help the understanding of the process, the overall lack of visual clutter is apparent. The proposed approach, therefore, seems to have the potential to automatically generate behaviorally accurate process models that are simple to read.

Table 1. Fitness values for the generated models

Procedural			Hybrid								
Alpha	Heuristic	ILP									
			Root	P1.1	P1.2	P1.3	P1.4	P2.1	P2.2	D1.1	D1.2
0.58	0.40	0.01	1.00	0.84	0.73	0.69	0.81	1.00	0.86	1.00	1.00

5   Related Work

Several approaches in the literature focus on the discovery of declarative process models [1,4,2,5,6,7,8]. The algorithms proposed in [4,2,6,8] are tailored to discover Declare specifications. In particular, the technique proposed in [4,2] is based on a two-step approach. First, the input event log is parsed to generate a knowledge base containing information useful to discover a Declare model. Then, in a second phase, the knowledge base is queried to find the set of constraints that hold on the input log. The work proposed in [6] is based on an Apriori algorithm for association rule mining and has been used in this paper for the discovery of the declarative sub-processes of a hybrid model. The approaches proposed in [1,5] are more general and allow for the specification of rules that go beyond the traditional Declare templates. However, these approaches can be hardly used in real-life settings since they are based on supervised learning techniques thus requiring negative examples that are difficult to be derived from real data. In the work proposed in [7], a first-order variant of LTL is used to specify a set of data-aware patterns. Such extended patterns are used as the target language for a process discovery algorithm to produce data-aware Declare constraints from raw event logs.

A recent implementation of a hybrid process modeling technique is made available in CPN Tools 4.0 [15]. Different than what is proposed in the paper at hand, a hybrid CPN net allows for the use of procedural and declarative modeling elements within the same sub-process. Already at an earlier stage, modeling approaches have been proposed that embrace "pockets of flexibility". Specifically, in [11] it is proposed to define at build-time in a workflow process pockets in a way that is highly similar to a declarative style to match their highly flexible behavior; at runtime one has to pick a specific procedural instantiation of the workflow that fits the definition. Two other approaches that combine procedural and declarative elements worth noting are Flexibility-as-a-Service (FAAS) [14] and the Guard-Stage-Milestone model [12]. It should be noted that for none of these approaches automated discovery techniques exist.

6   Conclusion

In this paper, we presented an automated discovery technique for hybrid process models. By analyzing the traces that are available in an event log and clustering them together according to their structure (or lack thereof), we are able to mine the structured and less structured pockets within a process with procedural and declarative mining algorithms, respectively. The result is a hierarchical process model with both procedural and declarative sub-processes. Our evaluation on a real-life event log suggests that the proposed technique is indeed capable of producing a much simpler representation of a process than traditional, purely procedural approaches can.

The proposed approach could be improved along theoretical, technical, and empirical angles. On a theoretical side, there is a need to establish proper metrics that tie to the established quality dimensions of fitness, precision, generalization and simplicity [13] for hybrid, hierarchical process models. At this point, it is not entirely clear how a quality measure for a subprocess propagates to the quality of the overall model. Establishing this will pave the way for a more thorough insight into the strengths and weaknesses of the proposed discovery technique. Technically, a step ahead would be to allow for *duplicate events*, i.e. the same event can be part of a procedural as well as a declarative sub-process. We did not allow for this at this point, but this could be done by identifying "recurrent" predecessors/successors even if these appear only in a certain percentage of cases. From an empirical angle, end users need to be confronted with hybrid models for a thorough evaluation of their usefulness and ease of use.

As to stimulate the uptake of hybrid process models, a number of other developments are called for as well. As we pointed out in our earlier work [10], modeling guidelines and tool support will be essential to allow for the manual creation and maintenance of hybrid process models. We are currently experimenting with such guidelines and our initial insights are that modelers with an intermediate experience with procedural modeling approaches do not find the composition of hybrid models all that difficult. We hope to report on more substantial insights in the near future.

References

1. Chesani, F., Lamma, E., Mello, P., Montali, M., Riguzzi, F., Storari, S.: Exploiting inductive logic programming techniques for declarative process mining. ToPNoC (2009)
2. Di Ciccio, C., Mecella, M.: A two-step fast algorithm for the automated discovery of declarative workflows. In: CIDM (2013)
3. Debois, S., Hildebrandt, T., Slaats, T.: Hierarchical declarative modelling with refinement and sub-processes. In: BPM (2014)
4. Di Ciccio, C., Mecella, M.: Mining constraints for artful processes. In: BIS (2012)
5. Lamma, E., Mello, P., Riguzzi, F., Storari, S.: Applying inductive logic programming to process mining. In: Blockeel, H., Ramon, J., Shavlik, J., Tadepalli, P. (eds.) ILP 2007. LNCS (LNAI), vol. 4894, pp. 132–146. Springer, Heidelberg (2008)
6. Maggi, F.M., Bose, R.P.J.C., van der Aalst, W.M.P.: Efficient discovery of understandable declarative process models from event logs. In: Ralyté, J., Franch, X., Brinkkemper, S., Wrycza, S. (eds.) CAiSE 2012. LNCS, vol. 7328, pp. 270–285. Springer, Heidelberg (2012)
7. Maggi, F.M., Dumas, M., García-Bañuelos, L., Montali, M.: Discovering data-aware declarative process models from event logs. In: Daniel, F., Wang, J., Weber, B. (eds.) BPM 2013. LNCS, vol. 8094, pp. 81–96. Springer, Heidelberg (2013)
8. Maggi, F.M., Mooij, A.J., van der Aalst, W.M.P.: User-guided discovery of declarative process models. In: CIDM, pp. 192–199 (2011)
9. Pesic, M., Schonenberg, H., van der Aalst, W.M.P.: DECLARE: Full Support for Loosely-Structured Processes. In: EDOC 2007, pp. 287–298 (2007)
10. Reijers, H.A., Slaats, T., Stahl, C.: Declarative modeling–an academic dream or the future for BPM? In: Daniel, F., Wang, J., Weber, B. (eds.) BPM 2013. LNCS, vol. 8094, pp. 307–322. Springer, Heidelberg (2013)
11. Sadiq, S.W., Orlowska, M.E., Sadiq, W.: Specification and validation of process constraints for flexible workflows. Information Systems 30(5), 349–378 (2005)
12. Vaculín, R., Hull, R., Heath, T., Cochran, C., Nigam, A., Sukaviriya, P.: Declarative business artifact centric modeling of decision and knowledge intensive business processes. In: EDOC, pp. 151–160 (2011)
13. van der Aalst, W.M.P.: Process Mining - Discovery, Conformance and Enhancement of Business Processes, pp. 1–352. Springer (2011)
14. van der Aalst, W.M.P., Adams, M., ter Hofstede, A.H.M., Pesic, M., Schonenberg, H.: Flexibility as a service. In: Chen, L., Liu, C., Liu, Q., Deng, K. (eds.) DASFAA 2009. LNCS, vol. 5667, pp. 319–333. Springer, Heidelberg (2009)
15. Westergaard, M., Slaats, T.: Mixing paradigms for more comprehensible models. In: Daniel, F., Wang, J., Weber, B. (eds.) BPM 2013. LNCS, vol. 8094, pp. 283–290. Springer, Heidelberg (2013)

Declarative Process Mining: Reducing Discovered Models Complexity by Pre-Processing Event Logs

Pedro H. Piccoli Richetti, Fernanda Araujo Baião[*], and Flávia Maria Santoro[*]

Department of Applied Informatics,
Federal University of the State of Rio de Janeiro, Rio de Janeiro, Brazil
{pedro.richetti,fernanda.baiao,flavia.santoro}@uniriotec.br

Abstract. The discovery of declarative process models by mining event logs aims to represent flexible or unstructured processes, making them visible to business and improving their manageability. Although promising, the declarative perspective may still produce models that are hard to understand, both due to their size and to the high number of restrictions of the process activities. This work presents an approach to reduce declarative model complexity by aggregating activities according to inclusion and hierarchy semantic relations. The approach was evaluated through a case study with an artificial event log and its results showed complexity reduction on the resulting hierarchical model.

Keywords: process mining, declarative modeling.

1 Introduction

Process mining techniques allow knowledge extraction from events stored by information systems. They are also an important connection between data mining and business process management. The interest on this topic has grown due to the advancement on computers technology and processes management, so even more events can be registered and more details about business process are available, and to the need for improving and supporting business processes in a competitive and rapidly changing environment [11].

Despite its benefits, process mining has some disadvantages. One of them is that discovered models tend to be large and complex, especially on flexible scenarios where process execution involves multiple alternatives. Because traditional techniques used on discovery try to model every possible process behavior, they result in a spaghetti-like model with an information overload that reduces model comprehensibility. Traditional imperative models are appropriate to represent well-structured models, because they provide better support for analysis and execution direction. On the other side of the continuum are the unstructured processes, where flexibility is needed to drive changes or deviations on the activities flow. van der Aalst et al. [12]

---

[*] Fernanda Araujo Baião and Flávia Maria Santoro are partially funded by the CNPq brazilian research council, respectively under the projects 309069/2013-0 and 307377/2011-3.

S. Sadiq, P. Soffer, and H. Völzer (Eds.): BPM 2014, LNCS 8659, pp. 400–407, 2014.
© Springer International Publishing Switzerland 2014

show how a declarative approach enables a better balance between flexibility and support. However, declarative process mining techniques may produce models with a high quantity of constraints, which may be incomprehensible for humans, as showed by Bose et al. [2].

In this work, we address the problem of high complexity of declarative models generated by automatic process mining. Our proposed approach reduces the model complexity by automatically generating process hierarchies in pre-processing time, in which proposed subprocesses aggregate activities according to semantic relations.

The rest of this work is structured as follows. Section 2 presents theoretical background and related work about declarative process modeling and mining, and about complexity reduction through activities abstraction. Section 3 explains the method to abstract activities through semantic relations. Section 4 presents the first ideas towards the proposal for preprocessing and mining event logs applying activity abstraction. Section 5 describes the case study, and its results are discussed in Section 6. Section 7 concludes the paper and points to future work.

2   Background and Related Work

A declarative approach focuses on the logic that governs interactions between the actions of a process, describing what can be done, restricting only the undesired behavior [14]. An example of declarative modeling language is Declare [12], which is grounded on constraint templates modelled in linear temporal logic (LTL). A set of Declare constraints is presented in [8]. An implementation for declarative process mining is the DeclareMiner [8], available as a ProM[2] plugin.

Haisjackl et al. [4] showed that the combination of constraints in a process model might generate new hidden dependencies, which are complex and difficult to be identified by humans. Reijers et al. [9] said that the increasing number of restrictions negatively impacts on the model quality.

Abstraction is seen as an effective approach to represent readable models, showing aggregated activities and hiding irrelevant details [10]. While on imperative models every process fragment ranging from a single entry and a single exit (SESE) can be grouped as a subprocess [13], on declarative models this structure is not informative enough, because the activities' sequence is not rigid. Hierarchies may be used to perform aggregation, thus reducing the mental effort to understand a model [14].

Zugal et al. [14] examined the effects of hierarchy on declarative models. As a result, they confirmed that structural grouping of activities is inadequate and, for declarative models, it should consider a common objective of the grouped activities. The transformation of hierarchical structures back to flat models is not always possible without changing the process structure and, possibly, its semantics. This possible loss can be compensated by the expressiveness enhancement [14].

Li et al. [7] proposed an approach to search for sequential patterns on event logs and replace them with abstract activities. For declarative models, sequential patterns

---

[2] The tool is available at http://www.processmining.org

identification is not enough to infer groups of activities. Baier et al. [1] presented a method to construct abstraction layers in process models by matching events and activities. Their clustering schema is based on timestamps to calculate minimal distances. On a declarative perspective, this approach is not very adequate because there are constraints that cannot be identified by looking for minimal temporal distances.

Bose et al. [16] demonstrated how to discover hierarchical process models based on pattern abstractions by preprocessing an event log and applying Fuzzy Miner to discover maps that represent process models with abstractions. They defined a taxonomy for abstractions that considers loops and conserved regions relative to sequences in event log traces, but no semantic concerns are considered to build hierarchies.

None of the above-mentioned approaches addresses abstraction techniques on declarative process models to reduce their complexity. Thus, the contribution of this paper is showing how to automatically generate subprocesses by looking for semantic relations from activities labels of an unstructured business process. The generated subprocesses are incorporated into the event log prior to the process mining phase. The expected result is to produce a less complex declarative model.

3   A Method to Abstract Activities through Semantic Relations

Inspired by the semantic approach of Leopold et al. [6] to name imperative process models and fragments, our approach applies natural language processing to identify common objectives between activity labels, and then abstracts these activities into hierarchies. Wordnet[3] was chosen to search for the hypernyms and holonyms semantic relations between the words in activity labels; differently from [6], we aim to search for common objectives that can be used to gather activities in a subprocess.

Algorithm 1 groups activities that have actions and objects related to abstract common senses. We keep track of how strongly a word is semantically related to its abstract concept according to the Lin metric, since its results are similar to human judgment [3]. The next step is to define how to adequately group activities into a subprocess. Algorithm 2 proposes a strategy for grouping based on a graph representation. A prototype for executing Algorithms 1 and 2 was implemented in Java language. Auxiliary Python NLTK3.0[4] scripts were used for the part-of-speech tagging step. PERL WordNet:SenseRelate::WordToSet[5] scripts were used to get the most adequate sense from a list of words to be disambiguated in a given context and Wordnet:Similarity[6] scripts provided the semantic similarity relatedness calculus.

---

[3] WordNet is available at http://wordnet.princeton.edu/

[4] The toolkit is available at http://www.nltk.org/

[5] Refer to http://search.cpan.org/~tpederse/
WordNet-SenseRelate-WordToSet-0.04/

[6] Refer to http://search.cpan.org/~tpederse/WordNet-Similarity-2.05/

4   Preprocessing and Mining Event Logs with Activity Abstractions

Bose et al. [15] stated that "Spaghettiness" of process models can be reduced by first mining common constructs or functionalities, abstract them and then discovering process models on the abstracted log. Given a list of activity groups found by Algorithm 2, each group may be represented by a complex activity that substitutes all occurrences of its grouped activities in an event log. For example, given the following trace from a flat model: $\{a,b,c,d,c,a,d,b\}$. Suppose we identify a subprocess e grouping the activities a and c. Substituting the activities by their subprocess, the modified trace will be: $\{e,b,e,d,e,e,d,b\}$. This preprocessed log can be used as input to existing declarative process mining algorithms.

After preprocessing, the declarative mining algorithm will be able to identify interactions only in the top-level process. To discover the constraints within a subprocess, the activities belonging to it should be filtered from the original event log and presented to the declarative mining algorithm. Removing all the other activities will imply in analyzing only the behavior of the subprocess activities.

Currently, our implemented approach is able to deal with only one layer of subprocesses, but this can be extended to handle deeper levels. However, the growth of level numbers may increase the fragmentation of the model and consequently increase the model complexity [14].

5   Case Study

The main objective of this case study was to observe if a declarative process model, discovered after replacing activities by subprocess directly on the event log, is less complex. The declarative process model "How to prepare oneself and materials for teaching pupils" was chosen from literature [4]. It has a flat and a hierarchical version, both manually designed.

The process was modeled and simulated in CPNTools[7], generating 5,000 traces. Using this event log, a list of unique activity labels of the process was used as input for Algorithm 1. After executing the first algorithm, a set of activity pairs with their respective average semantic similarity value was produced. Together with the previous output set, a semantic similarity threshold was defined to run Algorithm 2. This threshold is used to filter out pairs with low similarity values. In a user guided fashion, a 0.40 threshold value was chosen. The remaining pairs of activities are candidates to generate the subprocesses through Algorithm 2 execution.

Algorithm 2 provided two subprocesses as output: "Prepare and give lessons" containing the activities "Prepare lesson in detail", "Give lessons" and "Read about topic in more detail"; and "Decide and prepare teaching" containing: "Prepare teaching sequence" and "Decide on teaching method". The event log was modified by substituting every occurrence of an activity by its complex activity representing each

---

[7] The tool is available at http://cpntools.org/

suggested subprocess. Then, the preprocessed event log was imported into ProM and the DeclareMiner plugin was used to discover a hierarchical declarative process model (Fig. 1b). The plugin parameters were set to "Min. Support" = 50 and "alpha" = 50, no additional filters were applied after the discovery. To compare the results, the unmodified event log was also mined to discover a flat process model (Fig. 1a). In order to mine each subprocess behavior, the original event log was preprocessed once more to extract only the subprocess activities. The preprocessing and mining steps should be carried out for each subprocess. All plugin settings were the same used for the hierarchical model. Table 1 summarizes the results for these mined process models.

6   Evaluation

To evaluate the results from both flat and hierarchical models, some metrics related to model complexity applicable to declarative models were calculated based on La Rosa et al. [5]. In addition, the number of constraints was used as a metric because it influences the complexity of declarative models, as stated in [9].

Algorithm 1: Identify semantic related activities

Input: List of unique activity labels A, number of levels to search in Wordnet's hypernymy and holonymy tree k

Output: Set of activity pairs with their respective average similarity measure R

1 Initialize R with $\varnothing$
2 **foreach** *activity label a in A* **do**
3   Apply part-of-speech tagging to identify all verbs V and all nouns N in a
4   **foreach** *verb v in V* **do**
5   Identify all hypernyms for v until reach the kth level starting from v
6   **foreach** *noun n in N* **do**
7   Identify all hypernyms and holonyms for n until reach the kth level starting from n
8 Generate a set P_a with pairs of activities p_a(activity label $a1$, activity label $a2$) from the combination $\binom{A}{2}$
9 **foreach** *activity label pair p_a in P_a* **do**
10   Generate a set $V_{1,2}$ with pairs of verbs $p_v(v_1,v_2)$ from the combination of each verb v_1 in V_1 from a_1 and each verb v_2 in V_2 from a_2
11   **foreach** *pair p_v in $V_{1,2}$* **do**
12   Match all common hypernyms H_v between v_1 and v_2
13   Invoke WordNet::SenseRelate::WordToSet algorithm to define the most adequate hypernymy h_v from H_v, using A as context
14   Calculate Lin's semantic relatedness metric between v_1 and h_v and v_2 and h_v
15   Generate a set $N_{1,2}$ with pairs of nouns $p_n(n_1,n_2)$ from the combination of each noun n_1 in N_1 from a_1 and each noun n_2 in N_2 from a_2
16   **foreach** *pair p_n in $N_{1,2}$* **do**
17   Match all common hypernyms and holonyms H_n between n_1 and n_2
18   Invoke WordNet::SenseRelate::WordToSet algorithm to define the most adequate hypernymy or holonymy h_n from H_n, using A as context
19   Calculate Lin's semantic relatedness metric between n_1 and h_n and n_2 and h_n
20   Calculate average semantic relatedness value s considering all nouns in N_1, N_2 and verbs in V_1, V_2 to their most adequate hypernymy or holonymy
21   Add p_a and its s value to R
22 **return** R

Algorithm 2: Group semantic related activity labels

Input: List of unique activity labels *A*, Set of activity pairs with their respective average similarity
measure *R*, semantic similarity threshold *t*

Output: Set of activity labels groups *S*

1 Initialize *S* with ∅
2 Remove all activity pairs from *R* with average similarity measure below *t*
3 Create a undirected weighted graph *G(V,E)* where each vertex *v* is an activity label from *A* and
   each edge *e* relates to a pair from *R* whose weight is the average similarity measure of the pair
4 **while** *G has edges* **do**
5   Generate all possible vertex groups *P* where in a group each vertex relates to each other
6   **foreach** *group p in P* **do**
7 | Sum the weight of all edges of *p*
8   Identify the vertex group *h* with the highest weight sum
9   Add *h* to *S*
10   Remove all vertex in *h* from *G*
11 **return** *S*

Considering that the input event log was the same, the reduction on the total number of activities (8 in flat model to 5 in hierarchical model), together with the lower number of constraints on the second model, positively contribute for reducing the overall complexity and make it easier to understand the process with abstractions. When looking at the subprocesses, the fewer number of activities tends to make them easier to understand when compared to the full flat model. Even merging the metrics for the hierarchical model and its subprocesses, the constraint/activity ratio remained lower than in the flat model.

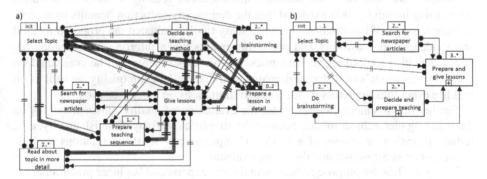

Fig. 1. Mined Declare models from the (a) flat and the (b) preprocessed event logs

We are aware that natural language processing may introduce some bias on identifying the grammatical types of words. Not always an activity label is written as a complete sentence, which may reduce the POS tagging accuracy. The predefined search level in the hypernymy and holonymy tree results is not considering common concepts that are beyond this limit. However, choosing a broader limit may bring uninteresting or too vague common synsets that will not help to increase semantic relatedness.

The resulting mined model could be compared to the a priori theoretical model presented in [4]. The hierarchical a priori model has only one subprocess, called "*Prepare lessons*", with three activities. Our automatic proposal discovered the subprocess "*Decide and prepare teaching*", that contains two common activities with the manually identified "*Prepare lessons*" subprocess ("Prepare teaching sequence" and "Decide on teaching method"). The "*Prepare and give lessons*" subprocess, which did not exist in the theoretical model, was found in our approach due to the affinity between its activities names ("Prepare lesson in detail", "Read about topic in more detail" and "Give lessons"). On manual modeling, other reasons besides the semantics can lead to activity aggregation, such as the execution sequence, or a deliberate decision based on personal judgment of the process modeler. The proposed automated method was able to produce less complex and easier to understand models.

Table 1. Complexity related metrics from the discovered process models

	Flat	Hierarchical only	Subprocess "Decide and Prepare Teaching"	Subprocess "Prepare and Give Lessons"	Hierarchical + subprocesses
No. of Activities	8	5	2	3	10
No. of Constraints	45	18	5	9	32
No. of Different Constraints	9	8	5	8	10
No. of Subprocessess	0	2	0	0	2
Contraint/Activity Ratio	5.63	3.60	2.50	3.00	3.20

7   Conclusion and Future Work

Although there may be some semantic modifications relating to model constraints when using hierarchy, it is expected that the complexity reduction benefits may compensate this loss of information. The case study firstly evaluated the proposed method and evidenced its feasibility and promising results when inferring relationships between activities by looking its semantics. Further experiments will be conducted on more process models of different domains with diverse labeling quality, as well as on real life event logs, to assess its success and limitations on other scenarios.

Further improvements will consider the evaluation of quality dimensions [11] on the resulting hierarchical model, because the simplification may diminish quality, e.g., reduce precision or fitness of a model. Complimentary semantic relations such as Least Common Subsumer are also being evaluated.

This work has the purpose to help domain non experts and beginner practitioners to better understand declarative process models by automatically suggesting subprocesses to make the models less complex and more legible. When there is no previous knowledge about the model to be discovered, the proposed method may show important views of a process model that can be comprehended and then revised or applied in process improvement.

References

1. Baier, T., Mendling, J.: Bridging abstraction layers in process mining by automated matching of events and activities. In: Daniel, F., Wang, J., Weber, B. (eds.) BPM 2013. LNCS, vol. 8094, pp. 17–32. Springer, Heidelberg (2013)

2. Bose, R.P.J.C., Maggi, F.M., van der Aalst, W.M.P.: Enhancing Declare Maps Based on Event Correlations. In: Daniel, F., Wang, J., Weber, B. (eds.) BPM 2013. LNCS, vol. 8094, pp. 97–112. Springer, Heidelberg (2013)
3. Lin, D.: An information-theoretic definition of similarity. In: ICML 1998 Proceedings of the Fifteenth International Conference on Machine Learning, vol. 98, pp. 296–304 (1998)
4. Haisjackl, C., Zugal, S., Soffer, P., Hadar, I., Reichert, M., Pinggera, J., Weber, B.: Making Sense of Declarative Process Models: Common Strategies and Typical Pitfalls. In: Nurcan, S., Proper, H.A., Soffer, P., Krogstie, J., Schmidt, R., Halpin, T., Bider, I. (eds.) BPMDS 2013 and EMMSAD 2013. LNBIP, vol. 147, pp. 2–17. Springer, Heidelberg (2013)
5. La Rosa, M., Wohed, P., Mendling, J., ter Hofstede, A.H.M., Reijers, H.A., Van der Aalst, W.M.P.: Managing Process Model Complexity Via Abstract Syntax Modifications. IEEE Transactions Industrial Informatics 7, 614–629 (2011)
6. Leopold, H., Mendling, J., Reijers, H., Rosa, M.: Simplifying process model abstraction: Techniques for generating model names. Information Systems 39, 134–151 (2014)
7. Li, J., Bose, R.P.J.C., van der Aalst, W.M.P.: Mining Context-Dependent and Interactive Business Process Maps Using Execution Patterns. In: Muehlen, M.Z., Su, J. (eds.) BPM 2010 Workshops. LNBIP, vol. 66, pp. 109–121. Springer, Heidelberg (2011)
8. Maggi, F.M., Mooij, A.J., van der Aalst, W.M.P.: User-Guided Discovery of Declarative Process Models. In: IEEE Symposium on Computational Intelligence and Data Mining, pp. 192–199. IEEE Computer Society (2011)
9. Reijers, H.A., Slaats, T., Stahl, C.: Declarative Modeling–An Academic Dream or the Future for BPM? In: Daniel, F., Wang, J., Weber, B. (eds.) BPM 2013. LNCS, vol. 8094, pp. 307–322. Springer, Heidelberg (2013)
10. Smirnov, S., Reijers, H.A., Weske, M.: A Semantic Approach for Business Process Model Abstraction. In: Mouratidis, H., Rolland, C. (eds.) CAiSE 2011. LNCS, vol. 6741, pp. 497–511. Springer, Heidelberg (2011)
11. van der Aalst, W., et al.: Process Mining Manifesto. In: Daniel, F., Barkaoui, K., Dustdar, S. (eds.) BPM Workshops 2011, Part I. LNBIP, vol. 99, pp. 169–194. Springer, Heidelberg (2012)
12. van der Aalst, W.M.P., Pesic, M., Schonenberg, H.: Declarative workflows: Balancing between flexibility and support. Computer Science - Research and Development 23, 99–113 (2009)
13. Weber, B., Reichert, M., Mendling, J., Reijers, H.A.: Refactoring large process model repositories. Computers in Industry 62, 467–486 (2011)
14. Zugal, S., Soffer, P., Haisjackl, C., Pinggera, J., Reichert, M., Weber, B.: Investigating expressiveness and understandability of hierarchy in declarative business process models. Software & Systems Modeling, 1–23 (2013)
15. Jagadeesh Chandra Bose, R.P., van der Aalst, W.M.P.: Abstractions in Process Mining: A Taxonomy of Patterns. In: Dayal, U., Eder, J., Koehler, J., Reijers, H.A. (eds.) BPM 2009. LNCS, vol. 5701, pp. 159–175. Springer, Heidelberg (2009)
16. Bose, R.P.J.C., Verbeek, E.H.M.W., van der Aalst, W.M.P.: Discovering Hierarchical Process Models Using ProM. In: Nurcan, S. (ed.) CAiSE Forum 2011. LNBIP, vol. 107, pp. 33–48. Springer, Heidelberg (2012)

SECPI: Searching for Explanations for Clustered Process Instances

Jochen De Weerdt and Seppe vanden Broucke

KU Leuven, Research Centre for Management Informatics (LIRIS)
Naamsestraat 69, B-3000 Leuven, Belgium
jochen.deweerdt@kuleuven.be

Abstract. This paper presents SECPI (Search for Explanations of Clusters of Process Instances), a technique that assists users with understanding a trace clustering solution by finding a minimal set of control-flow characteristics whose absence would prevent a process instance from remaining in its current cluster. As such, the shortcoming of current trace clustering techniques regarding the provision of insight into the computation of a particular partitioning is addressed by learning concise individual rules that clearly explain why a certain instance is part of a cluster.

Keywords: process discovery, trace clustering, user comprehension, instance-level explanations, support vector machines.

1 Introduction

Partitioning event logs into multiple groups of process instances is a convenient recipe for addressing the challenge of dealing with complex event logs, i.e. logs presenting a large amount of distinct process behaviour. In the literature, several trace clustering techniques have been described [1–9] that are capable of intelligently splitting up an event log into multiple groups of instances so that process discovery techniques can be applied to subsets of behaviour, with more accurate and comprehensible discovered models as a result. However, the application potential of trace clustering techniques is somewhat hampered by the low level of human comprehension. Concretely, there exist two major problems regarding trace clustering solutions. First of all, it is a non-trivial question to find out what the driving elements are that determine a clustering technique to split up the event log in a particular way. This is because most trace clustering techniques operate at a higher level of abstraction which makes that, for instance, the concept of *distance* between traces is not very insightful as a means to describing a clustering solution. Secondly, end users would like to be able to understand the differentiating characteristics between multiple clusters of process instances, preferably from a *domain perspective*, i.e. relying on control-flow characteristics that are present in the context of the process at hand.

A posteriori comprehension of a clustering solution plays a vital role for the usefulness of separating an event log into multiple subgroups. More specifically,

S. Sadiq, P. Soffer, and H. Völzer (Eds.): BPM 2014, LNCS 8659, pp. 408–415, 2014.

process analysts should be able to understand which factors determine the delineation of the discovered clusters in order to be able to give an interpretation to the solution. Currently available trace clustering techniques often lack the capability to provide insight into how a certain clustering solution is composed. Therefore, this paper presents a new technique which allows to find explanations that describe which control-flow characteristics of a certain process instance make that this instance pertains to a certain cluster. In the remainder of this paper, it is argued that instance-level explanations can overcome drawbacks of potential alternative explanation techniques, such as for example the visual analysis of the underlying process models. The novel technique, implemented as the *SVMExplainer-plugin* in ProM[1], is inspired by the work of Martens and Provost [10], who put forward an approach for explaining text document classifications. In the context of document classification, one is often confronted with limited comprehensibility of the predictive model, even despite using so-called *white box* techniques such as decision trees or logistic regression, which is mainly due to the high dimensionality. Similarly, such high dimensionality comes into play when characterising process instances by means of binary vectors representing control-flow characteristics.

Against this background, the main contribution of this paper is SECPI (Search for Explanations of Clusters of Process Instances), an algorithm that is capable of finding a minimal set of control-flow characteristics for a process instance, such that if these characteristics were not present, the process instance would not remain within its current cluster. Furthermore, the implementation allows to visualise explanations in the respective process models so that users can easily observe what characteristics make that a process instance belongs to a certain cluster.

2   Trace Clustering

Trace clustering is an interesting approach to deal with the problem that many event logs contain an extensive amount of distinct behaviour (i.e. process variants), because it allows the user to split up a log so that multiple distinct models can be learnt to describe the underlying business process.

2.1   State of the Art

In general, two distinct groups of trace clustering approaches can be discerned with on the one hand techniques that heavily rely on the principle of distance-based clustering, and on the other hand techniques that incorporate a model-driven approach. The first group consists of techniques such as presented in [1, 2, 4, 5, 9], which basically transform an input event log into a propositional format so as to apply well-known clustering techniques from the data mining domain. The technique presented in [4] is slightly different as the similarity between process instances is determined based on string edit operations, while the recently

---

[1] http://www.promtools.org/prom6/

presented technique in [9] adds a complexity-based procedure to determine the optimal number of clusters based on (approximate) clone detection. The latter group of trace clustering techniques [3, 6, 7] is different in the sense that they are model-driven by relying either on Markov models or Heuristic nets [7]. We refer to the latter paper for a more detailed description and analysis of trace clustering approaches.

2.2 Problem Statement

As indicated in the introduction, the problem with existing trace clustering techniques is that they provide little to no insight into the actual reasoning of partitioning an event log in a particular way. From a model learning perspective, the clustering bias of a trace clustering technique determines how a solution is constructed. Clustering techniques described in the process mining literature employ a wide variety of clustering biases. On the one hand, a subset of techniques relies on the concept of distance as a measure of instance similarity. Model-driven techniques on the other hand rely on maximum likelihood or fitness optimisation. Observe that the ex-post, aggregated fitness of the underlying models is an often employed quality measure for trace clustering solutions, see [4, 7].

For distance-based clustering, typical data mining techniques such as k-means or hierarchical clustering are applied. As such, the distance itself is a potential candidate for explaining a clustering result. For instance, one could visualise the instances in a networked graph or make use of comparative statistical analysis of the underlying variables that determine the inter- and intra-cluster distances. However, a projection of process instances onto process features will typically generate a large amount of variables (e.g. the combined number of 2- and 3-grams for a set of 20 labels is 8 400), which seriously complicates such an approach. To this, it should be added that due to the large amount of variables, distance-based techniques suffer from the curse of dimensionality problem [11]. As described in [12], conventional proximity metrics in high-dimensional space may not be qualitatively meaningful. Therefore, it is argued that the value of the distance concept for assisting users with understanding a trace clustering solution is low. As for model-driven techniques, the natural explanation method is a visual analysis of the resulting cluster models. However, this not only requires a high level of expertise, but is also impacted by the trade-off between recall, precision and generalisation as made by process discovery techniques.

3 Instance-Level Explanations with SECPI

3.1 Approach

This paper describes a completely new analysis approach for explaining the differences between clusters of process instances. The basic idea is shown in Figure 1. *Instead of providing a global explanation, concise if-then rules are learnt for each individual instance*, with a conjunction of control-flow characteristics (e.g. "sometimes directly follows"-relations) forming the antecedent and the cluster switch as consequence. As such, an explanation is a rule that stipulates which characteristics are the determining factors that make that a certain instance pertains to its current cluster. The goal of our technique is thus to learn accurate yet concise explanations.

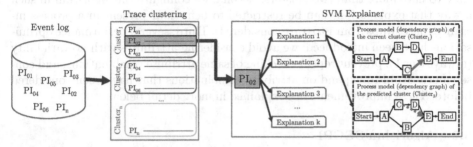

Explanation 1 for PI_{02}:   **IF** SometimesDirectlyFollows(C,E) = 0 **THEN** $Cluster_2$

Fig. 1. Overview of SECPI: for each process instance (PI) in the event log, one or more explanations are learnt and ranked according to their length. An explanation is a simple if-then rule with a conjunction of characteristics (as few as possible) which should not be present (i.e. set to zero) in order for the instance to rather belong to a different cluster. The SECPI-plugin in ProM is capable of visually reflecting these key determinants of cluster membership in the respective process models, as illustrated on the right hand side.

Constructing the Data Set: First, process instances are converted into feature vectors. The implementation supports several attribute templates (e.g. activity presence, always/sometimes weak order relations), however our initial experiments show that the "sometimes directly follows"-attribute template provides solid explanatory power from a control-flow perspective. The *SometimesDirectly Follows*(a, b) attribute for two activities a and b evaluates to true when these two activities both occur in the instance (potentially multiple times) and follow each other directly at least once, and to false otherwise (never follow each other directly or do not both occur). Note that it is out of scope of this study to investigate the optimal configuration of the featurisation step. The data set is completed by adding the appropriate cluster label to each instance. As such, a labeled data set is obtained to which supervised data mining techniques can be applied.

Deriving Explanations from a Support Vector Machine (SVM) Classifier: As stated earlier, our approach is inspired by [10] in which an algorithm is proposed to find explanations for document classifications. The most important similarity is the use of an SVM-based classifier as the base model from which explanations are derived. As for document classification, SVMs are ideally suited in our context because the use of multiple or complex attribute templates will quickly lead to massive dimensionality. By employing the well-known *liblinear* library for large-scale linear classification based on linear kernel SVMs, our approach can support data with millions of instances and features. For more details about SVMs, we refer to [13].

The main contribution of this paper consists in adapting the approach in [10] to the context of trace clustering with some key modifications. First, support for multi-class prediction has been developed because in our context it is highly plausible to have more than two clusters. Second, we configure the algorithm in such a way that explanations can be restricted to behaviour present in a process instance (only swaps from 1 to 0 are considered). Third, several performance optimisations have been introduced: we avoid considering attributes with no variability (always 0 or 1), prevent repeat checking of same attribute combinations, and consequently avoid to expand on attribute combinations that have been considered before. These improvements are explained in more detail below.

3.2   Algorithm SECPI

Algorithm 1 provides a formalised overview of the workings of the SECPI algorithm. As inputs, an instance to be explained (a process trace in a cluster) is given, defined as a sequence of binary attributes (generated using the attribute templates as discussed above). Next, a classifier is assumed to be trained over the data set which is able to, for a given feature vector, return a predicted class label and associated score (i.e. probability). Finally, three configuration options have to be set: *iterations* denotes the depth to search for explanations for the given instance. Increasing this value increases the run time but leads to more (albeit longer) explanations. The *zero_to_one* parameter denotes whether 0 to 1 attribute value swaps should be allowed. Since the instance attributes denote characteristics of the instance which *are* present (such as the direct following of two activities, for instance), it is recommended to set this parameter to *False*, as explanations denoting that a trace would not appear in its cluster when it did not present a specific characteristic are generally easier to interpret than explanations denoting that a trace should have a certain characteristic (as the question is then asked where and how exactly this characteristic would manifest itself within the trace). Additionally, since the multitude of all attributes for a trace are set to 0, the list of retrieved rules will be shorter and better fine-tuned to the actual behaviour as seen in the process instance. Finally, *require_support* denotes whether attribute value swaps should be taken into account for attributes which are always set to 0 or 1 (i.e. no variability). Again, it is recommended to set this to a *True* value, as providing explanations which require behaviour which is nowhere seen in the log are most likely less useable than those which do only incorporate seen behaviour.

As output, a set of explanatory rules is returned, formalised as a set of sets of attribute indices. Each set of indices represents a candidate explanation, and should be interpreted as follows: "this process instance would leave its current cluster when all the following attributes would be inverted" – or, in case where *zero_to_one* is set to *False*: "when it would not exhibit the behaviour as represented by these attributes". To construct this set of explanations, the algorithm

---

Algorithm 1. Formalisation of the SECPI algorithm (as explained in Sect. 4.1)

Input: $I := \langle I_i \in \{0,1\}, i = 1, 2, \ldots, |I| \rangle$ % Process instance $I \in$ event log L containing k clusters
Input: $C : L \mapsto \{1, 2, \ldots, k\}$ % Trained classifier with scoring function f_C
Input: $iterations := 30, zero\_to\_one := False, require\_support := True$ % Configuration
Output: Set of explanatory rules R

```
 1: function SECPI( I, C, iterations, zero_to_one, require_support )
 2:     c := C(I) % Predicted cluster
 3:     p := f_C(I) % Corresponding probability
 4:     R := {} % Set of instance explanations (set of sets)
 5:     E := {} % Combinations to expand on (set of sets)

 6:     % Search for single attribute explanations
 7:     for all i := 1 → |I| do
 8:         if IsAllowedSwap(I, i) then
 9:             I' := SwapAttributes(I, {i})
10:             c' := C(I') % New cluster label
11:             p' := f_C(I') % New probability
12:             if c' ≠ c then R := R ∪ {i}
13:             else E := E ∪ {i} end if
14:         end if
15:     end for

16:     % Iteratively search for multi attribute explanations
17:     for all iteration := 1 → iterations do
18:         combo := argmax_{A∈E}(p − f_C(SwapAttributes(I, A))) % Best combination
19:         combos' := {}
20:         for all i := 1 → |I| do % Expand combination
21:             combo' := combo ∪ {i}
22:             if combo ≠ combo' ∧ IsAllowedSwap(I, i) ∧ ¬IsSubsumed(R, combo') then
23:                 combos' := combos' ∪ {combo'}
24:             end if
25:         end for
26:         for all combo' ∈ combos' do
27:             I' := SwapAttributes(I, combo')
28:             c' := C(I') % New cluster label
29:             p' := f_C(I') % New probability
30:             if c' ≠ c then R := R ∪ combo'
31:             else E := E ∪ combo' end if
32:             E := E \ combo % Don't check this combination again
33:         end for
34:     end for
35:     return R
36: end function

37: function IsSubsumed(R, A)
38:     % Check whether attributes with indices ∈ A are subsumed by explanation in R
39:     for all E ∈ R do
40:         if E ∈ A then return True end if
41:     end for
42:     return False
43: end function

44: function IsAllowedSwap(I, a)
45:     % Check whether attribute with index a in instance I may be swapped
46:     a' := abs(I_a − 1)
47:     if ¬zero_to_one ∧ I_a = 0 then return False end if
48:     if require_support ∧ ∄J ∈ L : J_a = a' then return False end if
49:     return True
50: end function

51: function SwapAttributes(I, A)
52:     % Swap attributes with indices ∈ A in instance I
53:     I' := ⟨I'_i ∈ {0,1}, i = 1, 2, ..., |I| : I'_i = if i ∉ A then I_i else abs(I_i − 1)⟩
54:     return I'
55: end function
```

---

applies a heuristic, best-first search procedure with pruning. First, each candidate single attribute is evaluated (lines 7 to 15) to see whether rules composed of only one attribute can be found. If swapping an attribute's value does not lead to a class change, a combination of indices (in this case a single index) is added to E to be expanded in the next step.

Next, a number of iterations is performed (lines 17 to 34) as set by the *iterations* parameter. A best-first candidate selection from all currently available combinations to expand on is chosen, based on the classifier's scoring function (line 18). The goal is to first explore the set of attribute indices for which swapping their values moves the instance farthest away from its current class label (i.e. cluster). Expansions on this combination are created by creating a new set of combinations *combos'* by adding each allowed attribute to the set of *combo* (lines 20 to 25). Expansions which are equal to *combo* (i.e. the added attribute was already used in *combo*) or which are subsumed by an already existing explanation (the expansion contains all attribute indices of an existing explanation and thus adds no value) are not considered. Once all expansions are built, they are evaluated to see if they lead to a class change (lines 26 to 33). Expanded combinations are removed from E to prevent them being chosen again in the next iteration (line 32).

As a classification model, we use a combination of k (the number of clusters) SVM models to allow for multi-class classification with SVMs. To retrieve the predicted class label and score, we apply a winner-takes-all strategy as follows. An SVM model is built per cluster to predict whether an instance is in-cluster (label: 1) or out-of-cluster (label: 0). To predict the label and probability of an instance, the probability that the instance is out or in their respective cluster is evaluated for all SVMs (with probability p_k if predicted in-cluster and $1 - p_k$ if predicted out-of-cluster). The SVM model with the highest probability determines the label (and its corresponding probability). Note that other classifiers (such as decision tree or rule based classifiers) could, in theory, also be applied in the SECPI algorithm as long as a scoring function can be defined, and in fact could also return small-sized instance explanations – as is our goal – even though their model itself (in terms of number of rules or decision tree nodes for example) can still be large. However, the construction of such models becomes unwieldy when dealing with high dimensional data sets, so that SVMs remain a better suitable classifier for use within our proposed technique.

4   Conclusion

In this paper, SECPI (Search for Explanations of Clusters of Process Instances), a new technique assisting users with understanding trace clustering results was presented. The need for such a technique stems from the observation that typical trace clustering techniques do not provide sufficient insight into how a clustering solution is composed. In future work, we foresee to expand on a number of closely related topics. First, we plan to inspect the impact of the attribute templates used as they play a crucial role in representing the (control-flow) domain. Also, we aim at investigating the incorporation of non control-flow-based attributes.

Second, aggregation of instance-level explanations is a worthwhile research track as well. The current implementation already supports the investigation of shared explanations amongst groups of instances, which is a preliminary approach to bring our explanation technique to the global level. However, we plan to investigate more intelligent rule clustering and visualisation techniques for this purpose. Finally, we will focus on practical use cases in which SECPI might prove beneficial. User-driven discovery of process model collections from event data is one such area where it can support the feedback mechanism. Furthermore, SECPI is also perfectly capable of relating exogenously defined clusters, e.g. high versus low cost instances, to process-specific control-flow characteristics, a feature often desired in business process improvement cycles.

References

1. Greco, G., Guzzo, A., Pontieri, L., Saccà, D.: Discovering expressive process models by clustering log traces. IEEE Trans. Knowl. Data Eng. 18(8), 1010–1027 (2006)
2. Song, M., Günther, C.W., van der Aalst, W.M.P.: Trace clustering in process mining. In: Ardagna, D., Mecella, M., Yang, J. (eds.) Business Process Management Workshops. LNBIP, vol. 17, pp. 109–120. Springer, Heidelberg (2009)
3. Ferreira, D.R., Zacarias, M., Malheiros, M., Ferreira, P.: Approaching process mining with sequence clustering: Experiments and findings. In: Alonso, G., Dadam, P., Rosemann, M. (eds.) BPM 2007. LNCS, vol. 4714, pp. 360–374. Springer, Heidelberg (2007)
4. Bose, R.P.J.C., van der Aalst, W.M.P.: Context aware trace clustering: Towards improving process mining results. In: SDM, SIAM, pp. 401–412. SIAM (2009)
5. Bose, R.P.J.C., van der Aalst, W.M.P.: Trace clustering based on conserved patterns: Towards achieving better process models. In: Rinderle-Ma, S., Sadiq, S., Leymann, F. (eds.) BPM 2009. LNBIP, vol. 43, pp. 170–181. Springer, Heidelberg (2010)
6. Folino, F., Greco, G., Guzzo, A., Pontieri, L.: Mining usage scenarios in business processes: Outlier-aware discovery and run-time prediction. Data Knowl. Eng. 70(12), 1005–1029 (2011)
7. De Weerdt, J., Vanden Broucke, S.K.L.M., Vanthienen, J., Baesens, B.: Active trace clustering for improved process discovery. IEEE Trans. Knowl. Data Eng. 25(12), 2708–2720 (2013)
8. Song, M., Yang, H., Siadat, S., Pechenizkiy, M.: A comparative study of dimensionality reduction techniques to enhance trace clustering performances. Expert Systems with Applications 40(9), 3722–3737 (2013)
9. Ekanayake, C.C., Dumas, M., García-Bañuelos, L., La Rosa, M.: Slice, mine and dice: Complexity-aware automated discovery of business process models. In: Daniel, F., Wang, J., Weber, B. (eds.) BPM 2013. LNCS, vol. 8094, pp. 49–64. Springer, Heidelberg (2013)
10. Martens, D., Provost, F.: Explaining data-driven document classifications. MISQ 38(1), 73–99 (2014)
11. Bellman, R.E.: Adaptive control processes - A guided tour. Princeton University Press (1961)
12. Aggarwal, C., Hinneburg, A., Keim, D.: On the surprising behavior of distance metrics in high dimensional space. In: Van den Bussche, J., Vianu, V. (eds.) ICDT 2001. LNCS, vol. 1973, pp. 420–434. Springer, Heidelberg (2000)
13. Burges, C.J.C.: A tutorial on support vector machines for pattern recognition. Data Min. Knowl. Discov. 2(2), 121–167 (1998)

Business Monitoring Framework
for Process Discovery with Real-Life Logs

Mari Abe and Michiharu Kudo

IBM Research – Tokyo
5-6-52 Toyosu, Koto-ku, Tokyo, Japan
{maria,kudo}@jp.ibm.com

Abstract. Business analysis with processes extracted from real-life system logs has recently become important for improving business performance. Since business users desire to see the current situations of business with visualized process models from various perspective, we need an analysis platform that supports changes of viewpoint. We have developed a runtime monitoring framework for log analysis. Our framework can simultaneously extract process instances and derive appropriate metrics in a single pass through the logs. We tested our proposed framework with a real-life system log. The results for twenty days of data show synthesized process models along with an analysis axis. They were synthesized from the metric-annotated process instances generated by our framework.

1 Introduction

Process mining plays an important role in the business analysis of real-life logs generated from enterprise applications. The actual situation of an enterprise is visualized and analyzed based on extracted workflows to detect best practices. When consulting on the actual business situations of enterprises, analysis methods that include defining metrics for the analysis axes, extracting workflows based on the metrics, and analyzing them is practically a norm.

Our previous work describes business process analysis and associated client engagements [1,2] where we presented a technical approach with practical application scenarios. The most iterative and time-consuming work was the determination of metrics to discover processes that customers recognize the real processes of their business. Then they desire to see the discovered processes from different view points of the metrics as new analysis axes. For example, after customers recognize the processes of their business, they desire to compare the weekday processes with the weekend processes to find the causes of delays. Another example is customers want to compare purchasing processes for various product types with a duration within 10 minutes against over 10 minutes for the marketing strategies.

To change analysis axes according to the changes of the customer's requirements, we need to analyze the logs to extract the workflows again. It is an issue on the analysis method with process discovery that the analysis cycle is time-consuming and it causes belated results since a module of reading log and

S. Sadiq, P. Soffer, and H. Völzer (Eds.): BPM 2014, LNCS 8659, pp. 416–423, 2014.

extracting workflow must be reimplemented according to the metrics changed. This implies a need for a process discovery technology that can quickly extract workflows while reducing the time spent reading the logs so that the extracted results can be used even as the requirements of the customers are changing.

In this paper, we introduce a monitoring framework for process discovery. It simultaneously extracts the process instances and metrics of a single pass through the logs. We define the abstraction level of the monitoring context based on inclusion relationships of the correlation key definitions and present the monitoring algorithm based on the abstraction level. Instances of monitoring contexts are linked at runtime and that allows us to build process models. We tested our proposed approach with real-life logs and showed the process models that were synthesized with different values of an analysis axis.

2 Related Work

There are many proposed approaches for data warehousing that can analyze process logs [3,4]. Aalst [5] proposes "process cubes" that enable analyzing process logs by storing the results into data cubes that allow domain experts to execute online analytical processing (OLAP) operations such as drill-down, roll-up, and other operations for understanding the executed processes. We deal with real-life event logs from existing applications, so we are not limited to logs that are generated from particular workflow engines. Therefore, each event that we analyze is not always directly linked to a particular activity. An example of logs includes access history of external pages outside of the business flow. These logs can still be using as important as process logs if the domain experts want to see the causes of business performance degradation. Our advantage over these approaches is we expand the universe of inputs of the event base to event logs of legacy applications by leveraging our reverse engineering approach with business monitoring technology.

Liu et al. [6] propose complex event processing systems that support OLAP operations for multi-dimensional pattern analysis over event streams. Their solution improves computational efficiency for multi-dimensional event patterns by sharing the results among queries using a unified query plan. The difference in their approach is pattern-based event filtering versus our model-based filtering for event streams. However, optimization methods should also be beneficial for our method for efficient handling of events in real time.

Schiefer et al. [7] propose a solution for managing the performance data of business processes. Their system is intended for process-driven decision support and continuously improving business processes. It is important to drive decision support by analyzing both the process logs and other logs linked to processes.

The concepts and architectures of real-time business monitoring have been proposed for and applied to real customers [8,9]. The framework itself is a generic approach for an enterprise to improve its capabilities of sensing and responding to business situations. In our previous work [10], a model-driven mechanism of creating business monitoring applications was proposed. However, there are difficulties with such a purely top-down approach to build applications for enterprises that already have legacy applications for process management. We are now working on a novel approach for enhancing monitoring applications for agile business analysis with process discovery that can lead to a process model reflecting the actual behavior of users as recorded in the system logs. This re-engineering approach helps manage the lifecycle of business processes from the top-down to bottom-up and bridges the gap between business monitoring and process discovery.

3 Process Discovery from Real-Life Logs

Most real-life system logs are generated for system diagnoses including problem determination when there are abnormal situations such as server failures. The logs were not originally designed for reuse to create any secondary value. The characteristics of such logs make process discovery difficult to apply to real-life systems and our prior work [1,2,11] has attempted to address these problems. Fig. 1 is an extract from an example log for an insurance application that does premium calculations. Before discovering a process in the log, we must determine which parameters are correlated so we can extract tasks (activities) and process instances. In this example, a pair of parameters "pageid" for transaction type "response" and "sourcepageid" for "request" can be correlated to associate with the task. The column "user ID" can be used as a correlation key to extract a process. The semantics of these logs should be given by domain experts for our system of process discovery before the analysis.

To determine the metrics, we should select a column of the logs or some parameters that will eventually become our metrics or sources of metrics. In this example, the duration of each task can be derived using subtraction with

line #	Event type	User ID	Timestamp	Host	Request URL	Parameters
1	request	user1	2013-08-20T 08:30:33	sample.server.com	calc_premium	
2	request	user2	2013-08-20T 08:30:33	sample.server.com	logon	
3	response	user1	2013-08-20T 08:30:34	sample.server.com		pageid="calc_premium_page"...
4	request	user3	2013-08-20T 08:30:35	sample.server.com	logon	
5	response	user2	2013-08-20T 08:30:35	sample.server.com		pageid="logon_page"...
6	request	user1	2013-08-20T 08:30:48	sample.server.com	submit_condition	sourcepageid="calc_premium_page", birthday="1965/01/01", gender="male"
7	response	user1	2013-08-20T 08:30:49	sample.server.com		pageid="insurance_option_page", msg="input options next"
8	response	user3	2013-08-20T 08:30:50	sample.server.com		pageid="logon_page"...
9	request	user1	2013-08-20T 08:31:50	sample.server.com	submit_product	sourcepageid="insurance_option_page, product="life insurance", premium="$50", period="10 years"
10	response	user1	2013-08-20T 08:31:51	sample.server.com		pageid="simulation_result_page", msg="need physical check-up"
11	request	user1	2013_12-20T08::32:00	sample.server.com	save	sourcepageid="simulation_result_page"

Fig. 1. Example of input logs for insurance application

the timestamps of the response and request correlated by "pageid" and "sourcepageid" e.g. the duration is 14 seconds for "calc_premium_page" as calculated from the timestamps of Lines 3 and 6. Lines 1, 2, 4, and 5 are ignored if the users focus on the process of premium calculations. Similar metrics can be derived from other parameters. For example, "birthday" and "gender" are input to the insurance application on the "calc_premium_page" (Line 6) and "msg" is output to the "insurance_option_page" (Line 7). Process execution flow of the example is shown in Fig 2. The duration for each page is the metric for each task (14, 61, and 9 seconds). The input data and output data are also metrics for each task.

Monitoring business metrics in real time requires an event monitor runtime and event subscriber called a *monitoring context* [8,9,10,12]. We propose monitoring contexts and a runtime that allow extracting metrics and process instances simultaneously in a single pass through the logs described in the following subsections. Our approach offers two improvements over the existing approaches: (1) Associations of parent-child of the instances of the monitoring contexts are determined dynamically based on inclusion relationships of correlation key definitions and (2) The lifecycle of the instances of the monitoring contexts of the parents and children can be handled independently

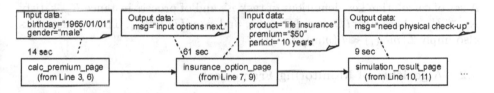

Fig. 2. A process instance for the insurance application of "user1"

3.1 Definition of Monitoring Context

We define "monitoring context" here for monitoring the events and calculating the metrics. Let E be an event sequence $\{e_1, \cdots e_n\}$. An event e is a tuple $e = \langle type_e, A \rangle$ where $type_e$ is a type of the event and A is a set of *attributes* for the event. An *attribute* is a tuple $a = \langle type_a, name, value \rangle$ where $type_a$ is a type of the attribute, *name* is a name of the attribute and *value* is its value.

Let X be a set of *variables*, including array variables. Let F be a set of *functions* for computing the values of X. Each value of variable x is derived from a function $f : t_1 \times t_2 \cdots \times t_n \to type_x$, where $type_x$ is a type for x. A *metric* is a specific *variable* that domain experts define with f and that will be used to query a process model in our method. A monitoring context mc is a tuple $mc = \langle E_i, K, E_o, C_e, X, F \rangle$ and an instance of mc is identified by a unique identifier. Each element of mc is defined as follows:

- E_i is a set of types of events occurred in E that can be monitored (inbound events). E_i does not necessarily include all of the types of events occurring in E. The *attributes* of an event are mapped to X with F.
- K is a set of variables derived from a set of mappings of E_i to uniquely identify an instance of mc (correlation keys). If there is no mc instance correlated with an inbound event and the event can be mapped to K, then an instance of mc is created and starts monitoring.
- E_o is a type for an event that can be generated from mc (outbound events). A generated event can be an input of other mcs.
- C_e is a set of conditions c that determines whether or not monitoring should be terminated. Each c is a specific f where the type of the variable derived from f is boolean. If all of the cs of an mc are set to *true*, then an instance of E_o is emitted to other mcs and monitoring is terminated.

We define the *abstraction level of the monitoring contexts* based on the relationships of the correlation keys. The mc that has K is denoted by mc_K. *An abstraction level of a monitoring context* $L(mc)$ is a positive integer and satisfies $L(mc_{K_0}) > L(mc_{K_1})$ if $K_1 \supset K_0$. It is a necessary condition for a monitoring context to generate hierarchical structures. Consider a process instance for the insurance application of "user1" (Fig. 2). The correlation key definitions of this task are "pageID" and "userID" while that of the process-instance is "userID". A set of correlation key definitions of task K_t and of process instance K_{pi} satisfy $K_t \supset K_{pi}$ where $userID, pageID \in K_t$, and $pageID \in K_{pi}$. These constraints also imply $L(mc_{K_t}) < L(mc_{K_{pi}})$.

3.2   Algorithm of Monitoring Framework

A monitoring context manager mgr manages the lifecycle of the instances of mc. It has a list of mcs for each abstraction level and knows how to serialize the mc instances when the instances terminate. The function "PROCESSEVENT" of mgr is the main flow of the event processing. We show the algorithm of "PROCESSEVENT" in Algorithm 1, which simply calls the "DOCORRELATION" and "DOEVENTPROCESSING" functions.

The mgr gets the correlating mc instance list by calling a function "GETCORRELATINGMC" in Line 6. In Lines 16 to 25 if this function, mgr gets the list of instances of mcs that is a higher level of abstraction than the event source. If the event source is a component for reading logs, then the list includes the lowest level of the instances of mcs, such as the instances of mc for mining tasks. If there are no instances of mcs listed, then mgr tries to instantiate mc from the event. A newly instantiated mc is registered in the mgr based on its abstraction level (from Lines 7 to 15). The next mgr has to do is to process the event. In the function DOEVENTPROCESSING from Lines 26 to 30, mgr simply calls processEvent of mc in the correlated list to update the variables of an instance of mc. If all of the variables of the instance of mc are set and the terminal condition C_e is true, then the instance emits an outbound event that includes the metrics. Then the instance recursively calls PROCESSEVENT of mgr.

Algorithm 1. event processing flow of mgr

```
 1: function PROCESSEVENT(e)                              ▷ e is an object of BusinessEvent
 2:     correlating_list ← DOCORRELATION(e)
 3:     DOEVENTPROCESSING(correlationg_list, e)
 4: end function
 5: function DOCORRELATION(e)
 6:     list ←GETCORRELATINGMC(e)
 7:     if list = empty then
 8:         instantiate MonitoringContext m from e
 9:         if m ≠ null then
10:             register m based on abstraction level
11:             list.add(m)
12:         end if
13:     end if
14:     return list
15: end function
16: function GETCORRELATINGMC(e)
17:     m0 ← e.getEventSource()
18:     list0 ← getList(m0)                    ▷ get monitoring contexts by abstraction level of m0
19:     for m in list0 do
20:         if m.correlate(e) then
21:             list.add(m)
22:         end if
23:     end for
24:     return list
25: end function
26: function DOEVENTPROCESSING(correlating_list, e)
27:     for m in correlating_list do
28:         m.processEvent(e)
29:     end for
30: end function
```

4 Experiment with Real-Life Logs

We tested our proposed framework on real-life system logs and verified the usefulness of the proposed approach. Table 1 shows some statistics for our experiment.
We tested the logs from 20 successive days of an application server. The number
of lines in the logs was 685,318.

The metrics for each task included four metrics, the task durations, the names
of products, the numbers of help pages accessed, and the status of the forms created (either new or update). The metrics for a process_instance included fifteen
metrics such as a list of pages, counts of help pages accessed, the status of process
started (either new or update) derived from mc for task, the status of process
termination (either save or cancel), and so on. The number of instances of mc for
the task was 260,568 and the total of process_instance was 25,781. There were
instances for a task that were not linked with any instances for process_instance
because they did not match the conditions for process start. Our framework

Table 1. Summary of the test data of the real-life logs and the results of the experiment

Test data				Result of experiment	
Period of logs	# of lines of logs	# of task metrics	# of proc_inst metrics	# of instances of mc for task	# of instances of mc for proc_inst
20 days	685,318	4	15	260,568	25,781

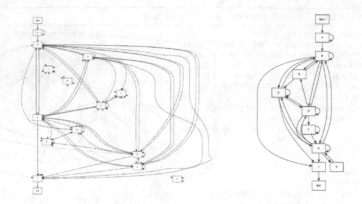

Fig. 3. The generated process models with different values of analysis axis

serialized the results into an MXML[13] file with metric annotations and an XSLT [14] file to extract the process instances.

Fig. 3 shows synthesized process models generated from our process discovery tool [2]. Each box indicates a page access as a task and the process flow starts from top to bottom. The help page are not included in the models as tasks because it is not a part of the business flow, but they appeared in the original logs. The left side is a process model in which the number of help page access is less than three. The right side is a model in which the number of help page access equals or is more than three. The difference is that users on the left are struggling with the process while users on the right are not. This result become one of data sources for domain experts to verify whether or not the help pages are effective.

5   Conclusion

In this paper, we proposed a monitoring framework for process discovery that simultaneously extracted the process instances and metrics of a single pass through the logs. We defined the abstraction level of the monitoring context based on inclusion relationships of the correlation key definitions and presented the monitoring algorithm based on the abstraction level. Instances of monitoring contexts were linked at runtime and that allows us to build process models. With the results, users could get process models from different metrics without reading huge log again. We tested our proposed framework with a real-life system log of twenty days and the results become one of data sources for domain experts to verify whether or not their system is used effectively.

References

1. Kudo, M.: Operational Work Pattern Discovery Based On Human Behavior Analysis. In: Service Research and Innovation Institute Global Conference (2014)

2. Kudo, M., Ishida, A., Sato, N.: Businesss Process Discovery by using Process Skeletonization. In: International Symposium on Data-Driven Process Discovery and Analysis (2013)
3. Kueng, P., Wettstein, T., List, B.: A Holistic Process Performance Analysis Through a Performance Data Warehouse. In: Proceedings of the Seventh Americas Conference on Information Systems (AMCIS 2001), pp. 349–356 (2001)
4. Mansmann, S., Neumuth, T., Scholl, M.H.: OLAP Technology for Business Process Intelligence: Challenges and Solutions. In: Song, I.-Y., Eder, J., Nguyen, T.M. (eds.) DaWaK 2007. LNCS, vol. 4654, pp. 111–122. Springer, Heidelberg (2007)
5. van der Aalst, W.M.P.: Process Cubes: Slicing, Dicing, Rolling Up and Drilling Down Event Data for Process Mining. In: Song, M., Wynn, M.T., Liu, J. (eds.) AP-BPM 2013. LNBIP, vol. 159, pp. 1–22. Springer, Heidelberg (2013)
6. Liu, M., Rundensteiner, E.A., Greenfield, K.: E-Cube: Multi-Dimensional Event Sequence Analysis Using Hierarchical Pattern Query Sharing. In: Proceedings of the 2011 ACM SIGMOD International Conference on Management of Data (SIGMOD 2011), pp. 889–900 (2011)
7. Schiefer, J., Jeng, J., Kapoor, S., Chowdhary, P.: Process Information Factory: A Data Management Approach for Enhancing Business Process Intelligence. In: Proceedings of the IEEE International Conference on E-Commerce Technology (CEC 2004), pp. 162–169 (2004)
8. Liu, R., Vaculín, R., Shan, Z., Nigam, A., Wu, F.: Business Artifact-Centric Modeling for Real-Time Performance Monitoring. In: Rinderle-Ma, S., Toumani, F., Wolf, K. (eds.) BPM 2011. LNCS, vol. 6896, pp. 265–280. Springer, Heidelberg (2011)
9. Chowdhary, P., Bhaskaran, K., Caswell, N., Chang, H., Chao, T., Chen, S., Dikun, M., Lei, H., Jeng, J., Kapoor, S., Lang, C., Mihaila, G., Stanoi, I., Zeng, L.: Model Driven Development for Business Performance Management. IBM Systems Journal 45, 735–749 (2006)
10. Abe, M., Jeng, J., Koyanagi, T.: Authoring Tool for Business Performance Monitoring and Control. In: Proceedings of IEEE International Conference on Service-Oriented Computing and Applications, SOCA 2007 (2007)
11. Kudo, M., Nogayama, T., Ishida, A., Abe, M.: Business Process Analysis and Real-world Application Scenarios. In: International Symposium on Data-Driven Process Discovery and Analysis (2013)
12. Momm, C., Gebhart, M., Abeck, S.: A Model-Driven Approach for Monitoring Business Performance in Web Service Compositions. In: Fourth International Conference on Internet and Web Applications and Services, pp. 343–350 (2009)
13. Process Mining Group, Math and CS department, Eindhoven University of Technology.: Mining eXtensible Markup Language, MXML (2003),
   http://www.processmining.org/logs/mxml
14. W3C Recommendation: XSL Transformations (XSLT) Version 2.0 (2007),
   http://www.w3.org/TR/xslt20/

Predictive Task Monitoring
for Business Processes[*]

Cristina Cabanillas[1], Claudio Di Ciccio[1],
Jan Mendling[1], and Anne Baumgrass[2]

[1] Institute for Information Business at Vienna
University of Economics and Business, Austria
{cristina.cabanillas,claudio.di.ciccio,jan.mendling}@wu.ac.at
[2] Hasso Plattner Institute at the University of Potsdam, Germany
anne.baumgrass@hpi.uni-potsdam.de

Abstract. Information sources providing real-time status of physical objects have drastically increased in recent times. So far, research in business process monitoring has mainly focused on checking the completion of tasks. However, the availability of real-time information allows for a more detailed tracking of individual business tasks. This paper describes a framework for controlling the safe execution of tasks and signalling possible misbehaviours at runtime. It outlines a real use case on smart logistics and the preliminary results of its application.

Keywords: Process Modelling, Process Monitoring, Support Vector Machines, Prediction, Event Processing.

1 Introduction

Increasing availability of event data from mobile and sensor devices provides various opportunities for improving business operations. Technologies such as the Global Positioning System (GPS) or Radio-Frequency Identification (RFID) have been designed to provide for a better geographical traceability of vehicles and physical objects. The generated data can be integrated with information systems to support process monitoring, and with other knowledge repositories to support decision making. In this line, Business Process Management Systems (BPMSs) can be extended from reactive towards predictive process execution.

Although some approaches contribute to the conceptual integration of event processing and processes at design time [1,10,11] and alerting at run time when undesired behaviours occur [15], only a few aim to leverage the predictive capabilities associated with event processing [18]. Moreover, these are restricted to events stemming directly from the execution within the BPMS, missing misbehaviour patterns on the level of singular tasks associated with external events.

In this paper, we address this research gap by developing a technique for defining rich alert patterns associated with specific task types for predictive

---

[*] The research leading to these results has received funding from the European Union's Seventh Framework Programme (FP7/2007-2013) under grant agreement 318275 (GET Service).

S. Sadiq, P. Soffer, and H. Völzer (Eds.): BPM 2014, LNCS 8659, pp. 424–432, 2014.

event monitoring in a BPMS. The feasibility of the framework is demonstrated by the help of a prototypical implementation on the basis of a real scenario on smart logistics with the task of transporting airfreight and alerting a diversion of the flight, which sets the basis to use it in different application scenarios.

The paper is structured as follows. Section 2 uses the case of airfreight transportation for identifying general challenges and requirements for a predictive system. Section 3 introduces the framework architecture. Section 4 defines an extension for task specifications in business processes, as basis for execution monitoring and prediction. Section 5 details the usage of supervised learning for realising predictive monitoring. Section 6 evaluates its feasibility. Section 7 discusses related work. Finally, Section 8 concludes the paper and envisions future research.

2 Predictive Monitoring of Continuous Tasks in Processes

Monitoring has mainly focused on identifying when tasks start and end. However, in various domains there are plenty of events recorded that can be utilised for the monitoring of a singular task, e.g., the task in charge of the shipment of goods in logistics chains. This type of tasks can be seen as *continuous* or *dynamic*, in contrast to *static* tasks such as signing a document or loading a container onto a truck. They require constant monitoring, as otherwise deviations from the expected behaviour might be detected too late, with undesirable consequences.

Let us describe part of a multimodal transport chain defined in the context of the EU-FP7 GET Service project. An aeroplane takes goods from the JFK International Airport (USA) to Amsterdam Airport Schiphol (NL), where they are transferred to a truck sent by a Logistics Service Provider (LSP) and transported to a destination in Utrecht (NL). The main goal of the LSP is to deliver the goods on time, for which the connection point in Amsterdam is especially critical. If the aeroplane has to divert and lands at a different airport (e.g., due to a thunderstorm near Amsterdam), the LSP has to cancel (or re-route) the truck that was sent to Schiphol, and in parallel reserve another vehicle to pick up the cargo at the new location. In order for these corrective actions to be effective, it is crucial that the LSP is aware of the aeroplane diversion as soon as possible, which implies constantly monitoring the task in charge of air transport.

Thus, the monitoring of dynamic tasks has implications that can be described in the form of challenges and, hence, requirements (RQ) for a predictive system:

RQ1 *Define monitoring points and expected behaviour.* The process model must be configured before enactment to introduce not only the monitoring points, but also the attributes to be considered, as well as the values desired for them.

RQ2 *Capture and process the information required for monitoring.* This information comes from different event and data sources. For instance, in the previous example, positioning information of the aeroplane can be obtained by connecting to data providers such as Flighradar24 or Flightstats. In case of road transport, it could be obtained from a GPS on-board device. In these cases, monitoring needs information external to the BPMS.

RQ3 *Normalise the information captured.* Relying on data sources implies that the information may arrive in different formats. Consequently, it must be first normalised in order to be jointly processed and generate valuable information.

RQ4 *Process event and data information.* Then, all the data must be processed and computed against the desired values configured in the executable model.

RQ5 *Identify and notify problems.* It is necessary to learn how to identify problems or abnormal behaviour as soon as they occur, and trigger proper alerts. Such an alerting mechanism can range from a yes/no notification indicating whether the behaviour is acceptable or not, to the detection of degrees of deviations, or root-cause analysis providing details of the problem.

RQ6 *Develop automatic support.* Support to deal with the previous challenges must be implemented and integrated into existing BPMSs.

3   Framework

Next, we describe the main components of a framework to monitor task execution and signal potential misbehaviours, addressing the aforementioned requirements. First, in a *modelling tool*, processes are modelled and tasks are annotated with predefined monitorable attributes (**RQ1**). Our approach for task annotation is described in Section 4. Second, a *process engine* calls external services to execute certain types of tasks, thus capturing the required data published by these sources (**RQ2**). This is available in engines such as Activiti. Third, a *Complex Event Processing (CEP) system* [10] is responsible for normalising events from different event sources, aggregating them to meaningful business events, and correlating them to task instances (**RQ3**). It must be capable of computing execution information against the specification set in the process model, too (**RQ4**), e.g., [3]. Fourth, a *deviation prediction system* aims at evaluating whether the task execution evolves as expected or deviates, and at informing proper participants (**RQ5**). Our approach to deal with this issue is explained in Section 5. The implementation of such a framework leads to the fulfilment of **RQ6**.

4   Definition of Monitorable tasks

In order to enable monitoring (**RQ1**), we propose to extend each task that needs to be monitored in a process model (hereinafter referred to as *monitorable tasks*) with a list of data attributes $\mathcal{T} = T_c \cup T_m \cup T_f$ divided into three groups: (i) constrained attributes T_c, for which each attribute t_c has an expected initial $\bar{t}_c^I$ and final $\bar{t}_c^F$ parameter, along with a threshold α; (ii) monitored attributes T_m, for which neither an initial nor a final parameter is meant to be provided, yet are monitored; and (iii) free attributes T_f, not monitored.

    Constrained attributes are a subclass of monitored attributes, which are a specialisation of free attributes. Constrained attributes and monitored attributes can be continuously monitored if and only if they belong to numeric types, or tuples of numeric types. In the latter case, the tuples must specify points that belong to an Euclidean space, e.g., longitude-latitude pairs. If the aforementioned conditions do not hold, continuous monitoring cannot be guaranteed. However, the initial and final parameters of constrained attributes can be confronted with the actual values, at the beginning and the end of the execution. We assume that the event sources (resp. external services) and their definition of event types are known. For instance, we know which values of an event indicate the position (e.g., longitude and latitude) and can use those to define rules.

5   Predictive Monitoring as a Classification Problem

Monitoring the execution of a task and checking its correct evolution corresponds to searching for possible anomalies in its behaviour. The current status of the execution is derived from the analysis of the task-related events. The gathered data are thus classified as safe or anomalous, i.e., whether they possibly lead to a successful completion or not. Such classification is based on a supervised learning model. To this extent, our approach adopts Support Vector Machines (SVMs).

SVMs [19,7] classify an input object on the basis of its position in a numeric hyperspace. The hyperspace dimensions depend on the objects' features that the analyst specifies as relevant for the classification. A *decision hyperplane* is adopted by SVMs to separate the hyperspace into two regions, thus dividing the objects into the classes to be assigned. SVMs are supervised learning models in that they learn how to define the decision hyperplane on the basis of previous data. The objective of the SVM is therefore to determine the decision hyperplane which is capable of correctly classifying an input object. The learning phase of the SVM is conducted on the basis of labelled input, i.e., a set of input objects that were already classified in advance. SVMs build the hyperplane according to specific parameters, defining the degree of acceptance of outliers (ν) and how fitting the hyperplane has to be with respect to the pre-classified objects (γ). The learning phase is thus associated with an evaluation phase, where the SVM is trained using different combinations of such parameters (*grid search*). The best tuning is calibrated on the basis of key factors that the analyst decides.

The training phase of SVMs is usually the most expensive in terms of computational effort, whereas the run-time classification is known to be fast. This is due to the compact representation of the hyperplane by means of its so-called support vectors, which are typically sparse. In fact, we opted for SVMs because not only are they a widely used tool for classification problems explicitly addressing the anomaly detection, but they also allow for a fast classification at run-time, which is a key factor in our scenario (**RQ5**). In our approach, a different specialised classifier is adopted for each monitorable task template.

5.1   Event Dynamic Feature Extraction

Our input objects for the classification are events and the evolution of a task execution is reflected in the history of events. SVMs classify single objects in a fixed-dimension space. Therefore, we adopted the following sub-sampling approach, aiming at representing the evolution of every monitored attribute as a scalar dimensionless value. In particular, this value corresponds to a normalised variation along a time interval. Each value represents one coordinate of the point in the feature hyperspace. The number of dimensions is thus fixed. Hence, the resulting point represents the dynamic change, and can be processed by the classifier, thus bridging the static analysis of single points in a feature space and the dynamicity of the task execution environment.

Let τ and τ' be two points in time, where $\tau' > \tau$, and $t_c(\tau)$ (resp. $t_m(\tau)$) the current value at time τ of a constrained attribute (resp. a monitored attribute). τ and τ' define an interval $I_\tau > 0$ during which the events are collected: $\tau' = \tau + I_\tau$. We define a new variable for monitored attribute, named *interval progress* ($\Delta \mathcal{P}_{t_m}^{\triangleright}$), as follows:

$$\Delta \mathcal{P}_{t_m}^{\triangleright} = \frac{\Delta\left(t_m(\tau), t_m(\tau')\right)}{\mathrm{avg}\left\{t_m(\tau), \ldots, t_m(\tau')\right\}}$$

The feature representing the rate of change of the monitored attribute is computed in terms of the increment during the time interval, $\Delta\left(t_m(\tau), t_m(\tau')\right)$, scaled by the average value during the interval, $\mathrm{avg}\left\{t_m(\tau), \ldots, t_m(\tau')\right\}$. We specify here that $\Delta(\cdot, \cdot)$ abstracts from the calculations needed to compute it. In the simplest case, it merely represents the subtraction between the passed values. Note, however, if the variables refer, e.g., to geographic coordinates, the increment has to be computed as a geodesic distance.

Constrained attributes are provided with initial and final values. The monitoring can thus be done on the basis of two more increments, with respect to *(i)* the final value, $\Delta\left(\bar{t}_c^F, t_c(\cdot)\right)$, and *(ii)* the initial value, $\Delta\left(\bar{t}_c^I, t_c(\cdot)\right)$. Therefore, we define two new variables for constrained attributes, named *progress from start* ($\Delta \mathcal{P}_{t_c}^{|\triangleright}$) and *progress to end* ($\Delta \mathcal{P}_{t_c}^{\triangleright|}$), as follows:

$$\Delta \mathcal{P}_{t_c}^{|\triangleright} = \frac{\Delta\left(\bar{t}_c^F, t_c(\tau')\right) - \Delta\left(\bar{t}_c^F, t_c(\tau)\right)}{\Delta\left(\bar{t}_c^I, \bar{t}_c^F\right)}$$

$$\Delta \mathcal{P}_{t_c}^{\triangleright|} = \frac{\Delta\left(\bar{t}_c^I, t_c(\tau')\right) - \Delta\left(\bar{t}_c^I, t_c(\tau)\right)}{\Delta\left(\bar{t}_c^I, \bar{t}_c^F\right)}$$

This reflects a perspective on the entire execution, as opposed to the interval progress, which considers an interval-focused view. The classification is hence made after events have been collected for I_τ time units. As a consequence, the anomaly refers to a single interval in time, whereas our approach aims at signalling whether the whole task is going to be disrupted. Consequently, there could be the need to wait more than one anomaly detection, before raising an alert. We indicate the number of consecutive anomaly detections as r.

The approach described so far covers not only the evolution of values for which a constraint was imposed at design time, but also for unconstrained monitorable attributes. This results in a more comprehensive observation of the evolution of task enactment.

5.2 Training the Classifier

Training data are gathered in our approach from a repository of event logs, in the form of stored sequences of events. Logs are pre-labelled as compliant or non-compliant according to the initial and final values for the constrained attributes: if and only if they are within the specified threshold for the activity, logs are considered as compliant.

The training of the SVM must be done not only based on its own parameters (ν and γ), but also with regards to the interval length I_τ and the number of sequential anomaly detections to accumulate before raising an alert, r. Section 6 exemplifies this joint training with a real use case.

As said, the objective of the training phase is to find the best tuning of parameters, in order to attain the best performance. In our case, the key drivers are accuracy and time-to-predict. Accuracy is assessed by Precision $\mathcal{P} = \frac{tp}{tp+fp}$, Recall $\mathcal{R} = \frac{tp}{tp+fn}$ and F-score $\mathcal{F} = 2 \cdot \frac{\mathcal{P} \cdot \mathcal{R}}{\mathcal{P}+\mathcal{R}}$ [14]. Respectively, true positives (tp) and false positives (fp) represent correct and incorrect classifications for tasks that are not respecting the constraints; true negatives (tn) and false negatives (fn) represent correct and incorrect classifications for tasks that are completing their execution according to the expected behaviour. Precision indicates the fraction of predicted anomalies that belong to the log of a misbehaving task. Recall denotes the fraction of misbehaviours that is classified as such. Finally, F-score is the harmonic mean of Precision and Recall measures. The time-to-predict (the second key driver in our approach), is computed as $I_\tau \cdot r$.

6 Evaluation

To study the effectiveness of our approach, we consider a real case study based on the monitorable task of airfreight transportation, as the one described in Section 2. In particular, we focus on alerting diversions, i.e., the signal to be raised when the aeroplane is going to land in an unplanned airport. This translates to the condition of violating the final coordinates of *aeroplane coordinates*, having the aeroplane position outside the *landing airport*.

In order to train the classifier, we collected 119 logs of events reporting flight data in the U.S. during May 2013 (98 regular flights, 21 diverted). Data were gathered from Flightstats, a data provider for air traffic information. Specifically, we automatically labelled as anomalous those traces ending in positions far from the expected destination. The remaining were compliant to the execution. The constrained attributes were *aeroplane position* (geographical coordinates), and the monitored attributes were the *aeroplane altitude* and *aeroplane speed*. Therefore, the classification was based on: *(i)* change rates in gained distance from the take-off airport (progress from start) and to the landing airport (progress to end), and *(ii)* interval-variations in *(a)* covered distance, *(b)* speed, and *(c)* altitude (interval progress) For the implementation, we adopted Esper as the CEP system and the Scikit-learn Python library's SVM as the automated classifier.

We performed a *grid search* in order to optimise the parameters described in Section 5. The ranges for parameter tuning were: *(i)* $I_\tau \in \{3, \ldots, 30\}$ min; *(ii)* $r \in \{1, \ldots, 15\}$; *(iii)* $\nu \in \{0.01, \ldots, 0.25\}$; *(iv)* $\gamma \in \{2^{-10}, 2^{-9}, \ldots, 2^3\}$. The best combination turned out to be based on 7-minute-long intervals, with 3 consecutive anomalies considered as eligible for an alert. The best performing ν and γ parameters, in this configuration, were resp. 0.01 and 0.5. Remarkably, the most accurate tuning was also among the most rapid in terms of time to predict (21 minutes). Test data consisted of 192 logs from Flightstats differing from the training set (170 regular flights, 22 diverted). The best F-score was obtained again with the 7-minute-long-intervals configuration: 87.8%.

The advantage for the process stakeholders is reflected by the possibility to be aware of a possible process disruption ahead of time. As explained in Section 2, this leads to increased possibilities to recover the process and, possibly, to tangible savings. Therefore, we analysed *(i)* the difference in time between the planned arrival and the diversion alert raising, and *(ii)* the difference in time between the actual landing (in an unexpected location) and the alert raising. These measures assess the time gained by the LSP to reorganise the road transport, originally assigned to pick up cargo at the planned arrival airport. The response time gained for the predicted diversions, indicates that the approach is on average able to raise an alert 104 minutes before the originally scheduled landing time, and 64 minutes before the actual landing time. This is a significant gain in comparison to the case where LSPs have to wait for a notification of the diversion, which sometimes occurs up to two hours past the actual landing time.

7   Related Work

To the best of our knowledge, there is not any framework for predictive task monitoring in business processes. However, some of the requirements described in Section 2 have been (partially) addressed. Regarding **RQ1**, a set of patterns describing relations and dependencies of events in processes that have to be captured in process models to observe the overall process context have been introduced [4]. Some approaches have also focused on the representation of CEP in business processes [9,11]. Continuous activities are typically defined in the logistics domain [6,12,16]. The approaches dealing with process monitoring usually aim at checking run-time compliance against rules [2,5,17,20]. They capture (**RQ2**) and process (**RQ4**) events related to the process, but external sources are disregarded and, thus, **RQ3** too. Unlike in our approach, rule violations are detected and notified when they occur but predictive capabilities are missing (**RQ5**). Further results in the application of CEP for Business Activity Monitoring (BAM) [13,8] present similar features as those related to compliance. Consequently, the existing automatic support referred by **RQ6** is partial.

8   Conclusion

In this paper, we presented a framework for monitoring the progress of task execution and predicting potential problems. To implement such a framework, an approach to configure monitorable tasks and a supervised learning model to detect behavioural deviations were introduced. Tests conducted on real data showed evidence of accuracy and timeliness in the misbehaviour detection.

We aim to extend our evaluation using different task types and event information, and to investigate the automatic definition and adjustment of the thresholds for safe task execution to improve the classification and alerting mechanisms.

References

1. Appel, S., Frischbier, S., Freudenreich, T., Buchmann, A.: Event Stream Processing Units in Business Processes. In: Daniel, F., Wang, J., Weber, B. (eds.) BPM 2013. LNCS, vol. 8094, pp. 187–202. Springer, Heidelberg (2013)
2. Awad, A., Decker, G., Weske, M.: Efficient Compliance Checking Using BPMN-Q and Temporal Logic. In: Dumas, M., Reichert, M., Shan, M.-C. (eds.) BPM 2008. LNCS, vol. 5240, pp. 326–341. Springer, Heidelberg (2008)
3. Backmann, M., Baumgrass, A., Herzberg, N., Meyer, A., Weske, M.: Model-Driven Event Query Generation for Business Process Monitoring. In: Lomuscio, A.R., Nepal, S., Patrizi, F., Benatallah, B., Brandić, I. (eds.) ICSOC 2013. LNCS, vol. 8377, pp. 406–418. Springer, Heidelberg (2014)
4. Barros, A., Decker, G., Grosskopf, A.: Complex Events in Business Processes. In: Abramowicz, W. (ed.) BIS 2007. LNCS, vol. 4439, pp. 29–40. Springer, Heidelberg (2007)
5. Birukou, A., et al.: An Integrated Solution for Runtime Compliance Governance in SOA. In: Maglio, P.P., Weske, M., Yang, J., Fantinato, M. (eds.) ICSOC 2010. LNCS, vol. 6470, pp. 706–707. Springer, Heidelberg (2010)
6. Cabanillas, C., Baumgrass, A., Mendling, J., Rogetzer, P., Bellovoda, B.: Towards the Enhancement of Business Process Monitoring for Complex Logistics Chains. In: Lohmann, N., et al. (eds.) BPM 2013 Workshops. LNBIP, vol. 171, pp. 305–317. Springer, Heidelberg (2013)
7. Cortes, C., Vapnik, V.: Support-Vector Networks. Machine Learning 20(3), 273–297 (1995)
8. Dahanayake, A., Welke, R., Cavalheiro, G.: Improving the Understanding of BAM Technology for Real-Time Decision Support. IJBIS 7(1) (December 2011)
9. Decker, G., Großkopf, A., Barros, A.P.: A Graphical Notation for Modeling Complex Events in Business Processes. In: EDOC, pp. 27–36. IEEE Computer Society (2007)
10. Herzberg, N., Meyer, A., Weske, M.: An Event Processing Platform for Business Process Management. In: Gasevic, D., Hatala, M., Nezhad, H.R.M., Reichert, M. (eds.) EDOC, pp. 107–116. IEEE (2013)
11. Kunz, S., Fickinger, T., Prescher, J., Spengler, K.: Managing Complex Event Processes with Business Process Modeling Notation. In: Mendling, J., Weidlich, M., Weske, M. (eds.) BPMN 2010. LNBIP, vol. 67, pp. 78–90. Springer, Heidelberg (2010)
12. Liao, F., Wang, J.L., Yang, G.-H.: Reliable Robust Flight Tracking Control: an LMI Approach. IEEE Trans. Control Systems Technology 10(1), 76–89 (2002)
13. Luckham, D.C.: The Power of Events: An Introduction to Complex Event Processing in Distributed Enterprise Systems. Addison-Wesley (2001)
14. Mitchell, T.M.: Machine Learning. McGraw-Hill (1997)

15. Montali, M., Maggi, F.M., Chesani, F., Mello, P., van der Aalst, W.M.P.: Monitoring Business Constraints with the Event Calculus. ACM TIST 5(1) (2013)
16. Pang, L.X., Chawla, S., Liu, W., Zheng, Y.: On Detection of Emerging Anomalous Traffic Patterns Using GPS Data. Data & Knowledge Engineering (2013)
17. Thullner, R., Rozsnyai, S., Schiefer, J., Obweger, H., Suntinger, M.: Proactive Business Process Compliance Monitoring with Event-Based Systems. In: EDOC Workshops. EDOCW 2011, pp. 429–437. IEEE Computer Society, Washington, DC (2011)
18. van der Aalst, W.M.P., Schonenberg, M.H., Song, M.: Time Prediction Based on Process Mining. Inf. Syst. 36(2) (2011)
19. Vapnik, V.: Estimation of Dependences Based on Empirical Data. Springer (1982)
20. Weidlich, M., Ziekow, H., Mendling, J., Günther, O., Weske, M., Desai, N.: Event-Based Monitoring of Process Execution Violations. In: Rinderle-Ma, S., Toumani, F., Wolf, K. (eds.) BPM 2011. LNCS, vol. 6896, pp. 182–198. Springer, Heidelberg (2011)

Author Index